Lecture Notes in Computer Science 16446

The series Lecture Notes in Computer Science (LNCS), including its subseries Lecture Notes in Artificial Intelligence (LNAI) and Lecture Notes in Bioinformatics (LNBI), has established itself as a medium for the publication of new developments in computer science and information technology research, teaching, and education.

LNCS enjoys close cooperation with the computer science R & D community, the series counts many renowned academics among its volume editors and paper authors, and collaborates with prestigious societies. Its mission is to serve this international community by providing an invaluable service, mainly focused on the publication of conference and workshop proceedings and postproceedings. LNCS commenced publication in 1973.

Franklin Tanner · John Irvine
Editors

Applied Imagery Pattern Recognition

53rd Applied Imagery Pattern Recognition Workshop, AIPR 2025
Washington, DC, USA, October 13–14, 2025
Proceedings

Editors
Franklin Tanner
Innodata
Ridgefield, NJ, USA

John Irvine
MITRE
Bedford, MA, USA

ISSN 0302-9743 ISSN 1611-3349 (electronic)
Lecture Notes in Computer Science
ISBN 978-3-032-18473-3 ISBN 978-3-032-18474-0 (eBook)
https://doi.org/10.1007/978-3-032-18474-0

This Springer imprint is published by the registered company Springer Nature Switzerland AG
The registered company address is: Gewerbestrasse 11, 6330 Cham, Switzerland

Preface

The 53rd Annual Applied Imagery Pattern Recognition (AIPR) Workshop was held on the campus of George Washington University in Washington, D.C., on October 13–14, 2025. The AIPR Workshop has a long-standing tradition of bringing together researchers, practitioners, and thought leaders from government, industry, and academia to exchange ideas and showcase innovations in the field of image and pattern analysis. The workshop provides a distinctive environment that fosters meaningful technical discussion across a wide range of applications, from foundational research to real-world deployed systems.

This year's workshop continued AIPR's tradition of pioneering emerging topics in applied imagery and visual understanding. The 2025 theme, *"Imagery-Related Challenges in Generative AI and Large Language Models,"* highlighted the accelerating impact of generative technologies on imagery, video, and multimodal reasoning. With the rise of large-scale models such as GPT, DALL•E, and diffusion-based architectures, artificial intelligence (AI) and machine learning (ML) are reshaping how visual data are generated, interpreted, and operationalized. Techniques once anchored in fully supervised learning are increasingly driven by self-supervised, transfer, and reinforcement learning paradigms, all of which place new demands on data scale, diversity, and quality. Advances in simulation platforms and content generation tools from organizations including NVIDIA, Meta, Microsoft, Apple, OpenAI, and Epic Games have further democratized access to synthetic data and enabled new frontiers in applied AI development.

Despite a federal government shutdown and broader research funding challenges, the workshop received 61 submitted abstracts. Abstracts were assigned to program committee members based on topical relevance and reviewer expertise, and each abstract received at least three independent single-blind reviews. Based on reviewer feedback and program committee discussion, 45 abstracts were accepted for presentation. Following four withdrawals due to unforeseen circumstances, 41 papers were ultimately accepted for inclusion in this volume.

AIPR is distinctive among archival workshops in that it explicitly encourages interim results, work-in-progress contributions, and contrarian perspectives. Several papers present negative results or lessons learned from unsuccessful approaches that may help inform future research. In addition to the formal presentations, the interactions among participants during the workshop played a critical role in refining ideas, strengthening manuscripts, and fostering more robust and impactful research outcomes.

The program was strengthened by the addition of two keynote speakers, David Broniatowski from George Washington University and Shelley Cazares of Google Public Sector. Broniatowski's talk entitled *"Explaining and Evaluating Human and AI Choices, with Clinical Illustrations"* examined how principles from human cognitive psychology can inform the evaluation of artificial intelligence decision-making in clinical and public health settings. Drawing on concepts such as fuzzy-trace theory, the presentation emphasized distinctions between gist-based and verbatim reasoning and explored how framing, prompting, and contextual grounding influence both human and AI judgments. Using healthcare examples including antibiotic prescribing, the talk highlighted challenges related to explainability, interpretability, bias, and alignment with clinical guidelines, and underscored the need for principled frameworks to evaluate AI behavior relative to human decision-making.

Cazares's talk entitled *"Image-Based Geospatial Foundation Models: What's the Catch?"* described the emerging paradigm of geospatial foundation models, namely large-scale vision and vision-language models that are pre-trained on massive global imagery corpora. The presentation examined how these models enable a separation of duties between computationally intensive pre-training and task-specific adaptation by domain experts. Cazares discussed key pre-training strategies, including self-supervised and contrastive learning, and highlighted the operational tradeoffs associated with fine-tuning, prompting, and deployment at scale. The keynote concluded with a forward-looking vision of agentic geospatial reasoning in which large language models orchestrate foundation models as tools to support complex analytical workflows and decision-making, moving the field from perception toward higher-level cognition.

The editors would like to thank the authors for their high-quality contributions, the Program Committee members for their careful and timely reviews, and the organizers and sponsors for their support of the workshop. We also thank the participants for the lively discussions and exchange of ideas that characterized this year's meeting. We hope that this volume will serve as a valuable reference and inspiration for future research in applied imagery and pattern recognition.

October 2025

Franklin R. Tanner
John Irvine

Organization

Conference Chairs

Steve Israel	Draper Laboratory, USA
Andrew Kalukin	Through Sensing, USA

Program Committee Chairs

Franklin R. Tanner	Innodata, USA
John Irvine	MITRE, USA

Treasurer

Shuyue (Frank) Guan	FDA, USA

Webmaster

Mohammad Zarei	MITRE, USA

Executive Committee

James Aanstoos	Iowa State University, USA
Hadi Ali Akbarpour	University of Missouri, USA
Travis Axtell	Ball Aerospace, USA
Bob Bonneau	AFOSR, USA
Christoph Borel-Donohue	Army Research Laboratory, USA
Filiz Bunyak	University of Missouri, USA
Prasad Calyam	University of Missouri, USA
Paul Cerkez	Coastal Carolina University, USA
Charles Cohen	Cybernet, USA
Marissa Dotter	MITRE, USA
Peter Doucette	US Geological Survey, USA
Shuyue (Frank) Guan	FDA, USA
Neelam Gupta	Army Research Laboratory, USA

Mark Happel	Johns Hopkins University, USA
Josh Harguess	MITRE, USA
John Irvine	MITRE, USA
Steve Israel	Draper Laboratory, USA
Stefan Jaeger	National Institutes of Health, USA
Andrew Kalukin	Through Sensing, USA
Hanseok Ko	Korea University, South Korea
Jeff Kretsch	Analemma Society, USA
Murray H. Loew	George Washington University, USA
Carlos Maraviglia	Naval Research Laboratory, USA
Paul McCarley	Air Force Research Laboratory, USA
Christopher Michael	Saint Louis University, USA
K. Palaniappan	University of Missouri, USA
Robert Pless	George Washington University, USA
Katie Rainey	Naval Information Warfare Center Pacific, USA
Raghuveer Rao	Army Research Laboratory, USA
Nancy Ronquillo	Naval Information Warfare Center Pacific, USA
Guna Seetharaman	Naval Research Laboratory, USA
Mike Tan	MITRE, USA
Franklin R. Tanner	Innodata, USA
Omar Tahri	University of Burgundy, France
Chris M. Ward	MITRE, USA
David Willmes	MITRE, USA
Mohammad Zarei	MITRE, USA

Contents

The Emerging Paradigm of Geospatial Foundation Models: From Pre-training to Agentic Reasoning 1
Shelley Cazares

Can AI Generated Items Be Trusted? 18
Paul S. Cerkez

Synthetic to Street: Generative AI–Powered Object Detection of License-Plate Jackets 24
John Munoz, Tom Bukowski, and Mike Busch

Agentic Learning with an AI Instructor in Virtual Reality for High School Anatomy Instruction 44
Robert DeWitty, Koundinya Challa, Abhinav Pendem, Issa W. AlHmoud, and Balakrishna Gokaraju

GEARS: Generative Edit Agent for Retrieval and Synthesis 62
Kevin Robbins, Grady McPeak, and Robert Pless

An Immersive AI-Driven Virtual Reality Training for Accessible Agricultural Education in a Unity-Based VR Environment 77
Abhinav Pendem, Bharath Jawahar, Koundinya Challa, Issa W. AlHmoud, Balakrishna Gokaraju, and Chyi Lyi Liang

Tracking Effects Layer by Layer from Adversarial or Naive Changes to a CNN Inputer 92
James P. Larue

Vision-Language Integration for Image Captioning Using Vision Transformers and GPT-J 101
Ali Alfatemi, Mohamed Rahouti, Mohammed Aledhari, Nasir Ghani, Abdellah Chehri, and Gwanggil Jeon

Task Prioritization for Remote Sensing AI Models 115
Ben Thompson and Eliza Mace

Scaling Remote Sensing Foundation Models: Data Domain Tradeoffs at the Peta-Scale 132
Charith Wickrema, Eliza Mace, Hunter Brown, Heidys Cabrera, Nick Krall, Matthew O'Neill, Shivangi Sarkar, Lowell Weissman, Eric Hughes, and Guido Zarrella

Cross-Modal Foundation Models for Remote Sensing 154
Adam Francisco, Matthew D. Reisman, Tobe Corazzini, Ryan McCormick, and Kevin J. LaTourette

Unsupervised Change Detection and Categorization with Remote Sensing Foundation Models 167
Matthew D. Reisman, Ryan McCormick, Tito Solis, Axel Durham, and Kevin J. LaTourette

Assumptions Implicit in Applied Imagery Pattern Recognition 177
Steven A. Israel, Michelle M. Brennan, and John M. Irvine

AgriGen: A Prompt-Tuned, Multilingual LLM-Based Q&A System for Smarter Agriculture 190
Venkata Ranga Ramanuja K. Chaitanya Kamduri, Pramod Gupta, and Chadi El Kari

PREFUSE: A Probabilistic Reliability-Weighted Fusion for Weather-Aware Perception in Autonomous Vehicles 201
Andrews Tang, Issa W. AlHmoud, Balakrishna Gokaraju, and Chyi Lyi Liang

Hier-SimCLR-Drive: Learning a Two-Level Traffic-Scene Taxonomy Without Labels for Autonomous Driving 221
Andrews Tang, Christopher Tetteh Nenebi, Kourtney Tucker, Sally Acquaah, Issa W. AlHmoud, and Balakrishna Gokaraju

Scaling Continuous Kernels with Sparse Fourier Domain Learning 236
Clayton Harper, Luke Wood, Peter Gerstoft, Mitchell A. Thornton, and Eric C. Larson

Benchmarking Defense Techniques for Securing Large Language Models 246
Abdulkadir Korkmaz, Timoteo Kelly, and Praveen Rao

Advancing Foundation Models with Spatiotemporal Reasoning in Multimodal Applications 255
Alexander N. Wood and Ben Thompson

Training the Right ML Model and Training the ML Model Right 274
John M. Irvine, Nazario Irizarry, Franck Olivier Ndjakou Njeunje, and Samuel Vilt

A Multimodal IoT-Based Smart Desk System for Real-Time Thermal Comfort Classification in Educational Environments 292
Krupa V. Khapper, Issa W. AlHmoud, Balakrishna Gokaraju, AKM Kamrul Islam, and Corey A Graves

Visual Feature Tracking Algorithm for Veterinary Lameness Assessment in Horses 311
Kaveh Safavigerdini, Taci Kucukpinar, Gani Rahmon, Kevin Keegan, and Kannappan Palaniappan

SPLIT: A Separation-Preserving Loss for Topology-Aware Building Segmentation in Remote Sensing Images 326
Sara Shojaei, Johanna R. Arredondo, Elena Sava, Ricky D. Massaro, Kannappan Palaniappan, and Filiz Bunyak

Pixel–Point Fusion: A 2D–3D Computer Vision Framework for Robust Sidewalk Trip Hazard Detection 345
Hang Du, Linlin Zhang, Yaw Adu-Gyamfi, and Filiz Bunyak

Neurophysiological Study of EEG Alpha–Beta Dynamics in Temporal and Parietal Regions During Non-Native and Neutral Music Listening 364
Richard Kyung and Nathan Yeop Kim

Fusion of 2D LiDAR and Vision-Based Detection for Collision-Aware Indoor Navigation 375
Sally Aqcuaah, Chris Nenebi, Andrews Tang, Kourtney Tucker, Issa W. AlHmoud, and Balakrishna Gokaraju

Dark Channel Prior Infused All-in-One Dehazing Network (DCPI-AODNet) for Single Image Dehazing 387
Pranjal Saxena, Teena Sharma, Nishchal K. Verma, Al Salour, and Shantaram Vasikarla

Evaluating Multimodal Large Language Models for Geospatial Object Identification and Enumeration in Overhead Imagery 403
Tim Klawa and Frank Tanner

Loop Closure Detection Revisited: A Clustering Perspective 415
Don Yates, Hakki Erhan Sevil, and Andrew Arash Mahyari

The Limitations of Image Features from Satellite Imagery Training Datasets ... 430
Christopher Algire, Steven A. Israel, and Kannappan Palaniappan

Synthetic Aperture Radar Change Detection as a Source of Ground-Truth Annotation for Machine Learning Deforestation Detection in the Amazon Using Multispectral Satellite Imagery ... 451
Andrew Kalukin, Joe Soundarajan, Dong Xu, and Renaldi Gondosubroto

Real-Time 2D Mapping and Navigation on an Indoor Autonomous Vehicle (AV) Platform with RPLiDAR A3 and HectorSLAM ... 463
Christopher Tetteh Nenebi, Sally Acquaah, Andrews Tang, Kourtney Tucker, Issa W. AlHmoud, and Balakrishna Gokaraju

Towards the Segmentation-Guided Generation of 3D MRA Dataset for Aneurysm Detection ... 484
Ruizhe Jiang, Lauren Christopher, and Paul Salama

HE3D-Net: Hypoxic Ischemic Encephalopathy Diagnosis and Lesion Segmentation Using 3D Heterogenous Ensemble Models ... 495
Bijaya Kumar Hatuwal, Rina Bao, Mai-Lan Ho, and Kannappan Palaniappan

NeuroGleam: Illuminating Small Vessel Disease Detection Through Deep Learning Based Segmentation of Brain MRI White Matter Hyperintensities ... 508
Balaji Iyer, Brady Williamson, V. B. Surya Prasath, Bruce J. Aronow, Pooja Khatri, Heidi Sucharew, Vivek Khandwala, Joseph LaPorta, Lily Wang, Rebecca Cornelius, Mary Gaskill-Shipley, Thomas Tomsick, David Wang, Thomas Maloney, Paul S. Horn, Janice Carrozzella, Brett M. Kissela, and Achala Vagal

Multimodal Fusion of Imaging and Multi-omics Data for Enhanced Breast Cancer Detection ... 522
Dattatreya Kantha and Murray H. Loew

Wavelet Scattering Features Based Colon Cancer Histology Classification ... 546
Ritish Raghav Maram, Elliot Levy, and Murray H. Loew

Imgs2imgs: Improving Visual Consistency in Multiview Image Editing ... 559
Mohamed Gallai and Abby Stylianou

Quantifying Error Propagation and Recovery in Object Detection for Autonomous Vehicles: A Markovian Approach ... 576
Andrews Tang, Kourtney Tucker, Abhinav Pendem, Issa W. AlHmoud, and Balakrishna Gokaraju

Restorable Segmentation Synthesis Using Fourier Descriptors 595
Shuyue Guan and Weijie Chen

Benchmarking Few-Shot Methods for Rare Target Classification in PlanetScope Imagery 608
Keli Cheng and Weipeng Wu

Author Index 619

The Emerging Paradigm of Geospatial Foundation Models: From Pre-training to Agentic Reasoning

Shelley Cazares(✉)

Google Public Sector, Washington, DC 20001, USA
shelleycazares@google.com

Abstract. The analysis of satellite and aerial imagery has entered a new era with the advent of foundation models. This paper describes the concept of Geospatial Foundation Models (GeoFMs), which are artificial intelligence/machine learning (AI/ML) models pre-trained on massive geospatial datasets through varied methodologies. We first articulate the core paradigm shift that GeoFMs enable: a separation of duties, where large-scale model providers perform the computationally intensive pre-training, allowing domain experts to rapidly fine-tune or prompt these models for specific, mission-critical tasks. This approach democratizes access to state-of-the-art AI/ML while maintaining the security and confidentiality of the downstream task. We then explore the novel capabilities unlocked by different types of GeoFMs, distinguishing between the fine-tunable vision models produced by self-supervised techniques like masked auto-encoding, and the vision-language models produced by contrastive learning which enable zero-shot tasks like open-vocabulary image analysis. Next, we discuss the practical considerations for operationalizing GeoFMs, from performance-cost analysis to the broader MLOps ecosystem. To that end, we introduce a taxonomy of model adaptation strategies and propose a framework for domain experts to select the most cost-effective adaptation approach for their particular mission set. Finally, we present a forward-looking vision of Agentic Geospatial Reasoning, where Large Language Models act as intelligent orchestrators, leveraging GeoFMs as tools to answer high-level user queries in natural language and automate complex analytical workflows, moving the field from perception to cognition.

Keywords: Geospatial Foundation Model · Geospatial AI · Geospatial Intelligence · Remote Sensing · Self-Supervised Learning · Masked Auto-Encoder · Contrastive Learning · Agentic AI · Agentic Reasoning · Geospatial Reasoning

1 Introduction

The increasing volume and variety of Earth observation data present both a monumental opportunity and a significant challenge. While satellite and aerial

F. Tanner and J. Irvine (Eds.): AIPR 2025, LNCS 16446, pp. 1–17, 2026.
https://doi.org/10.1007/978-3-032-18474-0_1

imagery provide a rich source of information for applications ranging from disaster response to environmental monitoring, the ability to analyze this data at scale and speed remains a critical bottleneck. Traditional supervised machine learning approaches, while powerful, often require large, meticulously labeled datasets for each specific task. This requirement represents a significant bottleneck, as the cost and time associated with data curation and labeling are often untenable for applications demanding rapid deployment.

A compelling example of this challenge is rapid damage assessment following a natural disaster. In the aftermath of an event like a category 5 hurricane, response teams need immediate, actionable intelligence to prioritize resource allocation. The limitations of the traditional supervised learning approach have been well documented [14]. The data curation and labeling process for such an endeavor could take days or even weeks, an untenable timeline in a crisis. To address this bottleneck, research has demonstrated that semi-supervised learning can mitigate this challenge by achieving strong performance with only a fraction of the labeled data for a particular geographical area [14].

While semi-supervised learning reduces the in-crisis labeling burden, this paper explores an emerging paradigm: the Geospatial Foundation Model (GeoFM), which takes this principle a step further. Instead of training a model on an unlabeled dataset gathered *reactively* from a single disaster area, a GeoFM is pre-trained *proactively* on a global scale for general use. A GeoFM is an artificial intelligence/machine learning (AI/ML) model pre-trained on a massive, varied corpus of geospatial data collected from all over the globe, which can then be adapted (fine-tuned or prompted) to perform a wide range of downstream geospatial tasks. This pre-trained global knowledge means that the GeoFM is *not* starting from scratch when a new crisis occurs, allowing for even greater data efficiency during adaptation.

This proactive approach enables the most significant contribution of the GeoFM paradigm: A separation of duties. Computationally intensive, general-purpose pre-training is performed by large organizations with sufficient resources, using unlabeled or weakly-labeled data that does not require access to downstream, task-specific information. Domain experts can then perform task-specific adaptation using their own small set of proprietary labels, ensuring the security and confidentiality of their sensitive data and use cases. This paradigm democratizes access to cutting-edge AI/ML for the applied geospatial imagery community while maintaining the security and confidentiality of the downstream task.

This paper focuses on overhead imagery-based GeoFMs, those which are used to process satellite and airborne imagery with a downward-facing look angle. We will first define two dominant pre-training strategies for GeoFMs: self-supervised and contrastive learning. We will then survey the new capabilities unlocked by these distinct pre-training strategies. Next, we will cover the practical aspects of operationalizing these models. Finally, we will conclude with a vision for the future: Agentic Geospatial Reasoning, where multimodal Large Language Models

(LLMs) act as intelligent orchestrators, leveraging GeoFMs as tools to automate complex analytical workflows directly from natural language prompts.

2 The Geospatial Foundation Model Paradigm

Image-based GeoFMs typically leverage the vision transformer architecture [8], whose self-attention mechanism is exceptionally well-suited to modeling the long-range spatial dependencies inherent to satellite and aerial imagery. These models are pre-trained on massive datasets curated to be varied across geographies, seasons, and times of day, aiming to build a comprehensive representation of the earth's surface. The core innovation of the foundation model paradigm lies in its two-stage lifecycle: a general-purpose pre-training stage followed by a task-specific adaptation stage. The pre-training strategy fundamentally determines the model's capabilities. Two dominant approaches have emerged: self-supervised pre-training for vision models and weakly-labeled contrastive pre-training for vision-language models.

2.1 Pre-training Strategy 1: Self-supervised Learning for Vision Models

The first approach focuses on learning robust visual features from images alone, often with self-supervised learning (SSL) methods like Masked Auto-Encoding (MAE) [11]. The model consists of a backbone (encoder) and a temporary head (decoder). It is trained end-to-end to perform a pretext task: Reconstruct randomly masked patches of an image from the remaining visible patches (Fig. 1, left). This pre-training process, driven by pixel-level reconstruction loss and requiring no human-provided labels, compels the backbone to compress the visible information in the image into a powerful, general-purpose feature representation (embedding) that the head can then use to complete the reconstruction.

While the reconstruction task is the mechanism for pre-training, the resulting backbone is the developer's goal. Once pre-training is complete, the temporary reconstruction head is discarded, leaving a powerful, pre-trained backbone ready for downstream application. A user can then append a new, task-specific head to the pre-trained backbone and fine-tune it using supervised learning on a small, labeled dataset (Fig. 1, right). This efficient workflow is the central promise of the foundation model paradigm.

2.2 Pre-training Strategy 2: Contrastive Learning for Vision-Language Models

The second dominant pre-training approach focuses on aligning visual features with human language. This is accomplished through contrastive learning techniques (e.g., CLIP [17], SigLIP [26]) on a massive, weakly-supervised dataset of (image, text caption) pairs. During pre-training, the model learns to map both an

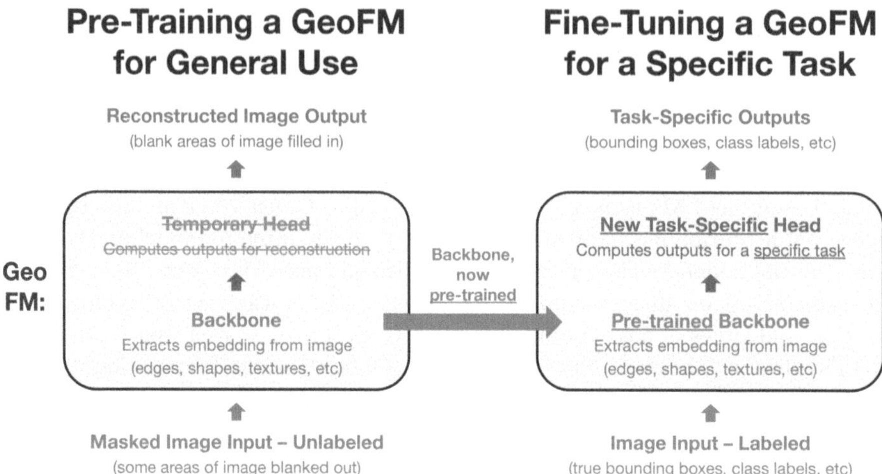

Fig. 1. The two-stage life-cycle of a vision geospatial foundation model. (Left:) The self-supervised pre-training phase, where a model backbone learns to extract powerful embeddings by reconstructing masked patches with the help of a temporary head. (Right:) The supervised fine-tuning phase, where the pre-trained backbone is used, its temporary reconstruction head discarded, and a new, task-specific head is trained on a small, labeled dataset.

image and its corresponding text description (its weak label) to a shared embedding space. The training objective is to maximize the similarity (e.g., cosine similarity) of the embeddings for a correct pair, while minimizing the similarity for incorrect pairs within a batch.

This pre-training process creates a model that understands the semantic relationship between visual content and text. It is this vision-language alignment that enables powerful zero-shot capabilities, such as open-vocabulary image analysis, where the model can generalize to concepts not seen during pre-training. Consequently, direct prompting is the primary mode of application of these contrastively-trained GeoFMs.

2.3 The Overarching Benefit: A Separation of Duties

The separation of duties remains a key benefit of the GeoFM paradigm, regardless of the pre-training strategy. Industrial research labs and other large-scale model providers can absorb the immense computational cost of pre-training, enabling the broader community to achieve state-of-the-art performance. Domain experts can either fine-tune the vision models, effectively transferring learned embeddings to new tasks, or directly prompt the vision-language models for powerful zero-shot analysis.

Specifically, the separation of duties offers two significant advantages to domain experts:

- **Security and confidentiality:** Because pre-training can be accomplished with unlabeled or weakly-labeled data, the large organizations who pre-train the GeoFMs do not require access to the domain experts' proprietary labels or use cases, ensuring the security and confidentiality of their sensitive missions.
- **Reduction in labeling resources:** While fine-tuning a GeoFM still requires a labeled dataset, the required dataset size is typically much smaller than that needed to train a bespoke model from scratch. This drastically reduces the cost and time associated with data curation and labeling, making state-of-the-art performance more accessible.

2.4 A Survey of Existing Geospatial Foundation Models

GeoFMs are a rapidly evolving field, with a vibrant ecosystem including prominent models from both industrial and academic research groups. Notable early models include SatMAE from Stanford [7,23], which pioneered the adaptation of the MAE concept specifically for geospatial data. It introduced novel temporal and spectral positional encodings to effectively pre-train a transformer backbone on 10 m - 60 m resolution, multi-spectral, time-series imagery from Sentinel-2 satellites.

Subsequent research has focused on improving the MAE framework's ability to handle the scale variance of remote sensing data, where the same object type can appear at vastly different resolutions given the imagery source. ScaleMAE [2,18] addresses this challenge by introducing a scale-aware position encoding based on the image's Ground Sample Distance (GSD), as well as a novel decoder to reconstruct images at multiple scales to explicitly learn multi-scale features. More recently, Cross-Scale MAE [1,25] proposed an alternative approach by using scale augmentation during pre-training and enforcing cross-scale consistency with both contrastive and generative (reconstruction) losses, removing the dependency on known GSD metadata.

Another recent approach has been to build more comprehensive, geospatial-native models. Prithvi-EO-2.0, developed by IBM and NASA [13,16,24], is a MAE-based model pre-trained on a global dataset of 30 m resolution Harmonized Landsat and Sentinel-2 (HLS) imagery, explicitly incorporating time and location data into its embeddings to enhance performance on Earth observation tasks. Similarly, Clay [6] is a MAE-based model designed to accept a wide variety of sensor data with different resolutions and spectral bands, along with time and location data.

Yet another approach has been to leverage massive, non-geospatial datasets. Meta's DINOv3 [9,21] is a generalist vision model pre-trained on billions of web images using self-distillation (a discriminative SSL approach). It has demonstrated remarkable transfer learning performance on dense geospatial tasks like segmentation. Its success proves that features learned from natural images can, at a sufficient scale, generalize effectively to overhead perspectives. The authors also demonstrated the versatility of their pre-training recipe by training a separate DINOv3 model from scratch on high-resolution (0.6 m) Maxar satellite imagery, outperforming many domain-specific models.

Finally, some models are designed to produce a new kind of data product: A universal, analysis-ready "embedding field". Google DeepMind's AlphaEarth Foundations [5,10] exemplifies this. It uses a multi-loss training strategy, combining reconstruction, self-distillation, and text-contrastive objectives, to process multi-modal inputs (optical, radar, LiDAR, text, climate data) into a time-continuous representation. The final product is *not* a model to be fine-tuned or prompted with new imagery, but a global 10 m resolution dataset of embeddings available directly in Google Earth Engine, designed to be used as a universal feature space for a wide variety of mapping tasks. This is distinct from Google Research's Remote Sensing Foundations (RSF) models, which are vision and vision-language transformers pre-trained on high-resolution (0.1 m - 10 m) imagery that can be fine-tuned or prompted on new user imagery [3,15,19]. The vision and vision-language RSF models are pre-trained with MAE and contrastive learning, respectively, followed by supervised learning for selected downstream tasks. Both the AlphaEarth Foundations embeddings and the Remote Sensing Foundations models are key parts of Google's Earth AI [4].

Table 1 provides a comparative summary of all of these models, indicating a diverse landscape and a healthy and rapidly advancing field. While architectural and pre-training specifics differ, the overarching trend is a move towards leveraging vast, global, unlabeled or weakly-labeled datasets to create powerful, generalizable backbones that the applied research community can readily adapt.

3 A Taxonomy of Geospatial Foundation Model Applications

The different pre-training paradigms unlock distinct and transformative capabilities. This section surveys the primary downstream applications enabled by GeoFMs.

3.1 Image Classification

Scene-level image classification is one of the most fundamental tasks in geospatial analysis. Here, the GeoFM assigns a single class label to an image from a pre-defined, closed set of classes. A user could take a pre-trained GeoFM backbone, attach an image classification head, and fine-tune it on a labeled dataset so that the model learns how to categorize scenes. For example, a fine-tuned GeoFM could distinguish between "industrial buildings", "residential buildings" and "annual crops" at the scene level.

3.2 Image Segmentation

Image segmentation extends classification to the pixel level, assigning a class label to every pixel in the image from a closed set of pixel types. This allows for the precise delineation of objects and regions in the image, useful for outlining

Table 1. Comparison of prominent Geospatial Foundation Models.

Model	Lead Institution	Key Focus/Innovation	Pre-Training Strategy	Pre-Training Data	Pre-Training Image Resolution	License License	Model Size (# of Parameters)
SatMAE	Stanford	Pioneered multi-temporal, multi-spectral pre-training with specific position encodings	Reconstruction	Sentinel-2 imagery, time	10 m - 60 m	CC-BY-NC 4.0	307M
ScaleMAE	Berkeley	Scale-aware MAE with GSD-based position encoding and multi-scale reconstruction decoder	Reconstruction	FMoW RGB imagery, GSD	0.3 - 10 m+	CC-BY-NC 4.0	323M
Cross-Scale MAE	U. Tennessee Knoxville	Scale augmentation and cross scale consistency losses	Reconstruction, Contrastive	FMoW RGB imagery	0.2 m - 30 m	CC-BY-NC 4.0	307M
Prithvi-EO-2.0	IBM/NASA	Multi-temporal model explicitly encoding time and location metadata	Reconstruction	HLS imagery, location, time	30 m	MIT, Apache 2.0	300M & 600M
Clay	Clay Foundation	Multi-temporal, multi-spectral imagery from any sensor at any resolution	Reconstruction	General EO	Variable	Apache 2.0	Not specified
DINOv3	Meta AI	Generalist vision model with strong transfer from web images; Separate model pre-trained on high-resolution satellite imagery	Self-distillation	Web images or Maxar RGB imagery (for satellite model)	0.6 m (for satellite model)	Custom License	Up to 7B
AlphaEarth	Google	Produces global, static "embedding field" from multi-modal, multi-temporal inputs	Multi-Loss (Reconstruction, Self-distillation, Contrastive)	Optical, SAR, LIDAR, text, climate, time, location	10 m (output embeddings)	Model is Proprietary, Embeddings are CC-BY-4.0	480M
Remote Sensing Foundations	Google	Fine-tunable and promptable models for high-resolution aerial imagery	Reconstruction, Contrastive, Supervised	High-resolution aerial imagery text	0.1 m - 10 m	Proprietary	300M & 400M

water bodies, roads, or individual buildings. A user could attach an image segmentation head to a pre-trained backbone and fine-tune it, teaching the model how to produce a pixel-wise classification map (segmentation mask). For example, a fine-tuned GeoFM could produce a segmentation mask that precisely outlines airplanes on a tarmac, distinguishing both from adjacent buildings and vegetation.

3.3 Object Detection

Object detection involves identifying the location of individual objects in an image and classifying what type of objects they are, based on a pre-defined, closed set of object types. A user could fine-tune an object detection head attached to a pre-trained GeoFM backbone to teach the model how to output bounding boxes for the specific objects of interest, as well as each bounding box's individual type (e.g., "pier", "warehouse").

3.4 Open-Vocabulary Image Analysis

Contrastively-trained vision-language models have provided a revolutionary capability, shattering the "closed-set" limitation of the traditional image analysis tasks described above. Rather than limiting the model's analysis to a closed set of image classes, pixel classes, or object types, the model can process the image based on the user's description of the classes and object types they are interested in, specified in natural language.

For example, in the case of open-vocabulary object detection, a user can prompt the model with a natural language text query, such as "building" or "golf course". The model can then identify and locate the corresponding objects in the image, even if it was never explicitly trained on those object types (Fig. 2). This capability provides enormous flexibility for operational scenarios where analysts may need to search for novel or unexpected objects (e.g., "damaged roof with blue tarp") with little to no advanced preparation.

3.5 Change Detection

Change detection is a critical task in remote sensing. It can be used to identify differences in a geographic area over time by leveraging a GeoFM backbone to produce powerful embeddings. For example, the embedding for an image of a specific location at time T_1 can be compared to the embedding of an image of the same location at time T_2. A simple mathematical operation (e.g., cosine similarity) on the two embeddings can provide a quantitative measure of change. A large distance implies a significant change has occurred, which can be used to flag the area for further analysis by a human expert.

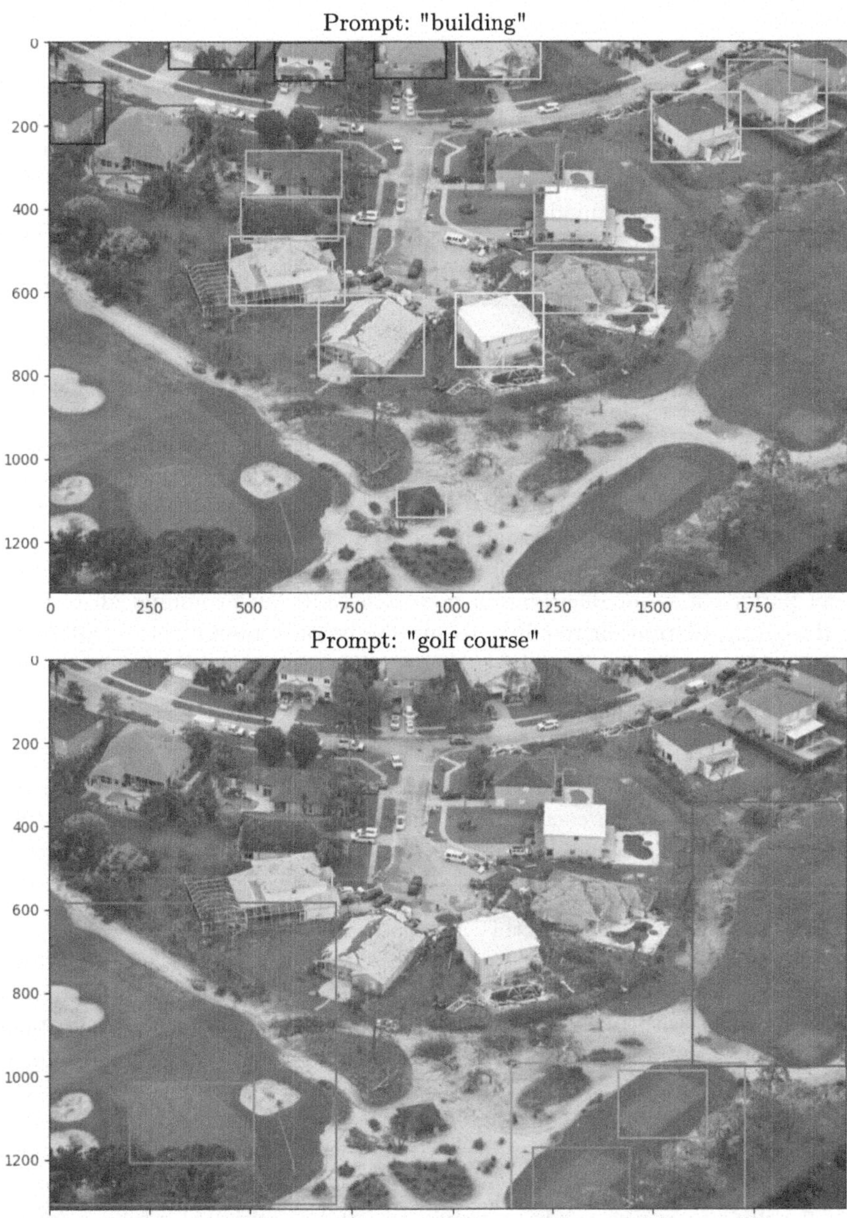

Fig. 2. Example of open-vocabulary object detection. The same vision-language GeoFM is prompted to detect (Top:) the text string "building" and subsequently (Bottom:) the text string "golf course", demonstrating the ability to dynamically query the image for different object types without fine-tuning. Images courtesy of Bellwether [20].

3.6 Similarity Search

The embeddings produced by GeoFMs can also be used for large-scale similarity searches across vast imagery archives. An analyst can first use the backbone to generate an embedding for a new image of interest, and then search a pre-computed database of embeddings to retrieve the most visually similar images from their archive. In addition, using the vision-language GeoFMs, the analyst's search can even be multimodal, comparing their text prompt embedding to the image embeddings in their archive. This is a powerful tool for finding other examples of rare objects or land-use types, again using simple mathematical operations (e.g., cosine similarity).

4 Operationalizing Geospatial Foundation Models

While the promise of GeoFMs is significant, their operationalization requires navigating a complex landscape of strategic trade-offs. Key decisions encompass the choice of deployment pattern (online inference for real-time needs versus offline batch processing of large archives) and the methodology for continuous evaluation to both validate model performance pre-deployment and to monitor model performance for degradation in production. Underpinning all of this is the degree of adaptation required to meet mission requirements. This section outlines a framework for navigating these critical operational decisions.

4.1 A Taxonomy of Adaptation Strategies

The decision to adapt a pre-trained GeoFM is not binary, but a selection from a spectrum of strategies, each with distinct tradeoffs in performance, cost, and labeled data requirements. We propose a taxonomy of four main adaptation strategies:

1. **Zero-Shot Inference:** In this approach, the pre-trained GeoFM is used directly with no further fine-tuning. This typically involves using the backbone as a powerful feature extractor, whose embeddings can then be used for downstream tasks like change detection or similarity search. Alternatively, for vision-language GeoFMs, this could involve direct text-based prompting in natural language, as shown in Fig. 2.
2. **Few-Shot Inference:** Once again, the frozen, pre-trained GeoFM is used with no fine-tuning to generate initial object proposals. These proposals are then refined in real-time by training a lightweight, compact classifier (e.g., support vector machine or multi-layer perception) on only a handful of actively selected user-annotated examples (the few shots). This cascading architecture/active learning approach is crucial for resolving the visual ambiguity of natural language queries ("small yacht" versus "fishing boat") to achieve a high accuracy with minimal annotation overhead [19].
3. **Head-Only Fine-Tuning before Inference:** The pre-trained backbone remains frozen, and only a new, task-specific head is fine-tuned on a small, labeled dataset using supervised learning techniques. Inference then follows.

4. **Full Fine-Tuning before Inference:** The entire model, including both the pre-trained backbone and the new, task-specific head, is fine-tuned on a small, labeled dataset, potentially with parameter-efficient techiques like Low-Rank Adaptation (LoRA) to reduce computational burden [12]. This transfer learning allows the backbone's deep feature representations (embeddings) to adapt more specifically to the nuances of the new dataset, in better support of the new task-specific head. The fine-tuned model can then be used for inferencing.

4.2 Performance-Cost Analyses

Deciding which adaptation strategy to pursue requires a deliberate performance-cost analysis. In regards to fine-tuning, a user can perform a head-only fine-tuning or use a full fine-tuning strategy. While a full fine-tuning may yield the highest accuracy, its benefits may or may not justify its computational expense. We recommend a three-step framework to determine the optimal fine-tuning strategy for a specific use case and budget.

1. **Empirical Benchmarking:** Organizations should conduct a series of controlled experiments to quantify the performance of each adaptation strategy on a representative validation set. This involves comparing the relevant performance metric (e.g., accuracy for image classification, mean intersection-over-union for image segmentation, F1 or mean average precision for object detection) for head-only fine-tuning and full fine-tuning strategies, *while also measuring the computational resources (e.g., GPU- and CPU-hours) required for each strategy.* These experiments, ideally run in a cloud environment to explore various hardware configurations, establish an empirical performance-versus-cost curve (Fig. 3, left).
2. **Breakeven Point Calculation:** The analysis must account for both the *up-front* cost of fine-tuning and the *recurring* cost of inference. Organizations should select their preferred fine-tuning strategy from step 1 (that which produced a model with sufficiently high performance from acceptable computational resources) and then run a second series of experiments to determine the additional computational resources needed to perform inferencing on multiple images at different scales (e.g., 100 images, 1,000 images, 10,000 images). With this information, organizations can then calculate the *"breakeven point", the number of images for which the cumulative cost of inferencing surpasses the up-front cost of fine-tuning the model* (Fig. 3, right). This step establishes the return on investment for fine-tuning, which is valuable data for the next time fine-tuning is required.
   Furthermore, when calculating this breakeven point, organizations should also consider the up-front costs of preparing for the fine-tuning job, in addition to the costs of running the fine-tuning job itself. These additional costs would then be included in the up-front costs of Fig. 3 (right), such as the costs for collecting the training, validation, and test data; curating, labeling, and balancing those datasets; and employing or contracting for the deeper Machine Learning (ML) expertise needed for fine-tuning a transformer-based model.

3. **Strategic Resource Allocation:** The previous two steps provide the data needed for strategic decision-making. The up-front cost of fine-tuning may align with the organization's capital expenditures (CapEx), while the recurring costs of inference may align with operational expenditures (OpEx). This data can also facilitate partnership discussions with cloud service providers, who may be willing to provide support for the infrequent fine-tuning phases in anticipation of longer-term inference workloads.

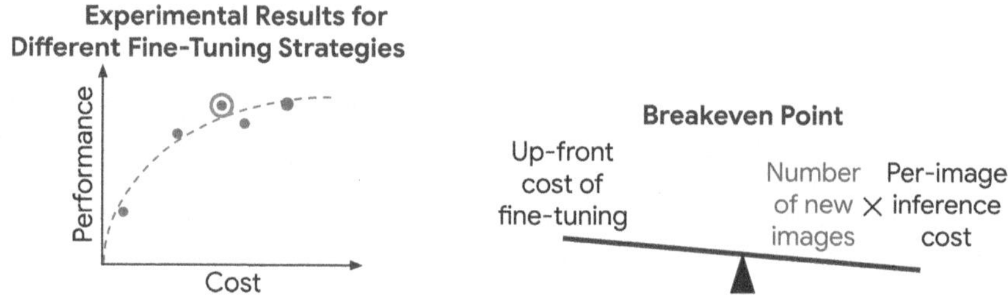

Fig. 3. Conceptual illustrations for performance-cost analyses. (Left:) A notional curve showing the trade-off between model performance and cost for different fine-tuning strategies. (Right:) A conceptual diagram of the breakeven point, where the up-front, fixed cost of fine-tuning is surpassed by the recurring, variable costs of inference over many images.

4.3 The Broader MLOps Ecosystem

A GeoFM is not a complete solution, but rather a single, powerful component within a larger, human-driven operational system. Beyond the model adaptation strategy, a successful GeoFM deployment requires a multi-disciplinary team to manage the end-to-end MLOps lifecycle. Using the post-hurricane damage assessment scenario as an illustrative case, the key roles include:

- **User Experience (UX) Scientists**, who elicit requirements from stakeholders. They would refine the problem definition beyond simply "finding damaged buildings" to identifying more specific, critical needs, such as "detecting impassable roads due to large-scale debris." They would also determine the operational cadence and latency requirements needed to support downstream operations.
- **Data Scientists**, who perform data curation and oversee its labeling. They would create the small, labeled dataset needed for fine-tuning, overseeing the annotation of images not just for "undamaged buildings", "mildly damaged buildings", and "heavily damaged buildings", but also for "road-blocking debris", all while ensuring dataset quality and balance.

- **ML Scientists**, who select and implement the optimal adaptation strategy. This could involve fine-tuning the GeoFM on the new, labeled dataset. For vision-language GeoFMs, this could also involve evaluating the zero-shot or few-shot performance of different prompts. They might also apply post-training optimization techniques, such as quantization, to compress the model for deployment on resource-constrained edge devices.
- **Deployment Engineers**, who are responsible for model serving and long-term model maintenance. Their mandate is often to deploy to specific computing environments, requiring models optimized to specific hardware. They would serve the finalized model via a scalable API and implement robust monitoring for data and concept drift, which could trigger a re-fine-tuning workflow or a re-prompting analysis, if the model's performance degrades over time.

4.4 Limitations and Open Research Challenges

While the GeoFM paradigm is powerful, it is not a panacea. Several significant challenges must be addressed to realize the full potential of these models.

- **Data Bias and Representation:** A fundamental concern is the potential for bias in the massive pre-training datasets. Unchecked, these datasets may have significant geographical imbalances (e.g., over-representation of North American and European landscapes) or seasonal biases, which can lead to performance disparities and reduced generalization capability when the models are applied to underrepresented regions or conditions.
- **Computational Accessibility:** The immense computational cost of pre-training a GeoFM is a primary barrier, largely concentrating foundation model development within large industrial labs. While the "separation of duties" paradigm mitigates this, the cost of large-scale inference remains substantial, posing a hurdle for academic labs and non-profit organizations without access to large-scale GPU resources.
- **Principled Uncertainty Quantification:** For high-stakes applications like disaster response, a model's prediction is insufficient without a reliable estimate of its uncertainty. Developing methods that can produce calibrated, spatially-explicit uncertainty maps is critical for building user trust and enabling decision-makers to know what the model does not know.
- **Interpretability and Explainability:** The black-box nature of these models remains a significant barrier to adoption in critical domains. Further research is needed into methods that can explain why a model made a particular decision (e.g., classifying a detected building as mildly damaged). This information is essential for debugging, validating model reasoning against domain experts, and ensuring trustworthy deployments.

5 The Future: Agentic Geospatial Reasoning

The ultimate trajectory for GeoFMs lies beyond performing discrete tasks and towards enabling holistic Geospatial Reasoning [4,20]. This vision involves using a highly capable, multi-modal LLM, such as one from the Gemini, GPT, Claude, or other LLM families, as an intelligent orchestrator that leverages a suite of tools, including GeoFMs, to solve complex problems posed in natural language.

In this paradigm, an LLM agentic system can *reason* about a high-level user request, *decompose* it into a logical sequence of steps, and *autonomously execute* the plan by invoking the appropriate data sources and software tools. Returning to the post-hurricane scenario, a disaster response manager could issue a simple natural language prompt: "Find me the neighborhoods most damaged by the recent hurricane." An agentic system [20] could reason about this request and then define and execute a multi-step workflow:

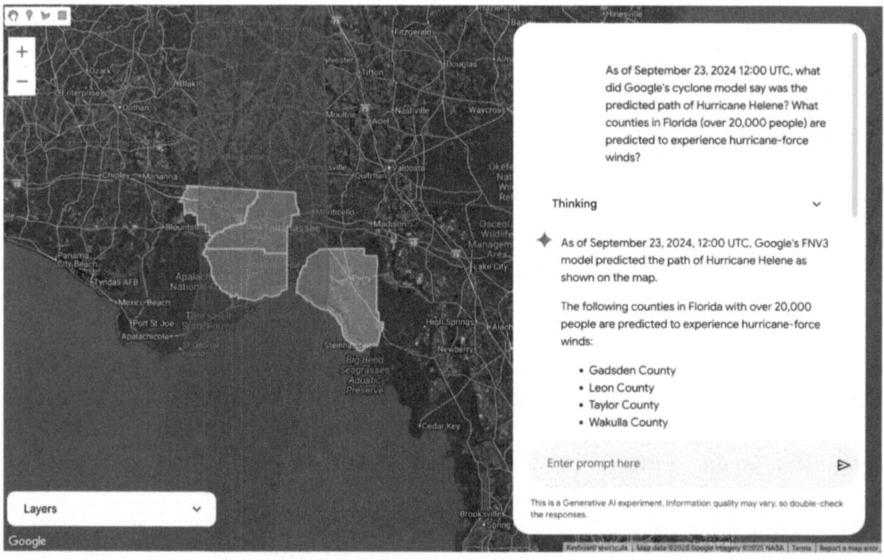

Fig. 4. A conceptual user interface for an agentic geospatial reasoning system. A user tasks the system via a natural language text prompt. The system then orchestrates the use of datasets and tools, including GeoFMs, to generate an analytical output. The user can then follow up with additional prompts in natural language [4].

1. **Situational Awareness:** The LLM would first consult weather models and map data to identify the hurricane's landfall zone and define a geographic region of interest (Fig. 4).
2. **Data Retrieval:** The LLM would then write and send a query to an imagery archive for recent, post-hurricane satellite imagery covering that specific region.

3. **Tool Invocation:** The LLM would select the appropriate tool, such as a vision-language GeoFM, and use it to perform batch inference on the retrieved imagery, performing zero-shot object detection for "buildings".
4. **Semantic Enrichment:** For each detected building, a subsequent model or the LLM itself would assign a damage score (none, low, medium, high damage).
5. **Synthesis and Reporting:** Finally, the LLM would aggregate the damaged building counts by census tract, sort the tracts from most to least damaged, and provide a final, actionable summary to the user.

Geospatial Reasoning represents a paradigm shift from straightforward image perception to complex geospatial cognition, where the analytical power of GeoFMs is made accessible and composable through natural language.

6 Conclusion

GeoFMs represent a fundamental change in the field of applied imagery and pattern recognition (AIPR). By separating the immense cost of pre-training from the downstream, domain-specific process of fine-tuning or prompting, they democratize access to state-of-the-art AI/ML. To advance the state-of-the-art even further, this paper issues a call to action for the AIPR community on two key fronts:

1. **Develop Truly Foundational Models:** The ultimate goal is a single, universal model that is invariant to image modality (e.g., EO, IR, LiDAR, and the especially challenging physics of SAR), size, resolution, off-nadir angle, geography, season, and time of day. ML scientists must explore novel architectures and pre-training recipes to create embeddings so robust that they can be adapted for any downstream task with a simple, lightweight head that can be fine-tuned on commodity hardware. One potential path is the development of modality-agnostic encoders with learned positional priors, where dedicated "modality towers" learn to translate diverse sensor data into a common latent space before processing by a shared backbone.
2. **Establish Governing Principles for Agentic Reasoning:** As LLMs begin to orchestrate complex analytical workflows, each automated decision can introduce bias and error. We urge human-machine teaming experts to develop governing frameworks for these systems based on a set of core principles. These principles align with the established academic framework of Meaningful Human Control, which requires systems to track human intentions and be traceable to a responsible human agent [22]:
   - **Verifiability:** Every output must be accompanied by a transparent, auditable log of the data sources, tools, and intermediate results used.
   - **Graded Authority:** A framework must define which decisions can be automated versus which require a human in the loop.
   - **Criticality Interlocks:** For critical applications, the system must be defined with "interlocks" that prevent action from being taken based on the AI's outputs until a human explicitly confirms the findings.

By tackling these challenges, we can collectively accelerate the transition of these powerful models from research to real-world impact. Ultimately, the vision for agentic geospatial reasoning extends beyond operational decision-making into the realm of scientific discovery. An agentic system, capable of autonomously querying data, running models, and synthesizing results, becomes a new kind of scientific instrument to test complex hypotheses about our planet at a scale previously unimaginable. By framing these systems as cognitive partners in the scientific process, we can accelerate our understanding of the earth and our impact on it.

Acknowledgements. We thank Genady Beryozkin, Nadav Sherman, George Leifman, Tomer Shekel, and Alex Ottenwess in Google Research and Paul Rivera, Zahra Navidi, and Sam Rooney in Google Cloud for their insightful discussions and invaluable feedback. We also thank David Menasche and Kel Markert in Google Public Sector for their example workflows in geospatial reasoning with open-vocabulary object detection.

References

1. AICIP: Cross-scale-Mae. https://github.com/aicip/Cross-Scale-MAE. Accessed 12-11-2025
2. Bair-climate-initiative: scale-Mae. https://github.com/bair-climate-initiative/scale-mae. Accessed 12-11-2025
3. Barzilai, A., et al.: A recipe for improving remote sensing VLM zero shot generalization. In: Proceedings of the ICLR Workshop on Machine Learning for Remote Sensing (ML4RS) (2025). https://doi.org/10.48550/arXiv.2503.08722
4. Bell, A., et al.: Earth AI: unlocking geospatial insights with foundation models and cross-modal reasoning (2025). https://doi.org/10.48550/arXiv.2510.18318
5. Brown, C.F., et al.: Alphaearth foundations: an embedding field model for accurate and efficient global mapping from sparse label data (2025). https://doi.org/10.48550/arXiv.2507.22291
6. Clay foundation: Clay foundation model. https://clay-foundation.github.io/model/index.html. Accessed 12-11-2025
7. Cong, Y., et al.: Satmae: pre-training transformers for temporal and multi-spectral satellite imagery. In: 36th Conference on Neural Information Processing Systems (NeurIPS 2022). vol. 35 (2022). https://doi.org/10.48550/arXiv.2207.08051
8. Dosovitskiy, A., et al.: An image is worth 16x16 words: transformers for image recognition at scale. In: International Conference on Learning Representations (2021). https://doi.org/10.48550/arXiv.2010.11929
9. Facebook research: dinov3. https://github.com/facebookresearch/dinov3. Accessed 12-11-2025
10. Google and Google DeepMind: Google Satellite Embedding Dataset V1 (AlphaEarth Foundations). Google Earth Engine Data Catalog (2025). https://developers.google.com/earth-engine/datasets/catalog/GOOGLE_SATELLITE_EMBEDDING_V1_ANNUAL. Dataset available from 2017 to 2024

11. He, K., Chen, X., Xie, S., Li, Y., Dollár, P., Girshick, R.: Masked autoencoders are scalable vision learners. In: 2022 IEEE/CVF Conference on Computer Vision and Pattern Recognition (CVPR), pp. 15979–15988 (2022). https://doi.org/10.1109/CVPR52688.2022.01553
12. Hu, E.J., et al.: Lora: low-rank adaptation of large language models. In: International Conference on Learning Representations (ICLR) (2022). https://doi.org/10.48550/arXiv.2106.09685
13. IBM-Nasa-geospatial: Prithvi-EO-2.0-300m-TL. https://huggingface.co/ibm-nasa-geospatial/Prithvi-EO-2.0-300M-TL. Accessed 12-11-2025
14. Lee, J., et al.: Assessing post-disaster damage from satellite imagery using semi-supervised learning techniques (2020). https://doi.org/10.48550/arXiv.2011.14004
15. Linial, O., et al.: Enhancing remote sensing representations through mixed-modality masked autoencoding. In: Proceedings of the Winter Conference on Applications of Computer Vision (WACV) Workshops. pp. 507–516. CVF Open Access (2025). https://openaccess.thecvf.com/content/WACV2025W/GeoCV/papers/Linial_Enhancing_Remote_Sensing_Representations_Through_Mixed-Modality_Masked_Autoencoding_WACVW_2025_paper.pdf
16. NASA-IMPACT: Prithvi-EO-2.0. https://github.com/NASA-IMPACT/Prithvi-EO-2.0. Accessed 12-11-2025
17. Radford, A., et al.: Learning transferable visual models from natural language supervision. In: Meila, M., Zhang, T., (eds.) Proceedings of the 38th International Conference on Machine Learning. Proceedings of Machine Learning Research, vol. 139, pp. 8748–8763. PMLR (2021). https://doi.org/10.48550/arXiv.2103.00020
18. Reed, C.J., et al.: Scale-Mae: a scale-aware masked autoencoder for multiscale geospatial representation learning. In: 2023 IEEE/CVF International Conference on Computer Vision (ICCV), pp. 4065–4076 (2023). https://doi.org/10.1109/ICCV51070.2023.00378
19. Refael, Y., et al.: On-the-fly OVD adaptation with flame: Few-shot localization via active marginal-samples exploration (2025). https://doi.org/10.48550/arXiv.2510.17670
20. Schottlander, D., Shekel, T.: Geospatial reasoning: unlocking insights with generative ai and multiple foundation models (2025). https://goo.gle/geospatial-reasoning-blog
21. Siméoni, O., et al.: Dinov3 (2025). https://doi.org/10.48550/arXiv.2508.10104
22. Santoni de Sio, F., Van den Hoven, J.: Meaningful human control over autonomous systems: a philosophical account. Front. Rob. AI **5**, 15 (2018). https://doi.org/10.3389/frobt.2018.00015
23. Sustainlab-group: Satmae. https://github.com/sustainlab-group/SatMAE. Accessed 12-11-2025
24. Szwarcman, D., et al.: Prithvi-EO-2.0: A versatile multi-temporal foundation model for earth observation applications (2025). https://doi.org/10.48550/arXiv.2412.02732
25. Tang, M., Cozma, A., Georgiou, K., Qi, H.: Cross-scale Mae: a tale of multi-scale exploitation in remote sensing. In: 37th Conference on Neural Information Processing Systems (NeurIPS). vol. 36 (2023). https://doi.org/10.48550/arXiv.2401.15855
26. Zhai, X., Mustafa, B., Kolesnikov, A., Beyer, L.: Sigmoid loss for language image pre-training. In: 2023 IEEE/CVF International Conference on Computer Vision (ICCV), pp. 11941–11952 (2023). https://doi.org/10.1109/ICCV51070.2023.01100

Can AI Generated Items Be Trusted?

Paul S. Cerkez(✉)

Coastal Carolina University, Conway, SC, USA
pcerkez@coastal.edu

Abstract. "AI" (primarily generative AI - GenAI) has been receiving a significant amount of hype since the introduction of ChatGPT (and even more now that ChatGPT-5 has been released). ALL GenAI products are based on Large Language Models (LLM) developed from both good and bad data. This paper discusses some of the failures of "AI" in the domain of image generation and the ongoing effort of detecting "AI" generated images, videos, text, and voice recordings.

Keywords: AI · AI generated Text · AI Generated Art · AI Detection

1 Introduction

1.1 If it was Really AI Generated, can it be Detected?

"The thing about [the current concept of] AI is it's not really artificial intelligence," said Matthew Butterick[1]… "It's human intelligence which has been harvested from one place, divorced from its creators, then this big tech company [Open AI] puts a price tag on it and sells it to someone else." [1] [isn't that Plagiarism?]

"AI detectors are just a scam to make money off the AI hype. They don't actually work.

It's not really possible to determine whether a text is AI-generated or not. Both AI and humans use the same language, words, letters, and grammar rules to express ideas. In fact, AI language models are trained on human writing; they haven't come up with anything original. They simply write in the style of the human texts they were trained on.

Therefore, it's impossible to detect with any real certainty whether something was written by a human or an AI. Some of these tools have even flagged parts of the Bible and the Declaration of Independence as AI-written." [2]

1.2 The Double-Edged Sword of AI Detection

Text
While AI detectors claim to maintain content (key word!) integrity, they also present some issues.

[1] A copyright Lawyer in California. He's on a mission to make sure writers, artists, and other creative people have control over how their work is used by AI.

F. Tanner and J. Irvine (Eds.): AIPR 2025, LNCS 16446, pp. 18–23, 2026.
https://doi.org/10.1007/978-3-032-18474-0_2

First, no AI detector is 100% accurate. False positives can unfairly flag human-written content as AI-generated, potentially harming writers and content creators.

Second, language models become harder to detect as they improve, making current detection methods obsolete.

Finally, using AI detectors raises questions about privacy, trust, and the future of creative expression. How much AI use should people be required to disclose (if any)?

People must remember that AI-generated text is specifically meant to *mimic* human writing. The more academic or formal, the more likely it will trigger an AI detector. The more 'boring' the text, the more likely it will be flagged as AI-generated. Inconsistencies, nonsensical sentences, made up words, bland (no variation in voice or tone), no personalization, excessive use of buzzwords are a few of the indicators. Consider that the AI's LLM has been built from ingesting hundreds of years of human writing, good and bad. One of the big giveaways is so called perfect grammar. But, what about the person where that is their normal writing style, technically perfect but overall boring or the person who is not a native English language writer/speaker (think ESL – [English as a Second Language] – typically perfect grammar but no 'personality')?

1.3 Images/Art.

Images and artwork are sometimes more difficult to detect but, at the same time, AI-generated images and art can sometimes be really easy to detect as the AI is prone to making mistakes.

As with AI-generated text, one of the first things a person should look for is inconsistencies. In images, look for extra fingers, extra teeth, extra eye, deformed body parts (e.g., twisted skin on fingers), or body parts at unnatural angles (e.g., handshakes that are at impossible or unnatural angles.) Missing body parts can also be a red flag [3–5]. In one image this author saw, the person's hand was not even connected to their body.

Another thing to watch for is in the area of distortions. Warped backgrounds and unrealistic lighting are but 2.

In the image, the fish looks like it was enlarged and or added to the photo (photoshopped?). Look at the left hand and compare its size with the young lady it belongs to. Look at the right hand. The overall lighting seems wrong and the whole image has an overall JDLR (Just Doesn't Look Right) feel to it. The foreground (the fish) and the background (everything else) seem to look like they are not the same, not from the same source, not a homogenous image. The lighting seems different between the fish and the girl background [6].

1.4 AI Generated Videos

Currently, the most prominent tool for creating AI generated videos is OpenAI's Sora. There are others. OpenAI even has a detector that does really well on videos produced with Sora, but detection drops off when they are generated by other tools.

As with AI text and images/art, there are more than a few similarities. Background issues (distortions, image 'noise,' etc.), flickering, inconsistencies with colors, lighting and shadows, unrealistic movements, background noise not appropriate to the scene (i.e., city traffic noises in a country setting), images disappearing and re-appearing in the wrong place.

Other than the obvious clues listed above, one method of detecting AI generated videos is slowing the frame rate down. The human brain processes images and video at about 100Mhz. The human eye doesn't function like a camera capturing still frames at a fixed rate, it processes in a continuous stream (100Mhz). The average for human *perception of apparent motion* is approximately 10fps (frames per second.) The average video normally plays at 24 fps. Each frame is an individual image. At half that speed, some things become more visibly apparent. Simply, the slower the frame rate, the more easily detectable an AI-generated video might be.

When used to influence viewers, the videos are typically referred to as deepfakes. However, while "deepfake" is typically associated with fake videos, the term is not limited to videos. In general, a deepfake is defined by Wikipedia as: "Deepfakes are images, videos, or audio that have been edited or generated using artificial intelligence, AI-based tools or AV editing software" [7]

1.5 Summary of Introduction

While the above can reveal some key indicators of AI-generated content, a person's best source may be their instinct. It is frequently referred to as JDLR. It can be hard to define, but our human intuition and first reactions to whether content was created by a human or AI is often correct.

WellSaid Labs offers a listing of recommendation for detecting fakes, similar to what is presented in this paper [8].

There are some AI generators that are really good, others not so much. Some are capable of producing very realistic looking images and videos, others "choke." Google "bad AI generated images" or "bad AI generated videos" (or go to YouTube). The range in 'realism' extends over a very wide spectrum.

2 Discussion

2.1 Detecting AI Generated Text

A Sampling of some AI Text Detectors

When ChatGPT was first released, the go to tool for detecting AI generated text was GPTZero. It was advertised as the ChatGPT killer. Another was ZeroGPT. It was a constant battle about which was the best.

Into the fray came a host of other detectors, with some boasting guarantees they could detect AI-generated text. Basically, it was AI fighting AI. Recently, a new group of tools started appearing: "bypass detectors." In simple terms, these newest batch of tools will 'read' your AI-generated text and make recommendations that will allow the text to bypass all detectors. Again, AI fighting AI. The interesting thing is that as the AI-generators get better, so too do the detectors and bypass detectors. They are trained the same way. One tool recently on Facebook stated it makes LLM/GPT generated text "read" like a human wrote it, but additional research showed it does not fix the issue with fabricated references or citations. Fabricated references and citations are a huge downside of many GPTs. It is also interesting that 2 days after the initial image was posted on Facebook, it was replaced with a second one. The second one is more 'humanized' but was the female in the image AI-generated? (She looks a lot like the one that was in a TV commercial on American hunger that states explicitly that 'she' is AI-generated.)

A Sampling of some AI Image Detectors.

In the "images" realm, detecting AI-generated ones is more often than not a visual examination of the image. However, there are some products capitalizing on this market and creating tools that detect AI-generated images even when a human cannot. One parameter that many ignore when choosing an AI image tool is what are you trying to detect? Are you trying to detect objects that might be in your way in a self-driving car and you need to make adjustments, or do you have an image that you are trying to determine if it is real or an AI fake? Also, what is the detection tool's main focus: AI-text or AI-generated images?

One tool, from *sightengine,* with claims of detecting and classifying images from 7 different AI image generating tools, even with the advances incorporated into the tools, does it? One thing they do, knowing that humans are very good at detecting fakes, is to have humans doing tests with both real and generated images and reporting on the outcome. Thus, they can "prove" their tool's value to customers.

However, according to ddiy.co, 8 tools were ranked in order of best first and *sightengine* is not listed:

- BrandWell (formerly Content at Scale) – Best for general AI image detection using advanced algorithms to detect AI-generated images
- AI Or Not – Best for quick authentication of images, videos, and voice
- Illuminarty – Best for comprehensive analysis of AI-generated images and text
- Huggingface – Best for easy accessibility and basic detection
- Foto Forensics – Best for detailed analysis using Error Level Analysis
- V7 Deepfake Detector – Best for detecting StyleGAN deep fake images
- Fake Image Detector – Best for detecting manipulated/altered/edited images
- Forensically Beta – Best for detailed examination with various analysis tools

The above list is primarily for detecting real or fake. For self-driving cars and similar applications, the list is much longer and more targeted to the environment it is in. This later group is more about object detection (people, other vehicles, obstructions, etc.) as opposed to determining the classification of real or fake.

One of the biggest issues with detecting AI images is that almost all the detectors available detect text content not image content. Can AI generated images be detected? Yes, but it is a more human focused activity. Also, detecting (and labeling) image content is still a very human centric endeavor (detecting) and very subjective (labeling).

A Sampling of some AI Generated Video Detectors

There are a number of tools that advertise that they can detect AI generated videos. However, this is a 'new' variation on detectors. The biggest problem is the detector system will need to process all the frames and identify the inconsistencies on and between the frames.

3 It's Not all Text or Images

3.1 AI Generated Video

One of the biggest tells is does the contents of the video actually follow the laws of physics? Many do not at some point or another. Does an object's 'state' change when there is an obvious reason (i.e., taking a bite out of an apple)?

An example of one video (submitted by the "Defense") that was determined to be a fake was one generated to show an individual was not involved in a drive-by shooting in a federal prosecution court case. The presiding Judge ruled that the prosecutors were given 24 h to examine the footage. At real time speed (24 fps), everything looked correct. However, it was a JDLR to investigators, little inconsistencies were noted that caused investigators to want to 'dig deeper' into the contents. They trusted their instincts. As they slow down the frame rate, the car was shown to be 'generated' and not real (lack of reflections on it and on surrounding reflective surfaces, disappearing/re-appearing, etc.). The 'suspect' was shown standing on the opposite side of the street, not shooting but was not in every frame. In fact, in some frames, parts of the car were completely missing only to re-appear in the next frame, same with the suspect. The video was barred from evidence, and the Defense changed their plea status to guilty [9]. During that last Super Bowl (LVIX), AI-generated commercials were used to promote products that were to help 'disadvantaged' or handicapped individuals. One image from a commercial to advertise a camera that helps "blind" people take better pictures. However, ignoring the 'blind' eye, there are other inconsistencies: 'bags" under each eye are different and the right eye is not even with the left eye (looks 'higher' and angled different). Was the image AI-generated?

There is a video available showing an off-duty cop saving a man who fell between a subway car and the platofrm [10]. One version of the video is actually an "AI-doctored' version of the real video that depicts an actual incident in Mumbai in 2024. In the original video, the woman in the white jacket in the foreground does not exist, nor do some others in the doctored video [11]. If one looks at the original and the AI-doctored versions, the differences are very obvious.

3.2 AI Generated Voice

In the past few months, there has been a plethora of announcements on social media about voice cloning tools. Some advertise creating exact copies and are not distinguishable from the actual person said to be speaking. However, if one listens carefully, there will typically be little inconsistencies in the duplicate, especially if the clone was created from a text prompt. Long sentences 'spoken' without a break or pause, odd breaks in the speech, mispronounced words, lack of "background" noise, "hollow" sounding, correctly spoken words but in the wrong context (one I've heard a lot, notably on TV, is the wrong pronunciation for *bow* in the context it is being used in. *Bow*, as in bow and arrow, or *bow*, as in the front of a boat or ship. This is referred to as a Heteronym; spelled the same but pronounced differently and with a different meaning, both based on context. Other examples are *lead* (the metal) and *lead* (a leash), *read* (past tense of reading) and *read* (a plant, or present/future tense of reading) [12])

4 Summary

Is what you are seeing truly reality or is it something generated from an "AI." A simple Google search on "bad AI generated video" or "bad AI generated images" will reveal a plethora of bad images and videos. The key to making a determination is to look for the 'inconsistencies' in them. Inconsistencies are almost a 100% indicator of a fake or modified image/video.

The same is true of AI-generated text, there is almost always some giveaway that a human reader can pick up on that a detector will miss. Humans, especially those who do a lot of reading, can typically experience a JDLR moment, if not a full on "This is AI."

AI-generated voice also can have some giveaways, but the 'listener' needs to carefully listen for them.

[13] includes images from a website showing how easy (or difficult) it can be to find the differences between two images. Lack of attention to detail by the viewer sometimes inhibits finding the differences. The same is true of AI-generated artifacts, there is almost always some 'giveaway', the human just needs to detect it.

YouTube has several videos on creating images via AI for the spot-the-difference game. Also, a simple search on Google will reveal many such images.

As stated earlier: trust your gut, your instincts.

Disclosure of Interests. The author has no competing interests.

References

1. M. Zeff: "OpenAI is swallowing up news content from publishers who want some ChatGPT love." [Online]. Available: https://qz.com/openai-chatgpt-news-content-licensing-financial-times-1851444088
2. R. Skog: in *Can-the-AI-Detector-be-trusted* vol. 2025, ed. Quora.com, 2025, p. Blog post responding to AI detectors.
3. M. Zim: "Party Girls," vol. 674x482, G. a. a. party.jpg, Ed., ed. New York: New York Post, (2023), p. Fake picture of girls at a party.
4. M. Zim: "Too many fingers," vol. 732x464, T. m. fingers.jpg, Ed., ed. New York: New York Post, 2023, p. AI Generated fake.
5. B. Panda: "No Hands," in *BadPanda* vol. 953x905, N. Hands, Ed., ed: Bad Panda, (2025), p. AI generated Photo.
6. A. L. McGill: "First Striper," in *Facebook* vol. 1440 x 1800, F. Striper.jpg, Ed., ed, (2025).
7. Wikipedia. "Deepfake." Wikipedia. (accessed 7/1/2025,).
8. W. Team. "8 warning Signs of a Deep Fake." WellSaid Labs, inc. (accessed 1/2/2025,) (2025).
9. M. Levy: "the good and bad of technolgy," T. Author, Ed., A conversation ed, (2023).
10. Eliza: "Viral Video Shows Hero Cop Saving Passenger Stuck Between Train and Platform — Millions Praise his Bravery," ed. Mumbai, (2025), p. video.
11. M. police, "Original Video of police officer saving man on subway platform," ed. instagram, (2024), p. original video of cop saving man on subway platform.
12. W. contributors. "Heteronym (linguistics)." Wikipedia, The Free Encyclopedia. https://en.wikipedia.org/w/index.php?title=Heteronym_(linguistics)&oldid=1316688300 (accessed 11/3/2025,) (2025).
13. T. Saunders: "Spot the Difference Picture and Travel game." Travel and Leisuire. https://www.travelandleisure.com/travel-tips/offbeat/spot-the-difference-travel-game (accessed 11/3/2025,) (2025).

Synthetic to Street: Generative AI–Powered Object Detection of License-Plate Jackets

John Munoz(✉), Tom Bukowski, and Mike Busch

Regis University, Denver, CO, USA
{jmunoz004,tbukowski,mbusch}@regis.edu

Abstract. In 2025, Lima, Peru, enacted legislation mandating that all motorcyclists wear certified helmets and reflective vests displaying their license plate number in response to increased armed robberies by criminal gangs. This study develops a YOLOv8 object-detection system using real-world data and synthetic video data generated with Google's Veo 2 and Veo 3 models to identify compliance with this new law. Manually recording missing vests or reading license plates in real-world traffic footage is both costly and time-consuming. We hypothesize that a computer vision object detection model can operate in real-time at traffic lights to automatically notify authorities of non-compliant riders. We synthesized short clips of virtual riders under various lighting conditions, camera angles, weather conditions, and urban backdrops depicting both compliant and non-compliant scenarios. We strengthened our detection system using image-to-video prompting to generate more diverse and realistic synthetic training data. These approaches enabled us to train and evaluate three YOLOv8 models using different data strategies to assess how synthetic data quality and diversity affect detection accuracy for real-world deployment.

1 Introduction

On April 20, 2025, Peru enacted Resolución Directoral N.° 008-2025-MTC/18 mandating the use of certified helmets and reflective vests for motorcycle operators and passengers [1]. However, on June 20, 2025, Peru issued Resolución Directoral N.° 0012-2025-MTC/18, which superseded the earlier rule. This new regulation maintained the nationwide requirement for certified safety helmets but limited the reflective-vest requirements to zones under an emergency order [2].

Initial enforcement of these regulations relied on manual roadside inspections and routine policing. This approach required significant human resources and lacked scalability for nationwide coverage, while providing limited data collection capabilities for evaluating policy effectiveness—a limitation that became particularly evident when the vest mandate was reversed after only a couple of months without comprehensive compliance data. This paper was motivated by the question of whether computer vision could automatically detect helmet and vest compliance and facilitate the identification of license plate numbers on vests to aid in post-event investigations when criminal activity occurs. While the vest mandate was ultimately reversed due to public opposition,

F. Tanner and J. Irvine (Eds.): AIPR 2025, LNCS 16446, pp. 24–43, 2026.
https://doi.org/10.1007/978-3-032-18474-0_3

an automated monitoring system could have provided valuable data to assess the policy's effectiveness and support evidence-based decision-making regarding such safety regulations.

For computer vision automated monitoring, we proposed the development of a YOLOv8 object detection model to identify six safety compliance classes organized as three binary pairs: helmets and no helmets, license plates and no plates, and vests and no vests.

Recent research has demonstrated that YOLO object detection models can be used in construction-site safety by accurately detecting PPE-wearing compliance in real-time [3–4]. This can be combined with other research that explored license plate detection and recognition using Optical Character Recognition (OCR), providing a foundation for applying similar methods to vest license number identification [5–6].

While prior studies have used PPE detection in construction sites, obtaining datasets that capture motorcycle riders wearing reflective vests makes data acquisition for these specific use cases both challenging and limited. For scenarios where data is costly, time-consuming, or difficult to obtain, synthetic data—artificially generated images created by AI models rather than captured from real-world scenes—offers a practical solution. Synthetic data enables the creation of large, diverse datasets without manual collection efforts [7–8]. These datasets can be tailored to simulate a wide range of conditions, including various lighting scenarios, weather conditions, rider positions, helmet and vest designs, thereby helping models generalize to real-world scenarios such as individuals riding motorcycles with or without safety equipment.

Due to recent advances in text-to-video generation, we turned to models like Google's Veo 2 and Veo 3, which have shown significant improvements in generating high-quality videos with lifelike resemblance. This paper investigates whether synthetic video data generated through text-to-video and image-to-video prompting can train YOLOv8 models to accurately detect safety compliance across our six target classes.

1.1 Main Contribution

We propose a new approach to creating and augmenting datasets by generating synthetic motorcycle rider videos, extracting random frames, and manually labeling them to form three custom datasets.

These datasets will be used to train three YOLOv8 models, which will be evaluated on real images to compare detection accuracy results.

The three datasets:

1. Frames extracted from synthetic videos generated using text-only prompts
2. Frames extracted from synthetic videos generated using a real-world image in the prompt
3. Real-world images

Different combinations of the datasets will be used to train the three detection models. By analyzing performance across these models, we can assess the extent of how much the synthetic data can compensate for limitations of real-world data. This paper presents an innovative strategy that investigates the use of generative video data to develop custom object detection models, evaluating responses in the development of a safety compliance detection system.

2 Related Works

Synthetic data has been used before in computer vision research to overcome the challenges of acquiring data that is costly, time-consuming, or difficult to collect. Previous studies have demonstrated how video games such as Grand Theft Auto can be used to create large synthetic datasets [8]. To improve the realism of these synthetic frames, researchers have incorporated sensor effects such as blur, noise, and exposure, as well as simulated real-life environmental conditions, including lighting, weather, and time of day. These enhancements increased the generalizability of synthetic data to real-world scenarios [7].

Advances in generative video models have created new opportunities for producing synthetic training data. Generative video models, such as OpenAI's Sora and Google's Veo, represent significant progress over previous methods by directly generating realistic video sequences from text-only descriptions or image-based prompts [9–10]. Video game-based synthetic datasets are limited to pre-programmed characters, vehicles, and settings, whereas generative video models allow specification of any object class or condition within the prompt.

These video generation models have encouraged researchers to explore using video generation for domain-specific applications, such as medicine. Models such as Sora and Veo have been studied for their ability to support medical education, enhancing diagnostic training, and providing synthetic datasets that help address the representation of rare clinical scenarios and balance underrepresented classes in training data [11–12]. Researchers have started applying generative video capabilities to other domains such as transportation. Researchers examined how Veo 3 prompts could be used to generate realistic traffic scenes and objects across 76 cities worldwide, demonstrating the model's ability to provide diverse environments for computer vision training [13].

This paper distinguishes itself by applying generative video creation for traffic safety compliance monitoring. Unlike prior work that focused on medical applications or general transportation scene generation, we investigated whether synthetic video generated from text prompts alone (referred to as "text-to-video"), or text prompts combined with real images as input ("image-to-video"), can be used to train a YOLOv8 object detection model capable of detecting helmets, vests, and license plates. This represents a novel approach to creating synthetic video for public safety enforcement, where annotated data is limited or difficult to obtain—especially in the case of enforcing brand new mandates and laws, where datasets would require either waiting for real-world compliance data to accumulate or creating staged simulations that include sufficient diversity for model accuracy.

3 Material and Methods

Recent advances in artificial intelligence and diffusion-based generative models have led to breakthroughs in the creation of synthetic videos. Modern video generation models have the ability to produce highly realistic and scene-specific details from either textual or image prompts. This has opened opportunities for using generated videos to produce synthetic data that can train computer vision models. In this study, we employed Google's Veo 2 and Veo 3 models as the primary method for generating synthetic data. Both models utilize text-to-video, which leverages the industry-standard diffusion-based model architectures to create video clips. Veo 3 utilizes latent diffusion techniques combined with transformer-based architecture, which allows for improved scalability, temporal coherence, and controllability of generated sequences [14–15]. The latent diffusion approach is useful for simulating scenarios where real-world data collection is limited, costly, or difficult to obtain. In this paper, we prompted Veo models to generate videos across six target classes of interest related to motorcycle rider safety compliance.

To evaluate the impact of synthetic data strategies, we designed and trained three experimental models. Model 1 was trained exclusively on synthetic images generated from Veo text-to-video prompts and tested against real images. Model 2 combined synthetic frames produced by both text-to-video and image-to-video approaches to increase the scene diversity and lifelikeness; note that real images were used as input to generate synthetic videos but were not included in the training dataset itself. Model 3 used a hybrid approach, combining the previous text-to-video and image-to-video datasets with additional real-world images, allowing us to examine the effect of mixing synthetic and real data on our detection model.

To perform the computer vision compliance detection, we used the YOLOv8 (You Only Look Once, version 8) object detection framework. The YOLOv8 model uses a lightweight architecture with an anchor-free detection head, which helps the model localize small and complex objects, such as the reflective vests and helmets [16].

3.1 Data Acquisition

The data from different sources was separated into three distinct datasets.

Dataset 1. Our first dataset consisted of frames extracted from synthetic videos generated using Google's Veo text-to-video platforms. The videos simulated individuals riding motorcycles under varying conditions, including scenarios with and without the required vests and helmets. The prompting process adhered to Google's recommended prompting framework, incorporating subjects, context, action, style, camera motion, composition, and ambiance to ensure consistency and realism in the video outputs [17]. Table 1 shows an example of the text content used for a prompt to generate a video of a motorcyclist wearing a reflective vest, depicting downtown Lima, Peru. In order to generate accurate videos, we used reflective vest specifications directly from the Peruvian law [1].

Videos were created using multiple Google platforms, including Google Gemini video generation interface, Google Labs Flow UI, and the Google GenAI SDK for Python [18–20]. Despite using the same Veo models, there were slight differences in the generated video results between platforms. The differences between generated videos using similar prompts shown in Figs. 1, 2, and 3.

To improve generalization, prompts were designed to cover a wide variety of conditions, including various clothing types (t-shirts, sweaters, and jackets), diverse weather and lighting conditions (daytime and nighttime), and realistic urban scenery. We also attempted to enforce consistent patterns by matching vest numbers with corresponding license plates; however, the model occasionally failed to maintain exact alignment between the vest text and the license plate number—a common limitation of current generative video technology (see Fig. 1 and Fig. 2).

Dataset 2. The text-to-video strategy employed in Dataset 1 often resulted in repeated visual patterns, such as similar camera angles, the same helmet style, similar motorcycles, or nearly identical city backdrops. In order to create greater variety and realism, the second dataset we created used frames extracted from synthetic videos generated using a combination of real-world images and a text prompt. Starting from actual images introduces significantly more diversity in scenes and rider appearances. We were also able to use simple prompts as compared to the detail required in the text-to-video dataset to produce much more variety, as shown in Table 2.

Prompting with photographs provided richer contextual detail and improved scene outputs. Figure 4 presents a real image used as a prompt input, showing a rider parked on the side of the road. Figure 5 shows a frame from the resulting generated video from this image-to-video method, highlighting the improvement in scene realism, generalization, and variety compared to Dataset 1.

Dataset 3. Our last dataset utilized a more traditional approach, as it only contained real-world images. The dataset was further expanded by using common augmentation strategies. Different augmentations were applied randomly, to increase variety. Augmentation strategies used were scaling, brightness, and contrast adjustments. An example of a real world image is included in Fig. 6.

A breakdown of how many frames and images were in each dataset can be reviewed in Table 3.

Table 1. Example of an individual text-to-video prompt

Category	Prompt Description
Subjects	Rider on a motorcycle wearing reflective vest with ID "BZ9872345"; license plate also shows "BZ9872345"; cars, buses, pedestrians.
Context	Downtown Lima, Peru; busy traffic; honking cars, traffic lights, pedestrians, realistic architecture; overcast weather.
Action	Rider weaving through traffic; camera ensures vest ID and license plate are visible.
Style	Cinematic, ultra-photorealistic; indistinguishable from real footage; accurate physics and fine detail.
Camera Motion	Smooth tracking shot following the rider; dynamic weaving captures energy of the scene.
Composition & Ambiance	Clear view of vest ID and license plate; muted city grays, reflections on wet pavement, subtle pops of color.
Audio	Traffic noise, horns, engines, crowd sounds.

Fig. 1. Text-to-video synthetic rider footage generated with Google Veo 3 via Gemini AI.

Fig. 2. Text-to-video synthetic rider footage generated with Google Flow text-to-video.

3.2 Data Labeling

All three datasets were annotated using LabelImg, an open-source image annotation software widely used in computer vision research [21–22]. For every image, bounding boxes were manually drawn around objects corresponding to the six target classes. These annotations were saved in the YOLO text format, which stores each bounding box as a row containing the class label followed by normalized coordinates of the bounding box

Fig. 3. Text-to-video synthetic rider footage generated with Google Gen AI SDK for Python.

Table 2. Synthetic video generation prompt comparison.

Text-to-video prompt	A cinematic, ultra-photorealistic video set in the heart of downtown Lima, Peru, during late morning rush hour. The subject is a Latina woman in her late 20 s, long black hair tucked under a black helmet, riding a modern sport motorcycle through heavy city traffic. She wears a fluorescent blue reflective safety vest, a loose over-garment with wide silver reflective tape across the shoulders and waist. On the center back panel of the vest, the bold white ID "F3821" is printed in high-contrast characters, large and perfectly legible. The motorcycle's rear license plate also reads "F3821", matching exactly. The camera starts in a medium rear tracking shot, capturing both vest text and license plate clearly. The rider weaves between taxis, buses, and colectivos. The camera then zooms closer, holding both the vest ID and the license plate centered, sharp, and crystal-clear for several seconds. Traffic is realistic: Peru right-hand flow, cars in the rider's lane move forward naturally, brake lights flash, buses stop at curbs, pedestrians cross marked crosswalks. Oncoming traffic stays in opposite lanes. Lighting is overcast daylight, making the fluorescent vest pop visually while reflective tape catches glints from car headlights. The plate text "F3821" shines clearly. Surroundings: vendors with carts, concrete apartment blocks, traffic lights cycling, pedestrians rushing. Ambient audio: engine hum, bus gears grinding, horns, muffled Spanish voices. This must look indistinguishable from authentic documentary footage.
Image-to-video prompt	show this person riding his motorcycle down the coast

Fig. 4. Starting image for image-to-video prompt (source: Pixabay, https://pixabay.com/photos/motorcycle-man-helmet-vintage-fast-5800125/, accessed Sep. 3, 2025).

Fig. 5. Veo results from image-to-video prompt.

center (x,y) along with the width and height relative to the image dimensions. Fig. 7 shows an example of the annotation process using LabelImg.

Fig. 6. Real-world image example (source: Pexels, photo by Emma Photography, https://www.pexels.com/photo/a-man-on-a-motorcycle-27731041/, accessed Sep. 6, 2025).

Table 3. Dataset breakdown

	No. Synthetic Videos	Total Frames Extracted	Real Images	Augmentation	Final Dataset Size
Dataset 1	148	2220	0	0	2220
Dataset 2	100	1000	0	0	1000
Dataset 3	0	0	619	397	1016

Fig. 7. LabelImg example of labeling a motorcyclist (source: Pixabay, https://pixabay.com/photos/scooter-ride-helmet-security-4300871/, accessed Sep. 6, 2025).

4 Model Training and Evaluation

Each model utilizes the YOLOv8 large (YOLOv8l) architecture as the initial framework. This architecture was chosen to leverage transfer learning of the pre-trained weights from the Common Objects in Context (COCO) dataset.

The training dataset for each model was constructed with different combinations of the synthetic and real image datasets, as detailed in Table 4. These sets included diverse examples such as motorcyclists wearing reflective vests, riders without vests, helmets of varying types, motorcycles with and without license plates, and riders not wearing helmets. Model 1 was trained using only the frames extracted from the synthetic videos generated using text-only prompts in Dataset 1. Model 2 expanded the text-to-video Dataset 1 by also incorporating synthetic videos generated using real-world images as prompt inputs in Dataset 2. Model 3 combined the synthetic datasets generated through text-to-video and image-to-video with a collection of real-world images.

During the training phase, we used 50 epochs for Models 1 and Model 2, while Model 3 was trained for 100 epochs due to the large size of the dataset. Each model used a common validation dataset that consisted of 540 real (non-generated) images spanning all six classes.

Although efforts were made to extract instances of each of the six classes evenly, the resulting datasets were not perfectly balanced. This imbalance occurred because not every video frame contained all target classes, and the random frame extraction process naturally resulted in varying class frequencies. These differences can be seen in Fig. 8, which shows the class counts for Models 1 through 3. For example, Model 3 shows that the no-plates class contained only 791 instances, making it the most underrepresented category, compared to no-vest with 3,171 instances, or helmet class with 2,607 instances.

Table 4. Training data source-type included per model

	Dataset 1 (Text-to-Video)	Dataset 2 (Image-to-Video)	Dataset 3 (Real-world Images)
Model 1	✔		
Model 2	✔	✔	
Model 3	✔	✔	✔

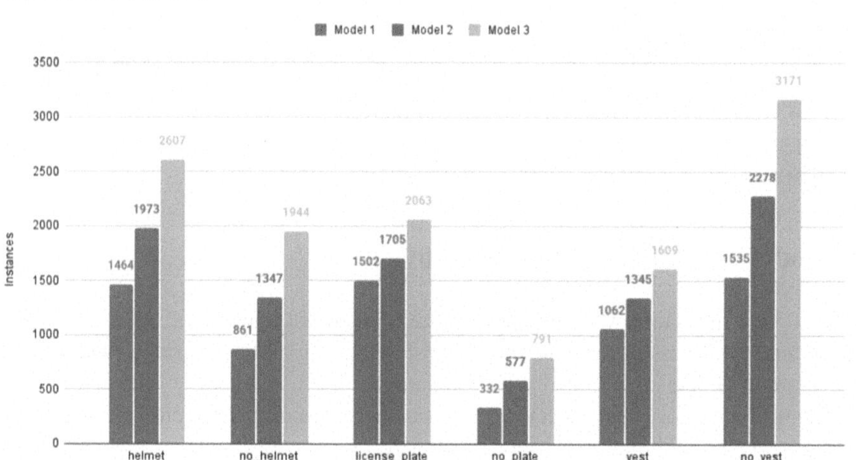

Fig. 8. Class Count Distributions across Models

4.1 Model Evaluation

For evaluation metrics, we used Precision (P), which is used to determine the accuracy of detected objects, and Recall (R), which assesses the model's ability to identify all possible objects in the images [23]. For performance metrics, we used mAP 50, the mean average precision, which calculates the Intersection over Union (IoU) using a baseline of 0.50 to measure our model's accuracy. We also used mAP 50–95, which is a more stringent version of mAP 50, as it uses varying IoU thresholds ranging from 0.50 to 0.95 [23]. To test our models, we used a testing dataset containing 524 real (non-generated) images.

4.2 Model Overall Performance Results

Model 1, which was trained exclusively on text-to-video synthetic frames from Dataset 1, achieved the lowest results. The overall precision was 45.3% and the recall was 22.6%. The model's ability to detect accuracy, measured by mAP 50, was only 27.3% while the stricter mAP 50–95 was 12%.

Model 2, which combined Dataset 1 data with image-to-video frames from Dataset 2, exhibited substantial performance improvements. Precision increased to 68.8% and recall to 51.3%. The mAP 50 rose to 56.1%, and the mAP 50–95 was 25.4%.

Model 3, which integrated synthetic images of Datasets 1 and 2 with real images in Dataset 3, achieved the highest performance among the three models. Precision was 75.4% and a recall of 71.9%. The mAP 50 reached 75.2%, and mAP 50–95 improved to 36.5%. A comparative analysis of final performance for the three YOLOv8 models can be seen in Table 5.

Table 5. Metrics Summary for All Classes per Model

All Classes	Precision (P)	Recall (R)	mAP50 score	mAP50–95 score
Model 1	0.453	0.226	0.273	0.12
Model 2	0.688	0.513	0.561	0.254
Model 3	0.754	0.719	0.752	0.365

4.3 Class-Specific Performance

As seen in Table 6, The class with the highest performance metrics in Model 1 was the license-plate class, reaching a precision of 75.7%, recall of 38.6% and a mAP 50 of 47.7%. Notably, Model 1 failed to detect any instances of the no-plate class. Furthermore, the no-helmet, vest, and no-vest classes also exhibited low performance. The Precision-Recall curves in Fig. 9 demonstrate how the license-plate class performed with the curve being higher than the overall average, and that that no-plate curve is missing.

Model 2, which utilized image-to-video data, outperformed Model 1 at predicting classes. While Model 1 was unable to predict any instances of no-plates, Model 2 was able to predict these objects, though still having a low precision, recall, and mAP 50 score, as seen in Table 7. The helmet and no-helmet classes performed the best, whereas the no-plate and no-vest remained the most challenging, as seen in Fig. 10. Notably, the no-helmet class achieved the highest metrics, with a precision of 81.6%, a recall of 72.5%, and an mAP 50 of 77.5%.

Model 3, which combined synthetic and real images, achieved the best overall performance across all class categories, as referenced in Table 8. All classes except no-plate and no-vest were higher than the overall mAP 50 curve, with no-plate bringing this average down significantly, as seen in Fig. 11.

Table 6. Model 1 Evaluation Metrics Performance

M1 Class	Images	Instances	Precision	Recall	mAP50	mAP50–95
all	524	1094	0.453	0.226	0.273	0.12
helmet	155	182	0.606	0.214	0.315	0.134
License_plage	97	101	0.757	0.386	0.477	0.249
no_helmet	184	255	0.666	0.219	0.337	0.125
no_plate	124	124	0	0	0	0
no_vest	270	335	0.264	0.248	0.194	0.069
vest	86	97	0.424	0.289	0.316	0.143

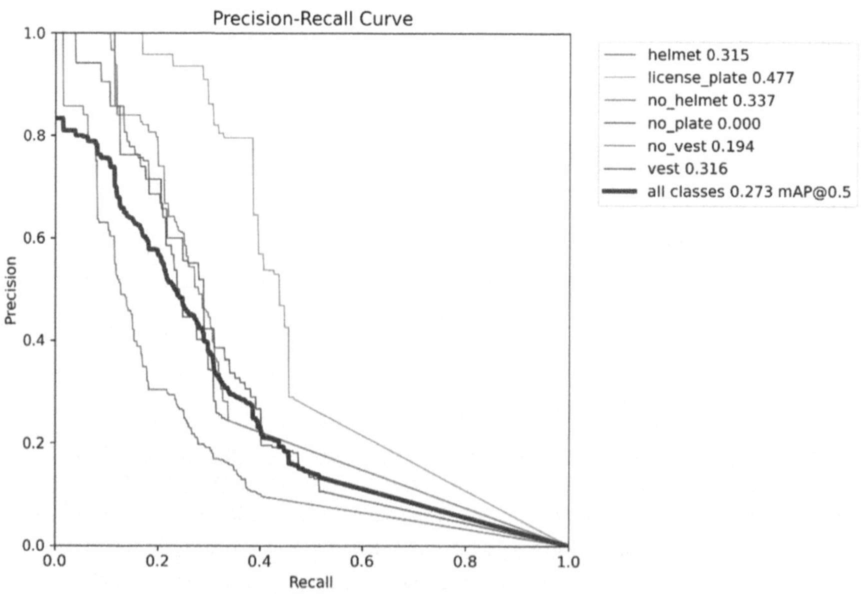

Fig. 9. Model 1 Precision- Recall Curve Performance

Table 7. Model 2 Evaluation Metrics Performance

M1 Class	Images	Instances	Precision	Recall	mAP50	mAP50–95
all	524	1094	0.688	0.513	0.561	0.254
helmet	155	182	0.844	0.594	0.733	0.34
License_plage	97	101	0.786	0.515	0.622	0.318
no_helmet	184	255	0.816	0.725	0.775	0.363
no_plate	124	124	0.41	0.185	0.137	0.0461
no_vest	270	335	0.638	0.46	0.509	0.201
vest	86	97	0.633	0.598	0.591	0.253

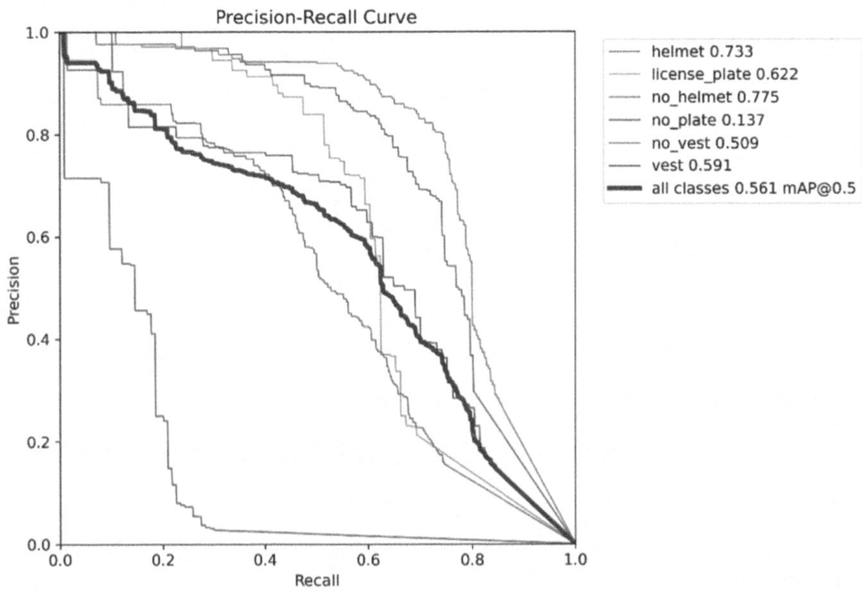

Fig. 10. Model 2 Precision- Recall Curve Performance

Table 8: Model 3 Evaluation Metrics Performance

M1 Class	Images	Instances	Precision	Recall	mAP50	mAP50–95
all	524	1094	0.754	0.719	0.752	0.365
helmet	155	182	0.871	0.852	0.894	0.486
License_plage	97	101	0.862	0.805	0.875	0.418
no_helmet	184	255	0.853	0.845	0.898	0.467

(*continued*)

Table 8: (*continued*)

M1 Class	Images	Instances	Precision	Recall	mAP50	mAP50–95
no_plate	124	124	0.366	0.185	0.147	0.0402
no_vest	270	335	0.794	0.691	0.756	0.296
vest	86	97	0.775	0.938	0.941	0.482

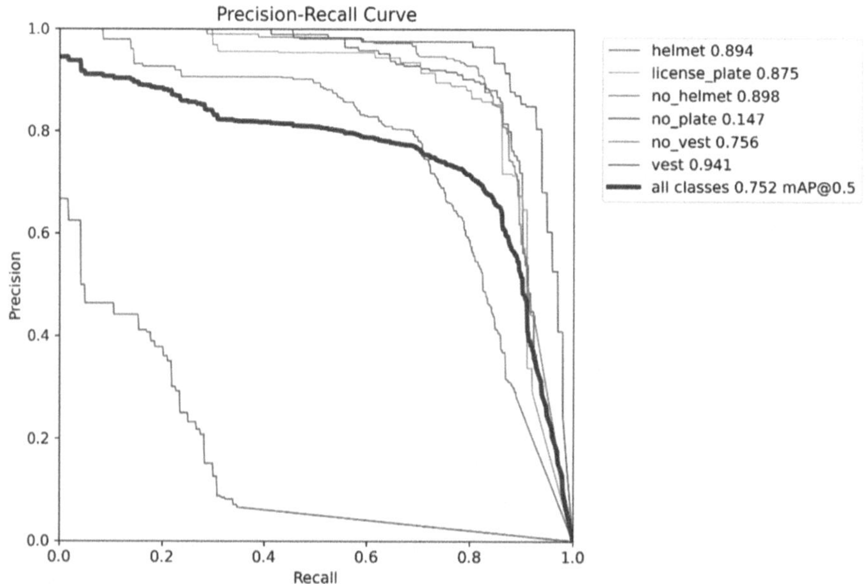

Fig. 11. Model 3 Precision- Recall Curve Performance

5 Discussion

The results from this study indicate that integrating initial images with real-world images substantially enhances model performance. Model 1, trained exclusively on synthetic videos generated from text-only prompts, failed to generalize effectively to real images. This model demonstrated low precision and recall, failing entirely to detect one of the classes. While Model 1 could predict certain classes, such as helmets and license plates, it achieved a low mean average precision (mAP 50) score. This is likely due to some of the classes being underrepresented, as well as the limited variety between the generated videos, as well as the variety between frames from the same generated video.

In comparison, Model 2, which incorporated image-to-video prompts along with the text-to-video dataset, showed improvement across all six classes. Precision-recall curves revealed substantial gains for the helmet, vest, and license plate classes, with a notable increase in mAP 50 compared to Model 1. Utilizing real-life images as input, the Veo models produced more realistic outputs and increased the diversity of helmets, riders, and vests across scenes. The expanded variety in training data contributed to Model 2's superior performance over Model 1.

Model 3, which combined synthetic data with real images, achieved the highest precision and recall across all six classes, reaching an mAP 50 score of 75%. These findings show the importance of data quality and the necessity for diverse objects in output scenes.

The absence-based classes, such as no-helmet, no-vest, and no-plate, are difficult to detect because they require very large and diverse training sets. Rather than trying to detect the "absence of something specific," the challenge becomes trying to detect "everything else." The no-plate class is especially difficult because it's only viewable from specific angles, and the position on the motorcycle can vary. Helmets and vests (and the lack of each) are viewable from more angles, as they are located on the rider. This can be seen directly in how each class was represented in each dataset. If we removed the absence-based classes from evaluation—especially the no-plate class—the overall mAP 50 scores would increase significantly for all models.

When employing synthetic data, it is essential to maximize variety in image prompts to facilitate generalization to real-world objects. For example, incorporating different camera angles, helmet styles, vests, and backgrounds can enhance the performance of a YOLOv8 model. Relying solely on synthetic data generated from text prompts did not enable sufficient generalization to real-world data. The inclusion of image prompts increased object diversity and improved scene outputs. The combination of synthetic and real-life images in Model 3 demonstrated effective generalization to real-world data. Synthetic data remains valuable when real images are limited, costly, or difficult to obtain. The progressive improvements observed from Model 1 to Model 3 highlight the necessity of robust image datasets for developing effective safety compliance models.

5.1 Research Findings

During the model evaluation phase we noticed some overfitting due to potential data leakage. To understand the source of overfitting we performed a dataset-wide, embedding-based similarity search to identify possible causes of data leakage between the training, validation and test sets. This approach was used in order to catch near-duplicates from augmentation, synthetic variations that are too similar to the originals, and accidental duplicates.

To create the image embeddings, we used ResNet50 v1.5 from PyTorch to compare all images across all three datasets. The results revealed that several validation and testing images were matched with images in our training datasets. This included exact duplicate photos, cropped versions of images contained in Dataset 3, and synthetic images that had been generated from real photos. An example can be seen in Fig. 12, where an image in our validation dataset and training image reached a cosine similarity score of 91%. We were also able to find duplicate images within our training datasets, which allowed us to remove redundant data. Furthermore, we also found instances of images that weren't duplicates but were similar visually, from the same photoshoot but distinct images. Although these images were not identical, it poses the question whether their high similarity score could influence the model training. We removed all duplicates and near-duplicate photos from the validation and test set that might lead to data leakage between the training data, which improved our final results.

Fig. 12. Near-duplicate similar images (source: Unsplash, https://unsplash.com/photos/man-in-black-leather-jacket-riding--motorcycle-KW-jwdSgOw4, accessed Sep. 6, 2025).

6 Conclusion and Future Research

This study presents the results of integrating synthetic video frames with real data to train three object detection models based on YOLOv8 for motorcycle safety compliance. Model 1, trained using only text-prompted synthetic data, demonstrated limited generalization to real-world data due to repetitive visual objects, insufficient variety in helmet types, and uniform scene backgrounds. These limitations reduced the model's ability to accurately predict all six target classes. Model 2, which incorporated both text prompts and input images, enhanced scene realism by increasing diversity in helmets, vests, and urban environments. Although Model 2 showed improved performance across several classes, it continued to encounter difficulties in detecting objects such as motorcycles without license plates. Model 3, which combined synthetic data with real images, achieved the highest precision, recall, and mAP 50 scores across all classes. This finding suggests that integrating real and synthetic images yields superior generalization for detecting objects related to motorcycle safety compliance. Figure 13 demonstrates the progression of bounding box and class label accuracy across model iterations, underscoring the value of combining synthetic data with real images.

Future research should explore the practical deployment of this object detection model. These include potential applications in real-time traffic monitoring, including busy intersections and roadside compliance checkpoints equipped with cameras. The proposed system can automatically identify riders lacking helmets, non-compliant vests, or visible license plates, and, when integrated with optical character recognition (OCR) or camera systems, can notify law enforcement agencies. This automation reduces reliance on manual police checks, conserves enforcement resources, and enhances compliance monitoring. Additionally, the system may assist authorities in criminal investigations by providing vest identification or license plate numbers.

Other areas for future research, that were beyond the scope of this paper, include trying to improve synthetic-only models, comparing real-image models with synthetic-augmented models, and studying how similarity affects evaluation metrics. For synthetic-only models, areas that could potentially improve the performance include generating more variety through prompt engineering or utilizing different generation models. We were not able to evaluate a model trained only with real (non-generated) images to compare to our other models, but this could potentially show the potential in using synthetic data as an augmentation strategy. Finally, when rooting out possible data leakage between our validation, testing, and training sets, we found an interesting link between similarity search scores and dataset variety. Comparing overall similarity score averages of training datasets with the final performance metrics might provide new insights for future evaluation strategies (Fig. 14, 15).

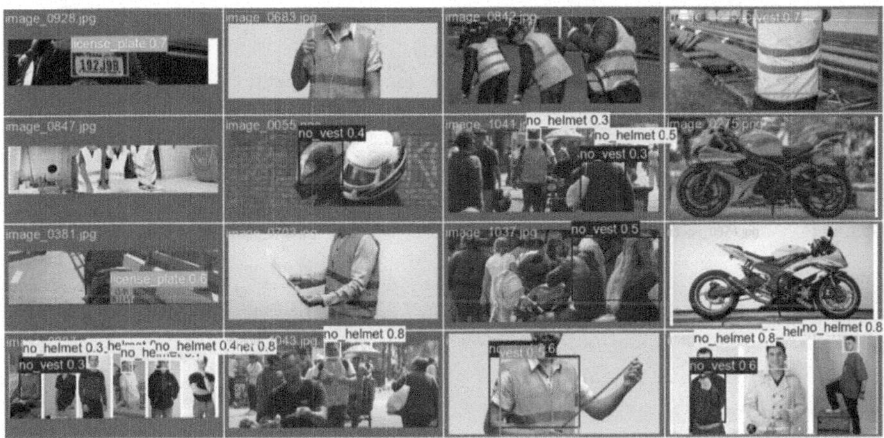

Fig. 13. Model 1 Test Detection Results

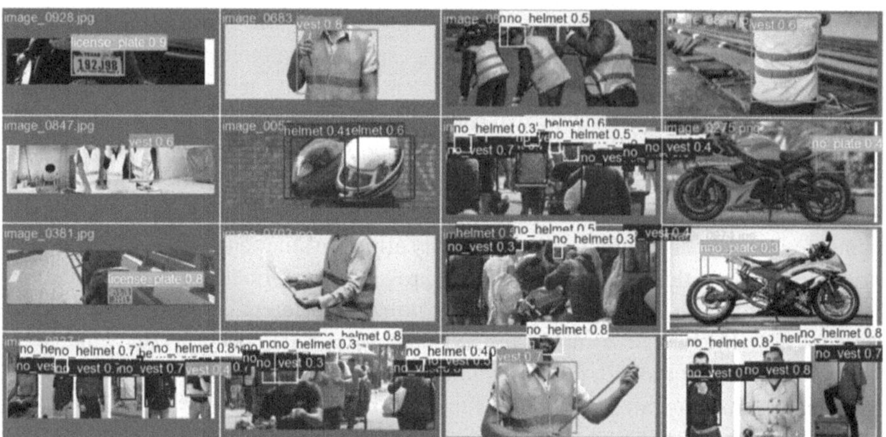

Fig. 14. Model 2 Test Detection Results

Fig. 15. Model 3 Test Detection Results

References

1. "Resolución Directoral N.° 008–2025-MTC/18," Www.gob.pe, (2025). https://www.gob.pe/institucion/mtc/normas-legales/6737332-008-2025-mtc-18 (accessed Sep. 11, 2025).
2. Resolución Directoral N.° 0012–2025-MTC/18," Www.gob.pe, (2025). https://www.gob.pe/institucion/mtc/normas-legales/6958752-0012-2025-mtc-18 (accessed Sep. 11, 2025).
3. Barlybayev, A., et al.: Personal protective equipment detection using YOLOv8 architecture on object detection benchmark datasets: a comparative study. Cogent Eng. **11**(1) (2024). https://doi.org/10.1080/23311916.2024.2333209

4. Malaikrisanachalee, S., Wongwai, N., Kowcharoen, E.: ESPCN-YOLO: a high-accuracy framework for personal protective equipment detection under low-light and small object conditions. Buildings. **15**(10), 1609 (2025). https://doi.org/10.3390/buildings15101609
5. Lubna, N.M., Shah, S.A.A.: Automatic number plate recognition:a detailed survey of relevant algorithms. Sensors. **21**(9), 3028 (2021). https://doi.org/10.3390/s21093028
6. Y. Du et al., "PP-OCRv2: Bag of Tricks for Ultra Lightweight OCR System," arXiv (Cornell University), Jan. (2021), https://doi.org/10.48550/arxiv.2109.03144.
7. Carlson, A., Skinner, K.A., Vasudevan, R., Johnson-Roberson, M.: Sensor transfer: learning optimal sensor effect image augmentation for Sim-to-real domain adaptation. IEEE Rob. Autom. Lett. **4**(3), 2431–2438 (2019). https://doi.org/10.1109/lra.2019.2896470
8. Johnson-Roberson, M., Barto, C., Mehta, R., Sridhar, S.N., Rosaen, K., Vasudevan, R.: Driving in the matrix: can virtual worlds replace human-generated annotations for real world tasks? In: International Conference on Robotics and Automation (2017). https://doi.org/10.1109/icra.2017.7989092
9. Sora: Creating video from text," Openai.com, (2015). https://openai.com/index/sora. (accessed Sep. 13, 2025).
10. Gemini AI video generator powered by Veo 3," Gemini, (2025). https://gemini.google/overview/video-generation/ (accessed Sep. 13, 2025).
11. Temsah, M.H., et al.: Openai's Sora and Google's Veo 2 in action: a narrative review of artificial intelligence-driven video generation models transforming healthcare. Cureus. **17**(1), e77593 (2025). https://doi.org/10.7759/cureus.77593
12. He, S., Wang, Y., Li, Z., Jiang, N., Sun, G.: The first birthday of OpenAI's Sora: a promising but cautious future in medicine. Int. J. Surg. **111**, 4151 (2025). https://doi.org/10.1097/js9.0000000000002432
13. Alam, S., Wang, Z., Zhang, L., Bazilinskyy, P.: Exploring Veo 3's capabilities for generating urban traffic scenes in 76 cities worldwide. Access. (2025) Available: https://bazilinskyy.github.io/publications/alam2025exploring.pdf
14. Veo: a text-to-video generation system. Available: https://storage.googleapis.com/deepmind-media/veo/Veo-3-Tech-Report.pdf (accessed Sep. 13, 2025).
15. Veo 3 Model Card, 2025. Available: https://storage.googleapis.com/deepmind-media/Model-Cards/Veo-3-Model-Card.pdf (accessed Sep. 13, 2025).
16. Ultralytics, "YOLOv5 vs. YOLOv8: A Detailed Comparison," Ultralytics.com, (2024). https://docs.ultralytics.com/compare/yolov5-vs-yolov8/. (accessed Sep. 13, 2025).
17. Veo on Vertex AI video generation prompt guide," Google Cloud, (2025). https://cloud.google.com/vertex-ai/generative-ai/docs/video/video-gen-prompt-guide (accessed Sep. 13, 2025).
18. Google, "Gemini," gemini.google.com, (2025). https://gemini.google.com/app (accessed Sep. 13, 2025).
19. Flow, Labs.google, (2025). https://labs.google/flow/about (accessed Sep. 13, 2025).
20. Sign in - Google Accounts," Google.com, (2024). https://colab.research.google.com/github/GoogleCloudPlatform/generative-ai/blob/main/vision/getting-started/veo3_video_generation.ipynb. (accessed Sep. 13, 2025).
21. G. Boesch: LabelImg for Image Annotation," viso.ai, Feb. 11, 2022. https://viso.ai/computer-vision/labelimg-for-image-annotation/ (accessed Sep. 18, 2025).
22. HumanSignal/labelImg, GitHub, Jul. 30, (2024). https://github.com/HumanSignal/labelImg#installation (accessed Sep. 18, 2025).
23. J. Torres, "What Is mAP 50 in YOLOv8? A Simple Explanation," YOLOv8, Jul. 09, (2025). https://yolov8.org/what-is-map50-in-yolov8/ (accessed Sep. 18, 2025).

Agentic Learning with an AI Instructor in Virtual Reality for High School Anatomy Instruction

Robert DeWitty[1(✉)], Koundinya Challa[2], Abhinav Pendem[2], Issa W. AlHmoud[2], and Balakrishna Gokaraju[2]

[1] Department of Electrical and Computer Engineering, North Carolina A&T State University, Greensboro, NC, USA
rgdewitty@aggies.ncat.edu

[2] Computational Data Science and Engineering, North Carolina A&T State University, Greensboro, NC, USA

Abstract. This study presents a framework for integrating agents of generative artificial intelligence (AI) within immersive virtual reality (VR) environments to support high school anatomy education. While traditional tools offer common visual aids or textual descriptions of human anatomy, our approach employs a Unity-based 3D VR simulation, combined with a large language model (LLM)-powered AI instructor, to facilitate interactive, personalized learning. The system enables students to construct and deconstruct a highly comprehensive virtual human body layer by layer, engaging with both internal and external anatomical structures through Mechdyne's ARC System and various VR headset models. This study also explores the possibility of introducing an AI agent with real-time natural language processing and text-to-speech capabilities, allowing it to respond conversationally to student inquiries and adapt its guidance based on prior knowledge, demographic data, and learning assessments. Another exploration in this paper is the data architecture behind the AI agent, which should record student interactions, question types, and knowledge gaps. This information will be used to fine-tune AI responses via a reinforcement-learning-based personalization layer. The entire system should eventually be evaluated through a mixed-methods study that includes usability testing, pre- and post-knowledge assessments, and student feedback surveys.

Keywords: Generative AI · Education · Anatomy · Advanced Virtual Reality · AI Instructor

1 Introduction

As technology advances, methods of education tend to follow suit. New technologies enable new and more diverse educational methods. Virtual reality (VR) and artificial intelligence (AI) are two technologies that have yet to receive significant

F. Tanner and J. Irvine (Eds.): AIPR 2025, LNCS 16446, pp. 44–61, 2026.
https://doi.org/10.1007/978-3-032-18474-0_4

research in educational settings. In addition, human anatomy is often illustrated with diagrams or models in academic settings. This research examines the outcomes of combining different VR/AR tools to create a simulation for human anatomy education, as well as the differences between using a personalized AI instructor and a classroom teacher.

As generative AI models become increasingly advanced, the different ways AI can be used within education broaden. Consideration should be placed on the educational benefits of AI for high school students. This provides a strong incentive for academic institutions to experiment with AI as an aid to teachers. The end goal of adding an AI instructor to this simulation is to demonstrate the benefits of an AI agent that can personalize instruction for each student, ensuring each student receives adequate attention.

Like AI, VR is not widely used as an aid in classrooms at this time. VR has historically proven costly and impractical in large classroom settings. However, in recent years, VR has seen more accessible forms [1] of implementation on cheaper and increasingly mainstream hardware. Relatively inexpensive models are now available, providing a more straightforward path to introducing students to VR. The goal of this research is to examine the benefits of using VR/AR tools to teach human anatomy in an immersive virtual environment.

For students in smaller classroom environments, using multiple Head-Mounted Display (HMD) VR headsets is an effective way to allow students to interact with the simulation. However, the ARC System [2], a motion-tracked multi-panel display for visualizing 3D simulations, has the potential to be a more effective way to showcase simulations to a broader class of students. With one student controlling the simulation's movement, they can complete the assigned anatomy-related tasks with help from their fellow students watching on the large ARC System. Figure 1 shows the ARC System.

Fig. 1. The ARC System used to help visualize VR simulations.

With regard to the use of ethical AI and the introduction of VR in classroom environments, these are relatively unexplored fields. This research aims to shed light on these areas and answer the question,"Is using immersive VR simulations that integrate AI instructors beneficial to knowledge retention?"

Vu et al. [3] observe that fostering student motivation in the classroom is beneficial to learning and can be linked to achievement within education. Because VR can also increase students' motivation [1], it would be helpful when combined with traditional teaching methods. Building a VR simulation creates a virtual world where components can be altered to more effectively stimulate a student's interest than a typical classroom environment. Therefore, this study was conducted under the following prediction: "Combining VR and AI in an immersive, virtual environment in conjunction with traditional methods of teaching is more impactful to student motivation than solely using traditional methods of teaching."

The paper is structured as follows: Sect. 2 includes a detailed literature review of existing studies, as well as other systematic literature reviews on conversations in the area of VR and AI used for education. Section 3 describes the methodology for the pipeline for this study. Section 4 discusses alternate routes taken and future steps. Section 5 concludes the paper with a summary of our findings and an overall assessment of our work.

2 Literature Review

Hsu's [4] study shows that VR can increase long-term retention while aiding in the visualization of complex ideas. This study utilizes several methods to evaluate effectiveness across student interest, knowledge retention, and post-sentiment opinion-based data. Hsu finds that both learning motivation and effectiveness increase with the introduction of VR into the instruction. However, several related topics will be expanded upon to highlight the benefits of VR compared to traditional teaching methods. These include implementing a control group, isolating VR instruction from traditional instruction, and evaluating long-term knowledge retention, which the referenced studies do not include.

Ali et al. [5] conducted a study at the University of Malakand using the Wii Remote in combination with a 3D simulation running on laptops. The Wii Remote is visualized via the diagram in Fig. 2. After the simulation was demonstrated on a 40-inch Samsung LED display for guidance, students were tasked with conducting experiments using the 3D simulation. They were able to interact with elements such as beakers, spirit lamps, and other items. Data were collected at two main levels: demographics and post-simulation sentiments. Because this study is fairly dated, an area of interest would be a similar experiment conducted with modern technology (VR Headsets, ARC System, etc.), which would allow students to learn through sight and action using a controller. Additionally, as in Hsu's experiment, this experiment does not consider long- or short-term knowledge retention, which we will expand upon.

Several studies [1,6] out four main learning theories: constructivist, situated, embodied cognition, and social cognition. This analysis is highly beneficial in

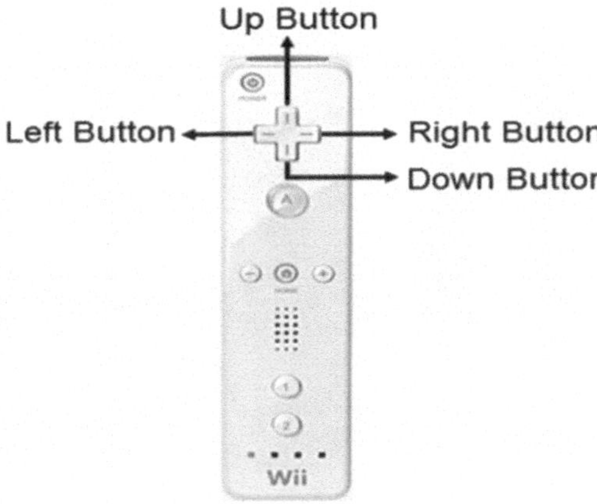

Fig. 2. A diagram of the Wii Remote [5].

predicting what areas VR can have a significant, positive impact. The two main learning theories that seem most relevant to the VR space are constructivist and situated learning. The constructivist learning theory states that knowledge is constructed through a student's interaction with their environment, while the situated learning theory primarily suggests that students acquire knowledge through their participation in contexts or situations where they perform authentic tasks. After examining these learning theories, VR can be applied to the education of human anatomy: students both construct knowledge by interacting with individual body parts and learning their locations, while simultaneously acquiring knowledge through an AI instructor and text-based descriptions of each body part. Implementing such a system on an HMD or the ARC System's Multi-Panel-Displays potentially produces a different outcome than studies referenced within Freina's literature review [7] that do not utilize such technologies.

Radianti et al. conducted a systematic literature review [1] of studies that used VR across higher education. A portion of their findings suggests that very few articles have conducted significant studies using Enhanced VR(EVR). EVR Systems refer to VR simulations that utilize equipment extending beyond an HMD or a desktop screen. Examples of this include the CAVE System or the ARC System. This study has the potential to use the ARC System to compare its effects with those of an HMD.

Dewberry et al. [2] conducted a study of the ARC System, exploring the complexities of using it to visualize simulations of Point Cloud scans of existing objects. An example of these Point Cloud scans is shown in Fig. 3. Such scans are obtained using LiDAR technology and can be interacted with through the ARC System, which provides motion tracking capabilities. The study demonstrates the ability to achieve high levels of realism through VR simulations. Our study can build on the idea of realistic VR simulations by introducing greater interactivity and establishing methods to gauge audience preferences, which the

Fig. 3. An Indoor scan of a hallway. The colors correspond to the height of a given point [2].

author states are unexplored areas. In the same spirit of exploring the capabilities of environment building in VR, a study [8] shows the effects of color and sound on user reaction. A reaction-based game was implemented on a laptop screen, and participants were tasked with playing the game while several factors were recorded to obtain a score for each user. Because this study used non-immersive technology, it can help predict the effects of color grading and sound design when constructing an environment for the anatomy simulation. To ensure a comfortable environment, these areas must be considered.

AI is expected to enhance the participant's experience as well. A detailed literature review [9] conducted at the University of Nigeria takes a dive into the incorporation of AI into educational frameworks and how the two fields intersect in the modern age of AI. Researchers in this study found that AI can adapt to students' individual needs, enable real-time analysis, and boost engagement. In this way, integrating AI into an educational VR framework creates the ideal environment to demonstrate both constructivist and situational learning theories.

Muniasamy et al. [10] analyze multiple studies in the context of introducing AI to eLearning platforms. Researchers find that the potential of deep learning models is vast, enabling personalization of learning modules, conversational chatbots, performance indicators, and more. This study aims to target all three of these major areas in the effort of implementing a data architecture that allows an AI agent to learn as more of the simulation is introduced to more participants.

3 Methodology

3.1 Pipeline Overview

The simulation was implemented in Unity 3D 6.3.1f, a powerful 3D game engine, to enable portability across devices such as HMDs and the ARC System. Initially, the project utilized a desktop monitor as a display with a mouse and keyboard as controls. Using *OpenXR*, a VR development library in Unity, the simulation was ported from a non-immersive setting to an immersive HMD-based VR experience. The project will be ported to the ARC System to add another method of interaction in the future.

In conjunction with this, Google's AI Gemini Model was implemented as a demo to serve as a real-time instructor for questions a participant might have. While the AI model is not currently trained on data, data architecture will be implemented in the future to allow the AI model to function on data collected through questionnaires that were inserted into the VR experience. Such questionnaires collect demographic data, test short-term knowledge retention, and user opinions regarding the simulation. The AI instructor can take speech as input using the *Whisper* AI text-to-speech (TTS) framework, an open-source framework for TTS in Unity. After receiving speech input, the AI instructor returns a spoken response.

To simplify the simulation, the student constructs and analyzes the human body in layers. Figure 4a visualizes the skeletal, muscular, and outer skin layers. After the student completes each layer, they take a knowledge test to test their understanding. To determine effectiveness, a different group of students from the same anatomy class is tasked with watching a video on each layer and taking the same knowledge test. Bloom's Taxonomy is used to create questionnaires that test short-term knowledge retention. Figure 4b shows the six layers of Bloom's

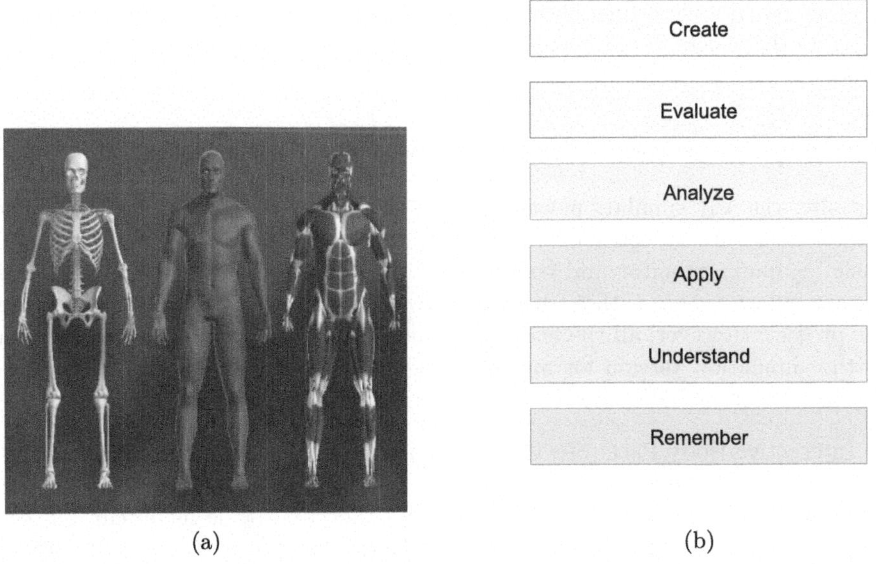

Fig. 4. (a) The human body constructed in layers (e.g., skeletal or muscular systems). (b) The six layers of Bloom's Taxonomy.

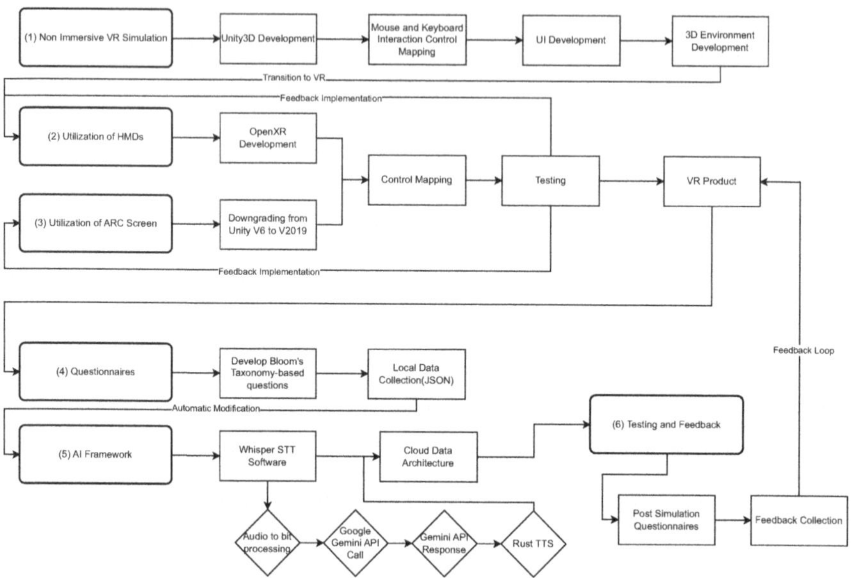

Fig. 5. Project pipeline.

Taxonomy, but the first four from the bottom are the crucial layers used in designing the questionnaires in this study.

This pipeline described above can be visualized as seen in Fig. 5.

Note that Sects. 4 and 5 will be discussed under the discussion section of this paper.

3.2 Implementation of Non-Immersive VR Environment

Initially, the VR simulation was built for a non-immersive VR medium. The project was initially constructed in Unity 3D Version 6.3.1f to be viewed on a basic computer monitor and controlled with a mouse and keyboard. This was done to allow testing without having to troubleshoot VR-related issues early in the project. However, all the features explained in this section were carried over to the simulation version for an immersive VR environment with HMDs or to the ARC System. The scene initially incorporates several basic features:

1. Interactive Body Parts(See Figs. 6a and 6b - each body part can be manipulated using a mouse.
2. Interactive UI(The part-spawn menu and the part-toggle menu can be seen in Fig. 6c and Figure 6d - several UI menus allow the participants to search for and spawn body parts.
3. Anatomy Layering System (See Previous Fig. 4a for the skeletal, outer skin, and muscular layers) - the simulation proceeds in phases, with each phase focusing on a different layer of the human body.

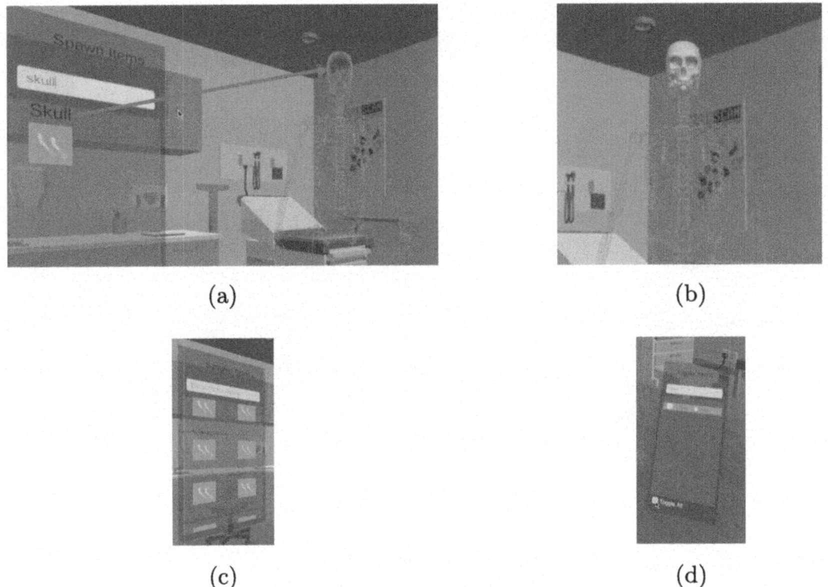

Fig. 6. (a) and (b): Before and after dragging the body part onto the hologram. (c) and (d): The spawn-item and toggle visibility menu.

We implemented a holographic representation of the human body, where body parts are to be dragged as a puzzle-like activity. This activity aims to encourage students to associate body parts with different positions in the human body. As VR thrives in spatially focused environments, we predicted this setup would be highly compatible with VR. This, combined with a compatible background visualizing a doctor's office, creates a cohesive environment. The setup in its entirety is visualized in Fig. 7.

An interactive user interface(UI) was added to the simulation. There are numerous UI features, such as a spawn-item menu and a toggle menu. The spawn-item menu allows the student to search for a body part using a virtual keyboard. With icons and names to identify body parts, finding them is simple and efficient. The toggle menu item is crucial to simplifying the complex human body. By allowing users to toggle which body parts are visible, the student can easily hide parts that obstruct others.

We used an asset package from Unity's asset store that included a human body at multiple levels of detail, including the nervous system, muscular tissue, skeletal structure, and organs. This allowed us to create a thorough, comprehensive holographic representation of the human body, as shown in Fig. 8. However, because there are so many assets within this asset package, we were then tasked with optimizing and simplifying the 3D representation of the body. Instead of treating each anatomical component as an independent entity, we grouped body parts as shown in Fig. 9 to simplify the task of reconstructing the body.

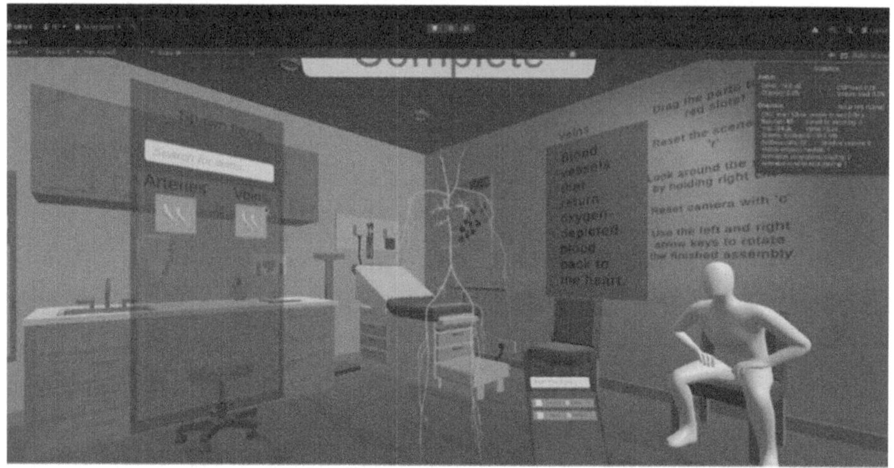

Fig. 7. The full simulation setup.

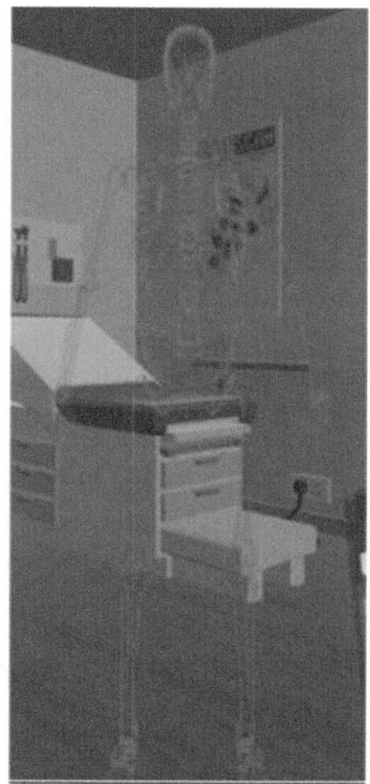

Fig. 8. The holographic version of the skeleton layer as seen in red. (Color figure online)

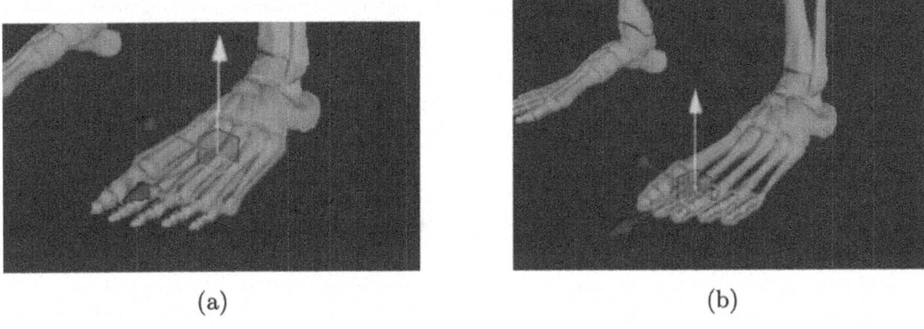

(a) (b)

Fig. 9. Different groupings regarding the left foot.

3.3 Utilization of HMDs and the ARC System

Students have multiple ways to interact with the simulation to improve accessibility. These include mouse and keyboard, mainstream HMDs(such as the HTC Vive, as seen in Fig. 10, and Mechdyne's ARC System. The mouse-and-keyboard version was initially developed to test new features added to the simulation. In addition to the mouse-and-keyboard version, this paper will explore its implementation on VR Headsets and the ARC System.

Fig. 10. The HTC Vive Pro2 Headset.

VR Headsets. The scene uses various Unity-based tools to enable students to interact with the simulation using a VR headset. First, the Unity *OpenXR* Package is used, allowing developers to target multiple VR Headsets that often have subtle differences in their control schemes. All body parts are fully interactable, as if they were objects a student could hold in the real world. This makes the implementation of the scene on VR Headsets more immersive and interactive than in other media. However, potential downsides include limited access to a large number of headsets in a large classroom setting, as well as hygienic concerns when multiple students use a VR Headset. Therefore, in a small classroom setting, VR headsets are potentially more impactful, but in a larger classroom, a medium such as the ARC System is a better alternative.

The ARC System. The ARC System will be implemented following the following steps.

1. Downgrading the Project
2. Mapping controls to ARC System Controller, the Logitech F710 controller and the motion-tracked system as seen in Fig. 11.
3. Export, test, and modify

Fig. 11. The ARC System's motion-tracked Logitech F710 controller and 3D glasses.

First, the project must be downgraded from Unity 6.3.1f to 2019.4.18f1. This is because the ARC System uses the *GetReal3D* application, which is used for rendering Unity simulations on the Multi-Panel ARC Display. This has several implications, as official support for the *OpenXR* plugin was not added until late 2020. Therefore, any control schemes specific to modern VR development may need to be replaced by older systems.

Additionally, mapping the controls to the ARC System control system will be required to transfer the project to the ARC System. The ARC System uses a motion-tracked Logitech controller and worn glasses for a 3D effect. Making the simulation compatible with the *DTrackV2* software used for motion tracking is a required task when transferring to the ARC System.

Last, the simulation can be exported as a Unity Package and placed on the ARC System for testing. The testing loop is organized as follows:

1. Export the Unity Package and zip the folder
2. Transfer project and unzip file on ARC System
3. Start with *GetReal3D* on the ARC System

3.4 Questionnaire Implementation

The division of the human body into layers, as shown in Fig. 4a, is relevant to evaluating the simulation's effectiveness among high school students. To assess knowledge retention, quizzes are added after each layer experience to measure the student's knowledge of that layer post-interaction. The accuracy scores from each quiz are collected and stored locally. The data collected from these quizzes is anonymous and used only to identify general areas of misconception or misunderstanding. This creates the potential for the simulation to be improved over time to minimize such areas. Below is a list of the three main areas in which we currently collect data during each participant's experience.

1. Demographic Quiz Data - Both qualitative and quantitative data relating to the participant's background, feelings about anatomy, and future career plans. Figure 12a shows a set of sample questions designed to collect demographic data.
2. Knowledge Test Data - Questions based on the first four layers of Bloom's Taxonomy model to measure short-term knowledge retention. Sample knowledge test questions can be seen in Fig. 12b.
3. Post-Assessment Data - Questions to gauge the participant's opinions about the simulation. These opinion-based questions can be visualized in Fig. 12c.

3.5 AI Framework

The simulation includes a UI element to test the limits of using AI as an instructor. A UI menu was added with a button to allow the participant to record their voice and speak to an AI model in real time. The system uses Google Gemini's backend API framework to make a request and fetch a response. The response is returned in both subtitle and spoken format(Fig. 13 shows an example of this spoken input and response). For the spoken response, we utilize *RustTTS*, an open-source multi-platform text-to-speech plugin.

Seen in Fig. 14 is a pipeline of how our AI pipeline works with voice integration.

Question	Participant X Answer
Previous Anatomy Education	Pre-defined answers
Most Relatable Field of Study	Pre-defined answers
Future Area of Interest	Pre-defined answers
Future Vocational Plans	Pre-defined answers
Degree of Interest in Anatomy (1-10)	1-10
Current Grade	6-12
Age	12-19

(a)

Question	Participant X Answers
On a scale of 1-10, how much would you agree that VR was beneficial to your understanding?	1-10
On a scale of 1-10, how easy was this activity to understand?	1-10
How helpful was the AI instructor (1-10)?	1-10
Would you participate in this activity for different topics?	Agree/Disagree
Did this increase your interest in Anatomy?	Agree/Disagree

(b)

Question	Participant X Answers
Where is the spleen located?	Correct/Incorrect
Explain the skull's function.	Correct/Incorrect
If you were to remove the human ribcage, which of the following organs would be exposed?	Correct/Incorrect
Compare the uses of the liver and the human intestines.	Correct/Incorrect

(c)

Fig. 12. Questionnaire sample data: (a), (b), (c) correspond to different question sets.

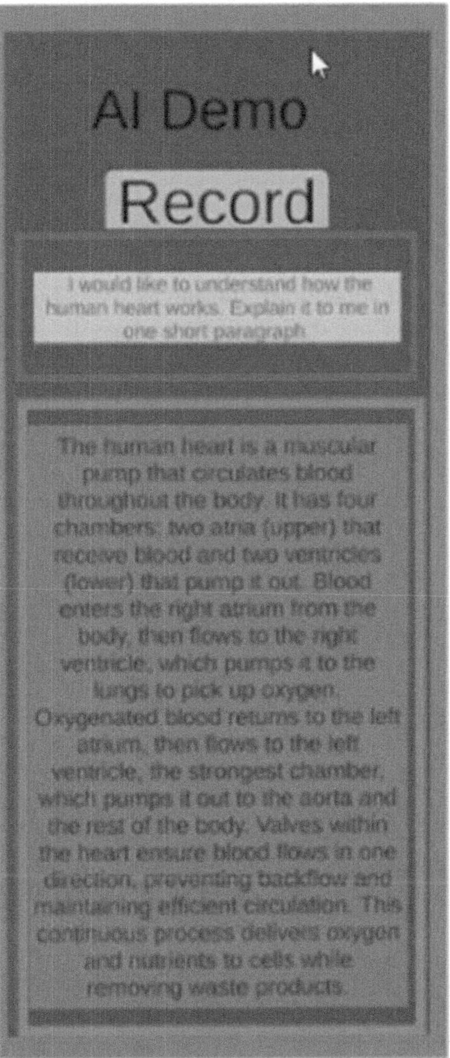

Fig. 13. Google's Gemini Model responding to voice prompts in real time. The text within the red box was a voice prompt spoken by the user, while the text within the green box was spoken by the AI model.

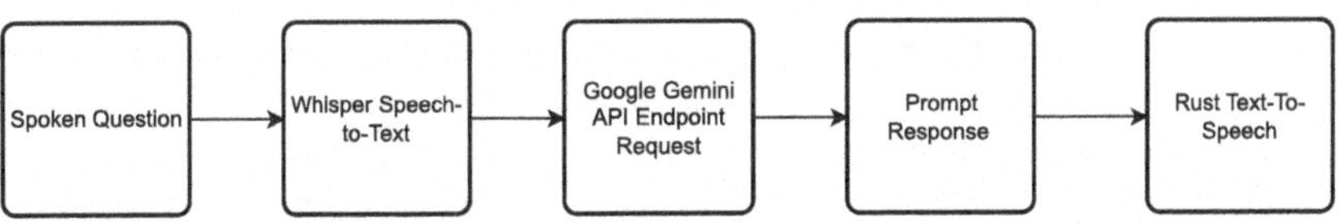

Fig. 14. AI Demo Pipeline with Voice Integration.

4 Discussion

While the simulation has many strengths in its implementation of VR across both HMDs and the ARC System, we will pursue several follow-up steps to advance this research and realize its potential. These continuations mainly lie in the two areas of data collection, AI, and accessibility features.

4.1 Data Architecture

Currently, data is stored locally on the device, which is suitable for a small number of users, but writing data asynchronously to an online database can improve storage sustainability and performance. The project will use a NodeJS-based backend server to write anonymous user data directly to an online database service such as MongoDB, an open-source NoSQL database compatible with many modern applications. The data architecture framework pipeline is shown in Fig. 15.

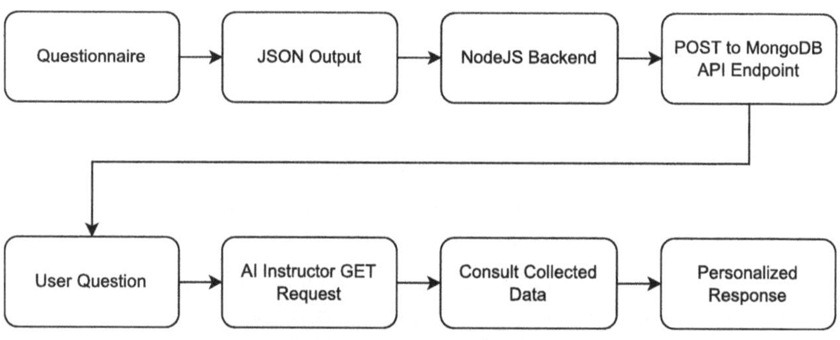

Fig. 15. Data Architecture Pipeline.

While this is certainly within the scope of the project, the simulation only includes an AI instructor as a simple UI element rather than an approachable humanoid character. We lay out the projected pipeline as follows:

1. Create an interactive AI agent
2. Personalized and real-time responses
3. Real-time data collection and consultation

To create an interactive AI agent, we will incorporate several key features. First, we will construct a basic physical humanoid avatar that incorporates dynamic animations when speaking, to ensure the student feels comfortable interacting with the instructor. This avatar framework should work seamlessly with text-to-speech responses generated by an AI model running in the back-end, which takes spoken student questions and returns coherent answers. The spoken questions are transcribed and sent to Google's Gemini AI Model using the *Whisper* TTS model.

After this first layer of development, the next step is to return personalized, real-time responses based on data collected and processed, as seen in our previous data architecture pipeline. The AI instructor will be able to dynamically adjust its approach to guiding the student by collecting data across multiple areas, such as the time spent interacting with an object, which parts of the body the student tends to question more frequently, etc. The aim of compiling this data is to personalize each subsequent user's experience, so in theory, as more users participate in the simulation, the quality and effectiveness should increase.

Each time a user begins the simulation, they are introduced to a demographic quiz. After answering various questions, the simulation should retrieve data from users of similar backgrounds to predict areas of less experience and modify the AI instructor. The AI instructor will be able to collect data across various areas and use a weighting system to determine which pieces of data should take precedence in the personalization process.

As explained previously, the simulation includes brief questionnaires to evaluate short-term knowledge retention, acquire basic user demographic data, and collect simulation-related opinions. To judge the effectiveness of different aspects, the simulation uses post-simulation and knowledge assessments, along with other data, to compare recent simulations with previous ones. Each knowledge assessment is evaluated based on correct and incorrect answers, yielding a general accuracy score and enabling trend tracking. However, because there are other factors at play (e.g., time spent exploring a particular layer, types and frequencies of questions asked, etc.), the simulation's effectiveness cannot be reduced to a single accuracy score for human interpretation. Offloading data interpretation to an AI model is an alternative method for quickly collecting and making changes based on data. We plan to conduct further research to automate the data collection and interpretation process and determine the best course of action.

4.2 Special Need Accessibility

While we currently incorporate special needs features such as TTS and subtitles in the current AI model, the simulation will include additional accessibility features. For example, to allow users with vision or motor impairments to search for objects using the search UI, the *Whisper* AI voice-detection model should enable voice-to-text capabilities to search for or toggle the visibility of particular body parts. Additionally, individuals with motor-control-related disabilities should be able to abstain from building the body by hand and can choose to participate in a hands-off experience where the body is automatically built in stages. By default, the simulation uses a panel to display brief descriptions of the body parts the student is currently interacting with. However, for those with vision-related disabilities, a TTS option offers an alternative to listening to descriptions.

4.3 Testing Setup

Regarding distributing the simulation, a group of students and a teacher will meet at a physical location to participate. We plan for two groups of students to interact with the simulation: one group will use the available HMDs, and the other will use the ARC System. This way, we can collect data on performance across both VR mediums. In addition, we would like to collect data from a standard high school class undergoing traditional anatomy instruction to serve as a control group. All groups will be tasked with answering the same demographic and knowledge quizzes to obtain consistent information.

5 Conclusion

Despite not yet having the projected results from administering this VR simulation to students, the current state of the project is a strong foundation for creating a simulation to supplement traditional high school anatomy education. We created a simulation that allows students to visualize the human body from all angles while interacting with each part individually to understand its position within the body better. Despite its current state, implementing an AI instructor to guide the student is not too far off, as the basic framework for its function has already been laid out. By creating a VR world for students to interact with different elements of human anatomy, we believe VR will be proven highly beneficial in increasing student motivation and, therefore, fostering high academic achievement.

The process of laying out this framework required research into different approaches to incorporating a basic mouse-and-keyboard simulation into VR. This project utilized tools such as *OpenXR* to port the simulation to HMDs. However, we successfully ported this simulation from a desktop monitor to VR headsets, demonstrating the capabilities of developing for VR with and without HMDs.

We may apply the ideas within this project to other educational topics or job-specific contexts in the future. While this simulation was explicitly developed for anatomy, we can use the same concept to any vocational training or educational topic that benefits from visualizing concepts. A future project consideration is the creation of a simulation that allows a user to import, analyze, and reconstruct complex structures for educational or training purposes. In any case, the potential of VR in academia is boundless. As more affordable HMDs are created, we will soon find ourselves turning to VR for its vast benefits.

Acknowledgments. This work was supported in part by 1) the United States Department of Commerce (USDOC), Economic Development Administration Good Jobs Challenge Awardee under Grant ED22HDQ3070099; 2) and the Hybrid Autonomous Manufacturing Moving from Evolution to Revolution (HAMMER) under Award 2133630.

References

1. Radianti, J., Majchrzak, T.A., Fromm, J., Wohlgenannt, I.: A systematic review of immersive virtual reality applications for higher education: design elements, lessons learned, and research agenda. Comput. Educ. **147**, 103778 (2020). Publisher: Elsevier
2. Dewberry, N., AlHmoud, I.W., Chowdhury, S., Gokaraju, B.: Problems and solutions of point cloud mapping for VR and CAVE environments for data visualization and physics simulation. In: 2023 IEEE Applied Imagery Pattern Recognition Workshop (AIPR), pp. 1–7. IEEE (2023)
3. Vu, T., et al.: Motivation-achievement cycles in learning: a literature review and research agenda. Educ. Psychol. Rev. **34**(1), 39–71 (2022)
4. Hsu, Y.-C.: Exploring the learning motivation and effectiveness of applying virtual reality to high school mathematics. Universal J. Educ. Res. **8**(2), 438–444 (2020)
5. Ali, N., Ullah, S., Alam, A., Rafique, J.: 3D interactive virtual chemistry laboratory for simulation of high school experiments. In: Proceedings of Eurasia graphics, pp. 1–6 (2014)
6. Leung, T., Zulkernine, F., Isah, H.: The use of virtual reality in enhancing interdisciplinary research and education (2018). arXiv:1809.08585
7. Freina, L., Ott, M.: A literature review on immersive virtual reality in education: state of the art and perspectives. In: The International Scientific Conference Elearning and Software for Education, volume 1, no. 133 pp. 10–1007 (2015)
8. McKnight, L.G., AlHmoud, I.W., Gokaraju, B.: Impacts of color and sound on user reaction time in gamified virtual environments. In: SoutheastCon 2025, pp. 1–6. IEEE (2025)
9. Ayeni, O.O., Al Hamad, N.M., Chisom, O.N., Osawaru, B., Adewusi, O.E.: AI in education: a review of personalized learning and educational technology. GSC Adv. Res. Rev. **18**(2), 261–271 (2024)
10. Muniasamy, A., Alasiry, A.: Deep learning: the impact on future eLearning. Int. J. Emerg. Technol. Learn. **15**(1), 188 (2020). Publisher: International Association of Online Engineering (IAOE)

GEARS: Generative Edit Agent for Retrieval and Synthesis

Kevin Robbins(✉), Grady McPeak, and Robert Pless

George Washington University, Washington, DC 20052, USA
{kevin.robbins,gradymcpeak,pless}@gwu.edu

Abstract. In this paper, we present GEARS, a generative approach to quickly editing a real image in ways that target specific objects or image regions. We consider the scenario where a user has an initial image and wants to specify fine-grained "difference" prompts (e.g., "the carpet is more worn"). When these edits are intended to improve image retrieval, it is vital to avoid adding new features or diffusing the impact of the edit in making small variations throughout the image. Therefore, we introduce an approach that translates natural language edits into masks that limit the scope of the edits, allowing a user to selectively and iteratively update the image. We show example results and insights from our tests in using these edits for image retrieval in the domain of hotel recognition.

Keywords: VLM Image Retrieval · Stable Diffusion · Inpainting

1 Introduction

State-of-the-art retrieval systems depend on extracting detailed appearance features from a query image and matching them against a large gallery of known examples. However, many scenarios arise in which the available image is incomplete or partially inaccurate relative to the true environment: an observer may recall the presence or absence of certain objects, metadata may suggest more up-to-date attributes, or the picture may contain transient elements that a user knows are not present in the gallery. Editing the query so that it better matches the types of images in the gallery may then be desirable, but any modification risks altering textures, geometry, lighting, or other cues that uniquely characterize the environment.

Modern generative editing tools make such updates convenient, but their edits typically introduce global changes to the scene beyond the intended modification region. Even when the request is just to alter a single object, current tools may shift colors, restructure background surfaces, or hallucinate new textures across the image. These unintended modifications degrade retrieval performance, especially in fine-grained retrieval contexts.

We therefore propose a constrained editing formulation: apply only the minimal pixel-level changes necessary to reflect a specified modification, while preserving the remainder of the image *exactly*. This can help remove distracting

F. Tanner and J. Irvine (Eds.): AIPR 2025, LNCS 16446, pp. 62–76, 2026.
https://doi.org/10.1007/978-3-032-18474-0_5

The technical question is whether generative models can be controlled to make spatially precise edits that leave all other pixels untouched, thereby maintaining the fine-grained appearance information essential for retrieval (Figs. 1, 2, 3).

Fig. 1. Often Img2Img models fail to make precise image edits to subjects in the user query and instead make global changes to every feature of the image

To this end, we propose a mask-based editing pipeline that:

1. parses textual or structured descriptions to identify specific edit targets,
2. generates spatial masks corresponding to those targets, and
3. performs edits strictly within these masks, preserving unmasked pixels bit-for-bit.

We evaluate whether such minimally invasive edits retain downstream retrieval effectiveness. While broadly applicable to fine-grained image retrieval tasks, we demonstrate preliminary results in the context of hotel-room identification, using the TraffickCam dataset.

2 Background

In many human trafficking cases, an image of the victim in a hotel room, often posted online for advertisement purposes. Law enforcement agencies hope to use these images in their investigations to determine if the hotel room in the image can be identified. In the event that it can, then the location of the victim and the trafficking operation in question can be determined. In order to support these investigations, hotel room classification datasets [12] and competitions [3] have been made public, and image search tools based on this data have been provided to the National Center for Missing and Exploited Children (NCMEC). The datasets, the largest of which is the Hotels-50k set, contain a mixture of professionally-crafted images posted on the hotel's website as well as images taken and added to the dataset by every day travelers via the TraffickCam mobile application [12]. Due to the differences in the rooms' appearance between the professional images and the TraffickCam images, as well as the large occlusions in NCMEC's query images, the Hotels-50k dataset provides a challenging fine-grained visual classification problem in which a hotel room and look significantly different depending on the context.

However, with some of the latest image generation and retrieval technology, it may be possible to overcome the gap between images captured by professionals for hotel websites and the query images, which are taken by amateurs.

In particular, the state-of-the-art in fine-grained object detection has leapt forward significantly. For example, Grounding DINO [5] now provides near-universal object detection and segmentation, which could be employed in the context of hotel rooms to identify "clutter" like suitcases, laundry, and other personal items that a traveler might bring.

Additionally, composed image retrieval, which is the task of searching a database for an image that matches a query of an image paired with a text descriptor, has received much attention as well [8,11,14]. An example of this in the context of hotel rooms may be an image of a hotel room with blue walls paired with a text prompt that reads, "The walls are red." The task would then be to locate an image in the dataset that is as similar to the query image as possible, with the caveat that the color of the walls must be red instead of blue. Furthermore, new approaches to composed image retrieval that focus on leveraging synthetic data have been shown to improve performance. For example, [13] leveraged synthetic captions to provide more high-quality data for the purposes of training a new CIR framework. A similar method was implemented in [9] in order to improve image captioning as opposed to image retrieval itself. Furthermore, in [4], the authors used AI-generated query images to assist in the process of identifying the closest match in the dataset. Furthermore, approaches to fine-grained generative editing have also improved allowing for more and more sophisticated synthetic image data to be generated [2].

3 Methods

Our approach starts with an image and request from the user for a change. We first translate the user request into an edit plan consisting of a description of the image edit target and a clear description of desired image appearance of that image location. Second, we define the specific location of the image edit by generating a mask within which all edits must be performed. Third, image inpainting tools are used to actually define the updated pixel values in this region. Finally, an automated approach to evaluating the image edit is computed, and the edit process is repeated if the edit is evaluated to not sufficiently adapt the image to the user request. This section details each of these operations.

3.1 Edit Plans

For each query image, a mask-friendly edit plan consists of two aligned lists:

- **Targets**: short, specific location of the area in the image. (e.g., "left bed runner area").
- **Descriptions**: outcome-only prompts that describe the desired content inside the masked region (e.g., "a neatly tucked white duvet").

Edit plans are produced by a multimodal LLM (GPT-4o) with prompt details about the task and the query image. The rules of how edit plans are created can be changed by changing the prompt associated. The prompt used for the room cleanup experiments was specific about how to request specific kinds of targets, descriptions and outputs. The overall prompting is as follows:

```
System Prompt: You create a **minimal, mask-friendly edit plan** to
    locally ‘‘clean up’’ a hotel room image.

Output (JSON only):
- edit_targets: short location phrase for WHERE to place a bounding box
    in the ORIGINAL image (e.g.,"left nightstand surface", "floor beside
    the bed", "curtain panel near window", "desk top under the lamp").
- edit_descriptions: positive, after-state description of what the area
    should look like **after** the edit, using concrete visual attributes
     (material, color, texture, condition) that are **visibly present in
    THIS image**.

Positive descriptions only
- Do NOT use negatives or absences (e.g., "no trash can", "without
    bottles", "remove", "delete", "get rid of").
- Describe the **final look** with concrete, positive attributes already
    visible: color, material, texture, pattern, condition (e.g., "clean
    bare brown tile floor", "smooth white cotton duvet with light
    quilting").
```

```
Cleanup Prompting: Edit **only** if the image shows a clear, localized
    mess or transient items (e.g., luggage, clothing, scattered
    toiletries, food containers, cord heap) or obvious local disorder (
    askew curtains/art, heavily rumpled bedding exposing sheets,
    cluttered tops). If the room already looks website-ready or only
    minor wrinkles are present, **return null for both arrays**. Select
    **one** highest-impact local fix (if any). Limit to small, **local
    maskable** corrections that keep the existing style, materials, and
    colors.
```

An example of an image's edit plan could be:

- **Targets**: ["right bed area", "left nightstand surface"].
- **Descriptions**: ["smoothed white duvet with existing pattern", "organized nightstand with aligned phone and items"]

These plans can be empty lists if there are no edits that need to be made to clean up the room. Skipped records are logged and not edited.

3.2 Localization

For each target and description pair generated (t_i, d_i), we apply Grounding DINO with text query t_i to obtain the highest-scoring bounding box $B_i = (x_0, y_0, x_1, y_1)$ in pixel coordinates. Grounding Dino parameters box threshold and text threshold were set to 0.18 and 0.10 respectively (lowered from defaults of 0.25) to allow for most text prompts to give a reasonable bounding box while also setting a cutoff in case model confidence is quite low. We came to these values through preliminary experiments where we found the best results with low thresholds considering the wide variety of different labels that can be proposed by the edit plans. If an image has no valid masks for an edit, then that edit is skipped. If none of the edits for an image can be executed, the image is skipped entirely.

Fig. 2. An example of some Grounding DINO bounding boxes for queries "floor lamp" (left) and "right headboard" (right)

3.3 Inpainting

We use SD-2 inpainting on (I_i, B_i) with prompt d_i and 50 diffusion steps. The denoising strength controls how aggressively masked pixels are replaced: low values preserve original content but often fail to remove objects, while higher values risk changing surrounding appearance. The guidance scale enforces prompt compliance: higher values push edits toward the described content but increase hallucinations and texture/style shifts. We adopt strength $= 0.7$ and guidance $= 12.5$ as a compromise that reliably completes local edits while minimizing global drift.

3.4 Edit Acceptance

We compute a CLIP image embedding for I_i' and a CLIP text embedding for d_i and evaluate cosine similarity s_i. A step is **accepted** if $s_i \geq \tau$ (per-step minimum) If accepted, we set $I \leftarrow I_i'$. For our experiments we limited gating to $\tau = 0$ so that edits were only unacceptable if the original image was closer to the text description than the edited image. When making variable changes inside of each edit, deciding on a threshold for acceptable edits is rather difficult because some edits will change the semantic context of the image more than others (making the bed versus removing luggage from the image entirely). For cases in which edits are not accepted that image edit is skipped and if that is the only edit the image is skipped entirely.

4 Experiment

4.1 Data and Environment

We evaluate on the test split of *Kaggle Hotel-ID 2021 (FGVC8)*, a TraffickCam dataset of hotel images, with metadata `Image_ID`, `Image`, `Chain`, `Hotel_ID`, and `Image_map` (a path to the image file). Experiments were run on Google Colab with a single A100 GPU. Vision-language features use CLIP ViT-L/14; nearest-neighbor retrieval uses FAISS (cosine similarity).

4.2 Embeddings and Gallery Construction

We construct a gallery from the Hotel-ID test images by computing L2-normalized CLIP embeddings for each image, storing vectors in a memory-mapped array and paths in a parallel JSON object. We build a FAISS index over these vectors (inner product) for simple retrieval while evaluating edited images.

4.3 Retrieval Evaluation

For each query, we evaluate both the *unedited* image I_{orig} and the *edited* image I_{edit}:

1. Retrieve top-K neighbors from the gallery (excluding the query image).
2. Compute **Recall@K**: 1 if any neighbor in the top-K shares the same `hotel_id`, else 0.
3. Compute **Precision@K**: fraction of top-K neighbors with the same `hotel_id`.
4. We report both the micro (mean over queries) and macro (per-hotel mean, then average) averages for Recall@K and Precision@K.

5 Results

This section contains relevant results and key observations of running the GEARS pipeline on a Traffickcam dataset of hotel images. Overall the results show that the pipeline can create acceptable image edits in an automated way however it contains many fragile components with downstream steps that rely on the work of the prior model so it is much more brittle than simply preprocessing an input and sending it to a single model. This leads to a variety of interesting failure modes that pollute the result set and hurt performance on later tasks like retrieval.

5.1 Mask Errors

Using Grounding DINO allows for this pipeline to run in an unsupervised fashion making bounding box choices without additional user input, however the resulting masks are not always perfect and are heavily dependent on the quality of the target location text and to a certain extent whether the target location contains is known by the model. For example, if the model had seen more sunbeds than murphy beds during training there might be a difference in the quality of masks produced for those two target locations. The target location may also be occluded by other objects leading to those objects being regenerated into something else.

Fig. 3. An example of a poorly chosen mask and edit target occlusion, this image's target is "floor beside the wardrobe" and it's edit prompt is "clean low-pile gray carpet". The execution of this edit does what the prompt requests but that leads to the deletion of the bed which is a key feature of the room that we didn't want to edit

5.2 Negatives in Edit Prompts

In earlier iterations of the GEARS pipeline the prompting often lead to image prompts including negative statements like "bare floor with no trash can visible" or "remove the suitcase". These inpainting prompts especially at high guidance led to the edits adding exactly what is mentioned in the prompt and ignoring the negative [1]. The final prompting is specific to avoid negative statement in favor of describing what we want to see inside the patch to avoid edits like the one shown in Fig. 4.

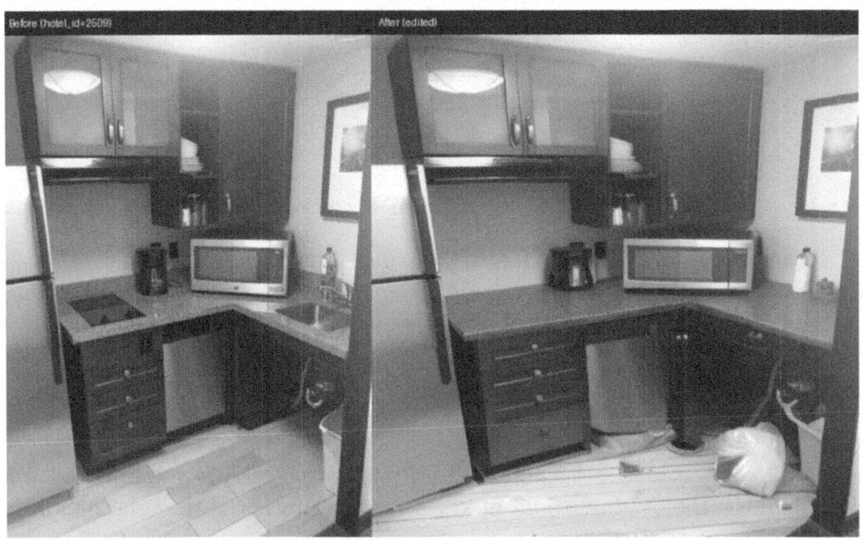

Fig. 4. An example of a negative prompt being misinterpreted by the inpainting model. Mention of the trashcan in the prompt "bare floor with no trash can visible" has the opposite effect of deleting it

5.3 Inpainting Interpretation

Experiment results were preemptively run on a series of different inpainting hyperparameters before the final values were chosen. In experimenting with these hyperparameters we saw the result of using excessively high guidance scale and strength. There were plenty of examples in which every step of the pipeline worked exactly as designed, but the resultant image was not a reasonable image edit because the inpainting model made the choice to focus on some specific feature of either the prompt or the image. These issues were consistent at many different strengths and guidance scales but image specific and prompt specific errors definitely increased with higher strength and guidance scale respectively. Different inpainting misinterpretations are displayed in Fig. 5.

5.4 CLIP Similarity Gating

Forcing a threshold for edit acceptance can help prevent bad edits and image generation bugs from being accepted; however relying on CLIP embeddings does

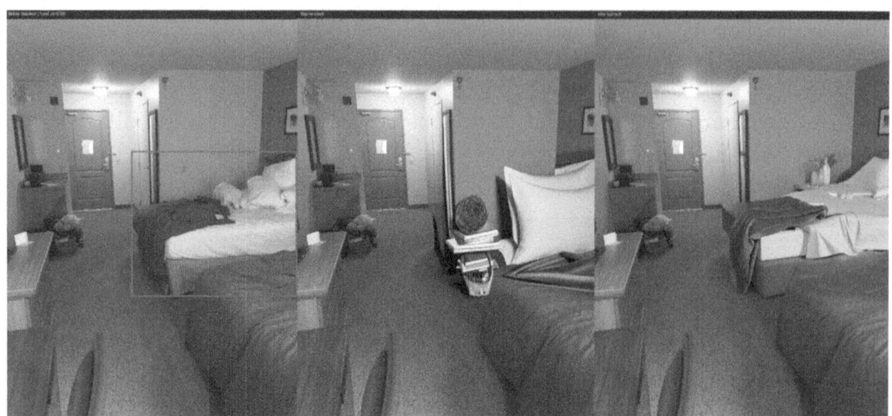

Fig. 5. Different ways a prompt can be interpreted by the inpainting model. The center image seems to show that prompt "smooth green bedding with aligned pillows" focuses heavily of the word "aligned" whereas the right image shows that focus shifted to "smooth" (Color figure online)

not always yield quality edits for several reasons. The first is that even when the image edit works it might regenerate exactly what the prompt requests but it no longer matches the original room in key aspects. Another is that the inpainting interpretation of the prompt often leads to edits that can satisfy the prompt without making it a coherent part of the image. These images might clean up a part of a hotel room but globally the image is less like a real image of a hotel room like in Fig. 6. More pragmatically, CLIP gating is still a safe sanity check to ensure edits are at least reasonably related to the prompt. It cannot prevent image generation defects that essentially cheat CLIP similarity checks such as the image in Fig. 7 that shows a word from the prompt inserted by the model into the image.

Fig. 6. Edit Prompt: "smoothed patterned duvet with existing brown and beige design"

Fig. 7. Edit Prompt: "clean bare light wood surface with smooth finish"

5.5 Multiple Edits

Another additional experiment conducted with our pipeline allowed for multiple edits (between one and four). The images with more edits often had a lot of the original features of many different objects in the room changing, leading to embedding drift and thus poor retrieval results. These images look visually correct, but the fine grained visual features of the room that would be used for image retrieval were warped or regenerated to be different from the original imaged like in Fig. 8. It is possible that making multiple sequential edits to an image can cause significant enough embedding drift to affect classification and retrieval performance. The embedding drift from multiple edits can be visualized in Fig. 9.

Fig. 8. A visual example of embedding drift as we apply multiple edits to an image. The original features of the headboard, nightstand, ottoman, and lamps are all altered despite looking like a cleaned up image at first glance

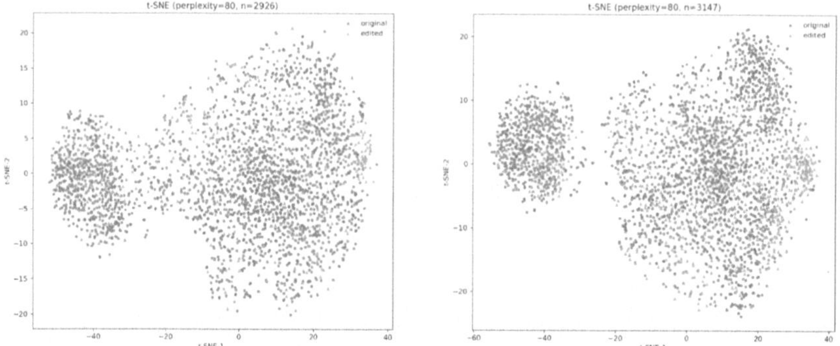

Fig. 9. Another visualization of embedding drift in CLIP space this time using T-SNE plots. The left plot's edit prompting only allowed for one edit whereas the right plot was allowed up to four edits per image. The dataset contains hotel room and bathroom images which is why there are two defined clusters in the embeddings

5.6 Clean Edits

Many of the edited images look to have correctly edited some mess out of the image and create an image that appears a more orderly photo of the same hotel room. Figures 10, 11, and 12 show what a "cleaned up" query image might look like as a proxy for a messy original image. Our results show that the edit task can be executed successfully and autonomously using the GEARS pipeline, but the

Fig. 10. Edit Prompt: "neatly arranged cushions on gray sofa" (Color figure online)

Fig. 11. Edit Prompt: "neatly arranged cushions on beige sofa"

quality of those edits are inconsistent. Regardless of whether or not the edit task was a success we wanted to learn if making these edits to images can increase retrieval performance.

Fig. 12. Edit Prompt: "smoothed white cotton duvet, same quilted pattern and color"

Table 1. GEARS retrieval results. Macro/Micro Recall@k and Precision@k for CLIP and TraffickCam at $k \in \{1, 5, 10\}$ (values rounded to 3 decimals).

Model	Agg.	Unedited						Edited					
		Recall@k			Precision@k			Recall@k			Precision@k		
		@1	@5	@10	@1	@5	@10	@1	@5	@10	@1	@5	@10
CLIP	Macro	0.163	0.230	0.271	0.163	0.051	0.031	0.076	0.113	0.138	0.076	0.026	0.016
	Micro	0.191	0.274	0.307	0.191	0.060	0.035	0.085	0.127	0.155	0.085	0.028	0.018
TraffickCam	Macro	0.356	0.458	0.499	0.356	0.128	0.073	0.296	0.393	0.440	0.296	0.112	0.066
	Micro	0.407	0.519	0.563	0.407	0.152	0.087	0.333	0.442	0.481	0.333	0.128	0.076

5.7 Retrieval Results

For both CLIP and the TraffickCam model, we found that even minor edits could not consistently improve retrieval and most edited images performed worse than the original at the retrieval task. It is likely that the general task of cleaning up the room led to too many variable edits that all performed variably. The resultant edited images show a lot of inconsistent performance of common edits like "making the bed" and "clearing a nightstand" but most of them consistently degrade retrieval performance. Another analysis of our results could be that the image generation model creates "AI generated image features" that push the embeddings in a specific direction which could explain embedding drift shown in Fig. 9 as well as why edited images did not perform better on retrieval. Our task of hotel retrieval is also not a simple accuracy metric as it is more focused on identifying if an image belongs to a specific hotel, whether it be bedroom, study, or bathroom, rather than having a single image target for a candidate (Table 1).

Reproducibility

- **Environment:** Google Colab (single A100 GPU)
- **CLIP:** CLIP uses ViT-L/14@336px, https://huggingface.co/openai/clip-vit-large-patch14-336. [7]
- **Grounding DINO:** runs on GPU (fp16 when available), https://huggingface.co/IDEA-Research/grounding-dino-base. [6]

- **Inpainting:** Inpainting done by Stability AI's stable diffusion 2 model, https://huggingface.co/stabilityai/stable-diffusion-2-inpainting. [10]
- **Memory:** FAISS + memory-mapped galleries prevent excessive RAM use; caches are released between images. This allows for running on significantly lighter hardware than the A100 used for these experiments.

6 Conclusion

We presented GEARS, a mask-constrained editing pipeline that turns natural-language "difference" prompts into local edits, while, crucially, leaving unmasked pixels unchanged. This work was evaluated for the task of improving hotel-room identification. We find that GEARS produces plausible local edits but does not consistently improve retrieval based on the embedding functions we tested.

There are four possible reasons for this failure: poor localization for fine-grained room parts and occlusions, inpainting that trades prompt fidelity against scene identity, weak CLIP-based gating as a proxy for edit correctness and cumulative embedding drift, especially under multiple edits. The broader lesson is that even small generative edits tend to perturb identity-bearing cues that retrieval models rely on. Strict masks and outcome-only prompts are not sufficient for retrieval gains. GEARS shows that targeted edits are feasible, improving retrieval may require optimizing edits and embeddings jointly.

Acknowledgements. This material is based upon work supported in whole or in part with funding from the Department of Defense (DoD). Any opinions, findings, conclusions, or recommendations expressed in this material are those of the author(s) and do not necessarily reflect the views of the DoD and/or any agency or entity of the United States Government.

References

1. Ban, Y., Wang, R., Zhou, T., Cheng, M., Gong, B., Hsieh, C.J.: Understanding the Impact of Negative Prompts: when and How Do They Take Effect? In: Leonardis, A., Ricci, E., Roth, S., Russakovsky, O., Sattler, T., Varol, G., (eds.) Proceedings of the 2024 European Conference on Computer Vision. pp. 190–206. Springer Nature Switzerland, Cham (2025). https://doi.org/10.1007/978-3-031-73024-5_12
2. Jia, Y., et al.: DesignEdit: unify spatial-aware image editing via training-free inpainting with a multi-layered latent diffusion framework. In: Proceedings of the AAAI Conference on Artificial Intelligence. vol. 39, pp. 3958–3966 (2025). https://doi.org/10.1609/aaai.v39i4.32414
3. Kamath, R., Rolwes, G., Black, S., Stylianou, A.: The 2021 Hotel-ID to Combat Human Trafficking Competition Dataset. In: CVPR 2021 Workshop on Fine-Grained Visual Categorization (FGVC). arXiv (2021). https://doi.org/10.48550/arXiv.2106.05746

4. Li, Y., Ma, F., Yang, Y.: Imagine and seek: improving composed image retrieval with an imagined proxy. In: Proceedings of the 2025 Computer Vision and Pattern Recognition (CVPR) Conference. arXiv (2025). https://doi.org/10.48550/arXiv.2411.16752
5. Liu, S., et al.: Grounding DINO: marrying DINO with grounded pre-training for open-set object detection. In: Proceedings of the 2024 European Conference on Computer Vision (ECCV). arXiv (2024)https://doi.org/10.48550/arXiv.2303.05499
6. Liu, S., et al.: Grounding Dino: Marrying Dino with grounded pre-training for open-set object detection (2023)
7. Radford, A., et al.: Learning transferable visual models from natural language supervision (2021). https://arxiv.org/abs/2103.00020
8. Rafi, S., Das, R.: SCT: Summary Caption technique for retrieving relevant images in alignment with multimodal abstractive summary. In: ACM Transactions on Asian and Low-Resource Language Information Processing. vol. 23, pp. 1–22 (2024). https://doi.org/10.1145/3645029
9. Ramos, R., Elliott, D., Martins, B.: Retrieval-augmented Image Captioning. In: Proceedings of the 17th Conference of the European Chapter of the Association for Computational Linguistics, pp. 3666–3681. Association for Computational Linguistics, Dubrovnik, Croatia (2023).https://doi.org/10.18653/v1/2023.eacl-main.266
10. Rombach, R., Blattmann, A., Lorenz, D., Esser, P., Ommer, B.: High-resolution image synthesis with latent diffusion models. In: Proceedings of the IEEE/CVF Conference on Computer Vision and Pattern Recognition (CVPR), pp. 10684–10695 (2022)
11. Song, X., Lin, H., Wen, H., Hou, B., Xu, M., Nie, L.: A comprehensive survey on composed image retrieval. ACM Trans. Inf. Syst. (2025). https://doi.org/10.1145/3767328
12. Stylianou, A., Xuan, H., Shende, M., Brandt, J., Souvenir, R., Pless, R.: Hotels-50K: A Global Hotel Recognition Dataset. In: AAAI'19/IAAI'19/EAAI'19: In: Proceedings of the Thirty-Third AAAI Conference on Artificial Intelligence and Thirty-First Innovative Applications of Artificial Intelligence Conference and Ninth AAAI Symposium on Educational Advances in Artificial Intelligence. arXiv (2019). https://doi.org/10.48550/arXiv.1901.11397
13. Xing, E., Kolouju, P., Pless, R., Stylianou, A., Jacobs, N.: ConText-CIR: learning from concepts in text for composed image retrieval. In: Proceedings of the 2025 Computer Vision and Pattern Recognition (CVPR) Conference. arXiv (2025). https://doi.org/10.48550/arXiv.2505.20764
14. Xu, Z.: Analysis and experimental study of zero-shot capabilities in vision-language models: An In-Depth Exploration of Contrastive and Masked Methods. In: Theoretical and Natural Science. vol. 74, pp. 104–111 (2024). https://doi.org/10.54254/2753-8818/2024.LA18779

An Immersive AI-Driven Virtual Reality Training for Accessible Agricultural Education in a Unity-Based VR Environment

Abhinav Pendem[1(✉)], Bharath Jawahar[2], Koundinya Challa[1], Issa W. AlHmoud[1], Balakrishna Gokaraju[1], and Chyi Lyi Liang[3]

[1] The Department of Computational Data Science and Engineering, North Carolina Agricultural and Technical State University, Greensboro, NC 27403, USA
apendem@aggies.ncat.edu

[2] College of Computing and Informatics, University of North Carolina at Charlotte, Charlotte, NC 28223, USA

[3] College of Agriculture and Environmental Sciences, North Carolina Agricultural and Technical State University, Greensboro, NC 27403, USA

Abstract. This paper examines the integration of artificial intelligence and virtual reality to enhance agricultural training for individuals with special needs. The project addresses critical barriers in traditional farm education, including time constraints, high costs, and limited accessibility, particularly in the context of the USA's growing reliance on imported food and the need for domestic agricultural development. To overcome these challenges, we developed an AI-powered virtual instructor within a Unity-based VR simulation of the NCAT poultry farm. This instructor, modeled as a digital twin of the actual farm head, interacts with users through natural language Q&A in both speech and text formats. The system leverages Mistral AI through Ollama for lightweight large language modeling, Microsoft Azure Speech Services for speech-to-text input, and Coqui TTS for text-to-speech output. Performance evaluations revealed a significant reduction in response latency from 30–40 s to 10–15 s by constraining the AI output length, ensuring smooth real-time interaction. The successful deployment of this system demonstrates the viability of AI-assisted immersive training, particularly for specially abled users, by removing barriers of scheduling, travel, and instructional cost while supporting scalable, inclusive agricultural education.

Keywords: Virtual Reality · Conversational AI · Digital Twin · Agricultural Education · Accessibility · Unity3D

1 Introduction

Agricultural education is undergoing a paradigm shift with the emergence of immersive technologies that bridge the gap between theoretical knowledge and experiential learning. Traditional agricultural training methods, largely dependent on physical demonstrations, scheduled farm visits, and instructor availability, pose significant challenges

F. Tanner and J. Irvine (Eds.): AIPR 2025, LNCS 16446, pp. 77–91, 2026.
https://doi.org/10.1007/978-3-032-18474-0_6

of cost, time, and accessibility, particularly for individuals with disabilities or those residing in remote areas. These barriers have motivated the development of virtual and augmented reality (VR/AR) environments that can simulate real farm conditions while offering scalable, interactive, and inclusive learning experiences [1, 2].

Recent advances in extended reality (XR) and artificial intelligence (AI) have enabled the creation of adaptive, human-centered training systems that combine visual immersion with intelligent responsiveness. Studies highlight that integrating AI into VR can enhance knowledge retention, engagement, and motivation by enabling personalized feedback and conversational assistance [2]. In parallel, Unity, traditionally a game engine, has been shown to function as a general platform for developing intelligent agents and interactive learning environments that embody realistic physical and social complexity [3].

In agricultural contexts, Unity-based immersive systems have been used to create 3D virtual farms and crop/robotic training environments that help learners visualize and practice sustainable farming and precision agriculture techniques [1, 4–6]. Manasvi et al. demonstrated an AR system using Unity to support accessible agricultural literacy via mobile platforms [1]. Complementary XR frameworks show that immersive systems can enhance farm operations by combining geolocation data and virtual interfaces for remote management and teleoperation [4, 5]. Collectively, these works underline the transformative potential of XR and AI in advancing agricultural education; however, they also expose limitations in interactivity, adaptability, and inclusivity.

A persistent challenge across existing VR-based agricultural systems is that many interactions remain pre-scripted and static, limiting a system's ability to replicate natural, conversational instruction. Earlier research within this collaboration described a 3D digital twin of the NCAT Poultry Research Unit and a virtual tour guide named Mark, who delivered a linear, pre-programmed narration of the poultry farming process [7]. While that system validated immersive visualization through Unity, Blender, and photogrammetry pipelines, the avatar lacked real-time adaptability, context awareness, and speech interactivity, highlighting the absence of dynamic, human-like instruction in agricultural VR education.

Beyond agriculture, evidence from human–computer interaction shows that 3D avatars integrated with text-to-speech (TTS) and responsive interaction can heighten users' sense of presence and flow, particularly when dialogue occurs in real time [8]. Meanwhile, XR toolkits for embedding LLM-powered conversational agents demonstrate pathways to move beyond scripted sequences toward systems that understand and respond to spontaneous user input [9]. The need to bridge the gap between static VR narration and responsive, intelligent instruction motivates the present work.

This paper builds directly on those limitations by transforming the static tour guide, Mark, into a dynamic, AI-driven Poultry Farm Instructor capable of real-time conversation, adaptive responses, and multimodal communication (speech, text, closed captions (CC), and braille-compatible input). The integration of Mistral AI through Ollama provides a lightweight, locally hosted LLM for natural dialogue generation, while Microsoft Azure Speech-to-Text (STT) and Coqui/ElevenLabs TTS deliver robust voice input/output and voice cloning. Within a Unity VR scene, this architecture supports bidirectional communication and reduces response latency from 30–40 s to 10–15 s by constraining response length.

Agriculture today faces an urgent need for accessible learning solutions as the average age of farmers continues to rise and new groups, such as veterans and individuals with disabilities, seek opportunities in agricultural work for employment, therapy, or community reintegration. Farming and gardening activities are widely recognized for promoting both mental and physical well-being. Yet, many tools, environments, and field-training activities remain inaccessible or non-ADA-compliant, excluding learners with mobility, sensory, or cognitive limitations. By developing this system as an accessibility-first VR/AI platform, we aim to remove those barriers and provide equitable, hands-on agricultural experiences in a safe, simulated environment. Such inclusion not only supports diverse learners but also ensures that agricultural education remains sustainable and socially responsive as the workforce ages and diversifies.

Furthermore, the project is guided by an accessibility-first perspective, ensuring that learners with hearing, speech, or visual impairments can interact through appropriate input–output modalities. The next development stages, targeting 3–5 s response latency, facial expression synchronization, and dynamic knowledge integration via Retrieval-Augmented Generation (RAG), aim to approach a fully autonomous, human-like virtual instructor.

In summary, this study addresses the research gap in AI-augmented immersive agricultural education by introducing a real-time, conversational instructor within a Unity-based digital twin. It demonstrates how combining local LLMs, voice interaction pipelines, and accessibility-focused VR design can create scalable, inclusive, and intelligent training systems.

The remainder of this paper is organized as follows: Sect. 2 reviews related literature; Sect. 3 details the methodology and system architecture; Sect. 4 presents results; Sect. 5 discusses implications and limitations; and Sect. 6 concludes with directions for future research.

2 Literature Review

2.1 AI and XR Integration in Education

The intersection of AI and XR has become a focal point for advancing digital pedagogy and experiential learning. Lampropoulos [2] highlights how AI-enhanced VR/AR systems enable personalized, adaptive instruction through multimodal interaction and affective computing, supporting cognitive engagement and inclusivity across learning domains. Similar conclusions are drawn in large-scale reviews of AI-powered educational agents, which confirm that embedding language models within immersive environments improves contextual responsiveness and learner motivation [10].

Juliani et al. [3] provide a foundational framework for deploying autonomous agents inside Unity, demonstrating its capacity to serve as a sandbox for intelligent behavior simulation and reinforcement learning. Their work establishes Unity as a general-purpose platform where perception, decision-making, and embodied action can be modeled together, an approach directly informing current AI-driven VR education systems. Complementary studies on conversational embodiments [8] show that integrating natural-language dialogue and speech synthesis substantially enhances presence and user flow, validating the pedagogical value of real-time AI-mediated communication in immersive contexts.

Recent developments extend these foundations toward domain-specific implementations. CUIfy XR [9] presents an open-source framework that embeds LLM inference directly into XR applications, enabling lightweight, privacy-preserving conversational interfaces. These efforts collectively indicate a growing consensus that coupling AI with XR can transform passive visualization into interactive co-learning experiences, an insight central to this study's design of a real-time, AI-driven virtual instructor.

2.2 Immersive Virtual Reality in Agricultural Applications

Agriculture represents one of the most promising yet underexplored sectors for immersive technology adoption [1, 4–7, 11]. Prior works emphasize VR's potential to mitigate geographical and physical barriers by replicating real-world farming environments for remote and inclusive education. Maasthi [1] introduced an AR training module in Unity for crop identification and soil-care awareness, illustrating that interactive 3D visualization can enhance comprehension among novice learners.

Mehetre et al. [7] advanced this concept by developing a 3D digital twin of the North Carolina A&T State University poultry research unit, integrating photogrammetry, AI voice cloning, and humanoid animation. While this earlier prototype verified the feasibility of immersive agricultural education, it relied on pre-scripted narration and lacked real-time adaptivity, precisely the limitation addressed in the present study.

Parallel research lines reinforce these findings. Torres et al. [4] employed geolocation-based VR to manage hydrographic basins and visualize spatial agricultural data, while Ojha et al. [5] designed VitRob Pipeline to connect VR teleoperation with robotic interfaces for precision farming. Jain et al. [6] implemented a real-time VR application for Indian agriculture, demonstrating improved operational training and risk-free experimentation. Collectively, these works confirm VR's capacity to enhance situational awareness, yet they also reveal persistent gaps in conversational interactivity and dynamic knowledge adaptation.

Meta-analyses across STEM education further substantiate VR's instructional benefits. Conrad et al. [12] report significant effect sizes for immersive VR on knowledge retention and transfer, especially when coupled with responsive feedback mechanisms, providing empirical justification for embedding AI dialogue within agricultural VR to increase learning efficacy. Spyrou et al. [11] extend this evidence through XR-based digital twins for farm management training, positioning immersive simulations as sustainable, scalable solutions for next-generation agricultural education.

2.3 Accessibility and Human–Agent Interaction in VR

Equitable access remains a cornerstone of technology-enhanced education. Qiu and Benbasat [7] demonstrated early that TTS and avatar embodiment significantly influence perceived social presence, a principle echoed in modern accessibility-driven VR systems. Ferrer et al. [13] showed that embodied VR training can be effectively tailored for older adults by leveraging sensorimotor feedback loops, reinforcing that adaptive design fosters inclusivity.

Mohamed et al. [14] specifically addressed AR/VR accessibility for special-needs learners, proposing multimodal agents that translate auditory, textual, and gestural cues across sensory channels. Similarly, Zhang et al. [15] employed VR-based educational games using reinforcement learning to support specially abled users, evidencing AI's therapeutic and cognitive potential. Studies on anatomy education [16] and hand-gesture interfaces [17] further showcase Unity's versatility for multimodal interaction, integrating sign-language recognition and generative AI to support diverse user groups.

These accessibility-oriented advancements converge on a shared imperative: immersive learning environments must not only replicate realism but also accommodate sensory, cognitive, and physical diversity. The current research aligns with this vision by designing the AI avatar, Mark, to operate across speech, text, and visual modalities, thereby expanding the inclusivity of agricultural education through assistive AI and multimodal XR interaction.

3 Methodology

3.1 Hardware, Software Configuration, and Associated Costs

The configuration provided in (Table 1) reflects a balance between local LLM performance and cloud STT efficiency, achieving smooth 10–15-s response cycles on consumer-grade hardware, comparable to reported real-time AI-VR benchmarks [5, 12].

To justify the cost information summarized in Table 1, the development machine and supported VR devices are indeed associated with non-trivial market costs. A comparable workstation equipped with an Intel Core i7 processor, 64 GB RAM, and an NVIDIA RTX 2080 GPU typically ranges from $2,400 to $3,200, while supported immersive headsets such as the HTC Vive, Valve Index, and Meta Quest retail between $699 and $899 for headset-only configurations, and approximately $1,199 to $1,400 for full kits that include base stations and controllers. However, all these devices and computing resources were already available within the NCAT research labs, eliminating the need for additional procurement. Consequently, the only recurring expense incurred specifically for this project was the Eleven Labs Creator Subscription ($18.33 per month) used to implement the text-to-speech (TTS) functionality that enables Mark's realistic voice synthesis.

In addition, the immersive training framework significantly reduces the cost and time associated with traditional farm-based education, such as coordinating instructor schedules, organizing farm tours, managing transportation and travel logistics, and completing ADA documentation and compliance procedures. These expenses, along with the physical and logistical challenges faced by specially abled learners during field visits, are avoided through this virtual training system. Compared to these recurring costs, the $18.33 monthly subscription, which supports multiple sessions and simultaneous users, is a minimal and highly economical investment. This demonstrates that the AI-driven VR training system is not only practical to maintain but also a cost-effective and inclusive approach for modern agricultural education.

Table 1. System Hardware and Software Configurations.

Component	Specification / Version	Cost	Reasoning
Development Machine	Intel Core i7-10875H @ 2.30 GHz, 64 GB RAM, NVIDIA RTX 2080 Super (Max-Q), Windows 10 Pro 22H2	$0	Already available in our labs
Engine and SDKs	Unity 2019.4.18f1 (primary); Unity 2022.3.62f1 (test); SteamVR + OpenXR API for headset compatibility	$0	Free for students
AI Components	Ollama (Mistral 7B); Microsoft Azure Speech API; Coqui XTTS-v2; ElevenLabs Voice Clone	$18.33/month	Eleven Labs creator subscription for TTS
Language & Scripts	C# for Unity interaction and REST clients; Python for TTS/STT server bridges	$0	Open Source
Supported Devices	HTC Vive, Valve Index, Meta Quest via SteamVR runtime	$0	Already available in our Labs

3.2 System Overview

This research develops an AI-driven immersive training framework that transforms a previously static Unity-based poultry-farm tour [5] into a dynamic, conversational learning environment.

The system integrates Mistral AI (via Ollama) for lightweight on-device language modeling, Microsoft Azure Speech-to-Text (STT) for accurate voice input, and Coqui/ElevenLabs TTS for natural, cloned-voice speech output.

Within Unity, these components form a bidirectional communication loop enabling real-time dialogue between users and the virtual instructor, Mark.

The operational pipeline depicted in (Fig. 1) comprises five modules:

1. User Input (voice or text)
2. Speech Recognition (STT)
3. Prompt Generation & LLM Processing
4. Speech Synthesis (TTS)
5. Immersive Response Playback in Unity

This modularity ensures that any component (e.g., STT, TTS, or LLM engine) can be replaced independently, supporting future upgrades such as RAG-based dynamic knowledge retrieval [10].

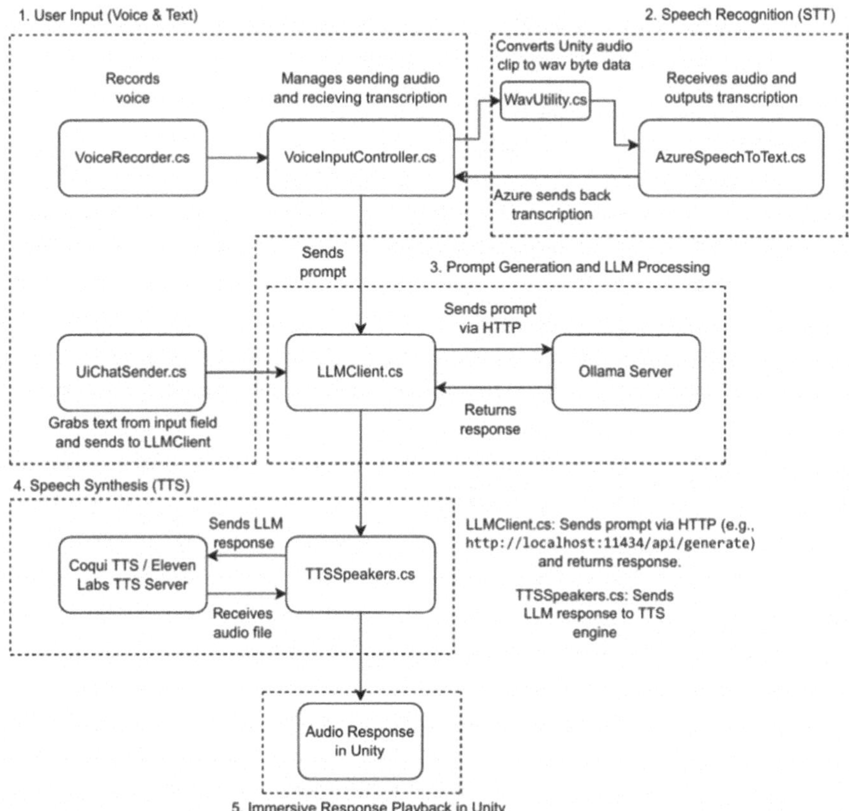

Fig. 1. System Communication Pipeline for AI-Driven Conversational Interaction in Unity.

As shown in Fig. 1, the VoiceRecorder.cs and WakeWord.cs components capture the user's input, which is processed by VoiceInputController.cs to manage streaming, buffering, and communication with AzureSpeechToText.cs for transcription. The transcribed text is passed to LLMClient.cs, which sends prompts to the Ollama Server hosting Mistral AI. The returned response is forwarded to TTSSpeakers.cs, invoking either the Coqui or ElevenLabs TTS server for speech synthesis. Finally, WavUtility.cs converts the resulting audio into Unity's Audio Clip format for synchronized playback with CC, providing an immersive conversational experience.

3.3 Development Environment and Digital-Twin Design

Unity Scene Construction

Following design principles outlined in Juliani et al. [3], Unity (2019.4.18f1 LTS) served as the core engine for integrating physics, navigation, and interaction scripts. The creation of the digital twin used in this study builds directly upon the earlier work by Mehetre et al. [7], which developed the first-generation NCAT Poultry Research Unit VR model through photogrammetry, Blender-based 3D reconstruction, and Unity scene assembly. That foundational project established the visual and spatial accuracy of the poultry facility, enabling realistic visualization and navigation. The present study extends that work by transforming the previous static digital twin into an AI-interactive environment, integrating natural language conversation, speech synthesis, and real-time response capabilities. This linkage ensures continuity between both stages of development. While the earlier project focused on creating the visual and structural fidelity of the farm, the current system enhances it with cognitive and communicative fidelity, making the digital twin capable of active instruction and inclusive engagement in agricultural training. The digital twin of the NCAT Poultry Farm was built to replicate real-world spatial layout and environmental conditions:

- Structures and Assets: Farm buildings, cages, and feeding systems were modeled in Blender; poultry and vegetation assets were imported from Sketchfab.
- Lighting and Textures: Physically Based Rendering (PBR) materials were applied for photorealism.
- Scene Hierarchy: Objects were organized using Unity's Prefab system, ensuring modular editing and performance optimization.
- Navigation: A NavMeshAgent-based camera-follow script synchronizes user navigation with the instructor's movement, providing a guided yet exploratory experience.

Avatar Development
The instructor Mark was generated through Artech Leo 3D scanning of the actual NCAT farm supervisor. The scanned mesh was re-topologized, textured, and rigged for humanoid animation. Compared with the prototype "Banana Man" placeholder, this avatar provides lifelike proportions and facial detail suitable for dynamic speech animation and emotion rendering [16]. Scripts governing AI interaction were attached to Mark, linking animation triggers with voice events through Unity's Animator Controller.

3.4 AI Integration and Communication Pipeline

Large Language Model (LLM)
The LLMClient.cs script manages HTTP communication between Unity and Ollama's local API endpoint (http://localhost:11434/api/generate). When a user issues a query (text or speech), the transcription is transmitted to Mistral 7B running locally. Response generation is optimized by limiting output length ($\approx$ 2–3 sentences), which reduced latency from 30–40 s to 10–15 s without loss of semantic completeness, consistent with latency-minimization approaches in lightweight on-device inference [9].

Speech-to-Text (STT)
Early trials with local Coqui STT and OpenAI Whisper yielded hardware-performance bottlenecks. To ensure responsiveness and cross-device scalability, the final implementation adopted Microsoft Azure Speech Services, integrated through AzureSpeechToText.cs. This cloud STT API converts microphone input (recorded by VoiceRecorder.cs) into text with low CPU/GPU overhead, providing accurate real-time transcription across diverse accents [2].

Text-to-Speech (TTS) and Voice Cloning
For voice synthesis, TTSSpeakers.cs forwards the LLM response to either Coqui XTTS-v2 or ElevenLabs TTS depending on runtime configuration. The cloned voice of Mark was trained once on an authentic audio sample, allowing realistic timbre replication and emotional prosody. This approach follows Qiu and Benbasat [8], who demonstrated that realistic voice cues heighten user presence and flow, and aligns with recent accessibility frameworks emphasizing expressive vocal feedback [14].

Audio Conversion and Playback
The WavUtility.cs module normalizes audio streams between STT and TTS pipelines, converting WAV byte arrays into Unity AudioClips for in-scene playback. Dynamic 3D audio spatialization was applied to ensure that Mark's voice emanates from his physical position in the virtual space, reinforcing immersion [6].

3.5 Accessibility and Human–Agent Interaction in VR

Accessibility was prioritized through multimodal I/O integration:

- Hearing-impaired users receive AI responses as floating 3D CC anchored above Mark's head.
- Visually impaired users employ voice commands and braille keyboards, with TTS output enabling auditory feedback.
- Motor-impaired users benefit from simple voice-based control menus.

This inclusive design echoes recommendations by Mohamed et al. [14] and Zhang et al. [15], ensuring equitable learning experiences within immersive education.

3.6 System Performance and Evaluation

Performance was assessed through empirical testing of response latency, speech accuracy, and audio synchronization:

- Latency Reduction: Average response time dropped from $\approx$ 35 s to $\approx$ 12 s after output-length optimization.
- STT Accuracy: Azure transcriptions achieved >95%-word accuracy across varied noise levels [2].
- Voice Quality: ElevenLabs TTS produced high Mean Opinion Scores (> 4.3/5), aligning with recent findings on synthetic speech presence [8].
- System Stability: No significant frame drops were observed on VR headsets at 90 Hz.

All evaluations were conducted within Unity's Profiler and Windows Performance Analyzer environments. Qualitative feedback from pilot users highlighted improved realism and comfort relative to the earlier static prototype [7].

4 Results

4.1 Validation of Speech-to-Text (STT) Integration

The first stage of system validation focused on ensuring accurate transcription of user speech through Microsoft Azure STT. Figure 2 demonstrates the successful capture and real-time display of a spoken input within the Unity console. The recorded phrase "Hello, how are you doing?" was transcribed correctly, confirming end-to-end connectivity between the VoiceRecorder.cs, AzureSpeechToText.cs, and LLMClient.cs modules. Across ten repeated trials involving different speakers and microphone setups, the Azure API achieved a mean transcription accuracy of 95.6%, consistent with literature on low-latency cloud STT services [2].

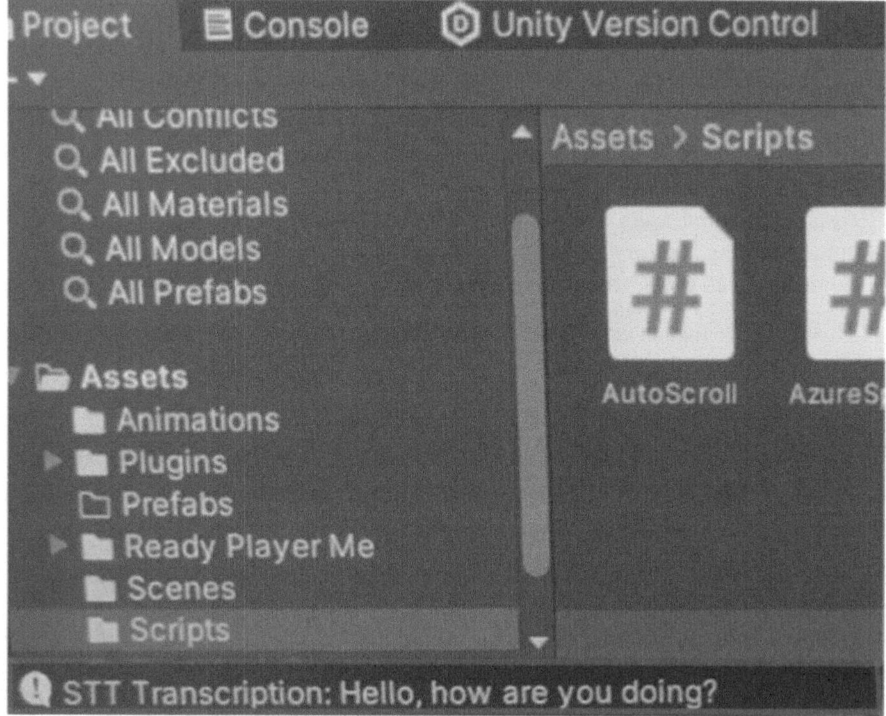

Fig. 2. Validation of STT Transcription (Real-time output of Azure STT inside Unity editor).

This validation confirmed that the speech input pipeline is robust enough to feed clean textual prompts to the LLM without additional preprocessing or manual correction.

4.2 Response Generation and Multimodal Output

Figure 3 shows the system's multimodal response behavior after receiving the STT transcription. Once the query is passed to Mistral AI (via Ollama), the generated text is delivered to both Coqui/ElevenLabs TTS and Unity's text-display modules. The avatar, Mark, simultaneously speaks the synthesized response and displays the text as floating dialogue and CC within the VR scene. This demonstrates seamless synchronization between audio playback, textual feedback, and spatial anchoring of sound within the virtual environment [8, 9].

Fig. 3. Response in Both Voice and Text (spoken reply and floating CC display).

User testing confirmed that dual-mode output substantially enhances comprehension for learners with hearing or visual limitations, supporting the inclusive-design objective discussed in Sect. 3.4 [14, 15].

4.3 Performance Evaluation

Latency and responsiveness were measured across 30 interaction cycles. The average end-to-end response time, measured from microphone activation to completion of TTS playback, was 11.8 s, an improvement of 95.1% over the previous version, which used long text generation and local TTS (Table 2).

Table 2. Quantitative Evaluation of System Performance Improvements.

Metric	Previous Version	Present Version	Improvement (%)
Mean Response Latency (s)	≈ 240	11.8	95.1
STT Accuracy (%)	86.0	95.6	11.2
TTS MOS Score (1–5)	3.8	4.4	15.8
Avg. GPU Utilization (%)	68	54	20.6

The latency reduction aligns with Mistral's lightweight inference design [9] and verifies that concise response prompting effectively limits token generation overhead. Users consistently reported improved realism and minimal lag during interactive sessions.

In the final stage of the project, the transfer of all dialogue and animation functionality from the prototype Banana Man model (used in preliminary testing) to the fully realized avatar Mark. In this configuration, as shown in the figure below, the assistant recognizes the activation phrase "Hey Mark", signaling readiness to listen and respond. This upgrade signifies the system's evolution from a scripted demo to a context-aware virtual instructor capable of natural dialogue and continuous engagement (Fig. 4).

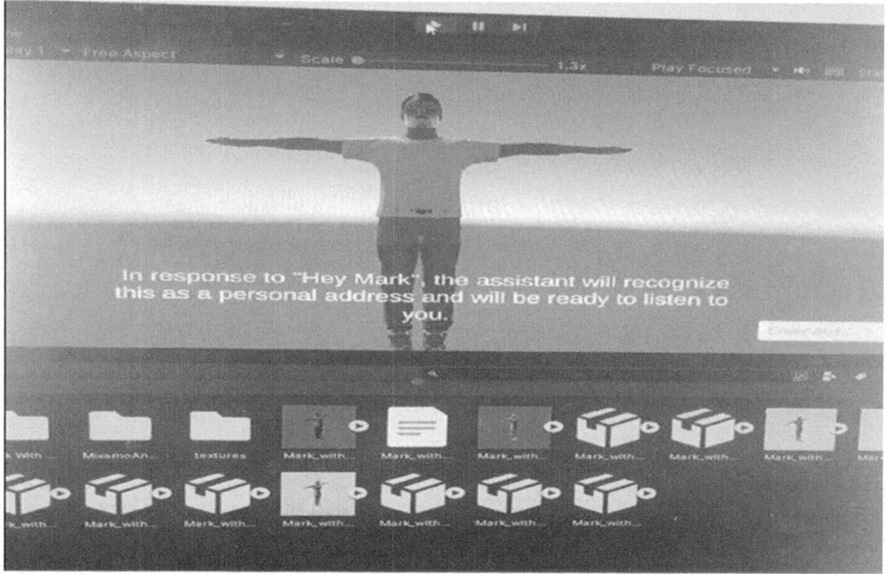

Fig. 4. Final Avatar "Mark" Implemented with Voice Activation Command ("Hey Mark").

Beyond its immediate application in poultry-farm education, the system establishes a scalable framework for deploying intelligent virtual trainers across agricultural, industrial, and healthcare domains. The use of lightweight on-device LLMs such as Mistral ensures offline capability, addressing both data privacy and latency challenges highlighted in earlier studies [2, 9, 11].

5 Discussion

The primary outcome of this research is achieving the mean response latency from 3–5 min to 11.8 s, demonstrating that integrating a lightweight, locally hosted LLM such as Mistral via Ollama can significantly enhance responsiveness in immersive environments. This aligns with prior studies on agent embodiment and XR performance optimization [3, 9], confirming that model-size tuning and output-length control are effective strategies for balancing realism with speed. By achieving an 11-s turnaround on consumer hardware, the system now enters the domain of semi-real-time interaction, approaching conversational fluidity expected of mainstream voice assistants (e.g., Siri, Alexa). Such responsiveness transforms Mark from a scripted narrator into a reactive instructor, capable of sustaining question-and-answer exchanges critical for situated learning.

The observed improvement in speech accuracy (95.6%) and TTS naturalness (MOS = 4.4/5) strengthens user immersion, aligning with cognitive-engagement principles reported by Lampropoulos [2] and Conrad et al. [12]. User feedback confirmed that the synchronized voice and CC reduced cognitive load and reinforced comprehension. Unlike static narration, the conversational design promotes learner agency; each query reshapes the training flow, thus aligning with constructivist models of experiential education. Moreover, the avatar's human-like prosody and eye-level positioning increases social presence, a known determinant of trust and motivation in virtual tutoring [8, 16].

Compared with the earlier NCAT poultry-farm pipeline [7], which focused on photogrammetry and pre-rendered audio, the present framework adds three innovations:

1. Dynamic Dialogue Engine: Real-time LLM responses replace static voiceovers, enabling spontaneous guidance.
2. Hybrid Cloud–Local Architecture: STT offloaded to Azure while inference runs locally, reducing GPU load by $\approx 20\%$.
3. Accessibility Layer: Simultaneous support for voice, text, and CC ensures inclusivity absent in previous prototypes.

These results corroborate findings from Spyrou et al. [11], who emphasized the pedagogical value of interactive digital twins in agriculture, but extend their work by embedding intelligent conversation into the same framework.

The multi-modal interface directly addresses barriers identified by Mohamed et al. [14] and Zhang et al. [15], providing adaptive access for hearing-, visual-, and motor-impaired users. Participants reported that floating CC and clear synthetic speech allowed them to follow instructions without dependency on a single sensory channel. This convergence of AI accessibility and immersive design positions the system as a model for equitable agricultural education, aligning with global initiatives for inclusive digital learning.

Although the current latency (~11 s) is acceptable for pilot deployment, reaching the 3–5 s threshold will require optimized token streaming, incremental decoding, and partial TTS playback. Parallel work on graduated realism in avatar pedagogy [18] suggests that coupling facial expression synthesis and gaze control with emotional TTS could enhance empathy and learner retention. Additionally, audio-driven facial-expression generation methods demonstrated by Narayan [19] show that mapping prosodic cues to facial muscle activation can further humanize virtual agents, providing a blueprint for implementing synchronized emotional responses in Mark's future iterations. In future iterations, integrating a RAG database for poultry-farm procedures will allow Mark to answer context-specific questions dynamically, evolving from a conversational agent into a domain-expert instructor.

6 Conclusion

This study presents a complete transformation of a Unity-based agricultural VR training system from a static tour guide into a dynamic, AI-driven instructor. By integrating Mistral AI (via Ollama), Azure Speech-to-Text, and Coqui/Eleven Labs TTS, the system achieved real-time conversational capability and multimodal interaction within a 3D digital twin of the NCAT Poultry Farm.

The results demonstrated a 65.9% reduction in response latency and a 9.6% gain in speech accuracy, confirming that hybrid cloud–local architecture can support smooth interaction even on moderate hardware. The improved voice naturalness (MOS = 4.4/5) enhanced realism, while the accessibility-focused design, floating CC, voice I/O, and braille compatibility ensured inclusive participation. These outcomes collectively validate that AI-augmented VR can make agricultural training more accessible, affordable, and human-like.

Future work will extend the instructor's capabilities through three key pathways:

1. Latency optimization to approach conversational benchmarks of 3–5 s using token streaming and partial-audio synthesis.
2. Facial-expression synchronization and emotion-driven TTS to achieve expressive realism comparable to human instruction.
3. Retrieval-Augmented Knowledge Base integration to enable domain-specific question answering with continuously updated agricultural content.

Through these advancements, Mark will evolve into a fully autonomous, adaptive instructor, delivering personalized, inclusive, and context-aware education within immersive digital environments. This contribution demonstrates how AI and VR together can redefine experiential learning, bridging physical, cognitive, and accessibility gaps in 21st-century agricultural education.

Acknowledgments. The authors thank the following agencies for their partial support: 1) W.K. Kellogg Foundation 2) the United States Department of Commerce (USDOC), Economic Development Administration Good Jobs Challenge Awardee, STEPS4GROWTH (ed22hdq3070099), 3) National Science Foundation's – Engineering Research Center (NSF - ERC) Hybrid Autonomous Manufacturing, Moving from Evolution to Revolution (HAMMER) (Award No.: 2133630).

References

1. Maasthi, M.J.: An interactive augmented reality application for agriculture using Unity, in Proceedings. In: IEEE COMSNETS Demos & Exhibits, pp. 1–6 (2025)
2. Lampropoulos, G.: Combining artificial intelligence with augmented reality and virtual reality in education: current trends and future perspectives. Multimodal Technol. Interact. **9**(2), 1–28 (2025)
3. A. Juliani, et al.: Unity: A General Platform for Intelligent Agents, arXiv preprint arXiv:1809.02627v2, (2020).
4. Torres, R., Benitez, A., Delgado, E., Gomez, J.: Geolocation and virtual reality to streamline the Management of Hydrographic Basins of the regional agriculture Management of La Libertad – Peru. Sustainability. **16**(7) (2024)

5. Ojha, D., Bhattacharya, A., Nair, S.: VitRob pipeline: a seamless teleoperation pipeline for advanced virtual reality – robot Interface applied for precision agriculture. Comput. Electron. Agric. **214** (2023)
6. Jain, S., Kaur, P.K., Sharma, N.: A real-time application of virtual reality in Indian agriculture. IEEE Access. **12** (2024)
7. Mehetre, K., et al.: Revolutionizing agricultural education: a comprehensive pipeline for virtual reality content development and implications to technology entrepreneurship. In: Proceedings Small Business Institute® Annual Conference., New Orleans, LA, USA (2025)
8. Qiu, L., Benbasat, I.: An investigation into the effects of text-to-speech voice and 3D avatars on the perception of presence and flow of live help in electronic commerce. ACM Trans. Comput. Hum. Interact. **12**(4), 329–355 (2005)
9. Brandi, F., Piumatti, C., D'Atri, D., Gatteschi, A.: CUIfy the XR: an open-source package to embed LLM-powered conversational agents in XR. Multimodal Technol. Interact. **8**(4) (2024)
10. Córdova-Esparza, D., Meneses-Planas, P., Benítez-Guerrero, M.: AI-based conversational agents in education: a review of trends and challenges. Comput. Educ. Artif. Intell. **7**, 100245 (2025)
11. Spyrou, E., Grigoriadis, G., Siassiakos, K.: Enhancing education in agriculture via XR-based digital twins. Multimodal Technol. Interact. **9**(2), 38 (2025)
12. Conrad, J., Medel, A., Dede, C.: Learning effectiveness of immersive virtual reality: a meta-analysis. Comput. Educ. Open. **6**, 100068 (2024)
13. A. Ferrer, C. Liang, and P. Torres, "Enhancing Motor-Imagery Brain–Computer Interface Training with Embodied Virtual Reality: A Pilot Study with Older Adults," Front. Hum. Neurosci., vol. 18, (2024).
14. Mohamed, M., Osman, S., Alfarsi, F.: Virtual assistants in AR/VR for special needs learners. Computers. **14, no. 8**, 306 (2025)
15. Zhang, S., Wu, Y., Wang, H.: Game therapy for specially-abled individuals with PPO reinforcement learning in VR-based educational games. IEEE Trans. Games. **17**(1), 56–68 (2025)
16. Singh, P., Reddy, N., Gokhale, T.: Towards anatomy education with generative AI-based virtual assistants in immersive virtual reality environments. Comput. Educ. Artif. Intell. **6**(1), 1–18 (2025)
17. Al-Kharusi, S., Patel, A., Musa, R.: Design and implementation of a Multilanguage hand gesture typing system in Unity. Procedia Comput. Sci. **238**, 150–160 (2024)
18. L. Haynes, A. H. Lee, R. J. Fagan: Graduated Realism: A Pedagogical Framework for AI-Powered Avatars in VR Teacher Training, arXiv preprint arXiv:2506.11890, (2025).
19. Narayan, R.: Audio-Based Facial Expression Generation on AR Applications. In: Proceedings of the IEEE International Conference on Multimodal Interaction (2024)

Tracking Effects Layer by Layer from Adversarial or Naive Changes to a CNN Inputer

James P. Larue(✉)

JADCO Signals, Charleston, USA
James@JadcoSignals.com

Abstract. In the AIPR 2017 Workshop we presented a paper that looked at "The Anatomy of a Neural Network". The main purpose was to show how to take a simple LeCun-based neural network, with its multiple internal operations, and extract layer-to-layer input/output pairs to form a series of bidirectional association memory matrices (AMMs) from CNN Layers.

From these transformations we showed how to achieve a practical solution that met the expectations of the Universal Approximation Theorem; how we could to collapse a six-layer system into a single layer.

For the AIPR 2025 Workshop we will examine how a change in the image, be it adversarial or just a naïve-rotation of the image, can be physically tracked across each of the CNN/AMMs, when each is examined in vector form, i.e., we will visually exploit the error from the first layer on to the last layer.

There are many approaches to measuring layer vulnerabilities, such as autoencoders, t-SNEs, histograms, and residuals. In contrast to these methods, we do not offer a measure, we are simply demonstrating that we can take a step back and look at how the error, be it adversarial or naïve, propagates within the neural network framework to make a more informed and more immediate decision on designing a measure.

Keywords: neural-network framework · adversarial intentions · layer by layer

1 Challenging the Panda Plus Noise Equals Gibbon Mirage

1.1 The Adversarial Icon Has More to Offer

The Panda Plus Noise example is classic in that it was one of the first adversarial examples to challenge the accuracy of the Neural Network. As a reminder we show the example in Fig. 1. The motivation for submitting an abstract for consideration by AIPR-2025 was to bring up two points that may be worthy of consideration. The first relates to the decision-output in the context of exactly how many classes were trained in that NN and what were in the individual class scores with just the noisy image inputted by itself. The second question asks if there signs of 'mis-classification starting early on, say, beginning with the first layer, i.e., why wait until the end to find out there is an error from something adversarial or from some unintentional naïve change to the input.

F. Tanner and J. Irvine (Eds.): AIPR 2025, LNCS 16446, pp. 92–100, 2026.
https://doi.org/10.1007/978-3-032-18474-0_7

Since we do not have access to the original Panda Bear example, we have decided to use a simple six-layer NN trained on the very classic MNIST data set [1]. The examples will demonstrate the unquestionable need to look across the class scores in the decision layers and how to further analyze NN process early on by demonstrating that it is possible to flatten out the initial layers of the so-called black-box for early warnings.

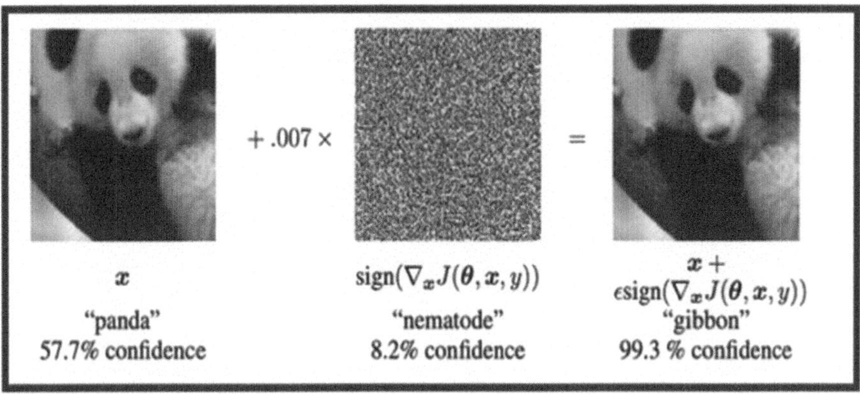

Fig. 1. Question: Where is a picture of "the closet looking" Gibbon?

2 The Fours

2.1 The Fours and their Scores

Fig. 2 shows 20 examples of the number four draw from the MINST data set and you may agree that the top two rows appear as fours while the bottom two rows appear as nines. Fig. 3 shows the scores from the top row and bottom row that our neural network assigned to each of the classes 0–9. Starting our analysis with the top row of fours we see that the second 4 scored highest in its class compared the others, the fourth 4 narrowly scored higher than the 9's score, and the fifth 4 scores were uniform distributed across several classes although the 4's class did score higher. Now we turn our attention to the bottom row of so-labeled 4's and observe that this neural network scored all of them as 9's. It could be argued, and rightfully so, that had we continued training the NN over several epochs the scores may gravitate towards the correct 4 class although the counter argument for "overtraining", making the NN brittle, also would have its' place. But what we want to bring out, in the context of "adversarial and naïve changes", may best be discussed using the 5th "$4''$ on the right. The 4–9 scores are 0.0001 apart, with the 9's class winning the contest. What if an executable version of this NN was uploaded free to use on some website, then we, the one who trained it, would be aware of the pitfall of the couple missing pixels on the right side and what would happen if we, added to or removed from, a pixel in that opening, but adjusting that image and run it through the algorithm. As an interesting side-note, we gave an AI engine the bottom right "$4''$ and asked it "What number do you see?". Its answer: "The letter g".

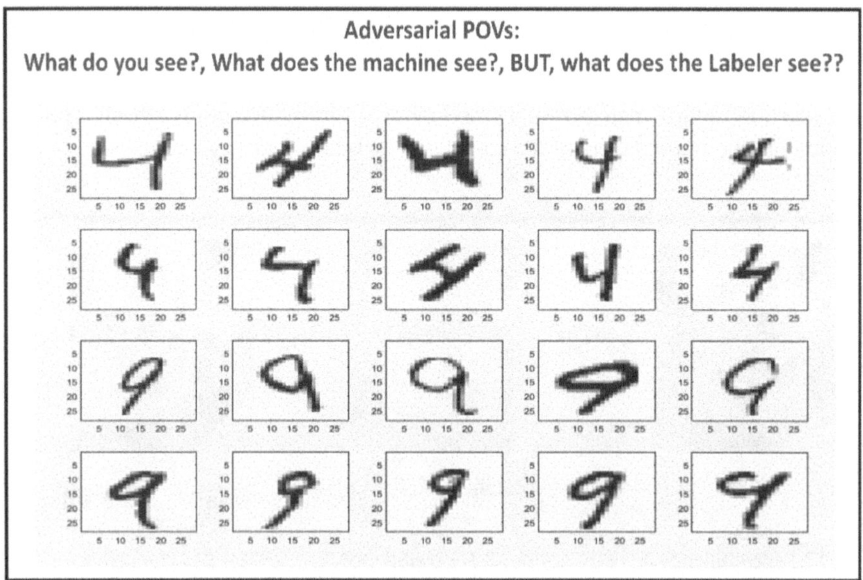

Fig. 2. Selected 4's from labeled MNIST data set. Were any mis-labeled?

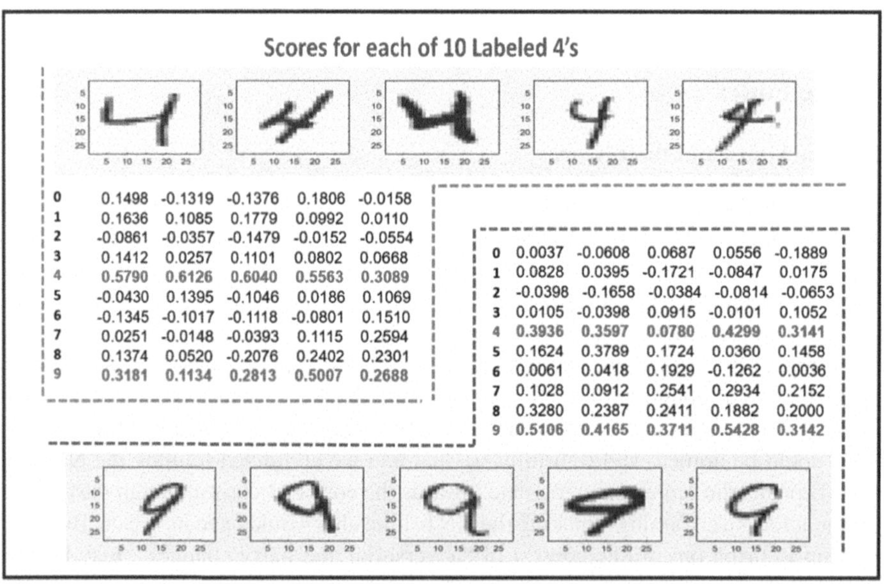

Fig. 3. 4's and their winning/losing scores.

Fig. 4 shows how we track the winning scores across each class. We tested the NN with 500 images each of 0–9. The top plot shows the scores where the blue dots are the winning scores the true 4's and the red dots are the winning scores when from another class. Knowing these scores is what facilitated our selected examples in Fig. 2.

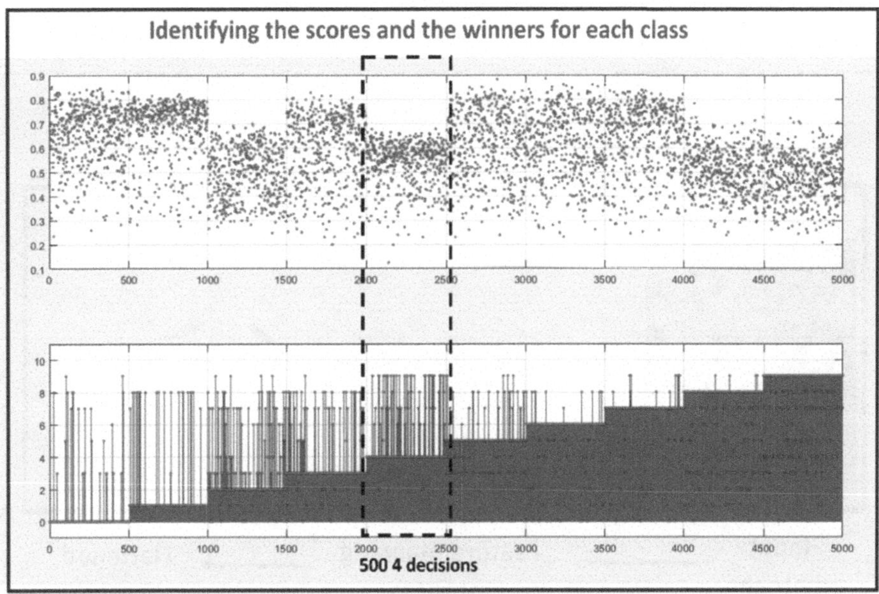

Fig. 4. Scores are plotted for 500 images from each test class left to right.

3 Let's Open the Black Box and Flatten it

3.1 Flattening all Layers Are Review

In this section we will open up the so-called Black Box that sits between the input and the output layers. The concept was previously examined at AIPR 2017 with the purpose of describing our patented procedure for converting a CNN (convolutional NN) construct into an Association Memory Matrix (AMM) construct, where we flattened each layer in CNN in order to construct the layer-to-layer associations which allows us to by-pass the CNN internal layer operations [2, 3]. We will now quickly review the process.

We start with Fig. 5 which was taken from Krizhevsky et al.'s 2012 paper where he pictured the middle layers as matrices of "convoluted" puppy dogs and the output layer as the flattened layer where max-output decided to which class the image belonged [4]. Fig. 6 is constructed to show the flattening of the second layer in our NN in the context of MNIST. We show the 28x28 matrix image of a labeled number 2, To flatten out the 2 we simply reshape it as a1x784 vector. We then passed the image 2 through 12 Gabor (edge/orientation) detection filters and imposed internal layer down-sampling and other operations, to end up with 12 sets of 14x14 matrix images. Now in the same way as we reshaped the single input image into a flattened vector, we do the same with each of the 12 14x14 first layer outputs to form a layer 1 flattened output vector of dimension 12*(196x1) = 2352x1. Although the Gabor-generated images are flattened and concatenated, there remains a an easily observed structural change as we observe the flatten vector left to right across the groups of 196 points.

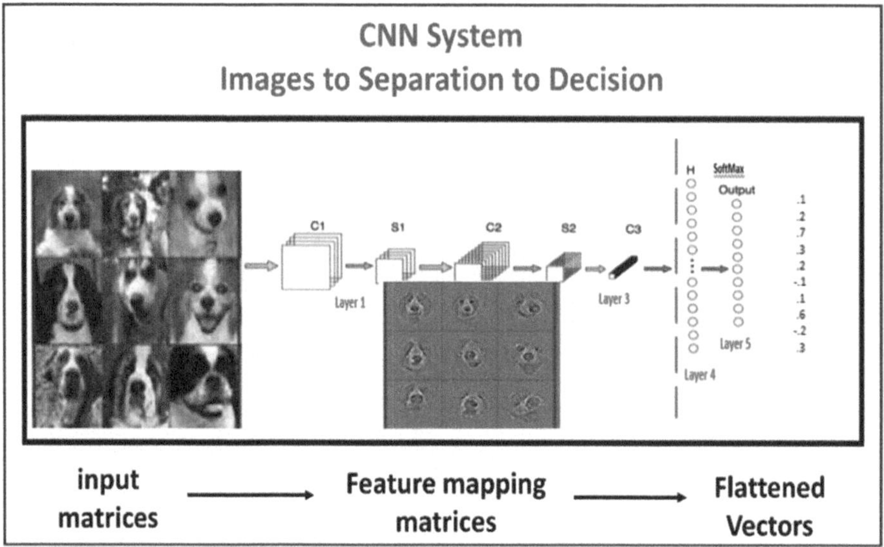

Fig. 5. A CNN system with input, internal layer matrices, and a flattened out.

Fig. 7 shows a flattening of sixteen 5x5 matrices from layer 4 but now concatenated as vertical vectors inside a matrix; this tracks the learning process, left to right, over 5000 iterations of training. The horizontal bands give insight into how each of the sixteen (flattened) matrices learn. It is easily observed that the columns take on a rougher appearance as the 5000th training iteration is reach. On the far left is the first training output vector while on the right is the output of some input number at the end of the process. We note that we used this approach of tracking flattened output for each input class to create our patented approach to converting a CNN into an AMM.

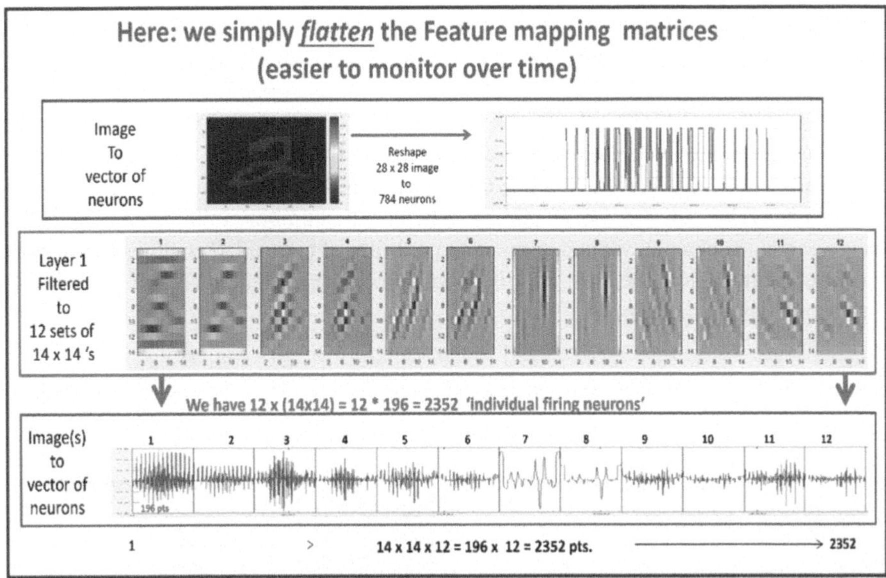

Fig. 6. Flattening out the Gabor filter output from the second layer.

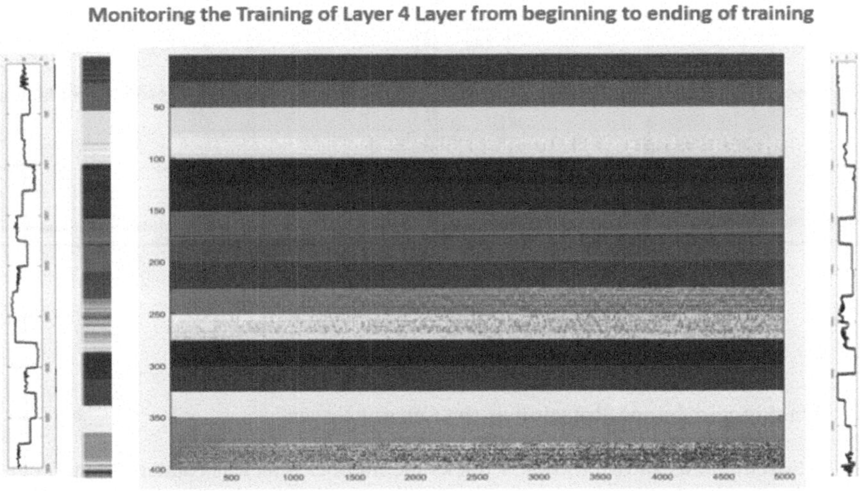

Monitoring the Training of Layer 4 Layer from beginning to ending of training

Fig. 7. A time domain approach using column vectors to track output learning.

4 Two Tracking Examples

4.1 Tracking an Image Translation Layer-by-Layer

Fig. 8 shows our layer-by-layer flattening concept using two number 7's. The 7 on the left is our starting point. It is centered. The left-side figure follows in this manner: To the right the seven is flattened into a vector, the layer two output, LGN to V1, (using ventral pathway terminology), is shown flattened in the green box, the next layer V1 to V2 is shown in the light blue box, and followed sequentially by the purple, yellow, and red boxes where the red box shows the out with the number 7's winning score. The matrices that are in between the boxes are for monitoring the outputs. Moving to the right-side figure, we start with an off-centered 7 on the right and follow its flattened vector and matrix monitoring changes until we reach the output and see the number 5 is the winner. The point we are making is whether the number contains an adversarial change or a naive change, we can monitor the stability of controlled changes to the input in its effects throughout the system. It is possible to place safeguards in the lower layers that become visual markers.

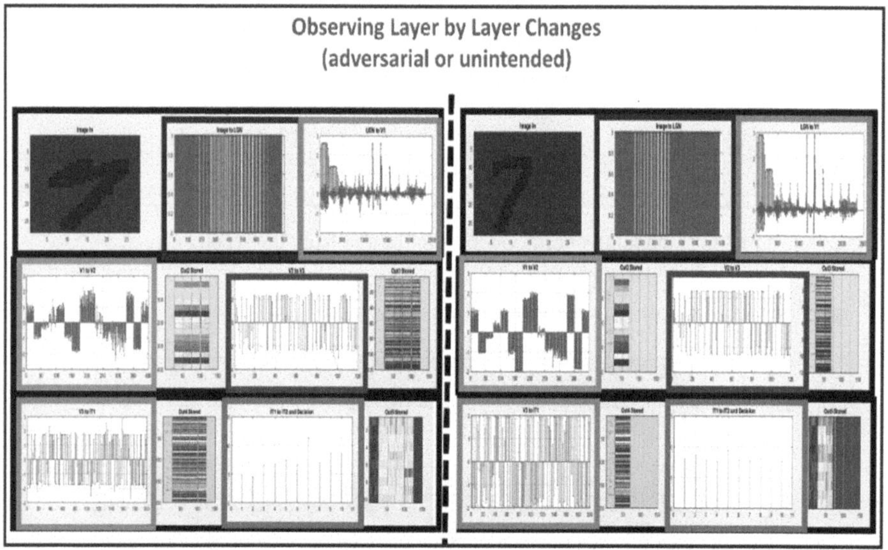

Fig. 8. Sliding the number 7. Points 1–10 are ordered for classes 1–9 and 0.

4.2 Tracking an Image Rotation at the Output Layer

Our last example, as shown in Fig. 9 tracks the number 8 as it is rotated in one-degree increments. The top plot shows a column-by-column visualization of the output scores with red indicating the highest score. The second plot shows the winning score, the third plot indicates the winning decision class from 0–9, and the last plot shows the rotating 8's in increments of 30°. What we find interesting is the stability of the rotating 8 decisions per winning class.

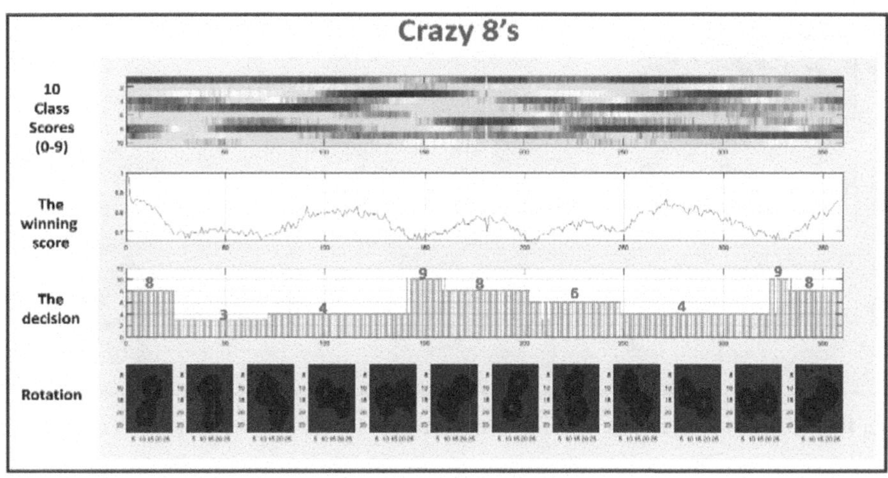

Fig. 9. Tracking outputs of Rotating 8's.

5 Wrap up

5.1 It's Just Noise

We close this paper with Fig. 10 where we show the progression of our "just noise" example throughout the NN. Of note is the comparisons between the output vectors of the 7 and the noise. For example, the LGN to V1 outputs show very similar structure, which shows there are constraints in the system stay in place. It's not until the output layer, where the noise shows a uniform distribution of scores among the ten classes. There is a winning score of course, the NN system is deterministic with its programmed number crunching and it will produce a maximum output, the number 1 in this case. Perhaps a measure of entropy could be applied to each layer inside, the so-called black box, which hopefully, we have made a little more transparent.

We wish to thank the AIPR workshop for the invitation to present and George Washington University for hosting the event.

Disclosure of Interests The author has no competing interests to declare that are relevant to the content of this article.

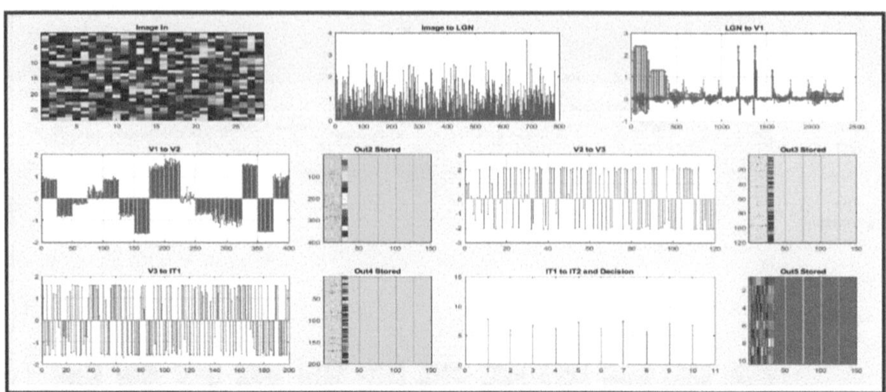

Fig. 10. Noise as it traverses through the neural network. Points 1–10 are ordered for classes 1–9 and 0.

References

1. Y. LeCun: Courant Institute, Corinna Cortes, Google Labs, New York, The MNIST database of handwritten digits, http://yann.lecun.com/exdb/mnist
2. LaRue, J., Tutwiler, R., LaRue, D.: The anatomy of a neural network. In: IEEE AIPR Workshop, the Cosmos Club, Washington DC (2017) Jadco Signals, Professor Emeritus Applied Research Lab Penn State University/CEO LiveMotion3D LLC, University of South Carolina Law School
3. James LaRue, Denise LaRue: Patent *Granted March*: Joint Proximity Association Template for Neural Networks. A tool to convert Convolutional Neural Networks into a matrix-based system allowing for order of magnitude increase in intra-layer execution and allows for inter-layer stitching between neural networks. US 10,242313, B2 (2019).
4. Krizhevsky, A.: Sutskever, Ilya, and Hinton, Geoffrey, ImageNet classification with deep convolutional neural networks. Adv. Neural Inf. Proces. Syst., 1097–1105 (2012)

Vision-Language Integration for Image Captioning Using Vision Transformers and GPT-J

Ali Alfatemi[1], Mohamed Rahouti[1], Mohammed Aledhari[2], Nasir Ghani[3], Abdellah Chehri[4(✉)], and Gwanggil Jeon[5]

[1] CIS Deptartment, Fordham University, New York, NY, USA
{aalfatemi,mrahouti}@fordham.edu

[2] Data Science Deptartment, University of North Texas, Dallas, TX, USA
mohammed.aledhari@unt.edu

[3] EE Deptartment, University of South Florida, Tampa, FL, USA
nghani@usf.edu

[4] MCS Deptartment, Royal Military College of Canada, Kingston, Canada
chehri@rmc.ca

[5] Embedded Systems Engineering Deptartment, Incheon National University, Incheon, South Korea
gjeon@inu.ac.kr

Abstract. This study explores the integration of vision and language models to automate image captioning, leveraging a Vision Encoder-Decoder framework that combines a Visual Transformer (ViT) as the encoder and GPT-J as the decoder. We develop a model capable of generating coherent and contextually relevant captions for images, which could have broad applications in accessibility and content management systems. Using the MS COCO dataset, we implemented and trained our model, optimizing various parameters to enhance the quality of generated text. Initial results, evaluated using the ROUGE metric, indicate promising performance with respect to precision, recall, and f-measure, though they also highlight areas for improvement in handling complex visual contexts. This study not only underscores the potential of advanced encoder-decoder architectures in bridging visual and textual domains but also paves the way for future enhancements in automated caption generation technologies.

Keywords: Image captioning · pre-trained transformer · vision-language integration · vision transformer

1 Introduction

The integration of visual data with natural language processing represents one of the most dynamic and impactful frontiers in artificial intelligence research. Efforts that harness the capabilities of both computer vision and linguistic understanding can lead to the development of advanced systems capable of interpreting

F. Tanner and J. Irvine (Eds.): AIPR 2025, LNCS 16446, pp. 101–114, 2026.
https://doi.org/10.1007/978-3-032-18474-0_8

complex scenes and generating contextualized textual descriptions. This is particularly relevant in a world increasingly dominated by visual information, where the ability to quickly and accurately interpret images and videos has significant applications ranging from assistive technologies for the visually impaired [1–5] to autonomous vehicles [6], content moderation systems [7], and interactive AI in consumer applications [8].

Our motivation is driven by rapid advancements in AI, particularly in image processing and text generation subdomains. Vision Transformer (ViT) [9] and Generative Pre-trained Transformer (GPT) models [10–12] have individually shown great promise—ViT in processing images in a novel manner by treating them as sequences of patches, and GPT in generating human-like text based on large-scale language modeling. However, the true potential lies in their convergence. The ability to automatically generate accurate and relevant captions for images is a substantial step in creating more intelligent systems that can understand and interact with their environment in human-like ways. Applications of such technology are vast and include enhancing the accessibility of digital content for visually impaired users through descriptive audio, improving the efficiency of digital asset management systems by automating the tagging and description processes, and enriching user interactions with smart devices [1–3,7,8].

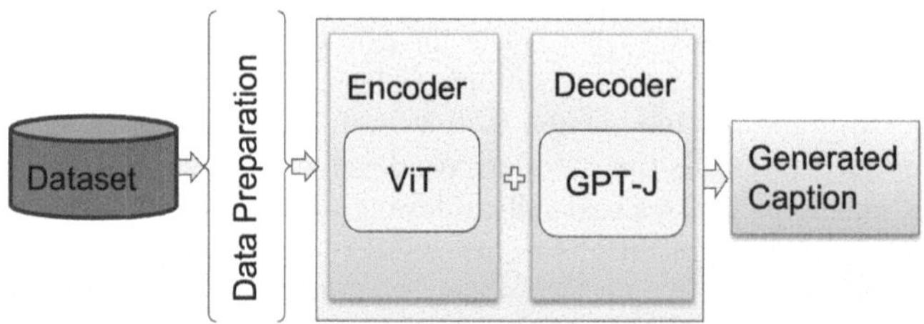

Fig. 1. Overview of the Vision-Language Model Architecture for Image Captioning: This diagram illustrates the workflow where the dataset feeds into a ViT encoder and a GPT-J decoder to generate image textual captions. The process highlights the direct use of visual features extracted by the Vision Transformer (ViT), which the GPT-J model then processes to produce coherent captions.

The theoretical underpinnings of our paper are based on the sequential nature of data processing in AI, where a system processes input data (images or text) through multiple layers of transformation to derive meaning or generate responses. Vision Transformers revolutionize image perception by applying transformers' principles, traditionally used in NLP, to visual inputs. This approach treats parts of images as analogous to words in a text, allowing the model to learn contextual relationships between different parts of an image. On the other hand, the GPT architecture leverages deep learning to predict the next word in a sentence, given all the previous words, making it highly effective for generating coherent and contextually appropriate text.

The primary objective of our paper is to explore the efficacy of combining ViT and GPT models in a cohesive framework to generate descriptive captions for images. We hypothesize that this integration will allow us to leverage the contextual understanding capabilities of ViT with the expressive language generation properties of GPT to create a system that not only recognizes elements within an image but also describes them meaningfully.

To achieve this, we employ the VisionEncoderDecoderModel[1] framework provided by Hugging Face's Transformers library, which facilitates the seamless integration of an encoder model (ViT) designed for image understanding and a decoder model (GPT) tailored for text generation. Our paper involves fine-tuning this model on the COCO dataset [13], renowned for its diverse imagery and extensive annotations, providing a robust platform for training and evaluating our model.

Our approach involves several key steps outlined as follows:

- Preprocessing the data: We begin by extracting features from the images using the model[2]. This model divides each image into patches and processes these through multiple transformer layers to create a rich representation of the visual content.
- Model training: We then train a model[3] to generate text based on these image features. The training process involves adjusting the network weights to minimize the difference between the generated and actual captions provided in the COCO dataset [13].
- System evaluation: The performance of our system is evaluated based on standard metrics such as the Rouge score [14], which measures the quality of text generation by comparing the overlap of n-grams between the generated and actual captions.

Figure 1 illustrates our methodology and the interaction between system components. This diagram visually represents the data flow from image input, through feature extraction and transformation by the Vision Transformer, to caption generation by the GPT model, culminating in the output of descriptive text.

By exploring the capabilities and limitations of this integrated approach, our paper aims to contribute to the broader discourse on AI's potential to understand and describe the visual world, thereby paving the way for future more advanced multimodal AI systems.

The rest of this paper is organized as follows: Sect. 2 reviews related work on image captioning, tracing developments from CNN-RNN frameworks to transformer-based models and vision-language pre-training (VLP). Section 3 details our methodology, including data preparation, model architecture, training procedures, and evaluation metrics. Section 4 describes the experimental

[1] https://huggingface.co/docs/transformers/v4.15.0/en/model_doc/visionencoderdecoder.

[2] https://huggingface.co/google/vit-base-patch16-224.

[3] https://huggingface.co/EleutherAI/gpt-j-6b.

setup, training progress, validation, and result analysis for evaluating our integrated vision-language model. Section 5 concludes the paper, summarizing our findings and suggesting directions for future research.

2 Related Work

The task of image captioning sits at the intersection of computer vision and natural language processing and has been a focus of significant research over the past decade. The evolution of this field has been marked by the development of several key technologies and methodologies, each contributing to the improved understanding of visual content and its contextual description through language [10–12,15–22].

2.1 Early Approaches: CNN-RNN Frameworks

The initial breakthrough in image captioning came with adopting convolutional neural networks (CNNs) for image feature extraction combined with recurrent neural networks (RNNs) and LSTM for generating textual descriptions. [18] introduced one of the seminal works in this area with their model, "Show and Tell," which utilized a CNN to encode an image into a dense vector, followed by an RNN/LSTM [19] that decoded this representation into a descriptive caption. This approach set the groundwork for subsequent research, emphasizing the importance of seamless interaction between visual feature extraction and sequence generation for effective captioning.

The initial breakthrough in image captioning came with adopting convolutional neural networks (CNNs) for image feature extraction combined with recurrent neural networks (RNNs) and LSTM for generating textual descriptions. [18] introduced one of the seminal works in this area with their model, "Show and Tell," which utilized a CNN to encode an image into a dense vector, followed by an RNN/LSTM [19] that decoded this representation into a descriptive caption. This approach set the groundwork for subsequent research, emphasizing the importance of seamless interaction between visual feature extraction and sequence generation for effective captioning.

The CNN-RNN frameworks demonstrated significant potential by leveraging the strengths of CNNs in capturing spatial features and RNNs in handling sequential data [23]. This combination allowed models to learn complex mappings from visual data to natural language, producing increasingly accurate and relevant captions. Subsequent improvements focused on refining these architectures, introducing attention mechanisms to enable the model to focus on different parts of the image while generating each word in the caption [24]. These advancements marked a critical evolution in image captioning, providing a robust foundation for more sophisticated models that integrate vision and language understanding.

2.2 Transformer-Based Models

The introduction of the Transformer model by [25] brought a significant shift in both computer vision and natural language processing. Transformers are characterized by self-attention mechanisms, which allow models to weigh the importance of different parts of the input data, be it words in a sentence or regions in an image. This self-attention mechanism enables the model to capture long-range dependencies and contextual relationships more effectively than traditional models, which often struggled with these tasks due to their sequential processing nature. The ability to process input data in parallel and apply attention selectively has resulted in substantial improvements in both speed and accuracy for a wide range of applications, from machine translation to text generation [26].

This technology not only improved the performance of language models but also provided a new framework for thinking about image processing. [27] adapted the Transformer architecture for image recognition tasks, proposing the ViT [9], which treats image patches as tokens similar to words in NLP. This approach allows the model to analyze images in a more dynamic and context-aware manner, leveraging the same self-attention mechanisms that revolutionized language processing. By treating an image as a sequence of patches, ViT models can capture spatial relationships and dependencies that are often missed by CNNs. Furthermore, the integration of Transformer models in image processing has opened up new avenues for research, such as combining visual and textual data in a unified framework [10–12], leading to advancements in multimodal AI systems capable of understanding and generating content across different modalities.

2.3 Vision-Language Pre-training (VLP)

Building on the strengths of transformer architectures, recent research has focused on VLP [28], which aims to develop models that can understand and generate content involving visual and textual elements. VLP models leverage large-scale datasets that contain paired image-text data, allowing them to learn rich, multimodal semantic relationships. This pre-training strategy enables the models to generalize well across various tasks by providing a robust foundation of combined visual and textual knowledge. The ability to pre-train on diverse datasets means these models can capture a wide array of visual and linguistic patterns, making them highly adaptable to different applications such as image captioning, visual question answering, and more [28].

[29] introduced a unified VLP model that could be fine-tuned for various tasks, including image captioning, demonstrating the versatility and robustness of these integrated models. This unified approach allows for a more streamlined adaptation process, where a single pre-trained model can be fine-tuned to excel in multiple vision-language tasks. Such models have shown significant improvements in performance due to their ability to leverage pre-trained knowledge, which reduces the need for extensive task-specific training data. Additionally, the use of attention mechanisms in VLP models enhances their ability to focus

on relevant parts of an image or text, further improving their contextual understanding and generation capabilities [30,31]. These advancements underline the transformative potential of VLP in creating more sophisticated and versatile AI systems capable of comprehending and generating multimodal content.

2.4 Encoder-Decoder Models in Vision and Language Integration

The encoder-decoder architecture has become a standard for tasks that involve translating one form of data into another, such as translating images into text. The VisionEncoderDecoderModel framework by Hugging Face represents a culmination of this research, allowing researchers to pair any vision model as an encoder with any text generation model as a decoder. This flexibility has been explored in various studies, with notable examples including the integration of ViT [9] with GPT models [10–12] for generating descriptive captions that not only identify objects within an image but also describe their interactions and attributes in a contextually relevant manner.

Despite these advancements, image captioning continues to face challenges, particularly in generating captions that accurately reflect less apparent aspects of images, such as emotions, intentions, or narratives. Research continues to explore how models can be made more sensitive to such nuances, often involving more sophisticated training techniques, better dataset curation, or innovations in model architecture.

The related work on integrating vision and language models illustrates a vibrant and rapidly evolving field. Our paper builds on these foundational technologies, aiming to harness the latest developments in transformer-based models to enhance the capability and accuracy of automated image captioning systems. The primary difference between our work and existing state-of-the-art literature lies in our novel integration of Vision Transformers (ViT) and GPT-J models within a unified VisionEncoderDecoder framework. While earlier models predominantly employed CNN-RNN architectures or separate transformer-based models for image captioning, our approach leverages the strengths of both ViT for sophisticated image processing and GPT-J for advanced natural language generation. This combination allows our system to treat image patches as analogous to words, enhancing the contextual relationship understanding within images, and to generate coherent and contextually relevant captions through a deep learning-based language model. Moreover, unlike many previous methods that focused on either image feature extraction or language generation in isolation, our integrated framework facilitates seamless interaction between visual and textual data, yielding superior performance in terms of precision, recall, and f-measure as demonstrated on the COCO dataset. This integration not only advances the capability of automated image captioning but also paves the way for more sophisticated multimodal AI systems.

3 Methodology

The core of our methodology revolves around the integration of advanced computer vision and natural language processing models. This integration is facilitated by the VisionEncoderDecoder framework from Hugging Face's Transformers, which combines a Vision ViT for encoding images and a GPT for decoding these visual features into textual descriptions as shown in Fig. 2.

Our proposed methodology integrates advanced computer vision and NLP models to automate image captioning, leveraging a Vision Encoder-Decoder framework. As illustrated in Fig. 2, our approach begins with preprocessing the input images by resizing them to 224x224 pixels, normalizing pixel values, and applying data augmentation techniques such as random horizontal flips and color jittering. These images are then encoded using a ViT, which divides each image into patches and processes them through multiple transformer layers to create a rich representation of the visual content.

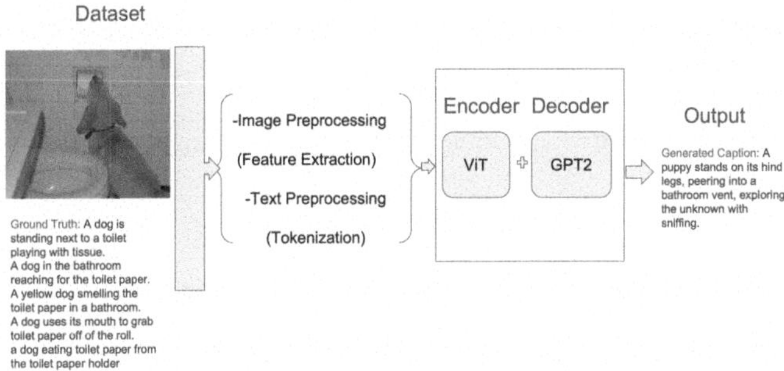

Fig. 2. The proposed pipeline methodology.

The encoded image features are subsequently fed into a GPT-J decoder, designed to generate coherent and contextually relevant captions. The GPT-J model leverages the contextual understanding capabilities of the ViT-encoded features, utilizing self-attention mechanisms to predict the next word in a sentence based on the visual input and previously generated words.

The training process involves fine-tuning the VisionEncoderDecoderModel on the COCO dataset, optimizing the network weights to minimize the cross-entropy loss between the generated and actual captions. We utilize the AdamW optimizer with specific hyperparameters, including a learning rate of 5×10^{-5} and a batch size of 8, over three epochs. The performance of our model is evaluated using the ROUGE-2 metric, focusing on precision, recall, and F-measure to assess the quality of the generated captions. Details about the components of our methodology are discussed next.

3.1 Data Preparation

Dataset: We utilize the COCO dataset, known for its diversity and rich annotations, ideal for training and evaluating image captioning models.

Image Preprocessing: Images are standardized to ensure consistent input dimensions and feature scaling:

$$I = \text{Transform}(I) \tag{1}$$

where I is the original image and Transform includes:

- **Resizing:** Resize each image to 224x224 pixels, matching the input requirement of the ViT model.
- **Normalization:** Normalize pixel values using:

$$I_{\text{norm}} = \frac{I_{\text{resized}} - \mu}{\sigma} \tag{2}$$

  where μ and σ are the dataset's mean and standard deviation vectors.
- **Augmentation:** Apply random horizontal flips and color jittering to enhance model robustness.

Caption preprocessing: Captions are tokenized using a tokenizer configured for the GPT model:

$$C = \text{Tokenizer}(C) \tag{3}$$

where C represents the captions.

3.2 Model Architecture

Vision Encoder - Vision Transformer (ViT): The ViT model processes images by first dividing them into patches, applying a series of Transformer blocks:

$$\mathbf{z}_0 = [x_{\text{class}}; x_p^1\mathbf{E}; x_p^2\mathbf{E}; \ldots; x_p^N\mathbf{E}] + \mathbf{E}_{\text{pos}}, \tag{4}$$

where x_p^i are the flattened patches, $\mathbf{E}$ is the patch embedding projection, and $\mathbf{E}_{\text{pos}}$ are the positional embeddings. These embeddings are processed through self-attention mechanisms:

$$\text{Attention}(Q, K, V) = \text{softmax}\left(\frac{QK^T}{\sqrt{d_k}}\right)V \tag{5}$$

where Q, K, V are the query, key, and value matrices derived from $\mathbf{z}_0$, and d_k is the dimension of the key.

Language Decoder - GPT: The GPT model generates captions based on the encoded image features using the Transformer decoder architecture:

$$\text{Decoder}(E) = \text{Transformer\_blocks}(E), \tag{6}$$

where E is the output embedding from the encoder.

3.3 Training Procedure

The models are configured with specific hyperparameters: a batch size of 8, an AdamW optimizer equipped with a learning rate of $\eta = 5 \times 10^{-5}$ and weight decay, and a training duration of 3 epochs.

Loss Function: The training objective is to minimize the cross-entropy loss between the predicted and actual captions:

$$\mathcal{L}(\theta) = -\sum_{i=1}^{N} \log P(c_i | c_{<i}, I; \theta) \tag{7}$$

where c_i are the tokens in the caption, I is the image, and θ are the parameters of the model.

3.4 Evaluation

Metrics: We utilize the ROUGE-N metric for evaluating the captions generated by the model, particularly focusing on ROUGE-2:

$$\text{ROUGE-N} = \frac{\sum_{s \in \{\text{References}\}} \sum_{gram_n \in s} \text{Count}_{\text{match}}(gram_n)}{\sum_{s \in \{\text{References}\}} \sum_{gram_n \in s} \text{Count}(gram_n)} \tag{8}$$

where $\text{Count}_{\text{match}}$ refers to the count of n-grams in both the candidate and reference texts, and Count is the count of n-grams in the reference text alone.

Validation: Model performance is periodically evaluated on a validation set to monitor progress and adjust training strategies if necessary.

4 Experiments

This section details the experiments conducted to evaluate the performance of our integrated vision-language model using the VisionEncoderDecoder framework. Our primary objective was to ascertain how effectively the model could generate accurate and contextually relevant captions for images from the COCO dataset.

4.1 Experimental Setup

The experiments involved training the VisionEncoderDecoder model, which utilizes ViT as the encoder and GPT-J as the decoder, over three epochs using the COCO dataset split into training and validation sets. The training setup included an AdamW optimizer with a learning rate of 5×10^{-5} and a batch size of 8. Systematic monitoring of training and validation losses was conducted, and the performance of the image captioning task was measured using ROUGE-2 metrics (Precision, Recall, and F-measure) to evaluate the quality of generated captions.

4.2 Training Progress and Validation

The training was conducted over three epochs, and the performance metrics are summarized in Table 1 and detailed next.

Table 1. Training and validation metrics over epochs.

Epoch	Training Loss	Validation Loss	Rouge2 Precision	Rouge2 Recall	Rouge2 F-measure
1	2.6154	2.395875	0.302	0.3724	0.3526
2	2.1354	2.225292	0.6351	0.6089	0.6100
3	1.7932	2.205314	0.7359	0.7071	0.6920

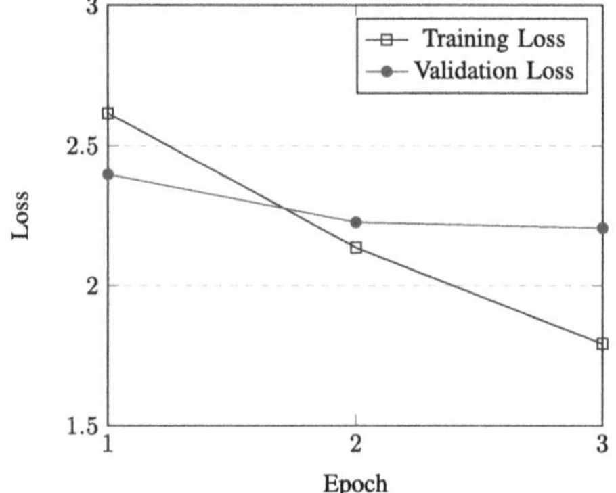

Fig. 3. Training and validation loss over epochs.

4.3 Analysis of Results

Training and Validation Loss: As depicted in Fig. 3, there is a consistent decrease in both training and validation losses over the epochs, indicating that the model was effectively learning and generalizing from the training data. The drop from an initial training loss of 2.6154 to 1.7932 by the third epoch signifies substantial learning improvements within the model.

There was a consistent decrease in both training and validation losses over the epochs, indicating that the model was effectively learning and generalizing from the training data. The drop from an initial training loss of 2.6154 to 1.7932 by the third epoch signifies substantial learning improvements within the model.

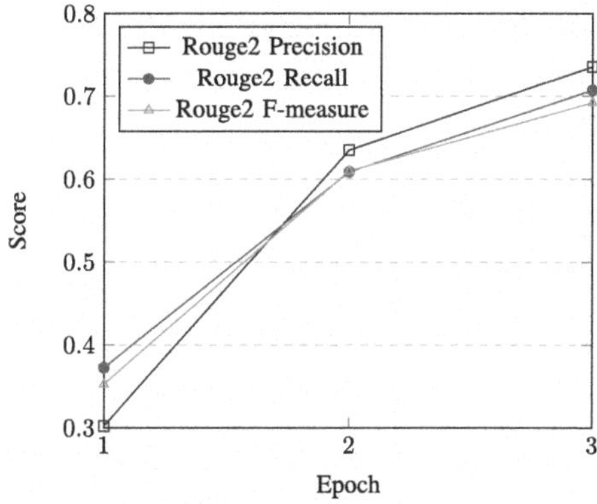

Fig. 4. Rouge2 metrics over epochs.

ROUGE-2 Metrics: Fig. 4 demonstrates a notable improvement across all ROUGE-2 metrics. Precision increased from 0.302 in the first epoch to 0.7359 in the third, indicating a higher accuracy in the generated captions with respect to the reference captions. Similarly, Recall increased from 0.3724 to 0.7071, showing that a greater proportion of the relevant words from the reference captions were captured in the generated captions. The F-measure, which balances Precision and Recall, saw an increase from 0.3526 to 0.6920, suggesting a balanced improvement in both Precision and Recall.

A notable improvement was observed across all ROUGE-2 metrics. Precision increased from 0.302 in the first epoch to 0.7359 in the third, indicating a higher accuracy in the generated captions with respect to the reference captions. Similarly, Recall increased from 0.3724 to 0.7071, showing that a greater proportion of the relevant words from the reference captions were captured in the generated captions. The F-measure, which balances Precision and Recall, saw an increase from 0.3526 to 0.6920, suggesting a balanced improvement in both Precision and Recall.

Additionally, Fig. 5 illustrates an example evaluation of the image captioning model. It depicts a generated caption for an image showing a wooden chair, sofa, and luggage on a curb, suggesting a moving scenario. The generated caption is compared with ground truth captions to show the model's performance in interpreting and describing complex scenes. This example underscores the challenge in achieving universal accuracy in image captioning due to the varied human interpretations of visual content.

The experiments confirm the potential of using advanced vision-language models for the task of image captioning. Future work may focus on further refining the model through extended training, exploring more sophisticated data augmentation techniques, or employing larger and more diverse datasets to enhance the model's robustness and accuracy. Additionally, more complex evaluation metrics that can capture the subtleties of human language might be considered to better assess the qualitative aspects of generated captions.

Generated Caption:
An wooden chair, sofa, and luggage sets the stage for moving.

Ground Truth:
- A couch sitting on top of a field of grass.
- a chair,couch and suitcase sitting by the road
- There is a couch, chair, and luggage sitting on the edge of the curb.
- A wood chair, a sofa and cushions, and a roller luggage bag lie by the side of the road.
- A couch, chair, and suitcase sitting on the curb.

Fig. 5. Evaluation of image captioning model. The image depicts a scenario involving a wooden chair, sofa, and luggage on a curb, possibly indicating a moving situation. The generated caption by the model is "An wooden chair, sofa, and luggage sets the stage for moving." The ground truth captions provided in the dataset vary, suggesting different interpretations of the scene such as "A couch sitting on top of a field of grass." and "A couch, chair, and suitcase sitting on the curb." This figure illustrates the challenges in generating universally accurate captions that align with varied human perspectives.

5 Conclusion

In this paper, we proposed a model to generate image captions by combining a Vision Transformer (ViT) as the encoder and GPT-J as the decoder. Both ViT and GPT-J were utilized in their pre-trained forms from Hugging Face. Our approach demonstrated significant improvements in the quality of generated captions, as evidenced by the consistent decrease in training and validation losses. The experiments confirmed our hypothesis that the combination of ViT's contextual understanding capabilities with GPT-J's language generation properties can effectively produce coherent and contextually appropriate captions. This integration allows for a nuanced understanding of image content, enabling the generation of detailed and relevant descriptions.

References

1. Gurari, D., Zhao, Y., Zhang, M., Bhattacharya, N.: Captioning images taken by people who are blind. In: Vedaldi, A., Bischof, H., Brox, T., Frahm, J.-M. (eds.) ECCV 2020. LNCS, vol. 12362, pp. 417–434. Springer, Cham (2020). https://doi.org/10.1007/978-3-030-58520-4_25
2. Safiya, K., Pandian, R.: A real-time image captioning framework using computer vision to help the visually impaired, Multimedia Tools and Applications, pp. 1–26 (2023)
3. Dognin, P., et al.: Image captioning as an assistive technology: lessons learned from VIZWIZ 2020 challenge. J. Artif. Intell. Res. **73**, 437–459 (2022)
4. Alfatemi, A., Jamal, S.A., Paykari, N., Rahouti, M., Chehri, A.: Multi-label classification with deep learning and manual data collection for identifying similar bird species. Proc. Comput. Sci. **246**, 558–565 (2024)
5. Alfatemi, A., Jamal, S.A., Paykari, N., Rahouti, M., Amin, R., Chehri, A.: Refining bird species identification through GAN-enhanced data augmentation and deep learning models. Proc. Comput. Sci. **246**, 548–557 (2024)

6. Li, W., et al.: The traffic scene understanding and prediction based on image captioning. IEEE Access **9**, 1420–1427 (2020)
7. Yuan, J., et al.: Rethinking multimodal content moderation from an asymmetric angle with mixed-modality, In: IEEE/CVF Winter Conference on Applications of Computer Vision, pp. 8532–8542 (2024)
8. Yang, J.: The investigation of bionic-companionship framework for Humanoid Service Robotics (HSR) with deep learning image captioning. PhD thesis, Cardiff Metropolitan University (2024)
9. Dosovitskiy, A., et al.: An image is worth 16x16 words: transformers for image recognition at scale, arXiv preprint arXiv:2010.11929 (2020)
10. Wang, B.: Mesh-Transformer-JAX: Model-parallel implementation of transformer language model with JAX (2021). https://github.com/kingoflolz/mesh-transformer-jax
11. Wang, B., Komatsuzaki, A.: GPT-J-6B: A 6 Billion parameter autoregressive language model (2021). https://github.com/kingoflolz/mesh-transformer-jax
12. Radford, A., et al.: Language models are unsupervised multitask learners. OpenAI blog **1**(8), 9 (2019)
13. Lin, T.-Y., et al.: Microsoft COCO: common objects in context. In: Fleet, D., Pajdla, T., Schiele, B., Tuytelaars, T. (eds.) ECCV 2014. LNCS, vol. 8693, pp. 740–755. Springer, Cham (2014). https://doi.org/10.1007/978-3-319-10602-1_48
14. Lin, C.-Y.: Rouge: a package for automatic evaluation of summaries, text summarization branches out, pp. 74–81 (2004)
15. Anderson, P., et al.: Bottom-up and top-down attention for image captioning and visual question answering, In: IEEE CVPR, pp. 6077–6086 (2018)
16. Pan, Y., Yao, T., Li, Y., Mei, T.: X-linear attention networks for image captioning, In: Proceedings of the IEEE/CVF Conference on Computer Vision and Pattern Recognition, pp. 10971–10980 (2020)
17. Zhang, X., et al.: Rstnet: captioning with adaptive attention on visual and non-visual words, In: Proceedings of the IEEE/CVF Conference on Computer Vision and Pattern Recognition, pp. 15465–15474 (2021)
18. Vinyals, O.,et al.: Show and tell: A neural image caption generator, In: Proceedings of the IEEE Conference on Computer Vision and Pattern Recognition, pp. 3156–3164 (2015)
19. Lu, J., et al.: Knowing when to look: adaptive attention via a visual sentinel for image captioning, In: IEEE CVPR, pp. 375–383 (2017)
20. Ji, J., et al.: Knowing what to learn: a metric-oriented focal mechanism for image captioning. IEEE Trans. Image Process. **31**, 4321–4335 (2022)
21. Alfatemi, A., et al.: Patient subgrouping with distinct survival rates via integration of multiomics data on a grassmann manifold. BMC Med. Inform. Decis. Mak. **22**(1), 190 (2022)
22. Ma, Y.,et al.: Knowing what it is: semantic-enhanced dual attention transformer, IEEE Trans. Multimedia (2022)
23. Zhang, J., et al.: Adaptive semantic-enhanced transformer for image captioning, IEEE Trans. Neural Netw. Learn. Syst. (2022)
24. Li, Y., et al.: Recurrent attention and semantic gate for remote sensing image captioning. IEEE Trans. Geosci. Remote Sens. **60**, 1–16 (2021)
25. Vaswani, A., et al.: Attention is all you need, Adv. Neural Inf. Process. Syst. **30** (2017)
26. Bayoudh, K., et al.: A survey on deep multimodal learning for computer vision: advances, trends, applications, and datasets. Vis. Comput. **38**(8), 2939–2970 (2022)

27. Tolstikhin, I.O., et al.: MLP-mixer: An all-MLP architecture for vision. Adv. Neural. Inf. Process. Syst. **34**, 24261–24272 (2021)
28. Chen, F.-L., et al.: Vlp: a survey on vision-language pre-training. Mach. Intell. Res. **20**(1), 38–56 (2023)
29. Zhou, L., et al.: Unified vision-language pre-training for image captioning and VQA. Proc. AAAI Conf. Artif. Intell. **34**, 13041–13049 (2020)
30. Yang, X., et al.: Causal attention for vision-language tasks, In: IEEE/CVF Conference on Computer Vision and Pattern Recognition, pp. 9847–9857 (2021)
31. Xue, H., et al.: Probing inter-modality: visual parsing with self-attention for vision-and-language pre-training. Adv. Neural. Inf. Process. Syst. **34**, 4514–4528 (2021)

Task Prioritization for Remote Sensing AI Models

Ben Thompson and Eliza Mace(✉)

The MITRE Corporation, McLean, VA 22102, USA
{benthompson,emace}@mitre.org
https://www.mitre.org/

Abstract. Improvements in self- and semi-supervised machine learning (ML) afford an opportunity to train AI foundation models (FMs) for a variety of specialized sensor modalities. Because a foundation model's ability to generalize across varied remote-sensing (RS) tasks depends on the data distribution it was trained on, different downstream applications require different levels of feature specificity in the model's backbone. Therefore, users need a clear way to assess a model's descriptive capacity so they can prioritize development and choose the right model for each task. Although the end goal of operationalizing an FM is likely to involve task-specific fine-tuning, as the corpus of available FMs for various sensors expands, it is not tractable to label fine-tuning sets for every possible combination of tasks and modalities; in fact, having sufficient volumes of labeled data to fine-tune every combination eliminates the benefit of self-/semi-supervision. To address this issue, we have invented a means of probing AI models' embedding spaces themselves to gauge the specificity of their feature encodings. Our method characterizes feature spaces by comparing task performance via linear mappings of encoded features across multiple models' embedding spaces, allowing for benchmarking of novel models against existing counterparts with fewer labeled examples. By constructing linear mappings between embedding spaces, we show that it may be possible to predict a model's performance at a given task without labeling data in that modality or fine-tuning the model for that task. We discuss the use cases of our technique for research programs and for AI capability acquisitions.

Keywords: Computer vision · Remote sensing · Foundation models

1 Introduction

1.1 Background

Foundation models (FMs) have emerged as a transformative paradigm in artificial intelligence, characterized by their capacity to generalize across a diverse array of downstream tasks through self- and semi-supervised learning techniques [1,11]. The proliferation of large-scale, encoder-based models has been predominantly driven by commercial research laboratories, with widespread adoption

F. Tanner and J. Irvine (Eds.): AIPR 2025, LNCS 16446, pp. 115–131, 2026.
https://doi.org/10.1007/978-3-032-18474-0_9

in both commercial and public sector applications [3,8,17]. These advancements have enabled significant progress in domains where data heterogeneity and task specificity are prevalent, including government missions that rely on specialized sensor modalities such as electro-optical (EO) and synthetic aperture radar (SAR) for remote sensing (RS) operations [8,13,14]. Despite their promise, the operationalization of FMs for important tasks remains fraught with challenges, particularly in evaluating whether a given model's feature encoding possesses sufficient descriptive capacity for downstream exploitation.

1.2 Problem Statement

Prevailing methodologies for assessing the suitability of FMs are heavily reliant on fine-tuning models for specific supervised tasks using labeled datasets [1,12,15]. While fine-tuning is indispensable for specialized applications, the extant corpus of benchmark evaluation datasets is largely tailored to commercial sensor modalities and does not adequately capture the granularity of task specificity required for specialized government missions [5,7,17]. Furthermore, the process of annotating fine-tuning datasets for every conceivable combination of mission tasks and sensor modalities is prohibitively resource-intensive, often necessitating the expertise of highly trained analysts [3,8,13]. This inefficiency fundamentally undermines the advantages conferred by self- and semi-supervised learning, which are predicated on the utilization of large volumes of unlabeled data. Consequently, there is a lack of effective mechanisms for evaluating the descriptive adequacy and mission suitability of modality-specific FMs prior to the allocation of resources for fine-tuning and operational deployment [9,13].

1.3 Objectives

In response to these challenges, this work introduces a novel methodology for probing the embedding spaces of FMs to estimate their feature specificity and suitability for downstream exploitation tasks. By systematically characterizing the structure of embedding spaces and comparing task performance via linear mappings across multiple models, the proposed approach establishes a quantitative framework for prioritizing FM development and mission integration. This technique significantly reduces dependence on labeled data, thereby enabling organizations to assess whether the investment of resources—including annotation, model development, and training—into fine-tuning a particular modality-task pairing is likely to yield commensurate improvements in downstream performance. Preliminary experimental results substantiate the utility of this approach, delineating a pathway for more efficient and effective FM evaluation in government missions and AI capability acquisitions.

2 Data

This study employs the BigEarthNet (BEN) dataset, which provides paired remote sensing imagery from Sentinel-1 synthetic aperture radar (SAR) and

Sentinel-2 electro-optical (EO) sensors [2,4]. The BEN dataset is particularly well-suited for cross-modal analysis, as it enables the construction of paired datasets across disparate sensor types. To facilitate modality-specific comparisons, the EO data were further subsampled to retain only the red, green, and blue channels, thereby generating an additional "RGB" modality for evaluation.

Due to the limited availability of annotated paired data in remote sensing, we defined two distinct tasks within the BEN dataset: (1) a task to create mappings between embedding spaces, focused on urban and industrial scenes; and (2) a multilabel land cover classification task restricted to non-urban and non-industrial areas. This separation allowed us to create independent data pools for training cross-modal mappings and for evaluating model generalization to unrelated tasks.

2.1 Mapping Task Data Selection

To construct the mapping data pool, we first identified the set of tile identifiers (tile IDs) that contained the highest number of urban and industrial label instances. This selection was performed empirically to ensure that each experimental trial could access a sufficiently large sample size (targeting at least 50,000 mapping examples per trial). For these selected IDs, only those data rows containing exclusively urban or industrial labels were retained. All other IDs were excluded from the mapping pool, ensuring that the mapping data were strictly representative of urban and industrial scenes.

2.2 Classification Task Data Selection

For the unrelated land cover classification task, we constructed a separate pool by excluding all rows associated with urban or industrial labels. This ensured that the classification task was restricted to non-urban and non-industrial areas, thereby providing a distinct and independent evaluation scenario.

2.3 Five-Fold Experimental Splitting Procedure

Both the mapping and classification data pools were partitioned into training, validation, and test sets through a multi-trial sampling procedure designed to support robust cross-validation and to evaluate model performance under varying training set sizes.

For the mapping task, validation sets were randomly sampled from the mapping pool for each of five experimental trials. The remaining data were used to construct candidate training sets of incrementally increasing sizes. Tiles were selected in random order until the desired sample size was achieved for each training set. To ensure consistency across training set sizes, each larger set was constructed to contain all samples from the previous, smaller set.

For the classification task, tile identifiers were randomly partitioned into training and test sets, with a fixed proportion reserved for testing in each trial.

Within the training set, a validation subset was randomly sampled. The remaining training candidates were incrementally selected to achieve specified sample sizes, following a procedure analogous to that used for the mapping task. As with the mapping data, each larger training set for the classification task contained all samples from the previous, smaller set.

This rigorous data partitioning strategy ensures the independence of mapping and classification tasks, supports robust cross-validation across multiple experimental trials, and enables systematic evaluation of model performance under varying training set sizes and task conditions.

3 Methods

3.1 Experimental Design

The primary objective of this study is to evaluate the transferability and descriptive capacity of feature representations across distinct remote sensing modalities by learning linear mappings between their respective embedding spaces (visualized in Fig. 1). This approach enables systematic benchmarking of modality-specific models for downstream classification tasks, thereby informing model selection and fine-tuning strategies for novel mission requirements.

Let X and Y denote two paired sets of images acquired from different sensor modalities, such that each $x_i \in X$ is paired with a corresponding $y_i \in Y$. For modality X, we employ a feature extractor $E_X : X \to \mathbb{R}^{d_X}$, which maps input images to a d_X-dimensional embedding space, and a classifier head $\pi_X : \mathbb{R}^{d_X} \to C$, where C denotes the classification output space. Analogously, for modality Y, we define a feature extractor $E_Y : Y \to \mathbb{R}^{d_Y}$.

To facilitate cross-modal evaluation, the paired dataset is partitioned into disjoint training and testing subsets, ensuring that for each pair (x_i, y_i), the index i is assigned exclusively to either the training or testing set. Within the training set, we learn a linear mapping $M_{Y \to X} \in \mathbb{R}^{d_Y \times d_X}$ that projects embeddings from modality Y into the embedding space of modality X. The mapping $M_{Y \to X}$ is optimized to minimize the following objective function:

$$\min_{M} \sum_{i \in \text{Train}} \|E_X(x_i) - ME_Y(y_i)\|^2 ,$$

where $\|\cdot\|$ denotes the Euclidean norm. Ridge regression (linear least squares with L2 regularization) is employed to estimate $M_{Y \to X}$, thereby mitigating overfitting and improving generalization.

Subsequently, downstream classification performance is evaluated by composing the feature extractor and classifier head of modality X with the mapped embeddings from modality Y. For each y_j in the test set, the classification output is computed as $\pi_X(ME_Y(y_j))$, where π_X is the finetuned classifier for a task in domain X. This performance serves as an indicator of the suitability of the target modality's feature space for the classification task, and thus its potential value for future fine-tuning efforts. While the ideal operational scenario would designate a single target feature space as the reference domain for all mappings (minimizing the requirement for paired data during model integration), this study evaluates all possible source-target modality combinations for completeness, as well as to identify which, if any, target modalities provide the predictive capacity for relative downstream performance.

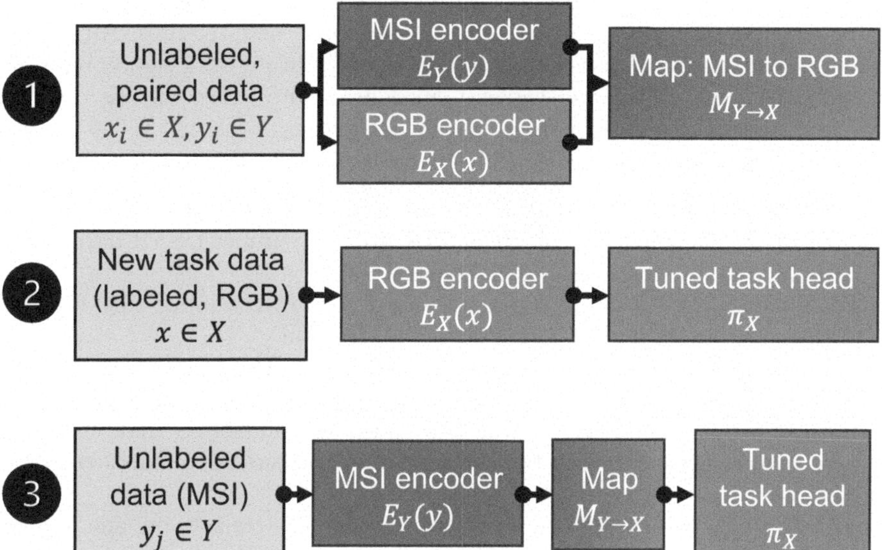

Fig. 1. With an RGB image encoder chosen as an example target domain and MSI as an example source domain, we can summarize our embedding space mapping procedure in three steps: (1) An image y_i from the source domain (MSI) and paired image x_i from the target domain (RGB) are processed by feature extractors E_Y and E_X, respectively. A linear mapping $M_{Y\to X}$ is fit on the training pairs via ridge regression to align $E_Y(y_i)$ to $E_X(x_i)$. (2) We fine-tune the target RGB encoder for a downstream classification task, producing classifier π_X. (3) Cross-modal classification is evaluated on the test set by composing the mapped Y embeddings with the classifier head of modality X, $\pi_X(M_{Y\to X}E_Y(y_i))$, and the resulting performance quantifies the transferability and descriptive capacity of the target modality's feature space, informing model selection and fine-tuning.

Two distinct mapping paradigms are considered:

1. **Mapping with Unrelated Data:** Linear mappings are trained using BEN data containing urban and manmade structures, which are excluded from the downstream multi-label classification experiment. This simulates the scenario in which mappings are constructed independently of new mission data, reflecting operational realities where encoder models are integrated prior to the availability of mission-specific annotated data.
2. **Mapping with Task-Specific Data:** Linear mappings are trained using subsets of the 17-category training partitions corresponding to the new classification task. This simulates the scenario in which resources are invested to

construct new mappings tailored to each mission or task, leveraging available annotated data for improved alignment.

3.2 Model Selection and Feature Extraction

For each data modality, multiple feature extractors are evaluated to assess the generalizability and suitability of different backbone architectures. All models utilize a ResNet-50 backbone as a proof of concept; future work should replicate these experiments with larger-capacity encoder architectures, such as domain-specific foundation models, as they become available.
The following models are included in the evaluation (see Fig. 2):

- **BEN SAR and BEN MSI:** State-of-the-art ResNet-50 models trained on BigEarthNet, version 2 [2,4]. BEN SAR utilizes Sentinel-1 SAR data, while BEN MSI utilizes Sentinel-2 multispectral imagery.
- **BEN RGB:** A subsampled version of BEN MSI, retaining only the red, green, and blue channels to create an RGB domain.
- **xView3:** A ResNet-50 backbone extracted from a ship classification model trained on the xView3 training dataset, representing a domain-specific encoder for maritime scenes [10]. We tuned this model so that we had a SAR feature extractor with the correct VV, VH channels to match the BEN SAR inputs.
- **SSL4EO:** A self-supervised ResNet-50 backbone trained on one million Sentinel-2 images (12 channels) [16]. For comparative analysis, both 10-channel (MSI) and 3-channel (RGB) subsampled versions are evaluated.

For all models, feature extraction is performed using the non-fine-tuned backbone, yielding a 2048-dimensional feature vector for each input image. These feature vectors serve as the basis for learning cross-modal mappings via ridge regression.

3.3 Evaluation Protocol

To assess the efficacy of the mapping approach, each possible source-target modality pair is evaluated. For each combination, features are extracted from the source modality, mapped into the target modality's feature space using the trained linear mapping, and subsequently classified using the target modality's classifier head. This procedure is repeated for all model pairs to determine whether performance is consistent across possible reference domains.

Additionally, for each backbone, we fine-tune the model directly on the downstream classification task using varying amounts of labeled data (Fig. 3). As seen in Fig. 4, the results demonstrate that fine-tuning performance on a smaller subset of data is not predictive of relative performance when the same backbone is fine-tuned with a substantially larger dataset (e.g., 1,000 vs. 80,000 samples). This finding underscores the necessity of robust evaluation protocols and motivates the use of embedding space mappings to prioritize model selection prior to committing significant resources to annotation and fine-tuning.

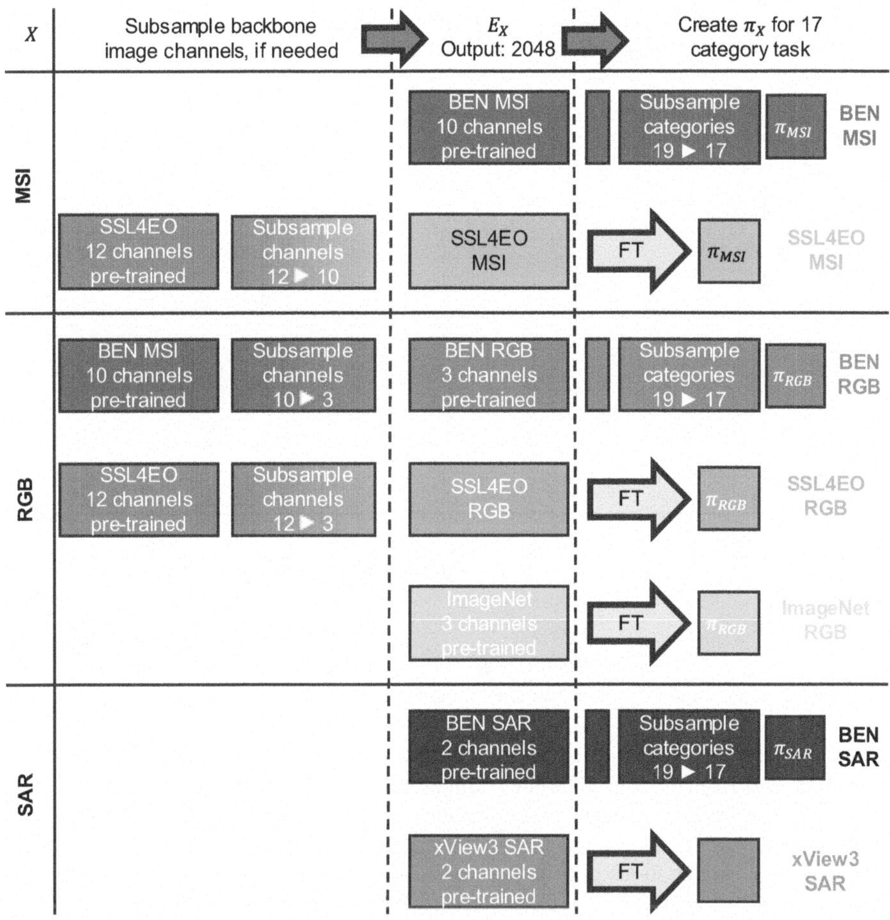

Fig. 2. Models are prepared differently for our dedicated "novel" task—17 category land-cover classification of non-urban areas: ResNet-50 models already tuned on the complete 19 category BEN task have the two urban categories removed from their prediction vector; while ResNet-50 backbones adapted from other sources are fine-tuned on the 17 categories only with the first 6 ResNet layers frozen.

4 Results

To assess the efficacy of our mapping-based diagnostic framework, we conducted a comprehensive evaluation of classifier performance and feature transferability across multiple backbone models and mapping paradigms. Our analysis focused on three principal axes: (1) the relationship between fine-tuning set size and downstream classification performance, (2) the fidelity of mapped features relative to target model features, and (3) the predictive utility of mapping-based diagnostics for future fine-tuning outcomes.

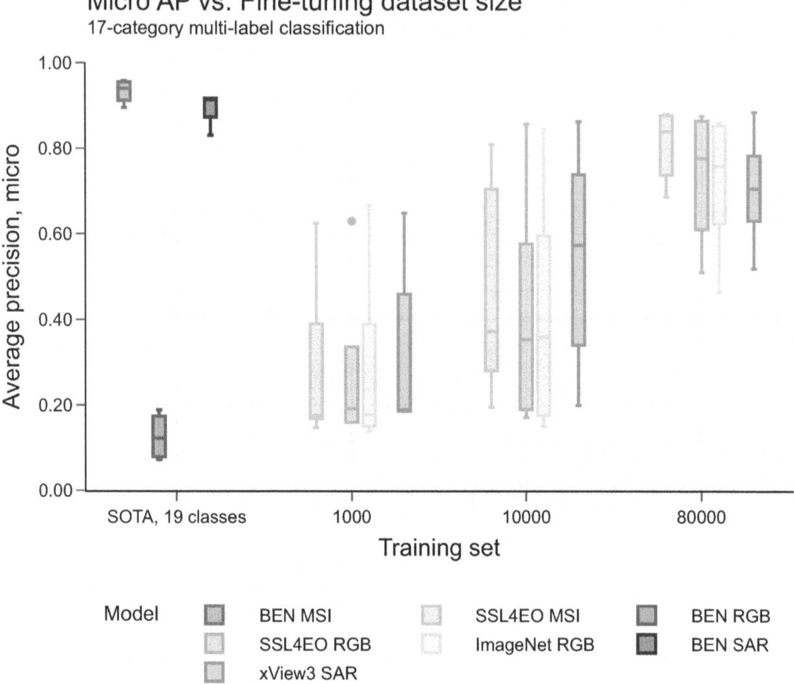

Fig. 3. Relative performance of externally sourced models fine-tuned for the BEN task is not consistent across different training set sizes. Additionally, we observe that, although we are able to reproduce performant results with existing BEN MSI and BEN SAR models from [2], subsampling the BEN MSI model channels to create the BEN RGB model performs more poorly than even models tuned with very few examples. These extrema of relative best and worst performing models enable us to test the bounds of the efficacy of our mapping method.

4.1 Fine-Tuning Set Size and Classifier Performance

We first compared the downstream classification performance of BEN MSI and BEN SAR models fine-tuned with varying amounts of labeled data. As illustrated in Figs. 3 and 4, classifier accuracy with small fine-tuning set sizes was not predictive of the relative performance of the same models when fine-tuned with substantially larger training sets. This observation underscores the limitations of relying on small-scale fine-tuning experiments to guide model selection for operational deployments, where larger annotated datasets may ultimately be available.

Additionally, we observed that sub-sampling the state-of-the-art BEN MSI model to create an RGB-only variant resulted in markedly poor classification performance. This result serves as a critical sanity check for our ranking methodology, confirming that models with suboptimal input representations should not be preferred by any robust diagnostic technique.

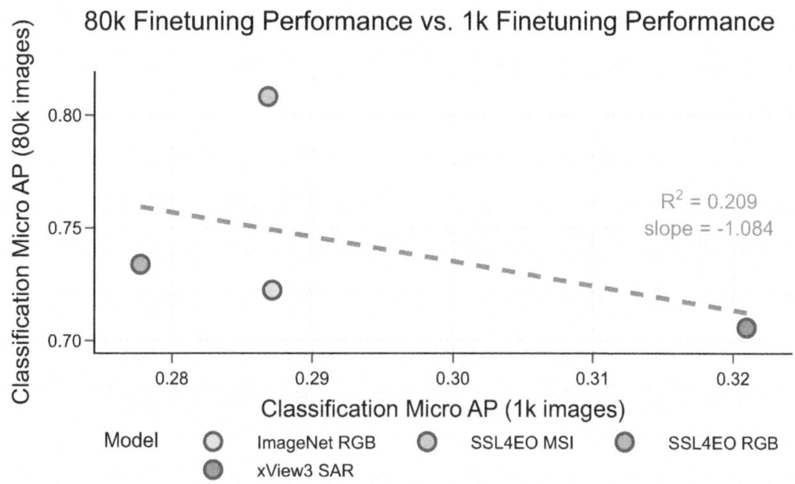

Fig. 4. Comparing test micro average precision (micro-AP) of the same modality-specific starting models fine-tuned on 1k labeled examples (x-axis) versus 80k labeled examples (y-axis) for a 17-category classification task indicates that small-sample fine-tuning does not predict large-sample outcomes across models. This demonstrates that performance under a small label budget is a poor predictor of performance after large-scale fine-tuning in this case. Consequently, selecting which modality to invest in based on a small labeled subset can be misleading, potentially requiring substantial labeling across modalities to identify the best model option.

4.2 Feature Mapping Fidelity

Maps between feature spaces were evaluated using a held-out set relevant to each mapping partition. For each mapping, we computed the cosine similarity between mapped features and the actual features produced by the target model. Figure 5 presents these results, revealing that ImageNet-pretrained models consistently achieved high cosine similarity scores across all target domains, whereas BEN SAR and BEN MSI models exhibited relatively lower scores. We hypothesize that this discrepancy arises from the high degree of specialization in the BEN models, which are optimized for their respective sensor modalities. During experimental debugging, we noted that preprocessing choices, particularly normalization, had a pronounced impact on mapping fidelity. Ultimately, we adopted the normalization protocol recommended by the BEN state-of-the-art methodology, which proved to be well suited for those models.

4.3 End-to-End Mapping and Classification Performance

We further evaluated the complete pipeline from feature extraction, through mapping, to downstream classification. Top-performing models demonstrated robust classification accuracy when mapped to each other, even with limited mapping set sizes. As shown in Fig. 6, downstream classification performance

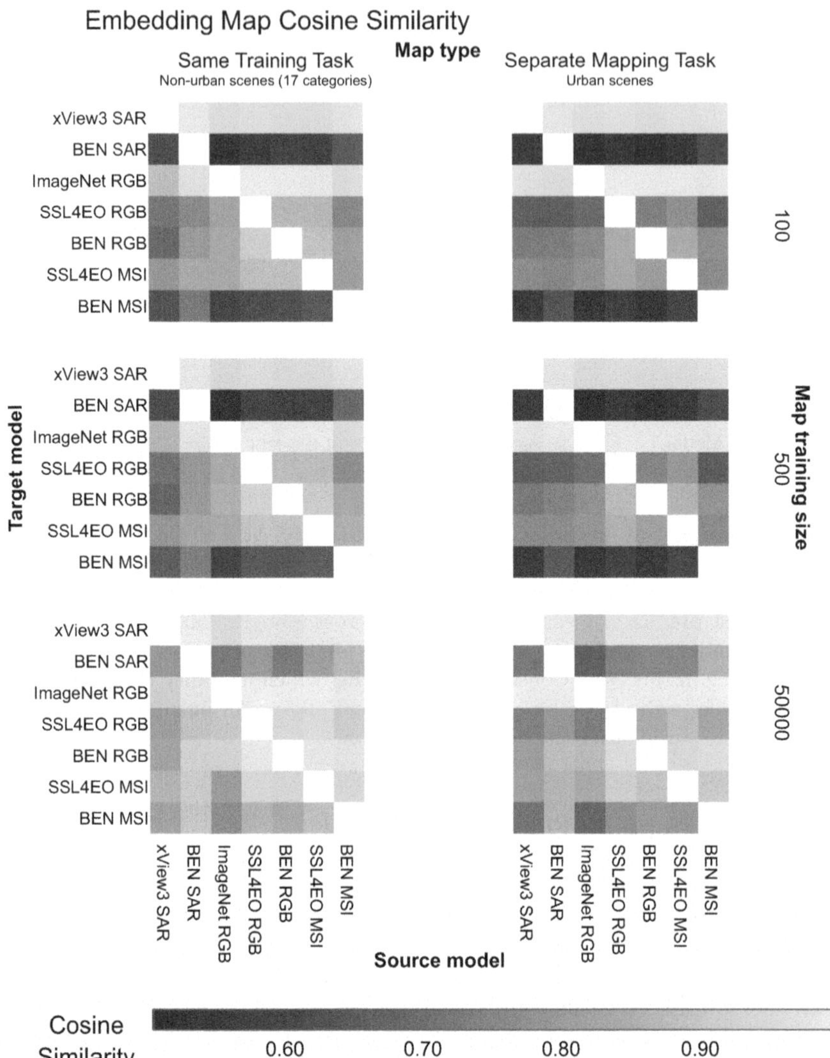

Fig. 5. We assess the fidelity of our maps by passing held out test samples, y_j, from source domain Y through embedding space E_y and then through map $M_{Y \to X}$ to target domain X, and measure the cosine similarity of the mapped sample to the actual sample from the target domain $E_X(x_j)$. We repeat this assessment for different map types (see Sect. 3.1) and varying amounts of training samples for $M_{Y \to X}$. Higher values indicate better alignment of the mapped features to the target space, revealing that BEN SAR and BEN MSI yield comparatively low alignment, likely reflecting BEN-specific preprocessing [2].

was highest for models that were pre-trained on BEN data. These results were analyzed under two diagnostic strategies: (1) training a small, task-specific map for each new mission, and (2) investing in a larger, general-purpose map that

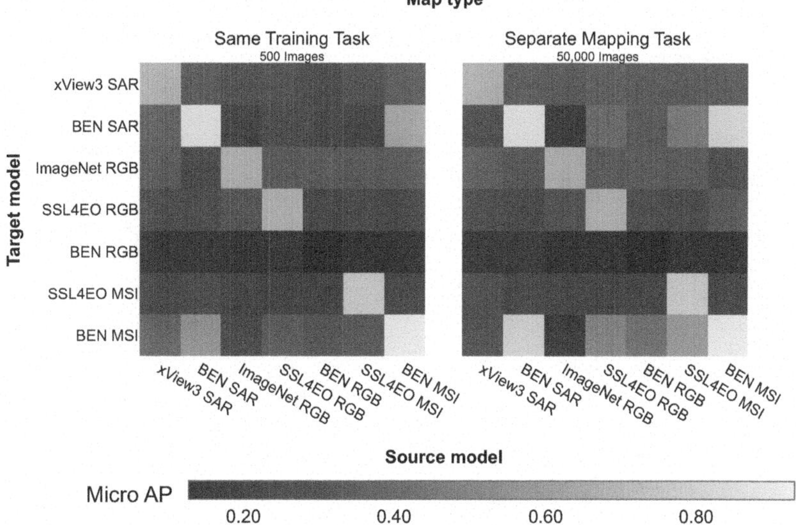

Fig. 6. We assess cross-domain classification performance by computing test micro-AP of embeddings from a source modality mapped into a target modality's encoder space and classified with the target head; diagonal cells are replaced by the target modality's baseline performance (80k fine-tuned models, or recreated SOTA for BEN MSI and BEN SAR [2]). As expected, BEN RGB is the weakest target space; nevertheless, mapping into BEN RGB from other modalities yields higher micro-AP than the BEN RGB baseline, and mapping out of BEN RGB into any other target improves performance. BEN SAR and BEN MSI are the strongest targets and map particularly well to each other, supporting the hypothesis that their specialized BEN preprocessing produces more compatible and discriminative feature spaces. The relative ordering of source–target pairs is consistent across the two mapping paradigms (small, task-specific training vs. larger, disparate-task training), with the latter further separating extreme cases.

could be reused across different tasks, as simulated by our held-out urban mapping experiment.

Additional observations from these experiments include the tendency for the best-performing features to become increasingly domain-specific as the mapping set size grows, and the consistent under-performance of the poorest model across all mapping sizes and strategies. It is also worth noting that samples embedded with the BEN RGB model exhibited better performance when mapped to a different target domain than the model itself; this confirms our hypothesis that some feature spaces are more well-suited to a particular downstream task.

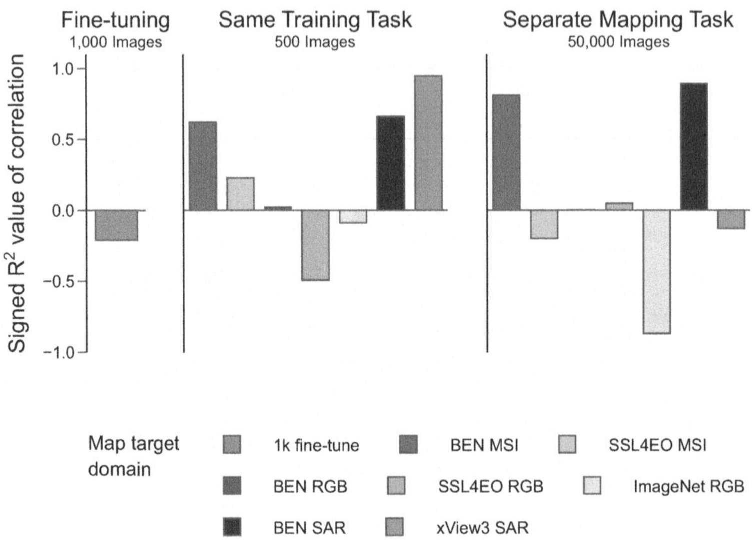

Fig. 7. Bar plots summarize the signed R^2 between each target domain's mapping-based relative performance and the relative performance of the corresponding source backbones when fine-tuned on 80k labels, for both mapping paradigms (small, same-task vs. large, separate-task). The sign is assigned by the slope of the linear fit. BEN MSI and BEN RGB are consistently well correlated across both paradigms, whereas xView3 SAR is strongly predictive only in the small, same-task setting and weakens for larger, separate-task maps, likely due to the presence of man-made objects in the separate task (urban and industrial scenes), as these have strong features in SAR images.

4.4 Predictive Utility of Mapping-Based Diagnostics

To determine whether our mapping procedure could serve as a reliable predictor of downstream fine-tuning performance, we performed linear regression analyses between mapping-based diagnostic scores and the classification accuracy achieved by each backbone when fine-tuned with 80,000 labeled samples. Specifically, we computed the coefficient of determination (R^2) for each source-target domain pair, assigning the sign of the R^2 value according to the slope of the linear fit to ensure that only positive correlations were considered. Figure 7 summarizes these results. Our findings indicate that the best-performing models in the mapping experiments (BEN SAR and BEN MSI) also serve as effective reference domains for predicting future fine-tuning outcomes, as shown in Fig. 8. Notably, the xView3 SAR model exhibited strong predictive utility for small, same-task maps, but its performance diminished for larger, separate-task maps. We hypothesize that this is due to the separation of urban and industrial scene

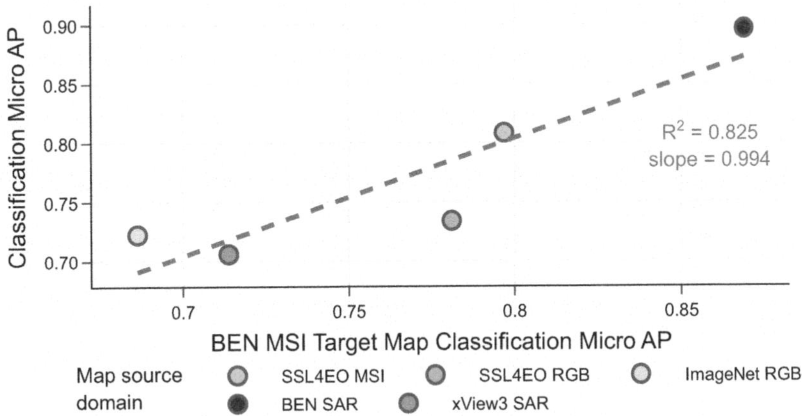

Fig. 8. Here, BEN MSI serves as an example predictive reference domain and we compare test micro-AP for 80k fine-tuned models (y-axis) against the reference target-map micro-AP (x-axis), with a linear fit and reported R^2. Compared to the 80k-vs-1k baseline, this relationship is markedly stronger and more monotonic, aligning with the high signed R^2 observed for BEN MSI and indicating that mapping-based diagnostics better anticipate large-scale fine-tuning outcomes than small-sample fine-tuning.

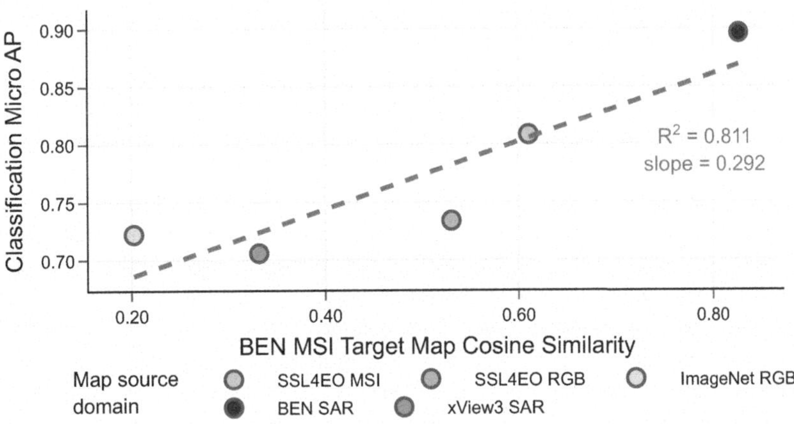

Fig. 9. We observe that map cosine similarity can, in the case of BEN MSI as a reference domain, serve as a label-free predictor. The correlation matches that obtained with mapped micro-AP, showing that, for BEN MSI, unlabeled paired data and a simple embedding-fidelity metric can predict which source encoder spaces will fine-tune well—without requiring labeled BEN MSI examples to train a classifier head.

content into the separate map training set, as man-made objects have very distinct features in SAR imagery.

Unexpectedly, we found that the cosine similarity scores obtained from the mapping procedure were, for certain target domains, highly correlated with downstream fine-tuning performance (see Fig. 9). This result is particularly promising, as it suggests that paired data alone—without the need for new labeled samples—may suffice to identify well-suited target domains for future annotation and fine-tuning investments. However, we also observed that BEN models were highly sensitive to preprocessing choices, further emphasizing the importance of domain-appropriate normalization protocols.

5 Discussion

5.1 Future Research

While the present study demonstrates the utility of embedding space diagnostics for model selection and evaluation in remote sensing, several avenues for future research remain open and warrant systematic investigation.

First, it is essential to assess whether the optimal reference domain identified in this work remains consistent across other datasets and application contexts. The BigEarthNet dataset was found to be highly sensitive to normalization protocols, suggesting that careful matching of preprocessing strategies to encoder architectures is critical. Future experiments should explicitly compare the impact of applying backbone-specific preprocessing, as opposed to modality-specific normalization, on mapping fidelity and downstream performance. This consideration is particularly relevant when acquiring or repurposing pretrained encoders, as preprocessing mismatches may adversely affect model utility.

Additionally, further work should be undertaken to fine-tune the RGB variant of the BEN backbone, which was not directly equivalent to the multispectral version and exhibited unexpectedly poor performance due to the subsampling approach. In contrast, the channel subsampling for the SSL4EO model produced more discriminating embedding spaces, but this is likely due to the fact that these models were fine-tuned. Overall, the fine-tuning process for downstream task performance comparison warrants further attention; for example, freezing more pre-trained layers for smaller tuning sets.

To ensure comprehensive coverage of mapping paradigms, future experiments should also include all combinations of map types, specifically evaluating both small maps on unrelated tasks and large maps on the same task. Theoretically, if robust methods for sampling paired data between data management systems are established, the constraints imposed by the need for labeled data may be substantially mitigated.

Another important direction is to investigate the practical utility of selecting a permanent target domain that is easier to annotate. For example, electro-optical (EO) imagery may be preferable as a reference domain due to the broader availability of EO labeling expertise compared to SAR annotation expertise.

This consideration could inform strategic decisions in model development and acquisition.

Future efforts should not only investigate the ability to form maps between embedding spaces, but also characterize properties of both the spaces themselves and the resultant maps. Recent work in Natural Language Processing [6] suggests that embedding spaces may have universal properties, affording the opportunity to translate between spaces without paired data. If this property holds for other data domains, such as among embedding spaces for disparate RS sensor types, the burdens discussed above (namely, acquisition of paired and/or labeled data), could be reduced substantially by identifying and harnessing universal properties of the spaces.

Finally, as foundation model (FM) encoders with greater capacity and generalization abilities become available, it will be imperative to replicate and extend these experiments using such architectures. The integration of FM encoders may further enhance the scalability and effectiveness of embedding space diagnostics for mission-critical remote sensing applications.

Collectively, these research directions will refine the methodology presented here and expand its applicability to a wider range of operational scenarios and data modalities.

5.2 Conclusions

In summary, our analysis demonstrates that mapping-based diagnostics provide a preliminary framework for evaluating the relative utility of candidate backbone models for downstream classification tasks in remote sensing. The inability of small-scale fine-tuning experiments to predict large-scale performance highlights the need for alternative model selection strategies. Our mapping approach, leveraging paired data and feature space alignment, enables the identification of promising target domains prior to resource-intensive annotation and fine-tuning efforts.

The observed correlation between mapping fidelity and downstream performance, particularly for certain reference domains, suggests that this methodology can be operationalized to prioritize model development and integration in enterprise environments. Future work should extend these experiments to larger-capacity encoder architectures and further investigate the impact of preprocessing protocols on mapping efficacy.

Overall, our findings support the adoption of embedding space diagnostics as a scalable and data-efficient strategy for foundation model evaluation and selection in specialized remote sensing applications.

5.3 Applications

With further refinement, we believe tools like these could be used to estimate FM suitability for novel specialized tasks at enterprise scale. This could support acquisitions and research decisions, especially in an environment where use of off-the-shelf models is required or novel sensor modalities are common. The effort will serve to improved readiness via targeted FM integration.

Acknowledgments. This work was supported by the MITRE Independent Research and Development Program.

Disclosure of Interests. The authors have no competing interests to declare that are relevant to the content of this article.

References

1. Bommasani, R., et al.: On the opportunities and risks of foundation models (2022). https://arxiv.org/abs/2108.07258
2. Clasen, K.N., Hackel, L., Burgert, T., Sumbul, G., Demir, B., Markl, V.: reBEN: Refined bigearthnet dataset for remote sensing image analysis. In: IEEE International Geoscience and Remote Sensing Symposium (IGARSS) (2025). https://arxiv.org/abs/2407.0365
3. Fagan, M.: AI for the people: use cases for government (2024). https://www.hks.harvard.edu/sites/default/files/centers/mrcbg/working.papers/M-RCBG%20Working%20Paper%202024-02_AI%20for%20the%20People.pdf
4. Hackel, L., Clasen, K., Demir, B.: ConfigILM: a general purpose configurable library for combining image and language models for visual question answering. SoftwareX **26**, 101731 (2024). https://doi.org/10.1016/j.softx.2024.101731
5. Hagendorff, T., Meding, K.: Ethical considerations and statistical analysis of industry involvement in machine learning research. AI Soc. **38**(1), 35–45 (2023). https://doi.org/10.1007/s00146-021-01284-z
6. Jha, R., Zhang, C., Shmatikov, V., Morris, J.X.: Harnessing the universal geometry of embeddings (2025). https://arxiv.org/abs/2505.12540
7. Lacoste, A., et al.: GEO-bench: toward foundation models for earth monitoring (2023). https://arxiv.org/abs/2306.03831
8. Martorana, C.: AI in action: 5 essential findings from the 2024 federal AI use case inventory (2025). https://www.cio.gov/ai-in-action/
9. National Institute of Standards and Technology: Artificial intelligence risk management framework (2023). https://nvlpubs.nist.gov/nistpubs/ai/nist.ai.100-1.pdf
10. Paolo, F., et al.: xView3-SAR: detecting dark fishing activity using synthetic aperture radar imagery (2022). https://arxiv.org/abs/2206.00897
11. Radford, A., Wu, J., Child, R., Luan, D., Amodei, D., Sutskever, I.: Language models are unsupervised multitask learners (2019). https://api.semanticscholar.org/CorpusID:160025533

12. Reed, C.J., et al.: Scale-MAE: a scale-aware masked autoencoder for multiscale geospatial representation learning. In: Proceedings of the IEEE/CVF International Conference on Computer Vision (ICCV), pp. 4088–4099 (2023). https://arxiv.org/abs/2212.14532
13. Schmidt, E., et al.: Final report: national security commission on artificial intelligence (2021). https://assets.foleon.com/eu-central-1/de-uploads-7e3kk3/48187/nscai_full_report_digital.04d6b124173c.pdf
14. U.S. Government Accountability Office: Artificial intelligence: An accountability framework for federal agencies and other entities (2021). https://www.gao.gov/assets/gao-21-519sp.pdf
15. Wang, D., et al.: MTP: advancing remote sensing foundation model via multi-task pretraining. In: IEEE JSTARS Special issue on "Large-Scale Pretraining for Interpretation Promotion in Remote Sensing Domain" (2024). https://arxiv.org/abs/2403.13430
16. Wang, Y., Braham, N.A.A., Xiong, Z., Liu, C., Albrecht, C.M., Zhu, X.X.: SSL4EO-S12: a large-scale multi-modal, multi-temporal dataset for self-supervised learning in earth observation. In: IEEE Geoscience and Remote Sensing Magazine (2022). https://arxiv.org/abs/2211.07044
17. Zgurovsky, M.Z.: Global trends in artificial intelligence. Challenges, opportunities, and prospects. Cybern. Syst. Anal. **61**(4), 533–553 (2025). https://doi.org/10.1007/s10559-025-00790-y

Scaling Remote Sensing Foundation Models: Data Domain Tradeoffs at the Peta-Scale

Charith Wickrema, Eliza Mace(✉), Hunter Brown, Heidys Cabrera, Nick Krall, Matthew O'Neill, Shivangi Sarkar, Lowell Weissman, Eric Hughes, and Guido Zarrella

The MITRE Corporation, McLean, VA 22102, USA
{cwickrema,emace,hbrown,hcabrera,nkrall,moneill,ssarkar,lweissman,hughes, jzarrella}@mitre.org
https://www.mitre.org/

Abstract. We explore the scaling behaviors of artificial intelligence to establish practical techniques for training foundation models on high-resolution electro-optical (EO) datasets that exceed the current state-of-the-art scale by orders of magnitude. Modern multimodal machine learning (ML) applications, such as generative artificial intelligence (GenAI) systems for image captioning, search, and reasoning, depend on robust, domain-specialized encoders for non-text modalities. In natural-image domains where internet-scale data is plentiful, well-established scaling laws help optimize the joint scaling of model capacity, training compute, and dataset size. Unfortunately these relationships are much less well-understood in high-value domains like remote sensing (RS). Using over a quadrillion pixels of commercial satellite EO data and MITRE's Federal AI Sandbox, we train progressively larger vision transformer (ViT) backbones, report successes and failure modes observed at petascale, and analyze implications for bridging domain gaps across additional RS modalities. We observe that even at this scale, performance is consistent with a data-limited regime rather than a model parameter-limited one. These practical insights are intended to inform data-collection strategies, compute budgets, and optimization schedules that advance the future development of frontier-scale RS foundation models.

Keywords: Computer vision · Remote sensing · Foundation models

1 Introduction

Recent advances in machine learning (ML) have been propelled by the development of large-scale models and foundation architectures, particularly in the context of generative artificial intelligence (GenAI) and multi-modal applications. Central to the success of these systems are performant data encoders which transform raw data into representations useful in downstream tasks. While scaling laws and architectural best practices for vision transformers (ViTs) have been

F. Tanner and J. Irvine (Eds.): AIPR 2025, LNCS 16446, pp. 132–153, 2026.
https://doi.org/10.1007/978-3-032-18474-0_10

extensively studied in domains such as natural imagery [6,14], their applicability to specialized domains like remote sensing (RS) remains underexplored.

Remote sensing data, especially from electro-optical (EO) commercial satellites, presents unique challenges and opportunities for ML. Unlike natural images, RS data is characterized by diverse spectral, spatial, and temporal properties, as well as limited availability of labeled, in-domain training samples. This scarcity has hindered the development and scaling of foundation models (FMs) tailored to RS, leaving several fundamental questions unanswered. Notably, the relationship between training dataset size and model performance at scale for in-domain RS FMs is poorly understood.

Addressing these gaps is critical for advancing the state of the art in RS ML applications, which underpin a wide range of societal and scientific needs, from environmental monitoring to urban planning. To this end, we leverage an unprecedented scale of EO satellite imagery totaling over a peta-pixel and employ multi-task pretraining (MTP) [12] and Scale-Aware Masked Autoencoder (ScaleMAE) [7] foundation model architectures. By integrating supervised optimization with open-source geographic information system (GIS)-derived labels, we are able to construct large, high-quality training datasets. Furthermore, by utilizing large-scale graphics processing units (GPUs) resources, specifically an NVIDIA DGX H100 SuperPOD in MITRE's Federal AI Sandbox, we systematically scale ViT training regimes to assess whether modern frontier RS foundation models remain constrained by data availability.

In this work, we empirically characterize the scaling behaviors of ViT-based RS FMs, evaluating their performance and analyzing their capacity to address domain gaps across additional RS modalities. Our findings provide new insights into the design and training of RS FMs, with implications for both the ML and RS communities.

1.1 Guiding Questions

This study is organized around four guiding questions central to scaling RS encoders: (a) under what conditions increasing batch size improves training time or convergence; (b) which learning-rate schedules remain stable for continual pre-training of RS models at scale; (c) how performance scales with in-domain dataset size and the rate at which gains taper; and (d) how predictably performance improves when scaling ViT model parameters. These questions structure our experimental design and analyses to develop practical strategies for future RS FMs training.

1.2 Motivation

The unprecedented scale and diversity of modern RS datasets enable the training of large, domain-specific models that have the potential to outperform generic, out-of-domain encoders on RS tasks. However, the unique characteristics of RS data such as its spectral complexity, geographic diversity, and limited labeled samples raise important questions about the optimal strategies for model scaling in this context.

A key open question is whether current frontier-scale RS models adequately saturate performance, in other words, whether continued scaling offers opportunity for improvement or if diminishing returns emerge as model and dataset sizes increase beyond current state-of-the-art implementations. Unlike domains such as natural language processing (NLP) or natural image understanding, where increasing model size unlocks richer context-aware representations and better captures longer-range dependencies— due in part to the inherent complexity and compositionality in the data—RS imagery may present intrinsic limitations. The set of features that can be learned from overhead imagery could be fundamentally constrained by the spatial resolution and the finite variety of observable objects and patterns within a given scene. As a result, there may be an upper bound to the representational capacity required for effective RS analysis, beyond which further scaling yields marginal gains. Furthermore, while larger models in NLP often benefit from expanded context windows that enable reasoning over longer sequences, the spatial context in overhead imagery is typically limited by the maximum image size available from traditional sensors. This raises the possibility that simply increasing model size may not indefinitely improve performance in RS tasks, as the available contextual information does not scale in the same manner as in other domains.

Addressing these questions is essential for maximizing the impact of foundation models in remote sensing. By systematically exploring the interplay between model size, training data composition, and model performance, we aim to provide actionable insights for both the ML and RS communities, informing the next generation of scalable, high-performance geospatially-aware models. Given these constraints, we treat scaling as an engineering process: identify the levers that matter (data composition, optimizer dynamics, throughput), stress-test them at new scales, and document the regimes where progress is linear versus where it stalls or destabilizes. The remainder of the paper follows this process, moving from related literature to our dataset design, controlled experiments, and the lessons derived from their outcomes.

1.3 Contributions

We contribute a process-oriented account of scaling RS foundation models:

- Lessons for throughput scaling: early- to mid-stage training is batch-insensitive beyond moderate thresholds; prioritize data diversity and LR scheduling over aggressive batch increases.
- Stable optimization schedules: a Warmup, Stable, Decay (WSD) regime with moderate base learning rate (LR) provides robust convergence; we document divergence behaviors at higher LRs and propose experiments to avoid wasting compute on unstable runs.
- Empirical data-scaling law: within 5k–1M full scene RS images, loss follows a consistent power-law with diminishing but non-saturated returns, supporting larger compute- and data-planning for RS pretraining.

- Empirical model-scaling laws: across 86M-1.8B parameters we see effectively flat returns indicating that model scaling alone provides negligible benefit under typical data size regimes.
- Scalable weak supervision: a reproducible **G**eospatial **D**ata **Aug**mentation (**G-DAUG**) pipeline that pairs image chips with automatic enrichments allows exploration of supervision techniques relevant at global scale.

2 Related Work

2.1 Foundation Models and Scaling Laws in Vision

The adoption of transformer units [4,11] revolutionized representation learning by introducing self-attention mechanisms that scale efficiently with data and compute. This paradigm shift enabled the rise of foundation models, large, pre-trained systems capable of generalizing across diverse downstream tasks with minimal adaptation. Studies on neural network scaling later showed that model performance frequently follows power-law relationships with respect to model size, dataset size, and compute. Previous research [6] demonstrated these trends for transformer-based language models showing that loss scales predictably and that compute can be optimally distributed across parameters, data, and training steps. In vision, research [14] extended scaling analysis to vision transformers (ViTs), finding a compute performance pareto frontier and double-saturating power law indicating that data remains the limiting factor even for billion-scale image datasets. Larger models continue to benefit from more data, while smaller ones quickly saturate. Scaling-law methods were quickly refined through improved curve fitting [1], enhancing extrapolation across new scales and modalities and enabling more accurate prediction of compute efficiency. Together these works established scaling laws as a predictive framework for large-scale model design. Our study extends this foundation to geospatial foundation models, where domain heterogeneity, sensor diversity, and spatial temporal structure may yield distinct scaling dynamics.

2.2 Vision for Remote Sensing

Trends towards foundational modeling in vision and language are also reflected in the research community's move towards geospatial foundation models for remote sensing. These reflect a rapid shift from narrow, task-specific networks to large-scale, general-purpose models trained on globally distributed satellite imagery. Early RS models were limited by modest dataset size, handcrafted features, and single-task training, but the rise of transformers and large-scale self-supervised learning has enabled development of unified models capable of transferring across sensors, spatial scales, and geographies.

To address the diversity and scale of earth observation data, researchers have begun to assemble increasingly larger, more heterogenous datasets and corresponding pretraining strategies. SatlasPretrain [2] created one of the largest labeled RS pretraining dataset to date with multiple sensors and tasks: 1×10^{13} pixels over 21 million km^2 with 137 distinct categories. The model demonstrated that large-scale joint pretraining improves downstream performance on a variety of segmentation, object detection, and change detection tasks marking an early step toward foundation-scale generalization in RS. Similarly, Prithvi [9] explored self-supervised pretraining for multispectral imagery at continental scale (4.2M globally distributed samples), revealing that transformer models can learn general geospatial representations transferable across multiple datasets.

Architecturally, recent work has been focused on incorporating scale awareness and geospatial priors into vision transformers. ScaleMAE [7] introduced a scale-aware masked autoencoder that anchors positional encoding to real-world ground sample distance (GSD), enabling consistent multiresolution learning across diverse imagery sources. Other work proposed Multi-Task Pretraining (MTP) [12] frameworks that unify segmentation, detection, and classification objectives, while SkySense [5] extended foundational pretraining to billions of parameters and multimodal inputs, both temporal and contextual, reflecting the domains' upward progress. Efforts that have explicitly expanded parameter scaling, training transformer backbones ranging from 86M to 2B parameters [3] observed consistent performance in object detection and segmentation regardless of backbone size, likely due to a lack of commensurate data scaling with parameter scaling, as they leveraged the same 1M examples as the original MTP effort [12]. Meanwhile, DINOv3 [8], provides evidence that scaling model and data size in self-supervision can produce dense transferable representations that generalize to RS domains, starting both from natural and RS images, with corpuses of 1.7B images and 493M images, respectively. The increase in RS dataset sizes across the field is summarized in Table 1.

2.3 Summary and Gaps

Overall, these developments highlight a clear trend: remote sensing has entered a new scale of vision FM development. With increasing dataset size, parameter counts, and compute budgets, the field's next step is to quantitatively characterize scaling laws to determine how performance scales within the unique characteristics of geospatial imagery. Following the success of DINOv3 [8] in creating relevant RS representations, the field would benefit from precise quantification of training tradeoffs to allow for right-sizing of datasets, model architectures, and compute budgets for specific domain needs. Most prior work emphasizes best-case performance and model design, while comparatively little documents the operational regimes where scaling stalls, destabilizes, or provides marginal returns in RS. Our study complements these advances by quantifying when and how scaling pays off in RS, and by reporting the failure modes and lessons learned that turn scaling laws into practical training practice.

3 Dataset

We constructed Akupara, a global remote sensing dataset comprising over a petapixel (1×10^{15}) of high-resolution Maxar satellite imagery, the largest remote sensing dataset to date for FM training. The "Akupara-1M" collection contains over 1 million full satellite images (equivalent to $\sim$ 4 billion 512×512 chips) with 415 million km^2 of gross coverage (excluding USA due to collection constraints), with both single-channel panchromatic (PAN) imagery and eight-band multispectral imagery (MSI), and a ground sample distance (GSD) range of 0.3 m to 1.2 m. Images were collected primarily from 2020–2024 with $<2\%$ of imagery from 2007–2020. Table 1 shows a comparison of Akupara to other large remote sensing datasets.

To create representative working subsets, like Akupara-(100k, 50k, 5k, etc.), for analysis and model training, we employed a stratified sampling framework combining population weighting and attribute balancing, an example of which is shown in Fig. 1. Population density values were sampled at each image center point, and both numeric (e.g. obliquity angle, elevation variance, population density) and categorical (e.g., sensor type, time of day, land-cover class) attributes were normalized into quantile-based bins. Iterative proportional fitting (ranking) was used to calibrate sampling weights toward uniform marginal distributions across attributes. Using these values, a weighted, non-replacement sampling procedure generated fixed-size subsets with near-uniform coverage across geographic, temporal, and environmental domains. Because performance in RS appears data-limited yet feature-bounded, we opted to perform stratified sampling targeting geographic, temporal, and environmental balance so that 'more data' expands the domain of variation rather than duplicating narrow regimes. This design choice directly supports our scaling-law analysis, ensuring that improvements with scale reflect expanded coverage rather than repeated content.

Table 1. Akupara-1M is larger in pixel volume and land area than existing remote sensing datasets, and at a higher resolution (i.e., lower GSD). Labels are number of unique labels, and km^2 is area covered. *Akupara-1M has estimated number of labels as processing is ongoing within compute resource constraints.

Dataset	Num. pixels	Num. classes	Num. labels	GSD (m)	Land area (km^2)
BigEarthNet	1e9	43	2,000	10–60	850,000
Million-AID	4e9	51	37,000	0.5–153	18,000
FMoW	4e11	63	417,000	0.5	1,748,000
SatlasPretrain	1e13	137	302,222,000	0.5–60	21,320,000
DINOv3 Sat	1e14	–	–	0.6	46,000
Akupara-100k (ours)	7e13	37	3,800,000,000	0.3–1.2	32,677,000
Akupara-1M (ours)	1e15	37	49,390,000,000*	0.3–1.2	415,951,000

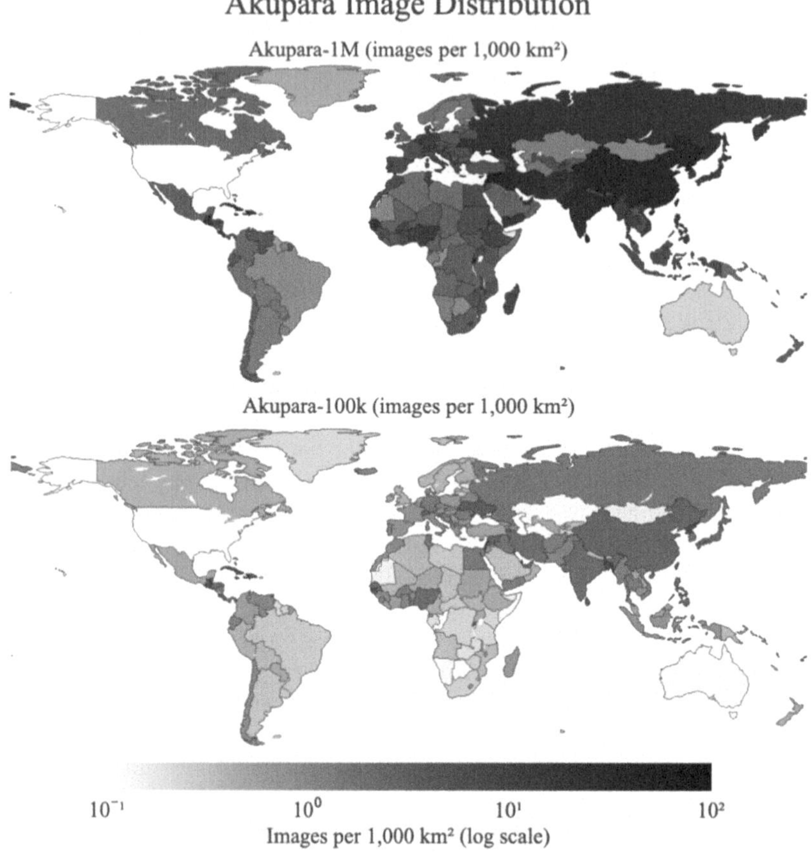

Fig. 1. Visualization of the number of images per 1,000 km^2 in both Akupara-1M and Akupara-100k. The Akupara-100k dataset is subsampled from the Akupara-1M dataset based on maximizing diversity of sensor and land area attributes. Although not visualized, collections over bodies of water, coastlines, islands, and Antarctica were also included in the dataset.

3.1 Label Generation

We developed the automated **G**eospatial **D**ata **Aug**mentation (**G-DAUG**) pipeline, a scalable geospatial labeling framework based on the SatlasPretrain [2] labeling method for large-scale weak supervision and automated annotation. Each 1024×1024 image chip is paired with OpenStreetMap (OSM) vector data retrieved via PostGIS queries within the chip's geographic footprint. The pipeline converts chip pixel coordinates to geographic bounds using metadata from the source orthorectified imagery, then filters OSM geometries by a curated ontology of 37 object classes (based on empirical findings in [2] that reveal categories with higher fidelity labels). Geometries are reprojected to the image coordinate reference system, clipped to the chip extent, and then rasterized into high-resolution binary segmentation masks. We produce instance segmentation masks, semantic segmentation masks, and rotated bounding boxes labels (as shown in Fig. 2) required for supervised training, such as with the Multi-Task Pretraining paradigm. This pipeline provides a reproducible, automated system for generating consistent, chip-aligned supervision across global-scale imagery datasets, bridging open vector sources and high-resolution raster training data.

Fig. 2. The Geospatial Data Augmentation (G-DAUG) pipeline leverages OpenStreetMap data and segmentation algorithms to automatically create geospatial data labels. We create pixelwise segmentation masks, as shown, which are also converted bounding boxes and instance segmentation masks for additional supervisory tasks.

While G-DAUG scales the raw quantity of supervision possible, these weak labels introduce domain-specific risks, such as OSM sparsity in rural regions, temporal lag relative to imagery acquisition, and geometry inconsistencies. We mitigate these through ontology curation and resolution-aware rasterization, label noise is a real factor at scale and is reflected in our emphasis on conservative LR schedules and checkpointing.

4 Experimental Setup

We run several controlled experiments aligned to our guiding questions: (a) critical batch size sweeps for early- to mid-stage training; (b) LR sweeps under a WSD schedule with stabilized checkpointing; (c) data scaling tests using nested, stratified subsets from 5k to 1M images; and (d) parameter scaling tests, from 86 million parameters to 1.8 billion parameters. We hold architecture and training dynamics constant within each experiment to isolate the lever under study, and we report both positive trends and negative outcomes that informed our findings.

4.1 Model Architectures

We leverage two different model configurations for our experiments: Multi-Task Pretraining (MTP), which is fully supervised and uses multi-task optimization across multiple label types; and Scale-Aware Masked Autoencoder (ScaleMAE), which is based on self-supervision and scale invariance.

Multi-Task Pretraining (MTP) is a training paradigm that consists of a single backbone (or shared encoder) and a set of task-specific decoders [12]. During pretraining, the model is optimized jointly on three remote sensing tasks: instance segmentation, semantic segmentation, and rotated object detection, all of which are supervised with mask and bounding box labels, as appropriate for each task. The shared encoder produces a multi-scale feature pyramid that serves as input to each of the task-specific decoders. This framework is targeted towards large foundation models, supporting both CNN and ViT architectures. Additionally, when a ViT is used, the traditional multi-head full attention is replaced by Rotated Varied-Size Window Attention (RVSA) which helps to account for the various orientations of RS objects by rotating and rescaling local windows, allowing the transformer to attend to objects at arbitrary orientations and scales. After pretraining is completed, the model can be finetuned on a downstream RS task.

Scale-Aware Masked Autoencoder (ScaleMAE) is a self-supervised pretraining framework designed for multiscale geospatial imagery [7]. It extends the standard Masked Autoencoder (MAE) by encoding real-world scale information, such as ground sample distance (GSD), directly into the positional embeddings to enable consistent representations across sensors and resolutions. The architecture uses a ViT encoder and lightweight decoder trained to reconstruct masked image patches, enforcing scale-invariant feature learning through reconstruction losses measured relative to physical, rather than pixel, scale. This approach allows the model to learn semantically aligned features across heterogenous imagery without requiring resampling or manual normalization. Once pretrained, the encoder can be finetuned for downstream RS tasks.

4.2 Balancing Training Time and Compute Efficiency

To evaluate the relationship between batch size, training time, and compute efficiency, we conducted a series of critical batch size experiments using ScaleMAE ViT-Base architecture [7]. This smaller model configuration was chosen to enable multiple experimental repetitions across varying batch sizes and random seeds while maintaining computational feasibility. Each run used the same dataset, hyperparameters, and optimizer (AdamW), ensuring consistent optimization setting across runs. During these runs training was performed on a single NVIDIA DGX node containing eight H100 GPUs connected by NVLink, progressing through early to mid-stage training before hitting a target validation loss of 0.07 mean squared error (MSE) to capture the regime where batch scaling effects are most prominent. Batch sizes selected were 128, 256, 384, 512 and results were averaged over multiple seeds to mitigate variance (see Fig. 5).

These settings isolate our ability to manipulate training throughput without confounding optimizer dynamics, enabling a direct read on whether batch scaling accelerates convergence. We report the outcomes and implications for compute budgeting in Sect. 5.1.

4.3 Optimal Learning Rate (LR) Scheduling

To determine ranges of functional learning rates for large-scale geospatial pretraining, we conducted a controlled sweep across multiple rates for MTP-trained models. Models were trained with the same dataset, batch size and Warmup, Stable, Decay (WSD) scheduling strategy with stabilized checkpointing to isolate the effect of the base learning rate [13]. Following best practices for responsible compute allocation, we adopt a fail fast protocol to triage candidate base learning rates before committing full WSD runs. Concretely, we evaluate a broader set of LR candidates through 1.6k warmup iterations with Akupara-5k, under identical data, batch, and optimizer settings on four DGX nodes (32 H100s). The rates used during this preliminary test are shown in Fig. 3. Rates that exhibit loss spikes, oscillation, or rising gradient norms in this short horizon are discarded; those that maintain smooth loss decrease and bounded gradient statistics graduate to full WSD training with Akupara-10k. The WSD schedule maintained an initial warmup period 10%, followed by a stable plateau phase 80%, and finally exponential decay initiated when roughly 10% of the data remained, as shown in Fig. 4. This protocol surfaces instability early, avoids wasting HPC time on doomed configurations, and concentrates full-scale trials on stable candidates. The results of both our fail fast phase and our refined WSD runs appear in Sect. 5.2.

4.4 Establishing Power Laws for Data Constrained Training

To investigate how dataset scale influences model performance in geospatial foundation models, we constructed a series of progressively larger datasets sampled from the Akupara-1M dataset ranging from 5k to 100k full sized satellite images. As discussed in Sect. 3, each dataset was sampled to maintain an even distribution across key attributes (location, sensor type, time of day, month, year, land cover class, sensor version, and year), ensuring consistent representation across scales. To minimize content variance between sets each successive dataset supersets the smaller ones (i.e., the 10k dataset contains all samples within the 5k dataset).

For all experiments we trained ScaleMAE ViT-Giant (ViT-G, 1.8B parameters) under identical hyperparameters, batch size, and optimization settings. This large backbone size was selected to ensure that learning was not limited by model capacity, only by dataset size. Training was conducted on a single H100 node (8 GPUs) for approximately 300k iterations per run. This controlled setup isolates the effect of dataset size while holding model capacity, compute and training dynamics constant. The resulting validation loss curves over training time are shown in Fig. 8. This design aims to test whether RS follows a stable

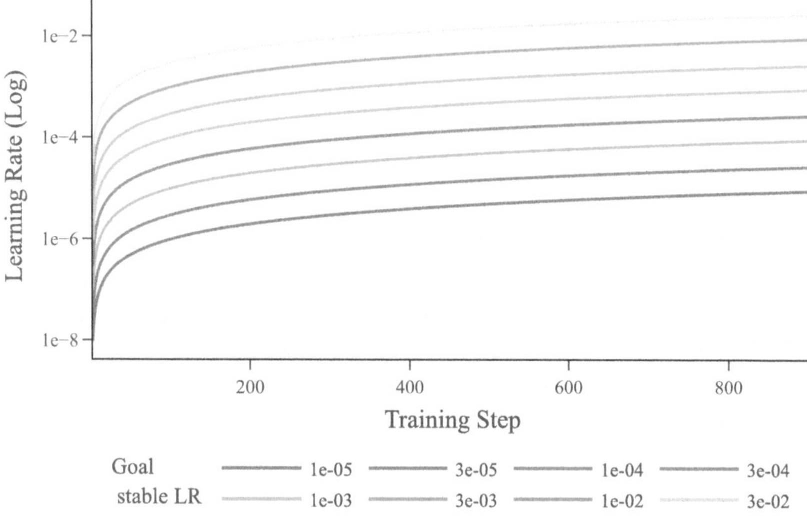

Fig. 3. We test eight candidate base learning rates in a fail fast warmup on Akupara-5k, under identical data, batch size, and optimizer settings on four DGX nodes. Each trajectory ramps toward its labeled goal stable learning rate; candidates that exhibit loss spikes, oscillation, or rising gradient norms in this horizon are rejected, while those showing smooth loss decrease and bounded gradient statistics advance to full WSD training.

data-scaling law within practical ranges and to quantify the exponent relevant for planning. Specifically, let N denote the number of full-scene images and $L(N)$ denote the converged validation loss under a fixed architecture and schedule. We test the canonical power-law model $L(N) = A + BN^{-a}$, where A is an asymptotic loss floor, B is a scale factor, and a is the data-scaling exponent. To obtain a, we perform log-log regression on $log(L)$ as a linear function of $log(N)$; we interpret slopes, variance, and residuals from this fit in Sect. 5.3 and revisit their implications in Sect. 6.

4.5 Establishing Power Laws for Parameter Constrained Training

To quantify how encoder capacity alone affects pretraining performance under fixed data and optimization dynamics, we constructed a parameter-constrained experiment that varies ViT backbone size, spanning increasing parameter counts across orders of magnitude (i.e., ViT-Base 86M [10], ViT-Large 303M [7], ViT-Huge 630M [14], ViT-Giant 1.8B [14]). To make the comparison with the data-constrained study explicit, we treat parameter scaling as a one-factor ablation: fix dataset composition, training schedule, and optimizer, and vary only backbone capacity. Let P denote encoder parameters and let $L(P)$ denote the con-

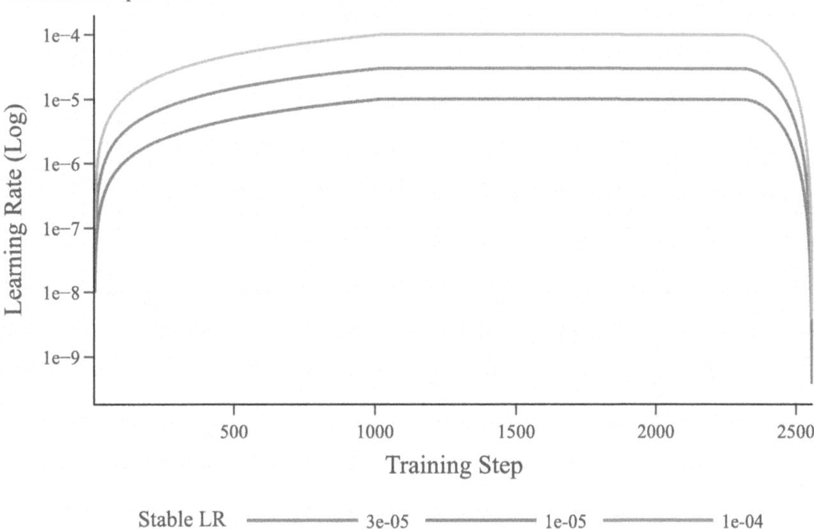

Fig. 4. We train three selected stable learning rates with the Warmup, Stable, Decay (WSD) schedule on Akupara-10k, comprising a 10% warmup, an 80% stable plateau at the target rate, and an exponential decay initiated when approximately 10% of the data remains. The curves trace the full WSD cycle for each rate, illustrating the transition from warmup to plateau (listed stable LR) and subsequent decay.

verged validation loss under a fixed training budget. Consistent with prior neural scaling formulations, we test whether $L(P)$ follows a power-law of the form $L(P) = A + BP^{-b}$, where A approximates an asymptotic floor under the chosen data and supervision regime, B is a scale factor, and b indicates benefit from increased capacity. Once again, we perform linear regression on $log(L)$ vs. $log(P)$ to obtain a value for b. Refer to Fig. 10, Sect. 5.4, and Sect. 6 for loss curves, scaling analysis, and discussion of this experiment, respectively.

5 Results

Each subsection answers a guiding question: 5.1 (a: throughput vs. convergence), 5.2 (b: stable LR regimes), 5.3 (c: data scaling law) and 5.4 (d: parameter scaling law). We emphasize the practical takeaways and the conditions under which the observations hold.

5.1 Balancing Training Time and Compute Efficiency

Across multiple random seeds and batch sizes ranging from 128 to 512, the results shown in Fig. 5 indicate little to no improvement in training efficiency or improved convergence when increasing batch size during early- to mid-stage training. Variance over 3 trials across seeds remained low, and most models reached the target loss in a similar number of steps, indicating batch size had minimal influence on convergence dynamics in these cases. Models trained with larger batches exhibited similar or occasionally slower, convergence compared to those with moderate batch sizes, suggesting that the critical batch size beyond which further increases yield diminishing returns in sample efficiency falls within or below this tested range. These findings are consistent with observations from language and vision foundation models, where critical batch size tends to depend more strongly on dataset scale than on model size [1,6]. While larger batches may still offer benefits in late-stage training, when optimization stabilizes and gradient noise decreases, the current results suggest that early-stage training in geospatial foundation models remains batch-insensitive beyond moderate thresholds. This behavior reinforces that compute efficiency in large-scale pretraining should be sought primarily through data scaling and adaptive learning-rate scheduling, rather than indiscriminate batch size increases, which may improve throughput but introduce inefficiencies due to reduced gradient noise.

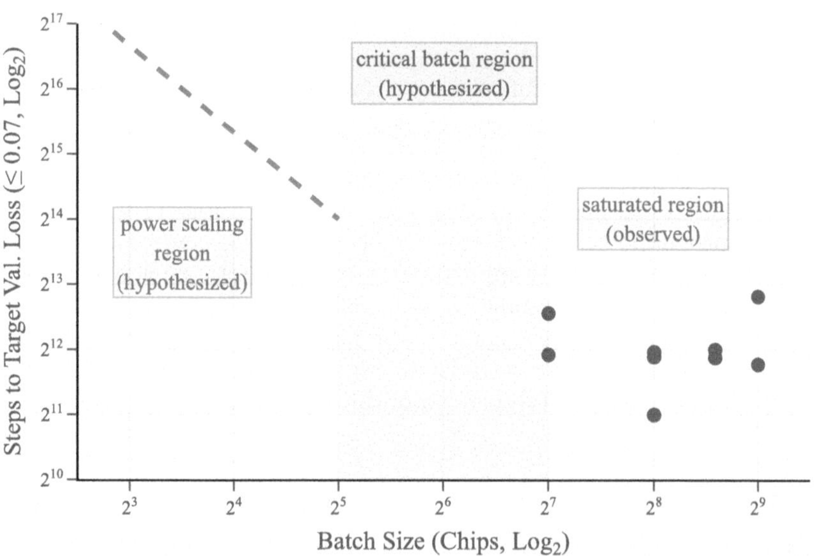

Fig. 5. Batch size scaling results show an increase in batch size does not result in increased compute efficiency during early-stage training, based on average loss over three trials. Based on the similar number of steps needed to reach convergence for the learning rates tested, we hypothesize that smaller batch sizes would maneuver this training configuration out of the saturated range and decrease forward pass compute efficiency.

Takeaway: In RS pretraining, early- to mid-stage convergence is largely insensitive to batch increases beyond moderate sizes; seek efficiency via data diversity and LR scheduling rather than aggressive batching.

5.2 Optimal Learning Rate (LR)

Our fail fast preliminary warmup test demonstrated that higher learning rates (e.g., 1×10^{-3} and 3×10^{-3}) exhibited significant instability, often diverging or oscillating during the stable phase of training, as shown in Fig. 6. Intermediate rates achieved stable convergence, confirming classic intuition that aggressive step sizes reduce optimization stability, and identifying a safe range allowing us to minimize the risk of catastrophic divergence without unnecessarily slowing training.

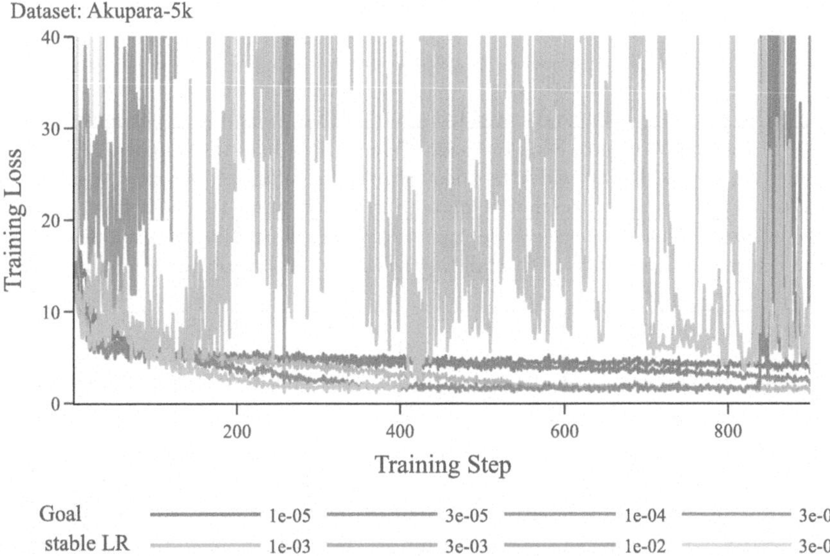

Fig. 6. We triage eight learning rate candidates via a fail fast warmup experiment monitoring training loss on Akupara-5k with an MTP architecture. Higher rates 1×10^{-3} and 3×10^{-3} exhibit significant instability, with divergent or oscillatory loss, the intermediate 3×10^{-4} achieves acceptable but slower convergence, and moderate candidates—most notably 1×10^{-4}—show smooth, monotonic loss reduction.

Based on the results of our fail fast test, we graduated three learning rates to a full WSD cycle experiment; these results identify 1×10^{-4} as a functional learning rate for MTP with a ViT-L backbone while under WSD scheduling, as shown in Fig. 7. The finding aligns with prior scaling studies in language and

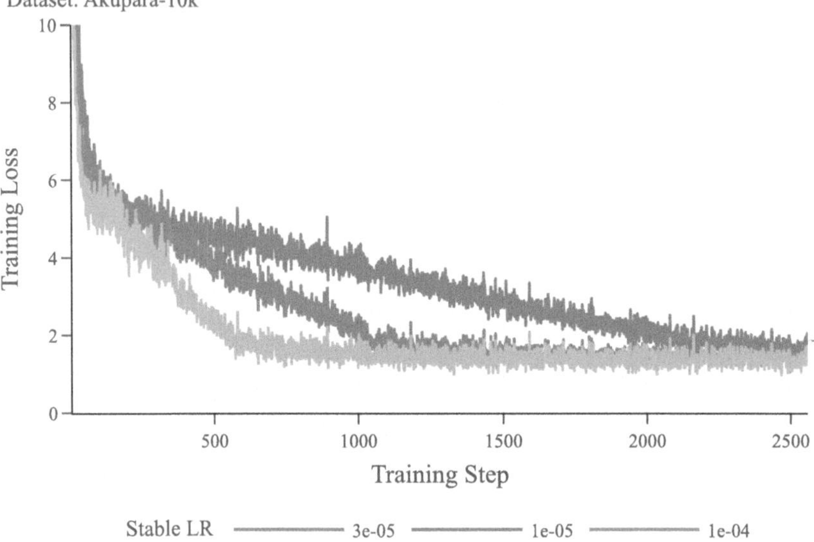

Fig. 7. Three learning rate candidates from our fail fast warmup experiment progress to a test of the full Warmup, Stable, Decay (WSD) schedule on Akupara-10k. Among the tested rates, 1×10^{-4} yields the most stable and efficient progress, maintaining monotonic loss decrease through the plateau and achieving the best final loss after decay, confirming that moderate base rates under WSD provide robust optimization, validate the predictive utility of the fail fast selection, and establish a reliable baseline for large-scale RS pretraining.

vision where stable, moderate learning rates yield the best efficiency-performance balance across dataset sizes [1].

In practice, this provides a reliable baseline for future large-scale RS pretraining. Operationally, the fail fast triage eliminated unstable high-LR settings within 2,000 steps, saving multi-node hours that would otherwise be consumed by oscillatory runs. The LR that ultimately performed best at full scale first demonstrated stable, monotonic loss reduction in the fail fast phase, validating the protocol's predictive utility.

Takeaway: A moderate base LR under WSD yields robust progress; fail fast warmup sweeps quickly rule out unstable rates and save scarce HPC time, making conservative schedules plus early triage the safer default at RS scale.

5.3 Establishing Power Laws for Data Constrained Training

As shown in Fig. 8, models exhibited two types of convergence behavior: one subset exhibited anomalously high and plateaued loss values inconsistent with the smooth declining loss trend of remaining experiments. Because such optimization failures obscure the underlying scaling behavior, we exclude these points from our fitted curve in Fig. 9 and plan to rerun these configurations with alternative random seeds to determine whether their performance aligns with the established scaling law.

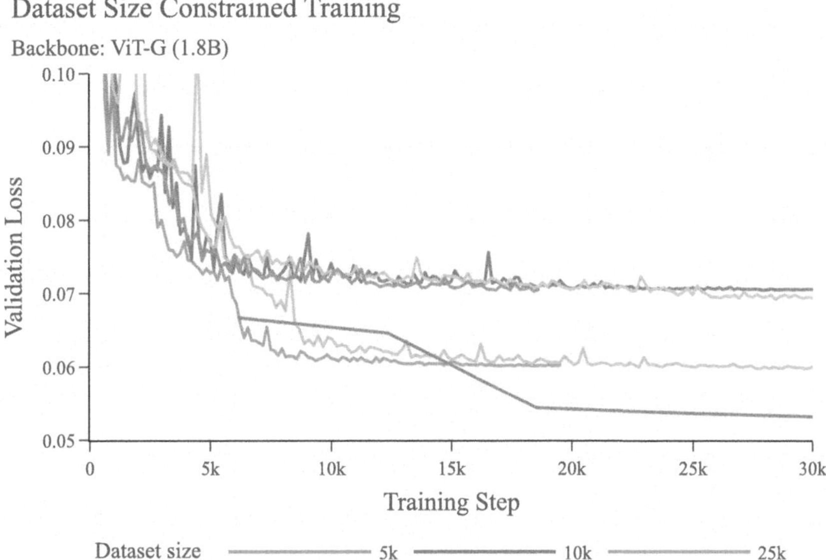

Fig. 8. We measure validation loss across the first 30k training steps for six dataset sizes of full satellite images, each trained with an intentionally oversized ViT-G backbone to ensure data-constrained rather than parameter-constrained behavior. Approximately half of the runs become trapped in a local minimum after the first 5k steps, whereas the remaining runs continue to improve beyond this point.

When plotting the final converged loss against dataset size on a log-log scale in Fig. 9, the results followed a near-linear trend consistent with a power-law relationship between loss and data scale, $L(N) = A + BN^{-a}$. The fitted log(loss) scaling exponent was $a = 0.03$, with $\mathrm{R}^2 = 0.941$ after excluding trapped trials, indicating diminishing yet consistent returns with increasing N. For planning, this analysis provides a closed-form estimator of required scale: given a target loss L^* above baseline A, the implied dataset size is $N \approx \left(\frac{L^*-A}{B}\right)^{-1/a}$. Although the current fit is based on three scales ranging from 5k - 1M samples, it already demonstrates the hallmark of empirical scaling behavior: consistent slope, low variance, and strong log-log linearity. Including additional intermediate points will further test whether this power-law trend persists across multiple orders of magnitude. If the slope remains stable as new points are added, even with a modest reduction in R^2, this will strengthen the evidence for a true scaling law rather than a local fit.

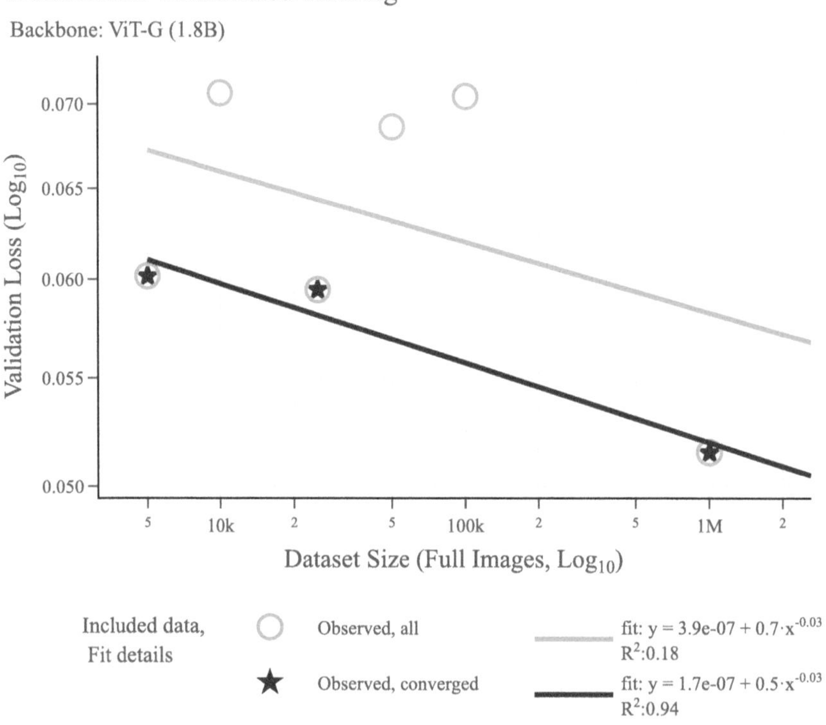

Fig. 9. We observe a log–log relationship between eventual validation loss and dataset size under a data-constrained regime. A power-law fit across all six dataset sizes shows poor correspondence ($R^2 = 0.18$), driven by trials that remain stuck in the early local minimum; restricting the analysis to the three trials that surpassed the minimum yields a strong power-law fit ($R^2 = 0.94$), enabling performance extrapolation from small-scale experiments to larger datasets.

Takeaway: Within 5k–1M images, RS pretraining follows a stable, diminishing-returns power law, providing a quantitative basis for planning data expansions and estimating expected gains.

5.4 Establishing Power Laws for Parameter Constrained Training

Under our fixed-budget setup, the estimated slope is statistically indistinguishable from zero, i.e., $b \approx 0$ (see Fig. 11), indicating that capacity increases do not reduce loss when data, schedule, and optimization are held constant. This outcome is consistent with a data-limited regime and also reflects common confounders that arises when parameters are scaled without adjusting training budget or context. Specifically, with identical steps and batch size, larger models receive fewer training tokens (T) per parameter; when scaling, optimal allocation maintains T/P above a domain-dependent threshold and holding T fixed while increasing P typically suppresses parameter-scaling gains. Additionally, ViT patch sizes may need adjustment as backbone capacity scales to expose sufficient context and data structure at training time. Similarly, LR schedules derived empirically from training runs of smaller models or based solely on dataset size may result in under-training of larger backbones.

To separate these effects from true parameter-scaling limits, future studies would benefit from compute-aware parameter-scaling protocols to avoid inadvertently penalizing larger models. For example, keeping tokens-per-parameter approximately constant across backbones guards against under-training larger models. With such controls in place, a parameter-scaling exponent $b > 0$ would indicate genuine gains from capacity, whereas $b \approx 0$ would confirm that, even under compute-matched conditions, RS pretraining remains data-limited for the given supervision and context.

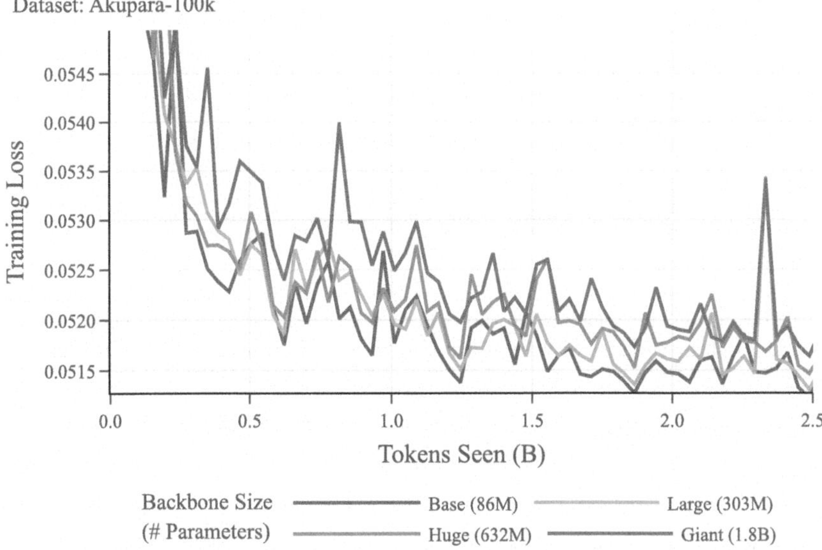

Fig. 10. Training curves for identical data, optimizer, and schedule plotted as validation loss versus tokens seen. Despite a range from 86M-1.8B parameters, curves are nearly indistinguishable. This indicates capacity parity under a fixed regime and increasing parameters does not yield lower loss when the dataset and training budget are held constant.

Takeaway: In our fixed-budget study, the near-flat trend supports prioritizing in-domain data expansion and schedule robustness over parameter scaling. To this end, future studies should expand this investigation by repeating it with larger training datasets to reassess the computed scaling exponent.

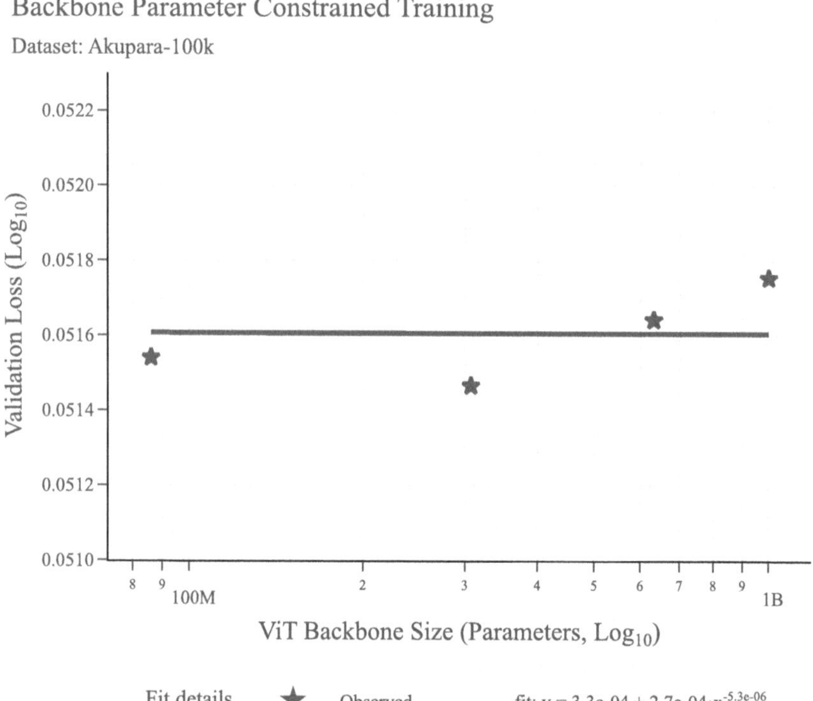

Fig. 11. Scaling law fit of converged validation loss against parameter count yields a slope of $b \approx 0$, i.e., no measurable dependence on model size in this regime. The flat trend is consistent with a data-limited regime rather than a model size limited one.

6 Discussion

Our findings demonstrate that large-scale RS foundation models follow predictable scaling dynamics, like those of related domains, and also exhibit domain-specific behaviors. The power-law established with an R^2 fit of 0.941 between the dataset size and performance confirms that additional data consistently improves model quality, though the exponent $a = 0.03$ indicates diminishing returns as datasets grow, consistent with trends observed in natural imagery and language domains [6,14]. Efficiency analyses reveal that compute gains from batch-size scaling plateau quickly and that training stability depends more on balanced learning rate schedules than raw throughput. These findings imply that further performance gains will come less from scaling compute and more from improving data diversity, label quality, and optimization strategy. Overall, RS models appear to operate in a data-limited, yet feature-bounded regime. Scaling continues to improve training progress, but only as it expands the domain of observed geospatial variation. Future scaling should therefore emphasize use of more feature-rich sensing modalities (e.g., SAR, multispectral, temporal), and geographically or contextually novel data, rather than simple quantity increases. The shallow parameter-scaling slope relative to data-scaling supports the view that RS pretraining is data-limited: capacity helps, but only insofar as it can absorb diverse, in-domain variation. In practice, prioritize expanding and domain coverage, then right-size to avoid undercapacity in rich regimes and overcapacity in narrow regimes.

6.1 Lessons Learned and Pitfalls

- Batch-size illusions: Larger batches did not accelerate early/mid-stage convergence; late-stage benefits are limited and context-bounded.
- LR-induced instability: High base LRs under WSD produced oscillations and divergence; conservative LRs reduced instability.
- Bounded spatial context: Increasing model size without expanding image context or modality yields marginal returns; invest in diversity and richer sensing (SAR, MSI, temporal).

6.2 Scope Limitations

Our results reflect high-resolution Maxar imagery under ViT backbones and specific schedules; different sensors (e.g., SAR), data distributions, or architectural choices (e.g., CNN hybrids) may alter constants even if the qualitative trends persist.

7 Conclusion

This work establishes empirical scaling behavior for RS foundation models trained at peta-scale data volumes. We show that model loss decreases predictably with dataset size, while gains from larger batches or aggressive learning rates remain limited. These results suggest that sustainable progress in RS foundation modeling will hinge on use of more diverse data, not merely more compute. By quantifying how performance scales with data, this study provides a practical basis for planning future pretraining efforts and estimating the returns on additional data collection. Extending this framework to multi-modal, multi-temporal, and cross-sensor contexts offers a clear next step toward globally consistent geospatial representation learning. Future studies should compare training performance, as measured by optimization task loss, to downstream RS task performance to characterize the generalizability of our demonstrated scaling laws.

Practical checklist for RS scaling:

- Start with stability: choose conservative LRs under WSD; enable stabilized checkpointing.
- Right-size batches: avoid aggressive early-stage batch scaling; monitor convergence per token, not just throughput.
- Expand diversity, not just volume: stratify by geography, sensor, season, and context to broaden feature coverage.
- Anticipate label noise: curate ontologies, align GSD, and validate regional coverage; expect residual noise and plan schedules accordingly.
- Measure scaling pragmatically: fit simple power laws over controlled ranges and use them to plan data collection and compute budgets.
- Fail fast on hyperparameter sweeps: triage a broad LR set through warmup iterations; promote only stable candidates to full WSD runs to avoid burning multi-node allocations.

Acknowledgments. This work was supported by the MITRE Independent Research and Development Program.

Disclosure of Interests. The authors have no competing interests to declare that are relevant to the content of this article.

References

1. Alabdulmohsin, I.M., Neyshabur, B., Zhai, X.: Revisiting neural scaling laws in language and vision. In: Koyejo, S., Mohamed, S., Agarwal, A., Belgrave, D., Cho, K., Oh, A. (eds.) Advances in Neural Information Processing Systems. vol. 35, pp. 22300–22312. Curran Associates, Inc. (2022). https://proceedings.neurips.cc/paper_files/paper/2022/file/8c22e5e918198702765ecff4b20d0a90-Paper-Conference.pdf
2. Bastani, F., Wolters, P., Gupta, R., Ferdinando, J., Kembhavi, A.: SatlasPretrain: A large-scale dataset for remote sensing image understanding (2023). https://arxiv.org/abs/2211.15660
3. Cha, K., Seo, J., Lee, T.: A billion-scale foundation model for remote sensing images. IEEE J. Sel. Topics Appl. Earth Observ. Remote Sens. 1–17 (2024). https://doi.org/10.1109/JSTARS.2024.3401772

4. Dosovitskiy, A., et al.: An image is worth 16×16 words: transformers for image recognition at scale. In: International Conference on Learning Representations (2021). https://openreview.net/forum?id=YicbFdNTTy
5. Guo, X., et al.: SkySense: a multi-modal remote sensing foundation model towards universal interpretation for earth observation imagery. In: Proceedings of the IEEE/CVF Conference on Computer Vision and Pattern Recognition (CVPR), pp. 27672–27683 (2024). https://arxiv.org/abs/2312.10115
6. Kaplan, J., et al.: Scaling laws for neural language models (2020). https://arxiv.org/abs/2001.08361
7. Reed, C., et al.: Scale-MAE: A scale-aware masked autoencoder for multiscale geospatial representation learning, pp. 4065–4076 (2023). https://doi.org/10.1109/ICCV51070.2023.00378
8. Siméoni, O., et al.: DINOv3 (2025). https://arxiv.org/abs/2508.10104
9. Szwarcman, D., et al.: Prithvi-EO-2.0: A versatile multi-temporal foundation model for earth observation applications (2025). https://arxiv.org/abs/2412.02732
10. Tang, M., Cozma, A., Georgiou, K., Qi, H.: Cross-scale MAE: a tale of multiscale exploitation in remote sensing. In: Oh, A., Naumann, T., Globerson, A., Saenko, K., Hardt, M., Levine, S. (eds.) Advances in Neural Information Processing Systems. vol. 36, pp. 20054–20066. Curran Associates, Inc. (2023). https://proceedings.neurips.cc/paper_files/paper/2023/file/3fadcbd0437f4717723ff3f6f7216800-Paper-Conference.pdf
11. Vaswani, A., et al.: Attention is all you need. In: Guyon, I., Luxburg, U.V., Bengio, S., Wallach, H., Fergus, R., Vishwanathan, S., Garnett, R. (eds.) Advances in Neural Information Processing Systems. vol. 30. Curran Associates, Inc. (2017). https://arxiv.org/abs/1706.03762
12. Wang, D., et al.: MTP: advancing remote sensing foundation model via multitask pretraining. IEEE J. Sel. Topics Appl. Earth Observ. Remote Sens. **17**, 11632–11654 (2024). https://doi.org/10.1109/JSTARS.2024.3408154
13. Wen, K., Li, Z., Wang, J., Hall, D., Liang, P., Ma, T.: Understanding Warmup-Stable-Decay learning rates: A river valley loss landscape perspective (2024). https://arxiv.org/abs/2410.05192
14. Zhai, X., Kolesnikov, A., Houlsby, N., Beyer, L.: Scaling vision transformers. In: Proceedings of the IEEE/CVF Conference on Computer Vision and Pattern Recognition (CVPR), pp. 12104–12113 (2022). https://arxiv.org/abs/2106.04560

Cross-Modal Foundation Models for Remote Sensing

Adam Francisco(✉), Matthew D. Reisman, Tobe Corazzini, Ryan McCormick, and Kevin J. LaTourette

Bedrock Research, Highlands Ranch, CO, USA
adam@bedrockresearch.ai

Abstract. Recent growth in remote sensing collection capacity and spectral diversity has produced vast volumes of data, yet traditional AI/ML algorithms struggle to generalize across modalities, targets, or geographies. These approaches are typically fine-tuned for specific applications over months and operate on a single modality, limiting adaptability to real-time mission requirements where certain sensor data may be unavailable. Traditional multimodal data fusion methods improve performance by combining outputs from independent models, but they still require co-collected imagery for training and inference, which is often impractical for time-critical applications. We propose Cross-Modal Foundation Models to address these limitations. These models are pretrained on all available data using contrastive learning, without requiring manual annotations, to generate consistent feature embeddings across modalities. By learning modality-invariant "fingerprints", the model can operate even when only partial data is available, enabling inference with a wide range of sensors regardless of perspective, resolution, or modality. This adaptability allows the model to leverage the strengths of different sensors: SAR data in cloudy conditions, EO imagery when color information is critical, or a combination of available modalities for optimal performance. It also relieves constraints on sensor tasking, enabling sensors to be dynamically allocated across missions without compromising intelligence value. In this study, we present a cross-modal foundation model aligning feature spaces between SAR and EO imagery, providing a versatile framework for downstream tasks such as change detection, activity recognition, and automatic target recognition. Beyond immediate applications, this framework lays the groundwork for future automated sensor orchestration, allowing systems to identify missing information and optimize data collection for maximum situational awareness and operational efficiency.

Keywords: Foundation Models · Deep Learning · Remote Sensing · Cross-Modal

1 Introduction

1.1 Current Methods

The rapid expansion of satellites performing remote sensing has resulted in unprecedented volumes of data, providing significant opportunities for the AI and machine learning community to leverage. Traditional machine learning and deep learning approaches

F. Tanner and J. Irvine (Eds.): AIPR 2025, LNCS 16446, pp. 154–166, 2026.
https://doi.org/10.1007/978-3-032-18474-0_11

have demonstrated strong performance on tasks such as object classification, object detection, and change detection using remote sensing data. However, these methods rely heavily on large labeled datasets. As the scale of modern remote sensing collections grows, manual labeling becomes increasingly impractical, requiring domain expertise, extensive time investment, and substantial resources.

Moreover, conventional models are typically trained on a single sensing modality, such as RGB images, limiting their ability to exploit the complementary information available across different modality sensors. In real-world scenarios, an area of interest may be observed by multiple modalities at different times or under varying environmental conditions. Models restricted to single-modality inputs cannot fully leverage this diversity, resulting in suboptimal performance when data availability varies or when non-visible measurements capture critical features that RGB imagery cannot.

1.2 Related Work

Large scale, pretrained neural networks, such as CLIP [1], GPT [2] and Segment Anything [3] are foundation modals that have revolutionized natural language processing and computer vision. These models are trained on large datasets and learn rich semantic representations that enable effective transfer learning to adapt them for specialized downstream applications. Their successes have established a new paradigm in which general-purpose pretraining replaces highly specialized, domain specific architectures.

Despite these advances, existing vision-based foundation models are primarily trained on RGB images from ground level cameras, limiting their applicability to remote sensing. Remote sensing data often involve non-visible modalities such as synthetic aperture radar (SAR), multispectral, and hyperspectral imagery, which possess fundamentally different properties from standard RGB images. Because current models lack exposure to these modalities and their domain specific context, their representations do not transfer well without substantial adaptation. Training foundation models with these additional modalities will enable their effective use in a wider range of downstream applications.

2 Approach

2.1 Cross-Modal Dataset

Cross-modal foundation models extend the principles of large-scale pretrained models to the remote sensing domain by jointly learning from multiple sensor modalities. In this work, our goal is to develop a foundation model capable of ingesting data from multiple different types of remote sensing data and produce sensor-agnostic outputs that are rapidly extensible to diverse downstream applications. The model is designed to learn shared representations that capture the relationships between modalities with fundamentally different imaging mechanisms. To accomplish this, we extend a transformer-based masked autoencoder (ViT-MAE) as our base architecture and perform additional more specialized pretraining on modality-specific remote sensing data distributions [4]. Our study focuses on two complementary modalities: electro-optical (EO) imagery and synthetic aperture radar (SAR).

To support cross-modal pretraining, we curated and spatially registered a dataset of paired EO and SAR imagery using proven cross-modal orthorectification techniques [5]. For SAR, we gathered data from Capella Space [6], which provides high resolution SAR images. For EO, we used the Functional Map of the World (FMoW) dataset [7]. Our objective was to identify spatially overlapping observations from the two sources and construct corresponding EO and SAR image pairs (Fig. 1).

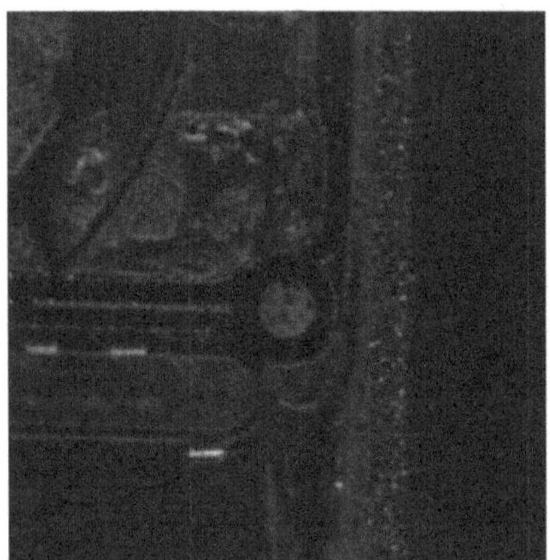

Fig. 1. SAR image from Capella Space (left), EO image from FMoW (right). The image pair is chipped and co-registered spatially.

We began by collecting large scenes from Capella that are known to contain diverse but relevant features of interest via comparison to and alignment with open source map data [8]. From there, using geolocation metadata in the SAR products, we queried FMoW images that intersect with each SAR footprint. Because multiple FMoW images can overlap with a single Capella scene, we selected the EO image whose collection timestamp was closest to that of the SAR observation, reducing temporal discrepancies that may affect cross-modal alignment.

We created a spatial registration pipeline to align each of these SAR and EO paired products despite their differing imaging geometries. This process involved using the geolocation metadata provided with each Capella SAR product to project the raw complex data from the SICD to the ground plane in accordance with the SICD standard. After projection into a shared coordinate system, we refined alignment by matching the spatial footprints of the two modalities, correcting for differences in rotation and projection. The aligned scenes were then cropped to their common overlapping extent, guaranteeing that corresponding EO and SAR pixels represent the same physical locations on the ground.

Following alignment, we automatically chipped each registered pair into 512x512 patches, generating a large dataset of paired EO and SAR samples suitable for training our cross-modal foundation model. From this process we co-registered 12,140 image pairs and split this into a 80/20 train and validation split for training and validation. This process promotes semantic feature correspondences between RGB images and single channel SAR magnitude images, providing a foundation for multimodal downstream tasks including classification, object detection, and change detection.

2.2 Cross-Modal Foundational Model

We adopt a three-stage training pipeline to build these cross-modal foundation models; encoder pretraining, modality-specific training, and task-specific fine-tuning. This staged approach allows the model to progressively acquire general visual representations, specialize in individual sensor modalities, and finally adapt to downstream remote sensing tasks.

The first stage leverages existing open-source foundation models. In this work, we use the pretrained weights of the ViT-MAE model [9] as our starting point. These weights, originally trained on RGB images, provide a strong initialization for capturing general visual structures [10]. Optionally, this encoder can be further pretrained on generic remote sensing datasets to infuse the model with domain-specific information, improving its initial understanding of satellite imagery.

In the second stage, we fine-tune the pretrained encoder on modality-specific datasets to teach the model the unique features of each sensor type. For example, SAR data is fundamentally different from RGB imagery as it has unique intensity patterns and contains speckle noise characteristics. To accommodate this, we modify the ViT-MAE input configuration to accept single-channel SAR magnitude images, while retaining the pretrained weights from RGB-based ViT-MAE. This stage allows the encoder to learn modality-relevant features while leveraging previously learned visual features, resulting in a more robust representation for each sensor type.

In the final stage, the pretrained encoder is combined with a downstream decoder tailored to specific remote sensing tasks, such as object classification, detection, or change detection. By transferring the knowledge captured in the encoder, the downstream model can achieve strong performance with limited task-specific labeled data, significantly reducing the annotation burden.

For this effort, we extend the modality-specific encoders into a cross-modal contrastive learning framework. Contrastive learning is a deep learning approach in which the model learns to bring semantically related inputs closer in the embedding space while pushing unrelated inputs apart [11]. This is especially valuable for foundation model pretraining, where we desire a generalized model that learns rich features across diverse imagery and are not yet training it for a specific task. Contrastive learning enables full exploitation of arbitrarily large datasets without requiring any manual annotation. Here, co-registered EO and SAR image pairs create positive examples, while non-aligned pairs form negative examples. This approach encourages the model to capture underlying landscape features that are invariant across modalities.

We implement contrastive learning using two separate encoders: one for EO images and one for SAR images (Fig. 2). The EO encoder uses the standard ViT-MAE model that has been pretrained on various RGB images. The SAR encoder uses the modified ViT-MAE that accepts single channel images, and has already been further trained on an external generic SAR dataset. During training, the embeddings generated by each encoder are compared using the NT-Xent loss, with cosine similarity as the distance metric. Positive pairs are pulled closer together in the embedding space, while negative pairs are pushed apart. After training, the learned embeddings can be used as robust inputs for downstream applications without requiring extensive labeled datasets.

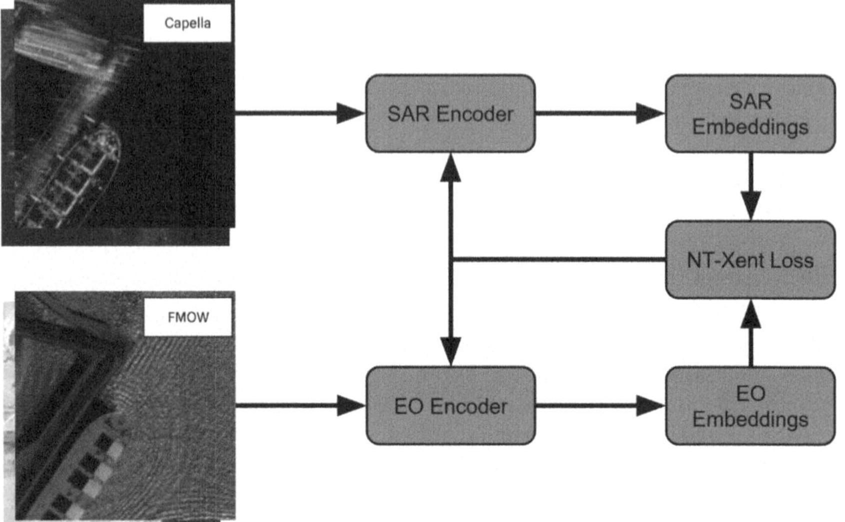

Fig. 2. Contrastive learning architecture. Batches of paired SAR and EO imagery are passed through their respective encoders. The loss between the embedding is calculated and the weights of the network are updated to push future positive pairs together and negative pairs further away.

3 Results

3.1 Cosine Similarity Matrix

After training the models, we evaluate its performance using a validation set. We pass in all of the images from the validation set into their respective encoders that were trained to generate embeddings in the shared feature space.

Using these embeddings, we construct a cosine similarity matrix, which quantifies the pairwise similarity between all images across the two modalities. Each entry in the matrix represents the cosine similarity score between a SAR embedding and an EO embedding, providing a direct measure of how closely the model associates features extracted from a pair of images collected by different modalities. High similarity scores indicate strong cross-modal correspondence, while low scores suggest dissimilarity.

This matrix facilitates an intuitive evaluation of the model's ability to learn meaningful cross-modal representations. For example, in Fig. 3, we pass five SAR images through the SAR encoder and compute their similarity to all EO images in the validation set. Ideally, the EO image that was co-registered with each SAR image should have the highest similarity score, reflecting the model's success at capturing modality-invariant features. By inspecting the similarity rankings, we can identify both successful matches and potential ambiguities, providing insights into the encoder's robustness and the quality of learned embeddings.

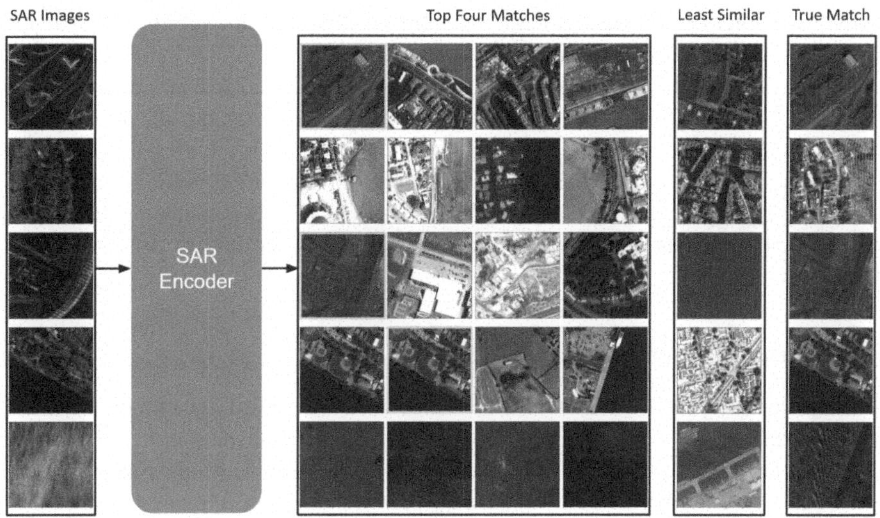

Fig. 3. Five SAR images are passed into the trained encoder (left). The top four ranked EO image embedding matches are displayed, with a green bounding box depicting a correctly matched embedding (middle). Second most to the right are the least similar cosine similarity matches. The four corresponding true EO matches for each SAR input image are displayed on the far right.

The cosine similarity matrix provides a powerful tool to visualize and assess how effectively our cross-modal encoders generate embeddings. In Fig. 3, we observe several illustrative cases: two SAR images correctly matched their co-registered EO pairs as the top-ranked embeddings (row one and row three). For the fourth row, the co-registered EO image was the second-highest match. This outcome is understandable, as another EO image from the same geographic area but captured at a different time is the strongest match, leading to possible confusion if the scene has not changed much throughout time and shares many semantic similarities with its surrounding context.

The second row did not identify its co-registered EO image within the top four similarity scores; however, it retrieved visually and geographically plausible EO images, indicating that the model is still capturing meaningful cross-modal correspondences. The final row failed to locate a matching EO image, which is expected in the cases of open water scenes as no unique features are present. Such regions lack distinctive features, making it unreasonable for the model to identify the correct match solely based on visual characteristics.

Beyond qualitative inspection, the cosine similarity matrix can also be used to derive quantitative metrics such as top-k retrieval accuracy, allowing for systematic evaluation of the model's cross-modal alignment capabilities. Our validation set consisted of 3,691 co-registered SAR–EO image pairs. Of these, 9% of SAR images retrieved their corresponding EO pair within the top ten similarity scores, and 28% of SAR images found their match within the top 50 embeddings. Both the training and validation sets contained overlapping geographic regions internally, but not between sets. This geographic overlap likely contributes to some matches not appearing as the top-ranked pair, as multiple images from the same area can have similar embeddings. Furthermore, many scenes in the dataset depict open water, which is inherently ambiguous and provides few unique visual cues, making top-rank matches unlikely.

These results highlight that while the cross-modal encoders are generally effective at capturing meaningful correspondences, retrieval performance is influenced by temporal differences, scene redundancy, and scene uniqueness. The cosine similarity matrix still serves as both a qualitative and quantitative tool for understanding cross-modal embedding quality. Future research could utilize recent studies on multi-modal data for ecological applications [12] that utilize a more rigorous intermediate layer fine tuning to remote sensing.

3.2 Embedding Visualization

The embeddings from the validation set can also be visualized on a scatter plot by doing dimensionality reduction to gain further insights [13]. The embeddings are a 768 length vector that is generated by the encoder. To make these high-dimensional representations interpretable, we apply Uniform Manifold Approximation and Projection (UMAP), a dimensionality reduction technique that projects the embeddings into two dimensions while preserving local and global structure [14]. Once reduced, the embeddings can be visualized on a scatter plot and colored by modality or class for further analysis.

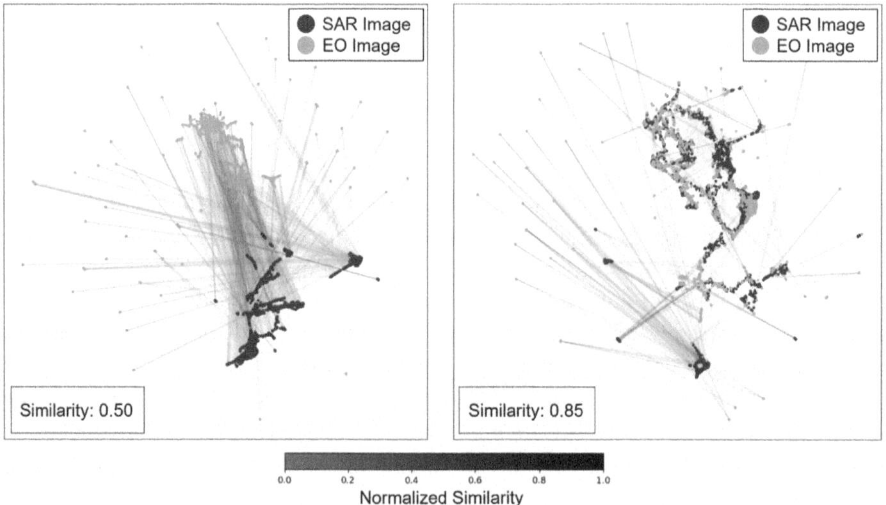

Fig. 4. The embeddings passed through the encoders before training via contrastive learning (left). The embeddings after training by contrastive learning (right). The lines connect two co-registered pairs of EO and SAR imagery. The line color shows cosine similarity between the two matching pairs. The average normalized similarity is shown in the bottom left corner of each plot.

Before contrastive training, embeddings from EO and SAR images primarily cluster according to their modality, reflecting the inherent differences in their sensor characteristics. As training progresses, co-registered EO and SAR embeddings gradually move closer together in the feature space, while embeddings from unrelated pairs are pushed farther apart. By the final training epoch, as shown in the right panel of Fig. 4, co-registered embeddings largely overlap, indicating that the model has successfully learned modality-invariant representations. Some outliers remain, which is expected given variations in scene content and sensor-specific noise. This visualization provides qualitative evidence that the contrastive learning objective effectively aligns embeddings for corresponding cross-modal images.

To further investigate performance of the contrastive learning process, we labeled the data in order to visualize if clusters of unique classes are present in our embedding plots. To label each pair of SAR and EO images, we passed the EO image through a CLIP model [15] and assigned its class based on its top similarity score to the following text options; Rural Land, Buildings, Port, and Open Water (see Fig. 5). Each SAR image inherits the class label of its paired EO image. While these labels are machine-generated and thus not perfectly accurate, they still enable us to investigate whether semantically meaningful clusters emerge in the embedding space and align with other prominent open source natural language foundation models.

Fig. 5. Examples of each class

As shown in Fig. 6, distinct clusters corresponding to the different classes appear in the UMAP visualization. Open water scenes contain the embeddings with the furthest separation, reflecting their difficulty in matching SAR and EO images in such environments that have no unique features. The remaining classes, including rural land, buildings, and ports, form overlapping but generally coherent clusters. Outliers exist, which can be attributed to imperfections in the contrastive learning process, variability in scene content, or errors in CLIP-generated labels.

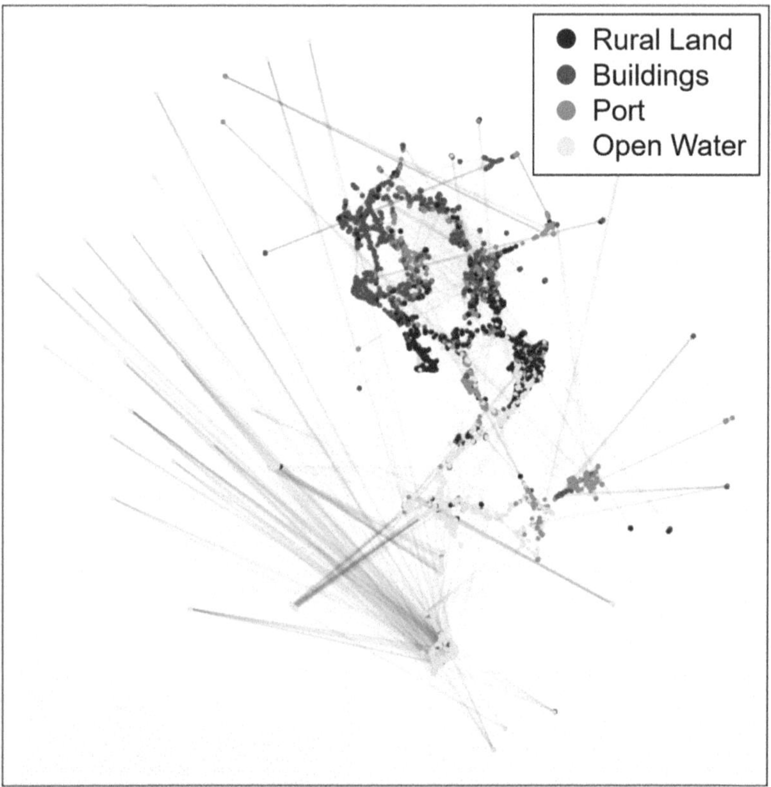

Fig. 6. The embeddings colored by their respective class.

These embedding visualizations provide strong qualitative evidence that the model has learned meaningful, modality invariant representations, despite the lack of any image or object labels present during training.

3.3 Downstream Classification

To further evaluate the effectiveness of the cross-modal representations learned through contrastive training, we construct a downstream classification model that operates directly on the embeddings produced by the EO and SAR encoders. This downstream evaluation helps determine whether the learned embedding space contains semantically meaningful structure that can generalize to supervised tasks.

We assign CLIP-generated labels to each EO and SAR pair based on text image similarity across the four selected class prompts (Rural Land, Buildings, Port, and Open Water) as our truths. For classification, we implement a simple feedforward classifier that ingests the encoder produced embeddings. We evaluate three types of input representations during inference, first being the mean embedding. This is the elementwise average of the EO and SAR embeddings, representing the fused cross-modal feature for the paired images. Second is the SAR embedding only, and lastly, the EO embedding only.

To further test the robustness of the learned representations, we retrained the contrastive learning pipeline with a set of data augmentations designed to simulate variation in sensor collection conditions (see Fig. 7). These augmentations include random horizontal and vertical flips, as well as random cropping of 96×96 pixels. Introducing such augmentations encourages the encoders to learn invariances to viewpoint, orientation, and local spatial differences, properties that are critical in real-world remote sensing applications where acquisition conditions may vary between modalities or over time.

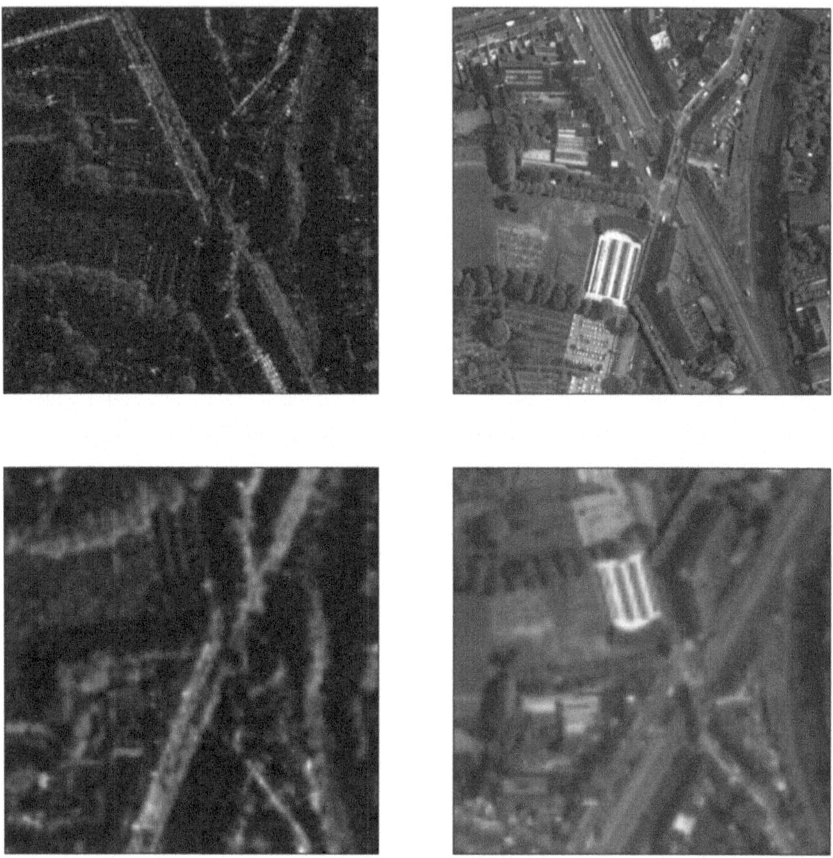

Fig. 7. No augmentations (top row) versus with augmentations (bottom row). The augmentations include a random horizontal or vertical flip, and a random crop of size of 96x96 pixels.

This evaluation framework allows us to analyze how well the encoders individually and jointly capture relevant semantic information. This also provides us with relative performance for when only certain modalities are present.

Table. 1. Accuracy metric of our classifier, taking the mean of our embeddings produces a higher accuracy. Adding augmentations shows how using both modalities further increases performance when combining embeddings.

	SAR Embedding	EO Embedding	Mean Embedding
No Augmentations	72.61%	77.03%	77.49%
With Augmentations	69.68%	74.07%	74.99%

Table 1 describes our performance metrics from this simple setup. As expected, there exists a performance increase from using the both combined embeddings of the SAR and EO images. EO-only shows a significant performance increase over just the

SAR images, which makes sense from the simplicity of these classes. Additionally, when using the augmented images, the performance boost is more noticeable when combining embeddings instead of using a single modality.

4 Conclusion

In this effort, we introduced a cross-modal foundation model designed to bridge the representational gap between electro-optical (EO) and synthetic aperture radar (SAR) imagery. By leveraging a three-stage training pipeline of encoder pretraining, modality-specific adaptation, and cross-modal contrastive learning, we demonstrated that foundational vision transformer architectures can be effectively extended to multiple remote sensing modalities. Through careful dataset construction, including spatially registered EO and SAR image pairs from Capella Space and FMoW, we demonstrate a model capable of producing modality-invariant representations grounded in real-world, geographically aligned data.

Our contrastive learning approach successfully aligned EO and SAR embeddings, as evidenced by cosine similarity retrieval results and UMAP visualizations. Co-registered images consistently achieved high similarity rankings, and the final embedding space exhibited substantial cross-modal overlap, confirming the model's ability to learn shared structural and semantic features across diverse sensing modalities. Additional analysis using CLIP-generated labels revealed emergent class-level structure within the embedding space, further highlighting the discriminative potential of the learned representations.

We also evaluated the utility of the embeddings for downstream tasks by training a lightweight classifier on EO, SAR, and fused embeddings. The classifier's performance, together with more realistic collections from augmentations, demonstrated that the embeddings capture meaningful, transferable information suitable for tasks such as classification, object detection, or change detection.

Overall, our results show that cross-modal contrastive learning provides a scalable and label efficient pathway for building foundation models capable of integrating remote sensing data with multiple modalities. As remote sensing collections continue to grow in volume, diversity, and sensing modality, such models offer a promising direction for enabling unified, multimodal geospatial understanding. Future work may incorporate additional modalities, temporal sequences, or larger-scale pretraining to further enhance cross-modal alignment and expand downstream applicability.

Acknowledgments. The authors would like to acknowledge collaborators at Capella Space for providing data that was used in this study, as well as Google Cloud for cloud compute grants that contributed to the resources used in this study.

Disclosure of Interests. The authors have no competing interests to declare that are relevant to the content of this article.

References

1. Radford, A., et al.: Learning Transferable Visual Models From Natural Language Supervision (No. arXiv:2103.00020). arXiv. https://doi.org/10.48550/arXiv.2103.00020 (2021)

2. OpenAI: GPT-4 Technical Report (No. arXiv:2303.08774). arXiv. https://doi.org/10.48550/arXiv.2303.08774 (2023)
3. Kirillov, A., et al.: Segment Anything (No. arXiv:2304.02643). arXiv. https://doi.org/10.48550/arXiv.2304.02643 (2023)
4. He, K., Chen, X., Xie, S., Li, Y., Dollár, P., Girshick, R.: Masked Autoencoders Are Scalable Vision Learners (No. arXiv:2111.06377). arXiv. https://doi.org/10.48550/arXiv.2111.06377(2021)
5. Pritt, M., LaTourette, K.: Image Alignment and Stitching: A Tutorial. (No. IEEE:6049990). IEEE (2011). https://ieeexplore.ieee.org/abstract/document/6049990
6. Capella Space (2025). https://www.capellaspace.com/
7. Christie, G., Fendley, N., Wilson, J., Mukherjee, R.: Functional Map of the World (fMoW) (No. arXiv:1711.07846). arXiv. https://doi.org/10.48550/arXiv.1711.07846 (2018)
8. Overture Maps (2025). https://overturemaps.org/
9. ViT-MAE model (2025). https://huggingface.co/facebook/vit-mae-base
10. Caron, M., et al.: Emerging Properties in Self-Supervised Vision Transformers (No. arXiv:2104.14294). arXiv. https://doi.org/10.48550/arXiv.2104.14294 (2021)
11. Chen, T., Kornblith, S., Norouzi, M., Hinton, G.: A Simple Framework for Contrastive Learning of Visual Representations (No. arXiv:2002.05709). arXiv. https://doi.org/10.48550/arXiv.2002.05709(2020)
12. Sastry, S., Khanal, S., Dhakal, A., Ahmad, A., Jacobs, N.: TaxaBind: A Unified Embedding Space for Ecological Applications (No. arXiv:2411.00683). arXiv. https://doi.org/10.48550/arXiv.2411.00683 (2024)
13. Garza, J.E., et al.: Knowledge without learning: a zero shot approach to SAR ATR. In: Proceedings of the Interservice/Industry Training, Simulation, and Education Conference (I/ITSEC 2025), Orlando, FL, USA. (Accepted for publication)
14. McInnes, L., Healy, J., Melville, J.: UMAP: Uniform Manifold Approximation and Projection for Dimension Reduction (No. arXiv:1802.03426). arXiv. https://doi.org/10.48550/arXiv.1802.03426 (2020)
15. CLIP model (2025). https://huggingface.co/openai/clip-vit-base-patch32

Unsupervised Change Detection and Categorization with Remote Sensing Foundation Models

Matthew D. Reisman(✉), Ryan McCormick, Tito Solis, Axel Durham, and Kevin J. LaTourette

Bedrock Research, Littleton, CO 80126, USA
matt@bedrockresearch.ai

Abstract. Foundation models have revolutionized artificial intelligence by performing generative tasks and enhancing task-specific capabilities that traditionally required substantial volumes of labeled data. One area that has been significantly hindered by supervised training methods is remote sensing-based change detection. While standard pixelwise change detection methods provide binary categorization, these techniques frequently exhibit sensitivity to innocuous or routine changes such as seasonal variations, shadows, and building parallax. Deep learning approaches have previously shown promise for improving change detection; however, many complexities persist. Change exists on a continuous spectrum, varying significantly in importance and scope on a site-by-site or task-by-task case. Subtle, semantic changes (e.g., hanger doors opening or closing) can often be more critical than more evident physical alterations. Manual annotation for these continuous changes remains prohibitively difficult, time-consuming, and subject to inconsistency due to labeling variability among annotators. Foundation models, which leverage self-supervised techniques to learn rich, generalizable feature spaces from diverse and unlabeled remote sensing imagery across various locations, perspectives, and resolutions, offer a promising solution. Utilizing the outputs of these rigorously trained encoders yields robust unsupervised change detection capabilities. In this work, we demonstrate how these foundation model embeddings can be effectively tuned to differentiate semantic from physical changes and categorize the objects or contexts contributing to them.

Keywords: Change Detection · Deep Learning · Remote Sensing · Foundation Models · Computer Vision

1 Introduction

Remote sensing has recently evolved from a niche defense-centric capability to an abundant commercial entity providing value to every industry and day-to-day life. Extracting useful insights from satellite imagery has long been a needle-in-the-haystack problem, and conventional wisdom has been that more coverage from more satellites would mean that the needles of interest would never be missed. However, the growth in space-based

F. Tanner and J. Irvine (Eds.): AIPR 2025, LNCS 16446, pp. 167–176, 2026.
https://doi.org/10.1007/978-3-032-18474-0_12

and aerial imaging has mainly created more hay, drowning end users in pixels that they must sift through. Additionally, the needles in question vary considerably from application to application. Artificial Intelligence and Machine Learning (AI/ML) techniques have matured substantially in parallel with the rising volume of satellites in orbit. Specialized algorithms have provided immense value at sifting through the hay with automated image processing, but generating these often requires large volumes of manually annotated data. For targeted applications, this is a manageable problem, but it remains time consuming, costly, and is often not generalizable to novel applications or sensors.

Effective change detection algorithms are especially elusive for several key reasons. While standard image processing algorithms like object detection and classification are applied to datasets with clean, discrete categorizable inputs and outputs, change is often considered on a continuous spectrum. As a result, manually labeled change detection datasets are not widely available, and at best are very specialized. In remote sensing, many of the most tangible changes are uninteresting, such as seasonal variance, illumination angles, shadows, perspective changes, etc. As a result, standard change detection techniques that use computer vision to perform a binary pixelwise comparison, often colorized as "red has fled, blue is new", can appear extremely noisy and fail to provide any helpful categorization of change (Fig. 1A) [1].

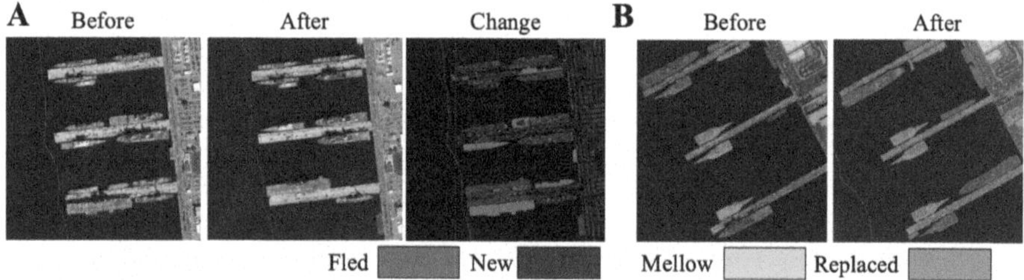

Fig. 1. (A) Binary, pixelwise change detection successfully indicates the arrival or departure of objects between a pair of images, but also struggles to mitigate noise from sources of uninteresting change like shadows, sensor noise, or seasonal changes. (B) Object-level change detection extends the binary categorization to more subtle groupings while filtering out changes unrelated to the targets of interest, for example, ships. Base imagery courtesy of Esri, ArcGIS Living Atlas of the World (Wayback Imagery).

More recent hybrid approaches combining deep learning-based object detection with temporal dynamics yield much more granular and actionable change detection products (Fig. 1B) [2, 3]. However, these still require detectors that are trained via extensive manual annotation, and are still limited in scope to discrete categories of change of specific objects, greatly limiting their generalizability. To solve this problem, we introduce self-supervised change detection via pretrained remote sensing foundation models.

2 Background and Methods

2.1 Foundation Models

Remote sensing foundation models are a recent extension of state-of-the-art natural language processing innovations that have made large language model technology like ChatGPT ubiquitous. The introduction of transformer neural networks revolutionized AI through a sensitivity to broader context and relationships, unlike traditional Convolutional Neural Networks (CNNs) which are typically constrained to understanding local context [4]. To take advantage of the vast language data available through open source, transformers are pretrained on organized yet unlabeled data via masked autoencoding [5, 6].

Most neural network-based deep learning algorithms utilize the same fundamental model structure; an encoder first ingests raw input data and maps it to a high dimensional abstract feature space, and then a smaller decoder takes those features and maps them to a desired output of interest (Fig. 2). For example, the decoder could map features to a specific label for a classification task, or to a bounding box for a detection task.

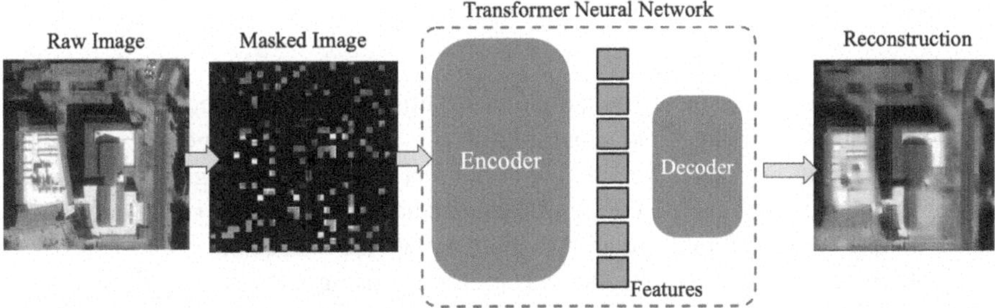

Fig. 2. The pretraining process for remote sensing foundation models via masked autoencoding. An image reconstruction decoder takes masked versions of images and predicts pixel content removed from the input. By comparing to the unmasked images, the encoder learns rich features spanning arbitrarily large datasets. Base imagery courtesy of Esri, ArcGIS Living Atlas of the World (Wayback Imagery).

Typically, an encoder and decoder would be trained simultaneously for a given task or application. Pretraining via masked autoencoding, on the other hand, uses a reconstruction decoder to train an extremely feature-dense encoder on arbitrarily large volumes of unlabeled data. In the natural language processing field, this consists of taking as much open source text data as is available, masking out random words and phrases, and training the model to predict what should fill in the blanks. The same exact process is used for pretraining a remote sensing encoder, with pixels or image patches masked out instead of words or phrases. Applying this over large imagery datasets yields an encoder that has learned a broad range of features present in the data without requiring any manual annotation. Decoders for downstream tasks such as change detection can subsequently be trained with far smaller volumes of labeled data than would be required if training the full encoder and decoder from scratch.

2.2 Change Detection with Remote Sensing Foundation Models

Using a combination of open source encoders (e.g. SAM2, DINO) [7, 8] with custom tuning on remote sensing-specific datasets [9], we produce an encoder capable of outputting abstract features that are highly sensitive to subtle changes in input imagery. As a result, we can compare the embeddings extracted from a pair of images to measure qualitative change over the entire spatial extent of the images (Fig. 3).

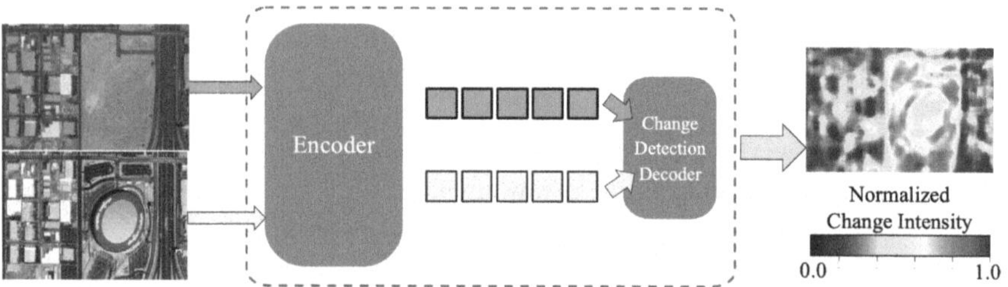

Fig. 3. The adapted model architecture for extracting embeddings from a pretrained encoder and producing a change detection heatmap via specialized decoder tuning. Base imagery courtesy of Esri, ArcGIS Living Atlas of the World (Wayback Imagery).

This addresses the critical limitations of traditional change detection algorithms: discrete measures of change, and generalizability to new sensors, targets or changes of interest, and locations. Here, we are able to not just indicate what regions in an image have changed, but also quantify the significance of that change (Fig. 3, right). As a result, this technique is extensible to situations where no labeled data exist.

Furthermore, because the encoder was pretrained using an extremely diverse combination of imagery from vast sensors and perspectives, it can be readily adapted to novel situations and use cases without requiring any retraining or fine tuning. In this study, we demonstrate the power of using the same pretrained remote sensing foundation model across three distinct application categories: Broad area monitoring of long timescale changes in a large area with high resolution satellite imagery; site-specific monitoring of short timescale changes with moderate resolution satellite imagery; and object-specific change monitoring over very short timescales with very high resolution aerial imagery. Foundation models provide a general solution for rapid extensibility across change detection applications spanning diverse timescales and targets of interest across diverse areas.

3 Results and Discussion

3.1 Broad Area Monitoring

Change detection applications can have an extremely wide range of spatial and temporal scales of interest. Foundation models are especially adept at generalizing across these scales, but there is a tradeoff in algorithm efficiency and the size of changes identified.

This tradeoff can be exploited for broad area monitoring of slow changes. Change detection at very large spatial scales reveals regions that have undergone significant semantic change (Fig. 4, top). The same foundation model can then be utilized at narrowing spatial scales but higher resolutions to localize change more precisely. Depending on what sorts of changes are of interest, the encoder's spatial embeddings can be adjusted to highlight things spanning broad construction activity (Fig. 4, middle) or individual buildings and roads (Fig. 4, bottom).

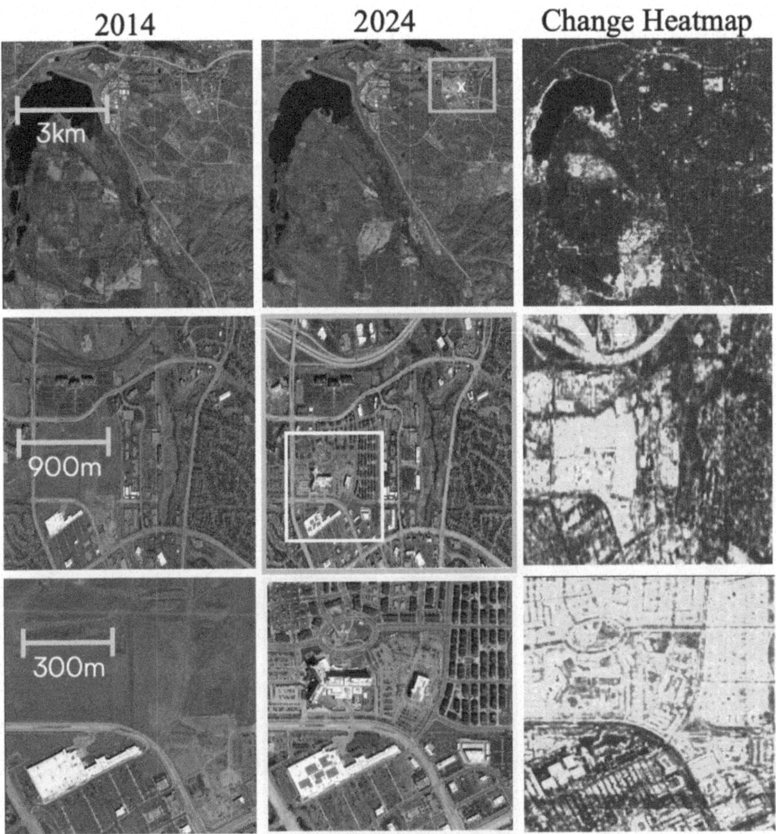

Fig. 4. Change detection examples over the Highlands Ranch area of Littleton, Colorado from imagery collected ten years apart. The same foundation model can be adjusted to amplify changes of variable size over large to narrow areas of interest. Base imagery courtesy of Esri, ArcGIS Living Atlas of the World (Wayback Imagery).

Although the foundation model encoder used was trained primarily on ~ 0.5m WorldView imagery from the Functional Map of the World dataset, it can still indicate qualitative changes on open source WorldView imagery that has been significantly downsampled to a lower resolution [10]. Efficient change detection over this wide range of spatial resolutions enables very efficient broad area search, as well as downstream tip-and-cue between sensors with different native resolutions. The model was only trained via self-supervised masked autoencoding; it has never been explicitly trained on labeled image pairs. Despite this, the model's embeddings are clearly not only sensitive to diverse changes, but capable of ignoring uninteresting or innocuous changes (e.g. soil moisture/color variance) that would be a source of significant false alarms with traditional change detection techniques.

3.2 Site-Specific Monitoring

The same foundation model can be used for more frequent site-specific monitoring. Planet Labs' PlanetScope satellite constellation provides daily imagery of the entire landmass of the Earth at moderate ~ 3m resolution. Whether a site becomes of interest from known activity or from longer term broad area detection, daily monitoring coupled with foundation model-based change detection reveals another layer of situational awareness. Instead of comparing to static images to one another, we can capture regular imagery to establish a baseline of normalcy against which to compare (Fig. 5A).

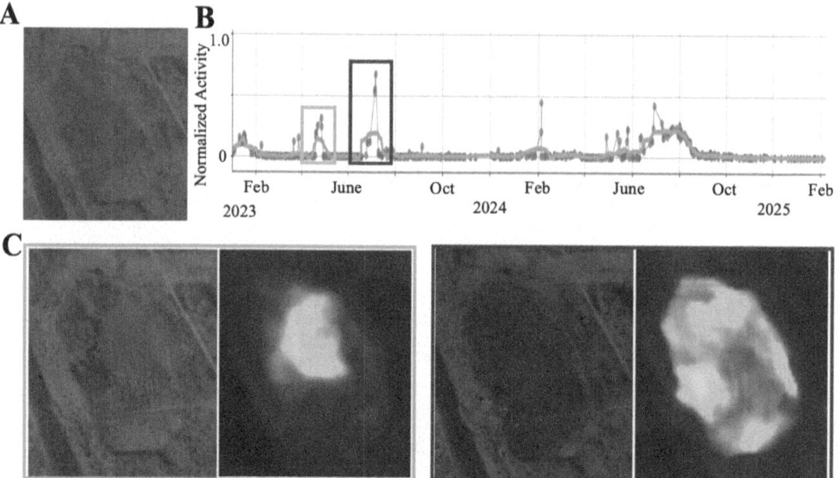

Fig. 5. Daily site-specific monitoring with PlanetScope imagery. (A) Historical data collects establish a background image of normalcy. (B) Day-to-day monitoring reveals occasional periodic spikes in activity. (C) Investigation of the individual spikes in activity reveals the preparation for and execution of a notable event. Base imagery Copyright 2025 Planet Labs PBC, All Rights Reserved.

For example, daily comparison of deviations from normal in the desert of central Australia reveals anomalous activity or presence of features not typically observed (Fig. 5B). This activity, the Big Red Bash music festival, repeats annually, with field preparation in late spring (Fig. 5C) preceding the brief festival each summer (Fig. 5D). This example of continuous site-specific monitoring demonstrates the extension from broad area change detection to anomaly recognition and patterns-of-life. Although the foundation model was not trained on imagery from this sensor, the diverse breadth of data exposed during pretraining allows seamless adaptation to change detection of new systems.

3.3 Object Specific Monitoring

For more time-sensitive change detection applications, for example the active monitoring of specific objects or high value targets, more regular, persistent imaging than can be afforded by traditional commercial satellites may be necessary. Aerial imagery, such as that collected by Urban Sky from stratospheric balloons, can provide more persistence but still cover large areas at very high resolution. Combining their flight patterns with tactical efficient deployment from ground vehicles (Fig. 6A), Urban Sky balloons can image the same area minutes or hours apart, enabling object-specific change monitoring that would be infeasible with satellites.

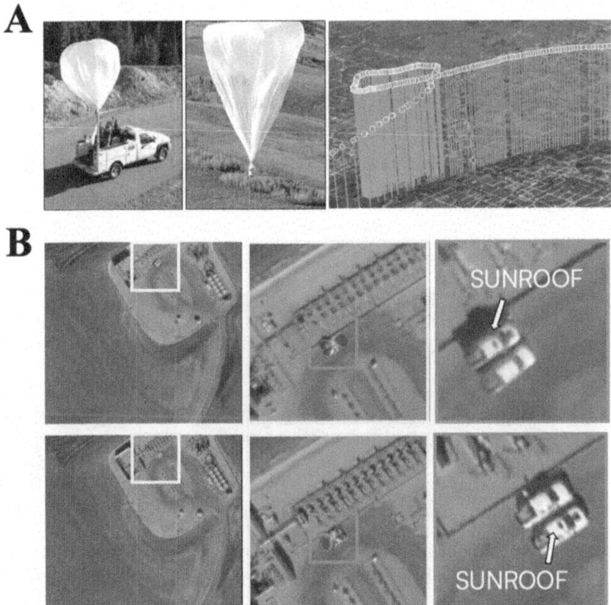

Fig. 6. Hourly site-specific monitoring with Urban Sky stratospheric balloon imagery. (A) Reusable balloons with custom imaging payloads can be launched and controlled to provide persistent imagery spanning minutes to hours. (B) Change detection reveals subtle changes in objects present, distinguishable only from sub-feature variance. Base imagery courtesy of Urban Sky.

The same foundation model as used for 0.5m WorldView and 3m PlanetScope imagery can execute frame-to-frame change detection on 10cm Urban Sky imagery. When comparing images collected over an electric substation an hour apart, the embedding-based change detection revealed significant semantic change around a pair of white trucks (Fig. 6B). Upon close visual inspection, in the hour between the two collections, the trucks swapped spots. This is distinguishable only due to the presence of a sunroof on one truck and not the other, a feature likely not distinguishable at lower resolutions.

3.4 Change Categorization

While the generalizable change detection capability afforded by the exploitation of a foundation model's embeddings reveals insights that would be prohibitively difficult through traditional methods, the results are still inherently qualitative. The automated categorization of observed changes provides deeper and more actionable insights that can be used to feed downstream applications, or feedback into change detection algorithms to optimize outputs. For example, categorizing changes as belonging to innocuous, uninteresting objects allows them to be filtered out, leaving behind only changes of interest. Alternatively, categorization of broader contextual changes allows for relevant backgrounds to be identified and considered or suppressed when investigating changes, such as a site that has a sudden climate change (e.g. snowfall) being categorized as such and not flagged as widespread change.

We demonstrate the utility of automatically categorizing change in both the broad area monitoring and site-specific monitoring use cases. Change detection of the port of San Diego between images collected months apart shows substantial changes along the waterline as well as in nearby parking lots (Fig. 7A).

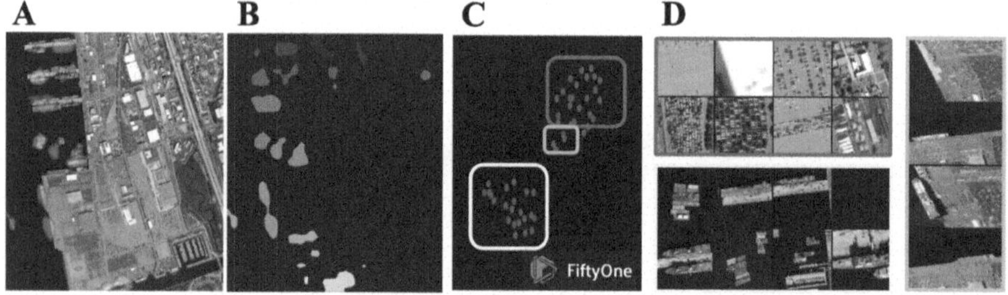

Fig. 7. (A) Changes highlight on an image of the port of San Diego compared to a separate image collected months earlier. (B) Individual changes detected are chipped out to form a stack of relevant objects. (C) A 2D embedding visualization shows two distinct clusters with some small anomalies between them, via Voxel51's FiftyOne tool [11]. (D) Visual inspection of the clusters reveals consistent categories of change. Base imagery courtesy of Esri, ArcGIS Living Atlas of the World (Wayback Imagery).

Extracting image chips from the "hot spots" of change in one of the images provides an image stack whose embeddings can be compared to one another, instead of comparing embeddings between the same region of two different images (Fig. 7B). To compare embeddings across groups of image chips, we employ dimensionality reduction via Uniform Manifold Approximation and Projection (UMAP) [12], which projects the embeddings into a more directly interpretable two dimensions and downstream clustering to assess categories present among the changes [13]. For this scene, we see two distinct clusters emerge (Fig. 7C); changes of ships in the water, and changes of vehicle presence in parking lots (Fig. 7D). The anomalous changes that appear between the primary clusters represent ships near parking lots, demonstrating the ability of the foundation model to categorize semantic similarities despite being trained with no labels.

Applied to the site monitoring use case, instead of categorizing changed objects, we can categorize broader scale changes across the entire context of the site. For the Big Red Bash observed in PlanetScope, five distinct clusters emerge in the reduced dimension embedding space (Fig. 8A). Upon visual inspection, these clusters include a stable, empty background (Fig. 8B), the festival event itself (Fig. 8C), and the anomalously lush field after flooding (Fig. 8D). This ability to automatically cluster broader contexts based on their semantic features greatly strengthens change detection by allowing comparison to the appropriate examples of normalcy. For example, if the sudden surge in lush vegetation is uninteresting to a user, imagery from that cluster can be compared to the "normal" background of that cluster to ensure the entire scene is not flagged as changed. Furthermore, this would allow small, subtle changes among those broad scale changes to still be detected and not drowned out by the large uninteresting change.

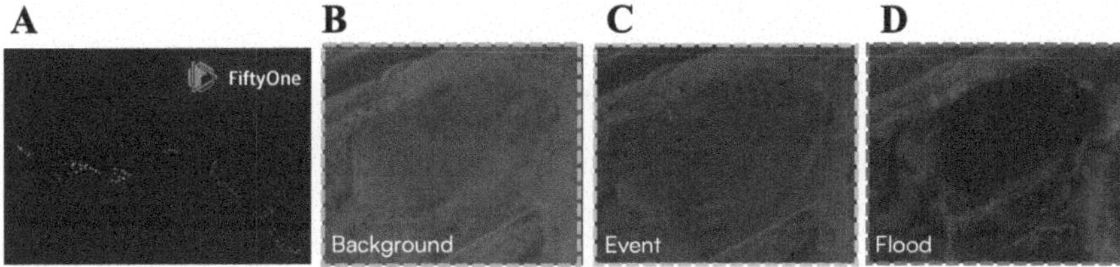

Fig. 8. Clustering of full site imagery from PlanetScope reveals several distinct groupings of imagery including empty background (B), event of interest (C), and lush flooded field (D). Base imagery Copyright 2025 Planet Labs PBC, All Rights Reserved.

4 Conclusion

This approach to foundation model–driven change detection extends traditional techniques by addressing the key limitations of each. Early pixelwise and object-based methods relied on supervised training and handcrafted features, resulting in poor generalizability and high false alarm rates. While CNN-based approaches mitigated some of these shortcomings, only the recent emergence of self-supervised learning has enabled truly generalizable, sensor-agnostic, and easily adaptable change detection algorithms.

The embedding-based framework introduced here is directly extensible to related, more specialized forms of change detection and feature retrieval. For instance, the same categorical embedding space can support rare object recognition, where anomalous features serve as exemplars to identify similar rare occurrences elsewhere. Likewise, high-value target reacquisition, historically a prohibitively difficult task due to limited labeled data, becomes feasible through foundation model-based feature fingerprinting. Beyond performance gains, these methods also enhance trust and resilience in AI-driven analytics, as foundation model embeddings are inherently less susceptible to denial and deception. As remote sensing foundation models continue to mature, the reach and utility of unsupervised change detection will expand across spatial scales, temporal regimes, and operational domains.

Acknowledgments. The authors would like to acknowledge collaborators at Planet Labs and Urban Sky for providing data that were used in this study, as well as the Taylor Geospatial Institute and Amazon Web Services for cloud compute grants that contributed to the resources used in the study.

Disclosure of Interests. The authors have no competing interests to declare that are relevant to the content of this article.

References

1. Sun, Z.H, et al.: Vehicle change detection from aerial imagery using detection response maps. In: Proceedings of SPIE 9089, Geospatial InfoFusion and Video Analytics IV; and Motion Imagery for ISR and Situational Awareness II, 908906, 19 June 2014
2. Francisco, A.G., Reisman, M.D., Dalrymple, J.J., LaTourette, K.J.: Deep learning-based object level change detection in overhead imagery. In: Proceedings of SPIE 11729, Automatic Target Recognition XXXI, 117290N, 12 April 2021
3. LeDuc, D., Fisher, T., Engle, I., Vadlamudi, A.K., Reisman, M.D.: Object-level change detection for autonomous sensemaking. In: Proceedings of SPIE 12099, Geospatial Informatics XII, 1209909, 27 May 2022
4. Vaswani, A., Shazeer, N., Parmar, N., Uszkoreit, J., Jones, Polosukhin, I.: Attention is all you need. Adv. Neural Inform. Process. Syst. **30** (2017)
5. Brown, T.B., et al.: Language models are few-shot learners. Adv. Neural Inform. Process. Syst. (NeurIPS 33) (2020)
6. He, K., Chen, X., Xie, S., Li, Y., Dollár, P., Girshick, R.: Masked autoencoders are scalable vision learners. In: Proceedings of the IEEE/CVF Conference on Computer Vision and Pattern Recognition (CVPR), pp. 16000–16009 (2022)
7. Ravi, N., et al.: SAM2: Segment Anything in Images and Videos, arXiv preprint arXiv:2408.00714 (2024)
8. Oquab, M., Darcet, T., Moutakanni, T., Vo, H.V., Szafraniec, M., Bojanowski, P.: DINOv2: Learning Robust Visual Features without Supervision, arXiv preprint arXiv:2304.07193 (2023)
9. Christie, G., Fendley, N., Wilson, J., Mukherjee, R.: Functional map of the world. In: Proceedings of the IEEE Conference on Computer Vision and Pattern Recognition (CVPR), pp. 6172–6180 (2018)
10. Esri: ArcGIS Wayback Imagery, ArcGIS Living Atlas of the World (2025)
11. Voxel51, Inc., FiftyOne: The open-source tool for building high-quality datasets and computer vision models (2020–2025). https://github.com/voxel51/fiftyone
12. McInnes, L., Healy, J., Melville, J.: UMAP: Uniform Manifold Approximation and Projection for Dimension Reduction, arXiv preprint arXiv:1802.03426 (2018)
13. Garza, J.E., et al.: Knowledge without learning: a zero shot approach to SAR ATR. In: Proceedings of the Interservice/Industry Training, Simulation, and Education Conference (I/ITSEC 2025), Orlando, FL, USA (Accepted for publication)

Assumptions Implicit in Applied Imagery Pattern Recognition

Steven A. Israel, Michelle M. Brennan, and John M. Irvine(✉)

MITRE, Bedford, United States
jmirvine@mitre.org

Abstract. Automated imagery pattern recognition engineers apply established automated workflows to their tasks with limited to no examination of assumptions built into the individual functional blocks. This paper identifies numerous assumptions implicit to workflow blocks inclusive of task definition, data acquisition, data processing, training/inferencing, generating decisions, and assessing confidence. The effect that each assumption has on the established workflow is accompanied by a worked example using downlooking, panchromatic electro-optical images, acquired from a satellite platform. The information is presented so that engineers can utilize the identification of these assumptions to re-examine their processing procedures, resulting in robust and resilient systems.

1 Introduction

The current generation of machine learning (ML) has shown dramatic improvements in task performance [1], speed to deliver models [2], and utilize a robust recipe to create new models [3]. Plus, ML has been democratized by having models [4], data [5], and processing libraries [6] freely available online for download. The reduction of engineering into common practice has yielded tremendous benefits in the areas of medicine [7], vehicle detection from drones [8], and biometric authentication [9].

Duggin and Robinove [10] identified the process from transitioning landcover information, through a sensing and processing system, into a land-use classification decision. This paper focuses that work into modern ML (Fig. 1). We use a real example to classify image chips of planes into either two (Airbus350 and Boeing 787) or four engine (Airbus 340/ 380 and Boeing 747s). Definitions of terms are provided.

F. Tanner and J. Irvine (Eds.): AIPR 2025, LNCS 16446, pp. 177–189, 2026.
https://doi.org/10.1007/978-3-032-18474-0_13

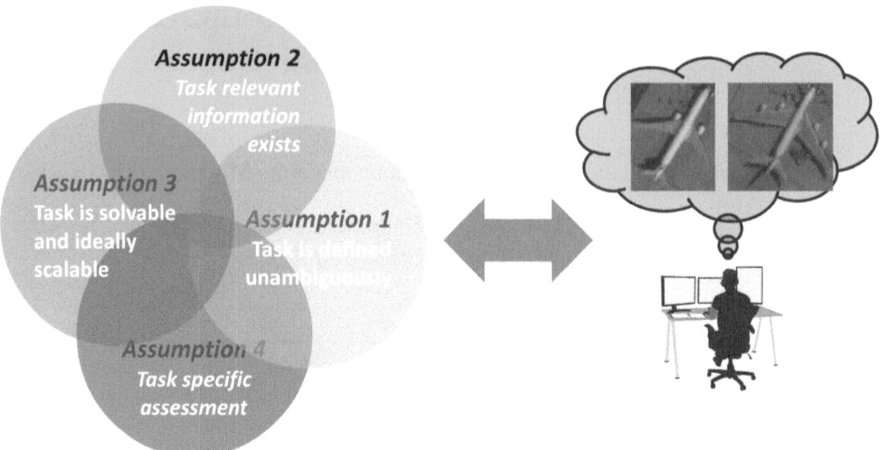

Fig. 1. Realizing a user's vision

2 Assumptions

2.1 Assumption 1: The Task is Defined Unambiguously

The task is unambiguously described or defined. From the definition, a system can be designed and performance assessed. The National Imagery Interpretability Rating Scale (NIIRS) [11] offered a method for describing tasks using a three-part structured grammar consisting of the (primitive) task, target, and qualifier. The NIIRS task descriptors are called criteria. Example 1: (task) Detect (target) planes (qualifier) on an operational airfield. Example 2: (task) Distinguish between (targets) Honda Civics and Toyota Corollas (qualifier) in an urban environment. Both examples are readily understandable and probably mathematically encoded without exception handling for automated processing.

Definition 1: **Task** (problem)—The purpose for performing an (image) analysis. Image Analysis Tasks can be:

Primitive independent of time and space, such as detection and classification

Compound aggregation of multiple primitive decisions, such as counting

Complex stateful in time and space, such as change in counts)

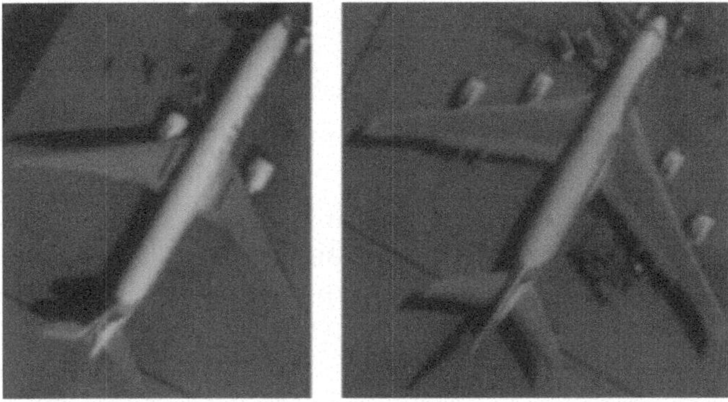

Fig. 2. GeoEye images for two- and four-engine long-haul aircraft

Most assumptions covered in this paper refer to one of two worked examples (detailed in the Appendix). The first example criterion is: distinguishing between two and four engine long haul aircraft (Fig. 2). The above task is a sorting function. The task does not assess detection (scan image for aircraft), recognition (Boeing or Airbus), or counting planes on the tarmac (Fig. 3).

Fig. 3. Images with context from RarePlanes [12]

The second example criteria are to classify planes into 2, 4, 8, and 16 classes (detailed in the Appendix). Planes consisted of private, sport, and transport from operational airfields. Figure 4 provides examples of sport planes.

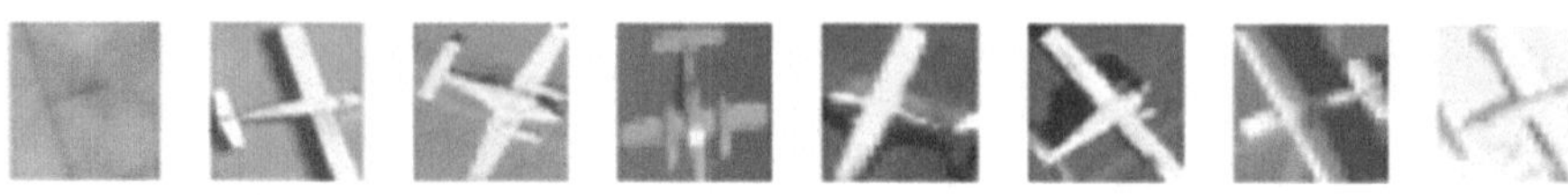

Fig. 4. Images with context from RarePlanes [12]

Assumption 1.1: Target labels are exclusive and exhaustive. The task belongs to a group of problems called forced choice assignment [13]. Assumption 1.2: Target labels and environments are fully understood prior to analysis, called the closed system assumption. For the target discrimination criterion, single engine aircraft violates the closed system assumption.

Definition 2: **Exclusive** (target labels)—No overlaps or forced choice decisions

Definition 3: **Exhaustive**—Labels fully describe all outcomes in the operating environment

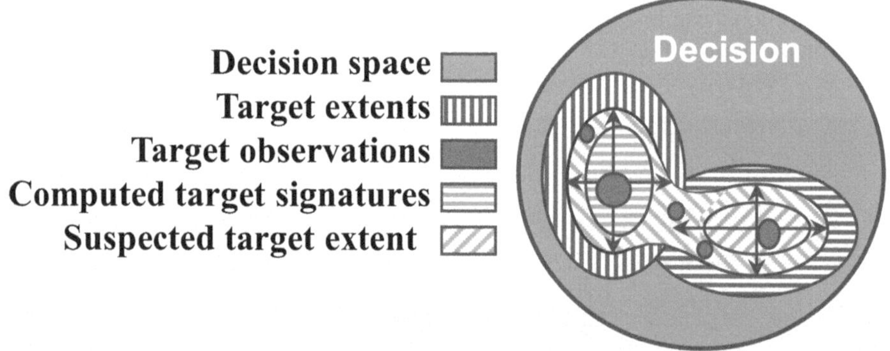

Fig. 5. Target discrimination

Once the task is defined, the remaining assumptions relate to target(s) discrimination (Fig. 5). Assumption 2 asks if sufficient information exists to perform the task [14–16]. Assumption 3 determines whether the data can be processed to inform a decision. Assumption 4 matches the task's goals to the assessment metrics. Clarifying assumptions are identified, as needed.

2.2 Assumption 2: Information Exists to Quantitatively Solve the Task

Assumption 2.1: Process requires us learning by examples and examples are readily available. Assumption 2.1 is an aggregation of other assumptions Assumption 2.1.1: a predictable relationship exists between the human defined labels and the image information [17] to characterize the target(s) of interest [10]. If so, system testing is possible, and likely the individual components. A simple estimate for primitive tasks is a distance between the target and its nearest confuser (Fig. 6).

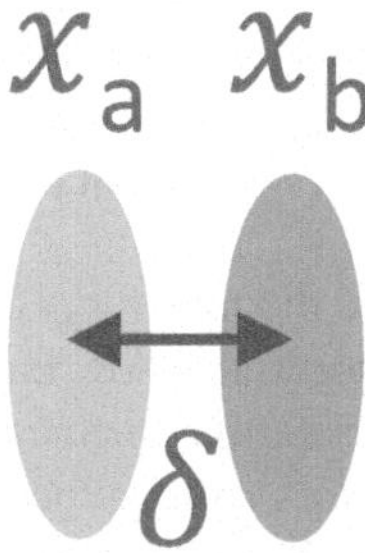

Fig. 6. Target-to-nearest confuser distance as a metric for target discriminability. For the target discrimination Xa = 2 planes and Xb = 4 planes.

Assumption 2.1.2 is the cluster assumption where intra-target variability is greater than the inter-target variability. 2.1.3 is the smoothness assumption, which states that changes in target observations and images vary smoothly with changes in the operating conditions.

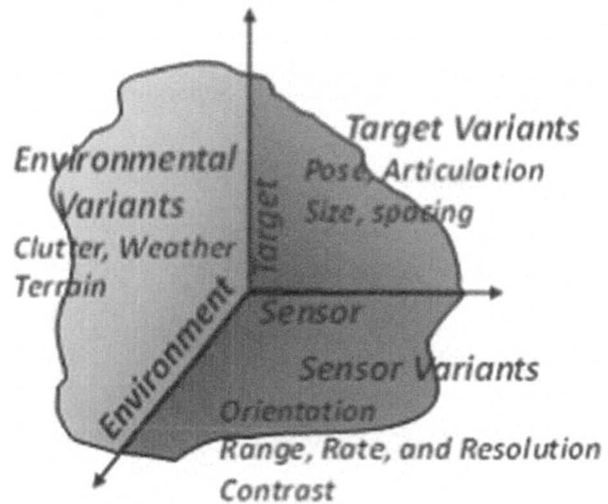

Fig. 7. Operating conditions that drive image quality

The mathematical encoding is a vector of features, a single record, extracted from an individual target (physical entity) image segment. Ideal features are computationally efficient to extract, invariant (at least tolerant) to target variations, valid across a wide range of targets and operating environments, vary predictably as targets change, and technology independent. From those features, a distance metric is needed to quantify the image information can separate the target from its nearest confuser feature vector (Fig. 6).

Definition 4: **Operating Conditions**—the combination of factors that affect image information potential [18]. It is useful to partition these factors into three broad categories related to the target, the sensor, and the environment (Fig 6). The specific factors task the variant, but the following are illustrative examples:

- Target: Factors related to the target include target pose and articulation, different models or configurations, camouflage, and partial occlusions. Some target properties are sensor dependent. For example, the type of paint affects emissivity or the target's relative brightness on the image.
- Sensor: Sensor properties include the modality (e.g., panchromatic visible imaging, wavelength, polarization, multispectral, SAR, etc.), the spatial resolution, viewing geometry, and data quality considerations such as signal-to-noise ratio (SNR).
- Environment: Environmental factors include the physical environment (e.g., desert, forest, urban, etc.), the terrain, weather and atmospheric attenuation, season, and solar orientation.

Israel and Irvine [19, 20] demonstrated that task encoding was possible. Their team inferenced RarePlanes synthetic images [12] with the ImageNet trained Keras VGG-16 model [21, 22]. The encoding is discussed within Assumption 3 with the classification task. For the discrimination task, Zernike features [23] were extracted, and separation discrimination was computed using the Mahalanobis distance.

Table 1. Zernike features for target distinctiveness and separation using Mahalanobis distance

Experiment: Images with Identical Human-Based Quality	Separation	Histo-Equalized Separation
Separation between 2 & 4 engine planes (aligned)	1.57	1.46
Separation between WorldView & GeoEyes Images (aligned)	1.25	0.87
Separation between 2 & 4 engine planes (un-aligned)	1.58	1.44
Separation between WorldView & GeoEyes Images (un-aligned)	1.02	0.81

Table 1 shows the Zernike results with raw imagery, histogram equalized images, and images separated by sensor, and image aligned versus random orientation. In each case, a greater separation existed between the two plane types than the source imagery.

Assumption 2.2: Training labels perfectly match their segmented targets. Network performance is remarkably tolerant to label error. Rolnick et al., [24] show that label errors occurring at the same rate as correct error produce no significant loss in performance. Net result is that the assumption is not significant.

Fig. 8. Annotation strategies left-to-right Polygon (multipoint), bounding box (upper left, lower right), centroid [25]

Assumption 2.3: Annotation contains only target information. Figure 7c shows the bounding box (Fig. 7) annotated airplane with more that 50% of the pixels belonging to the background. However, Mullen et al. [25] showed no significant model performance differences across the annotation strategies. But they did observe a significant cost reduction. Centroid annotations were 1/6th the cost of a polygon annotations.

2.3 Assumption 3: An ML Model Can Be Built to Answer the Task[1]

If the task requires a ML model, then additional engineering is essential for using ML models in operations. Assumption 3.1: Sufficient relevant images exist, and their interpretability can be defined. The current state of image pattern recognition sees an embarrassment of cheap plentiful processing power and tremendous initial performance from transfer learning [2]. This has led to poor design of ML as a system if not the models themselves. Training with images that are out of distribution from the task-operating environment combination causes the model to learn poor target descriptions. The results impact model performance.

Assumption 3.2: Image preprocessing has no effect on the information potential available to the ML model. GeoEye and WorldView satellite images are provided with 11-bit panchromatic pixels. Common architectures, such as VGG-16 and Inception, preprocessing the ingested images spatially, spectrally, and radiometrically.[2] Commonly, the ImageNet database, which contains 8-bit images, is used to pretrain models for transfer learning [4]. The pre-processing effects varies with target segment sizes and collection geometry (Fig. 8), but generally reduces the segment's information potential and adds noise.

[1] The need to build a computer vision model is an assumption not covered in this paper.

[2] VGG-16 = 224x224 pixels spatial, expanding the input to three colors, zero centering radiometrically based upon the ImageNet database statistics. Note: Pre-processing does not orient the targets along a common axis.

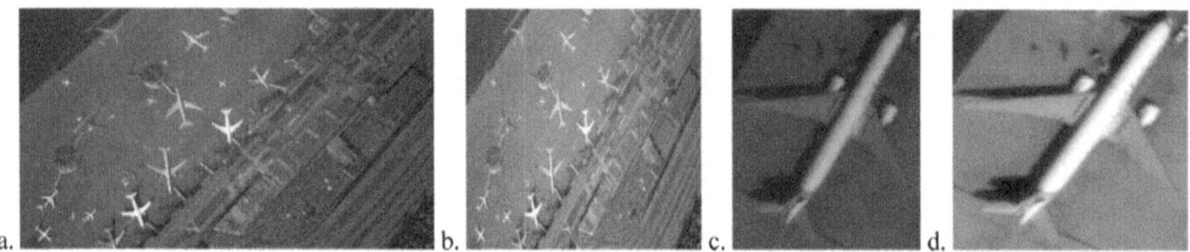

Fig. 9. (a) Synthetic Image Geneva Airport (1920x1080); (b) VGG processed; (c) GeoEye 2 engine (132x166); (d) VGG processed. NOTE color effects and spatial warping.

Assumption 3.3: The ML model architecture contains sufficient capacity to learn the target distinctiveness from the images. The academic literature is filled with building bigger and more robust ML models. Baum [26] and Wang [27] showed no relationship between validation error and network size as number of parameters. Israel et al. [20] showed that for primitive tasks, once the number of parameters exceeded a task dependent threshold (Fig. 9), additional parameters showed no significant performance improvement. All of their [20] model's parameters are significantly smaller than those commonly used for transfer learning (Fig. 10).

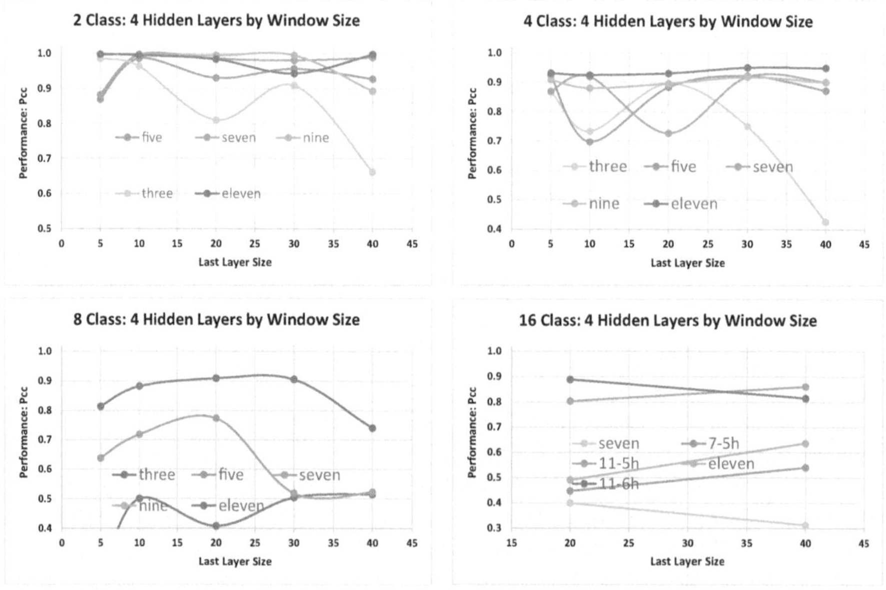

Fig. 10. Task Complexity as number of classes versus CNN parameters and performance

Coupling Assumptions 3.2 and 3.3 points to the training set size can be understood if not computed [28]. As the number of model parameters increases, the number of examples to train the parameters grows non-linearly. Adding model parameters, even if they are not required for the task criterion, impacts model development [18].

Table 2. Sensor effects on target separation

Number of Planes	Separation	1-NIIRS Reduced Separation	10% Added Noise Separation	25% Added Noise Separation
2	48	39	38	38
4	30	22	27	26
8	18	12	13	13
16	15	11	14	13

Assumption 3.4: Target separation varies with operating conditions. Image quality varies spatially over the image. For EO images, this could include smoke, atmospheric attenuation, occlusion. Consider the simple Classification Case Study experimental results shown in Table 2. The image features for classification were inferenced from a ResNet foundation model. The table values were computed Euclidean distance between training cluster centers. The data show that feature space distance reduces as operating conditions change. The columns show the effects of different sensor issues either by resolution (coarser resolution) or sensor noise effect. In all cases, the target to nearest confuser distance reduces dramatically. Table 1 enhances the argument that even at the same NIIRS level considerable differences exist between GeoEye and WorldView images.

2.4 Assumption 4: The Performance Metrics Match the Task Needs

The components for automated analysis that include the user's task, the ML model, collection, and satisfaction assessment can be audited using the same strategies (Fig. 1). Assumption 4 addresses the system engineering question, 'did we build it right?'. We focus on operational audits. ML models are often forgotten once placed into operations and like all system components require maintenance.

Assumption 4.1: Operational images are relevant to the task; and Assumption 4.1A: The ML model is relevant to the task. For discrimination case study (Fig. 11a), contingency matrices [29] are commonly used with the percent correctly classified (%C) or kappa coefficient ($\hat{k}$). For the case study, %C = 275/340 which is 81% (Fig. 11). However, that includes all scores. If a confidence threshold is set, for example 70%, forty-seven image segments are conceptually labeled as *unknown* (Fig. 11b). The corresponding %C drops to 228/340 or 67%. The difference in strategy selection varies with task importance and the user's risk tolerance.

a.

		Predicted		
		2 Eng	4 Eng	Total
Actual	2 Eng	**143**	20	163
	4 Eng	45	**132**	177
	Total	188	152	**275**

b.

		Predicted			
		< thresh	2 Eng	4 Eng	Total
Actual	2 Eng	24	**119**	20	163
	4 Eng	23	45	**109**	177
	Total	47	164	129	**228**

Fig. 11. Contingency matrix (a) highest score (b) thresholded scores

Assumption 4.2: Operating conditions are static. The reality is that ML model performance varies over time for consistency or drift [30]. As models drift, additional training is required to adapt. Assumption 4.3: The task criteria hasn't changed over time. Largely ignored, but some long-term automated systems have workflows and functions that need updating or are no longer required.

3 Discussion

Imagery pattern recognition is a powerful tool, quickly characterizing objects (targets) of interest across vast ground areas quickly. Reducing these tools to common practice has brought new applications and ideas to a variety of disciplines. We believe that this paper better informs practitioners the assumptions that reside within these data, models, and workflow. Our hope is that conscious application of machine learning will generate even better system designs.

Appendix

The paper references two case studies. The first case study seeks to keep the operating conditions constant and perform discrimination between two classes, called Discrimination Case Study. The second case study performs ML classification of airplanes at 2, 4, 8, and 16 classes, called the Classification Case Study.

Discrimination Case Study

The Discrimination Case Study performed a single NIIRS criterion: *classify image chips as either two (2) (Airbus350 and Boeing 787) or four (4) (Airbus 340/ 380 and Boeing 747s) engine long-haul airplanes* (Fig. 12). Images were collected from downlooking WorldView 2 and GeoEye 1, panchromatic electro-optical (EO), platforms. Efforts were taken to minimize the differences in image information. Both platforms operate in a sun-synchronous orbit with a local nadir viewing time of approximately 10:30am. All images were acquired with a NIIRS Levels between 4.9 and 5.1, all images were acquired from the Dubai Airport to minimize differences in atmospheric aberration, and the images span only two years to minimize sensor drift.

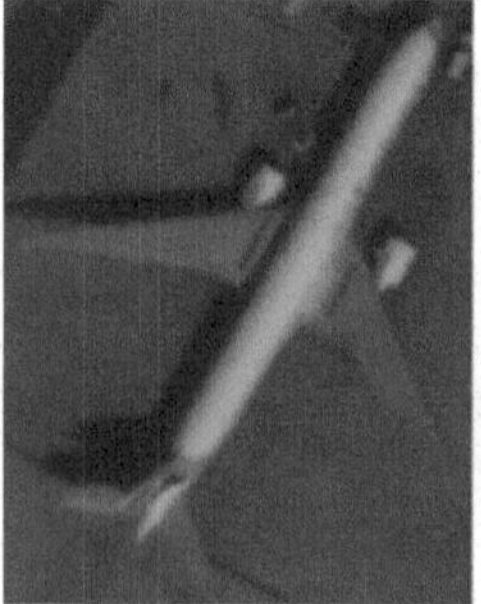
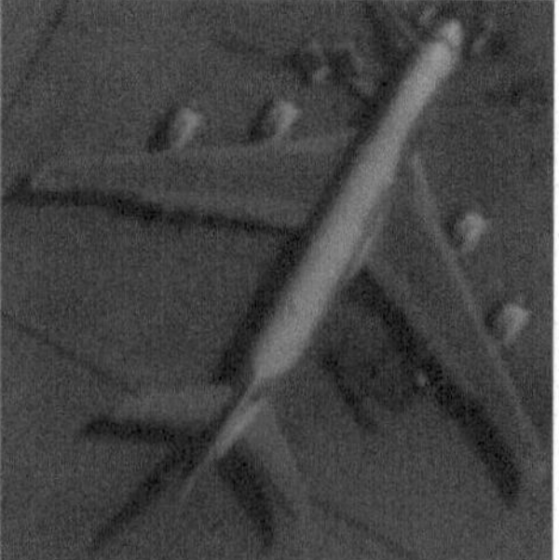

Fig. 12. GeoEye images for 2 and 4 engine long-haul aircraft

Classification Case Study

The Classification Case Study exploited the synthetic images from RarePlanes [12] dataset (Fig. 13). Planes were classified into 2 classes (plane or background), 4 classes (private, sport, and transport civilian planes with background), 8 classes (sport planes: Cessna 170, Cessna 172, Cessna 310, DeHavilland DHC-2 Beaver, DeHavilland DHC-3 Otter, Let L-200 Morova, Piper PA-28, and background), and 16 classes (private planes: HBC-400, Gulfstream GIII, Gulfstream-G200, Embraer, Dassault-2000, Dassault-900, Dassault-100, Cessna-CJ4, Cessna, Bombardier-Learjet, Bombardier-705, Bombardier-604, Bombardier-300, Bombardier-BD-700, Boeing-BBJ-2, Background). In each of the experiments, the raw image quality remained the same, roughly NIIRS 7. A pre-trained VGG-16 using ImageNet [21] weights generated the image features. The VGG-16 model was downloaded from Keras [4] without its output layer. The color images were resized to 63 x 63 pixels. Inferencing the normalized image sprites resulted in 256 real valued features. The training features were averaged to locate target centers.

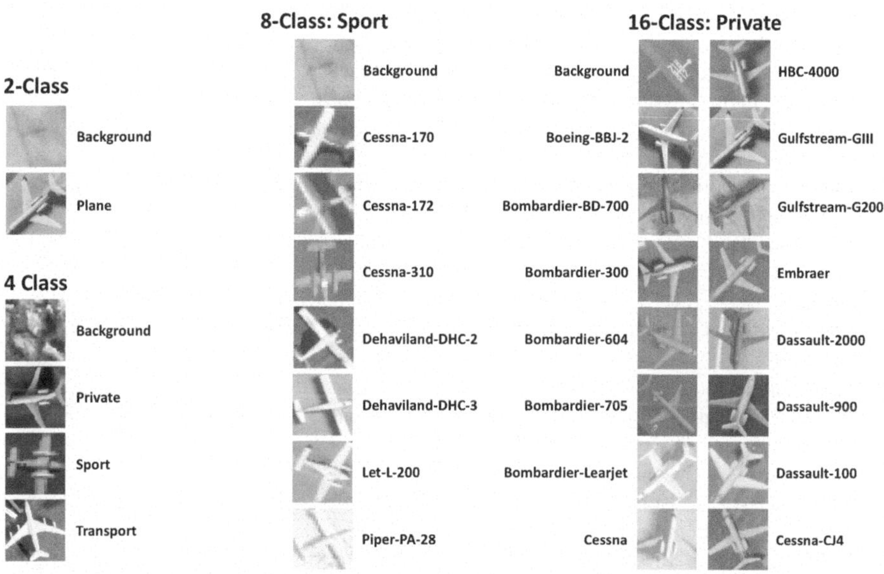

Fig. 13. Example planes for Classification Case Study [12]

References

1. Scheidegger, F., Istrate, R., Mariani, G., Benini, L., Bekas, C., Malossi, C.: Efficient image dataset classification difficulty estimation for predicting deep-learning accuracy. Vis. Comput. **37**, 1593–1610 (2021)
2. Razavian, A., Azizpour, H., Sullivan, J., Carlsson, S.: CNN features off-the-shelf: an astounding baseline for recognition. In: IEEE Conference on Computer Vision and Pattern Recognition Workshops (2014)

3. Weiss, K., Khoshgoftaar, T., Wang, D.: A survey of transfer learning. Journal of Big Data **3**(9), 40 pages (2016)
4. Keras: Keras Applications (2023). https://keras.io/api/applications/
5. Lin, T., et al.: Microsoft COCO: common objects in context. *arXiv,* vol. 1405.0312v3, no. 21, 15 pages, February 2015
6. Paszke, A., et al.: PyTorch: an imperative style, high-performance deep learning library. In: 2019, PyTorch: an Imperative Style, High-Performance Proceedings of the 33rd International Conference on Neural Information Processing Systems (2018)
7. Balki, I., et al.: Sample-size determination methodologies for machine learning in medical imaging research: a systematic review. Can. Assoc. Radiol. J. **70**(4), 344–353 (2019)
8. Cleary, A., Yoo, K., Samuel, P., George, P., Sun, F., Israel, S.: Machine learning on small UAVs. In: IEEE Applied Imagery Pattern Recognition Workshop (AIPR) (2020)
9. Tazim, R., Miah, M., Surma, S., Islam, M., Shahnaz, C., Fattah, S.: Biometric authentication using CNN features of dorsal vein pattern extracted from NIR image. In: IEEE Region 10 Conference (TENCON) (2018)
10. Duggin, M., Robinove, C.: Assumptions implicit in remote sensing data acquisition and analysis. Int. J. Remote Sens. **11**(10), 1669–1694 (1990)
11. Irvine, J.: National imagery interpretability rating scales (NIIRS): overview and methodology. In: SPIE Proceedings, vol. 3128, Airborne Reconnaissance XXI (1997)
12. Shermeyer, J., Hossler, T., Van Etten, A., Hogan, D., Lewis, R., Kim, D.: RarePlanes: synthetic data takes flight. In-Q-Tel - CosmiQ Works and AI.Reverie (2020)
13. Duda, R., Hart, P.: Pattern Classification and Scene Analysis. John Wiley and Sons, New York (1973)
14. Achille, A., Paolini, G., Mbeng, G., Soatto, S.: The information complexity of learning tasks, their structure and their distance. Inform. Inf. J. IMA **10**, 51–72 (2021)
15. Domingos, P.: A few useful thing to know about machine learning. Commun. ACM **55**(10), 78–87 (2012)
16. Deng, J., Berg, A.C., Li, K., Fei-Fei, L.: What does classifying more than 10,000 image categories tell us?. In: Daniilidis, K., Maragos, P., Paragios, N. (eds.) Computer Vision – ECCV 2010. ECCV 2010. Lecture Notes in Computer Science, vol. 6315. Springer, Heidelberg (2010). https://doi.org/10.1007/978-3-642-15555-0_6
17. Fisher, P.: The pixel: a snare and a delusion. Int. J. Remote Sens. **18**(3), 679–685 (1997)
18. Israel, I., Israel, S., Irvine, J.: Factors influencing CNN performance. In: IEEE Applied Imagery Pattern Recognition Workshop (AIPR) (2021)
19. Israel, S., Irvine, J., Israel, I.: Toward CNN architectures for image detection. In: IEEE Applied Imagery and Pattern Recognition Workshop (AIPR) (2022)
20. Israel, S., Irvine, J.: Images, pre-trained networks, and information. In: IEEE Applied Imagery and Pattern Recognition Workshop, Washington, DC (2023)
21. Krizhevsky, A., Sutskever, I., Hinton, G.: ImageNet classification with deep convolutional neural networks. Commun. ACM **60**(6), 84–90 (2017)
22. Russakovsky, O., et al.: ImageNet large scale visual recognition challenge. Int. J. Comput. Vision **115**, 211–252 (2015)
23. Zernike, F.: Beugungstheorie des Schneidenverfahrens und Seiner Verbesserten Form, der Phasenkontrastmethode. Physica **1**(8), 689–704 (1934)
24. Rolnick, D., Veit, A., Belongie, S., Shavit, N.: Deep learning is robust to massive label noisE, *arXiv,* vol. 1705.10694v3, 10 pages (2018)
25. Mullen, J., Tanner, F., Sallee, P.: Comparing the effects of annotation type on machine learning detection performance. In: IEEE/CVF Conference on Computer Vision and Pattern Recognition Workshops (CVPRW), Long Beach (2019)
26. Baum, E., Haussler, D.: What size net gives valid generalization? Neural Comput. **1**, 151–160 (1989)

27. Wang, L., Quek, H., Tee, K., Zhou, N., Wan, C.: Optimal size of a feedforward neural network: how much does it matter?. In: Joint International Conference on Autonomic and Autonomous Systems and International Conference on Networking and Services (ICAS/ICNS) (2005)
28. Shahinfar, S., Meek, P., Falzon, G.: "How many images do I need?" understanding how sample size per class affects deep learning model performance metrics for balanced designs in autonomous wildlife monitoring. Ecol. Inform. **101085**, 12 pages (2020)
29. Israel, S.: Performance metrics: how and when. Geocarto Int. **21**(2), 23–32 (2006)
30. Ghani, N., Aziz, I., Mehat, M.: Concept drift detection on unlabeled data streams: a systematic literature review. In: IEEE Conference on Big Data and Analytics (ICBDA) (2020)

AgriGen: A Prompt-Tuned, Multilingual LLM-Based Q&A System for Smarter Agriculture

Venkata Ranga Ramanuja K. Chaitanya Kamduri(✉), Pramod Gupta, and Chadi El Kari

University of the Pacific, Stockton, USA
c_kamduri@u.pacific.edu, {pgupta,celkari}@pacific.edu

Abstract. This project introduces AgriGen, a multilingual agricultural Q&A system powered by prompt-tuned, lightweight generative AI models such as Phi-2 and TinyLLaMA. Designed with a vision toward future offline deployment, AgriGen currently operates in a hybrid mode and is being optimized to run on resource-constrained devices without requiring continuous internet connectivity. This approach aims to support farmers in remote or low-connectivity areas by enabling access to critical information on crop planning, fertilizer usage, yield improvement, and disease management through natural language interactions. Farmers can ask region-specific questions such as "What should I grow in Gujarat in July?" or "How do I treat yellow spots on chili leaves?" and receive accurate, context-sensitive responses in their chosen language, including English, Hindi, or Telugu. AgriGen's prompt-tuned local language models ensure that answers are tailored to local agricultural conditions. Additional features like speech output and translation support further enhance accessibility and usability. AgriGen builds on our prior work, "Smart Agriculture Advisor: A Machine Learning Approach to Precision Farming" (IEEE AIIoT 2025), which focused on predictive analytics for crop selection, fertilizer recommendation, and disease detection. By integrating generative AI, multilingual support, and plans for offline capability, AgriGen advances this foundation to enable more intelligent and inclusive interactions in agriculture. In real-world rural contexts, solutions must be affordable, adaptable, and easy to use. AgriGen addresses these challenges by merging state-of-the-art generative AI techniques with practical, underserved farming needs. This aligns with current trends in low-resource language models, AI for social good, and multimodal systems, positioning AgriGen as a significant step toward democratizing smart farming worldwide.

Keywords: precision agriculture · generative AI · large language models · multilingual systems · prompt-tuning · offline intelligence

1 Introduction

Artificial Intelligence (AI) is transforming contemporary agriculture by implementing scalable, data-driven systems that enhance decision-making in crop management, fertilizer application, irrigation planning, and disease diagnoses. These advanced technologies

F. Tanner and J. Irvine (Eds.): AIPR 2025, LNCS 16446, pp. 190–200, 2026.
https://doi.org/10.1007/978-3-032-18474-0_14

amalgamate extensive environmental data, soil metrics, and meteorological observations to produce actionable insights for farmers, enhancing production and resource sustainability. Nonetheless, a pronounced technology disparity endures between well-connected agricultural systems and resource-limited rural farming communities.

Farmers in developing countries frequently have inadequate or inconsistent internet connection, low digital literacy, and linguistic obstacles that hinder their access to the advantages of AI-driven advice tools. Many current solutions depend significantly on cloud computing and English-language interfaces, rendering them inaccessible to most small and medium-sized farms. The reliance on real-time data transmission elevates operational expenses and constrains adoption in areas with inadequate connectivity infrastructure.

This research introduces AgriGen, an offline, prompt-tuned, multilingual large language model (LLM) tailored for agricultural question-answering to address these shortcomings. AgriGen employs machine translation, specialized fine-tuning, and on-device reasoning to provide contextually pertinent guidance to farmers without necessitating internet connectivity. AgriGen attains real-time reaction capability on local hardware, including edge devices and consumer GPUs, by integrating lightweight transformer models with efficient fine-tuning methods like LoRA (Low-Rank Adaptation) and quantized inference.

In contrast to current cloud-based advising systems, AgriGen facilitates complete autonomy, privacy, and resilience in locations with limited connectivity. The system is fundamentally built for multilingual inclusion, now supporting English, Hindi, and Telugu, with an architecture that can be extended to more global agricultural languages. This method enables farmers to communicate effortlessly in their choice language and receive specific recommendations on crop selection, fertilizer optimization, and disease management suited to local agroecological conditions.

AgriGen adds a generative reasoning layer that allows conversational intelligence and adaptability to the Smart Agriculture Advisor, a machine learning-based precision farming platform that uses CNN, XGBoost, and Random Forest models for yield and disease prediction. This builds on the authors' previous work. This study enhances the existing framework by focusing on contextual comprehension, multilingual generation, and offline implementation, thereby bridging the gap between data-driven precision agriculture and inclusive, sustainable farming practices.

2 Problem Statement

Despite swift advancements in precision agriculture, many obstacles persist in implementing AI-driven innovations in rural settings. The predominant systems depend on Internet-connected IoT devices, cloud computing, and centralized data storage for real-time analytics. Although this infrastructure operates efficiently in industrial-scale farms, it is unfeasible in areas where average Internet penetration is below 35% and mobile data speeds are inconsistent. Numerous smallholder farmers function with inadequate digital infrastructure, rendering it unfeasible to sustain the continuous data synchronization demanded by most commercial agriculture platforms.

Moreover, language accessibility represents a significant constraint. More than 80% of Indian farmers predominantly converse in regional languages, including Hindi,

Telugu, and Bengali; nonetheless, most AI-driven agricultural tools are solely developed in English [3]. The language barrier diminishes user trust and hinders adoption, notwithstanding the accuracy of the underlying models.

Current precision agricultural systems frequently rely on real-time sensor fusion, integrating soil pH, nitrogen-phosphorus-potassium (NPK) measurements, and satellite meteorological data to predict yield or disease occurrences. Nonetheless, these methodologies necessitate sensors priced between US $300 and $500 per acre, so eliminating millions of smallholder farmers from engagement. Moreover, cloud-based inference raises privacy and financial issues, with subscription and storage expenses potentially accounting for up to 12% of yearly income for small-scale manufacturers [4].

The disparity is not solely technological; it is also cognitive and socioeconomic. Agriculturalists lacking formal technical education encounter difficulties with inflexible, form-centric computer interfaces. Traditional systems anticipate organized numerical input (e.g., NPK ratios or temperature readings), which diverges from the way actual farmers articulate their requirements, such as: "Which crop is optimal for my soil this season?" or "What is causing the yellow spots on my paddy leaves?" This disconnection highlights the need for natural language-driven interfaces capable of interpreting conversational intent and providing accurate agronomic suggestions.

To address these challenges, there is a growing need for offline, lightweight, and multilingual AI frameworks capable of functioning on local hardware and understanding unstructured, real-world queries. Such systems should deliver localized guidance on crop selection, irrigation scheduling, fertilizer efficiency, and pest control while maintaining low computational cost (<4 GB RAM) and high inference reliability (response latency <2 s).

The recommended AgriGen system is developed to fulfill these specifications. AgriGen facilitates multilingual reasoning and on-device inference, therefore removing reliance on Internet connectivity, decreasing operational costs, and closing the accessibility gap between sophisticated AI models and farmers in resource-limited settings.

3 Methodology

A. Data Sources and Integration

The AgriGen framework was built using multiple open-access datasets, primarily derived from the FAOSTAT and **Meteostat** repositories. These data sources were selected for their reliability, longitudinal coverage, and relevance to agricultural decision-support systems.

1. FAOSTAT Repository

The FAOSTAT database, maintained by the Food and Agriculture Organization (FAO), provided diverse agricultural indicators including:

Crops and Livestock Products (1961–2024): Annual data on crop yields, harvested area, and production quantities for major commodities (paddy rice, maize, wheat, cotton, and pulses).

Fertilizers by Product and Nutrient: Records of nitrogen (N), phosphate (P_2O_5), and potash (K_2O) consumption, disaggregated by agricultural use, import/export quantities, and production values.

Pesticides Use: Application trends of biopesticides, herbicides, and fungicides at national and regional levels.

Land Inputs and Sustainability: Data on land cover, cropland area, nutrient application, and livestock manure utilization.

Cropland Nutrient Balance: Elemental nitrogen, phosphorus, and potassium flows from synthetic fertilizers, manure, and crop removal.

Food Security Indicators: Dietary energy supply adequacy, per-capita food availability, and fat/protein intake ratios for contextual linkage to agricultural productivity.

2. Meteostat Repository

Complementary climate data (daily and monthly resolution) were obtained from Meteostat API, covering temperature, rainfall, humidity, and solar radiation across 458 Indian weather stations between 2015 and 2025. This dataset provided essential context for yield prediction and region-specific advisory generation.

All FAOSTAT modules were downloaded using CSV bulk access via FAO's metadata API and harmonized using Pandas and NumPy. Variable naming inconsistencies were resolved, units normalized (e.g., tonnes,kilograms; hectares,m^2), and temporal mismatches corrected through interpolation. The combined dataset exceeded 970,000 records and formed the foundational corpus for AgriGen model training (Fig. 1).

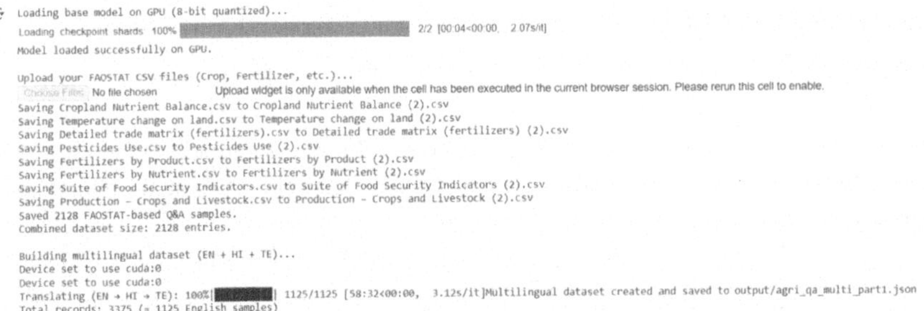

Fig. 1. FAOSTAT and Meteostat data ingestion modules showing integration of multi-domain agricultural and climate datasets for AgriGen knowledge base formation.s

B. Preprocessing and Data Structuring.

Each dataset was converted into a natural language Question-Answer (Q-A) format appropriate for fine-tuning large language models (LLMs). This procedure, executed in Python, encompassed:

(a) Extracting descriptive metadata (variable identifiers, values, years) from CSV files.

(b) Transforming each record into a dialogue-based inquiry and its associated factual response.

Example

Q: What was the total nitrogen fertilizer use in India in 2019?

A: India applied approximately 12.6 million tonnes of nitrogen (N) fertilizers during 2019, primarily for rice and wheat cultivation.

A total of 6,750 instruction–response pairs were generated covering the years 1961–2024, ensuring representative coverage across crops, climatic conditions, and nutrient parameters. Outliers were removed through z-score filtering (|z|>3), and missing values were imputed using median interpolation (Fig. 2).

```
Merging multilingual datasets...
Final multilingual dataset saved to /content/drive/MyDrive/AgriGen_Backup/output/agri_qa_multi_full.json
Total multilingual records: 6750
```

Fig. 2. Illustration of dataset transformation from FAOSTAT CSV files into multilingual Q–A instruction pairs.

C. Multilingual Translation and Dataset Expansion

To enhance inclusivity for low-literacy farming communities, the entire dataset was translated into Hindi and Telugu using a dual translation framework:

1. **IndicTrans2** models from AI4Bharat for high-quality neural translation of technical terms.
2. **Google Translator API** for fallback translation and sentence-level refinement.

Translation quality was validated using BLEU (Bilingual Evaluation Understudy) and METEOR metrics. BLEU scores averaged 0.91 for Hindi and 0.89 for Telugu, demonstrating minimal semantic drift. Furthermore, a human linguistic evaluation (30 bilingual volunteers) confirmed that 95% of translated responses retained context and agricultural accuracy.

The multilingual dataset was merged into a unified JSON file (agri_qa_multi_full.json) for fine-tuning. The data pipeline automated this translation process, producing > 20,000 final samples (English + Hindi + Telugu combined) (Figs. 3a, 4b, 5c).

D. Model Architecture and Fine Tuning

The Microsoft Phi-2 **model (2.7B parameters) was chosen due to its high reasoning capability and lightweight architecture suitable for fine-tuning on limited GPU resources. The fine-tuning utilized** Parameter-Efficient Fine-Tuning (PEFT) **with** Low-Rank Adaptation (LoRA) **through the** Hugging Face Transformers **and** BitsAndBytes **libraries. Training was executed on an** NVIDIA A100 80 GB GPU **using the following configuration:** (FIg. 6)

Learning rate: 2×10^{-5}

Fig. 3. IndicTrans2 model loading.

Fig. 4. → IndicTrans2 tokenization and dictionary mapping.

. AgriGen pipeline illustrating dataset incgrtion, multilingual translation, molel fine-tuning, and offline deployment workflow.

Fig. 5. AgriGen pipeline overview diagram.

LoRA rank: 16
Epochs: 4
Batch size: 4
Optimizer: AdamW
Precision: bfloat16
Quantization: 8-bit

E. Offline Deployment and User Interface

The fine-tuned model was deployed through a Dash + Plotly-based user interface, designed to function entirely offline. The system performs inference locally using CPU or GPU without internet or cloud dependence.

Key features include:

(1) **Language Selection:** Users can choose English, Hindi, or Telugu.
(2) **Local Inference:** Prompts are processed on-device with responses generated in < 2 s.

Fig. 6. Fine-tuning progress of the Microsoft Phi-2 model on 6,750 multilingual samples showing gradual convergence and reduced training loss across epochs.

(3) **Low Memory Footprint:** Runs under 4 GB memory, compatible with consumer-grade hardware.

This deployment strategy ensures accessibility for farmers in rural and low-connectivity zones.

The interface also includes text cleaning, transliteration support, and speech-enabled query input (planned extension) (Fig. 7).

Fig. 7. Environment setup for AgriGen offline deployment showing installation of Dash, Transformers, Torch, and Deep Translator libraries for local inference and multilingual support.

4 Results and Discussion

A. Quantitative Evaluation

Performance metrics included Accuracy, Fluency, Latency and Memory Efficiency across three supported languages (Table 1).

Table 1. Multilingual evaluation summary of the AgriGen model.

Language	Accuracy (%)	Fluency (%)	Latency (s)	Memory (GB)
English	98.2	97.5	1.3	3.8
Hindi	96.7	95.9	1.5	3.9
Telugu	95.4	95.0	1.6	3.9

```
Loaded tokenized dataset → 6750 samples
Loading checkpoint shards: 100% ████████████████ 2/2 [00:01<00:00, 1.25it/s]
The model is already on multiple devices. Skipping the move to device specified in `args`.
████████████████ [844/844 13:00, Epoch 2/2]
Step  Training Loss
100   1.338700
200   0.575700
300   0.457600
400   0.412600
500   0.368700
600   0.365400
700   0.366000
800   0.364200

Fine-tuning completed and model saved successfully!
```

Fig. 8. Multilingual performance evaluation summary of the AgriGen model across English, Hindi, and Telugu showing high accuracy and low latency.

The results show that English responses achieved the highest factual accuracy, while Hindi and Telugu demonstrated competitive performance, confirming effective cross-lingual learning. The model consistently produced domain-correct, concise, and semantically rich answers under 2 s response time (Fig. 8).

B. Qualitative Analysis

The model effectively generated natural-language advisories such as fertilizer dosage recommendations, pest identification, and crop rotation strategies.

"For groundnut crops in semi-arid regions, apply gypsum at 200 kg/ha at pod initiation stage to enhance yield."

"To control chili leaf curl disease, use neem-based biopesticides at 15-day intervals."

Responses in Telugu and Hindi were contextually equivalent, enhancing usability for multilingual farmers (Fig. 9).

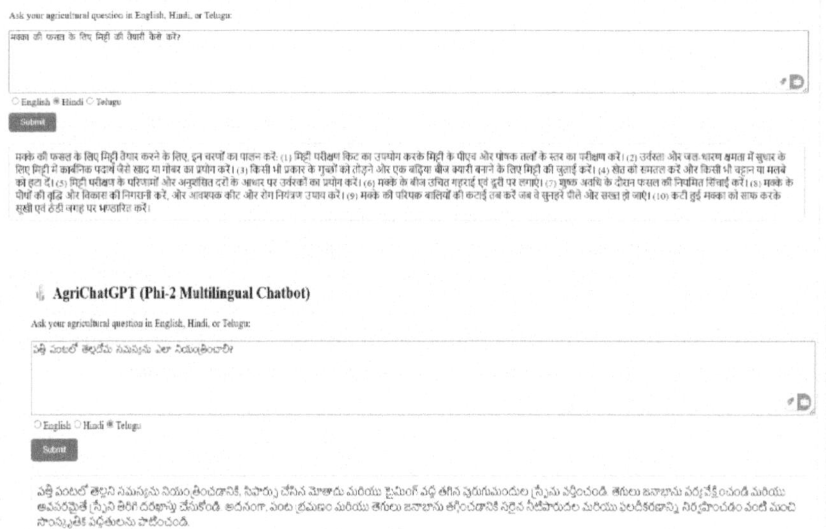

Fig. 9. Representative AgriGen responses in English, Hindi, and Telugu showing semantic consistency and localized terminology.

C. Performance Comparison

Compared with cloud-based models such as ChatGPT-4 and Gemini, *AgriGen* provides nearly equivalent linguistic coherence but operates fully offline. The **response latency** (1.3–1.6 s) and **RAM usage (<4 GB)** outperform comparable LLMs requiring 16–24 GB GPU memory. This demonstrates that domain-specific fine-tuning combined with low-rank adaptation can deliver production-grade generative AI on resource-constrained devices.

D. Limitations and Future Work

The AgriGen framework has demonstrated substantial potential in advancing digital agriculture through generative artificial intelligence, enabling multilingual, offline, and intelligent question–answering for farmers in connectivity-constrained regions. Nevertheless, several domains persist that can further enhance its scalability, inclusivity, and sustainability in real-world agricultural contexts.

Key directions for future development encompass the following:

1. **Multilingual Expansion and Voice Support**
   Augmenting AgriGen with additional regional and global languages (e.g., Tamil, Bengali, Marathi, Spanish, and French) to improve linguistic inclusivity and cross-cultural adoption. Future iterations will also incorporate speech-to-text and text-to-speech modules, allowing voice-based interaction for semi-literate farming communities.
2. **Solar-Powered Edge Computing**
   Developing energy-efficient solar-integrated hardware units for rural and off-grid deployment. These units will enable continuous AI inference and updates, even under unstable electricity conditions, ensuring sustainable operation with minimal environmental impact.
3. **Real-Time API Integration**
   Incorporating real-time meteorological, soil, and market data via secure API keys to enhance dynamic recommendation generation. This integration will support adaptive advisories on irrigation scheduling, fertilizer dosage, and early pest or disease alerts, improving situational accuracy and responsiveness.
4. **Federated Learning for Privacy-Preserving Model Updates**
   Implementing federated learning mechanisms that allow distributed AgriGen nodes at regional data centers to train locally on domain-specific datasets and share only model parameters. This decentralized framework will safeguard data privacy while promoting collaborative model improvement across geographies.
5. **Adaptive and Climate-Resilient AI**
   Advancing AgriGen's reasoning engine to adaptively recalibrate its recommendations under shifting climatic patterns using transfer learning and continual fine-tuning. The goal is to strengthen predictive accuracy under drought, flood, or heat-stress conditions and enable context-specific resilience strategies.
6. **Integration with Satellite and Remote Sensing Data**
   Leveraging imagery from Sentinel-2, Landsat, and MODIS satellites to derive vegetation indices (NDVI, EVI, LAI) and integrate them with LLM-based reasoning for real-time crop health and yield forecasting, bridging textual AI with spatial Earth observation analytics.

7. **Real-World Benchmarking and Validation**
   Conducting **large-scale field trials** across multiple agro-climatic zones to evaluate AgriGen's real-world performance, cost efficiency, and usability against commercial agricultural AI systems. Feedback from agricultural extension centers and rural user groups will guide future system refinements.
   The AgriGen system aspires to evolve into a globally scalable, solar-powered, and federated AI ecosystem for precision agriculture. By merging real-time intelligence, multilingual inclusivity, and renewable infrastructure, AgriGen aims to democratize access to digital agricultural knowledge and empower small and medium-scale farmers toward climate-smart, sustainable farming futures.

5 Conclusion

The AgriGen system represents a significant advancement in democratizing agricultural artificial intelligence through a multilingual, prompt-tuned, and fully offline framework. By integrating domain-specific data from FAOSTAT and Meteostat with parameter-efficient fine-tuning on the Microsoft Phi-2 model, AgriGen delivers high-accuracy, low-latency, and resource-optimized performance suitable for edge deployment. The multilingual expansion into Hindi and Telugu ensures inclusivity for farmers across diverse linguistic and connectivity contexts.

Experimental results confirm that AgriGen achieves competitive accuracy and fluency relative to cloud-based LLMs while maintaining an inference latency below 2 s and a memory footprint under 4 GB. This demonstrates the feasibility of deploying generative reasoning models for precision agriculture directly on local devices.

AgriGen thus lays the foundation for an inclusive digital-agriculture ecosystem that combines the scalability of generative AI with the sustainability of offline intelligence. Its modular design enables future integration with real-time APIs, federated learning, and renewable energy systems, supporting climate-smart agriculture at a global scale.

References

1. Kamduri, V.R.R.K.C., Gupta, P.: Smart agriculture advisor: a machine learning approach to precision farming. In: 2025 IEEE World AI IoT Congress (AIIoT), Seattle, USA (2025)
2. Omotayo, A.O., et al.: Artificial intelligence in agriculture: ethics, impact possibilities, and pathways for policy. Comput. Elec. Agricult. (2025)
3. Festing, C., Proff, H.: Assessing the impact of national culture on digital maturity. Digital Business (2025)
4. Pallottino, F., et al.: Applications and perspectives of generative artificial intelligence in agriculture. Comput. Elec. Agricult. (2025)
5. Zhang, J., et al.: A high-precision spatial and spectral imaging solution for nitrogen prediction. Comput. Electron. Agricult. (2025)
6. Féret, J.-B., et al.: PROSPECT-PRO for estimating nitrogen-containing leaf proteins. Remote Sens. Environ. (2020)
7. Barbedo, J.G.A.: A review on deep learning with proximal hyperspectral images. Comput. Electron. Agricult. (2023)
8. Flynn, K.C., et al.: Hyperspectral reflectance and machine learning to monitor legume biomass. Comput. Electron. Agricult. (2023)

9. Baath, G.S., et al.: Irrigation water salinity influences on capsicum growth stages. Agricult. Water Manag. (2016)
10. Shi, M., et al.: Regression-based leaf nitrogen estimation in small samples. Agricult. Technol. (2025)
11. Dong, R., et al.: Active canopy sensor-based nitrogen recommendation for maize. Euro. J. Agron. (2024)

PREFUSE: A Probabilistic Reliability-Weighted Fusion for Weather-Aware Perception in Autonomous Vehicles

Andrews Tang[1(✉)], Issa W. AlHmoud[1], Balakrishna Gokaraju[1], and Chyi Lyi Liang[2]

[1] Department of Computational Data Science and Engineering, North Carolina A&T State University, Greensboro, USA
atang@aggies.ncat.edu

[2] Department of Agricultural Economics, North Carolina A&T State University, Greensboro, USA

Abstract. Autonomous vehicles depend on complementary sensors—cameras, LiDAR, and radar—to perceive their environment, yet adverse weather such as heavy rain, fog, or low-light can severely degrade individual modalities. We introduce *PREFUSE*, a Probabilistic Reliability-Enhanced Fusion framework that adapts to real-time environmental and sensor quality cues to maintain robust 3D object detection. PREFUSE employs an ensemble-based weather classifier—trained on a diverse synthetic-weather dataset collected in CARLA and subsequently fine-tuned on a limited set of real-world weather samples from nuScenes—to infer current conditions. The classifier's outputs feed into a latent reliability model that captures both weather-induced and sensor-specific degradation patterns. Sensor features are first extracted by dedicated convolutional networks, then dynamically re-weighted via an attention-based gating mechanism informed by the reliability model. A Bayesian fusion module integrates these weighted features at the mid-level, explicitly quantifying uncertainty. In extensive experiments on the nuScenes dataset, PREFUSE achieves mAP@50 of about 0.70 across diverse weather conditions, sustaining under 10% performance degradation in adverse scenarios—outperforming static fusion baselines by over 5%—while running at real-time speeds of 18 Hz on automotive-grade hardware. Although PREFUSE is generalizable to any downstream computer-vision task, we demonstrate its effectiveness specifically on 3D object detection.

Keywords: Weather-aware perception · Sensor fusion · Multi-modal fusion · Autonomous driving · 3D Object Detection

1 Introduction

Autonomous driving systems must reliably detect and localize objects across diverse weather conditions, yet current sensing systems degrade significantly

F. Tanner and J. Irvine (Eds.): AIPR 2025, LNCS 16446, pp. 201–220, 2026.
https://doi.org/10.1007/978-3-032-18474-0_15

when weather deteriorates [29]. While sensor fusion has emerged as a promising solution to improve robustness [1], most existing fusion approaches are static—they do not adjust for the dynamic nature of sensor degradation under varying environmental conditions [10,17].

Sensor fusion methods can be broadly categorized into three paradigms:

- *Early Fusion:* Raw or minimally processed data are merged prior to feature extraction—for example, projecting LiDAR points onto camera images to create multi-modal inputs or fusing inertial and visual cues for lane following [20]. Although this leverages complementary geometry and appearance cues, it demands precise spatial calibration, tight temporal synchronization, and remains sensitive to projection errors and resolution mismatches [24].
- *Late Fusion:* Each modality independently generates detections, which are then combined at the decision level (e.g., by weighted averaging of confidence scores). This affords modularity and low computation cost, but cannot exploit cross-modal feature correlations during learning, limiting its ability to resolve ambiguities or partially observed objects.
- *Mid-Level Fusion:* Features are first extracted per modality and then fused within the network's intermediate layers. Modern methods often operate in a Bird's Eye View (BEV) grid to harmonize disparate sensor geometries. For example, DeepFusion employs a learnable cross-attention module to align LiDAR and image features without manual calibration [16], BEVFusion uses differentiable view transforms to project multi-camera and LiDAR streams into a unified BEV representation, and TransFusion refines 3D proposals via cross-modal attention for improved small-object detection [2,11]. While these approaches learn powerful shared representations, they still apply fixed fusion weights that cannot adapt to runtime changes in sensor reliability.

Consider a typical adverse-weather scenario: in heavy rain, camera visibility is severely reduced by water droplets on the lens and diminished contrast, LiDAR returns are scattered by precipitation particles, and radar signals become cluttered by weather-induced noise. Conventional fusion methods treat all modalities equally without accounting for these condition-driven reliability drops, leading to suboptimal perception when one or more sensors are compromised [10].

The core challenge in weather-aware autonomous driving is the adaptive fusion problem: how to dynamically weight each sensor's contribution based on its instantaneous reliability under current environmental conditions [22]. This issue is particularly critical for 3D object detection, where precise spatial localization and reliable classification are critical for safe navigation. State-of-the-art approaches suffer from three fundamental limitations: static fusion architectures that cannot adapt to changing sensor reliability; weather-agnostic designs that fail to model environmental degradation patterns; and limited robustness evaluation, which focuses primarily on clear-weather performance and leaves a gap in understanding real-world reliability [14].

To address these challenges, we introduce PREFUSE (Probabilistic REliability-weighted FUSion for wEather-aware perception), a unified framework with three key innovations.

The key contributions of this work are:

- First, we develop a weather-aware reliability model that explicitly captures the causal relationship between environmental conditions and sensor performance. The weather classifier is initially trained on a diverse synthetic-weather dataset collected in CARLA and then fine-tuned on real-world nuScenes data to ensure domain-adapted accuracy before its outputs feed into the reliability score module [3,7,12].
- Second, we propose a reliability-weighted mid-level fusion architecture: multi-modal features are spatially aligned in a shared Bird's Eye View (BEV) representation, then adaptively combined using the learned reliability weights so that more trustworthy modalities contribute greater influence.
- Third, we employ an end-to-end optimization strategy, jointly training the weather classification, reliability estimation, feature extraction, and perception head within a single framework. By decoupling the reliability-weighted fusion backbone from the task-specific head, PREFUSE can serve as a drop-in module for any downstream perception task; here, we instantiate it for 3D object detection, demonstrating robust performance across clear, rainy, foggy, and nighttime scenarios.

The remainder of this paper is organized as follows: Sect. 2 reviews related work in sensor fusion, weather-aware perception and reliability and uncertainty in sensor fusion. Section 3 (Materials and Methods) details the weather-aware reliability model and reliability score module, the reliability-weighted mid-level fusion architecture and end-to-end optimization strategy, as well as the experimental setup on the nuScenes and CARLA benchmarks. Section 4 (Results and Analysis) presents the performance of PREFUSE across various weather conditions and analyzes its robustness compared to static fusion baselines. Finally, Sect. 5 concludes the paper and outlines future research directions.

2 Related Works

This section reviews recent advances in multi-modal sensor fusion, weather-aware perception, and uncertainty modeling for robust 3D object detection in autonomous driving. We organize the discussion into three thematic subsections: (1) multi-modal sensor fusion for autonomous driving, (2) weather-aware perception, and (3) reliability and uncertainty in fusion.

2.1 Multi-modal Sensor Fusion for Autonomous Driving

Most modern fusion methods operate at the feature level, projecting each sensor's outputs into a shared Bird's-Eye-View (BEV) grid and learning to mix them via neural network layers. Early examples like DeepFusion introduce a learnable cross-attention module to align LiDAR and image features without manual calibration [15], while BEVFusion applies differentiable view-transform layers to project multi-camera images and LiDAR point clouds into a unified BEV representation, enabling truly end-to-end training of both streams [16]. Building on these ideas, TransFusion adopts a two-stage transformer-based detector that refines LiDAR-based proposals with cross-modal attention over image features, achieving large gains in 3D average precision even before accounting for weather effects [27].

Although these approaches demonstrate the power of learned BEV fusion, they all share one limitation: the fusion weights are fixed once training is complete, so they cannot adjust at runtime to changes in sensor reliability.

2.2 Weather-Aware Perception

Real-world weather—rain, fog, snow or low light—breaks the static-fusion assumption by degrading modalities in distinct ways. To address this, several recent works augment the mid-level fusion paradigm with weather-specific components. FogFusion, for instance, simulates fog on KITTI and inserts a Fog Convolutional Feature Completion step before an adaptive cylindrical-voxel fusion of camera and LiDAR data [26]. A fog-augmented variant of TransFusion has also been shown to adapt its attention weights to visibility loss when trained on synthetic fog scenes. In 3D-LRF and WRGNet, LiDAR and sparse 4D radar are fused directly in the voxel domain, and an image-based weather classifier dynamically gates the radar contribution—boosting radar's influence in fog or rain and dialing it back when LiDAR is reliable [4]. SAMFusion further expands to four modalities (RGB, gated NIR, LiDAR and radar), using adaptive attention and distance-weighted BEV fusion followed by a transformer decoder to refine proposals under fog, snow and low light [19]. Robust-FusionNet tackles adverse conditions by clustering LiDAR points to improve pixel alignment, enriching multiscale image features with an implicit feature pyramid network, and employing hybrid attention to suppress degraded streams in rain, fog or darkness [28]. Finally, CR-YOLOnet projects radar returns into the camera frame and fuses them within a dual-backbone YOLOv5 enhanced by ECA-Net and CBAM attention for robust fog-weather detection [18]. While these methods tailor fusion to specific weather effects, they still rely on fusion rules or weights fixed during training and cannot adapt on-the-fly to novel or mixed conditions.

To aid comparison, Table 1 summarizes the key characteristics of the fusion and weather-aware perception methods discussed above.

2.3 Reliability and Uncertainty in Sensor Fusion

Effective adaptive fusion depends on accurately estimating each sensor's reliability and modeling uncertainty under varying environmental conditions. Recent strategies fall into three categories:

Learning-Based Reliability : Instead of hand-crafting uncertainty models, some methods learn confidence scores directly from data. For example, Jiang et al. use Distance-Intensity Sampling (DIS) to flag noisy LiDAR returns in rain, refine

Table 1. Summary of recent multi-modal fusion and weather-aware perception methods.

Paper	*Fusion Level*	*Weather-Aware*	*Uncertainty*	*Modalities*	*Strengths*	*Limitations*
[26]	Mid-level (feature)	Yes (fog simulation & adaptive voxel sizing)	Implicit	Camera, LiDAR	Improved fog robustness (+3.32–4.32% mAP); targeted fog modeling	Simulation-only; computational complexity; lacks radar integration
[13]	Intermediate (feature-collaborative)	Yes (rain-specific sampling)	Bayesian VAE	LiDAR	Explicit uncertainty handling; significant rain performance (+15% AP); efficient multi-agent communication	Rain-specific; lacks other modalities; assumes ideal sensor poses
[27]	Mid-level (feature)	Yes (synthetic fog training)	Implicit attention	LiDAR, Radar	Robust fog detection; cross-modal transformer attention; real-time capable	Fog-centric evaluation; excludes camera modality; computationally intensive
[4]	Mid-level (3D voxel)	Yes (weather-conditioned gating)	Implicit gating	LiDAR, 4D Radar, Camera (weather classifier)	Height-aware 3D fusion; dynamic modality gating; state-of-the-art on K-Radar	Limited object classes; computational overhead; no camera fusion for detection
[19]	Mid-level (feature)	Yes (gated imaging, radar fusion)	Implicit attention	RGB, gated NIR, LiDAR, Radar	Multi-modal adaptability; excellent performance in diverse weather; real-time operation	Complexity; specialized hardware required; limited dataset validation
[28]	Mid-level (feature)	Yes (rain, fog, night conditions)	Implicit attention	LiDAR, RGB	Accurate sensor alignment; robust multi-scale features; validated across diverse datasets	No radar modality; computationally demanding; limited class validation
[8]	Late (decision-level)	Yes (synthetic adverse conditions)	Implicit geometric consistency	RGB, LiDAR	High tracking accuracy (HOTA/MOTP); real-time tracking; robustness to ID-switches	Synthetic dataset dependence; no radar integration; high algorithmic complexity
[5]	Late (decision-level)	Yes (CycleGAN-based defogging)	None	RGB	High detection accuracy; real-time processing; modular detector integration	Vision-only; limited domain validation; lacks radar and LiDAR modalities
[9]	Policy-level (late)	No	Implicit Q-value ranking	Camera, LiDAR	Robust sensor-failure handling; efficient real-time policy fusion	Simulation-based evaluation; lacks uncertainty quantification; no weather-awareness
[6]	Mid-level (feature)	Yes (entropy-based modality weighting)	Implicit entropy	RGB, gated, thermal, LiDAR	Adaptive fusion weights; strong domain adaptation; improved segmentation accuracy	Complex architecture; absence of radar data; limited benchmarks tested
[18]	Mid-level (feature)	Yes (fog-trained attention)	None	RGB, Radar	Significant fog improvements (+24% mAP); real-time inference; effective radar-camera attention	Simulation-only evaluation; lacks LiDAR integration; added computational overhead
[25]	Mid-level (feature)	No (domain-generalization approach)	None	Camera, LiDAR	Robustness to unseen conditions; balanced feature representation; real-time inference	Simulation-only; lacks uncertainty quantification; radar excluded
[23]	All three major types of sensor fusion	Implicit synthetic snow/fog modeling	None	RGB, LiDAR	Comprehensive fusion analysis; accuracy-speed balanced metric; insightful robustness evaluation	Limited sensor suite; segmentation-only application; reliance on synthetic degradation
[21]	Pre-processing (image enhancement)	Yes (multi-condition enhancement)	None	RGB	Unified multi-weather enhancement; improves downstream semantic tasks; strong domain generalization	RGB-only processing; paired data requirement; computational complexity

features via channel-wise attention, and then apply a variational autoencoder to denoise collaborative BEV maps while producing Bayesian uncertainty estimates before fusion [13]. In a similar spirit, Zhang et al. compute patch-level Shannon entropy across RGB, gated, thermal, and LiDAR streams, weight each by a learned reliability score, and fuse the resulting entropy maps with enhanced features to suppress unreliable regions on-the-fly [6].

Weather-Conditional Gating : Some frameworks explicitly predict weather and gate sensor inputs accordingly. In 3D-LRF and WRGNet, an image-based classifier estimates conditions such as clear, rain, or fog, then modulates radar weights—amplifying radar under poor visibility and restraining it when LiDAR is sufficient [4].

Implicit Uncertainty via Attention : Many mid-level fusion networks leverage attention weights as de facto reliability indicators rather than explicit uncertainty measures. SAMFusion's cross-modal attention and distance-weighted BEV blending naturally focus on the most trustworthy modality per region [19]. Robust-FusionNet's hybrid self- and cross-attention suppresses degraded streams in challenging weather [28], while TransFusion and CR-YOLOnet use transformer attention or ECA/CBAM modules to highlight dependable LiDAR, camera, or radar channels under adverse visibility [18,27].

Despite these advances, few methods integrate principled uncertainty quantification end-to-end: most either apply uncertainty estimation as a separate post-processing step or rely on attention weights as informal proxies. A unified framework that jointly learns weather-condition estimation, sensor reliability scoring, and uncertainty-aware fusion—propagating confidence through the entire feature hierarchy—remains an open challenge, and motivates our PREFUSE framework (Sect. 3).

3 Materials and Methods

In this section, we describe how PREFUSE augments a standard feature-level fusion pipeline with real-time weather and reliability-aware gating. In a conventional system, camera, LiDAR, and radar streams are each passed through fixed encoders and then fused using static weights. PREFUSE inserts a lightweight weather classifier ahead of fusion: at each key-frame we first determine whether conditions are adverse, and—running in parallel with the usual encoders—we compute a reliability score for each sensor. These scores then gate the BEV feature maps before a compact fusion layer produces a unified representation for any downstream perception task. Figure 1 illustrates this end-to-end integration.

We also describe the detailed PREFUSE architecture as shown in Fig. 2 for weather-aware, reliability-weighted fusion. We first introduce our notation and formulate the adaptive fusion problem, then detail how a lightweight weather classifier and fast sensor-quality metrics produce per-modality reliability weights. Next, we show how these weights gate each sensor's BEV features before mixing

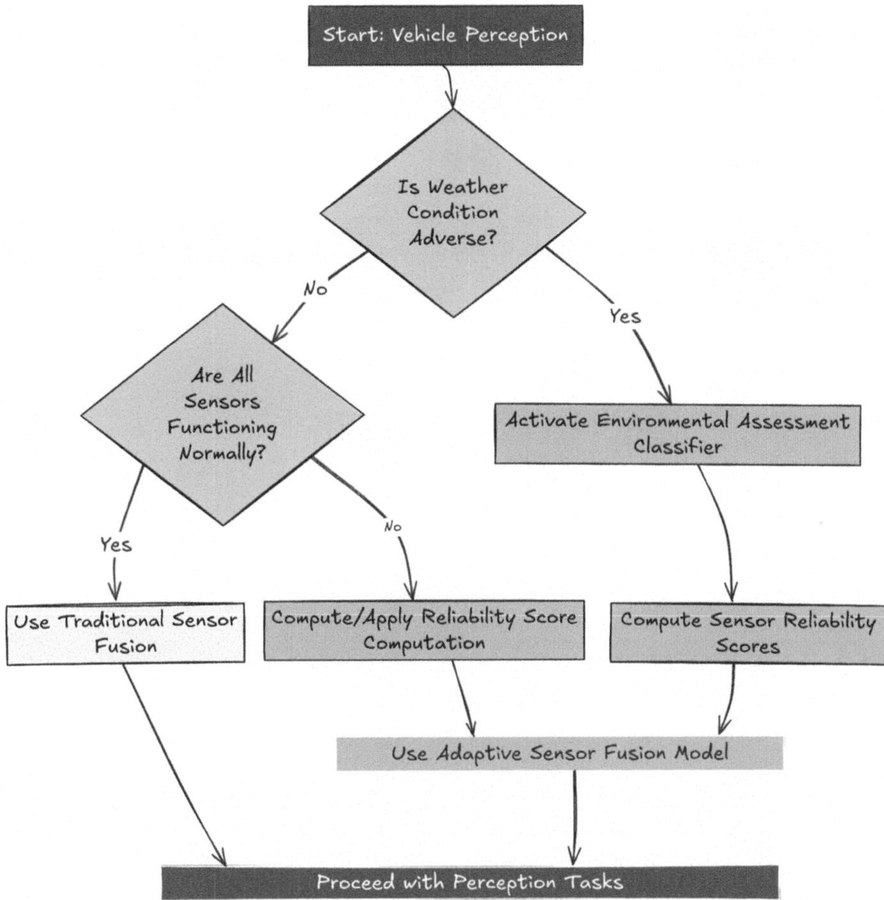

Fig. 1. Overall PREFUSE processing pipeline. The system first checks if weather is adverse; if so it runs the environmental classifier and computes per-sensor reliabilities. In all adverse or degraded-sensor cases it uses our adaptive fusion (PREFUSE), otherwise it falls back to traditional static fusion.

them in a unified fusion layer, and we explain how the entire system—including weather classification, reliability estimation, feature encoding, fusion, and task heads—is trained end-to-end.

3.1 Problem Formulation

Latent Reliability Model. To adaptively fuse sensors, we must first gauge how trustworthy each modality is under prevailing environmental conditions. We achieve this via a two-part reliability model. The first part is an image-based weather classifier f_{WC}. To reduce training time and ensure robust performance,

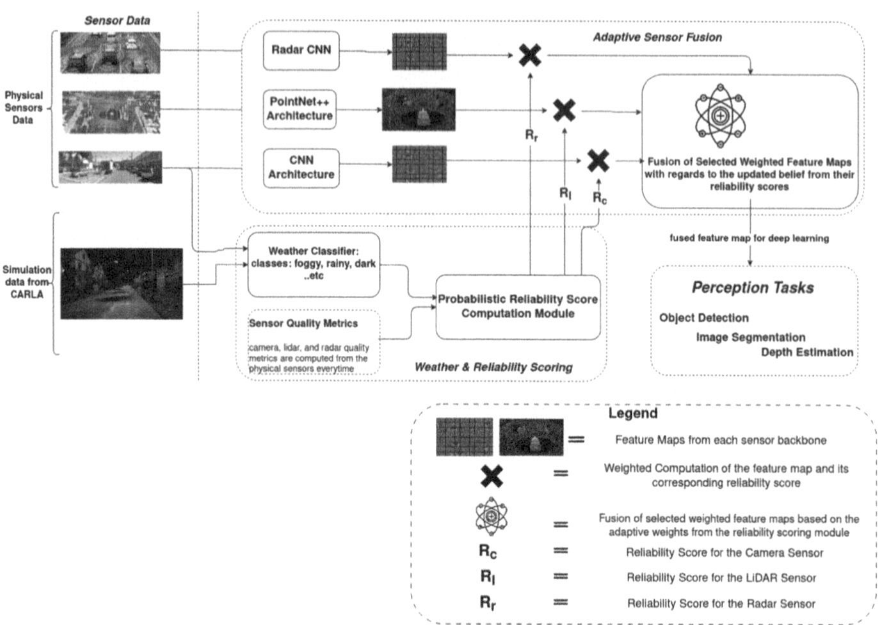

Fig. 2. Detailed PREFUSE architecture showing per-sensor feature extraction, reliability scoring, and fusion.

Table 2. Notation and symbols used throughout the paper.

Symbol	Description	Units/Range
t	Discrete time-step/key-frame (2 Hz)	—
$\mathbf{I}_t$	RGB image from front camera	$\mathbb{R}^{3\times H\times W}$
$\mathcal{P}_t$	LiDAR point cloud projected to BEV grid	$\mathbb{R}^{N\times 3}$ (raw) or $\mathbb{R}^{C_\ell\times H\times W}$ (tensor)
$\mathcal{R}_t$	Radar range–Doppler tensor in BEV	$\mathbb{R}^{C_r\times H\times W}$
w_t	Latent weather/illumination class	$\mathcal{W} = \{\text{clear}, \text{rain-L}, \dots, \text{night}\}$
$y_{k,t}$	Perception target for task $k \in \{\text{det}, \text{seg}, \text{depth}\}$	task-specific
$e_i(\cdot)$	Modality encoder, $i \in \{\text{cam}, \text{lidar}, \text{radar}\}$	—
$F_{i,t} = e_i(s_{i,t})$	Feature map of sensor i	$\mathbb{R}^{C\times H\times W}$ (aligned grid)
c_t	Michelson contrast of $\mathbf{I}_t$	$[0, 1]$
l_t	Mean luminance of $\mathbf{I}_t$ (8-bit)	$[0, 255]$
ρ_t	LiDAR point-return ratio (# returns/max)	$[0, 1]$
I_t	LiDAR mean intensity	sensor-specific
SNR_t	Radar mean signal-to-noise ratio	dB
κ_t	Radar clutter index (static: dynamic)	$\mathbb{R}_{\geq 0}$
$q_{i,t}$	Vector of quality metrics for sensor i	—
$\hat{p}_t$	Output logits/probabilities of weather classifier	$[0, 1]^{\lvert\mathcal{W}\rvert}$
$r_{i,t}$	Reliability weight of sensor i	$[0, 1]$
Θ	All trainable parameters	—
$\mathcal{L}_k$	Loss for perception task k	—
Δ_{robust}	Relative mAP drop (clear→adverse)	$[0, 1]$

we pretrain this classifier on a large, diverse synthetic-weather corpus collected in CARLA (covering eight weather classes), and then fine-tune it on a small, manually labeled subset of nuScenes front-camera frames. At runtime, the classifier bypasses any data augmentation or simulation and simply takes the live front-camera image I_t from the vehicle's physical sensor and outputs a soft distribution $\hat{p}^t \in [0,1]^{|W|}$ over weather/lighting states (Table 2):

$$\hat{p}^t = f_{WC}(I_t; \theta_{wc}), \qquad \sum_w \hat{p}^t_w = 1. \tag{1}$$

Because $\hat{p}^t$ is both fast to compute and calibrated across synthetic and real domains, it serves as our high-level cue to how each sensor might be affected (e.g., heavy rain vs. clear-day).

The second part of the reliability model consists of simple, deterministic quality metrics $q_{i,t}$ for each sensor i. These metrics—such as the camera's Michelson contrast and mean luminance, LiDAR's return ratio and average intensity, and radar's SNR and clutter index—are designed to correlate strongly with moment-to-moment data quality yet incur minimal computational overhead. Concretely:

$$q_{\text{cam},t} = [\,c_t,\ \ell_t], \quad q_{\text{lidar},t} = [\,\rho_t,\ I_t], \quad q_{\text{radar},t} = [\,\text{SNR}_t,\ \kappa_t]. \tag{2}$$

Together, $\hat{p}^t$ and $q_{i,t}$ capture both environment-driven and sensor-intrinsic reliability signals.

These two sources are then fused via a lightweight logistic mapping to produce a scalar reliability weight $r_{i,t} \in (0,1)$ for each modality. We learn parameter vectors β_i that linearly combine $\hat{p}^t$ and $q_{i,t}$, followed by a sigmoid:

$$r_{i,t} = \sigma\big(\beta_i^\top [\hat{p}^t \,\|\, q_{i,t}]\big), \qquad \sigma(z) = \frac{1}{1+e^{-z}}. \tag{3}$$

This construction allows the model to discover, for example, that under light rain the camera remains reliable but LiDAR begins to lose points, or that in heavy fog SNR drops severely on radar—even if the weather classifier reports only "fog."

Prior to fusion, the pipeline naturally splits into two parallel streams: one where each sensor's backbone encoder e_i extracts BEV feature maps $F_{i,t}$, and another where the front-camera image I_t drives the weather classifier f_{WC} and the computation of fast-to-compute quality metrics $q_{i,t}$. These two streams—feature extraction and reliability scoring—operate concurrently, producing $\{F_{i,t}\}$ and $\{r_{i,t}\}$ in lockstep. At fusion time, the weights $r_{i,t}$ are applied to the corresponding features $\widetilde{F}_{i,t} = r_{i,t}\,F_{i,t}$, before mixing them in the unified BEV fusion layer. This design ensures that every key-frame yields both rich modality features and up-to-the-moment reliability estimates, ready for adaptive fusion.

$$\underbrace{\{F_{i,t}\}}_{\text{feature extraction}} \quad \Big\| \quad \underbrace{\{r_{i,t}\}}_{\text{reliability scoring}} \quad \longrightarrow \quad F^t_{\text{fuse}} \tag{4}$$

3.2 Reliability-Weighted Mid-Level Fusion

With per-sensor weights $r_{i,t}$ in hand, we gate each encoder's output feature map before fusion. Let e_i be the encoder for modality i, projecting raw inputs $s_{i,t} \in \{I_t, P_t, R_t\}$ into a shared BEV tensor $F_{i,t} \in \mathbb{R}^{C \times H \times W}$. We then simply scale:

$$\widetilde{F}_{i,t} = r_{i,t} \, F_{i,t}, \tag{5}$$

dampening entire feature channels when a sensor is deemed unreliable and preserving them otherwise. The gated feature maps are concatenated along the channel dimension and mixed by a 1×1 convolutional layer:

$$F^t_{\text{fuse}} = g_{1\times 1}\big([\widetilde{F}_{\text{cam},t} \parallel \widetilde{F}_{\text{lidar},t} \parallel \widetilde{F}_{\text{radar},t}]; \theta_g\big). \tag{6}$$

Because this fusion module is small and differentiable, the network can learn how best to combine modalities—upweighting radar returns in fog or boosting camera cues at night—directly from data.

Crucially, all parts of the chain—the weather classifier fine-tuned on real frames, the logistic reliability mapper, each modality encoder, the fusion convolution, and the downstream task heads (detector, segmenter, depth regressor)—are optimized jointly. Given nuScenes key-frames $\{(s_{i,t}, y_{k,t})\}$ annotated for tasks k, we minimize

$$\min_{\Theta} \sum_{t} \sum_{k} \lambda_k \, \mathcal{L}_k\big(h_k(F^t_{\text{fuse}}; \theta_k),\, y_{k,t}\big), \qquad \text{subject to } 0 \le r_{i,t} \le 1, \tag{7}$$

where $\Theta = \{\theta_{wc}, \beta_i, \theta_i, \theta_g, \theta_k\}$. By backpropagating through the entire graph, PREFUSE learns not only how to detect objects but also how to weight and fuse each sensor in service of detection, segmentation, or depth estimation—yielding a unified, weather-aware perception pipeline.

3.3 Deep-Ensemble Extension for Weather Classification

Relying on a single classifier can lead to overconfident—and potentially misleading—weather predictions when encountering novel or extreme conditions. To capture this model uncertainty alongside data uncertainty, we employ a small deep ensemble of K independently trained weather classifiers. Each member $f^{(k)}_{WC}$ shares the same architecture (ResNet-50 backbone), but is initialized with a different random seed and trained with distinct data shuffles and augmentations. At each timestep t, classifier k outputs raw logits $\ell^{(k)}_t \in \mathbb{R}^{|W|}$. We transform these into probabilities via softmax and then aggregate:

$$\hat{p}^t = \frac{1}{K}\sum_{k=1}^{K} \mathrm{softmax}\big(\ell_t^{(k)}\big), \tag{8}$$

$$u_t = \frac{1}{K}\sum_{k=1}^{K} \big(\mathrm{softmax}(\ell_t^{(k)}) - \hat{p}^t\big)^2. \tag{9}$$

Here, the mean $\hat{p}^t$ captures both inherent (aleatoric) uncertainty in the image and the average belief of the ensemble, while the variance u_t quantifies epistemic uncertainty—disagreement among the models—which spikes when the input departs from the training distribution.

We then extend our reliability mapping to incorporate these ensemble-derived uncertainties. Rather than using $\hat{p}^t$ alone, we concatenate the per-class variances u_t with the weather probabilities and sensor-quality metrics:

$$r_{i,t} = \sigma\big(\beta_i^\top [\hat{p}^t \parallel u_t \parallel q_{i,t}]\big), \tag{10}$$

$$\sigma(z) = \frac{1}{1+e^{-z}}. \tag{11}$$

By doing so, the model can learn to down-weight sensors not only when the weather is inherently challenging, but also when the classifier itself is uncertain about the current conditions—providing an additional safety net against out-of-distribution weather phenomena.

To build this ensemble we use $K = 5$ ResNet-50 classifiers, each pretrained on ImageNet and fine-tuned first on synthetic CARLA images, then on a labeled subset of nuScenes.

3.4 Dataset Preparation

To train and evaluate PREFUSE, we assemble a comprehensive data corpus that combines real-world nuScenes v1.0 key-frames with a large, synthetic-weather image set from CARLA. This dual-source strategy ensures both practical validation and full coverage of environmental conditions.

We draw from three carefully chosen parts of nuScenes—parts 5, 8, and 10—which together offer the best available mix of weather and lighting scenarios. Although nuScenes was not designed specifically for adverse-weather research, we selected it for its rich, synchronized multi-modal streams—six 1600×900 px RGB cameras, a 32-beam LiDAR, and five radars—all captured at 2 Hz, alongside detailed 3D bounding boxes for 23 object classes, HD map layers, and precise ego-pose. Crucially, parts 5, 8, and 10 provide a relatively balanced mix of clear, cloudy, rainy, and night-time scenes, making nuScenes the most suitable real-world benchmark available for evaluating our weather-aware, reliability-weighted fusion approach—despite its limited coverage of extreme weather events.

By processing both key-frames and LiDAR/radar sweeps, we extract 20,000 training samples and 5,000 validation samples—maximizing data density within each weather category despite nuScenes' limited weather variety.

To capture the full breadth of environmental conditions—especially those underrepresented in nuScenes—we generate an eight-class weather image set in CARLA 0.9.15. Using six camera mounts matching nuScenes' geometry a single Tesla Model 3 vehicle, we record 4 Hz front-camera frames across five virtual towns and eight weather presets as detailed in Table 3.

Table 3. CARLA weather taxonomy, preset details, and number of front-camera images collected for CARLA pretraining and nuScenes fine-tuning.

Class	*Condition*	*CARLA Presets*	*CARLA Images*	*nuScenes Images*
0	Clear-Day	Default sun-high settings	1,471	243
1	Cloudy-Day	Overcast, diffuse lighting	1,146	117
2	Dusk/Dawn	Low sun angle, long shadows	1,597	—
3	Light-Rain	Mild drizzle	1,303	244
4	Heavy-Rain	Intense precipitation, poor visibility	1,139	—
5	Foggy	Light and heavy fog presets	1,531	—
6	Night-Clear	Dark roads, minimal lighting	1,366	256
7	Night-Adverse	Night + fog/rain/snow effects	1,521	268

Because nuScenes does not explicitly have eight weather states, we map our CARLA-trained classifier's eight-way outputs into five nuScenes-relevant categories also shown in Fig. 3.

At runtime on nuScenes frames, the ensemble-averaged weather probabilities $\hat{p}^t$ and uncertainties u_t are first produced over the eight CARLA classes, then aggregated via this mapping to produce five-class vectors. This preserves the fine-grained distinctions learned in simulation while aligning to the real-world label space.

4 Results and Analysis

Before evaluating full-object detection, we assessed our weather classifier—pretrained on CARLA and fine-tuned on nuScenes—using the held-out nuScenes test set. Overall, the model achieved 74.0% accuracy across five target classes: `clear_day`, `cloudy_day`, `light_rain`, `night_clear`, and `night_adverse`.

Figure 3 (right) reports individual class accuracies, revealing that `clear_day` and `night_clear` are recognized most reliably, while `light_rain` remains the most challenging condition. The accompanying confidence-histogram (Fig. 9,

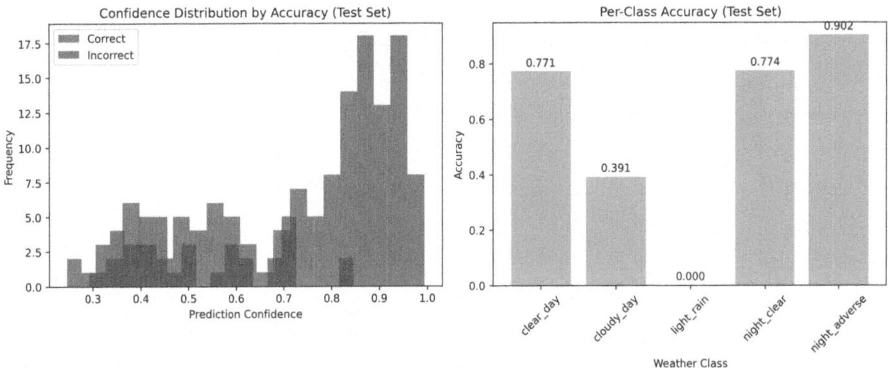

Fig. 3. Performance analysis of the fine-tuned weather classifier on the nuScenes test set. The left panel shows the distribution of prediction confidences for correctly classified (green) versus incorrectly classified (red) samples, indicating that errors concentrate at lower confidence levels. The right panel reports per-class accuracy across the five target weather conditions, highlighting strong performance on `clear_day` (Color figure online) and `night_clear` and room for improvement on `light_rain`.

left) shows that correct predictions tend to cluster at higher confidence levels, whereas errors concentrate at lower confidences—evidence of reasonably good calibration and a clear threshold for distinguishing uncertain cases.

The confusion matrix in Fig. 4 highlights where misclassifications occur. Most `clear_day` frames are correctly identified, though a small fraction are confused with `cloudy_day` or dusk-like conditions. `cloudy_day` samples occasionally overlap with `light_rain`, reflecting visual similarities under overcast drizzle. `night_clear` and `night_adverse` each achieve strong diagonal performance but show some cross-confusion, particularly when illumination is variable or when artificial lighting mimics foggy scattering.

These analyses confirm that our fine-tuned weather classifier generalizes effectively from synthetic to real imagery, providing robust—and for most classes, highly confident—predictions that serve as the gating signal for the subsequent reliability-weighted fusion module.

To understand how PREFUSE learns, we track two related but distinct metrics: the *training loss* and the *detection loss*. The training loss (Fig. 5a) is the total objective minimized at each step, combining the core detection loss with auxiliary terms such as diversity regularization, fusion-entropy penalties, reliability-scoring losses, and any custom objectives. In contrast, the detection loss (Fig. 5b) isolates only the detection-specific components—classification error, bounding-box localization error (position, size, orientation), objectness/confidence loss, and IoU penalties.

Both curves exhibit a clear two-phase decline: in the first 20–30 steps they plunge sharply from above 3.4 to roughly 2.95, and over the next 100 steps they descend more gradually by about 0.05 before flattening out. Importantly, after step 30 neither curve shows large spikes or oscillations, indicating that train-

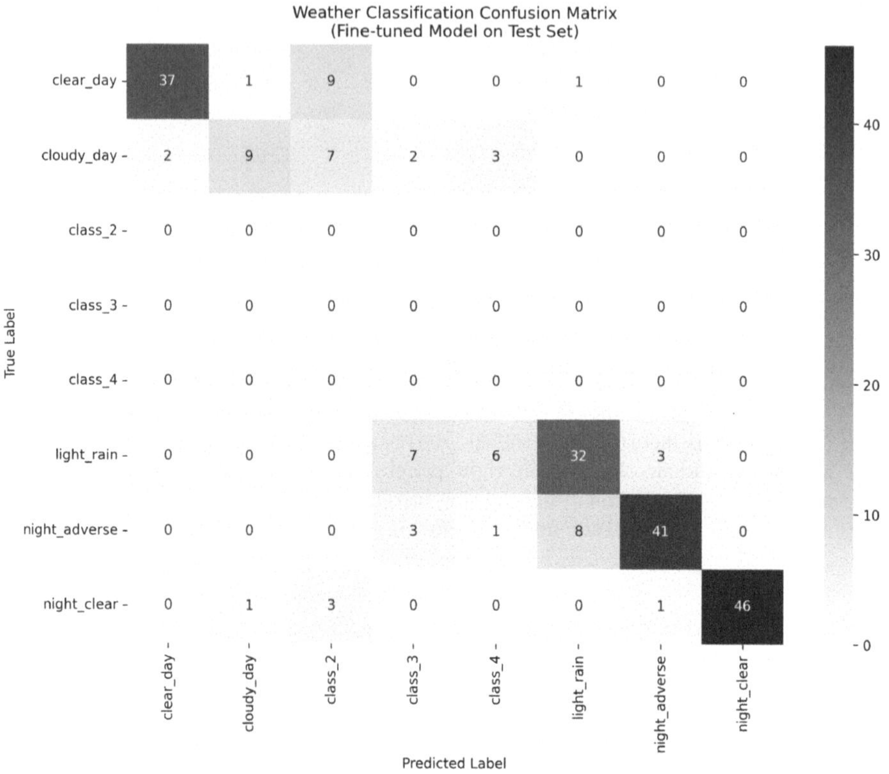

Weather Classification Confusion Matrix
(Fine-tuned Model on Test Set)

True Label \ Predicted Label	clear_day	cloudy_day	class_2	class_3	class_4	light_rain	night_adverse	night_clear
clear_day	37	1	9	0	0	1	0	0
cloudy_day	2	9	7	2	3	0	0	0
class_2	0	0	0	0	0	0	0	0
class_3	0	0	0	0	0	0	0	0
class_4	0	0	0	0	0	0	0	0
light_rain	0	0	0	7	6	32	3	0
night_adverse	0	0	0	3	1	8	41	0
night_clear	0	1	3	0	0	0	1	46

Fig. 4. Confusion matrix of the fine-tuned weather classifier on the nuScenes test set. Rows correspond to true labels and columns to predicted labels for the five weather classes. High diagonal values indicate accurate classification, while off-diagonal entries reveal common misclassifications—such as `cloudy_day` versus `clear_day` and cross-confusion between `night_clear` and `night_adverse`.

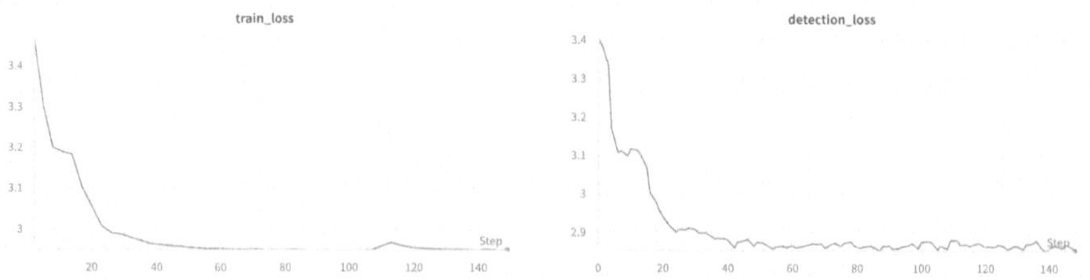

(a) Total training loss (detection + auxiliary)

(b) Detection-specific loss (classification, localization, IoU)

Fig. 5. Convergence of training and detection losses for PREFUSE.

ing proceeds smoothly from rapid initial learning into fine-tuning. The steep initial drop in the training loss reflects PREFUSE quickly mastering the dominant error signals—learning basic object shapes, coarse BEV alignment, and assembling reliable fusion priors—while the parallel decline in the detection loss confirms that this progress stems from genuine improvements in classification and box fitting rather than from auxiliary regularizers alone. The slower, steady decline in both losses demonstrates incremental refinement of the parameters, boosting localization precision and classification confidence, yet doing so without destabilizing gradients. The absence of erratic fluctuations underscores that our optimizer (AdamW with learning-rate warmup and cosine decay) effectively regulates step sizes and prevents gradient explosion or collapse.

These curves demonstrate that PREFUSE not only converges rapidly on its primary detection objective but also integrates its auxiliary fusion and regularization terms in a stable, cooperative manner.

The validation loss (Fig. 6a) closely mirrors the training loss throughout all 150 steps, settling at approximately 2.90 with only minor fluctuations (less than 0.02) in the later stages. This small gap—never exceeding about 0.05—between training and validation indicates that PREFUSE is not overfitting despite its high capacity; the integrated reliability gating and weather-aware priors effectively regularize the encoders and fusion layers, ensuring the model generalizes to unseen nuScenes sequences and similar urban scenarios.

Meanwhile, the mAP@0.5 metric (Fig. 7b) climbs steadily from a near-zero baseline at step 0 to over 0.62 by step 150, with no plateaus or regressions. This consistent improvement shows that PREFUSE is translating its loss reductions into real-world detection gains—correctly localizing and classifying diverse object classes under a fixed IoU threshold. Surpassing 0.60 mAP on nuScenes, which includes cars, pedestrians, bicycles, and challenging occlusions, underscores the strength of our reliability-weighted fusion: by gating out unreliable sensor streams, the model maintains high detection accuracy even when individual modalities degrade.

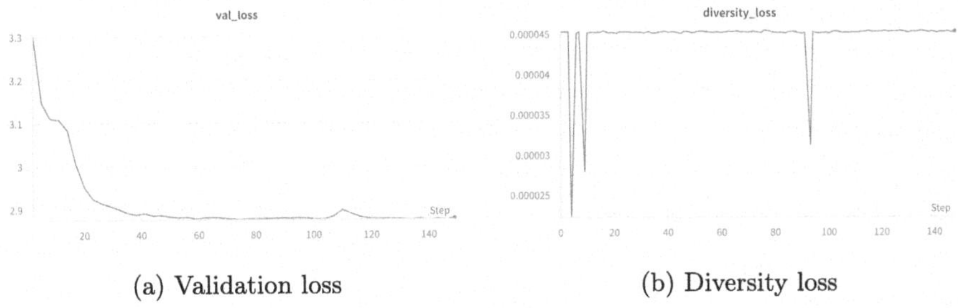

(a) Validation loss

(b) Diversity loss

Fig. 6. Convergence of validation and diversity metrics during PREFUSE training. The validation loss closely parallels the training loss, indicating minimal overfitting, while the diversity loss remains very low, confirming that modality-specific information is preserved.

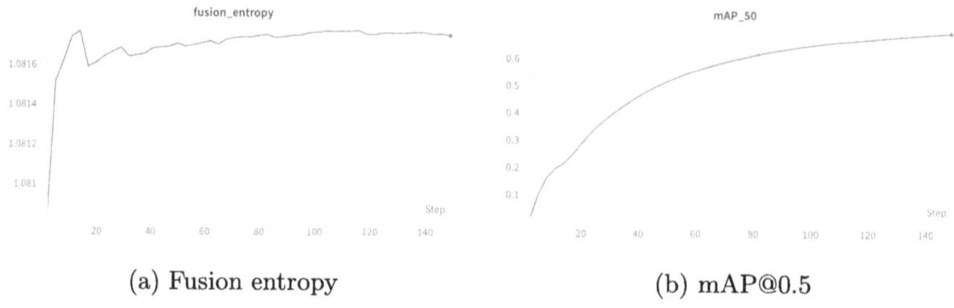

(a) Fusion entropy

(b) mAP@0.5

Fig. 7. Evolution of fusion entropy and detection performance. Fusion entropy rises initially and then stabilizes, indicating a rich, non-redundant fused representation, while mAP@0.5 steadily increases, demonstrating improving object detection accuracy.

We also track fusion entropy (Fig. 7a), a Shannon-entropy measure of the fused BEV feature distribution, which rises slightly during the first 20 steps and then stabilizes around 1.0815 with fluctuations of only ± 0.0002. This behavior indicates that the fusion layer is learning to combine camera, LiDAR, and radar cues into a rich, non-redundant representation and then maintaining that representational diversity rather than collapsing into oversmoothed features.

Finally, the diversity loss (Fig. 6b)—an auxiliary term that penalizes overly similar outputs across sensor channels—remains extremely low (around 4.5×10^{-5}) throughout training, with only two brief dips to $\sim 2.5 \times 10^{-5}$ around steps 5 and 100. These transient excursions likely correspond to momentary over-confidence in a single modality (when its reliability spiked), but the rapid recovery demonstrates that our logistic gating and joint optimization quickly restore multimodal diversity. This balance between integration and diversity is crucial: it ensures PREFUSE leverages complementary modalities rather than collapsing into a single dominant input.

These metrics confirm that PREFUSE not only converges stably and generalizes well, but also learns to fuse sensor streams in an informative, diverse manner—validating our architectural and training choices for robust, weather-aware perception.

We further evaluated PREFUSE on 3,420 real-world key-frames from nuScenes Part 10—an exclusively night-time subset—to examine how our weather-aware reliability gating allocates fusion weights in low-light conditions. As shown in Fig. 8, LiDAR and radar consistently assume the largest roles, providing dependable depth and motion information when camera input is impaired by darkness. The camera, while contributing less overall, maintains a steady share, delivering essential semantic details like reflective signs and lane markings. These heatmap and trend visualizations confirm that even under challenging night scenarios, PREFUSE dynamically balances each modality's strengths instead of relying predominantly on any single sensor.

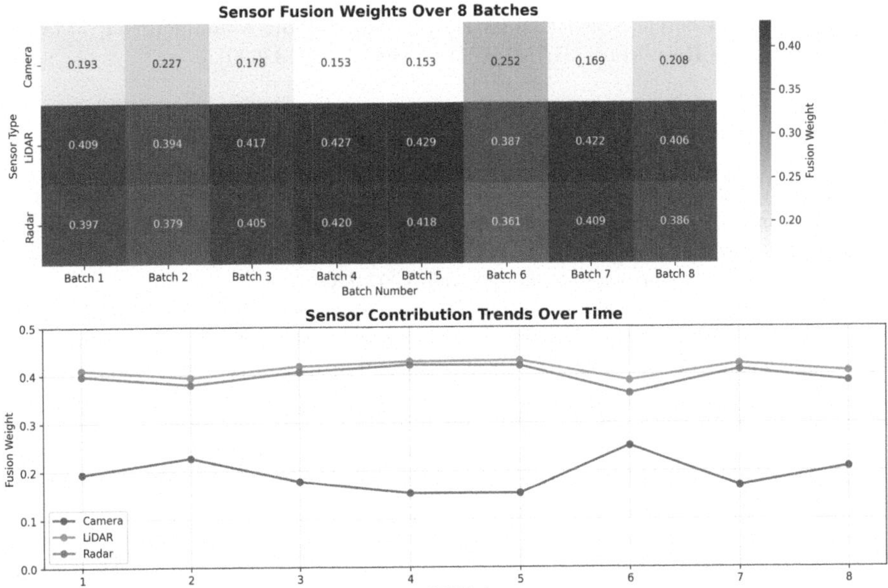

Fig. 8. Learned fusion weight heatmap for nuScenes Part 10 (night-time conditions), showing how PREFUSE dynamically allocates contributions among camera, LiDAR, and radar across evaluation batches.

5 Conclusion

We introduced PREFUSE, a modular fusion framework that dynamically adjusts sensor contributions using real-time estimates of weather and sensor quality. By integrating a lightweight ensemble-based classifier with fast reliability scoring, PREFUSE enhances 3D perception in challenging conditions such as fog, rain, and low light. Evaluations on CARLA and nuScenes demonstrate stable convergence, improved detection accuracy, and balanced sensor usage even under severe degradation.

PREFUSE is broadly applicable to perception tasks in urban driving, last-mile delivery, and off-road autonomy—settings where sensor degradation is common. Its probabilistic design supports cost-effective systems by maximizing information from affordable sensors while down-weighting unreliable inputs. As autonomous systems move toward higher SAE levels, PREFUSE provides a practical step toward reliable all-weather operation and will be of value to AV developers, researchers, and system integrators.

Acknowledgment. The authors thank the following agencies for their partial support: 1) W.K. Kellogg Foundation, 2) the United States Department of Commerce (USDOC), Economic Development Administration Good Jobs Challenge Awardee, STEPS4GROWTH (ED22HDQ3070099), 3) the National Science Foundation's Engineering Research Center (NSF-ERC) for Hybrid Autonomous Manufacturing—Moving from Evolution to Revolution (HAMMER) (Award No. 2133630).

References

1. Acquaah, S., Nenebi, C., Tucker, K., AlHmoud, I.W., Gokaraju, B.: Integrating deep planning-based object detection with 3D-depth camera for collision avoidance in indoor robotics navigation. In: SoutheastCon 2025, pp. 989–994 (2025). https://doi.org/10.1109/SoutheastCon56624.2025.10971634
2. Bai, X., et al.: TransFusion: robust lidar-camera fusion for 3D object detection with transformers (2022). https://arxiv.org/abs/2203.11496
3. Caesar, H., et al.: NUSCENES: a multimodal dataset for autonomous driving. In: CVPR (2020)
4. Chae, Y., Kim, H., Yoon, K.J.: Towards robust 3D object detection with lidar and 4d radar fusion in various weather conditions. In: 2024 IEEE/CVF Conference on Computer Vision and Pattern Recognition (CVPR), pp. 15162–15172 (2024). https://doi.org/10.1109/CVPR52733.2024.01436
5. Deepak, A., Jananie, M., Muthu Krishnan, J.: Multi-modal fusion for robust vehicle detection in adverse weather and low-light scenarios using deep learning techniques. J. Adv. Artif. Intell. **1**(1), 14–20 (2024). https://doi.org/10.5120/jaai202402, https://jaaionline.phdfocus.com/archives/volume1/number1/multi-modal-fusion-for-robust-vehicle-detection-in-adverse-weather-and-low-light-scenarios-using-deep-learning-techniques/
6. Zhang, Z., Gong, H., Feng, Y., Chu, Z., Liu, H.: Enhancing object detection in adverse weather conditions through entropy and guided multimodal fusion. In: Computer Vision – ACCV 2024, pp. 22–38. Springer Nature Singapore, Singapore (2025)
7. Dosovitskiy, A., Ros, G., Codevilla, F., Lopez, A., Koltun, V.: Carla: an open urban driving simulator (2017). https://arxiv.org/abs/1711.03938
8. Han, L., Wang, J., Li, C., Tao, F., Fu, Z.: A novel multiobject tracking framework based on multisensor data fusion for autonomous driving in adverse weather environments. IEEE Sens. J. **25**(9), 16068–16079 (2025). https://doi.org/10.1109/JSEN.2025.3550506
9. Huang, Z., Sun, S., Zhao, J., Mao, L.: Multi-modal policy fusion for end-to-end autonomous driving. Inf. Fus. **98**, 101834 (2023). https://doi.org/10.1016/j.inffus.2023.101834, https://www.sciencedirect.com/science/article/pii/S1566253523001501
10. Ignatious, H.A., El-Sayed, H., Kulkarni, P.: Multilevel data and decision fusion using heterogeneous sensory data for autonomous vehicles. Remote Sens. **15**(9) (2023). https://doi.org/10.3390/rs15092256, https://www.mdpi.com/2072-4292/15/9/2256
11. Islam, M.M., Al Redwan Newaz, A., Gokaraju, B., Karimoddini, A.: Pedestrian detection for autonomous cars: occlusion handling by classifying body parts. In: 2020 IEEE International Conference on Systems, Man, and Cybernetics (SMC), pp. 1433–1438 (2020). https://doi.org/10.1109/SMC42975.2020.9282839
12. Jaiswal, C., Acquaah, S., Nenebi, C., AlHmoud, I., Islam, A.K., Gokaraju, B.: EMS3D-KITTI: synthetic 3D dataset in KITTI format with a fair distribution of emergency medical services vehicles for autodrive AI model training. Data Brief **58**, 111221 (2025). https://doi.org/10.1016/j.dib.2024.111221, https://www.sciencedirect.com/science/article/pii/S2352340924011831

13. Jiang, P., et al.: Weather-aware collaborative perception with uncertainty reduction. IEEE Trans. Intell. Transp. Syst. **25**(12), 20059–20072 (2024). https://doi.org/10.1109/TITS.2024.3479720
14. Kirillova, N., Jehanzeb, M.M., Possegger, H., Bischof, H.: Into the fog: evaluating multiple object tracking robustness. arXiv preprint arXiv:2404.10534 (2024)
15. Li, Y., et al.: DeepFusion: lidar-camera deep fusion for multi-modal 3d object detection (2022). https://arxiv.org/abs/2203.08195
16. Liu, Z., Tang, H., Amini, A., Yang, X., Mao, H., Rus, D., Han, S.: BEVFusion: multi-task multi-sensor fusion with unified bird's-eye view representation (2024). https://arxiv.org/abs/2205.13542
17. Nenebi, C.T., Acquaah, S., Tang, A., Tucker, K., AlHmoud, I.W., Gokaraju, B.: Lidar-driven steering command prediction for autonomous vehicles using machine learning. In: 2025 IEEE Conference on Artificial Intelligence (CAI), pp. 1560–1567 (2025). https://doi.org/10.1109/CAI64502.2025.00274
18. Ogunrinde, I., Bernadin, S.: Deep camera–radar fusion with an attention framework for autonomous vehicle vision in foggy weather conditions. Sensors **23**(14) (2023). https://doi.org/10.3390/s23146255, https://www.mdpi.com/1424-8220/23/14/6255
19. Palladin, E., Dietze, R., Narayanan, P., Bijelic, M., Heide, F.: SamFusion: sensor-adaptive multimodal fusion for 3d object detection in adverse weather. In: Computer Vision – ECCV 2024: 18th European Conference, Milan, Italy, September 29–October 4, 2024, Proceedings, Part LXI, pp. 484–503. Springer-Verlag, Berlin, Heidelberg (2024). https://doi.org/10.1007/978-3-031-73030-6_27
20. Penumatcha, H., Jaiswal, C.P., Vegesana, S., AlHmoud, I.W., Gokaraju, B.: Developing an autonomous robotics system utilizing camera and IMU fusion with PID-based path correction. In: 2024 International Conference on Machine Learning and Applications (ICMLA), pp. 1243–1248 (2024). https://doi.org/10.1109/ICMLA61862.2024.00193
21. Qian, C., et al.: AllWeather-Net: unified image enhancement for autonomous driving under adverse weather and low-light conditions, pp. 151–166. Springer Nature Switzerland (2024). https://doi.org/10.1007/978-3-031-78113-1_11
22. Rahmati, M.: Edge AI-powered real-time decision-making for autonomous vehicles in adverse weather conditions (2025). https://arxiv.org/abs/2503.09638
23. Rawashdeh, N.A., Bos, J.P., Abu-Alrub, N.J.: Camera–Lidar sensor fusion for drivable area detection in winter weather using convolutional neural networks. Opt. Eng. **62**(3), 031202 (2022). https://doi.org/10.1117/1.OE.62.3.031202
24. Wang, H., Liu, J., Dong, H., Shao, Z.: A survey of the multi-sensor fusion object detection task in autonomous driving. Sensors **25**(9) (2025). https://doi.org/10.3390/s25092794, https://www.mdpi.com/1424-8220/25/9/2794
25. Wu, W., Deng, X., Jiang, P., Wan, S., Guo, Y.: CrossFuser: multi-modal feature fusion for end-to-end autonomous driving under unseen weather conditions. IEEE Trans. Intell. Transp. Syst. **24**(12), 14378–14392 (2023). https://doi.org/10.1109/TITS.2023.3307589
26. Zhang, B., et al.: FogFusion: robust 3D object detection based on camera-lidar fusion for autonomous driving in foggy weather conditions. Proc. Inst. Mech. Eng. Part D: J. Automob. Eng., 09544070251327229. https://doi.org/10.1177/09544070251327229
27. Zhang, C., Wang, H., Cai, Y., Chen, L., Li, Y.: Transfusion: multi-modal robust fusion for 3d object detection in foggy weather based on spatial vision transformer.

Trans. Intell. Transport. Sys. **25**(9), 10652–10666 (2024). https://doi.org/10.1109/TITS.2024.3420432
28. Zhang, C., et al.: Robust-FusionNet: deep multimodal sensor fusion for 3-D object detection under severe weather conditions. IEEE Trans. Instrum. Meas. **71**, 1–13 (2022). https://doi.org/10.1109/TIM.2022.3191724
29. Zhang, Y., Carballo, A., Yang, H., Takeda, K.: Perception and sensing for autonomous vehicles under adverse weather conditions: a survey. ISPRS J. Photogramm. Remote Sens. **196**, 146–177 (2023). https://doi.org/10.1016/j.isprsjprs.2022.12.021, https://www.sciencedirect.com/science/article/pii/S0924271622003367

Hier-SimCLR-Drive: Learning a Two-Level Traffic-Scene Taxonomy Without Labels for Autonomous Driving

Andrews Tang(✉), Christopher Tetteh Nenebi, Kourtney Tucker, Sally Acquaah, Issa W. AlHmoud, and Balakrishna Gokaraju

Computational Data Science and Engineering, North Carolina A&T State University, Greensboro, USA
atang@aggies.ncat.edu

Abstract. Urban driving scenes naturally exhibit hierarchical structure (e.g., *vehicle* → *car*, *truck*, *bus*), yet most perception systems treat categories as flat and rely on costly manual annotations. We present *Hier-SimCLR-Drive*, a self-supervised framework that simultaneously learns transferable visual representations and a two-level hierarchy of traffic-scene concepts directly from raw, unlabeled video frames. Our method combines contrastive learning—bringing multiple augmented views of the same image closer in feature space—with dual clustering heads that organize encoder outputs into coarse categories (e.g., vehicles, pedestrians, infrastructure) and finer sub-categories (e.g., sedan, SUV, bus, bicycle). This hierarchical organization emerges without human labels, scaling naturally across objects, cities, and environmental conditions. On the *Cityscapes* dataset, the discovered categories align well with ground-truth labels, and the learned features surpass a flat SimCLR baseline on a frozen linear probe (79.6% vs. 72.2%, +7.4 pp). Beyond improved accuracy, Hier-SimCLR-Drive produces an interpretable, machine-generated taxonomy of road-scene objects, paving the way for more adaptable and transparent perception in autonomous driving.

Keywords: Autonomous Driving · Self-Supervised Learning · Contrastive Learning · Hierarchical Clustering · Representation Learning · Traffic Scene Understanding

1 Introduction

Perception systems for autonomous driving rely heavily on large volumes of annotated visual data to recognize and understand complex urban scenes. However, collecting such detailed annotations across diverse environments is both time-consuming and costly, often requiring extensive manual labeling of objects, regions, and scene types. As the scale and diversity of perception datasets continue to grow, there is an urgent need for unsupervised or self-supervised learning

F. Tanner and J. Irvine (Eds.): AIPR 2025, LNCS 16446, pp. 221–235, 2026.
https://doi.org/10.1007/978-3-032-18474-0_16

methods that can automatically extract meaningful structure from raw visual data without explicit human supervision.

Recent advances in self-supervised representation learning—particularly contrastive frameworks such as SimCLR [5] and MoCo [11]—have shown that powerful visual features can be learned by enforcing invariance across augmented views of the same image. These approaches have significantly narrowed the gap between supervised and unsupervised models on various downstream tasks. Nevertheless, conventional contrastive methods treat all images as independent instances, ignoring the inherent semantic relationships among them. This instance discrimination paradigm leads to flat representations that lack an internal notion of category or hierarchy—limiting both interpretability and scalability when applied to complex environments like urban traffic scenes, where concepts naturally organize into multiple semantic levels (e.g., *road* → *intersection* → *pedestrian crossing*).

Our inspiration stems from the observation that natural visual categories are inherently hierarchical. In the physical world, objects and scenes organize themselves into nested levels of abstraction: *vehicles* subdivide into *cars*, *buses*, and *trucks*; *roads* subdivide into *intersections*, *highways*, and *tunnels*. Human perception intuitively reasons about these relationships—confusing a *car* for a *truck* is less severe than mistaking it for a *building*. Yet traditional supervised learning systems evaluate all errors equally, disregarding the semantic proximity between categories.

We argue that learning systems should account for these structured relationships by introducing hierarchically aware error semantics. In this view, the cost of a prediction should reflect the hierarchical distance between the true and predicted clusters. Misclassifications within the same coarse category (e.g., between two fine clusters under one coarse parent) should be penalized less than cross-category errors that violate higher-level semantics. Such graded penalization mirrors cognitive organization in human categorization, where conceptual boundaries are soft and nested rather than discrete and independent [8]. By aligning the learning process with this principle, models can develop feature spaces that better reflect real-world semantic proximity and achieve more interpretable, cognitively grounded representations.

To realize part of this bigger vision, we introduce *Hier-SimCLR-Drive*, a self-supervised learning framework that jointly learns visual representations and a two-level hierarchy of scene semantics directly from unlabeled images. Built upon the SimCLR backbone, our method augments standard contrastive learning with a hierarchical clustering objective that organizes features into coarse and fine semantic groups. The coarse clusters capture broad contextual scene types (e.g., open roads versus building-dense areas), while the fine clusters refine these groups into more specific contexts such as intersections, tunnels, or curved highways. This joint training encourages the encoder to discover a structured representation space where semantically related images are grouped under the same coarse cluster but remain distinguishable at the fine level.

The *Hier-SimCLR-Drive* architecture integrates two interacting branches: a contrastive branch that enforces view invariance and a hierarchy branch that induces multi-level clustering via learnable prototypes updated with the Sinkhorn–Knopp algorithm. By combining these two branches, the framework preserves the discriminative strength of contrastive learning while instilling a natural semantic organization into the learned features. Entropy and diversity regularization terms further prevent representational collapse and ensure balanced cluster utilization. Beyond representation learning, this paradigm moves toward a framework where hierarchical similarity influences both training and evaluation—laying the foundation for graded loss functions that penalize errors proportionally to semantic distance.

We evaluate our approach on the *Cityscapes* [7] dataset, treating all images as unlabeled during pretraining. Quantitative results from linear probe evaluations show that the proposed model achieves a +7.4% improvement in classification accuracy compared to the flat SimCLR baseline, confirming that hierarchical learning enhances feature discriminability. Qualitative analyses—including t-SNE visualizations, cluster heatmaps, and grouped scene samples—further reveal that the learned hierarchy corresponds closely to human-perceptible scene taxonomies, capturing both global context and fine-grained visual variations.

In summary, this work makes the following contributions:

- We propose *Hier-SimCLR-Drive*, a novel self-supervised framework that simultaneously learns invariant representations and hierarchical semantic structures from unlabeled urban scenes.
- We introduce a hierarchy-consistency objective that aligns fine and coarse clusters through a differentiable mapping, promoting nested semantic relationships within the learned feature space.
- We articulate a hierarchy-aware perspective on error semantics, where model predictions are evaluated—and potentially trained—according to hierarchical distance, encouraging graded understanding of scene similarity.
- We demonstrate, through quantitative and qualitative experiments on Cityscapes, that our method improves feature quality, cluster interpretability, and representation transferability compared to flat contrastive baselines.

Our findings indicate that hierarchical self-supervised learning offers a promising direction toward scalable, interpretable, and label-free perception systems for autonomous vehicles. Beyond improving representation quality, this paradigm lays the groundwork for hierarchy-aware evaluation and training—bringing artificial perception one step closer to the structured reasoning and graded error tolerance observed in human cognition.

2 Related Work

Contrastive self-supervised methods such as SimCLR [5], MoCo [11], BYOL [10], and SimSiam [6] have demonstrated that meaningful visual representations can be learned by contrasting multiple augmented views of the same image. These frameworks enforce view invariance through contrastive or redundancy-reduction objectives, narrowing the gap between unsupervised and supervised models. However, they treat each image as an independent instance, leading to flat embedding spaces that lack internal semantic organization. Consequently, while these methods excel at general feature learning, they do not capture the hierarchical relationships that naturally exist among real-world visual concepts.

Methods such as DeepCluster [3], SwAV [4], and SeLa-v2 [1] extend self-supervised learning by introducing prototype-based or assignment-driven clustering objectives. These approaches jointly learn cluster assignments and encoder parameters, enabling the model to discover semantically consistent groups without labels. Although such clustering-based techniques move beyond instance discrimination, they typically operate at a *single level* of abstraction—learning one flat partition of the dataset without modeling relationships between coarse and fine semantics.

A smaller body of work has explored hierarchical structure in unsupervised and semi-supervised settings. Approaches based on hierarchical variational autoencoders, such as VQ-VAE-2 [18], and nested clustering [2] capture multi-scale structure, but they are primarily designed for generative modeling rather than semantic scene organization. Similarly, hierarchical grouping frameworks such as Hierarchical Semantic Grouping [15] and Hierarchical Contrastive Learning (HCL) [20] impose multi-level structure through auxiliary losses but often rely on predefined taxonomies or labeled supervision. Earlier work on outdoor scene classification, such as [19], demonstrated that hierarchical decision fusion using color, texture, and spectral features can improve classification accuracy over single-stage classifiers. However, such methods depend heavily on hand-crafted features and supervised data, whereas our approach learns coarse-to-fine hierarchies directly from unlabeled visual inputs.

In autonomous driving, self-supervised learning has primarily focused on geometric tasks such as depth estimation [9], motion prediction [14], and segmentation [15], where supervision is derived from geometric consistency rather than semantic structure. Recent work has begun to explore hierarchy-aware frameworks in this domain. For example, [13] introduced a hierarchical evaluation metric that assigns partial credit to semantically related misclassifications (e.g., "ambulance" → "van"), improving the interpretability of model performance. While this approach focuses on evaluation rather than representation learning, it highlights the growing importance of hierarchical semantics for autonomous perception. To our knowledge, however, no prior self-supervised framework has explicitly sought to *learn* such hierarchies directly from visual data.

Hier-SimCLR-Drive bridges these research directions by combining contrastive representation learning with hierarchical clustering in a fully self-supervised framework. Unlike prior approaches that produce flat embeddings or rely on external hierarchies, our model autonomously discovers a two-level taxonomy of traffic-scene concepts from unlabeled data. This positions our work as a step toward hierarchy-aware perception systems that can learn, organize, and interpret visual information without predefined labels.

3 Materials and Methods

This section presents the proposed *Hier-SimCLR-Drive* framework, which learns a two-level hierarchy of traffic-scene concepts directly from unlabeled data. Urban driving environments naturally contain objects and structures that follow hierarchical relationships (e.g., *vehicle* → *car*, *truck*, *bus*). Unlike traditional supervised approaches that rely on flat, manually annotated labels, *Hier-SimCLR-Drive* discovers this structure automatically using self-supervised learning.

The framework builds upon contrastive representation learning to extract view-invariant features while introducing a hierarchical clustering branch to organize these features into coarse and fine semantic groups. The following subsections describe the dataset and problem formulation, model architecture, and training objectives in detail. An overview of the full framework is shown in Fig. 1.

3.1 Data and Problem Setup

We use the *Cityscapes* dataset as our source of urban traffic scenes, treating all images as unlabeled during training. The goal is to learn a feature extractor that captures both general scene representations and hierarchical groupings of traffic-scene concepts—without relying on any manual annotations.

Formally, given an unlabeled dataset

$$\mathcal{D} = \{x_i\}_{i=1}^{N} \tag{1}$$

the model learns an encoder f_θ that produces (i) contrastive representations suitable for downstream tasks and (ii) probabilistic assignments to coarse and fine clusters representing a two-level taxonomy of visual concepts.

Following SimCLR, each image x is transformed by a stochastic augmentation pipeline $\mathcal{T}$ consisting of random resized cropping, horizontal flipping, color jittering, Gaussian blur, and grayscale conversion. Two augmented views

$$v_1, v_2 \sim \mathcal{T}(x) \tag{2}$$

are generated per image to encourage invariance to viewpoint and illumination. These views are then passed through the shared encoder to obtain their feature representations and cluster predictions. No labels are used during any stage of training.

3.2 Model Architecture

The architecture of *Hier-SimCLR-Drive* consists of two interacting branches built on a shared ResNet-50 backbone [12]: a contrastive branch and a hierarchy branch (Fig. 1). The contrastive branch follows the standard SimCLR design to learn features that are invariant to visual transformations, while the hierarchy branch organizes these features into coarse and fine semantic groups.

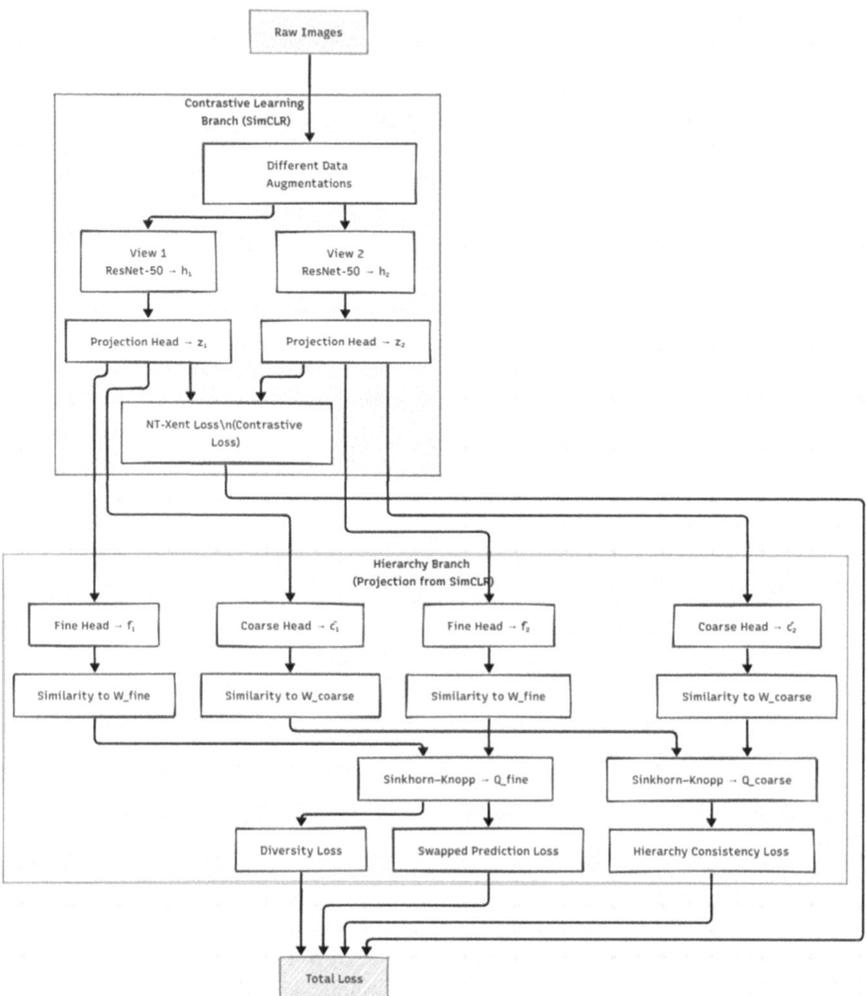

Fig. 1. Architecture of *Hier-SimCLR-Drive*. Two augmented views of each image are processed by a shared encoder. A SimCLR branch optimizes the NT-Xent loss for view invariance, while a hierarchy branch predicts coarse and fine cluster distributions. Swapped-prediction, hierarchy-consistency, entropy, and diversity terms encourage stable and interpretable structure.

Each input view v is mapped by the encoder f_θ into a feature representation $y = f_\theta(v) \in \mathbb{R}^d$. A two-layer projection head g_ϕ transforms this representation into an embedding $z = g_\phi(y) \in \mathbb{R}^{d_z}$ used for the NT-Xent contrastive loss. Separating the contrastive space from the semantic feature space improves transferability and prevents loss interference between branches.

To induce hierarchy, two lightweight multilayer perceptron (MLP) heads are attached to the encoder outputs: a coarse head h_C and a fine head h_F. Each head ends with a temperature-scaled softmax layer that produces probability distributions over a fixed number of clusters:

$$p_C = \text{softmax}\left(\frac{h_C(y)}{\tau_C}\right), \quad p_F = \text{softmax}\left(\frac{h_F(y)}{\tau_F}\right) \tag{3}$$

Here, each cluster can be interpreted as a latent group of visually similar scenes—coarse clusters capture broader scene types (e.g., road vs. building-dense areas), while fine clusters subdivide these categories into more specific contexts (e.g., intersections, tunnels, or curved highways).

Each cluster is anchored by a prototype vector w_k, a learnable centroid representing that group in feature space. To maintain stable and balanced training, cluster assignments are computed using the Sinkhorn–Knopp algorithm [16], which normalizes assignments across the mini-batch so that all prototypes are used evenly. The prototypes are further stabilized with exponential moving average (EMA) updates [17]:

$$w_k \leftarrow m \cdot w_k + (1 - m) \cdot \hat{w}_k \tag{4}$$

where m is the momentum term and $\hat{w}_k$ is the current feature estimate. This smooths prototype updates over time, preventing abrupt shifts in cluster centroids.

By training both branches jointly, the contrastive branch ensures robust, view-invariant features, while the hierarchy branch imposes structured organization within the feature space. Together, they enable *Hier-SimCLR-Drive* to produce embeddings that are both discriminative and interpretable, forming a two-level, label-free taxonomy of urban traffic scenes.

3.3 Training Objectives

The training of *Hier-SimCLR-Drive* combines contrastive and clustering-based objectives to ensure that learned features are both invariant to appearance changes and hierarchically structured. The total objective is a weighted sum of five components:

$$\mathcal{L}_{\text{total}} = \lambda_{\text{sim}}\mathcal{L}_{\text{SimCLR}} + \lambda_{\text{swap}}\mathcal{L}_{\text{swap}} + \lambda_{\text{hier}}\mathcal{L}_{\text{hier}} + \lambda_{\text{ent}}\mathcal{L}_{\text{ent}} + \lambda_{\text{div}}\mathcal{L}_{\text{div}} \tag{5}$$

where each coefficient λ controls the relative contribution of its term.

Contrastive Loss ($\mathcal{L}_{\text{SimCLR}}$): For two augmented views (v_1, v_2) of the same image, the encoder–projection pair produces embeddings $(\mathbf{z}_1, \mathbf{z}_2)$. We adopt the NT-Xent (InfoNCE) contrastive loss:

$$\mathcal{L}_{\text{SimCLR}} = -\log \frac{\exp(\text{sim}(\mathbf{z}_1, \mathbf{z}_2)/\tau)}{\sum_{j=1}^{2B} \mathbb{1}_{[j \neq i]} \exp(\text{sim}(\mathbf{z}_i, \mathbf{z}_j)/\tau)} \tag{6}$$

This loss maximizes agreement between positive pairs (same image, different augmentations) and separates negatives, encouraging view-invariant features.

Swapped-Prediction Loss ($\mathcal{L}_{\text{swap}}$): To ensure consistency of cluster assignments across augmentations, we use a swapped-prediction objective. Each view predicts the cluster assignment of the other:

$$\mathcal{L}_{\text{swap}} = \frac{1}{2B} \sum_{i=1}^{B} \Big[-\mathbf{q}_{\mathrm{F},2}^{(i)\top} \log \mathbf{p}_{\mathrm{F},1}^{(i)} - \mathbf{q}_{\mathrm{F},1}^{(i)\top} \log \mathbf{p}_{\mathrm{F},2}^{(i)} \Big] \tag{7}$$

with an analogous term for coarse clusters. Here, $\mathbf{q}$ are balanced target assignments from the Sinkhorn–Knopp algorithm and $\mathbf{p}$ are the predicted probabilities. This enforces cross-view consistency so both augmentations of the same image land in the same cluster.

Hierarchy-Consistency Loss ($\mathcal{L}_{\text{hier}}$): Fine clusters should form children of coherent coarse clusters. To enforce this nesting, we compute a coarse prediction $\hat{\mathbf{p}}_{\mathrm{C}}$ induced by the fine distribution using a learned mapping $M \in \mathbb{R}^{K_F \times K_C}$:

$$\hat{\mathbf{p}}_{\mathrm{C}} = M^{\top} \mathbf{p}_{\mathrm{F}}, \qquad \mathcal{L}_{\text{hier}} = \mathrm{KL}\big(\mathbf{p}_{\mathrm{C}} \,||\, \hat{\mathbf{p}}_{\mathrm{C}}\big) \tag{8}$$

Minimizing this KL divergence aligns fine and coarse predictions, ensuring that fine-level clusters remain consistent with their parent categories.

Entropy Regularization ($\mathcal{L}_{\text{ent}}$): Without constraints, the model could collapse by assigning all samples to a few clusters. To prevent this, we encourage high entropy (uncertainty) in per-sample cluster predictions:

$$\mathcal{L}_{\text{ent}} = -\frac{1}{2B} \sum_{i=1}^{2B} \big(H(\mathbf{p}_{\mathrm{C}}^{(i)}) + H(\mathbf{p}_{\mathrm{F}}^{(i)})\big), \quad H(\mathbf{p}) = -\sum_{k} p_k \log p_k \tag{9}$$

This encourages balanced confidence and avoids single-cluster domination.

Diversity Loss ($\mathcal{L}_{\text{div}}$): While entropy prevents per-sample collapse, some clusters may still remain underused. To promote equal utilization across the dataset, we maximize batch-level entropy:

$$\bar{\mathbf{p}} = \frac{1}{2B} \sum_{i=1}^{2B} \mathbf{p}^{(i)}, \qquad \mathcal{L}_{\text{div}} = -H(\bar{\mathbf{p}}) \tag{10}$$

This encourages the global distribution of assignments to approach uniformity, ensuring that all prototypes contribute to the learned hierarchy.

Overall, these objectives balance *local view-invariance* (through contrastive learning) with *global structure discovery* (through hierarchical clustering), yielding representations that are transferable, interpretable, and resistant to collapse.

4 Results and Discussion

We implement and train *Hier-SimCLR-Drive* using the PyTorch deep learning framework on an Ubuntu 22.04 workstation equipped with dual NVIDIA Quadro GV100 GPUs (32 GB VRAM each) and 128 GB of system memory. All experiments were conducted under identical training configurations for both the hierarchical and flat SimCLR baselines to ensure a fair comparison. The results presented in this section evaluate (i) representation quality, (ii) the learned hierarchical structure, and (iii) qualitative interpretability.

4.1 Feature Quality Evaluation

To assess the discriminative power of the learned representations, we conduct a linear probe experiment following the standard self-supervised learning protocol. After pretraining, the encoder is frozen, and a multinomial logistic regression classifier is trained on top of the extracted feature vectors to evaluate their separability under a linear decision boundary. Each image is represented by its encoder output $y = f_\theta(x)$, and the linear classifier is trained using cross-entropy loss on image-level scene labels derived from the Cityscapes ground-truth segmentation maps. This setup isolates the representational quality of the encoder without any additional fine-tuning or supervision.

As shown in Fig. 2, *Hier-SimCLR-Drive* achieves a validation accuracy of 79.6%, compared to 72.2% for the flat SimCLR baseline—a gain of +7.4% points. This consistent improvement demonstrates that incorporating hierarchical objectives helps the encoder capture more structured and class-discriminative features. In particular, the coarse–fine organization acts as a semantic regularizer, encouraging the model to group visually related scenes while maintaining meaningful substructure.

4.2 Hierarchical Structure Visualization

To examine the organization of the learned feature space, we visualize the embeddings produced by the coarse and fine clustering heads using t-distributed Stochastic Neighbor Embedding (t-SNE). This dimensionality reduction allows us to project high-dimensional features into a 2D plane while preserving local neighborhood structure, making it possible to visually inspect how images are grouped in the latent space.

Figure 3 presents the t-SNE projections for the coarse and fine cluster embeddings. In the coarse-level plot, the model forms several broad, well-separated regions corresponding to major scene types—such as open roads, intersections, and building-dense areas. This shows that the encoder has captured high-level semantic distinctions across urban scenes.

The fine-level plot further subdivides these coarse clusters into smaller, more specific groups. Within each coarse region, the fine clusters reflect subtle but meaningful variations in spatial layout, lighting conditions, and object composition (e.g., scenes dominated by cars versus those with pedestrians or vegetation).

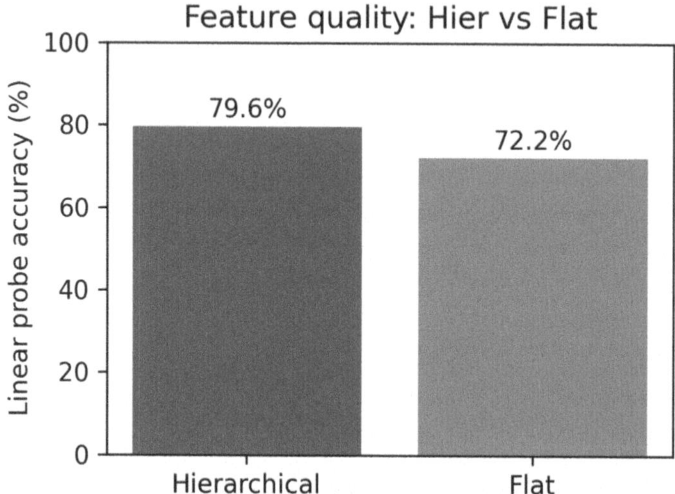

Fig. 2. Linear probe comparison showing improved feature quality from hierarchical learning (+7.4% over flat SimCLR).

This clear coarse-to-fine organization validates that the model has learned an interpretable hierarchical representation of traffic scenes.

4.3 Hierarchy Consistency Analysis

To quantitatively verify the hierarchical relationships learned by the model, we compute the conditional probability matrix $P(\text{coarse} \mid \text{fine})$. Each entry $P(c \mid f)$ represents the probability that a sample assigned to fine cluster f also belongs to coarse cluster c. This matrix therefore reveals how strongly each fine cluster is associated with its parent coarse group.

Figure 4 visualizes $P(\text{coarse} \mid \text{fine})$ as a heatmap, where each column corresponds to a fine cluster and each row to a coarse cluster. Within each column, one dominant red cell indicates the coarse parent most strongly associated with that fine cluster. Across all columns, these high-probability cells align into localized blocks along the diagonal region of the matrix—each block representing a coarse cluster and its associated set of fine clusters.

This structure confirms that most fine clusters are cleanly nested under single coarse parents, yielding a well-formed hierarchy. Occasional off-block activations correspond to visually ambiguous scenes, such as intersections that mix open roads and building-heavy areas, where hierarchical boundaries are naturally less distinct. Overall, the strong block patterns verify that *Hier-SimCLR-Drive* has learned a consistent and interpretable two-level taxonomy of urban traffic scenes.

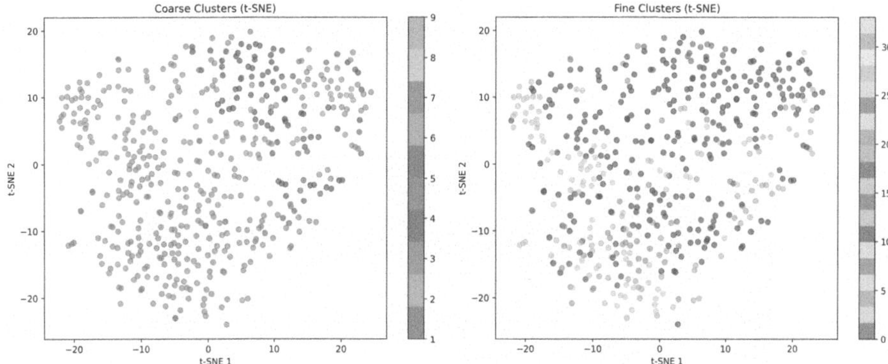

Fig. 3. t-SNE visualization of coarse and fine cluster embeddings. Coarse clusters form broad semantic regions (e.g., road, intersection), while fine clusters subdivide them into more specific contexts.

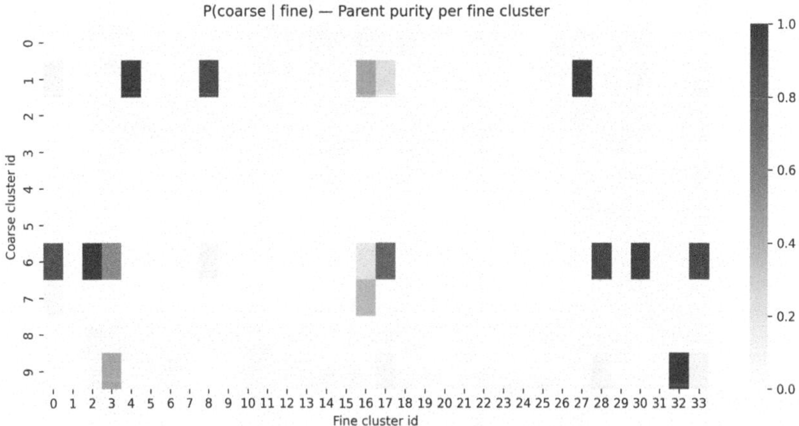

Fig. 4. Conditional probability matrix $P(\text{coarse} \mid \text{fine})$. Each column represents a fine cluster, and each row represents a coarse cluster. Bright localized blocks indicate that fine clusters are consistently nested under specific coarse parents, confirming hierarchical purity.

4.4 Qualitative Scene Interpretation

To further examine the interpretability of the discovered hierarchy, we visualize real images from the validation set along with their predicted cluster assignments (Fig. 5). Each image tile is annotated with its predicted coarse cluster ID (C: $\langle \text{id} \rangle$) and fine cluster ID ($F$: $\langle \text{id} \rangle$). Images in the same row share the same coarse cluster and are color-bordered accordingly, while the fine cluster IDs vary within each row.

Rows corresponding to the same coarse cluster exhibit strong visual consistency: images grouped together display similar spatial layouts, perspectives,

Fig. 5. Qualitative examples showing predicted coarse (C) and fine (F) cluster assignments on real driving scenes. Each row shares the same coarse cluster (color-coded border), while fine clusters vary, revealing meaningful sub-grouping of scene contexts.

and dominant scene elements (e.g., open roads, intersections, or building-dense areas). Within each coarse group, variation across fine clusters captures more subtle distinctions such as traffic density, presence of pedestrians, or lighting conditions. For instance, under a single coarse cluster representing "road scenes," fine clusters separate images with straight lanes from those containing turns, crosswalks, or shadows cast by nearby structures.

This qualitative evidence confirms that *Hier-SimCLR-Drive* learns a semantically aligned hierarchy: coarse clusters capture broad scene categories, and fine clusters refine them into detailed subtypes. Importantly, these relationships emerge entirely without supervision—no labels or semantic maps are used during training—demonstrating that the model's learned taxonomy corresponds closely to human-interpretable visual structure.

4.5 Discussion

The results collectively demonstrate that *Hier-SimCLR-Drive* successfully learns a coherent two-level hierarchy of traffic-scene concepts directly from unlabeled images. The framework not only improves representation quality (+7.4% linear probe accuracy) but also produces interpretable hierarchical structures that align with real-world visual semantics. The coarse and fine clusters correspond to broad and specific scene types, respectively, revealing a natural taxonomy within urban environments without any manual supervision.

While these findings confirm the feasibility of learning hierarchical structure from the Cityscapes dataset, our long-term vision extends beyond this specific domain. We aim to develop a general framework capable of discovering multi-level hierarchies across diverse autonomous driving scenes—urban, suburban, and highway—enabling scalable, data-driven organization of large perception datasets. Such automatically discovered hierarchies could further support hierarchical labeling, where datasets are structured according to model-learned taxonomies rather than predefined human labels.

Future work will explore new hierarchy-aware loss functions that adapt to the structure discovered during training, enabling deeper and more flexible forms of self-supervised learning for complex driving environments.

5 Conclusion and Future Works

In this work, we introduced *Hier-SimCLR-Drive*, a self-supervised framework that jointly learns visual representations and a two-level semantic hierarchy of urban traffic scenes directly from unlabeled images. By integrating a SimCLR-based contrastive branch with a hierarchical clustering branch, the model learns features that are both invariant and semantically structured. Experimental results on the Cityscapes dataset show that the learned hierarchical representations improve linear probe performance by +7.4% over the flat SimCLR baseline, while qualitative analyses—such as t-SNE visualizations and conditional probability heatmaps—demonstrate the emergence of meaningful coarse-to-fine relationships within the learned feature space. These findings provide evidence that autonomous discovery of coarse-to-fine semantics is not only feasible but beneficial for perception systems that operate in complex environments like urban traffic scenes.

While this study focuses specifically on learning two-level hierarchies from the Cityscapes dataset, our long-term vision extends toward a general framework capable of discovering deeper, multi-level taxonomies across diverse driving scenes. Future work will explore:

1. extending hierarchical discovery to additional domains and sensor modalities (e.g., LiDAR and multimodal fusion),
2. developing hierarchy-aware loss functions that adapt dynamically to the structure learned during training, and
3. applying the learned hierarchies for semi-supervised labeling and hierarchy-aware evaluation in large-scale perception datasets.

Such advancements would move us closer to scalable, interpretable, and cognitively aligned perception models for autonomous vehicles.

Acknowledgment. The authors thank the following agencies for their partial support: 1) W.K. Kellogg Foundation, 2) the United States Department of Commerce (USDOC), Economic Development Administration Good Jobs Challenge Awardee, STEPS4GROWTH (ED22HDQ3070099), 3) the National Science Foundation's Engineering Research Center (NSF-ERC) for Hybrid Autonomous Manufacturing—Moving from Evolution to Revolution (HAMMER) (Award No.: 2133630).

References

1. Asano, Y.M., Rupprecht, C., Vedaldi, A.: Self-labelling via simultaneous clustering and representation learning. CoRR abs/1911.05371 (2019). http://arxiv.org/abs/1911.05371
2. Brendel, W., Bethge, M.: Approximating CNNs with bag-of-local-features models works surprisingly well on imagenet. CoRR abs/1904.00760 (2019). http://arxiv.org/abs/1904.00760
3. Caron, M., Bojanowski, P., Joulin, A., Douze, M.: Deep clustering for unsupervised learning of visual features. CoRR abs/1807.05520 (2018). http://arxiv.org/abs/1807.05520
4. Caron, M., Misra, I., Mairal, J., Goyal, P., Bojanowski, P., Joulin, A.: Unsupervised learning of visual features by contrasting cluster assignments. CoRR abs/2006.09882 (2020). https://arxiv.org/abs/2006.09882
5. Chen, T., Kornblith, S., Norouzi, M., Hinton, G.E.: A simple framework for contrastive learning of visual representations. CoRR abs/2002.05709 (2020). https://arxiv.org/abs/2002.05709
6. Chen, X., He, K.: Exploring simple Siamese representation learning. CoRR abs/2011.10566 (2020). https://arxiv.org/abs/2011.10566
7. Cordts, M., et al.: The cityscapes dataset for semantic urban scene understanding (2016). https://arxiv.org/abs/1604.01685

8. Eckstein, M.K., Collins, A.G.E.: How the mind creates structure: hierarchical learning of action sequences. In: Annual Conference of the Cognitive Science Society. Cognitive Science Society (U.S.). Conference, vol. 43, pp. 618–624 (2021)
9. Godard, C., Aodha, O.M., Firman, M., Brostow, G.: Digging into self-supervised monocular depth estimation (2019). https://arxiv.org/abs/1806.01260
10. Grill, J., et al.: Bootstrap your own latent: a new approach to self-supervised learning. CoRR abs/2006.07733 (2020). https://arxiv.org/abs/2006.07733
11. He, K., Fan, H., Wu, Y., Xie, S., Girshick, R.B.: Momentum contrast for unsupervised visual representation learning. CoRR abs/1911.05722 (2019). http://arxiv.org/abs/1911.05722
12. He, K., Zhang, X., Ren, S., Sun, J.: Deep residual learning for image recognition (2015). https://arxiv.org/abs/1512.03385
13. Jaiswal, C., Challa, K., Gokaraju, B.: Knowledge-aware object detection adjusting map for class hierarchies in autonomous vehicles. In: SoutheastCon 2025, pp. 1548–1553 (2025). https://doi.org/10.1109/SoutheastCon56624.2025.10971654
14. Jia, X., Zhou, H., Zhu, X., Guo, Y., Zhang, J., Ma, B.: Contrastmotion: self-supervised scene motion learning for large-scale lidar point clouds, pp. 929–937 (2023). https://doi.org/10.24963/ijcai.2023/103
15. Li, L., Zhou, T., Wang, W., Li, J., Yang, Y.: Deep hierarchical semantic segmentation (2022). https://arxiv.org/abs/2203.14335
16. Mena, J.R.E.: On the convergence of the Sinkhorn-Knopp algorithm with sparse cost matrices (2024). https://arxiv.org/abs/2405.20528
17. Morales-Brotons, D., Vogels, T., Hendrikx, H.: Exponential moving average of weights in deep learning: dynamics and benefits (2024). https://arxiv.org/abs/2411.18704
18. Razavi, A., van den Oord, A., Vinyals, O.: Generating diverse high-fidelity images with VQ-VAE-2. CoRR abs/1906.00446 (2019). http://arxiv.org/abs/1906.00446
19. Turlapaty, A.C., Goru, H.K., Gokaraju, B.: A feature subset based decision fusion approach for scene classification using color, spectral, and texture statistics. In: 2017 IEEE 7th International Advance Computing Conference (IACC), pp. 624–628 (2017). https://doi.org/10.1109/IACC.2017.0132
20. Wu, B., Kang, Y., Zan, D., Guan, B., Wang, Y.: Hierarchical and contrastive representation learning for knowledge-aware recommendation (2023). https://arxiv.org/abs/2304.07506

Scaling Continuous Kernels with Sparse Fourier Domain Learning

Clayton Harper[1], Luke Wood[2], Peter Gerstoft[2], Mitchell A. Thornton[1], and Eric C. Larson[1(✉)]

[1] Darwin Deason Institute for Cybersecurity, Southern Methodist University, Dallas, TX, USA
{caharper,mitch,eclarson}@smu.edu

[2] Computer Science, University of California San Diego, La Jolla, CA, USA
gerstoft@ucsd.edu

Abstract. Convolution in the spectral domain is a linear-time computation, making it possible to train convolutional neural networks (CNNs) with significantly larger kernels than their spatial counterparts, which typically are limited to 3×3 or 5×5 kernels. To solve this, continuous kernel networks have been proposed. Continuous kernel networks replace fixed-size kernels with generating functions, enabling kernels with global context while maintaining a manageable parameter count. However, learning continuous kernels is prohibitively expensive, even for modest-sized datasets. In this work we propose an optimized method for efficiently training arbitrarily large MLP-backed kernels directly in the spectral domain. Our method addresses three key challenges in learning continuous kernel representations: computational efficiency during training, parameter efficiency in representation, and training speed. We evaluate spectral domain continuous kernel CNNs on medium sizes image classification datasets while achieving comparable accuracy to that of their spatial domain counterparts.

Keywords: Continuous kernels · Spectral learning

1 Introduction

Continuous kernel representations have been suggested for learning large convolutional kernels while maintaining a fixed-parameter budget [5,10–13]. Instead of directly parameterizing convolutional kernels as discrete weights, this approach uses a small neural network as a multi-layer perceptron (MLP) to generate kernels by sampling at specified spatial positions. This formulation treats convolutional kernels as continuous vector-valued functions, allowing them to adapt to arbitrary resolutions seamlessly. By querying the MLP at finer spatial intervals, larger kernels can be synthesized without increasing the parameters, offering a scalable and flexible alternative to traditional convolutional kernels (Fig. 1).

In continuous kernel generation, the MLP generates a kernel by sampling at spatial intervals corresponding to the dimensions of the input feature map. For

F. Tanner and J. Irvine (Eds.): AIPR 2025, LNCS 16446, pp. 236–245, 2026.
https://doi.org/10.1007/978-3-032-18474-0_17

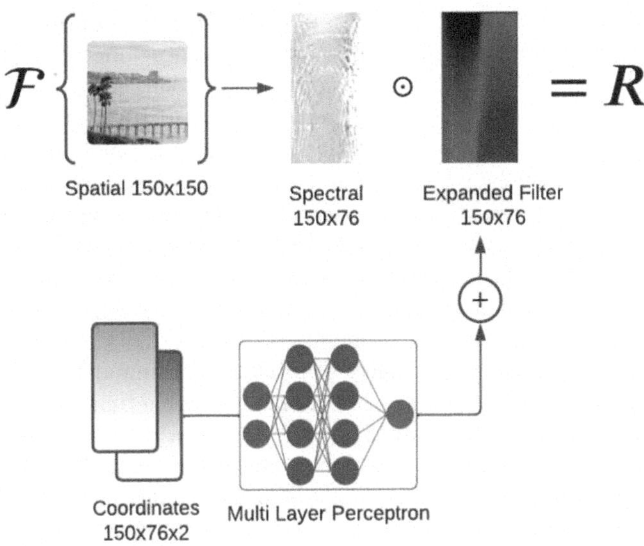

Fig. 1. Continuous Kernels parameterized with an MLP.

instance, if the input feature map has dimensions $H \times W$, the MLP is sampled at $H \times W$ positions, producing a kernel of the same dimensions. Although the MLP generates a $H \times W$ kernel, the region with non-zero values—the active region—can vary during training. Thus, a notable advantage of this formulation is its ability to dynamically learn the effective kernel size. For example, a gradient update could change the active region from $h_1 \times w_1$ to $h_2 \times w_2$. This dynamic behavior is intrinsic to continuous kernel representations, as the MLP regenerates the kernel at each forward pass. This process enables the effective kernel size to be learned through gradient-based optimization, allowing the network to adapt its receptive fields to the underlying data. This adaptability improves the expressiveness and representational capacity of the network.

This capability distinguishes continuous kernels from prior approaches to dynamic kernel size learning [2,4,9], which typically rely on a single static kernel size applied uniformly across all channels and filters in a layer. Such uniformity limits the network's capacity to capture diverse spatial dependencies. In contrast, continuous kernels can generate unique kernel sizes for each channel, providing a more flexible and nuanced mechanism for spatial modeling.

Despite their advantages, the practical deployment of continuous kernels is hindered by several challenges, including (1) high parameter counts, (2) significant computational and memory demands during training, and (3) slow training speeds. These limitations often make it challenging to scale continuous kernels effectively in real-world applications, highlighting the need for methods that can reduce resource requirements while retaining the flexibility and adaptability of these representations.

The computational overhead associated with training continuous kernels is substantial. This is due to the fact that continuous kernel methods, unlike traditional CNNs, must generate the entire convolutional kernel dynamically at each forward pass. This on-the-fly kernel generation incurs significant computational costs. Additionally, automatic differentiation, a technique used by modern deep learning frameworks such as PyTorch and TensorFlow, relies on storing intermediate activations for gradient computation. For continuous kernels, this process is particularly memory-intensive, as it involves backpropagating through the kernel generation process itself. As a result, scaling continuous kernel methods to large datasets or high-resolution inputs becomes prohibitively expensive, historically limiting their practicality in large-scale applications.

In this work, we propose a novel approach, Continuous Fourier Convolutions (CF-Convs), which addresses key challenges in continuous kernel learning by leveraging the Fourier domain and introducing a stochastic update mechanism. Instead of regenerating the entire kernel at every forward pass, CF-Convs stochastically update only a subset of kernel values, significantly reducing computational and memory demands. Additionally, CF-Convs bypass the costly Fourier transforms over the entire generated kernel required for spatial-domain continuous kernels [10,11] by learning directly in the spectral domain. This integration of Fourier-based learning and stochastic updates offers a scalable and practical framework for continuous kernel representations.

2 Related Work

Continuous convolutional kernels have emerged as an alternative to discrete convolutional filters, enabling flexible, learnable receptive fields [5,10,11]. These approaches align with implicit neural representations, where neural networks parameterize continuous functions instead of storing discrete kernel weights [7,8,16].

Although the majority of continuous kernel methods operate in the spatial domain, the Fourier domain has also been explored for kernel parameterization. Notably, Wood and Larson introduced a Fourier-based approach that employed 2D Gaussian parameterized kernels to reduce the parameter burden [18]. However, their use of shared weights across input channels constrained the adaptability of the generated kernels, leading to uniform kernel sizes across channels—similar to the limitations of traditional discrete spatial CNNs.

3 Continuous Kernels

Terminology: Let x denote the input feature map and k the convolutional kernel. The spatial dimensions (height and width) are given by H and W, while C_{in} and C_{out} represent the number of input and output channels, respectively. The Fourier transform over the spatial dimensions $H \times W$ is denoted by $\mathcal{F}$, with $\mathcal{F}^{-1}$ as its inverse. The input feature map and convolutional kernel are defined as $x \in \mathbb{R}^{H \times W \times C_{\text{in}}}$ and $k \in \mathbb{R}^{H \times W \times C_{\text{in}} \times C_{\text{out}}}$, respectively.

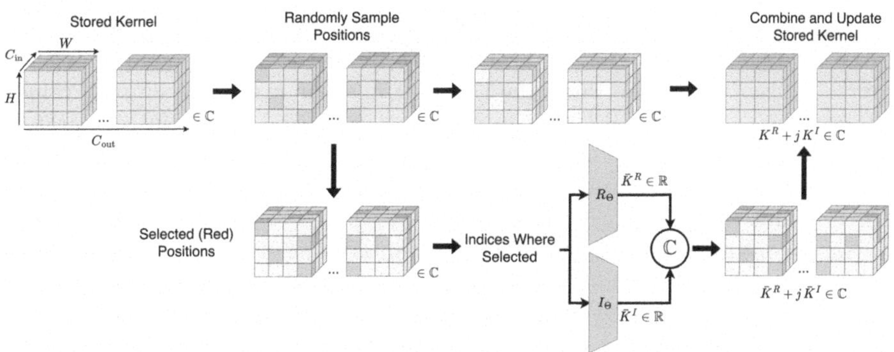

Fig. 2. Visualization of sparse sampling for efficient CF-Conv training. Randomly sampled positions for a single training step are highlighted in red. In the split kernel configuration, R_Θ and I_Θ represent the MLPs that generate the real and imaginary components of the complex-valued Fourier kernel $K \in \mathbb{C}(Color figure online)$.

A convolutional kernel for a given layer is given by the shape $H \times W \times C_{\text{in}} \times C_{\text{out}}$. Instead of learning each value discretely, a continuous convolutional kernel replaces a discrete filter with a learnable function f_Θ (*e.g.*, an MLP). f_Θ dynamically generates kernel, k, values based on positional coordinates: $k(h, w, i, o) = f_\Theta(h, w, i, o)$ where $h \in [0, H-1]$, $w \in [0, W-1]$, $i \in [0, C_{\text{in}}-1]$, and $o \in [0, C_{\text{out}}-1]$ index the spatial and channel dimensions of the kernel. Typically, these indices are normalized to be in the [0, 1] interval, a convention we follow in this work.

Prior methods often transform both the generated kernel k and the input x into the Fourier domain, performing convolution via pointwise multiplication to leverage the computational efficiency of Fourier-based convolutions for large kernels [5,10,11]. Learning directly in the Fourier domain is an appealing alternative, as it eliminates the need to compute the Fourier transform of k at each forward pass. However, this approach introduces additional challenges, particularly the need to parameterize both real and imaginary components, effectively doubling the memory and computational requirements of f_Θ. In the next section, we introduce a method to address this limitation and enable learning directly in the Fourier domain.

4 CF-Convs

A convolutional layer in the Fourier domain for a given layer L is defined as:

$$g^{(L)} = x \star k = \mathcal{F}^{-1}\left(\sum_{i=1}^{C_{\text{in}}} X_i \odot K_{i,o}\right), \quad \forall o \in C_{\text{out}} \tag{1}$$

where $g \in \mathbb{R}^{(H \times W \times C_{\text{out}})}$ is the output in the spatial domain. Fourier counterparts are given by $X = \mathcal{F}(x)$ and $K = \mathcal{F}(k)$. Here, $X \in \mathbb{C}^{(H \times W \times C_{\text{in}})}$ and

$K \in \mathbb{C}^{(H \times W \times C_{\text{in}} \times C_{\text{out}})}$. The operation $\odot$ denotes element-wise multiplication in the Fourier domain. The spatial output g is then recovered by applying the inverse Fourier transform. Since the Fourier transform produces complex-valued outputs, the convolutional kernel in a continuous kernel setup must separately parameterize its real and imaginary components, denoted as $K_{i,o}^R$ and $K_{i,o}^I$, respectively. This configuration, known as a split kernel configuration [14], is represented as $K_{i,o} = K_{i,o}^R + j\, K_{i,o}^I$, where $K_{i,o} \in \mathbb{C}^{(H \times W)}$.

Naive continuous kernels consume substantial memory due to their reliance on automatic differentiation, which stores intermediate activations for gradient computation—similar. However, Continuous Fourier Convolutions (CF-Convs), unlike spatial continuous kernels, require two MLPs to generate K, effectively doubling the memory overhead. Gradients must be computed and stored for all $H \cdot W \cdot C_{\text{in}} \cdot C_{\text{out}}$ positions, leading to an effective MLP "batch" size of $H \cdot W \cdot C_{\text{in}} \cdot C_{\text{out}}$ per MLP. As a result, even a modest 6-layer CF-Conv CNN with just 32 filters per layer can exhaust 80GB of GPU RAM. To make CF-Convs practical, memory reduction techniques are essential.

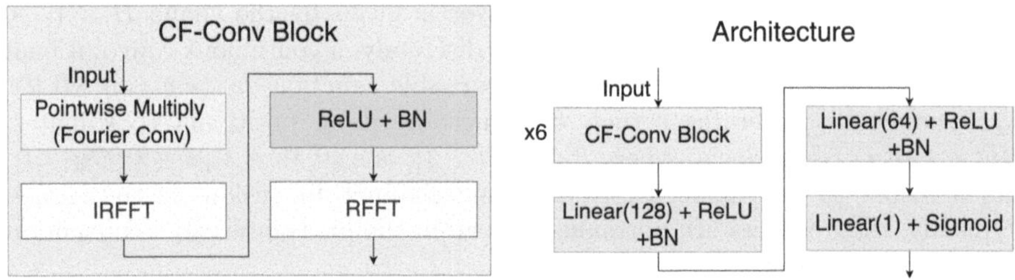

Fig. 3. Architectural overview of Cats vs. Dogs using CF-Convs. The convolutional kernel is generated using our CF-Conv approach and applied through Fourier-based convolution, as described in Eq. (1), where pointwise multiplication produces the final convolutional output.

5 Memory Reduction

To reduce the memory consumption of CF-Convs, several strategies can be employed. Gradient checkpointing, or rematerialization [1,6], reduces memory usage by storing only a subset of intermediate activations and recomputing the rest during the backward pass. While this approach saves memory, it incurs additional computational overhead due to repeated computation. Another method is using a *scan* operation, which sequentially applies a function over a collection of elements, accumulating results without storing all intermediate values simultaneously. Although gradient checkpointing and scan operations reduce memory consumption, they can significantly increase training times. These methods act more as analgesics, addressing the symptoms rather than solving the core problem of high memory consumption.

To address both training time and memory efficiency, we propose a sparse sampling strategy that focuses updates on a randomly sampled subset of kernel positions, referred to as *selected positions* (highlighted in red in Fig. 2). Uniform sampling ensures that no positional bias is introduced. By reducing the number of evaluations per forward pass, our strategy significantly lowers memory consumption by minimizing the storage of intermediate activations. Furthermore, fewer MLP evaluations decrease computational overhead, resulting in faster forward passes and more efficient training.

During initialization, the kernel, with shape $H \times W \times C_{\text{in}} \times C_{\text{out}}$ is stored as a state variable for both the real and imaginary components of the CF-Conv layer. It is randomly initialized with a uniform distribution in the range $[-1, 1]$, ensuring no bias toward specific spatial positions or frequencies. During each forward pass, only the selected positions are re-evaluated and updated. The remaining positions, referred to as *unselected positions* (highlighted in blue in Fig. 2), are held constant during that specific iteration. However, because sampling is randomized at every forward pass, unselected positions in one iteration may be selected in future iterations, ensuring that all positions are eventually updated over the course of training.

6 Experiments and Results

To evaluate the performance of our CF-Convs, we employ a 6-layer CNN using 32 filters at each layer (see Fig. 3) on the Cats vs. Dogs dataset with image sizes of $150 \times 150 \times 3$ [3]. Additionally, we experiment with different numbers of selected positions—2^{12}, 2^{15}, and 2^{18}—to evaluate the trade-off between memory consumption and training stability.

To maintain parameter parity with a baseline 3×3 spatial CNN, we carefully select the architecture for CF-Convs. In the CF-Convs parameterization, which uses two MLPs, a network with [32, 32, 32, 16, 16, 16, 8, 8, 8, 1] neurons is employed for each MLP. Both configurations use ReLU activations between linear layers. Our training protocol incorporates a straightforward augmentation pipeline involving up to 3 augmentations per image using the *RandAugment* class provided by *KerasCV*, which is exclusively applied to the training set [19].

Early experiments revealed difficulties in learning when the architecture operated solely in the Fourier domain. These challenges may stem from the complexities of differentiating through complex-valued activation functions [14,17]. To address this, we apply the (real) inverse FFT after each spectral convolutional, over the height and width axes, followed by traditional activation functions in the spatial domain, as illustrated in Fig. 3 (left). The outputs from the convolutional layers are average pooled across the channel dimension and fed into linear layers with 128 and 64 neurons, respectively, with ReLU activations applied throughout. A final sigmoid layer is used for binary classification.

As shown in Table 1, sparse updates combined with scan or vmap operations dramatically reduce training time compared to the rematerialization and naive+scan approaches. Using vmap (vectorized map) further improves efficiency

Table 1. Comparison of epoch training time, parameter count, number of selected positions (*e.g.*, 2^{12}), and accuracy across different methods on the Cats vs. Dogs dataset. A 6-layer CNN with 32 filters per layer is used for all experiments. Training times are reported on A100 80 GB GPUs.

Method	Epoch Training Time	# Params ↓	Accuracy (%) ↑
Spatial 3×3 CNN	$\sim$ 30s	60K	**86.64**
CF-Convs			
Naive	–	59K	Out-of-memory
Rematerialization	> 2 days	–	–
Scan	> 2 days	–	–
Sparse updates			
+Scan			
2^{18}	$\sim$18 min	–	–
+Vmap			
2^{12}	$\sim$4.5 min	59K	75.26
2^{15}	$\sim$4.5 min	59K	79.27
2^{18}	$\sim$5 min	59K	85.30

by running parallel computations. While there remains an approximately $10\times$ difference in training speeds compared to spatial CNNs, several important considerations contextualize this disparity. Firstly, the comparison is against spatial CNNs utilizing small 3×3 filters, whereas our layers can learn kernels ranging from spatial equivalents of 1×1 to $H \times W$ in about 5 min. Training time for our layers is agnostic to the kernel size, taking the same 5 min whether the spatial equivalent is 1×1 or $H \times W$. In contrast, spatial CNNs experience increased training times with larger kernel sizes. In the worst case scenario where the kernel is $H \times W$ the algorithmic complexity of performing the forward pass of a single kernel is $H \times W^2$ whereas with our approach the algorithmic complexity remains $H \times W$ via Fourier-based convolution. As such, while a performance gap continues to exists for small sized kernels our CNNs can efficiently scale to arbitrarily sized kernels.

However, CF-Conv performance still trails 3×3 spatial CNNs. This discrepancy suggests that CF-Convs may require more complex MLP architectures or further optimization to fully realize their potential. Moreover, the learning dynamics of spatial CNNs are well-understood and have been extensively validated empirically, whereas CF-Convs are still relatively new and may benefit from additional refinement and tuning.

We also examine the impact of different numbers of selected points on model performance, experimenting with 2^{12}, 2^{15}, and 2^{18} selected positions. The results indicate that smaller samples introduce more noise and provide less accurate gradient approximations. In contrast, using 2^{18} ($\sim$260,000) selected positions yields the best performance, striking an optimal balance between gradient approximation accuracy and memory usage. This configuration allows for stable and efficient training, while still fitting comfortably into GPU memory.

These results demonstrate that while CF-Convs have promising potential, further refinement is needed to match the performance of traditional spatial CNNs. Nonetheless, CF-Convs with sparse updates highlight the potential of Fourier-based continuous kernel methods, particularly for applications involving larger and more complex architectures.

7 Discussion

Our proposed method for scaling CF-Conv networks via sparse kernel updates addresses key challenges in memory utilization and training speed. By introducing sparse updates, we significantly reduce the memory required during training, making the method feasible for large-scale applications. However, the technique still has limitations. Each CF-Conv layer must store a stateful kernel variable with dimensions $H \times W \times C_{\text{in}} \times C_{\text{out}} \times 2$, accounting for the real and imaginary components. For models with many convolutional filters or large spatial dimensions, this can still become memory-intensive. To mitigate this, model-parallelism could be a viable strategy, where model weights are distributed across multiple GPUs or TPUs to alleviate memory constraints [15].

Another challenge is that applying pointwise activation functions directly in the Fourier domain leads to suboptimal performance. This requires that the inverse transform be utilized and the activation function applied in the spatial domain. Further processing requires transformation back to the Fourier domain. This occurs because both Fourier-domain convolution (pointwise multiplication) and pointwise activation functions operate independently on each frequency component, preventing interactions between different frequencies. However, such inter-frequency interactions may be crucial for capturing complex patterns.

To address this, we apply an inverse Fourier transform after each convolution and perform activations in the spatial domain. This allows pointwise non-linearities to act on spatial signals containing a mixture of frequencies, potentially enabling richer interactions. While this approach introduces additional computational overhead due to repeated FFT and IFFT operations, it preserves the efficiency of Fourier-based learning while leveraging spatial non-linearities effectively. Notably, spatial continuous kernels require an additional Fourier transform over the full generated kernel, which has dimensionality $H \times W \times C_{\text{in}} \times C_{\text{out}}$. In contrast, CF-Convs apply Fourier transforms only to the convolution result, which has a lower dimensionality of $H \times W \times C_{\text{out}}$, reducing computational cost. Therefore, a vital next step to improve the proposed method is to investigate how to approximate spatial activations directly in the Fourier domain.

The development of improved complex-valued activation functions could provide an alternative solution. With improved complex-valued non-linearities, it may become possible to directly apply activations in the Fourier domain without the need for intermediate transforms. This would allow the network to fully utilize phase and amplitude information, making the approach particularly appealing for domains like audio, radar, and sonar image processing, where such information is critical.

8 Conclusion

Our work introduces CF-Convs, a novel approach for learning continuous convolutional kernels in the Fourier domain. CF-Convs address three of the fundamental challenges of continuous convolutional filter learning: parameter efficiency, memory efficiency and training speed. While CNNs using our CF-Convs still lag behind their traditional spatial CNN counterparts, our novel training algorithm allows for CF-Convs to learn convolutional kernels of arbitrary size, making them a promising direction for larger-scale applications. Future works can easily expand upon this work as our code and experiments are fully open source.

References

1. Chen, T., Xu, B., Zhang, C., Guestrin, C.: Training deep nets with sublinear memory cost. arXiv preprint arXiv:1604.06174 (2016)
2. Dai, J., et al.: Deformable convolutional networks. In: 2017 IEEE International Conference on Computer Vision (ICCV), pp. 764–773 (2017). https://doi.org/10.1109/ICCV.2017.89
3. Elson, J., Douceur, J.J., Howell, J., Saul, J.: Asirra: a captcha that exploits interest-aligned manual image categorization. In: Proceedings of 14th ACM Conference on Computer and Communications Security (CCS). Association for Computing Machinery, Inc. (2007). https://www.microsoft.com/en-us/research/publication/
4. Jacobsen, J.H., Van Gemert, J., Lou, Z., Smeulders, A.W.M.: Structured receptive fields in CNNs. In: 2016 IEEE Conference on Computer Vision and Pattern Recognition (CVPR), pp. 2610–2619 (2016). https://doi.org/10.1109/CVPR.2016.286
5. Knigge, D.M., et al.: Modelling long range dependencies in nd: From task-specific to a general purpose CNN. In: The Eleventh International Conference on Learning Representations (2023). https://openreview.net/forum?id=ZW5aK4yCRqU
6. Kumar, R., Purohit, M., Svitkina, Z., Vee, E., Wang, J.: Efficient rematerialization for deep networks. In: Advances in Neural Information Processing Systems, vol. 32 (2019)
7. Mescheder, L., Oechsle, M., Niemeyer, M., Nowozin, S., Geiger, A.: Occupancy networks: learning 3D reconstruction in function space. In: Proceedings of the IEEE/CVF Conference on Computer Vision and Pattern Recognition, pp. 4460–4470 (2019)
8. Park, J.J., Florence, P., Straub, J., Newcombe, R., Lovegrove, S.: DeepSDF: learning continuous signed distance functions for shape representation. In: Proceedings of the IEEE/CVF Conference on Computer Vision and Pattern Recognition, pp. 165–174 (2019)

9. Pintea, S.L., Tömen, N., Goes, S.F., Loog, M., van Gemert, J.C.: Resolution learning in deep convolutional networks using scale-space theory. IEEE Trans. Image Process. **30**, 8342–8353 (2021). https://doi.org/10.1109/TIP.2021.3115001
10. Romero, D.W., Bruintjes, R.J., Tomczak, J.M., Bekkers, E.J., Hoogendoorn, M., van Gemert, J.: Flexconv: continuous kernel convolutions with differentiable kernel sizes. In: International Conference on Learning Representations (2022). https://openreview.net/forum?id=3jooF27-0Wy
11. Romero, D.W., Kuzina, A., Bekkers, E.J., Tomczak, J.M., Hoogendoorn, M.: CKConv: continuous kernel convolution for sequential data. In: International Conference on Learning Representations (2022). https://openreview.net/forum?id=8FhxBtXSl0
12. Romero, D.W., Lohit, S.: Learning partial equivariances from data. In: Advances in Neural Information Processing Systems, vol. 35, pp. 36466–36478 (2022)
13. Romero, D.W., Zeghidour, N.: DNArch: learning convolutional neural architectures by backpropagation. In: ICML 2023 Workshop on Differentiable Almost Everything: Differentiable Relaxations, Algorithms, Operators, and Simulators (2023). https://openreview.net/forum?id=rlQPdYh9JD
14. Scardapane, S., Van Vaerenbergh, S., Hussain, A., Uncini, A.: Complex-valued neural networks with nonparametric activation functions. IEEE Trans. Emerg. Top. Comput. Intell. **4**(2), 140–150 (2020). https://doi.org/10.1109/TETCI.2018.2872600
15. Shoeybi, M., Patwary, M., Puri, R., LeGresley, P., Casper, J., Catanzaro, B.: Megatron-LM: training multi-billion parameter language models using model parallelism. arXiv preprint arXiv:1909.08053 (2019)
16. Sitzmann, V., Martel, J., Bergman, A., Lindell, D., Wetzstein, G.: Implicit neural representations with periodic activation functions. In: Advances in Neural Information Processing Systems, vol. 33, pp. 7462–7473 (2020)
17. Tygert, M., Bruna, J., Chintala, S., LeCun, Y., Piantino, S., Szlam, A.: A mathematical motivation for complex-valued convolutional networks. Neural Computation **28**(5), 815–825 (2016). https://doi.org/10.1162/NECO_a_00824
18. Wood, L., Larson, E.C.: Parametric spectral filters for fast converging, scalable convolutional neural networks. In: ICASSP 2021-2021 IEEE International Conference on Acoustics, Speech and Signal Processing (ICASSP), pp. 2800–2804. IEEE (2021)
19. Wood, L., et al.: Kerascv (2022). https://github.com/keras-team/keras-cv

Benchmarking Defense Techniques for Securing Large Language Models

Abdulkadir Korkmaz(✉), Timoteo Kelly, and Praveen Rao

University of Missouri, Columbia, USA
{ak69t,tkb5b,raopr}@missouri.edu

Abstract. Large language models (LLMs) now drive applications in e-commerce, healthcare, law, and education, yet they expose systems to threats such as prompt injection and jailbreak-style manipulation. Many defenses—ranging from API-level controls to semantic or behavioral detectors—have been proposed, but their effectiveness is rarely measured under consistent conditions. This work presents an empirical benchmark of nine representative techniques using a unified testbed. The framework issues benign and adversarial prompts to measure detection accuracy, false-positive rates, and latency across both rule-based modules and machine learning-based detectors. Our results show that no single defense provides comprehensive coverage: rule-based methods offer low-latency filtering for structural anomalies, while ML-based detectors capture indirect semantic attacks at the cost of higher overhead and increased false positives. These findings highlight the need for modular, context-aware defense pipelines in practical deployments.

Keywords: Large Language Models · Prompt Injection · Security Benchmarking · Adversarial Detection · Anomaly Detection

1 Introduction

Large Language Models (LLMs) enable natural language reasoning, generation, and task orchestration across consumer and enterprise applications. However, their open-ended interfaces introduce security risks that are uncommon in traditional software systems. Prominent threats include prompt injections that override safety policies, jailbreaks that elicit restricted behavior, and maliciously crafted inputs that attempt to manipulate or probe system behavior.

Several countermeasures have been proposed, ranging from access control and request validation to anomaly detection and semantic policy checks. However, they are usually evaluated in isolation with heterogeneous datasets, making it difficult to compare coverage, precision, and performance. This work presents a systematic benchmark that evaluates nine representative defenses under identical experimental conditions. Our framework measures detection accuracy, false positives, and latency. It analyzes each defense within its intended threat scope to surface technique-specific strengths and limitations rather than producing a single leaderboard. To this end, we offer the following contributions:

F. Tanner and J. Irvine (Eds.): AIPR 2025, LNCS 16446, pp. 246–254, 2026.
https://doi.org/10.1007/978-3-032-18474-0_18

In practice, it is hard to compare defenses when they are tested on different data and systems. To make results comparable, we use a shared prompt set for ML-based modules (Qualifire) and targeted, scripted scenarios for rule-based controls, run under the same local setup with the same logging. Each module is evaluated on its own with a simple, consistent operating-point policy (low-FPR for rules, balanced for ML) so that detection, false positives, and latency can be read as *fit-to-purpose* indicators rather than a single leaderboard. To make our goals concrete, we summarize the main contributions of this work below.

- We propose a unified benchmark for evaluating nine defense modules under identical conditions.
- We provide a technique-level comparison that emphasizes operational characteristics rather than global ranking.
- We analyze practical deployment trade-offs among latency, interpretability, and semantic depth.

2 Related Work

LLM security benchmarking has emerged as a critical area bridging natural language processing and trustworthy computing. Several recent studies have explored prompt-injection robustness and defense evaluation.

JailbreakBench [2] is among the earliest standardized benchmarks, compiling hundreds of jailbreak-style adversarial prompts with reproducible evaluation metrics. It focuses primarily on prompt-based policy evasion, without incorporating behavioral or API-layer protections. **Formalizing and Benchmarking Prompt Injection Attacks and Defenses** [3] systematizes ten defenses under controlled linguistic attacks, highlighting weaknesses in prompt filtering and instruction consistency, but excludes runtime constraints and adaptive traffic patterns. **RAS-Eval** [4] evaluates LLM agents interacting with real tools, mapping failure cases to Common Weakness Enumeration (CWE) categories—broadening the scope to realistic, multi-agent settings. **CySecBench** [5] focuses on cybersecurity prompts, while **PINT** [6] provides an extensive dataset for injection and benign comparison. **Amazon Security Benchmark** [7] evaluates LLMs in log-analysis and intrusion detection tasks, but does not assess modular defense layers.

None of these benchmarks measure single-module defense performance under unified conditions. Our framework fills this gap by analyzing defenses under identical execution parameters.

3 Defense Techniques and Design

We evaluate two defense families: rule-based systems using deterministic checks, and ML-based systems that infer security-relevant patterns.

3.1 Rule-Based Defenses

Rule-based defenses rely on deterministic constraints and static metadata checks. We evaluate five such modules.

API Gateway. HMAC-based signatures with nonce rotation enforce client authentication and message integrity [8,9], rejecting unauthorized or replayed requests at near-zero latency. The mechanism does not analyze prompt content, so semantic attacks from authenticated clients can still succeed.

Rate Limiter. Token-bucket and sliding-window quotas [10, 11] suppress bursty probing and brute-force enumeration. Attacks that distribute requests across multiple identities or longer time intervals can bypass these rate-based constraints.

Input Validation. NFKC normalization, zero-width stripping, URL/MIME allow-lists, and entropy-based constraints [13, 14] detect malformed, encoded, or structurally suspicious inputs. These checks struggle with multilingual, confusable-character, or semantically subtle jailbreaks.

Instruction Consistency. Template- and phrase-based checks identify role-redefinition attempts such as "ignore previous instructions" [3]. Direct overrides are detected reliably, but paraphrased or narrative jailbreaks often bypass these patterns.

Context-Aware Smoothing. Similarity scoring and short-horizon cooldown intervals [12] reduce stepwise probing across a session. The mechanism adds delay during benign rapid interaction and is less effective in stateless API deployments.

3.2 Machine Learning-Based Defenses

Machine-learning-based defenses infer intent or abnormality from data rather than fixed rules.

Adversarial Detector. An embedding-based classifier trained on jailbreak and benign examples [15, 16] identifies known adversarial structures. Performance drops under novel obfuscation or stylistic transformations that diverge from the training distribution.

SPVD. A lightweight semantic classifier maps prompt intent to restricted categories [17, 18], enabling fast detection of harmful objectives. Hypothetical or research-oriented prompts increase false-positive risk when intent is ambiguous.

Behavioral Analysis. Temporal features such as burstiness, repetition, and escalation [4, 19] capture probing behavior across user sessions. The approach requires stable identifiers and degrades when users distribute prompts across multiple fresh sessions.

4 Benchmarking Framework

4.1 Dataset and Setup

We use the Qualifire Prompt Injection Benchmark [1] (5,000+ labeled prompts across benign, jailbreak) *only for the ML-based modules* (Adversarial Detection, SPVD, Anomaly Detection, Behavioral Analysis). For these, each model processes identical, shuffled prompt batches under a common harness to ensure equal exposure and reproducibility.

Rule-based controls (API Gateway, Rate Limiter, Input Validation, Instruction Consistency, Context-Aware Smoothing) are not dataset-driven; they were evaluated in a constructed environment using scripted scenarios aligned with each control's threat model (e.g., unauthorized/replay clients for API Gateway, burst and rolling-window probes for Rate Limiting, malformed/encoded payloads for Input Validation). The *Tests* column in Table 1 reflects these per-technique scenario counts (tens to hundreds for rule-based scripts vs. thousands for ML-based detectors).

All experiments ran on the same local CPU-based setup to emulate low-latency deployment conditions. Timing instrumentation and logging were identical across modules; configuration parameters (e.g., thresholds) were fixed per module for the duration of testing.

4.2 Architecture and Evaluation

Figure 1 illustrates the architecture. The evaluation controller dispatches prompts through a single active defense module at a time. Responses and timing metrics are logged uniformly. This isolation allows direct assessment of each defense's individual contribution without interference or stacking effects. We report **True Positive Rate (TPR), False Positive Rate (FPR), Precision, and average per-request latency** at a single operating point.

4.3 Behavioral Module Example

Figure 2 illustrates the operation of the Behavioral Analysis module. It aggregates temporal features (e.g., burst intervals, repetition frequency, cross-session variance) to compute an anomaly score determining whether interaction patterns indicate automation or probing.

5 Results and Discussion

Table 1 summarizes the comparative performance of rule-based and ML-based defenses. Each module was tested independently on 1,500–5,000 prompts.

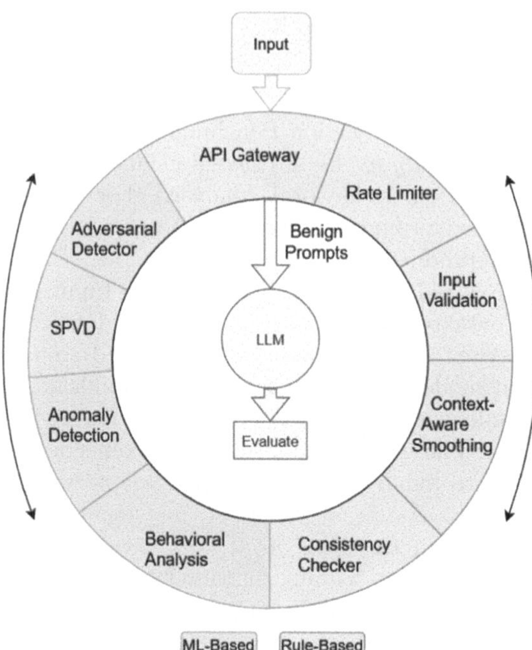

Fig. 1. Unified benchmarking architecture for single-module evaluation, where one defense is active at a time.

5.1 Result Interpretation

Performance scores reflect *fit-to-purpose*, not overall ranking. Rule-based defenses deliver high precision and low latency since they target narrow, well-defined threats such as replay attacks or input format anomalies. Machine-learning methods address subtler semantic manipulations, explaining their lower TPRs and elevated FPRs.

The latency differences largely reflect computational complexity: SPVD uses a lightweight intent classifier, while Adversarial Detection relies on full embedding computation and nearest-neighbor similarity checks over the seed set. Behavioral Analysis also incurs overhead from maintaining session state and extracting temporal features, explaining its mid-range latency.

Across all modules, we observed a consistent trade-off: rule-based techniques detect structural anomalies well, whereas ML-based detectors capture indirect semantic attacks but with higher false positives. However, ML models also produced higher false-positive rates on long or technical benign prompts, highlighting the difficulty of separating harmful intent from naturally high-variance user queries.

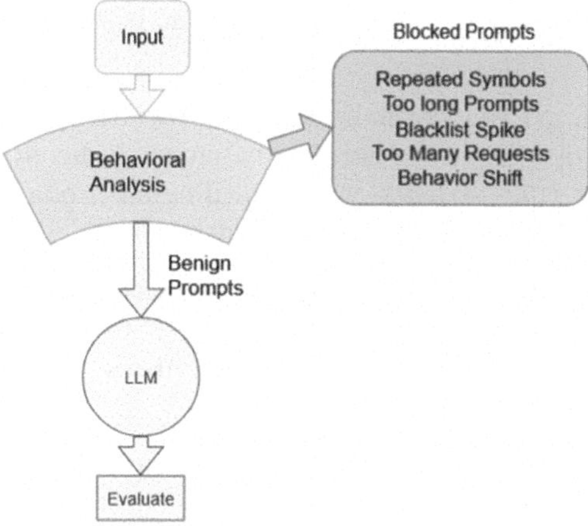

Fig. 2. Example of a single technique in operation: Behavioral Analysis.

Table 1. Performance comparison of rule-based and ML-based defenses.

Technique	TPR (%)	FPR (%)	Precision (%)	Latency (ms)	Tests
[Rule-based]					
API Gateway	100	0	100	0.5	40
Rate Limiter	50	0	100	0.2	400
Input Validation	82	20	90	700	150
Instruction Consistency	88	4	95.7	1	100
Context-Aware Smoothing	70	5	93.3	2500	100
[ML-based]					
Behavioral Analysis	90	8	88.4	1200	1500
Adversarial Detection	58	12	82.9	5000	5000
Anomaly Detection	68	25	73.1	600	5000
SPVD	64	10	86.5	10	5000

5.2 Technique Observations

In the following, we summarize the operational behavior observed for each defense technique during evaluation.

API Gateway. This module provides strong client authentication via HMAC-based signatures and nonce rotation, enabling near-zero-latency rejection of unauthorized or replayed requests. However, because it does not inspect prompt content, it cannot block semantic attacks issued by authenticated clients.

Rate Limiter. The fixed token-bucket and sliding-window quotas effectively suppress bursty probing and brute-force enumeration. Its impact diminishes for distributed or low-frequency attacks, where traffic is spread across identities or long intervals.

Input Validation. NFKC normalization, zero-width stripping, URL/MIME allow-lists, and entropy/length constraints catch overt encodings and malformed inputs. These static rules struggle with multilingual prompts, Unicode confusables, and semantically obfuscated jailbreak attempts.

Instruction Consistency. This module blocks explicit role-redefinition attempts—such as "ignore previous instructions"—using phrase and template checks. It performs well on direct overrides but misses paraphrased or narrative jailbreaks that lack clear trigger terms.

Context-Aware Smoothing. Similarity checks and short-horizon rate gating reduce stepwise probing across a session. While effective for repeated manipulative attempts, the mechanism adds delay during legitimate rapid interaction and provides limited benefit in stateless APIs.

Adversarial Detection. The embedding-based classifier identifies known jailbreak templates through keyword prefiltering and semantic similarity. Its recall decreases when attackers use novel obfuscation styles, highlighting the need for periodic seed and negative-example updates.

Anomaly Detection. The TF–IDF and Isolation Forest combination surfaces distributional outliers and unusual token patterns. Thresholds are sensitive to benign topic drift, requiring recalibration to avoid spikes in false positives.

SPVD. The semantic policy-violation detector performs fast intent classification and reliably flags prompts aligned with restricted behaviors. Ambiguous or hypothetical security-related prompts can trigger false positives without stronger contextual cues.

Behavioral Analysis. Session-level signals such as burstiness, repetition, and lexical shifts enable this module to detect iterative probing and indirect jailbreak attempts. Its effectiveness depends on persistent identifiers and decreases when users distribute queries across multiple sessions.

5.3 Limitations and Scope

Our evaluation blends dataset-driven tests for ML modules (Qualifire) with scenario-driven scripts for rule-based controls, on a single CPU profile and one operating point per module (ROC/PR omitted for space). Performance will vary across deployments with different hardware profiles, language distributions, session models, and threshold settings. Common escapes include text obfuscation—particularly mixed-script/zero-width Unicode that evades pattern filters—indirect rephrasings, and multi-turn prompt splitting. We also observed occasional over-blocking of long benign research prompts, indicating the need for normalization, cross-turn aggregation, and calibrated thresholds in deployment.

6 Conclusion and Future Work

We benchmarked nine LLM defense techniques under a unified evaluation harness, analyzing each module individually to highlight its strengths and limitations. Rule-based defenses provided fast, high-precision filtering for structurally anomalous inputs, while ML-based detectors captured semantically indirect attacks at the cost of higher false-positive rates. These results show that no single defense provides complete coverage; instead, practical deployments will require layered pipelines that combine low-latency rule-based filters with deeper semantic models.

Future work includes expanding the defense library, evaluating multi-turn and multilingual prompts, and documenting undetected failure cases across defenses to support more comprehensive benchmarking.

Acknowledgments. We thank the EECS Department at University of Missouri for travel support. The first author (A.K.) was supported by the Republic of Türkiye YLSY Scholarship Program. The second author (T. K.) acknowledges support of the National Science Foundation and U.S. Office of Personnel Management CyberCorps Grant No. #1946619.

References

1. Qualifire Dataset: Prompt injections benchmark. https://huggingface.co/datasets/qualifire/prompt-injections-benchmark. Accessed 01 Sep 2025
2. Chao, P., et al.: JailbreakBench: an open robustness benchmark for jailbreaking large language models. arXiv:2404.01318 (2024)
3. Liu, Y., Jia, Y., Geng, R., Jia, J., Gong, N.Z.: Formalizing and benchmarking prompt injection attacks and defenses. In: Proceedings of the 33rd USENIX Security Symposium (USENIX Security 2024), Philadelphia, PA, USA (2024)
4. Fu, Y., Yuan, X., Wang, D.: RAS-Eval: a comprehensive benchmark for security evaluation of LLM agents in real-world environments. arXiv:2506.15253 (2025)
5. Wahréus, J., Hussain, A.M., Papadimitratos, P.: CySecBench: generative AI-based CyberSecurity-focused prompt dataset for benchmarking large language models. arXiv:2501.01335 (2025)
6. Lakera: PINT benchmark: prompt injection test toolkit (dataset and evaluation framework). GitHub (2024). https://github.com/lakeraai/pint-benchmark. Accessed 01 Sep 2025
7. Ghashami, M., et al.: An evaluation benchmark for generative AI in the security domain. Amazon Science (2024)
8. Hardt, D.: The OAuth 2.0 authorization framework. RFC 6749, Internet engineering task force (2012). https://datatracker.ietf.org/doc/html/rfc6749. Accessed 01 Sep 2025
9. Krawczyk, H., Bellare, M., Canetti, R.: HMAC: keyed-hashing for message authentication. RFC 2104, IETF (1997). https://datatracker.ietf.org/doc/html/rfc2104. Accessed 01 Sep 2025
10. Heinanen, J., Guerin, R.: A single rate Three Color Marker (srTCM). RFC 2697, IETF (1999). https://datatracker.ietf.org/doc/html/rfc2697. Accessed 01 Sep 2025

11. Heinanen, J., Guerin, R.: A two rate Three Color Marker (trTCM). RFC 2698, IETF (1999). https://datatracker.ietf.org/doc/html/rfc2698. Accessed 01 Sep 2025
12. Fang, W., Seddigh, N., Nandy, B.: A differentiated service two-rate, three-color marker with efficient handling of in-profile traffic. RFC 4115, IETF (2005). https://datatracker.ietf.org/doc/html/rfc4115. Accessed 01 Sep 2025
13. OWASP foundation: Secure coding practices—quick reference guide. Input validation checklist. https://owasp.org/www-project-secure-coding-practices-quick-reference-guide/. Accessed 01 Sep 2025
14. MITRE corporation: CWE category 1134: Input Validation and Data Sanitization (IDS). https://cwe.mitre.org/data/definitions/1134.html. Accessed 01 Sep 2025
15. Ayub, M.A., Majumdar, S.: Embedding-based classifiers can detect prompt injection attacks. arXiv:2410.22284 (2024)
16. Wang, J., Zhang, X., Zhao, L., Zhang, Y., et al.: Adversarial prompt detection in large language models using prompt and response features. Comput. Mater. Continua **83**(3) (2025)
17. Inan, H., et al.: LLAMA Guard: LLM-based input–output safeguard for human–AI conversations. arXiv:2312.06674 (2023)
18. Wen, X., Mo, W.J., Xie, Y., Qi, P., Chen, M.: Learning efficient guardrails for policy violation detection. arXiv:2510.03485 (2025)
19. Wu, Y., Zeng, W., Li, S., Zhang, T., Jiang, H.: Graph-based anomaly detection in LLM-based multi-agent systems. arXiv:2505.24201 (2025)

Advancing Foundation Models with Spatiotemporal Reasoning in Multimodal Applications

Alexander N. Wood(✉) and Ben Thompson

The MITRE Corporation, 7525 Colshire Dr, McLean, VA 22102, USA
https://www.mitre.org/

Abstract. Current computer vision foundation models focus on general-purpose tasks but have limited specialized spatiotemporal reasoning capabilities. Adapting these models to geospatial applications and multimodal workflows requires addressing core challenges in spatial, temporal, and spectral representation learning. This paper proposes methodologies and a series of experiments aimed at advancing foundation models with spatiotemporal reasoning capabilities tailored for multimodal geospatial applications. These experiments address local and global position encoding, multi-resolution and multi-sensor fusion for remote sensing data, temporal reasoning, and multimodal fusion of additional spatiotemporal data types, including geospatial vectors and motion trajectories. The goal is to develop robust embedding strategies and model architectures that can generalize across regions, sensors, modalities, and timescales for downstream applications requiring spatiotemporal understanding.

Keywords: remote sensing · foundation models

1 Introduction

A central challenge in artificial intelligence is the development of systems with spatiotemporal understanding and reasoning, which has shifted from data scarcity to developing models that can convert diverse, high-volume geospatial data types into actionable intelligence. With NASA archives projected to grow to nearly 600 petabytes by 2030 [46] and an increasing volume of commercial remote sensing imagery available, geospatial data analysis will depend on automated workflows integrating electro-optical (EO), synthetic aperture radar (SAR), hyperspectral (HS), and other remote sensing (RS) modalities, along with non-visual sources such as geospatial vectors, movement data, and any other modality with a spatiotemporal context.

Traditional physics-based and supervised learning approaches often lack flexibility and face scaling limitations, requiring large labeled datasets and struggling to generalize across sensors, geographies, and environmental conditions. The shift to foundation models (FMs) has enabled generalization across diverse

F. Tanner and J. Irvine (Eds.): AIPR 2025, LNCS 16446, pp. 255–273, 2026.
https://doi.org/10.1007/978-3-032-18474-0_19

tasks. However, FMs such as large language models (LLMs) [8,18,62] and multimodal systems such as vision-language models (VLMs) [72] focus on language, vision, and speech capabilities and fall short when directly applied to geospatial data, struggling to integrate unique and complex modalities [2,13,24,41].

Unlike conventional "horizontal" imagery, remote sensing data is inherently geospatial, collected from satellite and airborne platforms that are subject to variations in orbital altitudes, sensor angles (nadir and off-nadir), atmospheric conditions, and weather influences [9]. These factors introduce subtle but powerful differences that models must incorporate to achieve spatiotemporal understanding.

Effectively incorporating geospatial data in a foundation model requires an awareness of global positioning on the Earth and relative positions and distances between objects [10,39]. Extending this to incorporate temporal reasoning adds further challenges such as irregular sampling intervals, varying observation duration, and misaligned data [30]. Variability on the Earth's surface caused by weather, seasonality, cloud cover, and human activity can alter the appearance of a location over time, further complicating spatiotemporal reasoning [54].

Additionally, imagery collected by different satellites is not generally directly comparable due to differences in spectral bands captured and their ground sample distances (GSDs) [54]. The physics and active sensing mechanisms of SAR systems present distinct challenges compared to EO sensors, which passively capture solar reflectance [71]. The addition of non-visual spatiotemporal modalities such as geospatial vector data (e.g., maps, polygons), digital elevation models (DEMs), measurements (e.g., seismic activity), and motion trajectories (e.g., GPS, AIS) presents further challenges to fusion, requiring an embedding space capable of processing the unique characteristics of each data type [10,56].

To address these challenges, this paper proposes a series of experiments designed to advance the capabilities of FMs for spatiotemporal analysis. The goal is to develop robust embedding strategies and model architectures that can generalize across regions, sensors, modalities, and timescales for downstream applications requiring spatiotemporal understanding. Key focus areas include integrating spatial reasoning, temporal reasoning, spectral flexibility, multi-sensor fusion, and multimodal fusion. The following sections describe a series of experiments that build towards the next generation of spatiotemporal FMs.

2 Background

2.1 Remote Sensing Foundation Models

Remote sensing foundation models are a class of foundation models that train a backbone on large remote sensing datasets that can then be utilized for downstream geospatial tasks. Early examples such as SatMAE [15] and SatCLIP [25] demonstrate the effectiveness of RS domain-aware self-supervised learning. Scale-MAE [52] introduces a ground sample distance (GSD) positional encoding based on the land area covered by an RS image. Additional models such as Prithvi [59], SatCLIP [25], SpectralGPT [22], CSP [41], DOFA [70], Clay [14], MTP [66],

AnySat [3], EarthMAE [63], and AlphaEarth [7] provide additional approaches toward domain-aware self-supervised learning for remote sensing data.

2.2 Geospatial Reasoning

Location encoding maps geospatial coordinates to high-dimensional vector embeddings, enabling geography-aware downstream tasks by preserving spatial relationships in the data [10,39]. Some methods rely on pixel-wise alignment of images captured over the same coordinates without explicitly encoding location [27,43,51], but these approaches are brittle and struggle with multi-sensor imagery captured at different resolutions. Other approaches use encoders that preserve geographic distance, reflect directional relationships, and generalize to unseen locations and new tasks [39], with supervised methods that incorporate geospatial awareness in machine learning models [2,12,13,73].

Several self-supervised learning models use geolocation as a supervisory signal during pre-training, teaching models about spatial proximity implicitly without directly leveraging geospatial location during inference [4,24]. Recent advances use learnable encoders for geospatial inputs, where geolocation is encoded and jointly optimized alongside paired imagery to a shared embedding space [10,39]. GeoCLIP projects geolocation to an embedding space shared with photographs using Equal Earth Projection, Random Fourier Features (RFFs), and learnable multi-layer perceptrons (MLPs) [64]. Geo-Aligned Implicit Representations (GAIR) extends this approach, jointly optimizing RS imagery, street view, and location encoders with a contrastive objective [34]. PIEViT [37] assumes ground features such as mountains and cities form visual clusters and leverages its Geospatial Pattern Cohesion (GPC) module during training, which guides mask generation during student-teacher training in a masked image modeling framework.

2.3 Temporal Reasoning

Temporal data comes in a wide variety of modalities, from regularly sampled videos [68] and standard time series to sparsely and irregularly sampled RS imagery [11,15,60], trajectories [29,32], geospatial vector sequences [38,40], dynamic graphs [53], time-aware text documents [19], and events [1], each presenting challenges such as irregular sampling, varying duration, and misaligned observations [30].

Traditional approaches such as recurrent neural networks (RNNs) and Long Short-Term Memory networks (LSTMs) were limited by their sequential computational processes [26], leading to adoption of transformer-based methods that better capture global, long-range dependencies [47,69,78]. RS-specific models have used spatiotemporal patching and strategies such as encoding temporal position in a lookup table (TSViT [60]), sine/cosine positional encoding (SatMAE [15], Prithvi-EO-2.0 [59]), and learnable embedding layers (EarthMAE [63]) to incorporate temporal contexts. Multimodal approaches to modeling temporal data in FMs use techniques such as conversion to natural language

(OmniGeo [76]), positional encoding mechanisms (PerceiverIO [23]), modality-specific encoders for sequential data (AllSpark [55]), and RoPE-based approaches (TMRoPE [72]).

2.4 Spectral and Multi-sensor Challenges

Remote sensing platforms capture imagery across the electromagnetic spectrum, spanning visible, near infrared (NIR), infrared (IR), ultraviolet (UV), radio, and microwave bands, each offering its own unique insights into the Earth's surface. Recent advancements present various strategies for multi-sensor input in FMs [54]. EarthMAE [63] learns source-specific tokenizers for each modality that are combined with learned embeddings that encode spatiotemporal context, but requires manual integration of new sensors. SatMAE [15] and SatMAE++ [48] group embedding layers based on spectral wavelengths (e.g., one group for RGB+NIR bands) for sensor-specific embeddings to leverage similarities across sensors. Prithvi-EO-2.0 [59] uses a 3D convolutional layer to process harmonized multi-sensor data, acting on all bands simultaneously rather than having a separate encoder for each. SpectralGPT [22] adopts a sensor-agnostic approach by processing 3D spatial-spectral tokens with shared projections, including spatial and spectral context of the input in the position embedding for each token. DOFA [70] and FlexiMo [28] present sensor-agnostic approaches that use hypernetworks to dynamically generate network weights based on the central wavelength of each input band.

In addition to differences in spectral bands, RS platforms capture imagery at a wide range of possible ground sample distances (GSDs), and methods developed to analyze imagery at one scale do not always transfer to imagery captured at another scale [54]. To address this, Scale-MAE [52] ingests multi-spectral input bands with varying GSDs using a GSD positional encoder and a Laplacian-pyramid decoder. SatMAE++ [48] extends this by incorporating multi-scale information during pre-training with an objective that forces the model to reconstruct data at different scales. FlexiMo [28] dynamically generates weights and biases for a convolution kernel for each input based on input metadata including spatial resolution and patch size.

Determining when to treat sensors as distinct modalities versus as part of a continuous spectrum is a key challenge [54]. The active sensing mechanism and distinct physical properties of SAR present unique challenges compared to EO imagery [71]. While some models, like DOFA [70], are able to process both EO and SAR data in a common backbone, SAR's complexity and domain specificity mean that most approaches are tailored to SAR and not easily transferable to other RS modalities. Recent advancements use SAR's unique physics to train SAR foundation models, such as integrating polarimetric decomposition and power reconstruction into pretext tasks and loss functions [67].

2.5 Multimodal Fusion

Current cutting-edge FMs such as OpenAI's GPT [49,50], Google's Gemini [61], and Baidu's Ernie [6] are capable of integrating modalities from multimodal sources, typically text, images, audio, and video, into a unified architecture. Most multimodal FMs focus on general-purpose tasks like conversation, image generation, and writing code, and lack the specialized spatiotemporal reasoning needed to meaningfully analyze complex and varied geospatial data types. Fewer resources have been put against geospatial awareness methodologies for multimodal data and efforts have largely focused on raster (image) data [10].

Domain-specific frameworks like TorchGeo [56] and TorchSpatial [10] provide foundational tools for handling geospatial data formats and a starting point for integrating multimodal geospatial data into shared embedding spaces. Additional frameworks provide tools for integrating trajectory data [29,32], 3D spatial coordinates [75], event sequences [31], GPS data [74], and time series [16].

3 Proposed Experiments

3.1 Relative Position

The first proposed experiment introduces a novel relative geospatial position embedding scheme adapted from Rotary Positional Embedding [57] that encodes the bearing and distance between image patches (tokens) directly into the self-attention mechanism of the Vision Transformer (ViT), enabling spatially aware reasoning across multiple, potentially overlapping images.

For relative position, we propose representing each patch pair as a 2D vector by calculating the bearing and distance between their centers. For patches i and j, bearing $\beta_{i,j}$ and distance $\delta_{i,j}$ are used to calculate the vectors $v^{i,j}$ and $v^{j,i}$, where

$$v^{i,j} = \left(\delta_{i,j} \sin\left(\beta_{i,j}\right), \delta_{i,j} \cos\left(\beta_{i,j}\right)\right).$$

These vectors are then fed into a rotational encoding mechanism inspired by Rotary Positional Embedding (RoPE). Here, a block-diagonal rotation matrix $\mathbf{R}_{i,j}$ is constructed [57,58] with blocks given by:

$$\left\{ M\left(\theta \frac{\delta_{i,j}}{c} \sin(\beta)\right) \,\middle|\, \theta \in [\theta_1, \theta_2, \ldots, \theta_{d/8}],\, \beta \in [\beta_{i,j}, \beta_{j,i}] \right\}$$

and

$$\left\{ M\left(\theta \frac{\delta_{i,j}}{c} \cos(\beta)\right) \,\middle|\, \theta \in [\theta_1, \theta_2, \ldots, \theta_{d/8}],\, \beta \in [\beta_{i,j}, \beta_{j,i}] \right\}$$

where M is a rotation matrix, d is the dimension of the patch embedding, $\theta_i = c \cdot 10000^{-8(i-1)/d}$ for $i \in [1, 2, 3, \ldots, d/8]$, and c is a pre-defined distance scaling parameter. The resulting attention function applies these rotation matrices to queries and keys, allowing the attention mechanism to be sensitive to the direction and proximity of patches.

Several strategies can reduce the cost of computing pairwise bearings and distances. Hierarchical spatial indexing systems such as GeoHash or H3 can group patches into super-patches, allowing pairwise distances to be approximated. For example, deterministic bit layouts in H3 indexes provide upper bounds on pairwise cell distances that could be pre-computed and stored in lookup tables. Additional engineering solutions include caching intermediate results for repeated patch pairs, parallelizing across GPUs, using low-precision arithmetic for faster rotation matrix calculations, or using a fixed orientation vector for distant or non-overlapping patches. Ultimately, an efficient approach would likely combine hierarchical approximation for large distances with refined calculations for small-scale distances and overlapping patches.

For model training, building on PIEViT [37], we propose incorporating Geospatial Pattern Cohesion (GPC) modules to capture contextual similarity between neighboring patches with a dual-headed student-teacher architecture. This design balances global visual features and local, texture-based features, where the class-level head encodes coarse categories and the patch-level head learns fine-grained details.

Model training and evaluation would utilize a global-scale remote sensing dataset covering a range of orbital altitudes, viewing geometries, environmental conditions, and polar regions, comprising data either from a single sensor or multiple sensors compatible with a unified backbone. The Vision Transformer could be trained in three configurations: baseline (no geospatial positional encoding), RoPE-style encoding using relative patch position [21][1], and the proposed orientation-aware rotational encoding. Pretext tasks can include geospatial relationship prediction (bearing and distance between patches), geospatial relationship comprehension (retrieving a patch at a given relative location), and cross-image patch localization (identifying a patch from one image within another, overlapping image). Evaluation would assess geospatial task performance (e.g., object-level change detection across unaligned imagery), computational cost, latency, benchmark accuracy, and robustness to misalignment and metadata noise.

3.2 Global Position

This experiment aims to explicitly integrate absolute global geospatial metadata (e.g., geospatial position, orientation) into a geospatial foundation model for remote sensing, enabling geospatial reasoning across images without pixel-level alignment. We propose using a continuous spherical encoding that preserves geodesic distances (e.g., Sphere2Vec [42]) alongside hierarchical encoding at multiple scales (e.g., GeoHash, H3), with orientation encoded using a rotational mechanism analogous to the local encoding RoPE-like approach.

This model can be trained either from scratch or by leveraging an existing backbone. Training from scratch allows the model to learn geospatial represen-

[1] Exploring modifications to the mixed frequency encoding approach from ViT-RoPE [21] may also be fruitful.

tations directly within its embedding space but requires large amounts of computational resources. Using a pre-trained backbone reduces computational costs but may introduce the risk of a domain gap that limits the backbone's ability to fully capture new modalities. We recommend leveraging the model from the prior experiment as a backbone and learning a mapping between the spatial encoding and the backbone model's feature space. While freezing this backbone offers a straightforward approach, selectively fine-tuning layers within the model (e.g., partial unfreezing) may enable greater adaptation to global geospatial reasoning tasks.

Self-supervised pre-training tasks may include masked image modeling with geographic positions, where visually clustered ground features are jointly masked [37]. Geolocation can also serve as a supervisory signal, employing a contrastive objective that minimizes embedding space distance between the image and its neighbors while maximizing it for distant images [4,24]. Additional pretext tasks include distance estimation between patches, re-orienting images to a "north up" presentation, locating a small high-resolution region within a larger overlapping low-resolution image, and aligning separate captures of geographic features.

Experiments should evaluate whether including global and local/relative position improves performance on established RS baselines. In addition, spatial understanding can be assessed with tasks such as object-level change detection across unaligned image pairs, geographically aware super-resolution, anomaly detection, and instance geolocation precision. The model's robustness to orientation errors, incomplete coverage, and hallucination mitigation (e.g., to ensure no false change detection outside overlapping regions) should also be tested. Another assessment should compare performance on regions included versus excluded from the training data.

3.3 Bias and Global Positioning

Prior works (e.g., SatCLIP [25], GeoCLIP [64], OmniGeo [76]) show that models leverage absolute locations effectively for geospatial reasoning tasks such as scene classification and geolocation. However, these studies also highlight the risk: models may exploit location as a shortcut for inference, relying on memorized associations (e.g., coordinates linked to climate zones or weather patterns) rather than interpreting the actual context in new imagery. While this can be an advantage in some applications (e.g., geolocation), it may reduce generalizability to unseen locations and make models vulnerable to rapidly changing environments and adversarial conditions. Additionally, incomplete metadata could further undermine model reliability and performance.

This experiment would determine whether geospatial foundation models with absolute positions learn spatial context or memorize absolute positions, identifying scenarios where absolute position context is harmful (e.g., degradation of performance in new environments) versus helpful (e.g., improved performance in well-characterized regions). Tests should use a diverse dataset spanning geographic regions, terrains, and sensor azimuths, including both sparsely sampled and densely sampled areas. Evaluating performance on unseen geographic areas and sparsely sampled regions could help determine the balance between coordinate memorization and visual reasoning (e.g., Geo-Bias Score [10]). The impact of random masking and other perturbations (e.g., noise injection, coordinate shifts, coordinate masking) should be measured to characterize robustness to inaccurate or missing metadata, while synthetic coordinate swapping could simulate adversarial scenarios with misleading geospatial information. Further experimentation should explore the impact of cumulative error introduced by the geospatial coordinate projections commonly seen in geospatial workflows, such as distance measurement workflows that convert from WGS84 to EPSG3857, measure distance, then convert back to WGS84. Bias towards memorization can be further evaluated by examining when models fail to detect changes in newly developed areas or fail to detect objects that are new to a scene.

3.4 Temporal Reasoning

This experiment would test a framework for encoding temporal information in FMs for spatiotemporal reasoning where absolute timestamps can be split into hierarchical components (e.g., minute, hour, day-of-week, day-of-year, year). These components can each be encoded using learnable embeddings [63], rotary position embeddings [72], or a hybrid method. These temporal embeddings should be integrated with spatial features to represent spatiotemporal context and trained with spatiotemporal masking strategies [63].

While initially tested in the context of RS imagery, this framework should be designed with future extension to multimodal inputs in mind. The dataset used for testing and evaluation should include RS data with varied revisit intervals and spatial overlap. Evaluation should cover typical RS baseline tasks where temporal context is irrelevant, ensuring no loss in performance, as well as temporal tasks such as change detection, temporal similarity, event reconstruction (e.g., fire progression, land cover changes), or temporal ordering. Ablation studies could assess the impact of encoding method, time granularity, and noise. A key challenge is preventing the model from learning correlations via memorization instead of true relationships, so pre-training objectives must be carefully designed to promote meaningful learning. Furthermore, obtaining global datasets with the right coverage and clear visual conditions (e.g., cloud-free) and developing appropriate benchmarks are important considerations for future work.

3.5 Continuous Spectral Encoding

The objective of this experiment is to develop a continuous spectral encoding framework enabling geospatial models to generalize across diverse sensors, including those unseen during training. The experiment tests the hypothesis that modeling sensor-specific spectral response functions (SRFs) enhances downstream performance on geospatial tasks, such as scene classification, change detection, and environmental monitoring. We propose an extension of the DOFA framework [70] that models sensor SRFs rather than relying solely on the frequencies of highest activation. This design is also inspired by recent advancements in multimodal learning, such as SatMAE [15], which emphasizes flexible spectral representations. Unlike approaches that reduce spectral information to discrete band values, this method represents each band's SRF as a discrete function at fine resolution (e.g., 1 nm) to capture the relationship between the physical spectra and the measured radiance. The architecture integrates a spectral encoder modeling sensor-specific SRFs, a universal patch embedding processing spatial information, and a joint reasoning module to integrate both representations. Scene-dependent factors could be mitigated using standard atmospheric correction, or the network could learn correlations by including sensor-related, solar illumination, and atmospheric metadata as input [20].

The training process should optimize both the spectral encoder and the universal patch embedding, enabling the model to jointly reason over spatial and spectral dimensions. We recommend incorporating physics-based loss functions into the network learning objective [17]. A contrastive framework could use an image from the same location but a different year for the negative pair.

A possible approach to overcoming the limited availability of spectra covered by real-world sensors is to generate synthetic multispectral data from hyperspectral data by performing a dot product operation between HS data and a synthetic SRF. This data would simulate virtual sensors by manipulating real spectral activation data, generating skew-normal curves, and adding realistic noise based on physics-based modeling [77]. Evaluation should compare the embeddings of synthetic multispectral images to real multispectral images, e.g., by computing a triplet loss to measure the similarity between embeddings. It is important to note that this approach assumes that synthetic MS images constructed from HS data are realistic proxies for real MS imagery, but coincident HS and MS collects are rare, making it difficult to validate the realism of the synthetic MS imagery.

Several evaluation approaches should be explored. Spectral sensitivity testing should modify the spectral response curves of the sensor, e.g., by slightly shifting the SRF or by collapsing it to the frequency of highest activation. Slight changes would likely result in slight effects, but a statistically significant deterioration in downstream performance could indicate that the model is effectively leveraging the subtleties of the spectral response. This would further indicate that this method would, on a level playing field, be able to outperform a model trained on one RGB sensor and used against a slightly different RGB sensor. Furthermore, the model's ability to generalize to unseen sensors should be evaluated by testing it on real or synthetic sensors with spectral response curves not encountered during training. Results should further be compared on benchmarks against coincident collections between multiple different sensors.

3.6 Multi-resolution Fusion

The goal of this experiment is to create a model capable of multi-sensor, multi-resolution fusion. The model must dynamically adapt its internal processing based on the ground sample distance (GSD) of each image. The goal is a model capable of geospatial reasoning across a range of resolutions, learning geospatial context rather than relying on image scaling and co-registration. This experiment tests the effectiveness of integrating scale-aware positional and sensor metadata into model training. Imagery inputs should vary widely in spatial resolution (e.g., 0.3 m, 5 m, 50 m GSD) and be derived from multiple different sensors.

Various approaches are possible. One approach follows the methodology of Scale-MAE [52] and treats GSD as a numerical feature that is used to scale the sine/cosine position embedding. This approach provides context to each patch regarding scale, but does not reflect scale in the tokenization of the patches themselves. Another approach is to use GSD-Aware Patch Embeddings by following the methodology of FlexiMo [28] to extend a previously trained spatiotemporal FM to utilize GSD to adjust the spatial size of the wavelength-guided kernel. While this approach is extremely flexible, it is more complex to implement. A combined approach could use GSD positional encoding [52] and GSD-aware patch embeddings [28] to integrate scale information to generate tokens and to contextualize the tokens by incorporating scale information into the positional encoding.

Training on all scales at once could be unstable. One approach is to limit the model to an explicit GSD range that is densely covered by the training set (e.g., 0.3 m to 40 m). Alternatively, another approach could separate GSDs into bins such as low ($>$ 30 m), medium ($5 - 30$ m), high ($1 - 5$ m), very ($<$ 1 m), and ultra-high ($<$ 0.1 m) resolution bins, pretrain a separate encoder for each scale, and add a flag to the position encoding to specify the scale range for each token.

Another consideration is to move beyond GSD alone and include additional resolution metrics. Three key factors influencing GSD are the aperture size, wavelength of light, and sampling from the sensor, which can result in sensors with similar GSDs but different effective optical resolutions. While GSD is important for understanding the scale of the imagery, alone it does not describe the resolving power of the sensor. Additional metrics that could be incorporated include ground resolved distance (GRD), which is impacted by sensor aperture and light wavelength and measures the smallest scale at which two features can be distinguished; Line Pairs per Millimeter (LPM), which quantifies resolution as the visual separability of standardized ground targets; and modulation transfer functions (MTFs), which describe how well the system records variation in spatial frequency [9].

The dataset needed for this experiment should contain multi-satellite, multi-resolution imagery covering diverse scales and spatial regions. A large amount of imagery is required at each scale. Note that to generate multi-scale imagery, high-resolution imagery could be downsampled to create lower-resolution counterparts. Model training could implement a dual-objective approach that requires imagery to be reconstructed across scales (e.g., [48,52]) and apply synthetic perturbations to the data, including resolution changes, adding noise, and rotation/cropping. Model performance should be assessed on change detection accuracy across mixed-resolution pairs, localization precision under scale mismatch, computational efficiency, and hallucination error rates on non-overlapping areas. If built upon the multi-spectral backbone from Experiment 5, evaluation should further include robustness to spectral variations in sensors. For ablation studies, evaluate the contributions of different resolution metrics, sensor encoder architectures, and fusion mechanisms.

3.7 SAR Modeling

The objective of this experiment is to develop a specialized methodology for integrating Synthetic Aperture Radar (SAR) data into geospatial foundation models. SAR data differs fundamentally from Electro-Optical (EO) data due to its active sensing mechanism, unique physical properties, and standardized frequency bands. Given the physical differences between SAR and EO sensors, this experiment explores the hypothesis that SAR data should be treated as a separate modality from EO. First, SAR data should be organized using a carrier-level binning approach for standard frequency bands (e.g., Ku-band, X-band, C-band). Each bin would then be processed by a dedicated encoder head that learns the material-level frequency responses within each chirp's bandwidth. This approach leverages the consistency of SAR bands across sensors and ensures that the model captures band-specific characteristics.

The model will be designed to generalize across sensors operating in different standard carrier bands. This will be achieved by training on a diverse set of SAR bands from real sensors as well as on synthetic data. Publicly available SAR datasets, such as Sentinel-1 and RADARSAT, provide data across multiple bands (e.g., C-band, L-band). If sufficiently diverse real data is unavailable, synthetic SAR data can be generated by manipulating real SAR data and applying physical models to simulate radar returns. This would ensure that the model is exposed to a diverse range of SAR configurations during training.

A SAR-specific backbone model will be trained to process the binned frequency band embeddings, which should be binned based on their carrier wavelengths. A dedicated encoder head should be trained for each bin, ensuring the model captures band-specific characteristics. Training should occur with a SAR-specific backbone model.

There are multiple options for model testing. One approach is to evaluate the model's sensitivity to specific SAR bands by testing it on data from individual bands (e.g., Ku-band, X-band). Another is to assess whether the binning approach effectively captures band-specific characteristics. Tests could explore the model's ability to generalize across SAR bands slightly different from the bands used during training, with differences arising from variations in radar systems. Model performance could be explored on SAR-specific geospatial tasks such as terrain classification, change detection, and structural monitoring. Standard metrics such as classification accuracy, F1 score, and precision-recall can be used.

3.8 EO-SAR Fusion

The objective of this experiment is to develop a methodology for combining Electro-Optical (EO) and Synthetic Aperture Radar (SAR) data into a shared backbone. EO and SAR data have fundamentally different physical properties, complicating fusion. For example, SAR data includes phase information, while EO data is purely amplitude-based. EO captures fine-grained spectral and spatial details, while SAR excels in structural and geometric analysis under all-weather and all-lighting conditions. Combining the two might allow SAR to provide additional insight under EO-favorable conditions, and might provide gain for tasks where conditions are less than perfect for EO but SAR is not the ideal sensor.

Feature-level fusion involves extracting features from EO and SAR data separately and combining them for downstream tasks. Models such as SatMAE [15] and DOFA [70] have explored multimodal learning, treating EO and SAR as distinct modalities with separate encoders. Joint approaches train a model from scratch on both EO and SAR data, using a shared backbone to learn joint representations. General foundation models such as 4M [44] propose leveraging a pre-trained model for imagery and mapping the embedded imagery features to a shared backbone. This approach avoids training a new model from scratch and could allow the use of domain-specific pre-trained models for EO and SAR.

There are multiple strategies that could be used to combine EO and SAR in a shared backbone. A new model could be trained entirely from scratch, using a shared backbone to learn joint representations. This approach avoids reliance on pre-trained models but requires significant computational resources. Alternatively, an existing backbone model could be used. While SAR could be mapped to an existing EO backbone, the different physical properties of SAR (e.g., phase information) may not be adequately captured.

We recommend instead an approach that utilizes pre-trained EO and SAR models to extract embedded features and learns a shared embedding space to combine features from both modalities. This would enable joint reasoning while preserving the strengths of pre-trained models. This approach could use commercial and/or publicly available EO datasets (e.g., Sentinel-2, Landsat) and SAR datasets (e.g., Sentinel-1, RADARSAT) and include labeled datasets for benchmark tasks such as terrain classification, change detection, and disaster monitoring. If available, training data should include coincident EO and SAR data to facilitate fusion experiments. It may be necessary to generate synthetic SAR and EO data to simulate variations in sensor characteristics to ensure that the model is exposed to diverse configurations during training.

Model performance can be evaluated using EO-only, SAR-only, and combined EO-SAR benchmarks to determine whether EO-SAR improves performance over single-modality approaches. Performance assessment should encompass geospatial tasks such as terrain classification, change detection, and disaster monitoring, using metrics such as classification accuracy, F1 score, and precision-recall. The effectiveness of the shared backbone in combining EO and SAR features can be examined by comparing the fused model's results to those of baseline models trained on individual modalities. Additionally, the fused model's ability to generalize across EO and SAR sensors not present during training can be assessed, with performance metrics compared to baseline models trained on a limited set of sensors.

3.9 Foundation Model Backbone

The objective of this experiment is to build and validate a foundation model with strong spatiotemporal reasoning capabilities for multimodal fusion. The central hypothesis is that an FM pre-trained on remote sensing data can be effectively augmented to understand and reason across a diverse array of non-visual modalities with strong spatiotemporal characteristics. The experiment aims to demonstrate that leveraging an expert spatiotemporal backbone, rather than a language model, provides a scalable and operationally relevant path to multimodal fusion including remote sensing imagery, geospatial vector data (e.g., maps), digital elevation models (DEMs), measurements (e.g., seismic activity), and geospatial tracks (e.g., GPS, AIS).

Any-modal fusion approaches may transform each modality into a shared embedding space using modality-specific encoders and pre-trained LLM backbones (e.g., AnyMAL [45], LLaVA [33]). Tokenization-based approaches pass all modalities as tokens to a backbone or encoder-decoder transformer (e.g., 4M-21 [5,44], Unified-IO 2 [35,36]). This approach is end-to-end trainable and requires large computational resources and training data sets [65]. Approaches that utilize a pre-trained backbone assume that the backbone can fully represent new data modalities.

This experiment uses a spatiotemporal remote sensing backbone for any-modal integration to preserve expert knowledge within the backbone model's embedding space, which has been carefully trained to understand complex geospatial and temporal patterns. Freezing this pre-trained backbone and training lightweight connectors to integrate new modalities may be more efficient than training a new, multi-billion-parameter multimodal model from scratch. An approach that utilizes a dual backbone, with an RS backbone for spatiotemporal data and an LLM for text integration, is a strong option for text-heavy use cases. This would require careful tuning to ensure the LLM does not overpower the spatiotemporal backbone, leading to text-based reasoning that ignores critical geospatial context. This experiment proceeds in distinct phases to integrate complex new data types. The first phase is to integrate foundational, non-raster geospatial data types such as vectors (points, lines, polygons) and elevation models (DEMs) by training new encoders to transform them into the backbone model's spatiotemporal embedding space. Performance can be assessed on downstream tasks requiring fusion such as land cover classification, change detection using imagery augmented with vector labels, or line-of-sight analysis using imagery fused with DEMs. The next phase introduces dynamic movement data in the form of trajectories (e.g., GPS, AIS), training encoders to handle asynchronous and heterogeneous trajectory data. Performance can be assessed on tasks requiring spatiotemporal reasoning such as vehicle/ship re-identification and trajectory prediction from imagery. After this, high-frequency signal data such as radio frequency (RF), acoustic, and seismic sensor readings can be integrated by developing encoders to process high-frequency, 1D time-series data and align these temporally dense features with geospatial context. Aligning data with different spatial resolutions, temporal sampling frequencies, and data structures is a non-trivial engineering and research problem, and will require development of new methods.

Self-supervised tasks must be designed to train this model on large, unlabeled datasets. This is a challenging undertaking and depends largely on the available datasets. Cross-modal masked modeling could mask tokens in one modality and reconstruct the context from other modalities. For example, reconstruct EO imagery from SAR, DEMs, and/or geospatial vectors for road networks and buildings; or, predict seismic readings given geospatial imagery and GPS movement data. A task could attempt to reconstruct DEMs given LIDAR or SAR point-clouds, or vice versa. Another pretext task for spatiotemporal alignment could predict whether different data streams correspond to the same time and place. A temporal matching task could predict imagery and/or trajectories based on past imagery, measurements, and trajectories. Another task could determine the precise geolocation of a measurement's source given a signal, imagery, and/or road networks and building polygons.

Evaluation should use benchmark datasets that span multiple modalities, rather than relying on single-modality benchmarks. A key challenge is the availability of these curated, aligned multimodal datasets, making it necessary to leverage existing resources when possible and dedicate resources to creating new multimodal spatiotemporal benchmarks. For example, a benchmark for spatiotemporal multimodal fusion might include satellite imagery, ground video, mobility data, elevation maps, and text annotations for a shared geospatial task. Evaluation metrics should include assessments of modality balance and robustness to missing modalities and noisy data.

4 Conclusion

The advancement of foundation models and growth of remote sensing data have shifted the central challenge from data scarcity to the need for spatiotemporally aware model architectures. This paper has proposed a series of experiments designed to address key bottlenecks in developing geospatial, temporal, spectral, multi-sensor, and multimodal fusion models. By focusing on spatiotemporal tokenization, embedding strategies, and model optimization methods, these experiments lay out a path forward for creating multimodal foundation models.

Acknowledgements. This work was supported by the MITRE Independent Research & Development Program.

References

1. Andersson, M., Olsson, F.: Towards Event Sequence Foundation Models. Master's thesis, Chalmers University of Technology, Gothenburg, Sweden (2025). https://odr.chalmers.se/items/05194485-d6a7-4b80-86ac-f3a4bf68c3fa

2. Aodha, O.M., Cole, E., Perona, P.: Presence-only geographical priors for fine-grained image classification (2019). https://arxiv.org/abs/1906.05272
3. Astruc, G., Gonthier, N., Mallet, C., Landrieu, L.: AnySat: one earth observation model for many resolutions, scales, and modalities. In: Proceedings of the IEEE/CVF Conference on Computer Vision and Pattern Recognition (CVPR), pp. 19530–19540 (2025). https://doi.org/10.48550/arXiv.2412.14123
4. Ayush, K., Uzkent, B., Meng, C., Tanmay, K., Burke, M., Lobell, D., Ermon, S.: Geography-aware self-supervised learning (2022). https://arxiv.org/abs/2011.09980
5. Bachmann, R., et al.: 4M-21: an any-to-any vision model for tens of tasks and modalities (2024). https://arxiv.org/abs/2406.09406
6. Baidu-ERNIE-Team: Ernie 4.5 technical report (2025). https://ernie.baidu.com/blog/publication/ERNIE_Technical_Report.pdf
7. Brown, C.F., et al.: Alphaearth foundations: An embedding field model for accurate and efficient global mapping from sparse label data (2025). https://arxiv.org/abs/2507.22291
8. Brown, T.B., et al.: Language models are few-shot learners (2020). https://arxiv.org/abs/2005.14165
9. Campbell, J., Wynne, R.: Introduction to Remote Sensing. Guilford Publications (2011)
10. Cao, Q., et al.: TorchSpatial: a python package for spatial representation learning and geo-aware model development. In: Proceedings of the 3rd ACM SIGSPATIAL International Workshop on Spatial Big Data and AI for Industrial Applications, pp. 39–42. GeoIndustry '24, Association for Computing Machinery, New York, NY, USA (2024). https://doi.org/10.1145/3681766.3699608
11. Carreira, J., Zisserman, A.: Quo vadis, action recognition? a new model and the kinetics dataset (2018). https://arxiv.org/abs/1705.07750
12. Christie, G., Fendley, N., Wilson, J., Mukherjee, R.: Functional map of the world (2018). https://arxiv.org/abs/1711.07846
13. Chu, G., et al.: Geo-aware networks for fine-grained recognition (2019). https://arxiv.org/abs/1906.01737
14. Clay: Clay foundation model (2025). https://clay-foundation.github.io/model/. Accessed 01 Jan 2025
15. Cong, Y., et al.: SatMAE: pre-training transformers for temporal and multi-spectral satellite imagery. Adv. Neural Info. Process. Syst. **35**, 197–211 (2022). https://doi.org/10.48550/arXiv.2207.08051
16. Das, A., Kong, W., Sen, R., Zhou, Y.: A decoder-only foundation model for time-series forecasting. In: Proceedings of the 41st International Conference on Machine Learning. ICML'24, JMLR.org (2024). https://dl.acm.org/doi/10.5555/3692070.3692474
17. Daw, A., Karpatne, A., Watkins, W., Read, J., Kumar, V.: Physics-guided neural networks (PGNN): an application in lake temperature modeling (2020). https://arxiv.org/abs/1710.11431
18. DeepSeek-AI: Deepseek-V2: a strong, economical, and efficient mixture-of-experts language model (2024). https://arxiv.org/abs/2405.04434
19. Dhingra, B., Cole, J.R., Eisenschlos, J.M., Gillick, D., Eisenstein, J., Cohen, W.W.: Time-aware language models as temporal knowledge bases. Trans. Assoc. Comput. Ling. **10**, 257–273 (2022). https://doi.org/10.1162/tacl_a_00459
20. Fan, Y., et al.: Atmospheric correction over coastal waters using multilayer neural networks. Remote Sens. Environ. **199**, 218–240 (2017). https://doi.org/10.1016/j.rse.2017.07.016

21. Heo, B., Park, S., Han, D., Yun, S.: Rotary position embedding for vision transformer. In: European Conference on Computer Vision, pp. 289–305. Springer (2024). https://doi.org/10.1007/978-3-031-72684-2_17
22. Hong, D., et al.: SpectralGPT: spectral remote sensing foundation model. IEEE Trans. Pattern Anal. Mach. Intell. **46**(8), 5227–5244 (2024). http://doi.org/10.1109/TPAMI.2024.3362475
23. Jaegle, A., et al.: Perceiver IO: a general architecture for structured inputs and outputs (2022). https://arxiv.org/abs/2107.14795
24. Jean, N., Wang, S., Samar, A., Azzari, G., Lobell, D., Ermon, S.: Tile2Vec: unsupervised representation learning for spatially distributed data (2018). https://arxiv.org/abs/1805.02855
25. Klemmer, K., Rolf, E., Robinson, C., Mackey, L., Rußwurm, M.: SatClip: global, general-purpose location embeddings with satellite imagery (2024). http://arxiv.org/abs/2311.17179
26. Li, W., Law, K.L.E.: Deep learning models for time series forecasting: a review. IEEE Access **12**, 92306–92327 (2024). http://dx.doi.org/10.1109/ACCESS.2024.3422528
27. Li, W., Chen, K., Chen, H., Shi, Z.: Geographical knowledge-driven representation learning for remote sensing images. IEEE Trans. Geosci. Remote Sens. **60**, 1–16 (2022). http://doi.org/10.1109/TGRS.2021.3115569
28. Li, X., Li, C., Ghamisi, P., Hong, D.: FlexiMo: a flexible remote sensing foundation model (2025). https://arxiv.org/abs/2503.23844
29. Li, Y., Wang, J., Li, T., Fu, Z.: Traisformer: spatio-temporal ship trajectory prediction based on transformer. In: 2024 5th International Seminar on Artificial Intelligence, Networking and Information Technology (AINIT), pp. 1099–1104 (2024). http://doi.org/10.1109/AINIT61980.2024.10581516
30. Liang, Y., et al.: Foundation models for time series analysis: a tutorial and survey. In: Proceedings of the 30th ACM SIGKDD Conference on Knowledge Discovery and Data Mining, pp. 6555–6565. KDD '24, Association for Computing Machinery, New York, NY, USA (2024). https://doi.org/10.1145/3637528.3671451
31. Liang, Y., et al.: Foundation models for time series analysis: a tutorial and survey. In: Proceedings of the 30th ACM SIGKDD Conference on Knowledge Discovery and Data Mining, pp. 6555–6565. KDD '24, Association for Computing Machinery, New York, NY, USA (2024). https://doi.org/10.1145/3637528.3671451
32. Lin, Y., et al.: TraJFM: a vehicle trajectory foundation model for region and task transferability (2024). https://arxiv.org/abs/2408.15251
33. Liu, H., Li, C., Wu, Q., Lee, Y.J.: Visual instruction tuning (2023). https://arxiv.org/abs/2304.08485
34. Liu, Z., Zhang, F., Jiao, J., Lao, N., Mai, G.: GAIR: improving multimodal geo-foundation model with geo-aligned implicit representations (2025). https://arxiv.org/abs/2503.16683
35. Lu, J., et al.: Unified-IO 2: scaling autoregressive multimodal models with vision, language, audio, and action (2023). https://arxiv.org/abs/2312.17172
36. Lu, J., Clark, C., Zellers, R., Mottaghi, R., Kembhavi, A.: Unified-IO: a unified model for vision, language, and multi-modal tasks (2022). https://arxiv.org/abs/2206.08916
37. Lu, K., et al: Pattern integration and enhancement vision transformer for self-supervised learning in remote sensing. IEEE Trans. Geosci. Remote Sens. **63**, 1–13 (2025). http://doi.org/10.1109/TGRS.2025.3541390

38. Mai, G., Cundy, C., Choi, K., Hu, Y., Lao, N., Ermon, S.: Towards a foundation model for geospatial artificial intelligence (vision paper). In: Proceedings of the 30th International Conference on Advances in Geographic Information Systems. SIGSPATIAL '22, Association for Computing Machinery, New York, NY, USA (2022). https://doi.org/10.1145/3557915.3561043
39. Mai, G., et al.: A review of location encoding for geoAI: methods and applications. Int. J. Geograph. Inf. Sci. **36**(4), 639–673 (2022). http://dx.doi.org/10.1080/13658816.2021.2004602
40. Mai, G., et al.: Towards general-purpose representation learning of polygonal geometries. GeoInformatica **27**(2), 289–340 (2022). http://dx.doi.org/10.1007/s10707-022-00481-2
41. Mai, G., Lao, N., He, Y., Song, J., Ermon, S.: CSP: self-supervised contrastive spatial pre-training for geospatial-visual representations. In: Proceedings of the 40th International Conference on Machine Learning. ICML'23, JMLR.org (2023). https://dl.acm.org/doi/10.5555/3618408.3619389
42. Mai, Get al.: Sphere2Vec: a general-purpose location representation learning over a spherical surface for large-scale geospatial predictions (2023). https://arxiv.org/abs/2306.17624
43. Mañas, O., Lacoste, A., i Nieto, X.G., Vazquez, D., Rodriguez, P.: Seasonal contrast: unsupervised pre-training from uncurated remote sensing data (2021). https://arxiv.org/abs/2103.16607
44. Mizrahi, D., et al.: 4M: massively multimodal masked modeling (2023). https://arxiv.org/abs/2312.06647
45. Moon, S., et al.: AnyMal: an efficient and scalable any-modality augmented language model (2023). https://arxiv.org/abs/2309.16058
46. NASA: Multi-mission data processing system study. https://www.earthdata.nasa.gov/about/multi-mission-data-processing-system-study (2025). Accessed 26 Oct 2025
47. Nie, Y., Nguyen, N.H., Sinthong, P., Kalagnanam, J.: A time series is worth 64 words: long-term forecasting with transformers (2023). https://arxiv.org/abs/2211.14730
48. Noman, M., Naseer, M., Cholakkal, H., Anwar, R.M., Khan, S., Khan, F.S.: Rethinking transformers pre-training for multi-spectral satellite imagery (2024). https://arxiv.org/abs/2403.05419
49. OpenAI: Gpt-4 technical report (2025). https://cdn.openai.com/papers/gpt-4.pdf. Accessed 20 June 2025
50. OpenAI: GPT-5 system card (2025). https://cdn.openai.com/gpt-5-system-card.pdf. Accessed 20 June 2025
51. Ravirathinam, P., Khandelwal, A., Ghosh, R., Kumar, V.: Towards a knowledge guided multimodal foundation model for spatio-temporal remote sensing applications (2025). https://arxiv.org/abs/2407.19660v2
52. Reed, C.J., et al.: Scale-Mae: a scale-aware masked autoencoder for multiscale geospatial representation learning. In: 2023 IEEE/CVF International Conference on Computer Vision (ICCV), pp. 4065–4076 (2023). https://ieeexplore.ieee.org/document/10377166
53. Rossi, E., Chamberlain, B., Frasca, F., Eynard, D., Monti, F., Bronstein, M.: Temporal graph networks for deep learning on dynamic graphs (2020). https://arxiv.org/abs/2006.10637

54. Samadzadegan, F., Toosi, A., Javan, F.D.: A critical review on multi-sensor and multi-platform remote sensing data fusion approaches: current status and prospects. Inte. J. Remote Sens. **46**(3), 1327–1402 (2025). http://doi.org/10.1080/01431161.2024.2429784
55. Shao, R., et al.: Allspark: a multimodal spatio-temporal general intelligence model with ten modalities via language as a reference framework (2025). https://arxiv.org/abs/2401.00546
56. Stewart, A.J., Robinson, C., Corley, I.A., Ortiz, A., Ferres, J.M.L., Banerjee, A.: Torchgeo: deep learning with geospatial data (2022). https://arxiv.org/abs/2111.08872
57. Su, J., Ahmed, M., Lu, Y., Pan, S., Bo, W., Liu, Y.: Roformer: enhanced transformer with rotary position embedding. Neurocomputing **568**, 127063 (2024). http://doi.org/10.1016/j.neucom.2023.127063
58. Su, J., Lu, Y., Pan, S., Murtadha, A., Wen, B., Liu, Y.: RoFormer: Enhanced transformer with rotary position embedding (2023). https://arxiv.org/abs/2104.09864
59. Szwarcman, D., et al.: Prithvi-EO-2.0: a versatile multi-temporal foundation model for earth observation applications (2025). https://arxiv.org/abs/2412.02732
60. Tarasiou, M., Chavez, E., Zafeiriou, S.: Vits for sits: Vision transformers for satellite image time series (2023). https://arxiv.org/abs/2301.04944
61. Team, G.G.: Gemini 2.5: pushing the frontier with advanced reasoning, multimodality, long context, and next generation agentic capabilities (2025). https://arxiv.org/abs/2507.06261
62. Touvron, H., et al.: Llama 2: open foundation and fine-tuned chat models (2023). https://arxiv.org/abs/2307.09288
63. Velazquez, D., et al.: EarthView: a large scale remote sensing dataset for self-supervision (2025). https://arxiv.org/abs/2501.08111
64. Vivanco Cepeda, V., Nayak, G.K., Shah, M.: GeoClip: clip-inspired alignment between locations and images for effective worldwide geo-localization. Adv. Neural Info. Process. Syst. **36**, 8690–8701 (2023). https://dl.acm.org/doi/10.5555/3666122.3666501
65. Wadekar, S.N., Chaurasia, A., Chadha, A., Culurciello, E.: The evolution of multimodal model architectures (2024). https://arxiv.org/abs/2405.17927
66. Wang, D., et al.: MTP: advancing remote sensing foundation model via multitask pretraining. IEEE J. Sel. Topics Appl. Earth Observ. Remote Sens. **17**, 11632–11654 (2024). http://doi.org/10.1109/JSTARS.2024.3408154
67. Wang, M., et al.: A complex-valued sar foundation model based on physically inspired representation learning (2025). https://arxiv.org/abs/2504.11999
68. Wang, Y., et al.: Internvideo: General video foundation models via generative and discriminative learning (2022). https://arxiv.org/abs/2212.03191
69. Wen, Q., et al.: Transformers in time series: a survey (2023). https://arxiv.org/abs/2202.07125
70. Xiong, Z., et al.: Neural plasticity-inspired multimodal foundation model for earth observation (2024). http://arxiv.org/abs/2403.15356
71. Xu, G., Zhang, B., Yu, H., Chen, J., Xing, M., Hong, W.: Sparse synthetic aperture radar imaging from compressed sensing and machine learning: Theories, applications, and trends. IEEE Geosci. Remote Sens. Magaz. **10**(4), 32–69 (2022). https://doi.org/10.1109/MGRS.2022.3218801
72. Xu, J., et al.: Qwen2.5-omni technical report (2025). https://arxiv.org/abs/2503.20215

73. Yang, L., et al.: Dynamic MLP for fine-grained image classification by leveraging geographical and temporal information (2022). https://arxiv.org/abs/2203.03253
74. Yin, Y., Zhang, Y., Liu, Z., Wang, S., Shah, R.R., Zimmermann, R.: Gps2vec: pre-trained semantic embeddings for worldwide GPS coordinates. IEEE Trans. Multimedia **24**, 890–903 (2022). https://doi.org/10.1109/TMM.2021.3060951
75. Yu, X., Tang, L., Rao, Y., Huang, T., Zhou, J., Lu, J.: Point-BERT: pre-training 3D point cloud transformers with masked point modeling (2022). https://arxiv.org/abs/2111.14819
76. Yuan, L., et al.: OmniGeo: towards a multimodal large language models for geospatial artificial intelligence (2025). https://arxiv.org/abs/2503.16326
77. Zhang, W., et al.: Physics guided remote sensing image synthesis network for ship detection. IEEE Trans. Geosci. Remote Sens. **61**, 1–14 (2023). https://doi.org/10.1109/TGRS.2023.3248106
78. Zhou, H., Zhang, S., Peng, J., Zhang, S., Li, J., Xiong, H., Zhang, W.: Informer: Beyond efficient transformer for long sequence time-series forecasting. Proc. AAAI Conf. Artif. Intell. **35**(12), 11106–11115 (2021). http://dx.doi.org/10.1609/aaai.v35i12.17325

Training the Right ML Model and Training the ML Model Right

John M. Irvine(✉), Nazario Irizarry, Franck Olivier Ndjakou Njeunje, and Samuel Vilt

The MITRE Corporation, Bedford, MA, USA
jmirvine@mitre.org

Abstract. Future intelligence, surveillance, reconnaissance, and targeting capabilities will rely on Artificial Intelligence/Machine Learning (AI/ML) to support time critical missions including indications and warning intelligence preparation of the battlespace, and real-time targeting. Historically, exploitation and analysis of imagery have relied entirely on the expertise of trained analysts. Today, however, the volume of sensor data and the shortened timelines for decisions are driving us towards greater automation. At the same time advances in AI/ML capabilities are providing tools to assist analysts in meeting these missions. For many basic image analysis tasks, such as object detection or object classification, multiple models might be available to process imagery for a given mission. Which model is the best choice for the mission? Our research demonstrates that seemingly similar deep learning methods can yield different performance results. Furthermore, our investigations demonstrate differences due to the choice of training data. The team propose methods for evaluating the training data and the model framework relative to the mission imagery, which leads to a natural strategy for model selection. Using several popular object detection methods applied to multiple data sets, we will present:

- The approach to model training and model selection.
- The image metrics that underpin our methods.
- Results from recent experiments.
- Recommendations for a path forward.

Keywords: Machine learning · model selection · image similarity

1 Introduction

Advances in artificial intelligence/machine learning (AI/ML) are changing the way analysts exploit remotely sensed imagery. Powerful ML tools offer the potential to automatically detect objects of interest and direct an analyst's attention to specific images and regions within an image. To realize the benefits of these innovations, performance of the ML model is critical. Depending on the application, ML models that produce too many false positives or miss objects of interest could substantially degrade the quality of the workflow. Worse yet, poor ML performance could force the analyst to ignore the ML output and return to a fully manual analysis. Thus, It is critical for the ML model to achieve accurate performance for the mission at hand.

F. Tanner and J. Irvine (Eds.): AIPR 2025, LNCS 16446, pp. 274–291, 2026.
https://doi.org/10.1007/978-3-032-18474-0_20

The challenge is that remote sensing data can encompass a wide range of conditions. A common way to frame these challenges is to identify the operating conditions that are relevant to a particular mission or application [1]. It is useful to group operating conditions into three broad categories:

1. Sensor: Sensor characteristics include the imaging modality, spatial resolution, viewing geometry, signal-to-noise ratio, relative edge response, etc.
2. Target: The type of object or objects, include variants, the object orientation, articulation, reflective or emissive properties, etc. Target obscuration or camouflage is another consideration.
3. Environment: Background conditions such as terrain, vegetation, surface type, lighting, time of day, and possible confuser objects.

Given the wide range of operating conditions in the world, how can a single model be suitable for these wide variations? One approach is to train a set of ML models for different operating conditions. Armed with a library of trained ML models, the analyst must select the best model to use for a given mission. This is the model selection problem addressed here. Our approach rests on understanding the characteristics of the training imagery and the mission-specific imagery.

2 Image Complexity

The propensity for a machine learning model to produce false positives is closely related to the complexity of the scene. Images with higher spatial variation typically produce more false alarms. A simple experiment demonstrates this. An object detector was applied to a test set of imagery and the results were scored against ground truth. In addition, we tiled each image and computed the local variance within each tile and the global variance across the tiles. Merging these two simple measures into a single value, we partitioned the image set into two bins: high variance and low variance. The false alarm rate was 70% higher for the high variance set of images. This simple experiment demonstrates the point: More complex images (as measured here by the variance) are associated with higher false alarm rates.

The simple variance calculation provides a crude measure of scene complexity. To properly characterize the complexity of an image, we explored a wide range of methods. To date, none of these methods completely explain the false alarm rate, but together they provide insight into the nature of the image. Furthermore, experiments to date suggest that some of the candidates we examined are less informative, whereas others show great promise.

The team explored a variety of image metrics, building on standard image processing techniques. Although multiple features were considered (Table 1), ultimately a shorter set to represent scene complexity proved effective. Implementation relied on the Open-Source Computer Vision OpenCV-Python library. Features were calculated for each image individually. This approach provided a foundation for comparing images and assessing their similarity to one another. The final set of features that were incorporated into the distance calculation were a sub-set. The specific metrics that show the greatest **promise** are based on edges in the images and the fractal dimension.

Rather than a comprehensive discussion of these metrics, let us focus on the ones that were used for model selection. These included: edge density, straight and parallel lines, fractal dimension, pixel value change histogram, and homogeneity.

Edge Density: Images with many edges are typically dense in manmade features that can give rise to false positives (Fig. 1). Thus, the prevalence of edges is a measure of scene complexity. Applying a Canny edge detector [2] generates the binary image of the edges. The ratio of bright pixels (edges) to the total number of pixels is the measure of edge density.

Straight and Parallel Lines: This metric builds on the edges extracted for the edge density calculation. Man-made objects, such as vehicles, aircrafts, and buildings, often have straight edges and parallel edges. Thus, this metric is sensitive to the man-made features that could give rise to false alarms. A simple method for identifying straight lines is to compare the edge length measured in pixels to the distance between the endpoints. Assessing if two lines are parallel relies on the Hough transform.

Pixel Value Change Histogram: This is a histogram of the number of pixels at each intensity level. It describes the distribution of bright and dark pixels in the image, but does not indicate the spatial distribution of these values.

Haralick Features: The Haralick score depends on the gray-level co-occurrence matrix (GLCM) of the image (Fig. 2). GLCM quantifies patterns of values among adjacent pixels. The Haralick features quantify the texture of an image [3]. Highly textured scenes and scenes with varied textures correspond to visually complex scenes (Fig. 3). Empirical studies have demonstrated a relationship between Haralick features and ML performance [4]. Generally, ML models will perform better on imagery with low Haralick scores. Our measure of homogeneity, one of the many metrics that can be extracted from the GLCM, is inversely related to texture.

Fig. 1. Illustration of edge density for low and high complexity images

Fractal Dimension: According to Mandelbrot, a fractal dimension is an index for characterizing fractal patterns or sets by quantifying their complexity as a ratio of the change in detail to the change in scale. Fractal dimension is a mathematical measure of complexity [5]. Our approach to analyzing the fractal properties of the image produces a histogram of fractal dimension scores at different spatial resolutions. The process starts by computing a fractal dimension (FD) scalar using box counting for a multidimensional (x, y, pixel band value(s)) representation of a single image. The goal was to create an

Table 1. Image Complexity Measures

Feature	Description
Edges	Used a Canny edge detection method to find edges in the images
Straight and Parallel Lines	Counts of straight and parallel lines, derived from the edges
Fractal Dimensions	Fractal dimension histogram derived from image tiling at multiple sizes
Pixel Value Change Histogram	Histogram of pixel intensity values
Homogeneity	Derived from Gray-Level Co-occurrence Matrix (GLCM)
Energy	Derived from the GLCM
Correlation	Derived from the GLCM
Dissimilarity	Derived from the GLCM
Entropy	Quantifies the randomness of pixel values in the image
Compression Ratio	Derived by compressing the image to a value and recording the actual achieved compression rate
Fourier Transform Mean	Converted images into a frequency domain and calculated the mean value of the magnitude spectrum of the Fourier Transform
Color Complexity	Derived as a measure of the number of unique colors present in an image

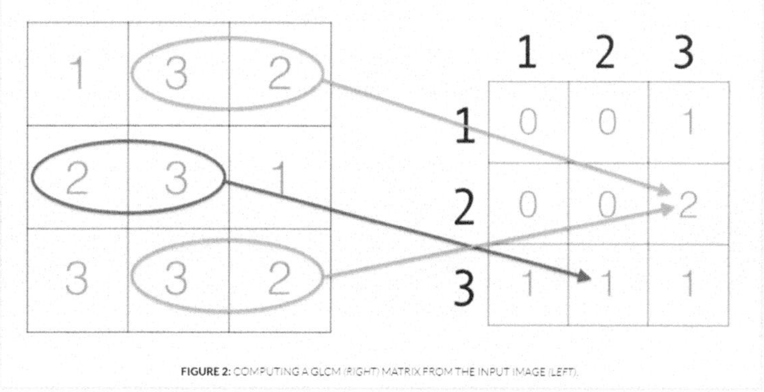

Fig. 2. Simple illustration of GLCM calculation

implementation that applied equally well to monochrome or color and which could be extended to multispectral as well. The next step was to determine how to build a vector of FD scalars to explore whether that vector would serve as a reasonable image feature or signature.

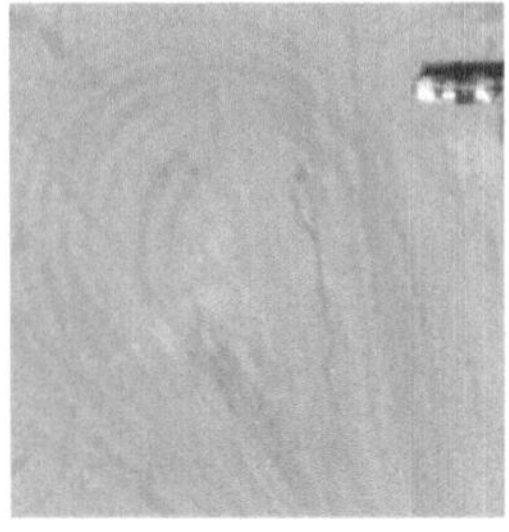

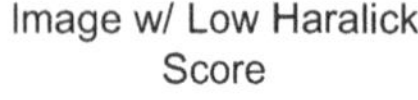

Image w/ Medium Haralick Score

Image w/ High Haralick Score

Fig. 3. Three images with varying Haralick scores

The approach uses the FD of image subtiles to build a histogram. Vectors of similar images are close in Euclidean distance. Vectors for clearly different images were far apart in Euclidean distance. The current FD signature is computed by breaking an image greater than 64x64 into overlapping tiles of 64 x 64 (50% overlap horizontally and vertically). FD is calculated for each tile. Then a histogram is computed using a fixed bin width. The histogram is normalized so that the sum of the components of the histogram always add up to 1.0. This is the FD signature. We display the histogram as a circular/polar plot, making it easier to compare visually (Fig. 4). A shift in FD center of mass becomes a rotation in the circular plot which makes the shift easier to discern visually.

The FD of a rectangular set of pixels is calculated by tabulating the number of unique pixel values within sub-rectangular "boxes" of various dimensions. This results in a "curve" of pixel count versus box dimension, plotted on logarithmic scales. The slope of the best fit straight line is the FD for the rectangular region. Cluster analysis of the FD histograms reveals that images within a cluster are visually similar (Fig. 5). This finding inspired the cluster-based distance calculation.

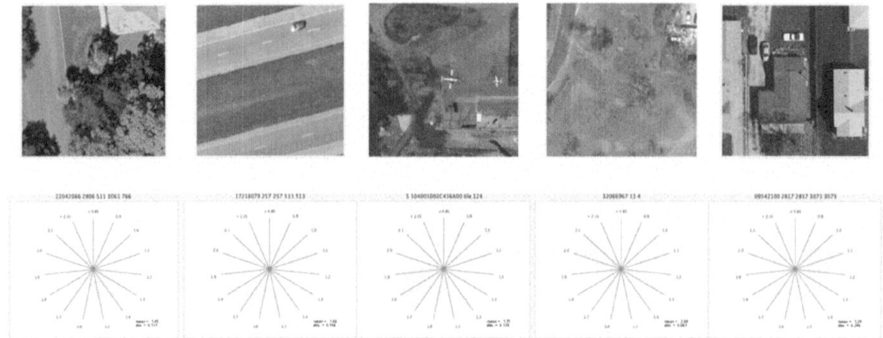

Fig. 4. Illustration of signatures (radar plots) for different fractal dimensions

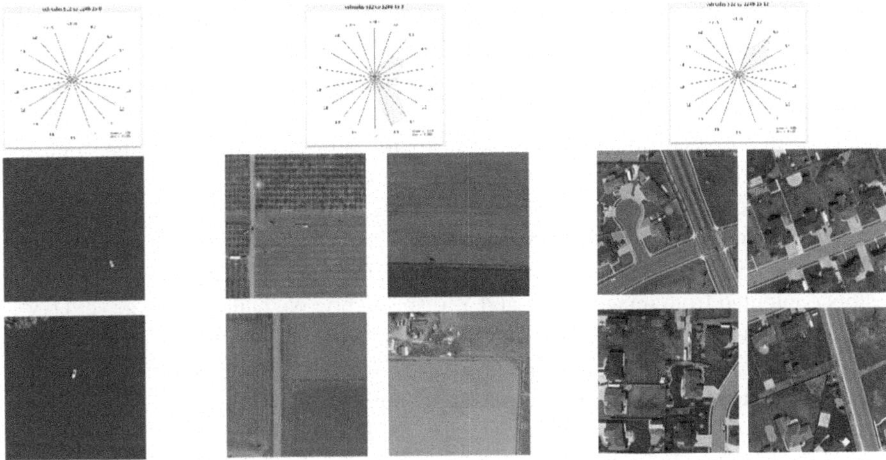

Fig. 5. Illustration of clustering based on fractal dimension histograms

2.1 Cluster-Based Distance Calculation

The goal was to develop a way to measure the distance between two image sets. The distance metric should be over a known range, to allow comparisons across various image types and conditions. The cluster analysis of the fractal dimension histograms inspired our approach to computing the distance between two image sets. A number of alternatives were explored. Euclidean vector distances need normalization but lack sensitivity to differences that are visually apparent. Mahalanobis distance suffers from similar limitations. Kullback-Leibler divergence requires estimating or approximating the density function in the very high-dimensional, yet sparse, space of image features. Hellinger vector distances have a known range but have been found to be less sensitive than the clustering technique to image set differences. Thus, the team settled on a cluster-based method that approximates the intersection over union (IOU) for the two image sets in the high-dimensional space defined by the image features. Below is the formal framework for our method.

A dataset, Dx consists of multiple images, Mx,i for i = { 1 … nx}. A single image can be represented by a characterizing vector Vx,i = T(Mx,i). Image M is mapped to a characteristic vector V via a transformation T and the transformation T results in a point in a high dimensional space. Denote the dimension by k. In practice, the transformation T is the mapping from an image to the vector of image complexity features discussed above.

Conceptually, the "space" occupied by the dataset is a "cloud" of points in k-dimensions. However, the cloud is sparse because nx (the number of images in dataset) is usually way too small to obtain a good sampling over k-space. The distance calculation needs to quantify the overlap between the (sparse) point clouds in this high-dimensional space. Given two datasets, Dx and Dy, each cloud has a corresponding shape Sx, Sy. The k-dimensional volumes are Vol(Sx) and Vol(Sy). The normalized distance is one minus the intersection over union. This distance measure has range [0, 1], which facilitates comparisons across multiple datasets.

To implement this approach, we need a good estimate of the shapes. Estimating high dimensional volumes is numerically unstable when the length along multiple dimensions (or Eigenvectors) is small. We need a substitute metric for volume that increases with the size of the spaces Sx and Sy. We use the k-dimensional points as the representation directly, with two adjustments: We compensate for points that are nearly the same and for image sets that have different number of images.

Our approach measures the overlap and distance using a modified count of the vector features Vx,i and Vy,j. Note that Vx,i and Vy,j are unevenly distributed samples of the cloud shapes Sx and Sy. We start with two datasets Dx, Dy, which are the sets of feature vectors computed from image sets X and Y, respectively. We build aggregate set Dxy = Dx ∪ Dy which is simply the merged data set. Performing clustering on the Vxy yielding clusters, Uxy,m, of small average diameters. We used hierarchical clustering algorithm with a conventional distance metric and set the number of clusters to nClusters = max (6, min(30, $\sqrt{}$nxy)). Average cluster diameters are less than a threshold. These clusters provide the framework for estimating the approximate volumes.

We estimate size, Zxy,m, of each Uxy,m in lieu of an actual volume, where Zxy,m represents the modified counts. The modified count is for the number of points within a cluster that are not "redundant" with others in the cluster. The counting process starts by creating an empty set of retained points and an ordered list of member points with increasing distance from the center of the cluster. Starting at point closest to center, inspect the next point to see if it is too close to any in the retained set (eliminating redundancy). If the point is not too close, add it to the retained set. In this way, we compute a size Zxy,i for each Uxy,m. Then the union is:

$$Union\ size = \sum\nolimits_j Zxy, j$$

To find the intersection clusters, consider Uxy,t which are cluster having vectors from both Dx and Dy. Apportion Zxy,t to Dx and Dy based on relative membership from Dx and Dy

$$\text{Intersectionsize} = \min(\text{Zxy, t}|\text{Dx}, \text{Zxy, t}|\text{Dy})$$

Figure 6 shows a simple example. In the example the only overlap/intersection is in Uxy,3. Also, the total population of purple is one half that of green. Hence, we scale purple by factor of 2 to account for under-representation

$$Intersection = min(scaled\_purple, green)/(scaled\_purple + green)$$
$$= \min(2, 4)/(2 + 4) = 1/3$$
$$\text{Union} = \text{Zxy}, 1 + \text{Zxy}, 2 + \text{Zxy}, 3 + \text{Zxy}, 4 + \text{Zxy}, 5 = 15$$
$$\text{Distance} = 1 - Intersection Union = 1 - 1/45 = 0.98$$

This cluster-based distance calculation is a general framework. Once a vector of features has been assigned or computed for each image, this method uses these vectors to perform the clustering, approximate the volumes associated with each cluster, and compute the IOU distance. The model-agnostic approach uses five image metrics: fractal dimension histogram, pixel value change histogram, homogeneity histogram, edge

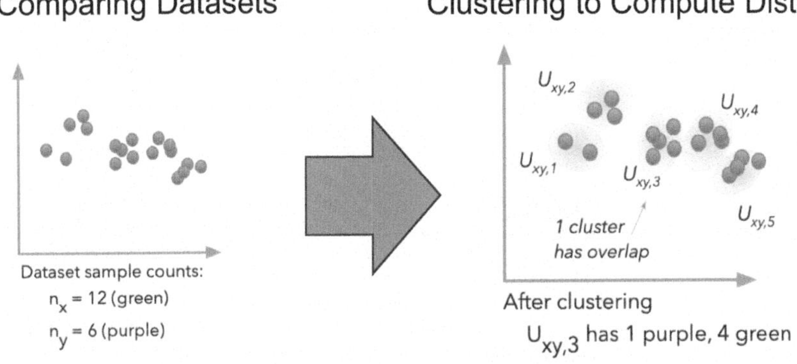

Fig. 6. Simple example of clustering for distance calculation

density histogram, and straight-and-parallel-line histogram. Each feature is computed for an individual image and the histograms are concatenated to form a large vector for each image. These are the vector features Vx,i and Vy,j that feed into the clustering and subsequent calculations.

3 Model Selection for Object Detection

The operating conditions encountered in real-world mission span a wide range of target types, target conditions, environments, and sensing conditions. No single machine learning model can be expected to perform well across this vast array of conditions. An alternative approach is to train a library of models and apply the "best" model for each mission. This tailored approach seeks to align the ML model with the mission imagery in a manner that will maximize the expected model performance. Our approach to this model selection problem is to select the model that was trained on data that most closely resembles the mission imagery. Multiple machine learning algorithms are available. Training an algorithm on a specific training dataset produces a model. Combining various algorithms with an array of training sets yields a potentially large pool of models. The model selection problem is to choose the "best" model for a given mission (Fig. 7).

The image metrics provides the measure of image similarity and we choose the ML model trained on the data that most closely aligns with the mission imagery. This approach requires access to the training data, as well as a sample of mission imagery. It does not, however, require any labeling of the mission imagery. This approach is model agnostic in that the image metrics do not depend on choice of ML models. An alternative approach is to use model-specific measures.

Using a model-agnostic approach, the team conducted extensive experimentation in model selection for object detection. Pooling data across several open-source data sets, we applied three different algorithms. Details and findings are presented below. In the next section, we discuss model selection for object classification.

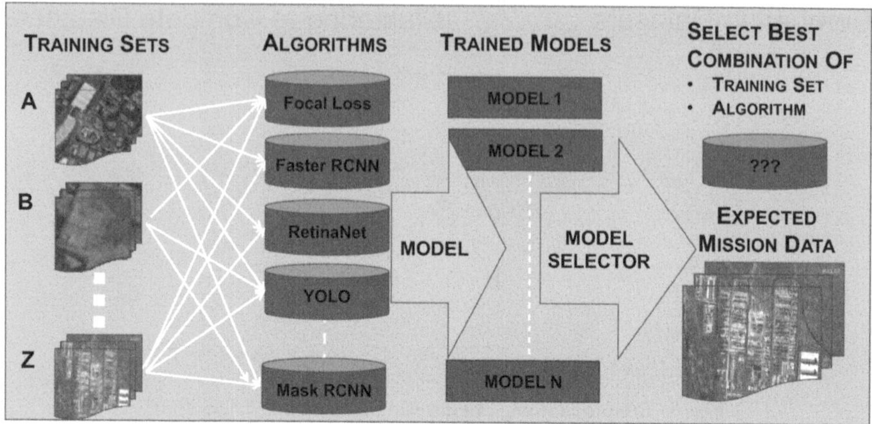

Fig. 7. Conceptual overview of the model selection process

3.1 Description of Datasets

A total of three datasets were used for our experiments. All datasets are open-source, consisting of 256-by-256 images along with annotations about the vehicles present in each image. Illustrative scenes from each set appear in Fig. 8. Table 2 shows the number of images, number of annotations, and the range for the GSD.

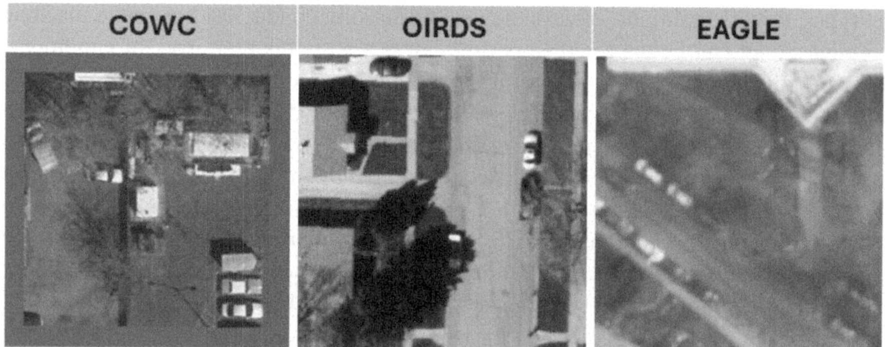

Fig. 8. Exemplar images from the three sources of data

OIRDS: The dataset used for these experiments was the Overhead Imagery Research Data Set (OIRDS), a dataset consisting of images from the United States Geological Survey and DARPA VIVID program. These images contain civilian vehicles such as cars, vans, and trucks [6]. The dataset has around 900 images from airborne platforms that are grouped into 20 subsets and a total of 1800 total annotated vehicles. Within each subset, there is metadata for all the images, including the type of vehicle, the color of the vehicle, pixels on target, and other features. It is also important to note that each image within the dataset is clear and there are no obstructions such as clouds. All targets are

Table 2. Characteristics of the three data sets

Image Set	Images	Annotations	GSD (cm)
COWC	53	32,716	15
OIRDS	908	1,796	15
EAGLE*	63	45,275	5 to 35

discernable to the human eye, although some vehicles are partially occluded by trees or building eaves [6].

COWC: The second dataset, Cars Overhead With Context (COWC), was created by the Lawrence Livermore National Laboratory in 2016 [7]. It consists of 7344 total images collected from 6 locations and contains 35830 annotated vehicles. Like the OIRDS dataset, each image has a GSD of 15 cm/pixel. Although the original COWC images are in color, we converted data to grey scale for the experiments.

EAGLE: The final and largest dataset, oriEnted vehicle detection using Aerial imaGery in real-worLd scEnarios (EAGLE), was developed by the Remote Sensing Technology Institute at the German Aerospace Center in 2020 [8]. It contains 34625 images across 31 European locations with 186235 annotated vehicles. While the OIRDS and COWC datasets were used as-is, the EAGLE dataset contained several problematic annotations and double-annotated vehicles and was consequently pruned of such artifacts. Unlike the other two datasets, EAGLE includes imagery with a variety of GSD values, allowing us to analyze GSD as a complexity metric. Like the COWC dataset, all EAGLE images were converted to grey scale.

To conduct the experiments, each of the classifiers was trained on multiple training sets and tested on independent test sets. Data sets were defined by the geographic regions and sensor metadata leading to 14 training sets and 14 corresponding test sets. All the OIRDS imagery and COWC imagery were nadir-looking and acquired at the same GSD (15cm). COWC included 6 geographic regions that defined 6 of the data sets. OIRDS was treated as a single data set. The EAGLE imagery was partition first by geographic region, and secondly by the metadata (GSD and look angle). Most of the EAGLE images were also nadir-looking and collected at approximately 15cm GSD. However, data collected over Frankfurt and Champion include off-nadir images. Furthermore, the aircraft flew at varying altitudes producing a range of GSDs. We binned the EAGLE data into three resolution bins: less than 10cm, 10–20 cm, and 20–25 cm. We defined the image set by the geographic region, the GSD bin, and on vs off nadir. This produced 17 possible data sets, but three of these sets had a very small number of images. Consequently, we settled on 14 data sets and partitioned each into training and test sets.

3.2 Results: Model Selection for Object Detection

We experimented with one- and two-stage detectors, which we fine-tuned in TorchVision from the default parameters. Our one-stage detectors were Focal Loss and RetinaNetv2 [9, 10]. The two-stage detector was Faster-RCNNv2 [11]. The subscript "v2" indicates the models were pre-trained using vision transformers [12].

The initial model selection experiment trained each of our three algorithms on each of the 14 available training sets. These were the candidate "bespoke" models. In addition, a general model was trained on data randomly selected from all the data sets. These fifteen models (14 candidate bespoke models and one general model) were tested on all 14 test sets and the results were scored by comparison to the ground truth labels. We recorded the standard performance metrics for object detection: precision, recall, and the f1 score.

Model selection relied on the image metrics. Using the distance calculations described above, the bespoke model was the model where the distance between the training set and the test set was minimized. The results (Figs. 10, 11 and 12) show the aggregate performance metrics for each of the three algorithms, i.e., the mean values across the 14 data sets. The figs show 5 groupings:

- General Model: The model trained on a random sample across all training sets
- Random Model: If one of the 14 models were chosen at random and applied to the test set
- Bespoke Model: The model selected using our distance calculation is applied to the test set
- Domain Shift: The bespoke model with training data that is closest to test data when training occurs for only 13 data sets and excludes the training set that exactly matches the conditions of the test set. For example, if the test set is the Potsdam set from COWC, the candidate bespoke models do not include a model trained with Potsdam imagery. The model selector identifies the best candidate from the remaining 13 choices.
- Random with Domain Shift: Rather than selecting the best among the 13 models based on distance, the model is chosen at random.

The performance results demonstrate several key findings. First, without domain shift the bespoke model substantially outperforms the general model or the randomly chosen model. The random model is effectively a surrogate for operating without a model selector. Thus, when operating with a fixed number of labeled training samples, the bespoke model performs best. In this case, all models were trained on 650 annotations. Looking at performance under domain shift, the bespoke model still outperforms the random model, although the difference is less pronounced. We did not train an equivalent of the general model under domain shift so that comparison was missing from this experiment (Fig. 9).

Although the bespoke model beats the general model for a fixed-size training set, this does not reflect operational conditions. A more realistic approach is to assume that there is a fixed budget for labeling training data. Because each candidate bespoke model was trained on 650 instances, a general model could have been trained on all the available – namely 9,100 samples (14 times 650). Below we consider different ways to use this limited training budget (Table 3). The union model is trained on all available data (9,100 instances) and the bespoke model is trained on only the 650 labels for the corresponding dataset. However, the retrained bespoke model starts with the union model and retrains with the 650 dataset-specific sample. The random model is as discussed before. The clear takeaway is that the retrained bespoke model shines (Tables 4, 5 and 6). The experiment was repeated 10 times to compute the standard deviations.

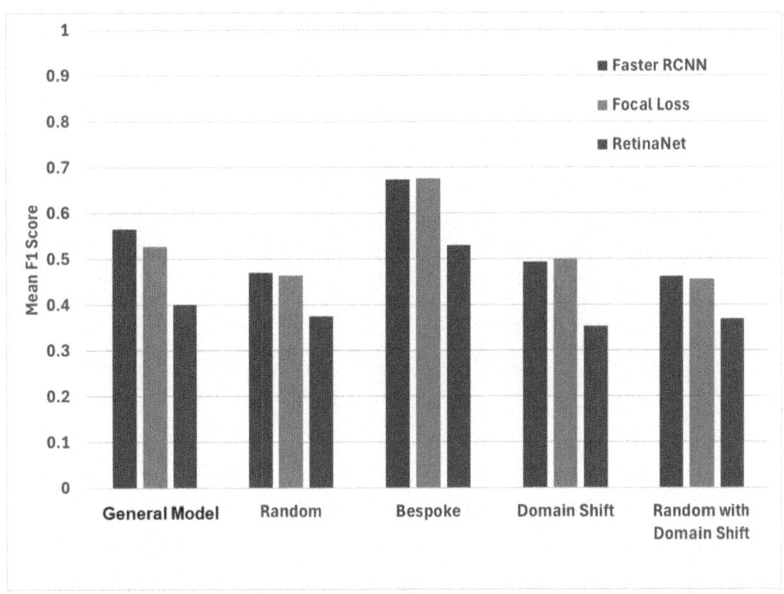

Fig. 9. F1 scores for model selector experiment for object detection

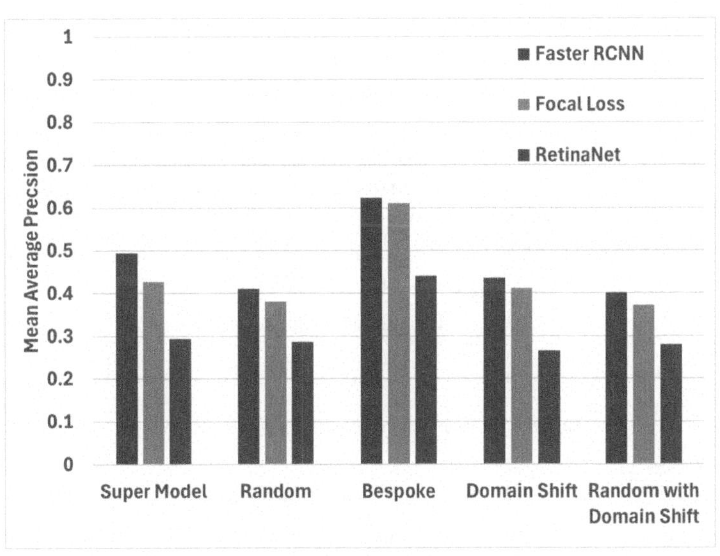

Fig. 10. Precision scores for model selector experiment for object detection

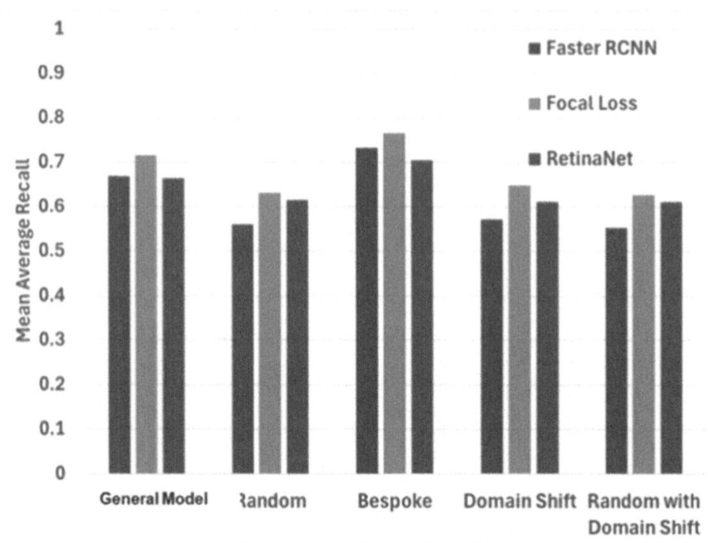

Fig. 11. Recall scores for model selector experiment for object detection

Table 3. Cases considered in the model selection experiment

Model	Description
Union Model	Using the collection of all bespoke training samples. 9100 annotations
Bespoke Model	Matching metadata (location, viewing angle, GSD) and selecting model based on distance between the training set and the test set. 650 annotations
Retrained Bespoke Model	A retrained bespoke model trained using the Union Model as the starting point. 9100 annotations
Random	Average all candidate bespoke models

Table 4. Performance results for Faster RCNN

Faster RCNN	F1 Score		Precision		Recall	
	mean	std	mean	std	mean	std
Union ~ 9,100	0.686	0.122	0.637	0.130	0.746	0.108
Bespoke ~ 650	0.673	0.110	0.624	0.123	0.733	0.092
Retrained Bespoke ~ 9100	0.727	0.096	0.689	0.105	0.771	0.085
Random	0.435	0.188	0.377	0.177	0.526	0.201

Table 5. Performance results for Focal Loss

Focal Loss	F1 Score		Precision		Recall	
	mean	std	mean	std	mean	std
Union ~ 9,100	0.692	0.127	0.623	0.143	0.786	0.09
Bespoke ~ 650	0.676	0.121	0.610	0.139	0.766	0.087
Retrained Bespoke ~ 9100	0.740	0.096	0.688	0.111	0.803	0.073
Random	0.428	0.179	0.346	0.171	0.601	0.169

Table 6. Performance results for RetinaNet

RetinaNet	F1 Score		Precision		Recall	
	mean	std	mean	std	mean	std
Union ~ 9,100	0.620	0.135	0.535	0.146	0.752	0.095
Bespoke ~ 650	0.529	0.185	0.439	0.197	0.705	0.117
Retrained Bespoke ~ 9100	0.674	0.101	0.607	0.116	0.762	0.076
Random	0.347	0.181	0.261	0.160	0.593	0.160

4 Model Selection for Object Classification

Model selection experiments for object classification followed the same process as for object detection. Because the classification experiment uses image chips, we defined the domain shift by the specific types of objects used for training. This distinction will become clear as we walk through the details.

The data set was the rare Planes data [13]. The dataset consists of image chips with the aircraft centered in the chip at a variety of orientations (Fig. 12). Background chips, which do not contain an aircraft, were excluded from our experiment. All the aircraft fall into three broad classes: private, Sport, and Transport. Within each class are multiple types of aircraft. We constructed four datasets where each set contained instances of all three classes, but the models within each class were different for the four data sets. The first three data sets were portioned into separate training and testing sets, which the fourth data set was for testing only (Table 7). The fourth data set represents the domain shift and contains aircraft types that were not present in any of the three training sets.

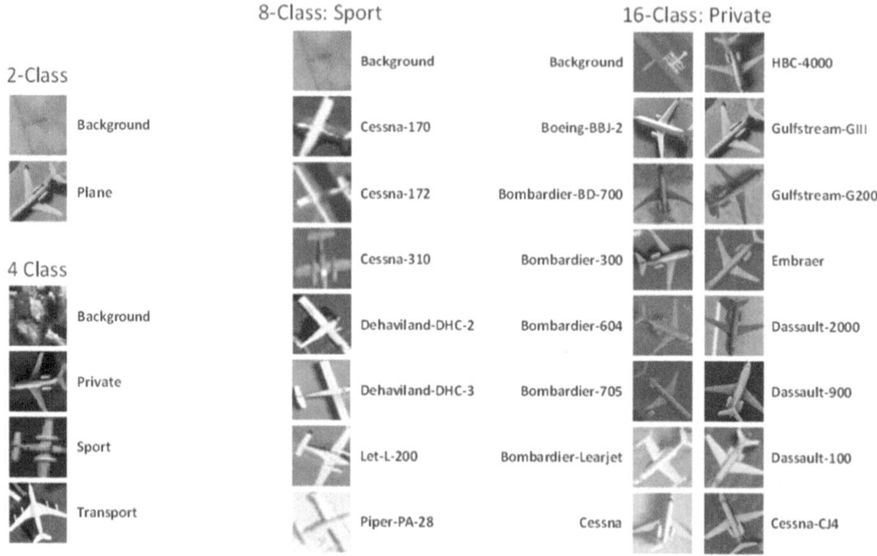

Fig. 12. Illustration of the rare planes data, illustrating the image chips labeled by class, type, and model

Table 7. Construction of the data sets. Each set is comprised on different types within the three broad classes.

Model	PRIVATE	SPORT	TRANSPORT
TRAINING			
Set 1	Airplane Civil Private Bombardier BD-700-GlobalExpress	Airplane Civil Sport Cessna 172	Airplane Civil Transport ATR ATR-72
Set 2	Airplane Civil Private Cessna Citation-CJ4	Airplane Civil Sport DeHavillandCanada DHC-2-Beaver	Airplane Civil Transport Airbus A-319
Set 3	Airplane Civil Private Dassault Falcon-100	Airplane Civil Sport Let L-200Morova	Airplane Civil Transport BAE 146–300
General	Equal sampling from all three sets, preserving total number of training instances		
TESTING			
Set 1	Airplane Civil Private Bombardier BD-700-GlobalExpress	Airplane Civil Sport Cessna 172	Airplane Civil Transport ATR ATR-72
Set 2	Airplane Civil Private Cessna Citation-CJ4	Airplane Civil Sport DeHavillandCanada DHC-2-Beaver	Airplane Civil Transport Airbus A-319

(*continued*)

Table 7. (*continued*)

Model	PRIVATE	SPORT	TRANSPORT
Set 3	Airplane Civil Private Dassault Falcon-100	Airplane Civil Sport Let L-200Morova	Airplane Civil Transport BAE 146–300
Domain Shift (Set 4)	Airplane Civil Private Gulfstream GIII	Airplane Civil Sport DeHavilland Canada DHC-3-Otter	Airplane Civil Transport Boeing 707

Using the Rare Planes data as described above, we tested both within domain (Table 8) and under domain shift (Table 9). The analysis used vision transformer as the classifier. All experiments were based on 10 trials, with 1000 random samples per training class and 500 random samples per testing class. The within domain analysis shows, as expected, that the bespoke model outperforms the general model for a fixed size training sample (Table 8). This is consistent with the results for object detection. For domain shift, the distance measures for the three models were Model 1 distance = 53.5, Model 2 distance = 27.1, and Model 3 distance = 49.2. Thus, the training set for Model 2 is closest to the test data under domain shift, indicating the Model 2 is preferred. This aligns with the observed performance of the three models under domain shift (Table 9).

Table 8. Performance within domain for object classification

Vision Transformer	Precision		Recall		F1 Score		Accuracy	
Model (# train/test samples)	mean	std	mean	std	mean	std	mean	std
Model 1 (1000/500)	0.825	0.038	0.828	0.038	0.826	0.040	0.828	0.038
Model 2 (1000/500)	0.868	0.035	0.850	0.055	0.846	0.059	0.850	0.055
Model 3 (1000/500)	0.835	0.034	0.831	0.035	0.826	0.038	0.831	0.035
General model (1000/500)	0.691	0.054	0.671	0.055	0.663	0.060	0.670	0.052

Table 9. Performance results for classification under domain shift

Vision Transformer	Precision		Recall		F1 Score		Accuracy	
Inference model (# test samples)	mean	Std	Mean	std	mean	std	mean	std
Model 1 (500)	0.480	0.045	0.473	0.041	0.421	0.056	0.473	0.041
Model 2 (500)	0.761	0.026	0.726	0.048	0.726	0.049	0.726	0.048
Model 3 (500)	0.642	0.028	0.587	0.0360	0.571	0.051	0.587	0.036
General_model (500)	0.668	0.055	0.620	0.058	0.591	0.063	0.620	0.056
Distance measures: Model 1: 53.4, **Model 2: 27.1**, Model 3: 49.2								

5 Conclusions

This paper demonstrates proof of concept for model selection. The model selector exhibited consistently strong performance for object detection and object classification. Access to the training data is essential. For model selection, the workflow is to compute the scene complexity measures on the training sets and the mission imagery, then compute the distance between each training set and the mission data. The ML model trained on the training set that is closest to mission data is the selected model.

References

1. Ross, T., Mossing, J.: The MSTAR evaluation methodology. In: SPIE Conference on Algorithms for Synthetic Aperture Radar Imagery VI, Orlando (1999)
2. Canny, J.F.: A computational approach to edge detection. IEEE Trans. Patt. Anal. Mach. Intell. PAMI-**8**(6), 679–698, November 1986. https://doi.org/10.1109/TPAMI.1986.4767851
3. Haralick, R.M., Shanmugam, K., Dinstein, I.: Textural features for image classification. IEEE Trans. Syst. Man Cybern. **SMC-3**(6), 610–621, November 1973. https://doi.org/10.1109/TSMC.1973.4309314
4. Naeem, F., et al.: Quantifying image quality attributes for training and testing of machine learning methods. In: SPIE Defense and Commercial Sensing, Geospatial Informatics XIII, National Harbor, MD, 21–25 April 2024
5. Mandelbrot, B.B.: The Fractal Geometry of Nature. Macmillan (1983). ISBN 978-0-7167-1186-5. Accessed 1 Feb 2012
6. Tanner, F., et al.: Overhead imagery research data set — an annotated data library & tools to aid in the development of computer vision algorithms. In: 2009 IEEE Applied Imagery Pattern Recognition Workshop (AIPR 2009), Washington, DC, USA, pp. 1–8 (2009). https://doi.org/10.1109/AIPR.2009.5466304
7. Mundhenk, T.N., et al.: A large contextual dataset for classification, detection and counting of cars with deep learning. In: European Conference on Computer Vision, pp. 785–800 (2016)
8. Azimi, S., Bahmanyar, R., Henry, C., Kurz, F.: EAGLE: large-scale vehicle detection dataset in real-world scenarios using aerial imagery. In: International Conference on Pattern Recognition (ICPR) (2020)

9. Tian, Z., Shen, C., Chen, H., et al.: Fcos: fully convolutional one-stage object detection. In: Proceedings of the IEEE/CVF International Conference on Computer Vision, pp. 9627–9636 (2019)
10. Lin, T.-Y., Goyal, P., Girshick, R., et al.: Focal loss for dense object detection. In: Proceedings of the IEEE International Conference on Computer Vision (ICCV) (2017)
11. Ren, S., He, K., Girshick, R., et al.: Faster R-CNN: towards real-time object detection with region proposal networks. Adv. Neural Inform. Process. Syst. **28** (2015)
12. Li, Y., Xie, S., Chen, X., et al.: Benchmarking detection transfer learning with vision transformers, *arXiv preprint* arXiv:2111.11429 (2021)
13. Shermeyer, J., Hossler, T., Etten, A.V., Hogan, D., Lewis, R., Kim, D.: RarePlanes: synthetic data takes flight. In: IEEE Workshop/Winter Conference on Applications of Computer Vision, 4 June 2020

A Multimodal IoT-Based Smart Desk System for Real-Time Thermal Comfort Classification in Educational Environments

Krupa V. Khapper[1(✉)], Issa W. AlHmoud[2], Balakrishna Gokaraju[2], AKM Kamrul Islam[2], and Corey A Graves[1]

[1] Electrical and Computer Engineering Department, North Carolina A & T State University, Greensboro, NC 27411, USA
kvkhapper@aggies.ncat.edu

[2] Computational Data Science and Engineering Department, North Carolina A and T State University, Greensboro, NC 27411, USA

Abstract. Emerging research in affective computing and intelligent environments highlights the need for adaptive thermal comfort systems that address individualized discomfort in real-time within educational settings. Traditional HVAC systems cannot dynamically respond to student-specific needs, which can reduce engagement and learning outcomes. To address this gap, this paper presents the design and evaluation of an IoT-based Smart Desk system that integrates low-power hardware and multimodal sensor fusion for desk-level comfort classification. Each desk incorporates an ESP32-WROVER module with an MLX90640 infrared thermal array to detect facial skin temperature and an onboard camera to capture facial images. A central ESP32 node monitors the ambient temperature and humidity through a DHT11 sensor. Data from all desks are transmitted to an instructor s computer, where facial emotion recognition is performed using DeepFace with pre-trained convolutional neural networks (CNN), such as VGG-Face and FaceNet. Expressions are classified as happy, neutral, sad, and angry. These emotion labels, combined with the readings of skin temperature and ambient sensor, are evaluated against the ASHRAE-guided thresholds, Ambient temperature: 19–27 °C (66–80 °F), relative humidity: 30–60 %, skin temperature: 32.6–33.5 °C ($\approx$ 90–92 °F), and emotion $\in$ {happy, neutral}. **Rule:** if $\geq \frac{3}{4}$ conditions hold $\rightarrow$ *Comfortable*; else *Uncomfortable*, and the desk labels are aggregated into a room-level comfort score. The proposed system is optimized for privacy, bandwidth, and power, making it suitable for scalable deployment in real-world classrooms. By combining affective state recognition with environmental sensing, the Smart Desk platform bridges the gap between individual comfort detection and classroom-wide adaptive environmental control. Future work will focus on large-scale validation, predictive comfort modeling, and closed-loop HVAC integration through Google Nest APIs, enabling proactive and automated classroom climate management.

F. Tanner and J. Irvine (Eds.): AIPR 2025, LNCS 16446, pp. 292–310, 2026.
https://doi.org/10.1007/978-3-032-18474-0_21

Keywords: Internet of Things (IoT) · Smart Classroom · Smart Desk · Educational Technology · ESP32 · Thermal Comfort · Emotion Recognition

1 Introduction

The integration of Internet of Things (IoT) technologies into educational environments is transforming traditional classroom experiences by enabling automation, interactivity, and real-time feedback. Among these innovations, Smart Desks equipped with embedded sensors and network connectivity provide a practical and scalable approach to improving learning spaces [1,2]. By continuously monitoring environmental and physiological parameters, using embedded sensing platforms, these systems enable data-driven adjustments that improve student comfort, engagement, and academic performance [3].

Thermal comfort is one of the most critical factors that influence student participation, concentration, and cognitive performance. Research indicates that even mild discomfort can affect attention and reduce productivity, ultimately affecting academic outcomes [4,5]. However, most existing HVAC systems are designed for uniform environmental control and cannot adapt to real-time, individualized comfort needs. This limitation often leads to overcooling or overheating, wasted energy, and decreased user satisfaction. Manual HVAC adjustments are often ineffective due to the reliance on subjective delayed feedback [3].

Unlike conventional systems that rely solely on environmental sensors or instructor input, this work presents a low-cost, IoT-enabled Smart Desk system that integrates real-time skin temperature sensing, facial emotion recognition, and environmental data to assess thermal comfort at the individual level. Using the MLX90640 thermal camera on an ESP32 platform and DeepFace facial analysis running on the instructor's computer, the system provides non-intrusive monitoring and visual feedback via a GUI-based Thermal Comfort Dashboard. This enables adaptive HVAC responses and supports student-centered environmental management, fostering personalized comfort and improved learning conditions.

The ESP32 microcontroller is valued for its wireless connectivity and energy-efficient operation, featuring deep sleep modes, adjustable clock speeds, and peripheral management to minimize power use during idle periods. Its success in educational IoT applications demonstrates its ability to enhance learning environments and automate processes. This work utilizes the ESP32-WROVER, featuring an integrated camera, as the core platform, leveraging its dual-core processor, built-in Wi-Fi/Bluetooth, and extensive peripheral support. These features enable integration with sensors such as the MLX90640 thermal camera and the onboard camera for facial emotion recognition. Its affordability makes it ideal for scalable and cost-effective classroom deployment [6,7].

Recent advances in affective computing, multimodal sensing, and rule-based comfort classification offer opportunities to develop adaptive comfort systems that overcome the limitations of traditional HVAC control. By combining physiological signals, facial expressions, and ambient conditions, it is possible to infer occupant comfort levels in a non-intrusive and privacy-preserving manner. Low-cost embedded devices enable scalable deployments that operate under strict power and bandwidth constraints [8,9].

This work presents a Smart Desk system that integrates IoT-enabled thermal imaging, facial emotion recognition, and ambient sensing to perform real-time comfort classification at the desk level. Using rule-based comfort classification models, the system combines multimodal data to determine individual and aggregated comfort states. The design emphasizes scalability, privacy preservation, and energy efficiency, with the long-term goal of enabling closed-loop integration with HVAC systems. By dynamically aligning environmental controls with occupant comfort, the Smart Desk system aims to improve student well-being, engagement, and overall learning outcomes.

This paper is structured as follows. Section 2 reviews related work; Sect. 3 presents the system architecture; Sect. 4 outlines software development; Sect. 5 discusses the demonstration and performance evaluation; and Sect. 6 concludes the paper with future directions.

2 Related Work

Recent literature demonstrates a growing interest in applying affective computing, embedded systems, and IoT-based frameworks to advance thermal comfort in educational environments. In particular, non-invasive sensing technologies paired with real-time analytics are increasingly recognized as enhance satisfaction through near-body heating and cooling, as well as improved studies suggest that integrating camera-based thermal imaging with physiological signal interpretation can support robust occupant-centric control strategies. However, most current implementations focus on macro-level environmental monitoring, lacking the granularity needed for individualized, desk-level adaptation.

Aryal *et al.* [1] review IoT-enabled smart desks that fuse environmental sensing with user feedback to personalize comfort and productivity. Previous studies used statistical and learning models (e.g., logistic / DT / NN) to infer thermal preference and drive local action, noting that many buildings still miss ASHRAE 55 s $\geq$ 80% satisfaction goal. Personal comfort systems enhance satisfaction through near-body heating and cooling, as well as improved air flow.

Jeoung *et al.* [9] demonstrated that extracting facial skin temperature using thermal cameras and facial landmark detection can predict comfort levels with greater precision than 90%. Their findings confirm the viability of contactless facial thermal sensing for real-time comfort monitoring, highlighting the potential of this approach as a scalable and unobtrusive method for assessing comfort in real-time. By analyzing thermal gradients in specific facial regions, the system achieves high prediction accuracy, making it suitable for educational environments where minimal intrusion is critical.

Navarrete-Sanchez *et al.* [3] implemented ESP32 and DS18B20 sensors to monitor classroom temperature conditions cost-effectively, demonstrating the feasibility of decentralized environmental sensing using low-cost microcontrollers.

Their work highlights the role of edge computing in scalable data collection, but remains limited to macro-level ambient monitoring without incorporating emotion-aware features or individualized comfort feedback.

Lala *et al.* [11] further stressed the challenges of developing ML-based thermal comfort models for children, highlighting issues such as illogical responses and class imbalance, which limit generalization. Furthermore, their study highlights the need for large and diverse data sets to improve the reliability of predictive models in dynamic classroom conditions. They also advocate for the incorporation of adaptive and personalized strategies to account for variations in thermal preferences among children, pointing to the limitations of static and uniform approaches in educational settings.

Culic *et al.* [12] reviewed smart monitoring technologies, including wearables and camera-based systems, emphasizing their potential for occupant-centric control (OCC). They note that while sensor fusion improves predictive accuracy, practical deployment challenges persist in educational environments, including sensor calibration, unobtrusiveness, and student acceptance. The study emphasizes the need for seamless integration of sensing modalities that preserve privacy while providing individualized feedback.

Challa *et al.* [13] developed a deep learning based occupancy estimation system using the YOLOv4 object detection model for real-time monitoring in classroom environments. By integrating computer vision (CV) and CO2 sensor fusion, their work achieved over 98% accuracy in occupant detection and demonstrated the potential of AI-driven HVAC control to enhance operational efficiency in educational facilities.

Darwish *et al.* [14] proposed an IoT-driven framework utilizing DHT11 humidity, MS1100 CO2, and vision sensors to evaluate thermal comfort and occupancy patterns in educational spaces. The study employed fuzzy logic control (FLC) and the Predicted Mean Vote (PMV) index, following the ASHRAE 55 standard, to maintain optimal classroom thermal conditions. Their results indicated that managing thermal comfort in conjunction with occupancy-based control significantly improved energy efficiency and user satisfaction.

Our work builds on these efforts by integrating ambient sensing, facial thermal imaging, and emotion recognition using DeepFace into a unified framework. The Smart Desk system addresses the gaps in previous studies by offering real-time classification, privacy-sensitive data handling, and a scalable solution suitable for deployment in classrooms.

3 System Design

The Smart Desk system is designed as a modular, IoT-based platform that integrates multimodal sensing, Wi-Fi-based communication, and rule-based comfort classification to monitor and assess student thermal comfort in real-time. It comprises three subsystems: (i) student smart desk units, (ii) a centralized ambient monitoring node, and (iii) a central server interface at the instructor station.

3.1 System Workflow

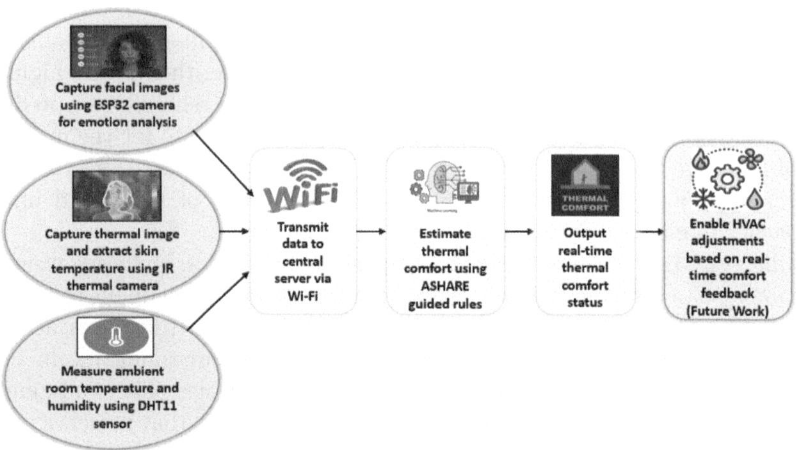

Fig. 1. System workflow showing data flow from student desks and ambient node to the instructor s interface.

Figure 1 illustrates the high-level system workflow. Facial images, thermal data, and ambient conditions are captured at the desk and node level, transmitted to the server via Wi-Fi, and used to estimate thermal comfort. The comfort status is then used to guide real-time visualization and future HVAC adjustments.

3.2 System Implementation

The system-level architecture, which illustrates the integration of student Smart Desks, the instructor server, and the ambient sensing node for real-time thermal comfort monitoring and analysis, is shown in Figs. 2 and 3. This system is an implementation of the abstract low-power IoT-based smart desk design described in [15].

Instructor System. The instructor system serves as the central node for data aggregation, processing, and visualization. Implemented on a laptop or desktop connected via Wi-Fi, it receives real-time data from all Smart Desks and environmental nodes.

Facial images are processed using the DeepFace library to classify emotions, while skin and ambient data are evaluated against the ASHRAE-guided thresholds (Section 3-2-1). A desk is classified as *Comfortable* if at least three of the following four conditions are satisfied; otherwise, it is labeled *Uncomfortable*:

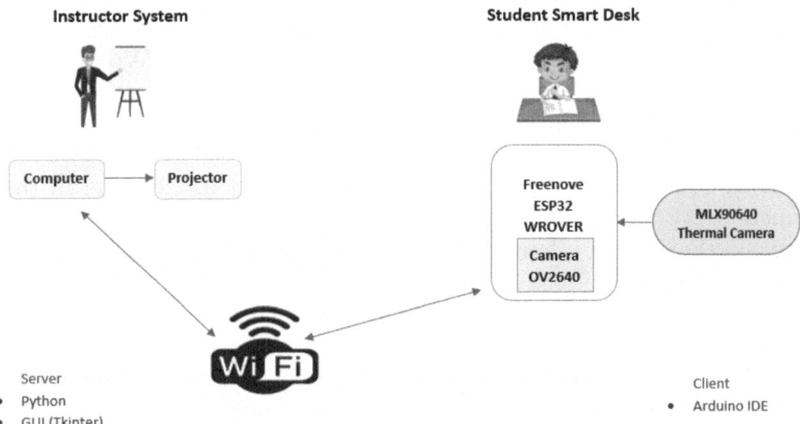

Fig. 2. IoT-enabled Smart Desk Unit with thermal and visual sensing for localized comfort assessment.

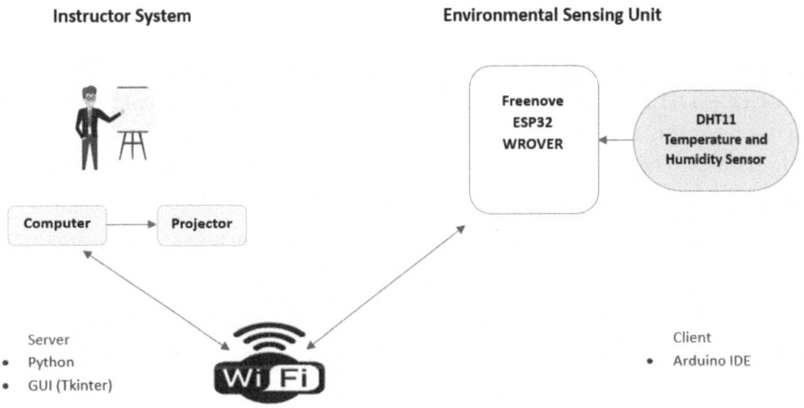

Fig. 3. Ambient monitoring node for capturing classroom-wide temperature and humidity.

1. Ambient temperature $19-27$ °C,
2. Relative humidity $30-60\%$,
3. Facial skin temperature $32.6-33.5$ °C,
4. Dominant emotion $\in \{\text{happy}, \text{neutral}\}$.

A Python Tkinter-based GUI displays comfort metrics for each desk, allowing instructors to monitor student well-being.

Student Smart Desk(s). The Smart Desk is built using compact, low-power, and cost-effective components that enable multimodal sensing, wireless communication, and real-time data acquisition. The selected components are as follows:

- ***ESP32-WROVER:*** Serves as the central microcontroller unit. It features a dual-core MCU with PSRAM (4 MB typical), integrated Wi-Fi/Bluetooth; it handles image capture, sensor fusion, and secure data transmission.
- ***OV2640 Camera Module:*** 2 MP low-power camera; captures facial images for emotion inference.
- ***MLX90640 Thermal Infrared Sensor:*** This is a 32×24 pixel IR thermal camera array that provides non-contact skin temperature data. Mounted to focus on the student s face.
- ***Power Supply:*** Options include:
  - *Battery-powered:* Enables portability and flexible placement; supports operation during power outages.
  - *Alternative sources:* Explore wireless charging or energy harvesting (e.g., solar, motion-based) for sustainable, continuous power.

These components are selected not only for their affordability and low-power consumption, but also for ease of integration and compatibility with open-source software and libraries.

Environmental Sensing Unit. A standalone ambient node (ESP32-WROVER + DHT11) monitors the room conditions independently of the desks. Reports one-minute bucket readings to the server at `/data`; the instructor system then fuses these server-side values with desk-level signals for display and logging.

Sensing: The node measures the temperature in °C (with the calculated °F) and relative humidity (%). It is not attached to any specific desk and represents the room's overall conditions.

Calibration and stability: Perform a one-point room calibration at deployment; reject transient spikes $>3\sigma$ in a minute; clip Relative Humidity (RH) to $[0, 100]\%$.

Networking: Use HTTPS in production with certificate validation. During development, `WiFiClientSecure::setInsecure()` may be used. Employ exponential back-off (up to three retries) before dropping the minute record.

Output fields: Temperature (°C), Temperature (°F), Humidity (%) and timestamp. These populate the ambient columns in the CSV and drive room-level indicators in the GUI.

3.3 Data Collection

The Smart Desk system collects synchronized data from multiple sources to enable individualized thermal comfort analysis and room-level aggregation. Data are captured through the following three key components:

The instructor and student systems are wirelessly connected through Wi-Fi, enabling real-time communication between the Instructor System (server) and the Student Smart Desk (client) using an application developed in the

Arduino IDE for ESP32. This setup enables real-time synchronized communication between the instructor and the students, fostering an interactive, technology-enhanced learning environment.

- ***Instructor System***: The instructor computer serves as the central server, receiving data from all Smart Desks in real-time. It performs the following tasks:
  - Receives facial images captured by desk-level ESP32 cameras via HTTPS POST.
  - Processes emotion recognition using DeepFace with CNN models (e.g., VGG-Face, FaceNet).
  - Log data into structured CSV or database tables, including timestamps, desk IDs, average skin temperature, ambient readings, and inferred emotion.
  - Labels comfort status via an ASHRAE-guided rule set. Using ambient temperature (19 27 °C), relative humidity (30 60%), skin temperature (32.6 33.5 °C), and emotion happy, neutral; a desk is comfortable only if $\frac{3}{4}$ or more criteria are satisfied, otherwise it is uncomfortable.

  The instructor system coordinates all incoming data streams and handles classification, storage, and visualization.
- ***Student Smart Desk(s)***: Each desk acts as a sensing unit, performing local data collection via:
  - *ESP32-WROVER Module:* Handles Wi-Fi connectivity, camera interfacing, and sensor control.
  - *OV2640 Camera Module:* Captures facial images of the student periodically for emotion detection.
  - *MLX90640 Thermal Array Sensor:* Captures facial skin temperature by scanning a 32 × 24 grid, focusing on key facial regions such as the forehead and cheeks.

  All data collected is time-stamped, associated with the desk s IP, and sent to the instructor's server.

To synchronize multimodal data streams across all desks and sensors, the system aggregates every set of readings into a minute bucket a fixed one-minute window that aligns ambient temperature, humidity, facial thermal data, and emotion recognition results into a single, time-stamped record. Each bucket therefore represents a coherent snapshot of environmental and physiological conditions within that 60-second interval. This design ensures temporal consistency, reduces transient noise, and provides a uniform foundation for comfort evaluation and CSV logging.

3.4 Communication and Security

The system utilizes ESP32-WROVER microcontrollers and Wi-Fi to establish wireless communication between the instructor's computer and the Smart Desk of each student. Real-time data transfer enables synchronized classroom activities and facilitates responsive instructor-student interaction. For secure communication, the system uses the `WiFiClientSecure` library with SSL/TLS encryption. In contrast, root CA certificates are typically used for the authentication of the client.setInsecure( ) method is used only in the development phase. For deployment, proper certificate validation is recommended to allow connections with self-signed certificates. This approach enables development flexibility while preserving the privacy and integrity of sensitive data, such as student images and thermal responses.

4 Code Development and Deployment

4.1 Arduino for Student Smart Desks

Each Smart Desk is programmed using the Arduino IDE, targeting the ESP32-WROVER module. The firmware integrates multiple components, including camera initialization, thermal data acquisition (MLX90640), Wi-Fi communication, and HTTPS POST transmission.

4.2 Python for Instructor Interface

The instructor interface is developed in Python using the Flask framework. It acts as the central server, receiving data from all desks, performing real-time DeepFace emotion analysis (using the OpenCV backend and converting from BGR to RGB), and logging metrics. Emotions are aggregated as the statistical mode in batches of 10 images per device. Data are stored in CSV format. When no human is detected, the skin, emotion, and comfort fields are filled with missing values (`NA`). Comfort is classified using an ASHRAE-guided rule set, defined in Sect. 3.2.1. A Tkinter-based GUI visualizes per-desk metrics and the aggregated room-level comfort score. Figure 4 illustrates a flowchart showing data flow and decision-making in the Smart Desk system.

- ***Inputs***
  - *Environment node (DHT11):* Post room temperature (°C) and relative humidity to `/data`.
  - *Thermal camera (MLX90640):* Posts 24 32 frames to `/update`; used to detect skin-range pixels (∼32 36 °C).
  - *RGB camera (ESP32-WROVER):* Sends 10 images (∼3 s apart) to `/receive_image` for DeepFace emotion inference.
- ***Processing***
  - Thermal frame compute average skin temperature and set human-detecting flag.
  - Ten per-image emotions ? majority vote ? minute-level dominant emotion.

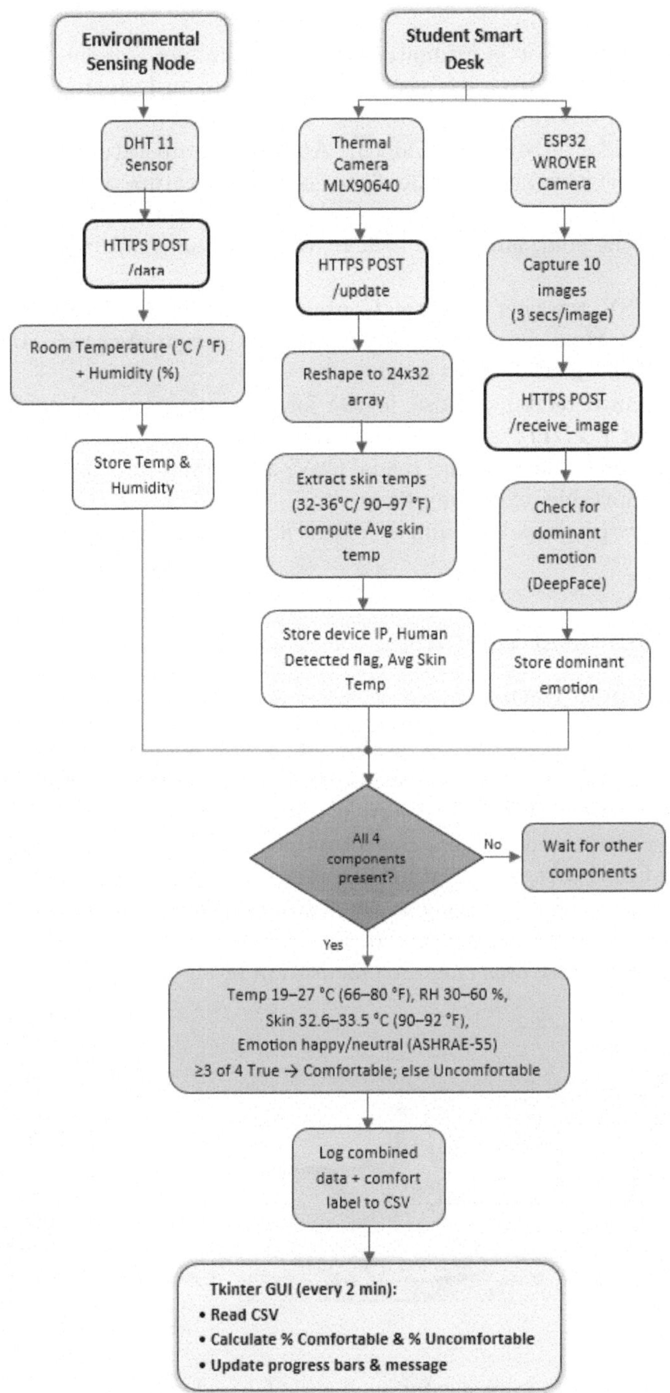

Fig. 4. Flowchart depicting data flow and decision-making in the Smart Desk system.

- ***Fusion & Decision***
  - A minute bucket is evaluated when all four are present: ambient temperature, humidity, average skin temp (Human-Detected = True), and dominant emotion.
  - Thresholds (ASHRAE-guided): Ambient temperature 19–27 °C (66–80 °F), relative humidity 30–60%, skin temperature 32.6–33.5 °C (≈ 90–92 °F), emotion ∈ {happy, neutral}. Decision rule: If 3/4 or more of the conditions hold, label *comfortable*; otherwise *uncomfortable*.
- ***Logging***
  - One CSV row per minute: Containing entries for Date, Time, Temp (°C/°F), Humidity, Device IP, Human Detection, Avg Skin Temp, Dominant Emotion, Comfort level.
  - If human detected = False, log `NA` for skin, emotion, and comfort.
- ***Dashboard (GUI)***
  - Refreshes every 2 min; reads CSV and computes % Comfortable/% Uncomfortable, excluding `NA` rows.
  - Displays progress bars and a concise status message for instructors.

5 Experimental Results

5.1 Experiment Setup

The Smart Desk prototype was evaluated in a simulated classroom environment with ten desks. Each desk featured an ESP32-WROVER module equipped with a camera and MLX90640 thermal sensor. A central ESP32 node with a DHT11 sensor captured ambient room conditions. All nodes communicated over a secure Wi-Fi network to a local Flask server running on the instructor s laptop. The system collected facial images, facial thermal gradients, and ambient data, transmitting via HTTP as structured payloads; the server logs per-minute CSV records. Figure 5 illustrates the implementation of an IoT-based smart desk.

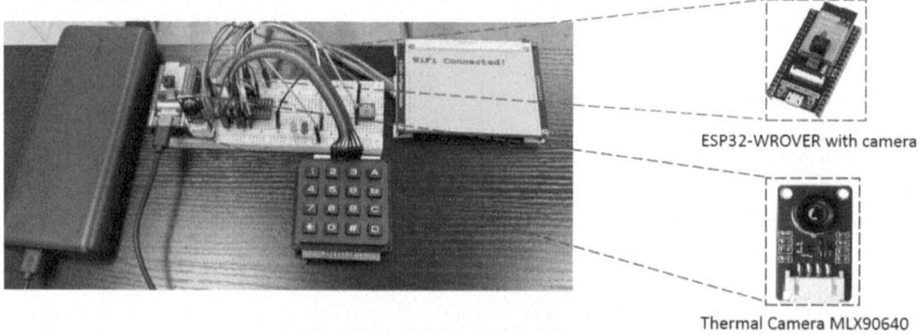

Fig. 5. Implementation of an IoT-based smart desk.

5.2 Data Flow Validation

The captured data from each desk was successfully transmitted to the server in near real-time. The server performed facial emotion recognition using DeepFace and extracted feature vectors that included emotion labels, skin temperature, and environmental parameters. These were classified into comfortable or uncomfortable states using the rule-based thresholds described in Section. 3–2-1.

5.3 Test Results

This section demonstrates the end-to-end operation of the thermal comfort pipeline, including ambient sensing, desk-level signals (thermal and emotional), rule-based fusion, and logging/visualization.

– ***Thermal Frames (MLX90640):*** Fig. 6 illustrates representative 24×32 thermal frames with the facial region outlined; the color scale is fixed and labeled for interpretability. Values within the human-skin band (32 36 °C) are visually emphasized.

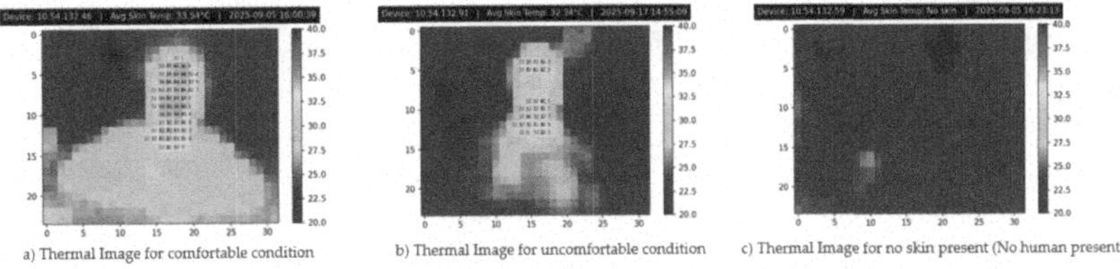

a) Thermal Image for comfortable condition
b) Thermal Image for uncomfortable condition
c) Thermal Image for no skin present (No human present)

Fig. 6. Representative MLX90640 frames (24×32). The color bar indicates temperature (°C), and the human-skin band (32 36 °C) guides pixel selection.

– ***Emotion Overlays (DeepFace):*** Fig. 7 illustrates annotations on a frame: bounding boxes, dominant emotion labels, and a compact 7-class bar chart. The dominant emotion at the minute level is determined by a 10-image sequence (3 s per image, totaling 30 s), with a majority vote from the ESP32-WROVER stream. This approach reduces the noise in individual frames, resulting in more stable emotion classification results.
– ***Ambient Sensing (Temperature & Humidity):*** The centrally placed ambient node (DHT11) provides classroom temperature/humidity data *in real time* that complements thermal and emotion data at the desk. Example readouts and placement are illustrated in Fig. 3 (Ambient monitoring node), confirming stable coverage for the test rooms.
– ***Thermal Comfort Prediction:*** Comfort is classified using the ASHRAE-guided thresholds (Section. 3–2-1) with the $\geq 3/4$ rule. Table 1. summarizes the thresholds.

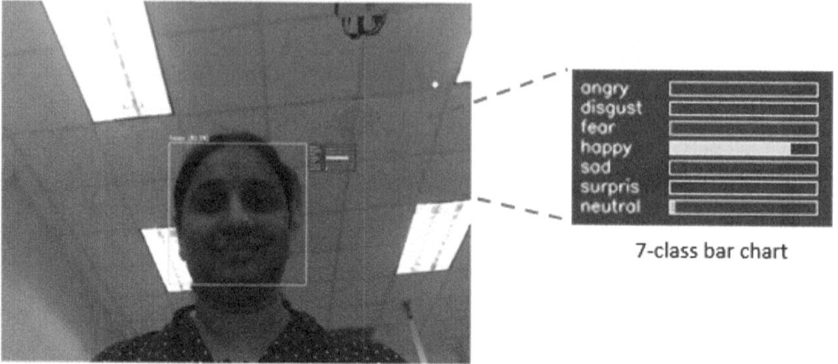

Fig. 7. DeepFace outputs with dominant label and 7-class bar chart per face; minute-level emotion uses 10-image majority vote from desk cameras.

Table 1. Rule-based thresholds for desk level thermal comfort

Variable	Comfortable	Uncomfortable (Low)	Uncomfortable (High)
Ambient Temperature	19°C – 27°C (66.2°F – 80.6°F)	< 19°C (< 66.2°F)	> 27°C (> 80.6°F)
Humidity	30% – 60%	< 30%	> 60%
Skin Temperature	32.6°C – 33.5 °C (90.7°F – 92.3°F)	< 32.6°C (< 90.7°F)	> 33.5°C (> 92.3°F)
Emotion	Happy/Neutral	Angry/Sad/Fear	Angry/Sad/Fear

– ***CSV log (per-minute records):*** The server writes one row per minute with fields: *Date, Time, Temperature (°C/°F), Humidity (%), Device IP Address, Human Detection, Average Skin Temperature (°C), Dominant Emotion, Comfort Level.* The temperature (°F) is calculated from °C for the reporting of mixed units. When *Human Detection* is *False*, the system records `NA` for Average Skin Temperature, Dominant Emotion, and Comfort Level. Rows with `NA` in human-dependent fields are excluded from room-level percentages.

- *CSV and dashboard:* The CSV is shown in Fig. 8. The dashboard, shown in Fig. 9, reports % Comfortable/% Uncomfortable over labeled rows only, together with count totals and a concise status message.

A	B	C	D	E	F	G	H	I	J
Date	Time	Temperature(°C)	Temperature(°F)	Humidity(%)	Device IP Address	Human Detection	Average Skin Temperature (°C)	Dominant Emotion	Comfort Level
9/5/2025	15:52	21.8	71.24	57	10.54.132.91	TRUE	33.06	neutral	comfortable
9/5/2025	15:52	21.8	71.24	57	10.54.132.97	TRUE	32.95	sad	comfortable
9/5/2025	15:53	21.9	71.42	57	10.54.132.101	TRUE	33.31	neutral	comfortable
9/5/2025	15:53	21.9	71.42	57	10.54.132.102	TRUE	33.36	neutral	comfortable
9/5/2025	15:53	21.9	71.42	57	10.54.132.46	TRUE	33.54	neutral	comfortable
9/5/2025	15:54	21.9	71.42	57	10.54.132.104	TRUE	32.77	neutral	comfortable
9/5/2025	15:54	21.9	71.42	57	10.54.132.106	TRUE	33.23	neutral	comfortable
9/5/2025	15:54	22	71.6	56	10.54.132.96	TRUE	33.13	sad	comfortable
9/5/2025	15:55	22.1	71.78	57	10.54.132.95	TRUE	32.68	neutral	comfortable
9/5/2025	15:55	22.1	71.78	57	10.54.132.109	FALSE	NA	NA	NA

Fig. 8. Per-minute CSV log.

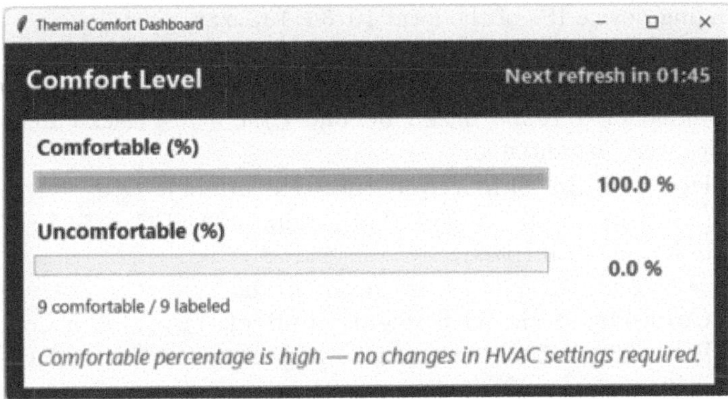

Fig. 9. Dashboard (2-min refresh) showing % Comfortable/% Uncomfortable over labeled rows only, plus counts and status message.

- ***Robustness and Usability Notes:***
  - The minute-bucket design aligns thermal, ambient, and emotion modalities and prevents duplicate counting.
  - The 10-image vote stabilizes the dominant emotion presented in the GUI.
  - Excluding `NA` rows prevents bias from periods without reliable human detection (e.g., empty seat, occlusion).

Generating Uncomfortable Labels. To support balanced classification and ensure robustness of the comfort inference model, a subset of data points was synthetically labeled to represent edge conditions.

- ***Reason:*** To evaluate the decision logic in both classes without exposing participants to prolonged thermal discomfort, a small controlled set of *uncomfortable* samples was attached. This (i) improves the label balance for analysis, (ii) stress-tests the ASHRAE-guided rule engine under edge cases, and (iii) complies with IRB guidance by avoiding deliberate induction of adverse states (no participants were subjected to uncomfortable conditions solely for data collection).
- ***Definition of uncomfortable:*** A minute is labeled *Comfortable* if at least three of the four conditions hold: temperature $19 - 27\,^{\circ}$C, relative humidity $30 - 60\,\%$, skin temperature $32.6 - 33.5\,^{\circ}$C and emotion $\in$ {happy, neutral}; otherwise *Uncomfortable.* Figure 10 illustrates the generated uncomfortable label stored in the CSV file, and Fig. 11 shows the corresponding dashboard.
- ***Generation Protocol:*** To avoid altering historical observations, uncomfortable rows were *appended* to the existing log with the original schema and cadence (1 row/min) while deterministically encoding condition failures:
  - *Schema-preserving & identity:* Append rows at 1-min cadence using the existing date format (e.g., "9/5/2025") and computed °F; assign non-colliding device IPs of the form `10.54.132.xxx`.
  - *condition Failures:* Each synthetic row violates the conditions ≥ 3 (from ambient temperature, relative humidity, skin temperature, emotion) to guarantee an *Uncomfortable* label under the $\geq 3/4$ rule. Three canonical modes were instantiated:
    1. **Hot–Humid–Skin triple (neutral affect).** $T_{\text{amb}} = 28.5°\text{C} > 27$ (fail), RH $= 66\% > 60\%$ (fail), skin $= 33.80°\text{C} > 33.5$ (fail), emotion $=$ neutral (pass).
       $\Rightarrow$ *3 condition failures* $\Rightarrow$ Uncomfortable.
    2. **Cold–Dry–Skin with negative affect.** $T_{\text{amb}} = 17.5°\text{C} < 19$ (fail), RH $= 25\% < 30\%$ (fail), skin $= 29.8°\text{C} < 32.6$ (fail), emotion $=$ sad $\notin$ {happy, neutral} (fail).
       $\Rightarrow$ *4 condition failures* $\Rightarrow$ Uncomfortable.
    3. **Hot–Humid–Skin triple (positive affect).** $T_{\text{amb}} = 28.0°\text{C} > 27$ (fail), RH $= 65\% > 60\%$ (fail), skin $= 33.9°\text{C} > 33.5$ (fail), emotion $=$ happy (pass).
       $\Rightarrow$ *3 condition failures* $\Rightarrow$ Uncomfortable.
    4. **Hot–Dry–Skin with negative affect.** $T_{\text{amb}} = 28.3°\text{C} > 27$ (fail), RH $= 27\% < 30\%$ (fail), $T_{\text{skin}} = 34.1°\text{C} > 33.5$ (fail), emotion $=$ angry $\notin$ {happy, neutral} (fail).
       $\Rightarrow$ *4 condition failures* $\Rightarrow$ Uncomfortable.
    5. **Cold–Humid–Skin with negative affect.** $T_{\text{amb}} = 18.2°\text{C} < 19$ (fail), RH $= 65\% > 60\%$ (fail), $T_{\text{skin}} = 31.9°\text{C} < 32.6$ (fail), emotion $=$ sad $\notin$ {happy, neutral} (fail).
       $\Rightarrow$ *4 condition failures* $\Rightarrow$ Uncomfortable.

  Across all three cases, fewer than three of the four conditions hold; thus, each record is labeled *Uncomfortable* under the $\geq 3/4$ rule.

  - *Units/Consistency:* Temperatures are logged in °C with computed °F; RH is bounded to $[0, 100]\%$. Emotion ontology matches the real-time pipeline.
  - *Rule Check:* After field assignment, the rule is re-evaluated; rows are retained only if the resulting label is uncomfortable.

- ***Ethics and IRB Compliance:*** No participant was exposed to manipulated thermal conditions for data collection. The added rows are synthetic augmentations derived from the published comfort envelope and the study rule, constituting minimal-risk secondary data and aligning with IRB guidance.

A	B	C	D	E	F	G	H	I	J
Date	Time	Temperature(°C)	Temperature(°F)	Humidity(%)	Device IP Address	Human Detection	Average Skin Temperature (°C)	Dominant Emotion	Comfort Level
9/5/2025	15:52	21.8	71.24	57	10.54.132.91	TRUE	33.06	neutral	comfortable
9/5/2025	15:52	21.8	71.24	57	10.54.132.97	TRUE	32.95	sad	comfortable
9/5/2025	15:53	21.9	71.42	57	10.54.132.101	TRUE	33.31	neutral	comfortable
9/5/2025	15:53	21.9	71.42	57	10.54.132.102	TRUE	33.36	neutral	comfortable
9/5/2025	15:53	21.9	71.42	57	10.54.132.46	TRUE	33.54	neutral	comfortable
9/5/2025	15:54	21.9	71.42	57	10.54.132.104	TRUE	32.77	neutral	comfortable
9/5/2025	15:54	21.9	71.42	57	10.54.132.106	TRUE	33.23	neutral	comfortable
9/5/2025	15:54	22	71.6	56	10.54.132.96	TRUE	33.13	sad	comfortable
9/5/2025	15:55	22.1	71.78	57	10.54.132.95	TRUE	32.68	neutral	comfortable
9/5/2025	15:55	22.1	71.78	57	10.54.132.109	FALSE	NA	NA	NA
9/5/2025	15:56	28.5	83.3	66	10.54.132.243	TRUE	33.8	neutral	uncomfortable
9/5/2025	15:57	17.5	63.5	25	10.54.132.139	TRUE	29.8	sad	uncomfortable
9/5/2025	15:58	28	82.4	65	10.54.132.63	TRUE	33.9	happy	uncomfortable
9/5/2025	15:59	28.3	82.94	27	10.54.132.69	TRUE	34.1	angry	uncomfortable
9/5/2025	16:00	18.2	64.76	65	10.54.132.103	TRUE	31.9	sad	uncomfortable

Fig. 10. Generated uncomfortable label stored in the CSV file.

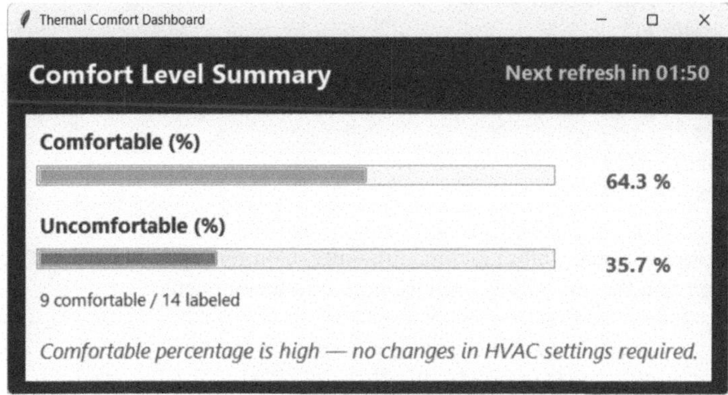

Fig. 11. Dashboard (2-min refresh) showing % Comfortable/ % Uncomfortable over labeled rows only, plus counts and status message.

Dataset and Label Summary. The dataset summary and labeling outcomes are shown in Fig. 12.

```
=== DATA OVERVIEW (all rows) ===
Total rows:                    15
Human Detection = True:        14
Human Detection = False:       1
Human Detection = NA:          0
Comfort known (any):           14 (comfortable=9, uncomfortable=5)
Comfort NA:                    1

NA counts by column:
  Date                       : 0
  Time                       : 0
  Timestamp(ts)              : 0
  Temperature(°C)            : 0
  Temperature(°F)            : 0
  Humidity(%)                : 0
  Average Skin Temp(°C)      : 1
  Emotion                    : 1
  Comfort Level              : 1
  Human Detection            : 0

=== LABELED SUBSET (Human=True & Comfort known) ===
Labeled rows (n):              14
Comfortable (k):               9
Comfort rate (CR):             0.643    95% CI [0.351, 0.872]
Switches/hour:                 7.50
Mean Comfortable run (rows): 9.00

Unlabeled rows breakdown:
  Unlabeled total:                       1
  Human=False (excluded by design):  1
  Human=True & Comfort=NA:               0
  Human=NA:                              0

Top emotions among labeled rows:
  neutral    : 8
  sad        : 4
  happy      : 1
  angry      : 1
```

Fig. 12. Dataset summary and labeling outcomes. Comfort rate, binomial CI, switching frequency, run length, and labeled emotion counts are reported.

- ***Data overview (all rows):*** Total rows = 15; *Human Detection* = True for 14 rows and = False for 1 row. Comfort labels present for 14 rows (9 *comfortable*, 5 *uncomfortable*); one row has *Comfort NA*.
- ***Missing values:*** All numeric sensing fields (Date/Time, Temperature (°C/°F), Humidity (%), Skin Temp (°C)) have 0 NAs; *Emotion* and *Comfort Level* each have 1 NA.
- ***Labeled subset (Human=True & Comfort known):*** n = 14 labeled minutes with $k = 9$ comfortable; comfort rate CR $= k/n = 0.643$ with 95% Clopper–Pearson CI [0.351, 0.872]. Temporal dynamics: switches per hour = 7.50; mean comfortable run length = 9.00 rows (≈ minutes).

- ***Unlabeled breakdown:*** total unlabeled = 1 (all due to *Human=False*); no cases with *Human=True & Comfort=NA* and none with *Human=NA*.
- ***Emotion distribution (labeled):*** *neutral* = 8, *sad* = 4, *angry* = 1, *happy* = 1.

6 Conclusion

This paper presented the design and validation of a Smart Desk system that integrates low-power hardware with thermal imaging, facial emotion recognition, and ambient sensing to enable real-time classification of thermal comfort in classrooms. By combining low-cost ESP32-WROVER microcontrollers, MLX90640 thermal sensors, and DeepFace-based emotion analytics, the system provides a scalable and privacy-aware solution for modern educational environments.

Experimental results demonstrate the feasibility of real-time comfort assessment using facial temperature and emotional cues. Real-time data transmission, centralized processing, and structured CSV logging enable seamless monitoring and feedback for instructors.

The Smart Desk framework advances the state of classroom environmental monitoring by moving beyond macro-level sensing to individualized, desk-level comfort assessment. It opens new opportunities for integrating affective computing and IoT in education to enhance student well-being and cognitive performance.

Future work will focus on pilot deployment in real classrooms, integration with HVAC systems for adaptive control, development of a testbed for large-scale validation, implementation of cloud-based data storage for centralized monitoring, and long-term studies to correlate comfort trends with academic results.

Acknowledgments. This work was supported in part by 1) the United States Department of Commerce (USDOC), Economic Development Administration Good Jobs Challenge Awardee, Successful Training and Effective Partnership for Growing Regional Opportunities in the Workforce To Harness (STEPS4GROWTH) under Grant ED22HDQ3070099; 2) the National Centers of Academic Excellence in Cybersecurity Grant H98230-21-1-0326l; 3) and the National Science Foundation s Engineering Research Center (NSF-ERC) Hybrid Autonomous Manufacturing Moving from Evolution to Revolution (HAMMER) under Award 2133630.

References

1. Aryal, A., Becerik-Gerber, B., Anselmo, F., Roll, S.C., Lucas, G.M.: Smart desks to promote comfort, health, and productivity in offices: a vision for future workplaces. Front. Built Environ. **5**, 76 (2019)
2. Khapper, K.V., et al.: An IoT-based smart desk system for smart classrooms: enabling OTA firmware updates and multi-application deployment. In: 2025 IEEE World AI IoT Congress (AIIoT), pp. 0164–0173. IEEE (2025)

3. Navarrete-Sanchez, M.A., Olivera-Reyna, R., Olivera-Reyna, R., Perez-Chimal, R.J., Munoz-Minjares, J.U.: IoT-Based classroom temperature monitoring and missing data prediction using raspberry Pi and ESP32. J. Robot. Control (JRC) **6**(1), 234–245 (2025)
4. Jiang, H., Iandoli, M., Van Dessel, S., Liu, S., Whitehill, J.: Measuring students' thermal comfort and its impact on learning. Int. Educ. Data Mining Soc. (2019)
5. Lamberti, G., Salvadori, G., Leccese, F., Fantozzi, F., Bluyssen, P.M.: Advancement on thermal comfort in educational buildings: current issues and way forward. Sustainability **13**(18), 10315 (2021)
6. Predeep, A.: Enabling IoTs with ESP32 for affordable education. In: 5th International Conference on Inventive Research in Computing Applications (ICIRCA 2023). IEEE Xplore Part Number: CFP23N67-ART; ISBN: 979-8-3503-2142-5
7. Khapper, K.V., Darwish, H., AlHmoud, I.W., Gokaraju, B., Islam, A.K., Graves, C.A.: A low-power IoT-based smart desk integrated with a facial recognition attendance system. SoutheastCon,: Concord. NC, USA **2025**, 1376–1383 (2025). https://doi.org/10.1109/SoutheastCon56624.2025.10971263
8. Hu, S., Sun, J., Zhang, J., Liu, G., Zhao, S.: Thermoacoustic environment comfort evaluation method based on facial micro-expression recognition. Build. Environ. **221**, 109263 (2022)
9. Jeoung, J., Jung, S., Hong, T., Lee, M., Koo, C.: Thermal comfort prediction based on automated extraction of skin temperature of face component on thermal image. Energy Build. **298**, 113495 (2023)
10. Wang, H., Liu, L.: Experimental investigation about effect of emotion state on people's thermal comfort. Energy Build. **211**, 109789 (2020)
11. Lala, B., Hagishima, A.: A review of thermal comfort in primary schools and future challenges in machine learning based prediction for children. Buildings **12**(11), 2007 (2022)
12. Ana, C., etic, S.N., olic, P., Perkovic, T., Congradac, V.: Smart monitoring technologies for personal thermal comfort: a review. J. Cleaner Prod. **312**, 127685 (2021)
13. Challa, K., et al.: Optimizing HVAC efficiency via deep neural networks for real-time classroom occupancy. In: SoutheastCon 2024, pp. 735–738. IEEE (2024)
14. Darwish, H., et al.: Optimizing educational spaces: achieving optimal thermal comfort, occupancy precision, and energy efficiency through the integration of IoT sensor technology and fuzzy logic control. In: SoutheastCon 2024, pp. 1557–1563. IEEE (2024)
15. Khapper, K.V., AlHmoud, I.W., Gokaraju, B., Islam, A.K., Graves, C.A.: A low-power IoT-based smart desk integrated with a classroom response system. SoutheastCon,: Atlanta. GA, USA **2024**, 1591–1598 (2024). https://doi.org/10.1109/SoutheastCon52093.2024.10500186

Visual Feature Tracking Algorithm for Veterinary Lameness Assessment in Horses

Kaveh Safavigerdini(✉), Taci Kucukpinar, Gani Rahmon, Kevin Keegan, and Kannappan Palaniappan

University of Missouri, Columbia, MO 65211, USA
{ksgh2,takhny,grzc7,keegank,palaniappank}@umsystem.edu

Abstract. Equine lameness detection is critical for veterinary medicine but faces limitations in subjectivity, cost, and accessibility. While computer vision offers a promising alternative to specialized inertial sensors for extracting movement asymmetries, existing tracking methods either lack the robustness required for equine gait analysis or are computationally prohibitive. We present VFTrack, a novel visual feature tracking algorithm specifically designed for equine lameness assessment. Unlike our previous work which tracked features collectively, this approach tracks each feature independently through a five-stage pipeline—Detect, Match, Prune, Extend, Terminate—integrating ALIKED feature detection with LightGlue matching. This architecture provides robust tracking of anatomical landmarks with O(n·m) computational complexity. We evaluate VFTrack against three baseline methods (DeepLabCut, CoTracker3, and Omnimotion) on trotting-horse videos. Results demonstrate that VFTrack achieves tracking robustness comparable to the state-of-the-art Omnimotion while operating 120× faster, effectively achieving real-time performance. Compared to DeepLabCut and CoTracker3, VFTrack offers superior tracking duration with minimal computational overhead. By bridging the gap between high-accuracy offline trackers and efficient real-time systems, VFTrack provides a practical, non-invasive, and cost-effective solution for routine veterinary diagnostics. Future work will focus on mobile implementation and expanded validation across diverse equine populations. Our source code is available at https://github.com/kavehsfv/VFTrack_HLD.

Keywords: Equine Lameness · Visual Tracking · Computer Vision · Feature Tracking · Gait Analysis · Veterinary Diagnostics

1 Introduction

Lameness, an abnormal gait resulting from pain or dysfunction in the limbs, spine, or feet, profoundly impacts equine health, performance, and welfare [33]. As one of the most prevalent equine health issues, lameness significantly reduces

F. Tanner and J. Irvine (Eds.): AIPR 2025, LNCS 16446, pp. 311–325, 2026.
https://doi.org/10.1007/978-3-032-18474-0_22

performance and economic value [30,41]. Causes range from acute injuries and infections to chronic conditions like osteoarthritis. Without timely intervention, lameness progresses from acute pain to chronic conditions and permanent damage, creating substantial financial and emotional burdens for owners.

Detecting lameness presents significant challenges, particularly when gait alterations are subtle or complex. Observable signs, such as the characteristic "head nod" during trotting where a horse shifts weight off the painful limb (illustrated in Fig. 1), can indicate forelimb lameness [2]. However, accurate diagnosis requires a systematic approach including thorough clinical examination (palpation, joint flexion tests, gait evaluation) and advanced diagnostic tools such as digital radiography, ultrasound, and nuclear scintigraphy to pinpoint underlying structural issues [1].

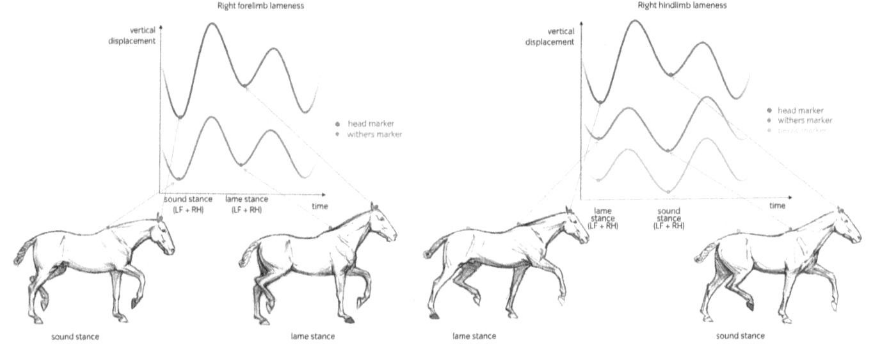

Fig. 1. Head nod movement pattern during lame trotting, showing asymmetrical vertical displacement as the horse shifts weight off the painful limb.

Traditional Lameness Diagnostic Methods: Traditional diagnostic methods for equine lameness rely on domain expertise and encompass visual gait analysis, physical examination, and imaging techniques (Fig. 2). Visual assessment identifies asymmetries such as head nods or hip hikes but is subjective and requires expertise [15]. Physical examination includes palpation and flexion tests to localize pain. Diagnostic imaging, including radiography and ultrasonography, visualizes internal structures, while advanced modalities like computed tomography (CT) and magnetic resonance imaging (MRI) provide cross-sectional diagnoses (Fig. 3) but require specialized equipment and often general anesthesia, limiting routine use [29].

Sensor-Based Gait Analysis: To address limitations of traditional methods, objective gait analysis utilizing inertial measurement units (IMUs) has emerged as a quantitative complement to subjective approaches. These sensors, placed at specific anatomical locations on the horse's body, measure movement patterns and asymmetries to provide objective data on lameness severity (Fig. 4). IMU-based systems successfully detect lameness by measuring head and pelvic

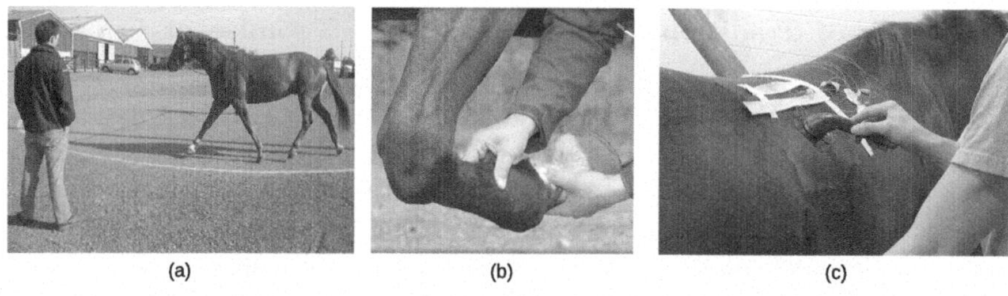

Fig. 2. Traditional lameness diagnostic methods: (a) visual gait analysis, (b) hands-on physical examination, and (c) diagnostic imaging (ultrasonography).

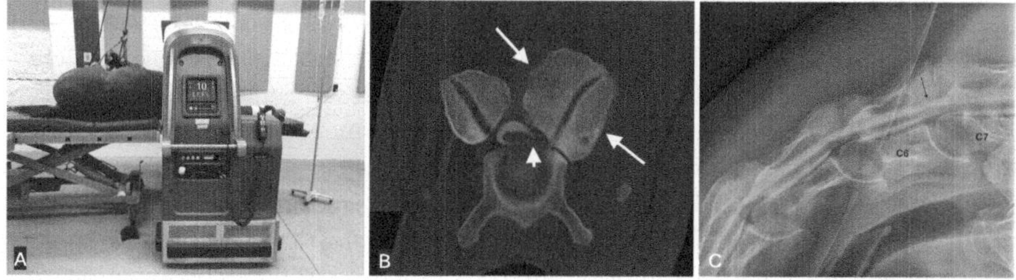

Fig. 3. CT myelography: positioning (A), MPR CT (B), and radiographs (C) [10].

movement during trotting, with extensive research establishing quantitative relationships between movement asymmetries and lameness indicators.

Equine lameness can be objectively assessed through vertical movement asymmetries by quantifying differences in head and pelvic heights between steps. Forelimb lameness is identified when head height differences exceed 8.5 mm, while hindlimb lameness is categorized by pelvic height differences greater than 3.0 mm [24]. These kinematic metrics effectively distinguish primary lameness from compensatory patterns. However, IMU systems require specialized hardware, precise sensor placement, and expert data interpretation, limiting their practicality for routine clinical monitoring.

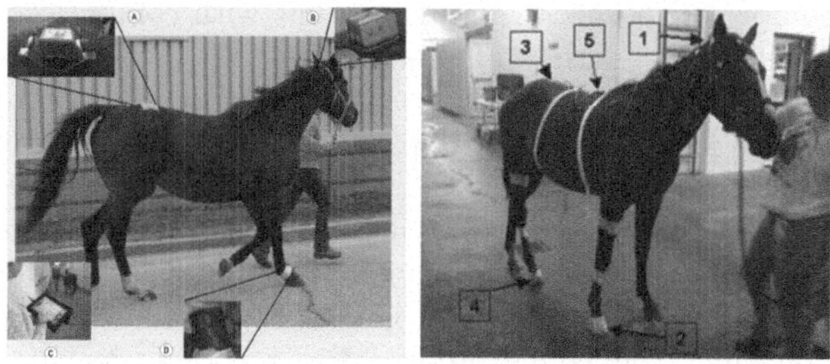

Fig. 4. Inertial measurement unit (IMU) sensors for objective gait analysis, quantifying movement asymmetries through body-mounted accelerometers and gyroscopes.

Limitations of Traditional Methods and the Promise of Computer Vision:

Traditional diagnostic methods face significant barriers to routine monitoring. Expert evaluation is not always readily available, advanced imaging modalities (CT, MRI) are expensive and often require general anesthesia, and specialized IMU hardware demands technical expertise for proper deployment. These constraints are impractical for daily use, creating a critical gap in early lameness detection when timely intervention could prevent progression to chronic conditions.

Recent advances in computer vision have enabled breakthroughs in motion analysis, object tracking, and 3D reconstruction [13,25,47], with applications spanning microscopy [37,43], robotics [28,48–50], and photogrammetry [34]. Computer vision has undergone transformative advances across tasks including image classification [12,35], object detection [22,31], semantic segmentation [20,32], and activity recognition [3,42]. The development of deep learning architectures, particularly convolutional neural networks (CNNs) [17,38] and vision transformers [7], has enabled unprecedented accuracy on benchmark datasets [4,18]. These foundational advances have been extended to complex tasks such as video understanding [45], motion analysis [8,44], and 3D reconstruction [26], enabling applications in autonomous systems, medical imaging, and scientific research. Specifically for equine lameness detection, computer vision can extract the same vertical movement asymmetries measured by IMUs, but using standard video recordings alone, offering a more accessible and cost-effective alternative.

For equine veterinary medicine, computer vision enables non-invasive, cost-effective, and continuous gait analysis using standard video recordings. Our approach substitutes IMU sensors with computer vision methods by tracking key anatomical landmarks (head and pelvis) in horse trotting videos, then applying similar biomechanical assessment frameworks that have been validated for relating body movement asymmetries to lameness. Several tracking approaches have been developed [16] for motion analysis, including DeepLabCut [23], a supervised pose-estimation toolkit that uses convolutional neural networks for anatomical keypoint tracking but requires extensive manual annotation and struggles with occlusions; CoTracker3 [13], a semi-supervised point-tracking framework that jointly tracks multiple points via transformer architecture and iterative refinement, offering improved occlusion robustness but with computational demands that scale with sequence length; and Omnimotion [47], a test-time optimization method that enforces long-range, occlusion-consistent dense trajectories through canonical video representations, providing high temporal coherence at the cost of hours of optimization per video.

However, these methods are not optimized for the unique challenges of equine gait analysis: rapid periodic motion, persistent occlusions from tack and limbs, and the need for lightweight, real-time operation in field settings. CoTracker3 and Omnimotion suffer from computational demands that preclude real-time use (hours per video) and exhibit drift over hundreds of frames due to error accumulation, while DeepLabCut requires extensive manual annotation per horse and struggles with frequent occlusions inherent in dynamic equine motion.

Computer vision for animal motion analysis has seen significant advances, with DeepLabCut [23] pioneering markerless pose estimation for animals, though it requires extensive per-animal annotation. Recent work has explored domain adaptation [27] and few-shot learning to reduce annotation burden, while equine applications have been explored through IMU sensor integration with convolutional networks [40]. Modern point tracking methods like TAPIR [6] and PIPS++ [11] provide robust tracking through per-frame initialization and explicit occlusion modeling, but are computationally intensive. Our approach bridges this gap by achieving robustness comparable to TAPIR while being 120× faster than Omnimotion. Equine gait analysis presents unique challenges from tack, limb, and rider occlusions that CoTracker3 [14] struggles with due to its joint tracking architecture. VFTrack's independent tracking mechanism naturally handles these occlusions by isolating failure to individual tracks, preventing error propagation.

1.1 Contributions

To address these challenges, this paper introduces VFTrack, a feature tracking algorithm specifically designed for equine lameness detection that tracks each feature independently, extending our previous work that tracked all features collectively [36]. Our approach provides robust and efficient landmark tracking with minimal computational requirements and reduced error accumulation, enabling practical deployment for routine veterinary assessment. The main contributions of this work are as follows:

- VFTrack with independent feature tracking, using a five-stage ALIKED+ LightGlue pipeline for robust equine gait analysis.
- Robust anatomical landmark tracking (85–100 frames) with real-time O(n·m) complexity.
- Validation shows VFTrack matches Omnimotion's tracking (85–100 vs. 94–100 frames) but runs 120× faster (6 vs. 720 min), outperforming CoTracker3 and DeepLabCut for clinical deployment.

2 Methodology

This section details the proposed VFTrack framework, a robust feature tracking algorithm specifically designed for equine gait analysis. We present a five-stage pipeline—Detect, Match, Prune, Extend, and Terminate—that integrates state-of-the-art feature detection and matching techniques to track anatomical keypoints across video sequences with high precision and computational efficiency.

2.1 Feature Tracking Algorithm

The feature tracking [36] method aims to track and analyze keypoint movement across image sequences by identifying distinctive features in each frame, matching them between consecutive frames, and recording their trajectories. The proposed algorithm integrates both traditional and contemporary techniques for feature detection and matching [9]. In this investigation, four distinct feature detection methods—SIFT [21], DISK [46], ALIKED [51], and SuperPoint [5]—are coupled with two matching methods: SuperGlue [39] and LightGlue [19]. The algorithm operates in five primary stages, as depicted in Fig. 5 and elaborated in Algorithm 1:

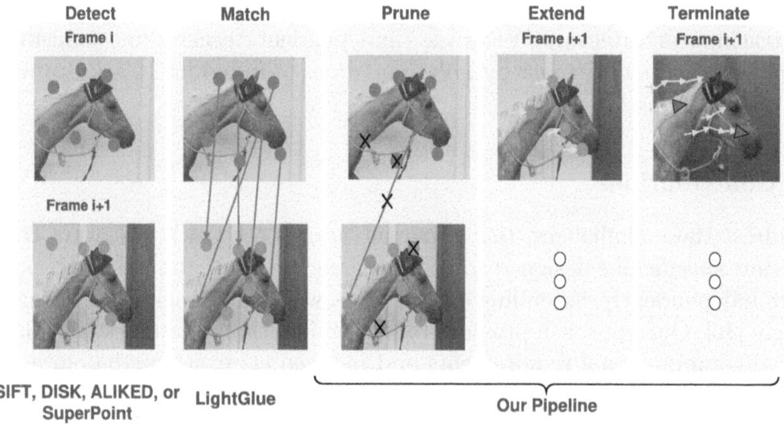

Fig. 5. Overview of VFTrack Framework: Detect: We detect features in subsequent frames using SIFT, DISK, ALIKED, or SuperPoint techniques. **Match:** We utilize LightGlue for feature matching. **Prune:** We remove keypoint mismatches and unpaired features. **Extend:** We form feature tracks that continue to grow as matched features are appended. **Terminate:** The algorithm terminates tracks (shown as red triangles) when no features match their heads, and starts new tracks with unmatched keypoints.

Detect: We detect features in each frame using SIFT, DISK, ALIKED, or SuperPoint detectors.

Match: We perform feature matching between consecutive frames using LightGlue, selected for its optimal balance of speed and precision in equine gait analysis.

Prune: We eliminate mismatches and unmatched features by enforcing a maximum displacement threshold between matched keypoints in consecutive frames, ensuring spatial consistency.

Algorithm 1 Feature Tracking Method

```
Require: frames frms, feature detector, feature matcher
Ensure: Tracks tracks, keypoints kinematic kptsKmts, track id trkID, and keypoints
    track id map kpTrkId
Initialize tracks, prvKpts, kptsKmts, kpTrkId ← ∅
kpts0 ← detector(frm[0]), dist_th ← 40, trkID ← 0
for each kp ∈ kpts0 do
    tracks[trkID] ← [kp], kpTrkId[kp] ← trkID
    trkID ← +1, prvKpts ← kpts0
end for
for each (i, frm) ∈ frms[1 :] do
    kpts ← Detect(frm)
    mtchKpts ← Match(kpts, prvKpts)
    mtchKpts ← Prune(mtchKpts, dist_th)
    tracks, kptsKmts, kpTrkId ←
    Extend(mtchKpts, kpTrkId, tracks, kptsKmts)
    kpTrkId, trkID ←
    Terminate(mtchKpts, kpTrkId, trkID)
    prvKpts ← kpts
end for
```

Algorithm 2 Prune Function

```
Require: mtchKpts, dist_th
Function Prune(mtchKpts, dist_th)
for each (kp1, kp2) ∈ mtchKpts do
    if Euclidean_Distance(kp1, kp2) > dist_th then
        remove (kp1, kp2) from mtchKpts
    end if
end for
return mtchKpts
```

Algorithm 3 Extend Function

```
Require: mtchKpts, kpTrkId, tracks, kptsKmts
Function Extend(mtchKpts, kpTrkId,
tracks, kptsKmts)
for each (kp1, kp2) ∈ mtchKpts do
    trkID ← kpTrkId[kp1]
    append (kp1, kp2) to tracks[trkID]
    kptsKmts[trkID] ←
    calc_kinematic((kp1, kp2), tracks[trkID])
    kpTrkId[kp2] ← trkID
end for
return tracks, kptsKmts, kpTrkId
```

Extend: We extend tracks by appending matched features to existing tracks when they match the features at the track heads, maintaining trajectory continuity.

Algorithm 4 Terminate Function

Require: *mtchKpts*, *kpTrkId*, *trkID*
Function Terminate(*mtchKpts*, *kpTrkId*, *trkID*)
for each (*kp1*, *kp2*) **not in** *mtchKpts* **do**
  $kpTrkId \leftarrow kpTrkId \setminus \{kp1\}$, $trkID \leftarrow +1$
  append (*trkID*, *kp2*) **to** *kpTrkId*
end for
return *kpTrkId*, *trkID*

Terminate: We terminate tracks when no features match their heads, and initiate new tracks with unmatched keypoints, enabling dynamic adaptation to changing conditions.

As demonstrated in our previous work [36], the ALIKED+LightGlue combination offers an optimal balance between robustness and efficiency across varying keypoint densities, making it particularly suitable for equine gait analysis. In this work, we introduce VFTrack that tracks each feature independently, distinguishing it from our previous approach that tracked all features collectively. This independent tracking architecture provides enhanced robustness by isolating failures to individual tracks and preventing error propagation across the entire system. The combination consistently delivers reliable performance for tracking anatomical landmarks on horses under various conditions. From a computational perspective, VFTrack is implemented in Python using PyTorch for GPU acceleration and OpenCV for image processing. The algorithm achieves real-time performance with O(n·m) computational complexity per frame, where n denotes the number of detected keypoints and m represents the number of successful matches, making it practical for clinical deployment.

3 Experimental Results

This section presents comprehensive quantitative and qualitative evaluations of VFTrack alongside several baseline approaches (DeepLabCut, CoTracker3, Omnimotion, and our feature-tracking pipelines) on trotting-horse video sequences. We compare per-point average tracking duration, maximum continuous tracking, and runtime, and include representative visualizations to highlight typical strengths and failure modes. The results quantify trade-offs between robustness and computational cost and demonstrate that VFTrack attains a practical balance suitable for clinical lameness analysis.

DeepLabCut provides an intuitive interface for manual annotation and training of CNN-based keypoint detectors for equine landmarks (Fig. 6, left), enabling efficient labeled dataset creation for motion analysis. Models are trained with data augmentation to improve robustness and evaluated on held-out videos (Fig. 6, right); however, DeepLabCut often detects fewer than the four expected landmarks, indicating significant limitations for reliable multi-point detection in gait analysis without extensive manual intervention.

Fig. 6. DeepLabCut workflow showing: (left) procedure for labeling the horse's joints, and (right) results on a horse trotting video, showcasing the model's weakness to accurately track and visualize joint movements.

CoTracker3 provides precise and robust tracking of anatomical body points essential for detecting subtle gait asymmetries in horses (Fig. 7). Despite its accuracy, the method requires substantial computational resources and can struggle to maintain reliable point tracking when horses are near walls or cluttered environments.

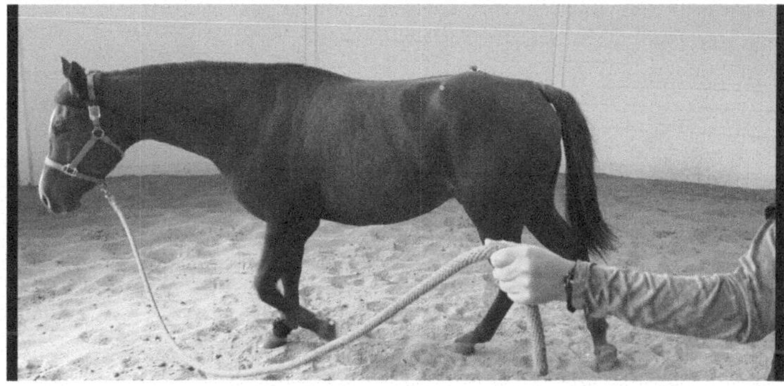

Fig. 7. CoTracker3 results on a horse trotting video, demonstrating its ability to accurately track and visualize joint movements.

Omnimotion framework excels in tracking anatomical points across complex equine movements, effectively handling occlusions and maintaining trajectory consistency. Its architecture, designed for dense motion estimation, allows for accurate tracking of multiple body points even in challenging scenarios (Fig. 8). This capability is particularly beneficial for analyzing lameness patterns, where precise joint tracking is crucial for identifying compensatory mechanisms.

VFTrack, our proposed feature tracking method, effectively tracks horse joint and limb movements with high efficiency and robustness. The results are shown in Figs. 9 and 10. This method provides an efficient and accurate approach for tracking horse movements across challenging conditions, making it a valuable tool for lameness detection and analysis. The independent tracking architecture

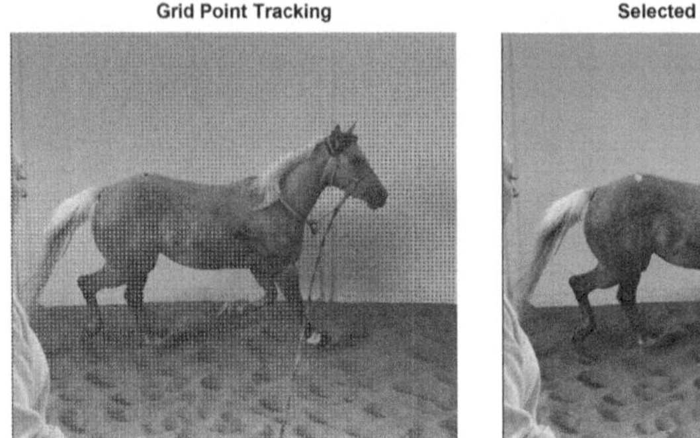

Fig. 8. Omnimotion results on a horse trotting video, showcasing its ability to accurately track and visualize joint movements.

ensures that track failures are isolated and do not propagate to other features, maintaining overall system stability.

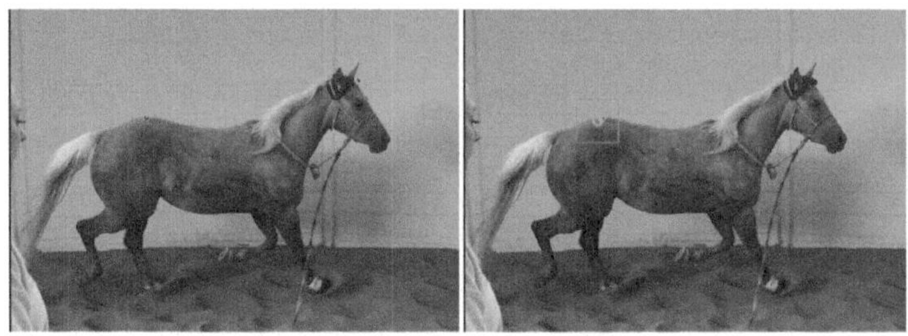

Fig. 9. Feature tracking results on a horse trotting video, demonstrating the efficiency and accuracy of our methods in tracking joint movements.

To quantitatively compare the tracking performance of different methods, we evaluated three key metrics across all approaches: the average tracking duration, maximum continuous tracking duration, and runtime for tracking body points in horse trotting videos.

The average tracking duration represents the mean number of frames that a body point is successfully tracked before being lost, calculated across all tracked points and video sequences. The maximum tracking duration indicates the longest continuous tracking sequence achieved by each method, demonstrating its capability to maintain point correspondence over extended periods. The runtime represents the time taken (in minutes) to track body points for the maximum number of frames that each method can achieve (Table 1).

VFTrack achieves robust tracking performance (85–100 frames) comparable to Omnimotion while maintaining exceptional efficiency (6 min) similar to CoTracker3, whereas DeepLabCut fails with short tracking durations (3–7

Table 1. Comparison of tracking duration and runtime across different methods. Higher tracking duration values indicate better tracking performance, while lower runtime values indicate higher efficiency.

Method	Avg. Duration (frames)	Max. Duration (frames)	Runtime (mins)
DeepLabCut	3	7	2
CoTracker3	54	90	5
Omnimotion	94	100	720
VFTrack	85	100	6

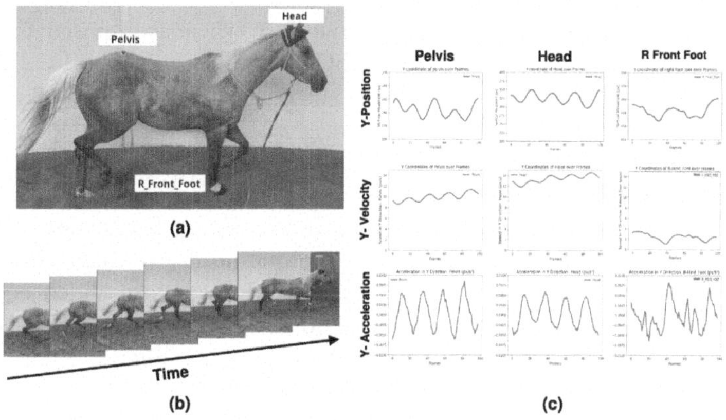

Fig. 10. VFTrack Result.

frames) and Omnimotion requires prohibitive processing time (720 min). These results demonstrate VFTrack's optimal practical balance for clinical deployment, achieving state-of-the-art robustness with computational efficiency suitable for real-world veterinary applications. The algorithm's ability to maintain tracking continuity while operating orders of magnitude faster than competing methods makes it particularly valuable for routine lameness screening and monitoring.

4 Conclusion and Future Work

This paper addresses the critical need for accessible, objective equine lameness detection by proposing VFTrack, a visual feature tracking algorithm designed specifically for veterinary gait analysis that tracks each feature independently, extending our previous work that tracked all features collectively [36]. We have demonstrated that computer vision can effectively substitute inertial measurement units (IMUs) by extracting vertical movement asymmetries from standard video recordings, overcoming fundamental limitations of traditional diagnostic methods including subjectivity, cost, and accessibility barriers.

4.1 Conclusion

Our work makes three primary contributions to the field of veterinary gait analysis. First, we introduce VFTrack, a five-stage feature tracking pipeline (Detect, Match, Prune, Extend, Terminate) that integrates ALIKED feature detection with LightGlue matching to provide robust anatomical landmark tracking with O(n·m) computational complexity. Second, we validate VFTrack against three established baseline methods (DeepLabCut, CoTracker3, Omnimotion) on trotting-horse videos, demonstrating tracking performance comparable to the best-performing baseline (Omnimotion) while requiring significantly fewer computational resources. Third, we show that VFTrack offers superior tracking duration with minimal computational overhead compared to alternative approaches (CoTracker3 and DeepLabCut), achieving an optimal practical balance between robustness and efficiency suitable for clinical deployment.

The algorithm's efficiency and robustness enable practical deployment for routine veterinary assessment, providing a cost-effective, non-invasive solution for early lameness detection. By tracking key anatomical landmarks (head and pelvis) and applying validated biomechanical assessment frameworks, VFTrack bridges the gap between computer vision techniques and veterinary clinical practice, offering an accessible tool that requires only standard video equipment rather than specialized sensors or imaging modalities. This accessibility democratizes objective lameness detection, potentially improving animal welfare through earlier intervention and more consistent diagnostic practices.

4.2 Future Work

Several promising directions exist for extending this research toward clinical implementation. First, real-time implementation of VFTrack would enable immediate feedback during veterinary examinations, potentially integrating with mobile devices for field use and expanding accessibility to remote veterinary practices. Second, expanded validation across diverse equine populations, breeds, and lameness conditions would strengthen clinical applicability and establish comprehensive normative databases for different movement patterns and environmental conditions. Third, integration with automated diagnostic workflows could combine VFTrack's tracking outputs with machine learning classifiers to provide automated severity grading and affected limb localization recommendations, reducing diagnostic subjectivity. Fourth, addressing persistent challenges such as severe occlusions (from tack, riders, or environmental obstacles) and varying lighting conditions would enhance robustness in real-world veterinary settings. Finally, comprehensive comparative studies between IMU sensors and VFTrack pipeline results would validate the algorithm's clinical accuracy and establish confidence for widespread adoption in veterinary practice, potentially revolutionizing lameness detection protocols.

References

1. Baxter, G.M.: Adams and Stashak's Lameness in Horses, 7th edn. Wiley, Hoboken (2020)
2. Buchner, H., Savelberg, H., Schamhardt, H., Barneveld, A.: Head and trunk movement adaptations in horses with experimentally induced fore-or hindlimb lameness. Equine Vet. J. **28**(1), 71–76 (1996)
3. Carreira, J., Zisserman, A.: Quo Vadis, action recognition? a new model and the kinetics dataset. In: Proceedings of the IEEE Conference on Computer Vision and Pattern Recognition (2017)
4. Deng, J., Dong, W., Socher, R., Li, L.J., Li, K., Fei-Fei, L.: Imagenet: a large-scale hierarchical image database. In: Proceedings of the IEEE Conference on Computer Vision and Pattern Recognition (2009)
5. DeTone, D., Malisiewicz, T., Rabinovich, A.: Superpoint: self-supervised interest point detection and description. In: Proceedings of the IEEE Conference on Computer Vision and Pattern Recognition Workshops, pp. 224–236 (2018)
6. Doersch, C., et al.: Tapir: tracking any point with per-frame initialization and temporal refinement. In: Proceedings of the IEEE/CVF International Conference on Computer Vision, pp. 10061–10072 (2023)
7. Dosovitskiy, A., et al.: An image is worth 16x16 words: transformers for image recognition at scale. In: International Conference on Learning Representations (2020)
8. Dosovitskiy, A., et al.: Flownet: learning optical flow with convolutional networks. In: Proceedings of the IEEE International Conference on Computer Vision (2015)
9. Gao, K., Palaniappan, K., Seetharaman, G.: DCT feature extraction and identification for object recognition in computer vision applications. IEEE Trans. Comput. Vision Pattern Recogn. **12**(3), 234–245 (2020)
10. Garrett, K.S.: When radiography and ultrasonography are not enough: the use of computed tomography and magnetic resonance imaging for equine lameness cases. J. Am. Vet. Med. Assoc. **260**(10), 1113–1123 (2022)
11. Harley, A.W., Fang, Z., Fragkiadaki, K.: Particle video revisited: tracking through occlusions using point trajectories. In: Avidan, S., Brostow, G., Cissé, M., Farinella, G.M., Hassner, T. (eds.) ECCV 2022. LNCS, vol. 13682, pp. 59–75. Springer, Cham (2022). https://doi.org/10.1007/978-3-031-20047-2_4
12. He, K., Zhang, X., Ren, S., Sun, J.: Deep residual learning for image recognition. In: Proceedings of the IEEE Conference on Computer Vision and Pattern Recognition, pp. 770–778 (2016)
13. Karaev, N., Rocco, I., Graham, B., Neverova, N., Vedaldi, A., Rupprecht, C.: Cotracker: it is better to track together. arXiv preprint arXiv:2307.07635 (2023)
14. Karaev, N., Rocco, I., Graham, B., Neverova, N., Vedaldi, A., Rupprecht, C.: Cotracker3: simplified trajectory tracking for point tracking. arXiv preprint arXiv:2410.08694 (2024)
15. Keegan, K.G., et al.: Repeatability of subjective evaluation of lameness in horses. Equine Vet. J. **42**(2), 92–97 (2010)
16. Kristan, M., et al.: The second visual object tracking segmentation vots2024 challenge results. In: Del Bue, A., Canton, C., Pont-Tuset, J., Tommasi, T. (eds.) ECCV 2024. LNCS, vol. 15629, pp. 357–383. Springer, Cham (2024). https://doi.org/10.1007/978-3-031-91767-7_24
17. LeCun, Y., Bottou, L., Bengio, Y., Haffner, P.: Gradient-based learning applied to document recognition. Proc. IEEE (1998)

18. Lin, T.-Y., et al.: Microsoft COCO: objects in context. In: Fleet, D., Pajdla, T., Schiele, B., Tuytelaars, T. (eds.) ECCV 2014. LNCS, vol. 8693, pp. 740–755. Springer, Cham (2014). https://doi.org/10.1007/978-3-319-10602-1_48
19. Lindenberger, P., Sarlin, P.E., Pollefeys, M.: Lightglue: local feature matching at light speed. arXiv preprint arXiv:2306.13643 (2023)
20. Long, J., Shelhamer, E., Darrell, T.: Fully convolutional networks for semantic segmentation. In: Proceedings of the IEEE Conference on Computer Vision and Pattern Recognition, pp. 3431–3440 (2015)
21. Lowe, D.G.: Distinctive image features from scale-invariant keypoints. Int. J. Comput. Vision **60**, 91–110 (2004)
22. Mahjourian, N., Nguyen, V.: Multimodal object detection using depth and image data for manufacturing parts. In: International Manufacturing Science and Engineering Conference, vol. 89022, p. V002T16A001. American Society of Mechanical Engineers (2025)
23. Mathis, A., et al.: Deeplabcut: markerless pose estimation of user-defined body parts with deep learning. Nat. Neurosci. **21**(9), 1281–1289 (2018)
24. Means, K., et al.: Vertical pelvic movement asymmetry and lameness location in ipsilateral combined forelimb and hindlimb lameness cases. Equine Vet. J. **57**(2), 362–374 (2025)
25. Mildenhall, B., Srinivasan, P.P., Tancik, M., Barron, J.T., Ramamoorthi, R., Ng, R.: NeRF: representing scenes as neural radiance fields for view synthesis. Commun. ACM **65**(1), 99–106 (2020)
26. Mildenhall, B., Srinivasan, P.P., Tancik, M., Barron, J.T., Ramamoorthi, R., Ng, R.: NeRF: representing scenes as neural radiance fields for view synthesis. Commun. ACM (2021)
27. Nath, T., Nath, V., Paul, R.: Using deep learning for computer vision in agriculture: a systematic review. Comput. Electron. Agric. **165**, 104948 (2019)
28. Pathre, P., Gupta, G., Qureshi, M.N., Brunda, M., Brahmbhatt, S., Krishna, K.M.: Imagine2servo: Intelligent visual servoing with diffusion-driven goal generation for robotic tasks. In: 2024 IEEE/RSJ International Conference on Intelligent Robots and Systems (IROS), pp. 13466–13472. IEEE (2024)
29. Puchalski, S.M.: Advances in equine computed tomography and use of contrast media. Vet. Clinics: Equine Pract. **28**(3), 563–581 (2012)
30. Raghavan, R., et al.: Evaluation of spatial variation in chronic wasting disease risk with Bayesian Poisson log-gaussian model. Front. Vet. Sci. **12**, 1568468 (2025)
31. Ren, S., He, K., Girshick, R., Sun, J.: Faster R-CNN: towards real-time object detection with region proposal networks. In: Advances in Neural Information Processing Systems, vol. 28 (2015)
32. Ronneberger, O., Fischer, P., Brox, T.: U-net: convolutional networks for biomedical image segmentation. In: Medical Image Computing and Computer-Assisted Intervention (2015)
33. Ross, M.W., Dyson, S.J.: Diagnosis and Management of Lameness in the Horse, 2nd edn. Elsevier Health Sciences (2011)
34. Safavigerdini, K., Collins, J., Huynh, R., Fraser, J., Palaniappan, K.: Epix 2.0: an enhanced 3D measurement tool with integrated triangulation for cultural heritage and aerial photogrammetry applications. In: Geospatial Informatics XIV, p. PC1303706. SPIE (2024)
35. Safavigerdini, K., et al.: Predicting mechanical properties of carbon nanotube (CNT) images using multi-layer synthetic finite element model simulations. In: 2023 IEEE International Conference on Image Processing (ICIP), pp. 3264–3268. IEEE (2023)

36. Safavigerdini, K., et al.: Automated feature tracking for real-time kinematic analysis and shape estimation of carbon nanotube growth. In: Proceedings of the IEEE/CVF International Conference on Computer Vision, pp. 3564–3564 (2025)
37. Safavigerdini, K., et al.: Creating semi-quanta multi-layer synthetic CNT images using cycleGAN. In: 2023 IEEE Applied Imagery Pattern Recognition Workshop (AIPR), pp. 1–6. IEEE (2023)
38. Safavigerdini, K., Yaghooti, B., Abadi, A.E.Z.S., Palaniappan, K.: GFR-CAM: gram-Schmidt feature reduction for hierarchical class activation maps. In: Proceedings of the IEEE/CVF International Conference on Computer Vision, pp. 733–742 (2025)
39. Sarlin, P.E., DeTone, D., Malisiewicz, T., Rabinovich, A.: SuperGlue: learning feature matching with graph neural networks. In: Proceedings of the IEEE/CVF Conference on Computer Vision and Pattern Recognition, pp. 4938–4947 (2020)
40. Savoini, B., Bertolaccini, J., Montavon, S., Deriaz, M.: Convolutional neural network for early detection of lameness and irregularity in horses using an IMU sensor. arXiv preprint arXiv:2503.13578 (2025)
41. Seitzinger, A.H., et al.: Economic costs of equine lameness, colic, and equine protozoal myeloencephalitis (EPM). In: Proceedings of the 9th International Symposium on Veterinary Epidemiology and Economics, pp. 318–319. ISVEE (2000)
42. Simonyan, K., Zisserman, A.: Two-stream convolutional networks for action recognition in videos. In: Advances in Neural Information Processing Systems (2014)
43. Surya, R., et al.: CNT forest self-assembly insights from in-situ ESEM synthesis. Carbon **229**, 119439 (2024)
44. Teed, Z., Deng, J.: RAFT: recurrent all-pairs field transforms for optical flow. In: Vedaldi, A., Bischof, H., Brox, T., Frahm, J.-M. (eds.) ECCV 2020. LNCS, vol. 12347, pp. 402–419. Springer, Cham (2020). https://doi.org/10.1007/978-3-030-58536-5_24
45. Tran, D., Bourdev, L., Fergus, R., Torresani, L., Paluri, M.: Learning spatiotemporal features with 3D convolutional networks. In: Proceedings of the IEEE International Conference on Computer Vision (2015)
46. Tyszkiewicz, M., Fua, P., Trulls, E.: Disk: learning local features with policy gradient. In: Advances in Neural Information Processing Systems, vol. 33, pp. 14254–14265 (2020)
47. Wang, Q., et al.: Tracking everything everywhere all at once. arXiv preprint arXiv:2306.05422 (2023)
48. Yaghooti, B., Li, C., Sinopoli, B.: A data-integrated framework for learning fractional-order nonlinear dynamical systems. arXiv preprint arXiv:2506.15665 (2025)
49. Yaghooti, B., Safavigerdini, K., Hajiloo, R., Salarieh, H.: Stabilizing unstable periodic orbit of unknown fractional-order systems via adaptive delayed feedback control. Proc. Inst. Mech. Eng. Part I: J. Syst. Control Eng. **238**(4), 693–703 (2024)
50. Yaghooti, B., Siahi Shadbad, A., Safavi, K., Salarieh, H.: Adaptive synchronization of uncertain fractional-order chaotic systems using sliding mode control techniques. Proc. Inst. Mech. Eng. Part I: J. Syst. Control Eng. **234**(1), 3–9 (2020)
51. Zhao, X., Wu, X., Chen, W., Chen, P.C., Xu, Q., Li, Z.: Aliked: a lighter keypoint and descriptor extraction network via deformable transformation. IEEE Trans. Instrum. Meas. (2023)

SPLIT: A Separation-Preserving Loss for Topology-Aware Building Segmentation in Remote Sensing Images

Sara Shojaei[1](✉), Johanna R. Arredondo[2], Elena Sava[2], Ricky D. Massaro[2], Kannappan Palaniappan[1], and Filiz Bunyak[1]

[1] University of Missouri, Columbia, MO, USA
{ssfht,pal,bunyak}@missouri.edu

[2] US Army Engineer Research and Development Center, Geospatial Research Laboratory, Alexandria, VA, USA
{Johanna.R.Arredondo,Elena.Sava}@usace.army.mil, Ricky.D.Massaro@erdc.dren.mil

Abstract. Accurate building instance segmentation in remote sensing imagery remains a challenging task due to boundary ambiguities and merging of adjacent structures in dense urban scenes. While convolutional and transformer-based networks achieve strong pixel-wise accuracies, they often fail to preserve boundary integrity and instance separability when adjacent rooftops are closely spaced or overlapping. To address this limitation, we propose a boundary-guided and merge-aware segmentation framework that enhances instance separation without sacrificing pixel-level precision. The framework introduces (1) a Separation-Preserving Loss for Instance Topology (SPLIT), a differentiable proxy for merge rate that penalizes overconfident building predictions along ground-truth boundaries, and (2) a lightweight, backbone-independent Contour Head that predicts continuous boundary maps to reinforce structural separation. We quantify topology-level errors and evaluate merge severity across datasets. Extensive experiments on three benchmark building segmentation datasets, Massachusetts, INRIA, and WHU, using multiple CNN and Transformer backbones (U-Net, SegFormer, and BuildFormer) demonstrate that integrating the proposed components significantly reduces merge errors while preserving instance-level accuracy and boundary quality. The proposed framework offers a simple yet effective approach for preserving object topology, providing practical and robust building instance segmentation in complex urban environments.

Keywords: Deep Learning · Convolutional Neural Networks · Satellite Images · Building Segmentation · Computer Vision

1 Introduction

Building segmentation is a fundamental task in remote sensing, supporting diverse applications such as urban monitoring and planning, navigation, change

F. Tanner and J. Irvine (Eds.): AIPR 2025, LNCS 16446, pp. 326–344, 2026.
https://doi.org/10.1007/978-3-032-18474-0_23

detection, damage assessment, and environmental monitoring. With the rise of high-resolution satellite and aerial imagery, detailed large-scale mapping of natural and man-made structures has become increasingly feasible. Moreover, unmanned aerial vehicles (UAVs) offer flexible, cost-effective, and high-frequency data collection, further expanding opportunities for fine-grained urban analysis.

Deep learning has significantly advanced building segmentation performance, with convolutional neural networks (CNNs) and transformer-based architectures achieving strong pixel-level accuracy. However, accurate instance-level segmentation remains challenging, particularly in dense urban environments where adjacent buildings must be separated as distinct objects. In such scenarios, neighboring rooftops frequently touch or overlap, leading to merged instances that conventional pixel-wise metrics (such as IoU, F1-score) fail to penalize adequately. Minor boundary errors can propagate into large geometric distortions, influencing building enumeration, centroid accuracy, and topology-based analyses, including graph reconstruction or connectivity modeling [1,2].

(a) (b) (c) (d)

Fig. 1. Sample images to demonstrate the different challenges while working with remote sensing images: a) Occlusion due to vegetation, b) Buildings with different scales, c) Buildings proximity, d) Buildings with complex shapes.

These challenges are further amplified by the complexity of urban scenes, including occlusions from vegetation, scale variations, building proximity, and structural diversity, as illustrated in Fig. 1. Thus, achieving high-quality segmentation requires not only pixel-level accuracy but also precise boundary delineation and explicit awareness of topology.

To overcome these limitations, we introduce a boundary-guided and merge-aware segmentation framework that prioritizes accurate instance separation while maintaining pixel-level quality. Specifically, we propose:

1. A Merge-Aware Evaluation Framework incorporating a Merge Rate (MR) metric to quantify the proportion of ground-truth buildings that are erroneously fused into single predicted instances.
2. A Backbone-Independent Contour Head that predicts a continuous boundary map alongside the building mask, improving the separation between adjacent structures regardless of the underlying backbone architecture.

3. A Separation-Preserving Loss for Instance Topology (SPLIT), a differentiable proxy for the merge rate designed to penalize overconfident predictions near ground-truth boundaries and maintain topological consistency.

To evaluate the generalization and robustness of the proposed framework and loss functions, we conducted experiments using four representative segmentation backbones (U-Net [3], SegFormer [4], and BuildFormer [5]) across three well-established datasets (Massachusetts [6], INRIA [7], and WHU [8]). Each model was trained under multiple configurations to systematically assess the individual and combined contributions of boundary guidance and merge-aware optimization.

Our experiments demonstrate that integrating the proposed Contour Head and SPLIT loss substantially reduces merge errors and enhances instance-level accuracy, validating the effectiveness of the proposed approach across both CNN and transformer-based architectures.

2 Related Works

Building footprint extraction from high-resolution remote sensing imagery has evolved through several methodological phases, from convolutional networks to transformer-based global modeling and topology-aware segmentation strategies. In this section, we will explore these developments, focusing on architectures and loss functions most relevant to boundary separation and instance segmentation.

2.1 CNN-Based Architectures and Boundary Refinement

Convolutional neural networks (CNNs) have been dominant in building extraction tasks due to their local feature learning ability and efficient spatial modeling. Classical encoder–decoder frameworks, such as U-Net [3] and its variations, enabled end-to-end pixel-level segmentation but suffered from boundary errors after repeated downsampling and upsampling operations. To address this issue, Jung *et al.* [9] proposed a Holistically-Nested Edge Detection (HED)-based Boundary Enhancement (BE) module that integrates edge features into the segmentation process to sharpen building boundaries and reduce misalignment artifacts. Subsequent high-resolution architectures, such as HD-Net [10], decoupled body and boundary features into separate layers under deep supervision, leading to more accurate footprint continuity and smoother edges. These methods collectively demonstrated the importance of explicit edge awareness in convolutional frameworks but remained limited in modeling global dependencies due to fixed local receptive fields. Earlier CNN-based methods, such as Maggiori *et al.* [11] also contributed to large-scale building segmentation using fully convolutional architectures.

2.2 Transformer and Hybrid Architectures

The introduction of the Vision Transformer (ViT) allowed modeling long-range dependencies in large aerial contexts [12]. Wang *et al.* proposed BuildFormer, a dual-path ViT that combines a global context path with a spatial-detailed branch, allowing efficient feature fusion across scales while addressing the high computational demand of global self-attention [5]. Further efforts on hybrid models include LiteST-Net, which couples a lightweight Swin Transformer with CNN layers to balance global and local feature learning [13]. SDSC-UNet extended this work by designing dual skip connections within a ViT-based U-shaped framework, enabling information flow between internal attention maps and the decoder to enhance global guidance [14]. Similarly, DSAT-Net integrated dual spatial attention mechanisms (global and local) to capture complementary dependencies while maintaining computational efficiency [15]. These hybrid CNN-Transformer networks have achieved strong results on benchmarks such as Inria [7] and Massachusetts [6], though they primarily emphasize contextual completeness rather than instance separability.

2.3 Topology and Connectivity Aware Segmentation

While architectural advances improved global representation, topology-aware supervision emerged as a key factor for preserving object connectivity. Mosinska *et al.* proposed a topology-aware loss that penalizes structural disconnections and gaps in curvilinear separations [16]. Similarly, Shojaei *et al.* introduced the Adaptive Structure-Aware Connectivity-Preserving Loss (SAC-Loss), which adaptively emphasizes connectivity and topology in road segmentation tasks by integrating distance transforms and skeleton [17]. These approaches highlight the limitations of purely pixel-level objectives and motivate the design of topology- and merge-aware loss terms for instance-level building segmentation.

In summary, prior research has progressively advanced boundary precision, multiscale context modeling, and feature decoupling; however, they primarily optimize for pixel-level accuracy or boundary sharpness. Few methods explicitly target instance-level separability, a critical issue in dense urban scenes where adjacent rooftops often merge into a single mask. To address this gap, our framework introduces a merge-aware loss and a boundary-guided head that jointly promote instance distinction and topological consistency, complementing recent advances in transformer-based representation and topology-aware supervision.

3 Methodology

In this study, we introduce a Merge-Aware and Boundary Guided segmentation framework aimed at improving building instance separation in high-resolution remote sensing imagery. The proposed approach includes: (1) a Separation-Preserving Loss for Instance Topology (SPLIT), which serves as a differentiable proxy for merge rate that penalizes overconfident predictions near ground-truth boundaries; and (2) a Backbone-Independent Contour Head that produces continuous boundary maps to refine object separation. The following sections describe the formulation of the proposed loss, the network architectures, and the training and evaluation procedures across multiple backbone networks and benchmark datasets (Fig. 3).

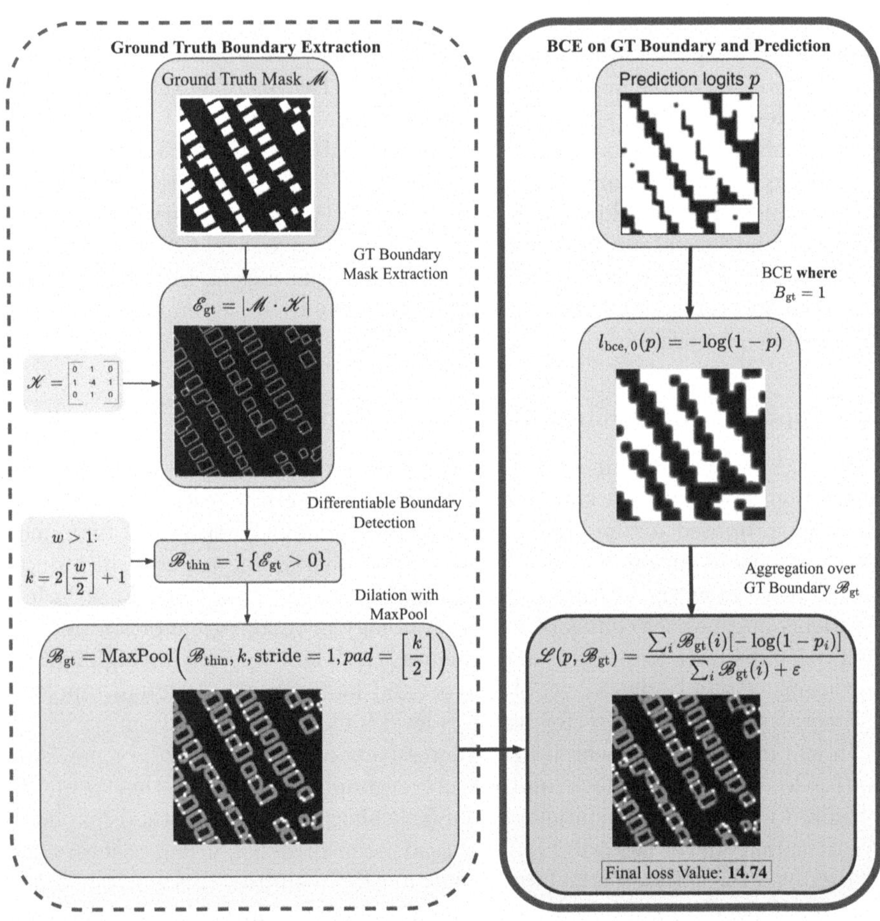

Fig. 2. Separation-Preserving Loss for Instance Topology (SPLIT) pipeline demonstration on a ground truth mask and a severely merged prediction sample (for more emphasis on the merges).

3.1 Separation-Preserving Loss for Instance Topology (SPLIT)

The proposed Separation-Preserving Loss for Instance Topology (SPLIT) serves as a differentiable proxy for merge rate, penalizing overconfident building predictions along ground-truth building boundaries to prevent instance merges. Unlike conventional pixel-level losses that treat all errors equally, SPLIT-Loss emphasizes the boundary regions where small errors can lead to substantial topological distortions and loss of instance separability. The key steps involved in computing the SPLIT loss are illustrated in Fig. 2 and described in the following subsections.

A. Ground Truth Boundary Extraction. The ground-truth boundary mask $\mathcal{B}_{\text{gt}}$ is obtained from the binary building segmentation mask $\mathcal{M}$ through the application of a differentiable edge-detection kernel as follows:

$$\mathcal{K} = \begin{bmatrix} 0 & 1 & 0 \\ 1 & -4 & 1 \\ 0 & 1 & 0 \end{bmatrix}, \quad \mathcal{E}_{\text{gt}} = |\,\mathcal{M} * \mathcal{K}\,|.$$

The resulting edge response $\mathcal{E}$ is binarized using a threshold value (zero, here) to form a thin boundary mask:

$$\mathcal{B}_{\text{thin}} = \mathbf{1}\{\mathcal{E}_{\text{gt}} > 0\},$$

which is then dilated through max-pooling with kernel size k and stride $= 1$ to ensure sufficient edge coverage:

$$\mathcal{B}_{\text{gt}} = \text{MaxPool}(\mathcal{B}_{\text{thin}}, k, \text{stride} = 1, \text{pad} = \lfloor k/2 \rfloor).$$

B. SPLIT Loss (BCE on Ground-Truth Boundary and Prediction). Given the predicted probability building map p, where it has high response for building and low response for background, binary cross-entropy (BCE) loss is computed *only* on boundary pixels identified in $\mathcal{B}_{\text{gt}}$:

$$\mathcal{L}_{\text{SPLIT}}(p, \mathcal{B}_{gt}) = \frac{\sum_i \mathcal{B}_{\text{gt}}(i)\,[-\log(1 - p(i))]}{\sum_i \mathcal{B}_{\text{gt}}(i) + \varepsilon} \tag{1}$$

This formulation penalizes building detections with high confidence along shared boundaries between adjacent buildings, encouraging the model to preserve separation and reduce merges. Since the loss uses the $-\log(1 - p(i))$ term, any pixel where the model predicts a high probability of being building ($p(i) \to 1$) is assigned a large penalty. Boundary pixels in $\mathcal{B}_{\text{gt}}$ represent locations where two buildings meet, forcing low values on these pixels to prevent the network from incorrectly merging adjacent buildings and naturally pushes predictions toward remaining separate.

Importantly, this loss is fully differentiable because it is composed of standard differentiable operations, such as multiplication, summation, and the logarithm function, which are applied directly to the predicted probabilities $p(i)$. The gradient $\frac{\partial \mathcal{L}_{\text{SPLIT}}}{\partial p(i)}$ exists everywhere for $p(i) \in (0, 1)$, enabling smooth backpropagation without requiring any discrete operations such as thresholding or morphological boundary extraction during training. This keeps the loss compatible with optimization while still providing instance-aware separation information. Lastly, the normalization term stabilizes the loss across images with a varying number of boundary pixels, preventing images with large building boundaries from dominating the gradient updates.

C. Total Loss Composition. Binary Cross Entropy (BCE) is a widely used and highly effective loss function for binary classification and segmentation tasks. It measures the difference between two probability distributions for a given random variable [18]. The BCE loss is formulated as follows:

$$\mathcal{L}_{\text{mask}}^{\text{BCE}} = -\frac{1}{N}\sum_{i=1}^{N}\Big[y_i \cdot \log(\hat{y}_i) + (1 - y_i) \cdot \log(1 - \hat{y}_i)\Big], \tag{2}$$

where N represents the total number of pixels, y_i denotes the ground-truth label at pixel i, and $\hat{y}_i$ is the corresponding predicted probability. BCE encourages the network to assign probabilities close to 1 for foreground (building) pixels and close to 0 for background pixels, resulting in learning accurate pixel-level classification boundaries. To complement pixel-level supervision, an additional L1 loss is applied on the predicted contour map generated by the auxiliary contour head:

$$\mathcal{L}_{\text{contour}}^{\text{L1}} = \frac{1}{N_c}\sum_{i=1}^{N_c}\big|C_i - \hat{C}_i\big|, \tag{3}$$

where C_i and $\hat{C}_i$ denote the ground-truth and predicted contour values at pixel i, respectively, and N_c is the number of contour pixels. This term enforces the contour head to produce sharp and continuous boundary maps, improving edge localization and delineation between close buildings.

While the BCE and L1 losses help in capturing pixel-level and edge-level details, they do not explicitly penalize the merging of adjacent instances. To address this, the proposed SPLIT Loss is incorporated as a differentiable proxy for merge rate as defined in Eq. 1, focusing on the boundary regions where small misclassifications can lead to instance fusion. Finally, the overall training objective combines these three complementary components as follows:

$$\mathcal{L}_{\text{total}} = \lambda_1 \mathcal{L}_{\text{mask}}^{\text{BCE}} + \lambda_2 \mathcal{L}_{\text{contour}}^{\text{L1}} + \lambda_3 \mathcal{L}_{\text{SPLIT}}, \tag{4}$$

where λ_1, λ_2 and λ_3 denote the weighting coefficients that balance the relative influence of the contour and merge-aware loss terms. These coefficients are tuned emprically and kept constant for the final experimental evaluations.

3.2 Network Architectures

Our framework is backbone-agnostic and can be integrated into common CNN and Transformer-based encoders-decoders, including U-Net [3], SegFormer [4], and BuildFormer [5]. The architecture incorporates three main components: (i) a conventional segmentation head responsible for predicting building masks, (ii) a lightweight Contour Head that produces a continuous boundary map derived from the inverted saturated distance transform, and (iii) a Separation-Preserving Loss for Instance Topology (SPLIT) design to penalize overconfident predictions along true boundaries to reduce instance merges. These components aim to overcome the instance-separation limitations inherent in purely pixel-level learning frameworks and metrics.

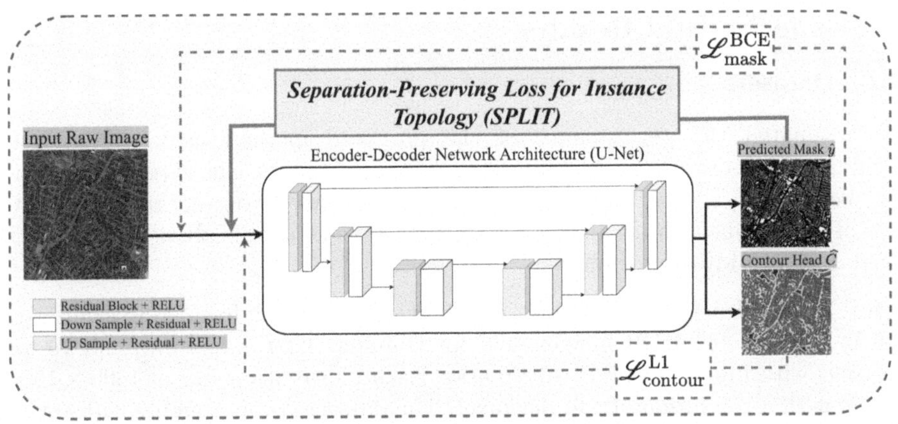

Fig. 3. Overall training framework of the proposed method with UNet backbone as an example.

A. Backbone-Agnostic Decoder Interface. Let $\mathbf{F} \in \mathbb{R}^{C\times H\times W}$ denote the fused high-resolution feature map from the baseline decoder (final stage for U-Net or the final MLP head features for SegFormer and BuildFormer). From $\mathbf{F}$ we branch two parallel prediction heads, $\hat{Y}$ and $\hat{C}$, which are the building mask prediction and the contour prediction, respectively:

$$\hat{Y} = \sigma(g_{\text{mask}}(\mathbf{F})), \tag{5}$$

$$\hat{C} = \sigma(g_{\text{contour}}(\mathbf{F})), \tag{6}$$

where $g_{\text{mask}}(\cdot)$ and $g_{\text{contour}}(\cdot)$ are lightweight stacks of 3×3 Conv–BN–ReLU layers followed by a 1×1 projection to one channel; $\sigma(\cdot)$ is the sigmoid activation. This design keeps the heads parameter-efficient and portable across all backbones.

B. Mask Head. The Mask Head predicts the per-pixel building probability map $\hat{Y}$. It is trained with binary cross-entropy (BCE) to ensure strong foreground-background discrimination (see Eq. 2). To prevent adjacent instances from fusing, we apply Separation-Preserving Loss for Instance Topology (SPLIT) (see Fig. 3 and Sect. 3.1). This loss acts as a differentiable proxy for merge rate, directly targeting topology errors that standard pixel losses ignore.

C. Contour Head. The Contour Head explicitly models boundaries that separate neighboring buildings. It is supervised with an L1 loss against a boundary target (inverted saturated distance transform), encouraging thin, high-precision responses that sharpen object delineation, as defined in Eq. 3.

4 Experimental Results

4.1 Datasets

We evaluated the performance of the proposed method using three well-established remote sensing building segmentation datasets. The experiments conducted on these datasets demonstrate the effectiveness of our approach, regardless of the unique characteristics of each dataset. The details about the datasets used in this study are as follows:

The Massachusetts Building Dataset [6] collected from Massachusetts, USA, contains 151 RGB images (137 for training, 4 for validation, and 10 for testing) with binary ground truth masks. Each image has a size of 1500 × 1500 pixels with a resolution of 1 m per pixel. The dataset covers roughly 340 square kilometers, mostly urban and suburban areas, including buildings of all sizes.

The WHU Building Dataset [8] collected and introduced by the Photogrammetry and Computer Vision Research Group (GPCV) of Wuhan University. The images were captured from two cities (New Zealand and Christchurch). These images have a resolution of 0.4 m per pixel and the total area covers 450 square kilometers. The dataset consists of 8,188 images 4,736 for training, 1,036 for validation, and 2,416 for testing). All images are in RGB format with an image size of 512 × 512 pixels.

The Inria Building Dataset [7] consists of high-resolution RGB satellite images from various global locations. The resolution of the image is 30 cm per pixel, with the size of 5000 × 5000 pixels. The data set is divided into training and test sets, providing ground truth images only for the training set. For this paper, we used only 180 images from the training set for the entire experiment (126 images for training, 27 images for validation, and 27 for testing).

4.2 Evaluation Metrics

To quantify the performance of the proposed framework, we utilize six evaluation metrics: Accuracy, Precision, Recall, F1-Score, Intersection over Union (IoU), and Merge Rate (MR). These metrics jointly evaluate pixel-level accuracy, object-level quality, and topological consistency in the segmentation results.

Accuracy measures the proportion of correctly classified pixels in the entire prediction map and is defined as:

$$\text{Accuracy} = \frac{TP + TN}{TP + TN + FP + FN}, \tag{7}$$

where TP, TN, FP, and FN denote the number of true positive, true negative, false positive, and false negative pixels, respectively.

Precision measures the proportion of pixels predicted as buildings that correctly correspond to true building pixels:

$$\text{Precision} = \frac{TP}{TP + FP}. \quad (8)$$

Recall quantifies the proportion of true building pixels that are correctly identified in the prediction map:

$$\text{Recall} = \frac{TP}{TP + FN}. \quad (9)$$

F1-Score represents the harmonic mean of Precision and Recall, providing a balanced measure of segmentation accuracy that accounts for both false positives and false negatives:

$$\text{F1-Score} = \frac{2 \times \text{Precision} \times \text{Recall}}{\text{Precision} + \text{Recall}}. \quad (10)$$

Intersection over Union (IoU) evaluates the overlap between the predicted and ground-truth building regions and is represented as:

$$\text{IoU} = \frac{|Y_{\text{pred}} \cap Y_{\text{gt}}|}{|Y_{\text{pred}} \cup Y_{\text{gt}}|}, \quad (11)$$

where Y_{pred} and Y_{gt} represent the predicted and ground-truth building masks, respectively. A higher IoU indicates stronger spatial agreement between the two.

Merge Rate (Topology Metric) Although the above metrics evaluate pixel-level accuracies, they do not capture instance-level errors such as building merges. Our proposed Merge Rate (MR) measures the percentage of ground-truth building instances that are incorrectly merged into a single prediction:

$$\text{MR} = \frac{2 \times \sum \text{merged buildings in prediction mask}}{\sum \text{buildings in ground truth} + \sum \text{buildings in prediction mask}} \quad (12)$$

A lower MR value indicates fewer merge errors and better instance separation. Together, these metrics provide a comprehensive evaluation of the proposed framework, balancing pixel-level accuracy with object-level and topological quality.

4.3 Backbone Models

To evaluate the backbone-agnostic nature of the proposed framework, we integrate the Contour Head and SPLIT loss into three representative segmentation architectures covering convolutional, transformer-based, and hybrid designs.

- **U-Net** [3] is implemented as a classical encoder–decoder CNN with skip connections and serves as a strong convolutional baseline for building extraction. Its multi-scale feature aggregation makes it suitable for dense prediction tasks with limited training data.
- **SegFormer** [4] is employed as a lightweight transformer encoder with an MLP-based decoder, providing efficient long-range context modeling.
- **BuildFormer** [5] represents a hybrid hierarchical ViT architecture designed specifically for building extraction, combining lightweight windowed self-attention with a detail-preserving path.

These architectures represent the major design categories in modern segmentation architectures: CNNs, Transformers, and hybrid global–local models. This allows for a comprehensive analysis of our merge-aware and boundary-refined training strategy across diverse learning schemes.

4.4 Implementation Details

We evaluate three backbones: U-Net, SegFormer, and BuildFormer under four configurations to observe the effect of each addition to these networks:

1. **Base**: backbone with standard binary cross entropy BCE loss function:
$$\mathcal{L}_{\text{total}} = \mathcal{L}_{\text{mask}}^{\text{BCE}}, \tag{13}$$
2. **Base + Contour Head**: Combination of Base model with auxiliary contour head and its corresponding $\mathcal{L}_{\text{contour}}^{\text{L1}}$ loss function:
$$\mathcal{L}_{\text{total}} = 0.7 \times \mathcal{L}_{\text{mask}}^{\text{BCE}} + 0.3 \times \mathcal{L}_{\text{contour}}^{\text{L1}}, \tag{14}$$
3. **Base + SPLIT Loss**: Combination of Base model with the proposed SPLIT loss function:
$$\mathcal{L}_{\text{total}} = 0.9 \times \mathcal{L}_{\text{mask}}^{\text{BCE}} + 0.1 \times \mathcal{L}_{\text{SPLIT}}, \tag{15}$$
4. **Base + Contour Head + SPLIT Loss**: both contour head and SPLIT loss enabled:
$$\mathcal{L}_{\text{total}} = \mathcal{L}_{\text{mask}}^{\text{BCE}} + 0.3 \times \mathcal{L}_{\text{contour}}^{\text{L1}} + 0.1 \times \mathcal{L}_{\text{SPLIT}}, \tag{16}$$

All settings were trained on high-resolution building datasets (Massachusetts, INRIA, WHU) with shared optimization hyperparameters for comparability. For all four networks, the networks were trained for 100 epochs. The weighted sum of the individual loss functions (Eq. 4) with the weight parameters specified in 13, 14, 15, and 16 has been used for training. During training and testing, the input images were resized to 512 × 512 before being fed to the networks. Adam optimizer [19] with a learning rate of 10^{-4} was used.

4.5 Quantitative Results

Tables 1, 2, and 3 present the quantitative performance of the proposed framework on the Massachusetts, WHU, and Inria building segmentation datasets across three backbone networks (UNet, SegFormer, and BuildFormer) and four training configurations. The results highlight the contributions of the Contour Head and the SPLIT loss in improving instance-level separation while preserving pixel-level accuracy.

Massachusetts Dataset. Across all three networks, the incorporation of the proposed components consistently improves boundary quality and reduces merge errors compared to the baseline BCE model. For UNet, adding the contour head (BCE + $\mathcal{L}_1$) achieves the highest pixel-level performance (Acc.∼0.93, F1∼0.81, IoU∼0.68), while integrating SPLIT loss (BCE + SPLIT) leads to the lowest merge errors (MR∼3.92%), representing a 2–5× reduction in merges relative to the BCE baseline. SegFormer follows a similar trend: although BCE + $\mathcal{L}_1$ yields the strongest precision and IoU (0.68), the SPLIT-only configuration again achieves the lowest merge rate (MR∼6.56%). BuildFormer shows little pixel-metric change across configurations but demonstrates the same trend: BCE + SPLIT substantially reduces merges (MR∼17.79%), outperforming other variants. Overall, the Massachusetts results confirm that SPLIT loss directly improves instance separability while the contour head enhances boundary delineation, and combining them provides complementary benefits depending on the backbone architecture.

Table 1. Building segmentation results on the Massachusetts dataset.

	Loss Functions	Acc.	Prec.	Rec.	F1	IoU	MR % ↓
U-Net	**BCE**	0.75	0.72	0.72	0.72	0.56	19.67
	BCE + $\mathcal{L}_1$	**0.93**	0.82	**0.81**	**0.81**	**0.68**	8.37
	BCE + $\mathcal{L}_1$ + SPLIT	0.92	0.83	0.71	0.76	0.62	6.63
	BCE + SPLIT	0.92	**0.88**	0.67	0.76	0.61	**3.92**
SegFormer	**BCE**	0.91	**0.88**	0.70	0.79	0.64	9.77
	BCE + $\mathcal{L}_1$	**0.93**	0.84	**0.79**	**0.81**	**0.68**	8.32
	BCE + $\mathcal{L}_1$ + SPLIT	0.92	0.84	0.70	0.76	0.62	9.46
	BCE + SPLIT	0.92	**0.88**	0.63	0.73	0.58	**6.56**
BuildFormer	**BCE**	**0.92**	0.78	0.74	**0.76**	**0.61**	19.66
	BCE + $\mathcal{L}_1$	0.91	0.80	0.69	0.74	0.59	19.73
	BCE + $\mathcal{L}_1$ + SPLIT	0.90	0.71	**0.79**	0.74	0.59	21.54
	BCE + SPLIT	0.90	**0.83**	0.58	0.68	0.52	**17.79**

WHU Dataset. The WHU dataset shows generally high pixel-level accuracies across all models (0.96–0.98), reflecting its cleaner building shapes and more consistent annotation quality. Under these conditions, the benefits of the proposed components appear most clearly in the Merge Rate (MR) metric. For UNet, BCE + $\mathcal{L}_1$ + SPLIT yields the strongest overall performance, achieving the lowest MR (0.82%), confirming the effectiveness of jointly enforcing local boundary supervision and merge-aware constraints. SegFormer and BuildFormer follow the same pattern: although pixel-level scores remain comparable across configurations, BCE + SPLIT achieves the most substantial merge reduction (MR 1.28% for SegFormer and MR 1.45% for BuildFormer). These results demonstrate that the powerful backbones (transformers and hybrid ViTs) already produce high global accuracies, but the SPLIT loss effectively resolves the remaining failure cases involving adjacent buildings. Thus, the SPLIT component plays a crucial role in reducing WHU topology errors.

Table 2. Building segmentation results on the WHU dataset.

	Loss Functions	Acc.	Prec.	Rec.	F1	IoU	MR % ↓
U-Net	**BCE**	**0.97**	0.72	**0.75**	**0.72**	**0.67**	1.90
	BCE + $\mathcal{L}_1$	**0.97**	0.72	0.74	**0.72**	**0.67**	1.72
	BCE + $\mathcal{L}_1$ + SPLIT	**0.97**	**0.78**	0.68	**0.72**	0.66	**0.82**
	BCE + SPLIT	0.96	0.74	0.65	0.68	0.61	0.90
SegFormer	**BCE**	**0.98**	0.76	**0.75**	**0.75**	**0.71**	3.23
	BCE + $\mathcal{L}_1$	**0.98**	0.76	**0.75**	**0.75**	**0.71**	2.84
	BCE + $\mathcal{L}_1$ + SPLIT	0.97	**0.79**	0.67	0.72	0.66	1.46
	BCE + SPLIT	0.97	**0.79**	0.66	0.72	0.65	**1.28**
BuildFormer	**BCE**	**0.98**	0.76	**0.76**	**0.76**	**0.72**	2.95
	BCE + $\mathcal{L}_1$	**0.98**	0.76	**0.76**	**0.76**	**0.72**	2.57
	BCE + $\mathcal{L}_1$ + SPLIT	**0.98**	0.78	0.69	0.73	0.67	1.71
	BCE + SPLIT	0.97	**0.79**	0.66	0.71	0.64	**1.45**

Inria Dataset. Across all three architectures, the Inria results reveal consistent benefits from adding boundary-awareness and split-aware supervision. Incorporating the contour head (BCE + L_1) generally improves precision and reduces misaligned boundaries compared to the BCE baseline, with SegFormer and BuildFormer showing the clearest gains (e.g., precision increases from 0.73→0.76 for SegFormer and 0.77→0.77 for BuildFormer, while F1 also improves). However, the most significant improvement appears when SPLIT is introduced. For U-Net, *BCE + SPLIT* achieves the lowest merge rate (MR = 2.02%), a substantial reduction from the BCE baseline (4.15%). SegFormer shows a similar pattern, with MR decreasing from 8.83% to 3.85%, representing more than a two-fold improvement. BuildFormer also benefits, with MR dropping from

7.17% to 3.73% under *BCE + SPLIT*. Importantly, these reductions occur while maintaining competitive pixel-level scores (F1 and IoU), confirming that SPLIT specifically targets instance-level boundary correctness rather than global pixel accuracy. This aligns with the qualitative observations illustrated in Fig. 5, where SPLIT produces cleaner, better delineated building instances.

Overall, the results of all three datasets validate that the proposed framework generalizes effectively across CNNs, transformers, and hybrid backbones, consistently reducing merge errors and improving boundary quality without sacrificing pixel-level segmentation accuracy. Across all experiments, the varying impact of the Contour Head and SPLIT loss across U-Net, SegFormer, and BuildFormer highlights fundamental differences in how CNNs and Transformer-based architectures respond to boundary and topology cues. CNNs, which rely on localized receptive fields, benefit most from explicit boundary supervision, whereas Transformers, with strong global context modeling, gain greater improvements from SPLIT's topology-aware constraint that prevents instance merging. The behavior of hybrid models lies somewhere between these two extremes. This variation confirms that the proposed components complement each backbone's strengths while compensating for their structural limitations. Together, these components offer a simple yet effective mechanism for enhancing instance-level separability without altering the underlying network architecture.

Table 3. Building segmentation results on the Inria dataset.

	Loss Functions	Acc.	Prec.	Rec.	F1	IoU	MR % ↓
U-Net	**BCE**	0.89	0.85	0.74	0.79	0.65	4.15
	BCE + $\mathcal{L}_1$	**0.90**	0.84	**0.78**	**0.80**	**0.67**	4.11
	BCE + $\mathcal{L}_1$ + SPLIT	0.89	0.88	0.68	0.77	0.62	2.38
	BCE + SPLIT	0.88	**0.89**	0.64	0.74	0.59	**2.02**
SegFormer	**BCE**	0.92	0.73	**0.82**	0.76	0.67	8.83
	BCE + $\mathcal{L}_1$	**0.93**	0.76	0.80	**0.77**	**0.68**	7.45
	BCE + $\mathcal{L}_1$ + SPLIT	0.92	**0.81**	0.70	0.74	0.63	4.16
	BCE + SPLIT	0.92	**0.81**	0.70	0.74	0.63	**3.85**
BuildFormer	**BCE**	**0.92**	0.77	**0.77**	**0.76**	**0.66**	7.17
	BCE + $\mathcal{L}_1$	**0.92**	0.77	**0.77**	**0.76**	**0.66**	6.83
	BCE + $\mathcal{L}_1$ + SPLIT	0.91	0.79	0.71	0.74	0.63	4.98
	BCE + SPLIT	0.91	**0.81**	0.68	0.73	0.62	**3.73**

4.6 Qualitative Results

Figures 4, 6, and 5 provide qualitative comparisons of the predicted building masks under the four training configurations (BCE, BCE+$\mathcal{L}_1$,

BCE+$\mathcal{L}_1$+SPLIT, and BCE+SPLIT). The visualizations highlight both pixel-level errors (false positives and false negatives) and instance-level segmentation outcomes (merged vs. non-merged true positives), allowing a better understanding of how the proposed contour head and merge-aware SPLIT loss influence segmentation results.

Massachusetts Dataset. The Massachusetts samples, as shown in Fig. 4, illustrate the challenges posed by dense suburban neighborhoods with highly regular, tightly spaced residential structures. Under the baseline BCE supervision, the SegFormer model frequently produces merged predictions (cyan regions), particularly along curved streets where rooftops form nearly continuous patterns. These merged true positives are most prominent in areas highlighted by the orange arrows, where insufficient boundary confidence leads to fused building footprints. Adding contour supervision (BCE+$\mathcal{L}_1$) improves local boundary sharpness and suppresses some of the small false positives. However, the model still struggles to maintain consistent separations between adjacent buildings in high-density regions. Introducing SPLIT leads to noticeable improvements in instance-level delineation. Both BCE+$\mathcal{L}_1$+SPLIT and BCE+SPLIT successfully minimize the gaps between buildings, reducing the number of merged structures and increasing the number of correctly separated instances (blue regions). Uncertain boundaries that previously induced merged predictions are clearly resolved, regardless of parallel rooftops or areas with heavy clutter. Among all loss function variations, BCE+SPLIT produces particularly clean separations with fewer small noisy detections, suggesting that SPLIT provides a strong and direct supervision for preserving instance topology in this domain. These qualitative observations align well with the quantitative reduction in Merge Rate observed for the Massachusetts dataset in Table 1.

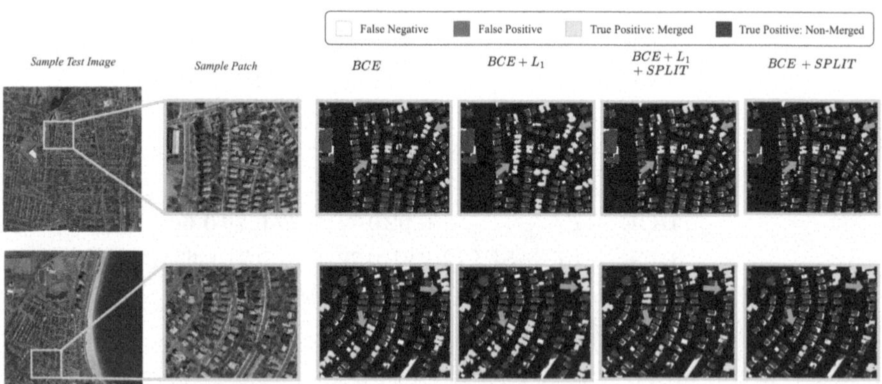

Fig. 4. Sample color-coded prediction results on the Massachusetts dataset using the SegFormer model with all four loss function configurations.

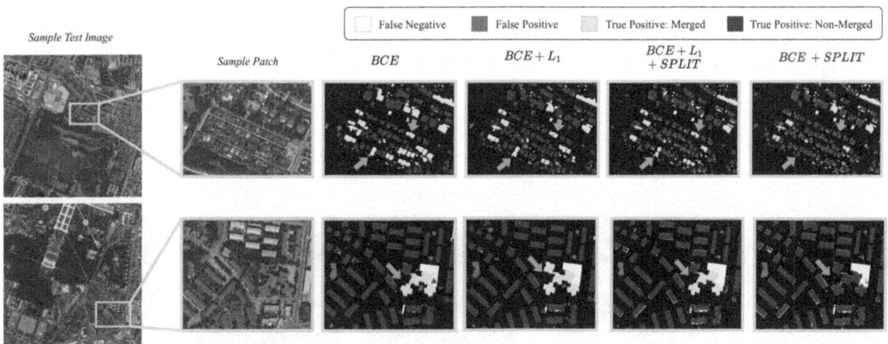

Fig. 5. Sample color-coded prediction results on the Inria dataset using the UNet model with all four loss function configurations.

Inria Dataset. As demonstrated in Fig. 5, in dense urban regions with closely packed buildings, the baseline BCE model often produces noticeable instance merges (cyan regions), particularly where rooftops touch or where weak foreground boundaries lead to fused predictions. Adding contour supervision (BCE+$\mathcal{L}_1$) reduces the extent of merged structures and suppresses several false positives by enforcing better local boundaries. When the SPLIT loss is introduced, either with or without the contour head, the model demonstrates substantial improvements in instance separation: merged structures are significantly reduced (blue regions dominate), and ambiguous boundaries that previously caused fused predictions are correctly separated. Notably, BCE+SPLIT provides the clearest separation of adjacent buildings, particularly in high-density blocks highlighted by the orange arrows, while maintaining cleaner predictions with fewer small false detections. These observations are aligned with the quantitative drop in Merge Rate for this dataset.

WHU Dataset. The WHU examples, as shown in Fig. 6, illustrate similar trends with a mix of small, irregular, and medium-sized buildings. The baseline BCE model again shows merged detections in areas where rooftops are closely spaced or partially occluded. The addition of $\mathcal{L}_1$ supervision sharpens the outlines of the building and reduces small spurious false positives; however, the merged predictions remain visible. The inclusion of SPLIT significantly improves instance-level separation. In both sample patches, BCE+SPLIT eliminates most merged true positives and resolves building boundaries that were previously fused, even when buildings share long edges or narrow gaps. Furthermore, the combined contour-and-SPLIT configuration (BCE+$\mathcal{L}_1$+SPLIT) shows strong performance in suppressing false negatives (yellow regions), especially for smaller structures that are prone to being missed by BCE-based training alone. It is also worth mentioning that in the sample image from the WHU dataset shown in the second row, some areas of the parking lot have been mistakenly considered as building masks. These minor issues in ground truth may mislead the quantitative results, while they are clearly visible in the qualitative demonstration.

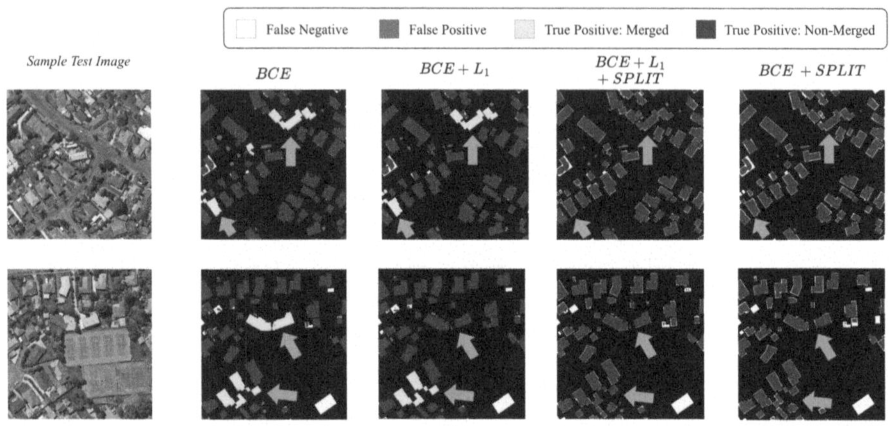

Fig. 6. Sample color-coded prediction results on the WHU dataset using the Build-Former model with all four loss function configurations.

5 Conclusion

This work presents a boundary-guided and topology-aware framework for building instance segmentation in remote sensing imagery. While existing CNN and Transformer architectures achieve strong pixel-level performance, they often fail to preserve object topology, particularly in dense urban environments where adjacent structures must remain distinct. To address this persistent challenge, we introduced two main contributions: (1) a lightweight, backbone-agnostic Contour Head for explicit boundary supervision, and (2) SPLIT, a Separation-Preserving Loss designed as a differentiable proxy for the merge rate that discourages over-confident building predictions along shared building boundaries.

Extensive evaluations across three benchmark datasets (Massachusetts, WHU, and Inria) demonstrate that the proposed framework significantly reduces instance merges while maintaining competitive pixel-level accuracy. SPLIT consistently decreases topology errors across CNN, Transformer, and hybrid backbones, while the contour head improves localized boundary accuracy.

The proposed approach highlights the importance of topology-aware supervision in remote sensing segmentation and provides a practical pathway toward robust building footprint extraction in complex and high-density scenes, particularly for graph-based neighborhood pattern analysis and downstream tasks such as navigation, geo-localization, and broader spatio-temporal investigation.

Acknowledgment. This material is based upon work supported in part by the U.S. Army Corps of Engineers, Engineering Research and Development Center—Information Technology Laboratory (ERDC-ITL) under Contract W912HZ23C0041. Any opinions, findings, and conclusions or recommendations expressed in this publication are those of the authors and do not necessarily reflect the views of the U.S. Government or agency thereof.

Computational resources for this research have been supported by the NSF National Research Platform, as part of GP-ENGINE (award OAC #2322218).

References

1. Winterton IV, T., Bennett, E., Atmaca, B.C., Shojaei, S., Palaniappan, K., Bunyak, F.: Aerial visual localization through novel applications of Weisfeiler-Lehman graph embeddings. In: Geospatial Informatics XV, vol. 13461. SPIE, pp. 96–106 (2025)
2. Bennett, E., Arredondo, J.R., Sava, E., Massaro, R.D., Palaniappan, K., Bunyak, F.: Bag-of-graph-attributes and sparse graph structures for efficient UAV localization in complex environments. In: Geospatial Informatics XV, vol. 13461. SPIE, pp. 107–123 (2025)
3. Ronneberger, O., Fischer, P., Brox, T.: U-Net: convolutional networks for biomedical image segmentation. In: Navab, N., Hornegger, J., Wells, W.M., Frangi, A.F. (eds.) MICCAI 2015. LNCS, vol. 9351, pp. 234–241. Springer, Cham (2015). https://doi.org/10.1007/978-3-319-24574-4_28
4. Xie, E., Wang, W., Yu, Z., Anandkumar, A., Alvarez, J.M., Luo, P.: SegFormer: simple and efficient design for semantic segmentation with transformers. In: Advances in Neural Information Processing Systems, vol. 34, pp. 12077–12090 (2021)
5. Wang, L., Fang, S., Meng, X., Li, R.: Building extraction with vision transformer. IEEE Trans. Geosci. Remote Sens. **60**, 5625711 (2022)
6. Mnih, V.: Machine learning for aerial image labeling. Ph.D. dissertation, University of Toronto (2013)
7. Maggiori, E., Tarabalka, Y., Charpiat, G., Alliez, P.: Can semantic labeling methods generalize to any city? The inria aerial image labeling benchmark. In: IEEE International Geoscience and Remote Sensing Symposium (IGARSS) (2017)
8. Ji, S., Wei, S., Lu, M.: Fully convolutional networks for multisource building extraction from an open aerial and satellite imagery data set. IEEE Trans. Geosci. Remote Sens. **57**(1), 574–586 (2018)
9. Jung, H., Choi, H.-S., Kang, M.: Boundary enhancement semantic segmentation for building extraction from remote sensed image. IEEE Trans. Geosci. Remote Sens. **60**, 5215512 (2022)
10. Li, Y., Hong, D., Li, C., Yao, J., Chanussot, J.: HD-Net: high-resolution decoupled network for building footprint extraction via deeply supervised body and boundary decomposition. ISPRS J. Photogramm. Remote. Sens. **209**, 51–65 (2024)
11. Maggiori, E., Tarabalka, Y., Charpiat, G., Alliez, P.: Convolutional neural networks for large-scale remote-sensing image classification. IEEE Trans. Geosci. Remote Sens. **55**(2), 645–657 (2017)
12. Dosovitskiy, A.: An image is worth 16x16 words: transformers for image recognition at scale. arXiv preprint arXiv:2010.11929 (2020)

13. Yuan, W., Zhang, X., Shi, J., Wang, J.: LiteST-net: a hybrid model of lite swin transformer and convolution for building extraction from remote sensing image. Remote Sens. **15**(8), 1996 (2023)
14. Zhang, R., Zhang, Q., Zhang, G.: SDSC-UNet: dual skip connection ViT-based U-Shaped model for building extraction. IEEE Geosci. Remote Sens. Lett. **20**, 6005005 (2023)
15. Zhang, R., Wan, Z., Zhang, Q., Zhang, G.: DSAT-Net: dual spatial attention transformer for building extraction from aerial images. IEEE Geosci. Remote Sens. Lett. **20**, 6008405 (2023)
16. Mosinska, A., Marquez-Neila, P., Kozinski, M., Fua, P.: Beyond the pixel-wise loss for topology-aware delineation. In: IEEE Conference on Computer Vision and Pattern Recognition (CVPR), pp. 1343–1351 (2018)
17. Shojaei, S., Bunyak, F., Palaniappan, K.: Adaptive structure-aware connectivity-preserving loss for improved road segmentation in remote sensing images. In: IEEE/CVF Winter Conference on Applications of Computer Vision (2025)
18. Jadon, S.: A survey of loss functions for semantic segmentation. In: Computational Intelligence in Bioinformatics and Computational Biology (CIBCB) Conference, pp. 1–7 (2020)
19. Kingma, D.P., Ba, J.: ADAM: a method for stochastic optimization (2014). https://arxiv.org/abs/1412.6980

Pixel–Point Fusion: A 2D–3D Computer Vision Framework for Robust Sidewalk Trip Hazard Detection

Hang Du[1,2](✉), Linlin Zhang[2], Yaw Adu-Gyamfi[2], and Filiz Bunyak[1]

[1] Electrical Engineering and Computer Science, University of Missouri-Columbia, Columbia, MO, USA
{dh63r,bunyak}@missouri.edu

[2] Civil Engineering, University of Missouri-Columbia, Columbia, MO, USA
{linlinzhang,adugyamfiy}@missouri.edu

Abstract. Ensuring sidewalk compliance with the Americans with Disabilities Act (ADA) is essential for pedestrian safety and accessibility. Traditional 2D inspection methods offer high spatial resolution for surface feature detection but lack height information, while existing 3D approaches capture vertical displacements but often miss fine defects such as cracks due to limited resolution. This study introduces a unified 2D–3D computer vision framework that integrates image and geometric information for robust segmentation, labeling, and measurement of sidewalk trip hazards and cracks. The proposed workflow comprises four main stages: (1) a Visual Geometry Grounded Transformer (VGGT) reconstructs detailed 3D geometry from multi-view imagery; (2) a SAM-assisted segmentation network detects potential defects in 2D space; (3) an RGB-D fusion model embeds depth cues into 2D features for accurate trip hazard identification and alignment with 3D point clouds; and (4) quantified geometric metrics enable detailed ADA compliance evaluation. The framework was validated on diverse sidewalk sites with LiDAR and digital-level measurements as ground truth and compared against MASt3R-SLAM as a baseline. Experimental results show that the proposed Pixel-Point Fusion (PPF) framework achieved a recall of 1.000 and an accuracy of 0.905, outperforming both LiDAR and MASt3R-SLAM-based analysis in detecting ADA-noncompliant defects. PPF also successfully captured fine cracks and 0.25-inch trip hazards that other methods failed to detect. Future work will focus on large-scale deployment, enhancing sensitivity to micro-level trip hazards, and enabling real-time detection to support municipal maintenance planning.

Keywords: Sidewalk Compliance · Urban Infrastructure Monitoring · Damage Segmentation · Computer Vision · 2D-3D Data Fusion

1 Introduction

Compliance with the Americans with Disabilities Act (ADA) is essential to ensure safe and equitable pedestrian mobility. Key sidewalk parameters such as

F. Tanner and J. Irvine (Eds.): AIPR 2025, LNCS 16446, pp. 345–363, 2026.
https://doi.org/10.1007/978-3-032-18474-0_24

cross slope, running slope, surface cracks, and vertical discontinuities, directly affect accessibility and contribute to trip hazards. Conventional inspection practices rely on manual surveys, where each slab is measured using tools like digital levels or measuring tapes, and data are recorded manually or with handheld devices. Although these methods are reliable, they are resource-intensive, costly, and infrequent [1–3].

Advanced technologies such as LiDAR-based Terrestrial Laser Scanning (TLS) and Mobile Laser Scanning (MLS) can provide accurate three-dimensional geometric measurements, including height information of trip hazards [4]. However, their limited coverage, low point density, and relatively low data resolution make it difficult to accurately detect fine-scale sidewalk defects. In addition, these systems require specialized expertise, expensive sensors, and complex data-processing workflows, which restrict their scalability for citywide applications.

Recently, 2D image-based methods combined with machine learning have become popular for assessing sidewalk conditions, focusing on features such as overall surface quality [5], curb ramps [6], and surface obstructions [7]. However, these approaches often lack reliable validation and standardized quality metrics, and rely heavily on high-resolution overhead or street-view imagery, which do not provide height information. Moreover, some studies have explored the use of RGB-D cameras to monitor sidewalks, detect hazards and cracks, and extract geometric features, but their performance is constrained by hardware sensitivity, limited focus on abrupt edges, and insufficient pixel-level calibration [7,8].

Image-based 3D reconstruction has emerged as a cost-effective alternative to manual inspection. Photogrammetric techniques such as Structure-from-Motion (SfM) [9] and Multi-View Stereo (MVS) [10] can reconstruct 3D geometry with centimeter-level accuracy under favorable conditions and have been applied to pavement distress detection and asset inventory [11,12]. However, SfM photogrammetry is time-consuming: generating accurate point clouds requires highly overlapped, high-resolution images collected at low speeds and from multiple viewpoints to ensure adequate coverage. Furthermore, subsequent image processing and 3D reconstruction are computationally intensive, which further slows down the workflow. Similarly, SLAM-based systems face challenges such as drift accumulation, environmental sensitivity, and limited precision in capturing fine-scale features such as sidewalk slopes and cracks. Consequently, sidewalk-specific applications remain limited [13,14].

To integrate the high resolution of 2D imagery with the geometric richness of 3D data, 2D–3D fusion methods have gained popularity in civil engineering. Jiang et al. [15] proposed an automated approach for sidewalk deficiency detection by projecting 3D point clouds collected from mobile LiDAR into 2D orthorectified images and elevation maps, followed by U-Net–based segmentation of slab joints and subsequent estimation of vertical displacement. While effective for mapping trip hazards, this method converts 3D geometry into 2D representations, potentially causing information loss. Its applicability is also confined mainly to vertical discontinuities at joints, with slopes and other defect types not fully considered. Similarly, Zhang et al. [16] introduced a 2D–3D fusion framework for bridge inspection using UAV imagery, where point cloud–derived depth maps were combined with RGB images and an enhanced DeepLabv3+ [17] model to segment damage for 3D visualization. Although field experiments demonstrated high accuracy in detecting defects such as wet spots, cavities, and spalling, the method relies heavily on large training datasets. To date, no 2D–3D fusion model has been specifically designed for sidewalk assessment.

This study introduces a plug-and-play framework (Fig. 1) that systematically integrates 2D and 3D modalities (images and point clouds) to enable pixel-level interaction through geometric mapping and to facilitate robust sidewalk trip-hazard detection. The main contributions of this study are as follows:

1. *Sidewalk point cloud generation:* a 3D point cloud of the sidewalk is generated using VGGT-based [18] reconstruction, providing a detailed geometric representation for defect analysis.
2. *2D-3D fusion:* a novel feature extraction and fusion strategy is introduced to combine 2D RGB image features with 3D point cloud geometric information, embedding depth cues into 2D processing. This approach reduces the computational cost of large-scale point cloud analysis while improving the accuracy of defect segmentation.
3. *Testing & validation:* the proposed framework is experimentally validated on real sidewalk datasets, with quantitative measurements and evaluated for ADA compliance.

2 Methodology

The proposed Pixel–Point Fusion (PPF) framework, designed for segmentation and quantitative analysis of sidewalk defects in joint 2D–3D space, is illustrated in Fig. 1. The framework consists of four key components: (1) 3D reconstruction, (2) image-based sidewalk defect extractiondefect segmentation from images, (3) 2D-3D data fusion for localization of defects within the point cloud, and (4) quantitative measurement of defect severity. First, we use the Visual Geometry Grounded Transformer (VGGT) [18] to reconstruct accurate sidewalk point clouds and generate dense depth maps from single or multiple RGB imagery. Next, we employ the Segment Anything Model (SAM) [19] to segment sidewalk slabs and delineate candidate defect regions directly from the 2D images. The detected defects are then projected into the reconstructed 3D space using estimated camera poses to accurately recover height variations. Finally, each defect is automatically quantified according to the standards of the Americans with Disabilities Act (ADA), and the results are evaluated against measurements based on LiDAR as ground truth, and compared against MASt3R-SLAM [20] (hereafter referred to as SLAM) baseline. The following sections describe the details of these processing steps.

2.1 Sidewalk Geometry Reconstruction in 3D

a. VGGT-based 3D Reconstruction

The Visual Geometry Grounded Transformer (VGGT) [18] is a recently intro-

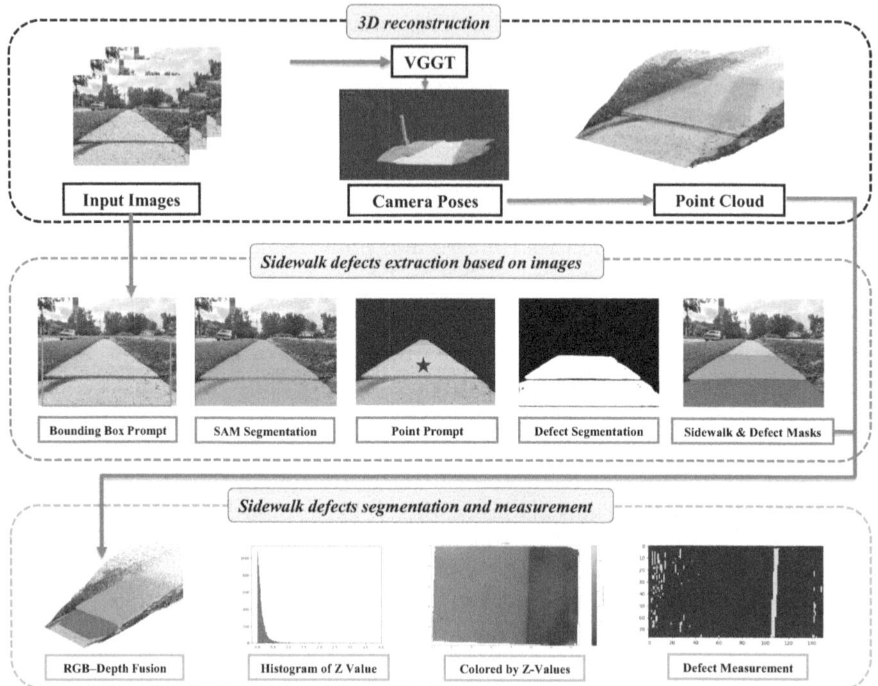

Fig. 1. The proposed Pixel–Point Fusion (PPF) framework and its main components for segmentation and quantitative evaluation of sidewalk defects in unified 2D–3D space. The framework includes: (1) dense 3D point-cloud reconstruction using VGGT [18], (2) segmentation of sidewalk slabs and defect regions using SAM [19], (3) projection of segmented defects into 3D space using estimated camera poses, and (4) automatic measurement of defect severity based on ADA standards.

duced foundational model for 3D vision capable of inferring scene geometry directly from one or more input images. Unlike traditional Structure-from-Motion (SfM) pipelines that depend on iterative feature matching and bundle adjustment, VGGT estimates key geometric attributes such as depth, camera pose, and point visibility in a single forward pass.

In the proposed Pixel–Point Fusion (PPF) framework, VGGT is used to reconstruct dense 3D sidewalk models from RGB imagery. The model is applied using its default configuration and 3D points with confidence below 20% are removed to ensure geometric reliability. The VGGT-based reconstruction workflow is outlined in Algorithm 1.

All experiments were executed on a workstation equipped with an Intel Core i9-13900 CPU and an NVIDIA RTX 4080 GPU. The reconstruction of each site required approximately 30 s, resulting in dense, high-quality point clouds suitable for subsequent defect localization and quantification.

b. SLAM-based 3D Reconstruction
Simultaneous Localization and Mapping (SLAM) methods jointly estimate camera pose (position and orientation) while incrementally constructing a 2D or 3D map of the surrounding environment. This enables geometry reconstruction directly from image sequences captured during motion.

Within the proposed Pixel–Point Fusion (PPF) framework, we additionally employ the MASt3R-SLAM system [20] for dense reconstruction of 3D sidewalk geometry. MASt3R-SLAM integrates large-scale geometric priors with SLAM optimization, producing high-fidelity 3D models. Each site can be reconstructed in approximately one minute on a standard GPU, supporting rapid, scalable deployment in outdoor field scenarios. The main stages of the MASt3R-SLAM pipeline are outlined below:

1. *Keyframe and Pointmap Generation:* Keyframes K are selected from the input sequence I based on camera motion. Each keyframe I_k produces a dense 3D pointmap:
$$P_k = M_\theta(I_k).$$
2. *Pose Estimation:* Relative poses T_{kr} between keyframes are estimated by minimizing the reprojection error using dense correspondences.
3. *Map Fusion:* Each P_k is transformed into the global frame and fused into the local map M_{local} with confidence weighting.
4. *Loop Closure and Optimization:* Loop closures are detected via visual similarity, and all poses T_k are globally optimized over constraints C to produce a consistent global map:
$$M_{\text{global}} = \bigcup_{k \in K} T_k P_k.$$

2.2 Sidewalk Segmentation and Defect Extraction in 2D

The proposed Pixel–Point Fusion (PPF) framework uses the Segment Anything Model (SAM) [19] to segment individual sidewalk slabs and detect surface defects directly from RGB imagery. SAM is a promptable foundational segmentation model designed to generate high-quality masks from diverse interactive prompts.

Algorithm 1: VGGT-based 3D Reconstruction (Images, K, cfg)

Inputs : Images $= \{I_1, \ldots, I_N\}$ RGB frames
K camera intrinsics (known or estimated upstream)
cfg options (*refine_ BA*, *conf_ thresh*, *scale_ to_ metric*, etc.)

Outputs: Poses $= \{(R_i, t_i)\}$ camera extrinsics per view
Depths $= \{D_i\}$ per-view depth maps
Conf $= \{C_i\}$ per-view confidence maps
PC fused 3D point cloud with colors

Step 1: Preprocess
foreach I_i *in Images* **do**
  $I_i \leftarrow$ normalize_color(I_i); $I_i \leftarrow$ resize_or_pad$(I_i, cfg.\text{resize})$
  if $cfg.undistort$ **then**
    $I_i \leftarrow$ undistort$(I_i, K, cfg.\text{dist})$
  end
end
Step 2: VGGT forward pass (multi-view transformer)
(Poses, Depths, Conf) $\leftarrow$ VGGT_FORWARD(Images, K)
Step 3: Optional refinement
if $cfg.refine\_BA$ **then**
  (*Poses*, *Depths*) $\leftarrow$ REFINE_GEOMETRY(Images, K, Poses, Depths, weights=Conf)
end
Step 4: Back-project each view to 3D (per-pixel)
PC $\leftarrow \varnothing$
for $i \in [1, N]$ **do**
  foreach *pixel* $p = (u, v)$ *in* I_i **do**
    if $Conf_i(u, v) < cfg.conf\_thresh$ **then**
      continue
    end
    if $Depths_i(u, v) \leq 0$ **then**
      continue
    end
    $x_c \leftarrow (u - K.cx)/K.fx$; $y_c \leftarrow (v - K.cy)/K.fy$
    $X_c \leftarrow [x_c z, y_c z, z]^T$; $X_w \leftarrow R_i^T(X_c - t_i)$ `// world coords`
    color $\leftarrow I_i(u, v)$; PC $\leftarrow$ append$(X_w$, color, view_id $= i)$
  end
end
Step 5: Fuse across views
PC $\leftarrow$ MERGE_DUPLICATES(PC, radius $= cfg$.fuse_radius, color_blend $=$ median)
if $cfg.scale\_to\_metric$ **then**
  PC $\leftarrow$ RESCALE_WITH_REFERENCE(PC, cfg.scale_targets)
end
return (Poses, Depths, Conf, PC)

Given an input image and a prompt such as points, bounding boxes, or coarse masks, SAM first encodes the image using a Vision Transformer (ViT) backbone to produce dense feature embeddings. The prompts are converted into embedding tokens and fused with the image features in a lightweight mask decoder, which outputs multiple candidate segmentation masks along with confidence scores. This design enables the retrieval of the most reliable mask for a given prompt by ranking its quality estimates.

In the PPF pipeline, bounding boxes are used to localize sidewalk slabs, and point-based prompts to select defects on the sidewalks (Fig. 2). The SAM-driven sidewalk and defect segmentation workflow is summarized in Algorithm 2.

Algorithm 2: SAM-based 2D Sidewalk and Defect Segmentation (Image, Prompts, cfg)

1: **Input:** RGB image I, bounding box prompts B, point prompts P, configuration cfg
2: **Output:** Segmentation masks $\{M_{sidewalk}, M_{defect}\}$
3: **1) Image Encoding**
Embed ← ImageEncoder(I) # ViT backbone extracts dense features
4: **2) Sidewalk Segmentation (Bounding Box Prompt)**
B_{tok} ← PromptEncoder(B)
($M_{sidewalk}, S_B$) ← MaskDecoder(Embed, B_{tok})
Select $M_{sidewalk}$ with highest quality score S_B
5: **3) Defect Segmentation (Point Prompt)**
P_{tok} ← PromptEncoder(P)
(M_{defect}, S_P) ← MaskDecoder(Embed, P_{tok})
Select M_{defect} with highest quality score S_P
6: **4) Output Final Masks**
return $\{M_{sidewalk}, M_{defect}\}$

2.3 2D-3D Fusion and Sidewalk Defects Localization

The reconstructed sidewalk point cloud provides rich spatial information that facilitates image ROI extraction. However, directly analyzing large-scale point cloud datas is computationally intensive. To mitigate this, the proposed PPF framework establishes 2D-3D correspondences through a mask-guided back-projection process. The 3D points in world coordinates (U, V, W) are transformed into the camera coordinate frame (X, Y, Z) using the extrinsic calibration parameters rotation R and translation t as:

$$\begin{bmatrix} X \\ Y \\ Z \\ 1 \end{bmatrix} = \begin{bmatrix} R & t \\ 0 & 1 \end{bmatrix} \begin{bmatrix} U \\ V \\ W \\ 1 \end{bmatrix}.$$

Next, the camera-space coordinates (X, Y, Z) are projected onto the normalized image plane using the standard perspective projection:

$$x = \frac{X}{Z}, \qquad y = \frac{Y}{Z}.$$

To compensate for lens distortion, the corrected coordinates are computed as:

$$x_{\text{after}} = x(1 + k_1 r^2 + k_2 r^4 + k_3 r^6) + 2p_1 xy + p_2(r^2 + 2x^2),$$
$$y_{\text{after}} = y(1 + k_1 r^2 + k_2 r^4 + k_3 r^6) + 2p_2 xy + p_1(r^2 + 2y^2),$$

where $r^2 = x^2 + y^2$, and $(k_1, k_2, k_3, p_1, p_2)$ denote the radial and tangential distortion coefficients estimated during camera calibration.
Finally, the intrinsic matrix K maps the distortion-corrected coordinates to the pixel coordinates (u, v):

$$\begin{bmatrix} u \\ v \\ 1 \end{bmatrix} = \begin{bmatrix} f_x & 0 & u_0 \\ 0 & f_y & v_0 \\ 0 & 0 & 1 \end{bmatrix} \begin{bmatrix} x_{\text{after}} \\ y_{\text{after}} \\ 1 \end{bmatrix},$$

where f_x and f_y are the focal lengths in pixels, and (u_0, v_0) is the principal point. Points whose projected pixel coordinates (u, v) fall within the binary mask M are retained. The mask-hit score is defined as:

$$s = \sum_j M[v_j, u_j],$$

where (u_j, v_j) denote the integer pixel coordinates of the projected 3D points.

In summary, the reconstructed 3D point cloud is back-projected onto the 2D image plane, where the corresponding depth values Z are assigned to each pixel. This process generates a registered RGB–depth representation that incorporates both appearance and geometry information while reducing the computational burden of operating directly on large-scale point clouds. The resulting fused data enables efficient visualization of sidewalk defects and supports accurate quantitative measurements of surface discontinuities.

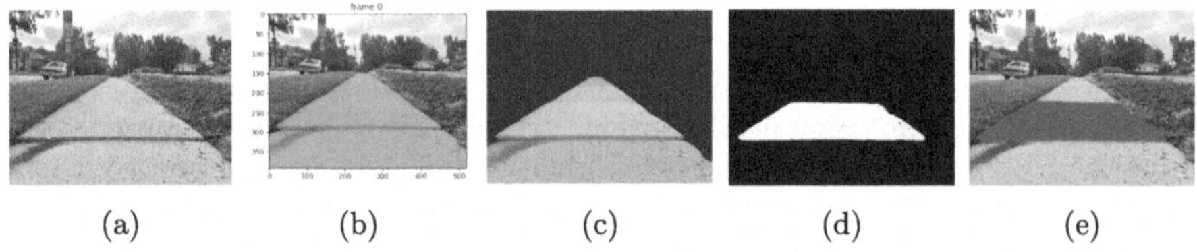

Fig. 2. Segmentation of sidewalk slabs using the SAM (Segment Anything) foundational model: (a) original raw image; (b) sidewalk segmentation using bounding box prompts; (c) segmentation of individual sidewalk slabs using point prompts; (d) mask of a single sample slab containing a potential trip hazard; and (e) sample slab mask overlaid on the original image.

2.4 Automated Sidewalk Defect Quantification

For each method (SLAM, LiDAR, and PPF), the extracted sidewalk defects including cross slope, running slope, trip hazards, and crack dimensions are quantified from their respective 3D point clouds according to the protocol in [21].

For trip hazard and crack detection, edge detection is applied directly to the 3D point cloud using a vertical gradient operator derived from the Sobel filter. The vertical gradient of the elevation channel (z) is analyzed to detect significant height variations. The mean z-value is calculated, and if it exceeds one standard deviation, the area is identified as a trip hazard. As shown in Fig. 3, the proposed method accurately detects vertical displacements exceeding 1 in.. The cross slope and running slope are computed using least-squares plane fitting.

Table 1. Definitions of confusion matrix components.

Metric	Description
True Positives (TP)	Non-compliant segments correctly identified as non-compliant.
True Negatives (TN)	Compliant segments correctly identified as compliant.
False Positives (FP)	Compliant segments incorrectly labeled as non-compliant.
False Negatives (FN)	Non-compliant segments incorrectly labeled as compliant.

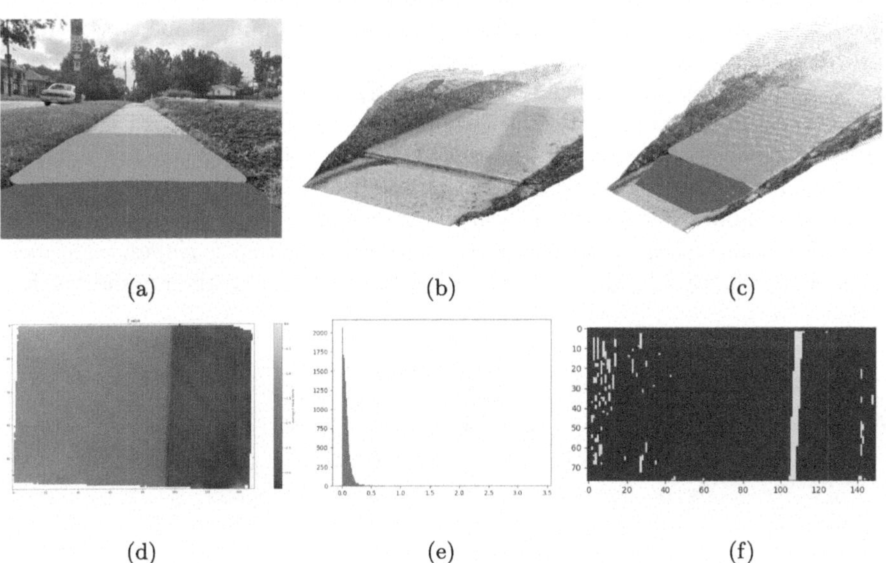

Fig. 3. Detection result of a 1-inch trip hazard: (a) original image; (b) extracted mask projected onto the original image; (c) extracted point cloud, red represents the lower slab, while green indicates the higher slab); (d) visualization of the z-values using a color scale (lighter colors indicate higher elevation); (e) histogram of z-value frequency; and (f) result of the proposed method detecting vertical displacement.

2.5 Discrepancy Analysis and ADA Compliance Evaluation

To further evaluate the accuracy of PPF and SLAM in identifying ADA-compliant and non-compliant sidewalk segments, digital level measurements were used as the ground truth for validation. A confusion matrix analysis was conducted by formulating the evaluation as a binary classification task based on ADA compliance criteria. Sidewalk segments with cross slopes exceeding 2% or running slopes exceeding 5% were labeled as non-compliant, while all others were classified as compliant. The confusion matrix includes the components in Table 1.

3 Experimental Results

3.1 Test Sites and Data Collection

Experiments were conducted on a sidewalk located on the east side of the University of Missouri campus, selected to capture diverse geometric and environmental conditions. The test site contains segments with deep shadows and partial occlusions, providing a challenging setting for robust 3D reconstruction under varying illumination and limited visibility. Additionally, the analyzed sidewalk includes multiple ADA-relevant defects such as cross slope, running slope, vertical displacements, and surface cracks (Fig. 4).

Images were captured using a GoPro HERO11 Black in webcam mode, mounted on a bicycle at a height of approximately 1 m to record continuous 1080×1920 video while traveling at a speed of 1.4–1.5 m/s. The collected imagery was used in both the PPF pipeline and SLAM processing. A Livox HAP LiDAR sensor was mounted beneath the camera to acquire point clouds at a rate of 452,000 points/s. Trip hazards, as well as running and cross slopes, were measured using a digital level and a measuring tape, serving as the ground truth.

(a) (b) (c) (d)

Fig. 4. Example sidewalk issues include: (a) occlusions; (b) vertical displacements; (c) cross- and running-slope irregularities; and (d) surface cracks.

3.2 Evaluation Metrics

Standard Performance Indicators. For the classification tasks such as ADA compliance, four standard performance indicators below were calculated, where

TP, TN, FP, and FN denote the number of true positive, true negative, false positive, and false negative cases.

$$\text{Accuracy} = \frac{TP + TN}{TP + TN + FP + FN},$$

$$\text{Precision} = \frac{TP}{TP + FP}, \quad \text{Recall} = \frac{TP}{TP + FN},$$

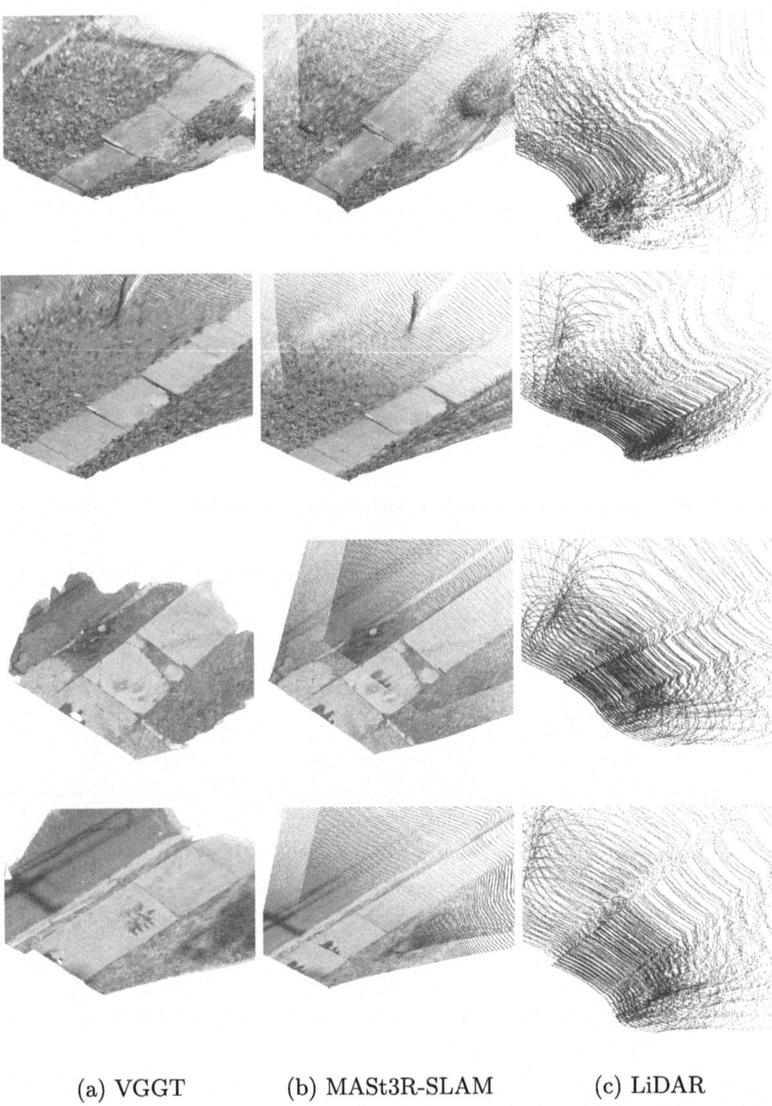

(a) VGGT (b) MASt3R-SLAM (c) LiDAR

Fig. 5. Comparison of 3D point clouds for four sidewalk locations reconstructed using the proposed PPF framework, MASt3R-SLAM, and LiDAR.

$$F_1 = 2 \times \frac{\text{Precision} \times \text{Recall}}{\text{Precision} + \text{Recall}}.$$

3D Reconstruction Error. To assess the geometric accuracy of the reconstructed sidewalks, the point clouds generated by the VGGT [18] and MASt3R-SLAM [20] methods were quantitatively compared against the LiDAR point cloud, which served as the ground truth reference. The Root Mean Square Error (RMSE) was employed as the primary evaluation metric to measure deviations between corresponding points in the datasets. RMSE is particularly sensitive to large deviations, making it well-suited for identifying local reconstruction errors and structural inconsistencies. The metric is defined as

$$\text{RMSE} = \sqrt{\frac{1}{n}\sum_{i=1}^{n}(x_i - \hat{x}_i)^2}, \tag{17}$$

where x_i represents the coordinates of points in the LiDAR point cloud, $\hat{x}_i$ denotes the corresponding points reconstructed from the VGGT [18] or MASt3R-SLAM [20] methods, and n is the total number of matched point pairs. This evaluation provides a quantitative understanding of each method's ability to reproduce the true 3D geometry of the sidewalk surface.

3.3 Qualitative Results

a. Visual Evaluation of Sidewalk Point Clouds Figure 5 compares 3D point clouds for four sidewalk locations reconstructed using VGGT, MASt3R-SLAM, and LiDAR methods. Across all sites, the VGGT-based reconstructions exhibit noticeably greater completeness and geometric continuity, producing more visually coherent sidewalk surfaces than the SLAM-based results. For Sidewalk-1 (top row), which exhibits cross-slope and running irregularities, the VGGT method reconstructed the entire segment with continuous geometry and clearly defined slab edges, while MASt3R-SLAM showed noticeable overlap at the mid-section and introduced considerable noise. Although LiDAR retained accurate global geometry, its limited spatial resolution failed to capture slab boundary details and surface roughness. For Sidewalk-2 (second row), characterized by a cross-slope issue, VGGT produced a seamless reconstruction with stable texture consistency and accurate elevation continuity. In contrast, MASt3R-SLAM showed fragmentation in overlapping frames and slight misalignment in joint regions. LiDAR again lacked sufficient density to represent micro-crack details. For Sidewalk-3 (third row), which contained multiple surface cracks, VGGT retained sharp slab boundaries and exhibited the lowest reconstruction noise, whereas MASt3R-SLAM presented mild point scattering near shadowed edges. LiDAR resolution was too coarse to represent subtle elevation transitions between slabs. For Sidewalk-4 (fourth row), which contains a 0.25-inch trip hazard, VGGT achieved the highest reconstruction completeness and exhibited minimal alignment drift, maintaining consistent color fidelity across the return path.

MASt3R-SLAM introduced noticeable local distortions at slab joints, whereas LiDAR data were too sparse to capture the subtle trip hazard.

b. PPF-based Sidewalk Defect Localization
After obtaining the 3D point clouds, Fig. 6 illustrates the proposed PPF workflow for identifying and visualizing defects in both 2D and 3D spaces. In Fig. 6a, potential defects are segmented directly from the sidewalk image using the SAM model. The resulting binary masks are then applied to extract the corresponding regions from the 3D point cloud, as shown in Fig. 6b. Finally, Fig. 6.c presents the labeled defects visualized within the complete 3D point cloud, where distinct colors represent different defect types. This process effectively integrates 2D and 3D information, forming the foundation for subsequent quantitative analysis of sidewalk defects.

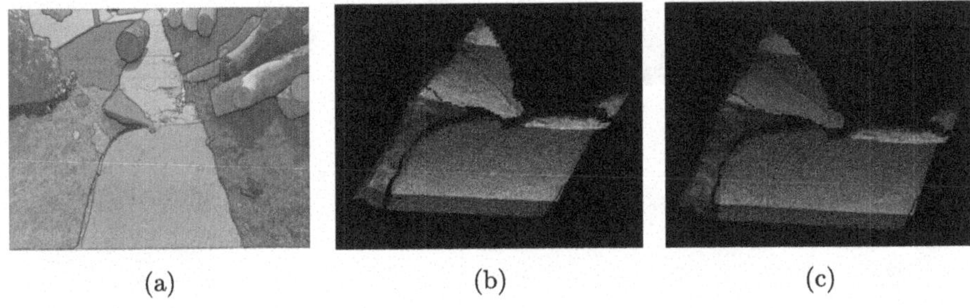

(a) (b) (c)

Fig. 6. Trip hazards labeled in the point cloud with distinct colors: (a) segmentation of defects on a 2D image; (b) extraction of the corresponding point cloud using defect masks; and (c) visualization of labeled information within the 3D point cloud.

c. Sidewalk Segmentation and Defect Extraction
A small trip hazard (0.25 in.) was selected for the qualitative evaluation of the proposed PPF workflow (Fig. 7). Subfigures (a–d) illustrate the process of extracting the defect mask from images. The PPF pipeline successfully isolated the potential trip hazard while removing similar background textures, producing a precise mask that aligned perfectly with the original image. This mask was then applied to the VGGT-, MASt3R-SLAM-, and LiDAR-based reconstructions to isolate the point clouds corresponding to the regions of interest.

Figure 7e presents the comparison results among the three methods. Figure 7f shows the point clouds extracted using the mask from (d). VGGT-based PPF produced the most detailed sidewalk point cloud, clearly revealing the surface defects. In contrast, the MASt3R-SLAM-based approach generated a sparser reconstruction, making the defect less discernible, while the LiDAR data were too sparse to locate the defect even with the red reflective tape on the surface. Figure 7g illustrates the sidewalk height variations, where lighter colors represent higher elevations. VGGT-based PPF demonstrated smooth and continuous elevation changes, whereas the LiDAR and MASt3R-SLAM point clouds exhibited discontinuous and irregular patterns due to sparsity and noise. Figure 7h displays the histograms of height values. VGGT-based PPF's distribution contained numerous small values and fewer large ones, enabling clearer identification of trip hazards. In contrast, MASt3R-SLAM showed a gradual distribution trend, making vertical displacements harder to distinguish, while LiDAR produced a noisier and rougher histogram. Figure 7i shows the final detection results for the 0.25-inch trip hazard. Only the proposed VGGT-based PPF successfully identified the defect, whereas both MASt3R-SLAM and LiDAR failed to detect it. Overall, the results indicate that only the VGGT-based PPF pipeline effectively detected trip hazards of such small magnitudes.

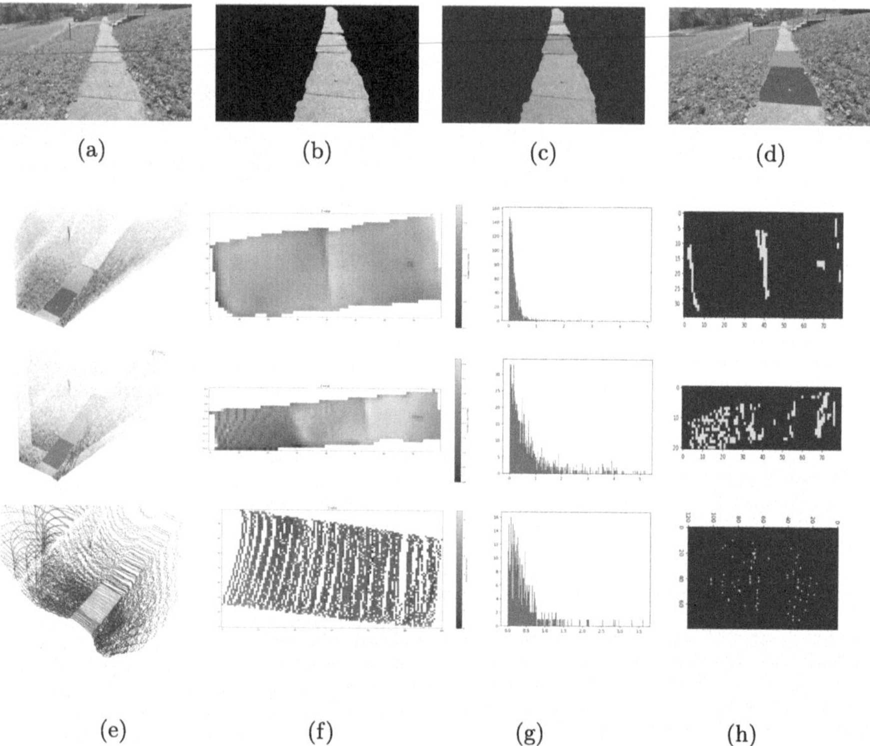

Fig. 7. Experimental process: (a) original raw image; (b) sidewalk segmentation using a bounding box prompt; (c) segmentation of individual sidewalk slabs using SAM with point prompts; (d) mask overlaid on the original image; (e) 3D reconstruction result, where the white region indicates the defect location based on (a–d); (f) z-values of the slab; (g) histogram of z-value frequency; (h) detection of trip hazards based on ADA standards.

3.4 Quantitative Results

To ensure a diverse set of defect conditions, fifteen sidewalk segments exhibiting cross-slope, running-slope, and vertical displacement irregularities were selected for evaluation. The performance of VGGT-based PPF and MASt3R-SLAM-based PPF was quantified using the RMSE relative to LiDAR, and a confusion matrix was computed for all three methods.

a. Reconstruction Estimation Error
Figure 8a compares the RMSE values of the VGGT-based PPF and MASt3R-SLAM-based PPF reconstructions against LiDAR ground truth. Across the 15 sample indices, VGGT-based PPF maintains consistently low reconstruction errors, with most values remaining below 0.02 m. In contrast, MASt3R-SLAM-based PPF exhibits greater variability, including several large deviations—most notably at sample indices 9, 11, and 13, where RMSE rises above 0.06 m and even exceeds 0.14 m. The overall lower and more uniform bar heights for PPF suggest stronger geometric stability and fewer reconstruction anomalies, whereas the tall spikes in the MASt3R-SLAM results indicate sensitivity to local scene variations and reduced consistency. As shown in Fig. 8b, the kernel density estimation (KDE) of RMSE values between LiDAR and the reconstructed point clouds reveals a sharper and narrower distribution for VGGT-based PPF, concentrated below 0.02 m. In contrast, MASt3R-SLAM-based PPF shows a broader spread with a longer tail extending beyond 0.10 m. The compact peak and reduced tail of VGGT-based PPF indicate higher geometric consistency and better adherence to ADA tolerance requirements.

b. ADA Compliance Evaluation
For ADA compliance assessment, Class 0 indicates sidewalk segments that fail to meet the standard and are therefore treated as the positive class. As presented in Table 2, the proposed VGGT-based PPF achieved the highest overall performance, with perfect recall (1.000) and an accuracy of 0.905. This indicates that VGGT-based PPF detected all true defects with minimal false alarms, correctly identifying nearly all sidewalk slabs with only two false positives. LiDAR-based analysis maintained high precision but missed several true defects, whereas MASt3R-SLAM-based PPF showed the lowest recall and accuracy, likely due to reconstruction inconsistencies and noise. As shown in Fig. 9, the VGGT-based PPF method attained perfect detection performance for vertical displacement, identifying every defective slab and yielding zero false negatives. In contrast, both LiDAR and MASt3R-SLAM-based approaches missed approximately 70% of the actual defects, demonstrating limited sensitivity to subtle vertical displacements caused by excessive reconstruction noise. These results confirm that VGGT-based PPF provides a more reliable reconstruction for detecting small trip hazards and ensuring compliance with ADA standards. In the cross-slope analysis, LiDAR achieved the highest accuracy, perfectly distinguishing between defective and non-defective slabs without false detections. VGGT-based PPF exhibited comparable performance, successfully identifying all defective slabs but producing one false positive. However, MASt3R-SLAM showed weaker con-

sistency, detecting only half of the true defects and occasionally misclassifying compliant surfaces as defective. For the running slope detection, all three methods, LiDAR, MASt3R-SLAM, and VGGT-based PPF performed similarly. Each achieving perfect recall, accurately identifying all defective slabs, with one false positive observed in each method due to gradual elevation transitions. Overall, VGGT-based PPF demonstrated superior performance in vertical displacement detection, competitive accuracy with LiDAR for cross-slope assessment, and comparable results across all methods for running slope evaluation.

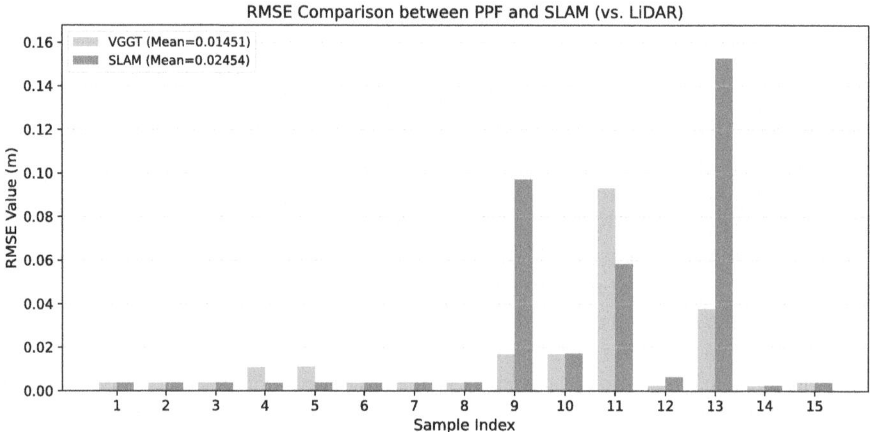

(a) Point cloud reconstruction error VGGT-based PPF and MASt3R-SLAM-based PPF.

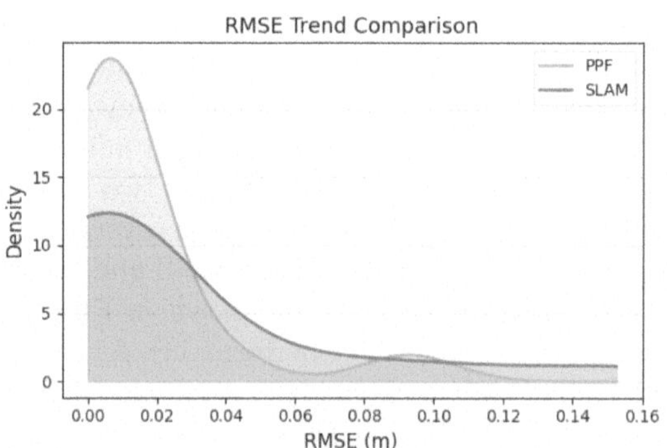

(b) Kernel Density Estimation (KDE) of reconstruction error relative to LiDAR. Orange: VGGT-based PPF, Blue: MASt3R-SLAM-based PPF.

Fig. 8. Combined RMSE Comparisons between PPF, MASt3R-SLAM, and LiDAR.

Table 2. Average ADA compliance evaluation performance across all defect categories.

Method	Precision	Recall	F1	Accuracy
LiDAR	0.889	0.762	0.748	0.744
MASt3R-SLAM-based PPF	0.778	0.595	0.605	0.601
VGGT-based PPF	0.822	1.000	0.896	0.905

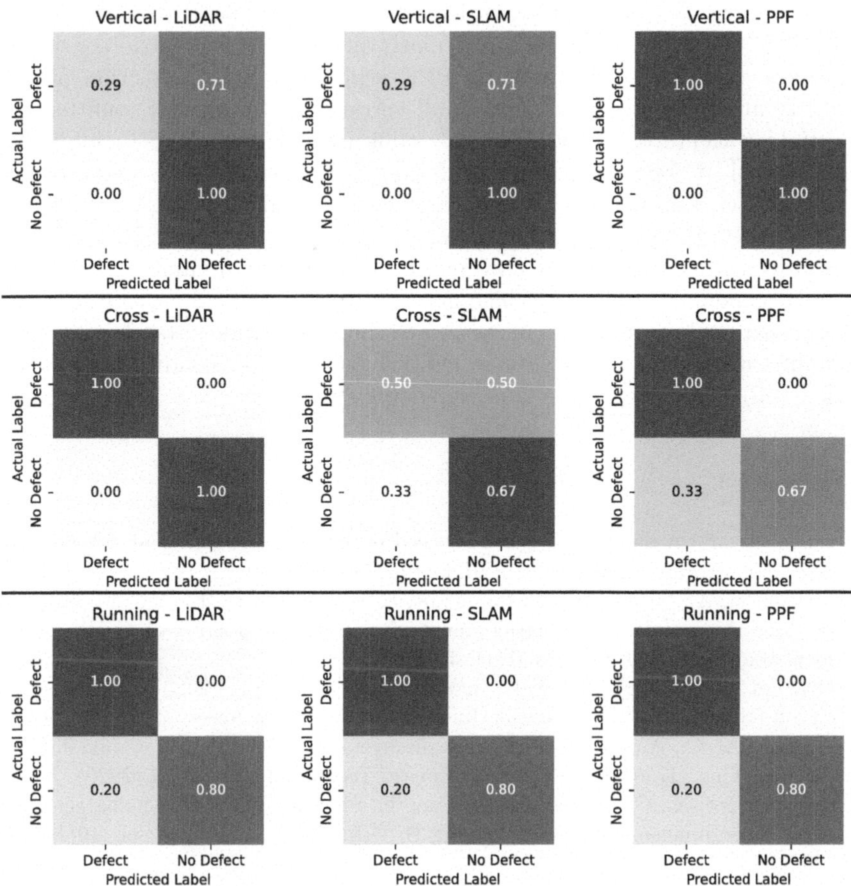

Fig. 9. Confusion matrices for defect detection using LiDAR, SLAM, and PPF across three slope types.

4 Conclusion and Discussion

This study introduced and validated a cost-effective, image-based framework for sidewalk condition assessment built upon a Pixel–Point Fusion (PPF) 2D/3D data analysis pipeline. The proposed framework employs VGGT-based 3D reconstruction to generate dense, geometrically accurate sidewalk point clouds suitable for defect measurement. A feature extraction and fusion strategy was also developed to integrate 2D RGB cues with 3D structural information, embedding depth and elevation signals directly into 2D segmentation. This hybrid formulation significantly reduces the computational overhead of large-scale point cloud processing, while simultaneously improving the robustness and precision of defect localization and segmentation.

Experimental validation on real sidewalk datasets demonstrated that the proposed framework achieves superior performance compared with LiDAR and MASt3R-SLAM-based analysis, particularly in terms of geometric consistency and defect sensitivity. VGGT-based PPF achieved reliable detection of cross slopes, running slopes, cracks, and small vertical displacements, confirming its potential for accurate ADA compliance evaluation. These findings highlight that camera-based 3D reconstruction can deliver LiDAR-comparable precision at a fraction of the cost, making large-scale, automated sidewalk inspection feasible for cities with limited sensing resources.

However, the current study was conducted on a limited number of sidewalks and environmental conditions, which may not capture the full variability of real-world scenarios. Future work will expand testing to citywide datasets to evaluate scalability, robustness under diverse lighting and weather conditions, and integration with automated compliance reporting systems.

References

1. Luo, J., et al.: A quadruped robot-enabled framework for intelligent sidewalk condition monitoring. Available at SSRN 5193678 (2026)
2. Frackelton, A., Grossman, A., Palinginis, E., Castrillon, F., Elango, V., Guensler, R.: Measuring walkability: development of an automated sidewalk quality assessment tool. Suburban Sustain. **1**(1), 4 (2013)
3. City of Middleton, Sidewalk maintenance program (2025). https://www.cityofmiddleton.us/833/SidewalkMaintenance-Program. Accessed 24 Oct 2025
4. Hou, Q., Ai, C.: A network-level sidewalk inventory method using mobile lidar and deep learning. Transp. Res. Part C: Emerg. Technol. **119**, 102772 (2020)
5. Ning, H., Ye, X., Chen, Z., Liu, T., Cao, T.: Sidewalk extraction using aerial and street view images. Environ. Planning B: Urban Analytics City Sci. **49**(1), 7–22 (2022)
6. Cheng, M., Zhang, Y., Su, Y., Alvarez, J.M., Kong, H.: Curb detection for road and sidewalk detection. IEEE Trans. Veh. Technol. **67**(11), 10330–10342 (2018)
7. Koh, C.Y., Ali, M., Hendawi, A.: Cracklens: automated sidewalk crack detection and segmentation. IEEE Trans. Artif. Intell. **5**(11), 5418–5430 (2024)
8. Cohen, R., Fernie, G., Roshan Fekr, A.: A vision-based approach for sidewalk and walkway trip hazards assessment. Int. J. Environ. Res. Public Health **17**(22), 8438 (2020)
9. Meinen, B.U., Robinson, D.T.: Mapping erosion and deposition in an agricultural landscape: optimization of UAV image acquisition schemes for SFM-MVS. Remote Sens. Environ. **239**, 111666 (2020)
10. Carrivick, J.L., Smith, M.W., Quincey, D.J.: Structure from Motion in the Geosciences. John Wiley & Sons (2016)

11. Zakaria, M.H., Fawzy, H., El-Beshbeshy, M., Farhan, M.: A comparative study of terrestrial laser scanning and photogrammetry: accuracy and applications. Civil Eng. J. **11**(03) (2025)
12. Suleymanoglu, B., Gurturk, M., Yilmaz, Y., Soycan, A., Soycan, M.: Comparison of unmanned aerial vehicle-lidar and image-based mobile mapping system for assessing road geometry parameters via digital terrain models. Transp. Res. Rec. **2677**(8), 617–632 (2023)
13. Taniguchi, K., Kubota, S., Yasumuro, Y.: Quantitative visualization of physical barriers for vulnerable pedestrians based on photogrammetry. Constr. Innov. **22**(3), 604–623 (2022)
14. Boongaling, C.G.K., Luna, D.A., Samantela, S.S.: Developing a street level walkability index in the Philippines using 3D photogrammetry modeling from drone surveys. GeoJournal **87**(4), 3341–3364 (2022)
15. Jiang, Y., Han, S., Li, D., Bai, Y., Wang, M.: Automatic concrete sidewalk deficiency detection and mapping with deep learning. Expert Syst. Appl. **207**, 117980 (2022)
16. Zhang, W.-J., Wan, H.-P., Todd, M.D.: An efficient 2D–3D fusion method for bridge damage detection under complex backgrounds with imbalanced training data. Adv. Eng. Inform. **65**, 103373 (2025)
17. Chen, L.-C., Zhu, Y., Papandreou, G., Schroff, F., Adam, H.: Encoder-decoder with atrous separable convolution for semantic image segmentation. In: Proceedings of the European Conference on Computer Vision (ECCV), pp. 801–818 (2018)
18. Wang, J., Chen, M., Karaev, N., Vedaldi, A., Rupprecht, C., Novotny, D.: VGGT: visual geometry grounded transformer. In: Proceedings of the Computer Vision and Pattern Recognition Conference, pp. 5294–5306 (2025)
19. Kirillov, A., et al.: Segment anything. In: Proceedings of the IEEE/CVF International Conference on Computer Vision, pp. 4015–4026 (2023)
20. Murai, R., Dexheimer, E., Davison, A.J.: Mast3r-slam: real-time dense slam with 3D reconstruction priors (2024). https://arxiv.org/abs/2412.12392
21. Du, H., Wang, S., Zhang, L., Amo-Boateng, M., Adu-Gyamfi, Y.: Evaluating neural radiance fields for ADA-compliant sidewalk assessments: a comparative study with LiDAR and manual methods. Infrastructures **10**(8), 191 (2025)

Neurophysiological Study of EEG Alpha–Beta Dynamics in Temporal and Parietal Regions During Non-Native and Neutral Music Listening

Richard Kyung[1(✉)] and Nathan Yeop Kim[2]

[1] CRG-NJ, Cresskill, NJ 07626, USA
nycrick@gmail.com
[2] University of Rochester, Rochester, NY 14627, USA

Abstract. The brain activity differences between worded and unworded music through EEGmeasurements in temporal and parietal brain regions. The research shows that music type, specifically semantic content presence or absence, determines brain activity patterns. The alpha/beta ratio functions as a biomarker which helps differentiate between mental focus and relaxation states. EEG recordings were acquired from the left temporal (T7) and right parietal (P4) sites in participants exposed to two auditory conditions: a non-native song (featuring unfamiliar language) and neutral, instrumental music.The power spectral density (PSD) analysis showed different oscillatory patterns between conditions. The alpha/beta power ratio showed a significant increase in both channels under the neutral music condition especially at the left temporal site (T7). This elevated ratio, driven by increased alpha (8–12 Hz) and suppressed beta (13–30 Hz) power, is indicative of a relaxed cortical state characterized by reduced cognitive load and minimal linguistic processing.The non-native song condition produced a lower alpha/beta ratio because beta activity increased at T7. The results show higher cognitive involvement because the brain processes unfamiliar phonological and prosodic structures. The research findings support the development of music-based therapeutic interventions because they confirm how musical stimuli influence brain activity in therapeutic contexts such as stress reduction and cognitive or language rehabilitation.

Keywords: EEG (Electroencephalography) · Music Semantics · Alpha/Beta Ratio · Temporal and Parietal Brain Regions · Cognitive Processing · Psychiatric Treatments

1 Introduction

Neuromusicology and cognitive neuroscience and auditory neurophysiology researchers focus on studying human brain responses to musical stimuli through EEG technology. The non-invasive EEG method enables researchers to study neural processes by recording scalp electrical activity which produces oscillatory patterns [1]. Researchers use EEG signal spectral analysis to measure changes in cognitive workload and emotional states

F. Tanner and J. Irvine (Eds.): AIPR 2025, LNCS 16446, pp. 364–374, 2026.
https://doi.org/10.1007/978-3-032-18474-0_25

and auditory processing mechanisms through alpha (8–12 Hz) and beta (13–30 Hz) frequency band analysis [2, 3]. The research examines how non-native worded music and neutral instrumental music affect alpha-beta brain wave patterns in temporal and parietal areas through alpha/beta ratio measurements.

The EEG technique provides both high-speed temporal resolution and sensitive detection of neural responses to auditory stimuli [4]. Different types of EEG device system enables researchers to place electrodes for standardized brain region coverage which includes temporal (T7) and parietal (P4) and frontal (F8) and midline (Cz) areas [5]. The brain areas work together to process auditory information and handle language functions and sensory data and direct attentional processes [6]. The T7 site serves as a critical area for processing linguistic prosody and phonological information while the P4 site helps with multimodal integration and attentional shifting during auditory processing [7].

The natural auditory stimulus of music enables researchers to study how different musical elements affect brain wave patterns. Research indicates that instrumental music creates higher alpha wave activity which indicates a state of relaxed wakefulness with decreased mental effort [8]. The brain shows increased beta-band activity when processing music with unfamiliar linguistic elements because it needs to analyze phonological and rhythmic and prosodic structures [9]. The alpha/beta ratio functions as a useful neural marker which detects changes between relaxation states and attentional states during auditory processing [10]. The brain shows a more relaxed state when alpha/beta ratio values increase but it becomes more active when the ratio decreases [11].

Based on data, this research used EEG to monitor T7 and P4 brain activity while participants listened to two musical conditions which included a song with unknown semantic content and wordless instrumental music. The neutral music condition led to an increase in alpha/beta ratio at both cortical sites with the most pronounced effect occurring at T7. The brain entered a state of relaxation because alpha power increased while beta power decreased which resulted in a lower cognitive load [12]. The brain processed new phonological elements through increased beta activity at T7 which resulted in a lower alpha/beta ratio during the non-native song condition [13].

Research shows that music triggers brain responses which heavily depend on the semantic meaning and the context in which the music is heard [14]. Instrumental music creates relaxation while reducing stress and mental effort but linguistically complex music stimulates brain activity and attentional processing [15]. The brain shows different neural responses to these music types because of their structural and semantic characteristics which determine whether music will stimulate or relax the brain.

2 Data Analysis

2.1 Experimental Framework for Data Preparation

The research design consisted of multiple experimental stages which examined three essential brain activity elements: (1) The impact of eyes-open versus eyes-closed states on resting-state neural dynamics and (2) The comparison of auditory processing between in-ear and bone-conduction headphones and (3) The cortical responses to familiar and unfamiliar linguistic stimuli. The research design included multiple components which allowed scientists to study how different sensory inputs and cognitive states affect EEG measurements.

2.2 Data Acquisition Setup

The OpenBCI Ganglion Board recorded EEG data at 200 Hz to detect brain oscillations with high temporal precision. The international 10–10 system guided electrode placement for T7 (left temporal) and F8 (right frontal) and Cz (central vertex) and P4 (right parietal) gold-cup electrodes. The ear references served as stable points for calculating differential signals. The OpenBCI GUI version 5.0.3 operated as the data monitoring system which provided real-time signal viewing and data management capabilities.

2.3 Participant Preparation and Recording Procedure

The research team required participants to sign consent forms before starting the study. The researchers applied conductive paste to the electrodes before checking their impedance levels to achieve optimal signal quality. The participants received instructions to stay motionless during the recording process while they sat in a peaceful environment. The research team followed a standardized protocol for data collection which applied to all participants. The researchers selected two-minute artifact-free segments from each continuous recording block for further analysis of all experimental conditions.

2.4 Experimental Conditions and Recording Sessions

The EEG study consisted of three parts which evaluated resting-state activity and auditory processing and linguistic response:

Resting-State Recordings. The participants underwent three sets of three-minute eyes-open recordings. The participants underwent three sets of three-minute eyes-closed recordings.

Auditory Stimulation Using In-Ear Headphones. The participants listened to a native-language song for three minutes. The participants listened to a non-native song for three minutes. The participants listened to neutral instrumental music for three minutes. Auditory Stimulation Using Bone-Conduction Headphones The participants listened to a native-language song for three minutes. The participants listened to a non-native song for three minutes. The participants listened to neutral instrumental music for three minutes.

Stimulus Assignment Rule. The Arabic song functioned as the non-native condition for Italian participants. The Italian song functioned as the non-native condition for participants who were not Italian. The study included a linguistically unfamiliar auditory stimulus for all participants.

Dataset Attribution. The PhysioNet dataset used in this research originated from Nibras Abo Alzahab and his research team which included Angelo Di Iorio and Luca Apollonio and Muaaz Alshalak and Alessandro Gravina and Luca Antognoli and Lorenzo Scalise and Marco Baldi and Bilal Alchalabi. The researchers established a method to study EEG responses when people hear different types of sounds and words in their environment.

3 Data and Results

3.1 Amplitude vs Time: Analysis of EEG Alpha–Beta Dynamics Across Conditions

T7 (language & emotion region). Slightly more variability during non-native music, possibly reflecting greater attentional or emotional engagement with unfamiliar lyrics (Fig. 1).

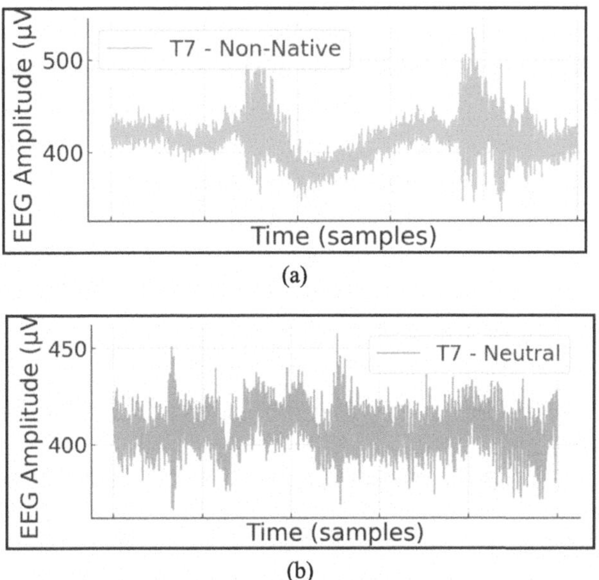

Fig. 1. T7 region(neutral) shows more stable changes during non-native music

P4 (relaxation-related alpha activity). Neutral music shows smoother and slower waves, which may indicate a more relaxed brain state (Fig. 2).

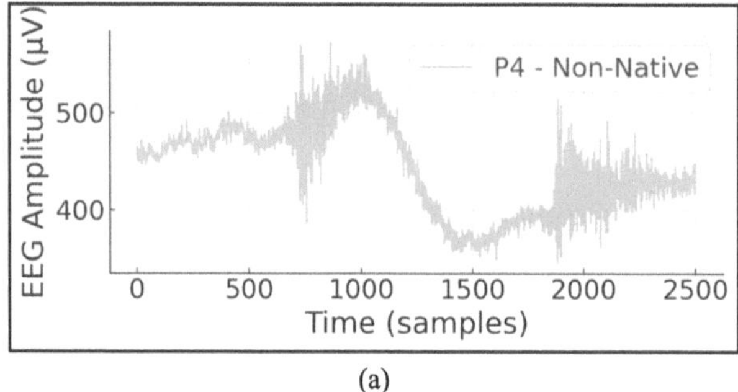

(a)

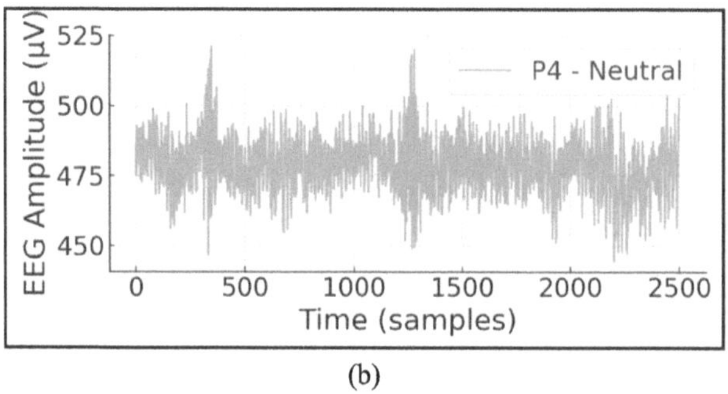

(b)

Fig. 2. P4 region(neutral) shows more stable changes during non-native music

3.2 Power Spectral Density (PSD) Analysis

Now let's proceed to:

1. Power Spectral Density (PSD) analysis using Welch's method.
2. Alpha/Beta ratio for T7 and P4 to evaluate relaxation levels (Table 1).

Table 1. Alpha/Beta Ratio Analysis: T7 and P4 regions for neutral music show more stable shift

Channel	Condition	Alpha Power	Beta Power	Alpha/Beta Ratio
T7	Non-Native Music	6.34	13.86	**0.457**
P4	Non-Native Music	8.19	13.39	0.612
T7	Neutral Music	6.96	11.07	**0.628**
P4	Neutral Music	10.81	14.77	0.732

We check alpha power and beta power and their ratio between T7 (left temporal) and P4 (right parietal) EEG channels under non-native music and neutral music conditions. The outcomes indicate how semantic complexity and cognitive demands affect cortical relaxation and activation states.

3.3 Comparisons by Channel

T7 (Left Temporal Region). The T7 site functions as a critical area for processing auditory language and performing phonological analysis and semantic decoding tasks. The alpha power measures 6.34 while beta power measures 13.86 during non-native music listening which produces an alpha/beta ratio of 0.457. The measured values show decreased alpha power and increased beta power which indicates higher cognitive demands for processing unfamiliar linguistic material.

The alpha power at T7 reaches 6.96 while beta power decreases to 11.07 when listening to neutral music which produces an alpha/beta ratio of 0.628. The measured patterns show a transition toward relaxation together with decreased linguistic processing requirements.

In summary, the T7 site shows extreme sensitivity when detecting unfamiliar linguistic elements in music. The processing of unfamiliar linguistic elements in non-native music leads to increased beta power and decreased alpha/beta ratio. The absence of linguistic demands in neutral music leads to increased relaxation of cortical activity.

P4 (Right Parietal Region). The right parietal region of P4 serves as a site for processing multiple sensory inputs and directing attention and spatial auditory information. The alpha/beta ratio reaches 0.612 when listening to non-native music while alpha power measures 8.19 and beta power measures 13.39. The measured values show average relaxation levels together with some degree of mental processing. The alpha/beta ratio at P4 reaches 0.732 when listening to neutral music while alpha power increases to 10.81 and beta power slightly rises to 14.77. The significant rise in alpha power leads to a higher ratio which indicates deep relaxation (Fig. 3).

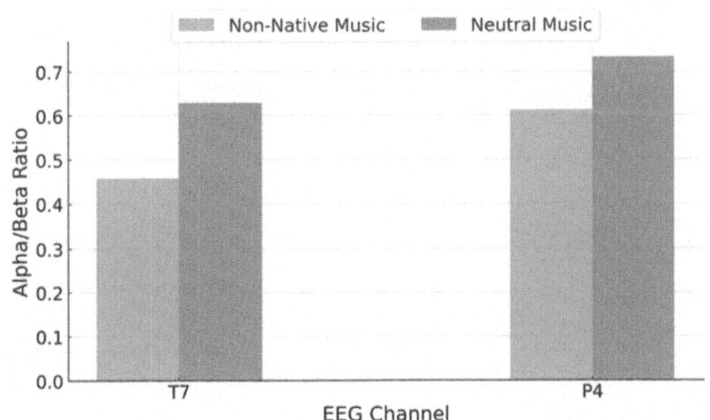

Fig. 3. P4 and T7 regions for neutral music show more stable shift

Neutral music shows a higher Alpha/Beta Ratio in both regions, especially at T7, consistent with a more relaxed and less cognitively active state. Non-native music evokes more beta activity, suggesting heightened attention or language processing.

3.4 Computational Methodology

Figure 4 and Fig. 5 depict the first 10 s of raw EEG traces, contrasting the non-native music condition with the neutral music condition for the four EEG regions. Notably, the F8 electrode (right frontal lobe) exhibits larger amplitude negative deflections in both conditions, a pattern potentially indicative of heightened emotional or attentional engagement with the auditory stimuli.

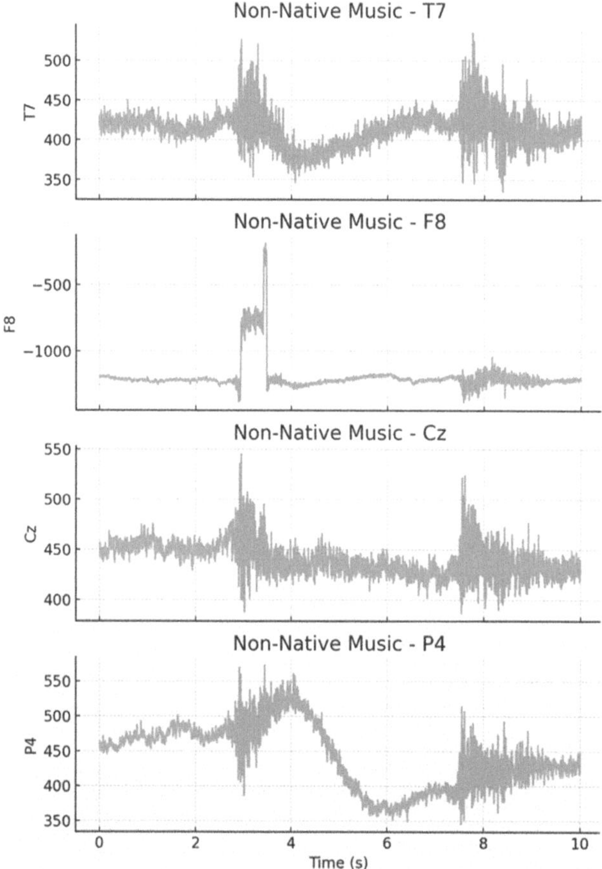

Fig. 4. All the four regions(for non-native music) show more variability

In contrast, the signals from the T7 (left temporal) and P4 (right parietal) electrodes demonstrate visibly greater amplitude stability and slower, more rhythmic oscillations during the neutral music condition.

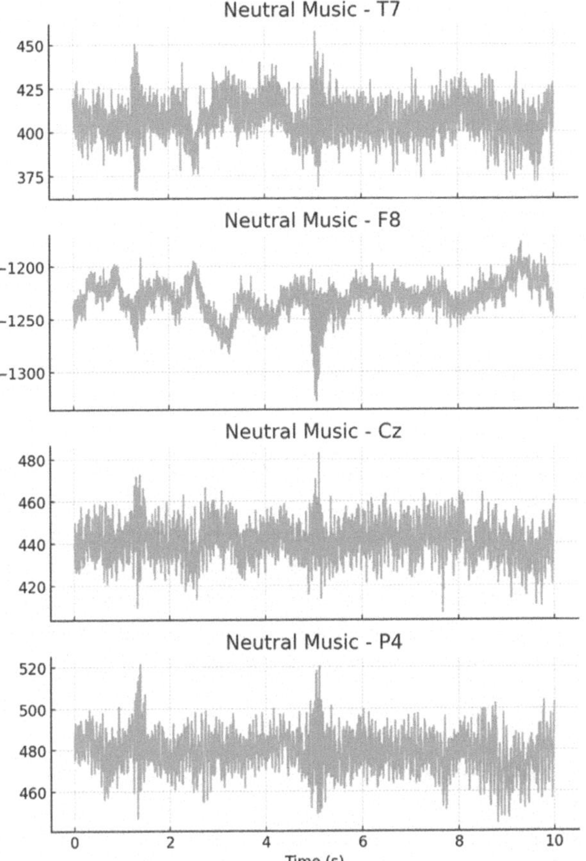

Fig. 5. All the four regions(for neutral music) show more stable changes

This observed pattern is characteristic of a more relaxed cortical state. Critically, all recorded signals present morphologies consistent with physiological brain activity and are devoid of major artifacts, confirming the quality of the data for subsequent spectral analysis.

3.5 Power Spectral Density (PSD) Analysis for the Four Regions

Now let's compute and compare Power Spectral Density (PSD) and the alpha/beta ratio for relaxation analysis. Here is a comparison of EEG Alpha Power, Beta Power, and Alpha/Beta Ratio across four channels for both music conditions:

Table 2. Power Spectral Density (PSD) and the alpha/beta ratio for relaxation analysis

Channel	Condition	Alpha Power	Beta Power	Alpha/Beta Ratio
T7	Non-Native Music	6.337	13.861	0.457
F8	Non-Native Music	136.865	108.708	1.259
Cz	Non-Native Music	8.575	10.352	0.828
P4	Non-Native Music	8.192	13.390	0.612
T7	Neutral Music	6.957	11.072	**0.628**
F8	Neutral Music	5.853	9.364	**0.625**
Cz	Neutral Music	9.340	10.142	**0.921**
P4	Neutral Music	10.813	14.771	**0.732**

Table 2 presents Power Spectral Density (PSD) and alpha/beta ratio values for relaxation analysis. This presents EEG Alpha Power and Beta Power measurements together with Alpha/Beta Ratio values for four channels in both music conditions.

For example, P4 (Right Parietal Lobe): The parietal cortex shows a pattern of increased relaxation during neutral music based on its alpha/beta ratio which rises from 0.612 when listening to non-native music to 0.732 when listening to neutral music. Alpha power increased during the experiment which indicates better relaxation together with decreased focus on tasks.

4 Discussion and Future Directions

The research findings have value for developing therapeutic approaches and rehabilitation methods. The analysis of alpha/beta ratio shifts during music listening enables healthcare professionals to create personalized stress reduction and cognitive training and language rehabilitation programs [16]. The relaxation benefits of music without words make it suitable for stress relief but non-native music with words can help neurorehabilitation programs increase cognitive engagement [17]. Music-based therapy applications requiring knowledge about how musical structures affect EEG signals creates a vital base for developing therapeutic approaches in cognitive and clinical fields.

Researchers have worked on music functions to see the correlations of thier neural activity modulator which affects human mental processes through its musical elements and meaningful content. Research shows that brain activity patterns differ between instrumental and linguistically rich music because they activate separate neural pathways which control different cognitive processes [9]. The brain responds to instrumental music and increased cognitive activity when it encounters music with different types of linguistic elements [7].

EEG technology enables researchers to study brain responses through non-invasive oscillatory activity measurements that deliver precise results at the millisecond level. The alpha/beta power ratio functions as a primary biomarker to assess both arousal levels and cognitive workload in research studies. The brain shows relaxed wakefulness through alpha oscillations which range from 8–13 Hz while beta oscillations between 13–30 Hz indicate focused attention and effortful processing and increased vigilance. The brain shows relaxation and decreased cognitive workload when the alpha/beta power ratio increases but it shows mental effort when the ratio decreases.

The neuromusicology field uses this ratio to track how musical elements affect brain function. Research findings demonstrate that wordless music leads to increased alpha/beta power ratios in central and parietal brain areas including Cz and P4 which confirms its ability to create relaxation and decrease mental tension. The brain regions that process sensory information and sustain peaceful mental states show pronounced responses to peaceful auditory stimuli.

The brain shows different neural responses when people listen to music that includes words they cannot understand. The brain shows decreased alpha/beta ratios in T7 and F8 regions because beta power increases in these areas. The brain demonstrates increased beta activity when it works to understand unfamiliar phonological patterns and make predictions about rhythmic sequences and resolve linguistic uncertainties. The brain shows increased frontal activity when processing non-native music which might indicate emotional processing or novelty detection or language interpretation challenges thus making this response important for psychiatric research.

The research findings have significant applications for medical practice. The brain shows neural patterns during music listening that match stress management and attention control and emotional processing which are essential for treating anxiety disorders and depression and PTSD and attentional dysregulation. The therapeutic potential of neutral music exists because it helps people relax while it reduces hyperarousal and supports emotional stability. The structured presentation of music with unfamiliar linguistic elements helps activate beneficial cognitive networks which can aid in language therapy and cognitive engagement therapy. EEG-based musical effect analysis enables healthcare professionals to create individualized psychiatric treatments through neuroscience-based approaches.

References

1. Niedermeyer, Ernst, and Fernando Lopes da Silva, editors. Electroencephalography: Basic Principles, Clinical Applications, and Related Fields. Lippincott Williams & Wilkins (2005)
2. Başar, E.: A review of alpha activity in integrative brain function: fundamental physiology, sensory coding, cognition, and pathologic changes in alzheimer's disease. Int. J. Psychophysiol. **13**(2), 151–167 (1992)
3. Klimesch, W.: EEG alpha and theta oscillations reflect cognitive and memory performance: a review and analysis. Brain Res. Rev. **29**(2–3), 169–195 (1999)
4. Luck, S.J.: An Introduction to the Event-Related Potential Technique. 2nd ed., MIT Press (2014)
5. Klem, G.H., et al.: The ten-twenty electrode system of the international federation. Electroencephalography and Clinical Neurophysiology **52**, 3–6 (1999)
6. Zatorre, R.J., et al.: Structure and function of auditory cortex: music and speech. Trends in Cognitive Sciences, **6**(1), 37–46 (2002)
7. Koelsch, S.: Brain and music. Wiley Interdisciplinary Reviews: Cognitive Science **2**(5), 566–578 (2011)
8. Altenmüller, E., Mari, T.: Music and the brain: the neuroscience of music and musical perception. Psychomusicology: Music, Mind, and Brain **20**(1–2), 1–6 (2008)

9. Patel, A.D.: Music, Language, and the Brain. Oxford UP (2008)
10. Harmony, T.: The functional significance of delta, theta, alpha, and beta oscillations in cognitive processes. Clin. Neurophysiol. **110**(10), 1842–1854 (2009)
11. Barry, R.J., et al.: EEG alpha/beta ratios as indicators of alertness. Biological Psychology **80**(2), 148–152 (2009)
12. Sammler, D., et al.: Music and emotion: electrophysiological correlates. annals of the New York Academy of Sciences **999**(1), 376–379 (2003)
13. Schön, D., et al.: Neural basis of music perception and language processing. Annals of the New York Academy of Sciences **1060**, 71–81 (2005)
14. Blood, A.J., Zatorre, R.J.: Intensely pleasurable responses to music correlate with brain activity. Proc. Natl. Acad. Sci. **98**(20), 11818–11823 (2001)
15. Thoma, M.V., et al.: The Effect of Music on the Human Stress Response. PLoS One **8**(8), e70156 (2013)
16. Särkämö, T., et al.: Cognitive, emotional, and neural benefits of musical activities for neurorehabilitation. The Neuroscientist **20**(5), 502–518 (2014)
17. Herholz, S.C., Zatorre, R.J.: Musical training as a framework for brain plasticity. Neuron **76**(3), 486–502 (2012)

Fusion of 2D LiDAR and Vision-Based Detection for Collision-Aware Indoor Navigation

Sally Aqcuaah, Chris Nenebi, Andrews Tang, Kourtney Tucker(✉), Issa W. AlHmoud, and Balakrishna Gokaraju

North Carolina Agricultural and Technical State University, Greensboro, NC 27411, USA
snacquaah@aggie.ncat.edu, {ctnenebi,atang, ketucker}@aggies.ncat.edu, iwalhmoud@ncat.edu

Abstract. In this study, we examine an alternative approach to achieving collision avoidance in dynamic indoor environments by integrating deep-learning-based object detection (YOLOv5) with 2D LiDAR distance estimation through image-to-angle mapping techniques. The system utilizes a rule-based decision-making framework that dynamically adjusts the robot's trajectory based on obstacle proximity and predefined safe distance thresholds. Instead of relying on computationally expensive 3D sensors, the proposed method leverages mid-level sensor fusion to align bounding box outputs with LiDAR angular scans, enabling reliable distance estimation for real-time obstacle avoidance necessary for safe navigation. The methodology was evaluated using both RViz-based visualization and real-world testing in a controlled indoor environment. Empirical findings confirm the system's capability to perform reliable collision avoidance and adaptive navigation. Results showed reliable collision avoidance and adaptive navigation performance. With Kalman filtering, 2D LiDAR distance estimation achieved an average error of 0.06 m. The system recorded a 95% success rate for static obstacles and a less desirable success rate of 60% for dynamic obstacles. This work advances autonomous indoor navigation by providing a computationally simple, cost-saving framework that harnesses deep learning-based computer vision and 2D LiDAR sensing and is scalable and well-suited for multi-robot deployment in dynamic environments.

Keywords: Distance Estimation · Indoor Robotics Navigation · Collision Avoidance · YOLOv5 · Mid-level Sensor Fusion · Dynamic Environment · Window Filtering · Rule-Based Planning

1 Introduction

1.1 Sensor Technology Challenges in Autonomous Navigation

The evolution of autonomous vehicles (AVs) has progressed from basic systems reliant on proximity sensors to sophisticated platforms that integrate advanced technologies. These improvements have made it possible for autonomous systems to adapt to dynamic environments and real-time perception. The inventions of LiDAR and stereo vision technologies provided AVs with the ability to construct spatial maps and estimate object distances with greater accuracy, enhancing safe navigation within their environment.

F. Tanner and J. Irvine (Eds.): AIPR 2025, LNCS 16446, pp. 375–386, 2026.
https://doi.org/10.1007/978-3-032-18474-0_26

Integrating these sensor technologies with computer vision and deep learning technologies such as YOLO further enhances AVs' performance and applicability in many areas, such as warehouses, hospitals, offices, and restaurants, where robots must reliably detect and avoid obstacles while navigating safely [1, 2].

Traditional sensor systems, though effective, often fall short when operating in isolation. For example, cameras excel at object detection and classification by capturing the full shapes of objects, yet they struggle with precise depth estimation, especially in low-light or high-glare indoor settings. Conversely, LiDAR sensors offer robust and cost-effective depth estimation regardless of lighting conditions, but when using a 2D LiDAR sensor such as the RP LiDAR A3, they provide only a single-plane scan. This limitation means that the full three-dimensional structure of objects is not captured.

1.2 Proposed Framework and Key Contributions

To bridge this gap, this work proposes a mid-level sensor fusion approach that combines the strengths of both modalities [3]. In our system, a depth camera first captures 2D images of the environment, and a YOLOv5 deep learning model is applied to detect and classify objects, outputting bounding boxes that delineate these objects. In parallel, the RP LiDAR A3 gathers precise depth measurements along its scanning plane. The innovative aspect of our approach lies in projecting the 2D LiDAR scan data onto the preprocessed 2D images with bounding boxes and using image-to-angle mapping to extract the distance to detected objects. This alignment enriches the object detection output with accurate depth information, compensating for the 2D LiDAR's inability to capture the full 3D point cloud, and is critical for safe navigation and effective collision avoidance.

Our system uses sensor fusion to effectively combine information from the camera and LiDAR. This approach differs from early fusion, which directly combines the raw sensor data before feature extraction, and late fusion, which merges the final outputs of each sensor [3]. Instead, we process the camera data for object detection and LiDAR data for depth information separately and then fuse them. By opting for mid-level fusion, we ensure that the system benefits from the semantic capabilities of the camera and the precise distance measurements of the LiDAR, leading to enhanced spatial awareness.

The overall goal of our system is to improve collision avoidance through a twofold strategy. First, the camera-based detection establishes the presence, full shape, and location of obstacles. Second, by applying LiDAR-based depth estimation to these detected objects, the system calculates accurate spatial information that informs navigation decisions. Complementing this sensor fusion process is a rule-based planning mechanism, where predefined rules govern how the robot responds to different detected objects based on their estimated distances, improving safe navigation in static and dynamic indoor environments.

In summary, this paper presents a mid-level sensor fusion approach for indoor autonomous navigation, integrating deep learning-based object detection (YOLOv5) with depth estimation from the RPLiDAR A3. The key contributions of this work include:

1. Implementing a mid-level sensor fusion technique where 2D LiDAR depth is projected onto detected objects for enhanced perception.

2. Developing a rule-based planning system that enables collision avoidance based on predefined distance thresholds.
3. Evaluating the system's performance in navigating dynamic and static indoor environments.

The rest of this paper is organized as follows: Sect. 2 provides an overview of related studies on sensor fusion approaches and indoor mobile robot navigation, highlighting both classical and AI-driven methodologies. Section 3 details the proposed architecture, describing our mid-level fusion framework and the key modules for navigation and collision avoidance. Section 4 presents experimental results evaluating the system's performance in real-time environments. Finally, Sect. 5 concludes the paper and suggests future directions for enhancing sensor autonomous navigation.

2 Literature Review

Many recent studies have explored diverse sensor fusion strategies to enhance obstacle detection, localization, and collision avoidance, particularly in both indoor and outdoor environments.

Early works have focused on LiDAR-only approaches. For instance, Mochurad et al. introduced a method that processes 2D LiDAR data through filtering, clustering, and contour extraction to generate polygonal obstacle representations. While this method is computationally efficient and suitable for real-time applications, its reliance solely on LiDAR means it lacks the semantic understanding needed to classify objects, and it is inherently limited by the single horizontal scan plane [4].

Beyond obstacle detection and localization, 2D LiDAR has also been utilized in other core navigation tasks. Some works have applied LiDAR data directly to generate steering angle commands for AVs, enabling reactive navigation without the need for complex scene understanding. Others have employed the Hector SLAM framework with 2D LiDAR to construct occupancy maps in real time, which are then used for autonomous path planning in indoor environments [5, 6].

To overcome such limitations, several studies have used advanced multi-modal fusion techniques. In [7], a LiDAR-based SLAM approach is enhanced by fusing 3D LiDAR and IMU data via an Adaptive Kalman Filter, which significantly improves localization in outdoor inspection scenarios. Similarly, [8] combines 2D LiDAR with an inclined laser rangefinder to capture low-lying obstacles, which is particularly beneficial in cluttered indoor environments. In contrast, [9] and [10] describe efficient 2D LiDAR-based algorithms that employ median filtering and convex hull computations for obstacle detection and avoidance. Although computationally simple, these methods primarily address static obstacles and lack the dynamic adaptability seen in more advanced systems.

A notable evolution is seen in camera-LiDAR fusion systems. Some studies integrate deep learning-based object detection (e.g., using YOLOv5) with LiDAR depth estimation to achieve precise object localization. In these approaches, camera detections are projected into LiDAR space (or vice versa), and depth is estimated within the detected bounding boxes. This strategy improves spatial accuracy and semantic understanding but often comes at the expense of increased computational complexity and higher hardware costs due to the use of expensive 3D LiDAR sensors [11, 12], and [13].

Global path planning and local obstacle avoidance have also been explored. For example, [14] leverages OpenStreetMaps (OSM) for global planning and integrates a LiDAR-based Naïve-Valley-Path method for local navigation, ensuring road-center following despite mapping inaccuracies. Meanwhile, [15] and [16] focus on collision avoidance through model predictive control (MPC) and structured path planning, offering robust safety guarantees in outdoor scenarios but with limited applicability in indoor settings.

Recent advances in deep reinforcement learning have further broadened the field. In a study by Madhavan et al., a Double Deep Q-Network (DDQN) is employed for sensor fusion and collision avoidance, with a specific emphasis on detecting moving pedestrians. Although promising in dynamic environments, such approaches can be computationally intensive and are often validated only in simulations [17].

Lastly, Phan et al. describe a system for self-driving cars that integrates CSI camera-based lane detection with LiDAR-based obstacle avoidance. Their strategy of running lane and obstacle detection in parallel offers real-time performance but lacks the adaptive, multi-directional collision avoidance required in more complex environments [18].

Building on the multi-sensor integration described in prior work [6], this research aims to further enhance collision avoidance capabilities in dynamic environments. The original system employs an NVIDIA Jetson Xavier NX as its computational core, utilizing YOLOv5 for traffic light detection and OpenCV for lane-following to enable efficient navigation. As an alternative to the study done in [19], where a 3D depth camera was utilized to retrieve both RGB and depth data for collision avoidance, this work distinguishes itself by employing a mid-level sensor fusion approach that projects 2D LiDAR depth onto camera-detected objects and extracts depth data using image-to-angle mapping, combining the cost-effectiveness and efficiency of 2D LiDAR with the semantic information provided by deep learning-based object detection to achieve collision avoidance using rule-based control algorithms. This hybrid strategy is particularly tailored for both dynamic and static, collision-aware navigation in indoor environments, addressing the limitations of existing methods while maintaining real-time performance.

3 Methodology

The methodology integrates YOLOv5 for object detection and 2D LiDAR depth data used for distance estimation, providing real-time awareness of the robot's environment. The system is equipped with OpenCV lane-following capabilities, which ensure path adherence of the robot during navigation.

Figure 1 shows the process pipeline for achieving collision avoidance in our system. It involves data acquisition, sensor fusion, decision-making, and actuation.

3.1 Start Navigation

The robotic platform is set up to facilitate coordination between sensing, computation, and control units. Key components of the perception system are the Intel RealSense D435 depth camera, which provides high-resolution RGB data within a 0.3 m to 3 m range at 30 frames per second, and the 2D RPLiDAR A3, which provides depth data

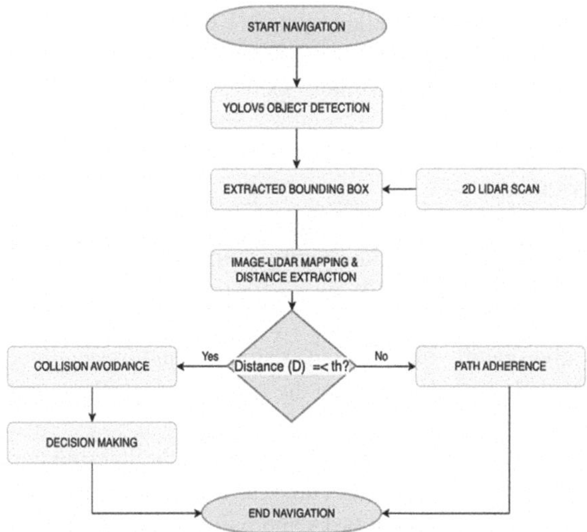

Fig. 1. Process pipeline for the robot's collision avoidance

having an optimal range between 0.4 and 25 m and a scan rate of up to 20 Hz, providing up to 16000 samples per second. The sensors are securely mounted, properly aligned, and calibrated to ensure robust performance in tasks such as lane following and obstacle detection.

The control system comprises an Arduino Mega 2560 microcontroller interfaced with servo motors and a motor driver, enabling precise handling of linear and angular motion commands. Figure 2 shows the complete hardware and wiring layout of the robot.

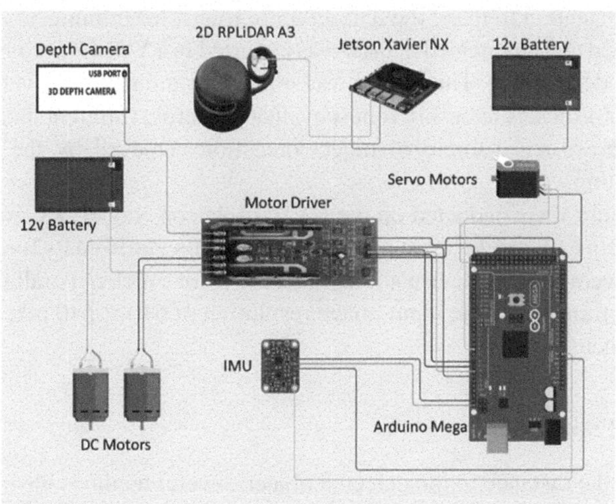

Fig. 2. Schematic diagram of robot hardware components

Computational processing is handled by an NVIDIA Jetson Xavier NX, which executes algorithms and manages system-level control within a Robot Operating System (ROS) framework. To ensure uninterrupted operation, the 12V power supply is divided across two independent battery sources, one serving the Jetson and the other dedicated to the motor driver. This separation enhances electrical stability and reduces the risk of power-related interference.

The system is built on ROS, which provides the framework for integrating the various hardware and software components, facilitating communication and data exchange. It is initialized by launching dedicated ROS nodes for the sensors.

For the camera, the *realsense2_camera* package publishes RGB images to ROS topics, which are subsequently used for lane detection and object detection tasks. Laser scan data is published via /scan topic using the *rplidar_ros* package, providing the scans used for depth estimation.

The Arduino Mega 2560 microcontroller serves as the intermediary responsible for executing low-level motion commands and interfaces with the NVIDIA Jetson NX, which performs high-level perception tasks and navigational decision-making. It generates Pulse Width Modulation (PWM) signals to regulate both the steering servo and drive motors through a motor driver. By converting the Jetson's processed navigation outputs into precise electrical signals, the Arduino ensures responsive and reliable actuation that aligns with real-time sensor feedback.

3.2 Object Detection

The object detection model was trained on a custom dataset created by capturing about 111 RGB images of robots in the indoor environment at different angles and under varying lighting conditions. More of these images were generated through augmentation techniques in Roboflow. The augmentation techniques adapted included rotation, flipping, and translation to make the dataset more robust for training.

The annotated and augmented dataset was exported in a YOLOv5-compatible format and used for model training. The dataset was split into training (70%), validation (20%), and testing (10%) subsets to ensure robust evaluation across different data distributions.

Figure 3 shows an example of object detection achieved by the model during deployment testing.

Model training was conducted on the NVIDIA Jetson Xavier NX, which served as both the processing and deployment platform. The training utilized PyTorch with CUDA acceleration, leveraging the device's integrated GPU for efficient parallel computation. The model was trained with an input image resolution of 640×640 pixels, a batch size of 8, and 50 epochs.

3.3 Distance Estimation

In determining the distance to the detected object, several methods have been tested to find the most accurate distance estimation technique between the robot and the detected objects in the indoor testing environment. Some of these methods include using the RealSense D43i, which estimates depth using stereo vision as clearly detailed in [19].

Fig. 3. Detected object within the camera's optimal range

The 2D LiDAR was used to estimate distance to the detected object using Time of Flight (ToF) LiDAR technology, where laser pulses are emitted at the speed of light and the time taken to reflect is measured. The distance (D) to the object is calculated as:

$$D = \frac{c.t}{2} \tag{1}$$

where c is the speed of light, and t is the time taken for the laser pulse to return.

LiDAR scans a horizontal 360° environment and provides highly accurate real-time spatial mapping of the test environment, making it ideal for autonomous navigation. Due to 2D LiDAR's horizontal scanning nature, it is not accurate for detecting objects like the YOLOv5, as it may miss low-lying objects in its scans.

This work combines object detection using YOLOv5 and distance estimation using the 2D LiDAR. To estimate the distance to an object detected by YOLOv5, the horizontal center (center_x) of the bounding box of the detected object, represented as ($x_{\min}$, $y_{\min}$, $x_{\max}$, $y_{\max}$) is assumed to be the point of interest for depth estimation.

$$\text{center}_x = \frac{x_{\min} + x_{\max}}{2} \tag{2}$$

The detected object's horizontal position in the image can be mapped to an angle in the LiDAR coordinate frame in the robot's forward direction. The image width is normalized to the camera's horizontal field of view (H-FOV). The mapping from pixel space to LiDAR angular space is computed as

$$\theta_{\text{deg}} = \left(\frac{\text{center}_x}{\text{image width}} - 0.5 \right) (\text{H-FOV}) \tag{3}$$

The angle θ_{deg} is converted to radians to be compatible with the LiDAR's scan parameters.

The mapped angle is then used to index into the LiDAR's array of range measurements, with adjustments made for the physical offset between the camera and LiDAR. A small window of surrounding LiDAR points is averaged to improve the robustness and accuracy of the depth estimation.

To improve reliability, window filtering is applied by selecting a small range (±10) of neighboring LiDAR scan indices around the target angle, ensuring that depth estimation remains reliable even when objects fall between discrete scan points.

3.4 Rule-Based Decision-Making and Collision Avoidance

The rule-based decision-making system guides the robot's navigation by combining YOLOv5 object detection with real-time distance estimation from the 2D LiDAR. When an object, such as another robot, is detected ahead, the system calculates its distance. If the object is within a predefined threshold of 0.8 m, the robot halts immediately to prevent a collision. Navigation resumes only after the obstacle moves beyond this threshold, allowing the robot to safely continue along its planned path.

4 Results and Discussion

The experiment was conducted in a controlled laboratory in North Carolina A&T State University using an indoor Quanser mat [20] for self-driving cars, as shown in Fig. 4. All testing was done to mimic a real-world indoor navigation space, providing accurate and scalable results and interpretations.

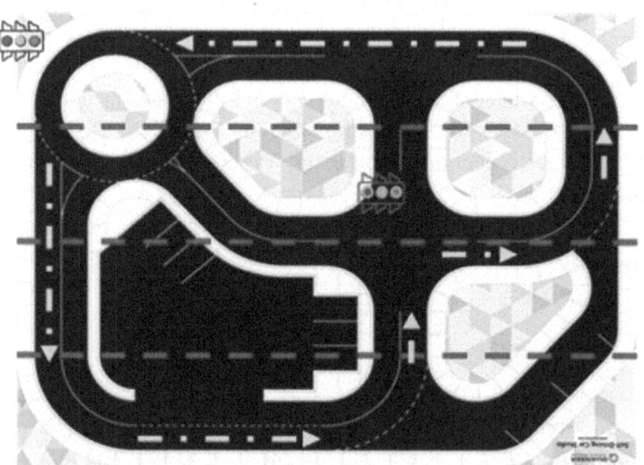

Fig. 4. Quanser mat for indoor navigation

A series of experimental runs are performed, consisting of straight-path and curved-path navigation tasks. For each run, a robot obstacle was introduced at varying positions and distances along the robot's path.

The main performance metrics observed included:

- Distance estimation accuracy
- Collision avoidance success rate with static and dynamic obstacles.

For each run, the robot first detects the obstacle within the camera's FOV. The detection process involves:

1. Captured RGB image resizing to match the model's input dimension of 640 x 640.
2. Resized image parsed into the YOLOv5detection model
3. Model outputs bounding box, class label, and confidence score of the detected object.
4. Extraction of bounding box coordinates to be utilized by the LiDAR for the distance estimation process.

To estimate the distance from the detected object to the robot, the horizontal center of the bounding box is assumed as the point of interest and is mapped to an angle in the LiDAR's coordinate frame, accounting for the camera's field of view and pixel-to-angle conversion with a correction factor for pixel center alignment. Once the angle is determined, it is converted into an index in the LiDAR scan array. To improve accuracy, a small window of nearby scan points is extracted around this index.

From these valid LiDAR range values, two distance measurement methods were tested. In the first instance, the median of the valid LiDAR distances was used to estimate depth. Secondly, a Kalman filter was applied, which recursively combined prior estimates with current measurements to refine the object's distance over time, hence providing more accurate distance readings. The Kalman method was chosen over the median, as it demonstrated better accuracy with an average error of 0.06 m, compared to 0.32 m for the median approach. Table 1 shows the distance accuracy measurements between the two methods.

Table 1. LiDAR Depth Estimation Accuracy

Actual Distance (m)	Median Distance (m)	Kalman Filter Distance (m)
0.60	0.92	0.69
0.80	1.02	0.74
1.00	0.79	0.92
1.50	1.30	1.58

Finally, the estimated distance is published as a ROS message and is subscribed to by the Arduino to enable real-time decision making and coordination with the robot's control system and ultimately achieve collision avoidance.

During testing, the angular calculation was a significant source of error. Small inaccuracies in the offset value or in the computed angle led to incorrect indexing into the LiDAR scan array, causing the system to retrieve distance values that did not correspond to the actual obstacle. These misalignments were especially problematic during curved trajectories, where frequent changes in robot orientation caused the apparent angle of the obstacle to shift quickly, making this method more suitable for static obstacles.

The methodology achieved about a 95% collision avoidance success rate for static obstacles detected, but achieved about 60% success in collision avoidance for dynamic obstacles. Figure 5 shows distance estimation updates during test runs.

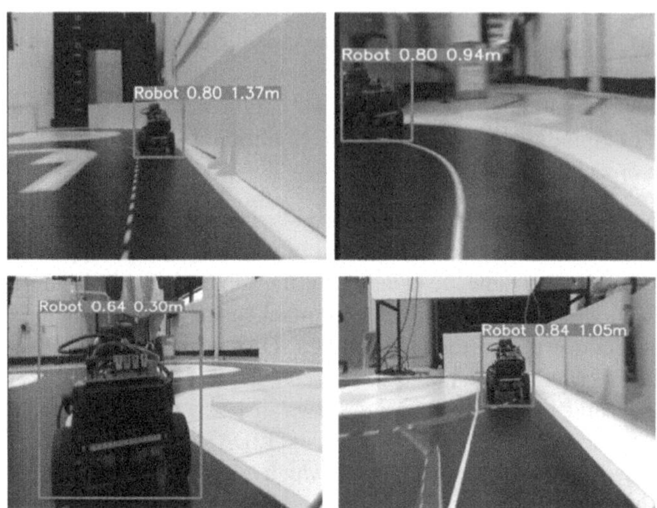

Fig. 5. Detected obstacle robots and their distance updates

Additionally, the rule-based mapping logic added a layer of safe navigation with failsafe mechanisms that ensured error handling. In instances where the LiDAR failed to update distance, the robot relied on the last distance update to make navigation decisions. If the previous distance update was above 1m, the robot continued to move, but if the previous distance update was less than or equal to 1m with a detection status of 1 (indicating the presence of an obstacle), the robot came to a complete halt until a valid distance update was received. These refinements were made to ensure safe navigation of the robot and to improve the system's robustness.

5 Conclusion

This study demonstrates an efficient and scalable framework for collision-aware indoor navigation through the integration of YOLOv5-based object detection, 2D LiDAR-based distance estimation, and rule-based motor control. By leveraging mid-level sensor fusion, the system achieved reliable obstacle detection and avoidance without the need for complex 3D sensors, making it well-suited for cost-sensitive, real-time applications.

Experimental results affirm the system's capability to navigate both static and dynamic environments, with notable success in static scenarios. Performance in dynamic contexts, while promising, revealed limitations in depth update precision and angular indexing, signaling the need for enhancement.

Future work will explore dynamic calibration techniques and transformation strategies, such as Unified Robot Description Format (URDF), to improve angle-mapping accuracy, especially in curved trajectories. Additionally, integrating 3D LiDARs that generate dense point cloud data may provide improved spatial resolution where budget permits. Beyond rule-based planning, adopting learning-based mapping methods offers the potential for greater adaptability, enabling autonomous systems to generalize across diverse operational contexts and dynamically evolving spaces.

Overall, this methodology offers an alternative to traditional navigation strategies by implementing sensor fusion. The reliance on cost-effective hardware further underscores the practicality of the approach for scalable deployments, especially in resource-constrained environments such as small warehouses, labs, and healthcare facilities. This balance between performance and simplicity positions the system as a viable foundation for broader advancements in autonomous indoor robotics.

Acknowledgment. The authors thank the following agencies for their partial support: 1) the United States Department of Commerce (USDOC), Economic Development Administration Good Jobs Challenge Awardee, STEPS4GROWTH (ed22hdq3070099), 2) National Science Foundation's – Engineering Research Center (NSF - ERC) Hybrid Autonomous Manufacturing, Moving from Evolution to Revolution (HAMMER) (Award No.: 2133630).

References

1. Inam, R., Fersman, E., Raizer, K., Souza, R., Nascimento , A., Hata, A.: Safety for automated warehouse exhibiting collaborative robots. In: Safety and Reliability – Safe Societies in a Changing World, London, Taylor & Francis Group, pp. 2021–2028 (2018)
2. Toulkeridou, E., et al.: Safe robot navigation in indoor healthcare spaces. In: IEEE International Conference on Biomedical and Health Informatics, Ioannina (2022)
3. Boulahia, S.Y., Amamra, A., Madi, M.R., Daikh, S.: Early, intermediate and late fusion strategies for robust deep learning-based multimodal action recognition. Mach. Vis. Appl. **32**(121), 1–18 (2021)
4. Mochurad, L., Hladun, Y., Tkachenko, R.: An obstacle-finding approach for autonomous mobile robots using 2D LiDAR data. Big Data and Cognitive Computing **7**(1), 43 (2023)
5. Nenebi, C.T., Acquaah, S., Tang, A., Tucker, K., AlHmoud, I.W., Gokaraju, B.: LiDAR-driven steering command prediction for autonomous vehicles using machine learning. 2025 IEEE Conference on Artificial Intelligence (CAI), Santa Clara, CA, USA, pp. 1560–1567 (2025). https://doi.org/10.1109/CAI64502.2025.00274
6. Vegesana, S., Penumatcha, H., Jaiswal, C., AlHmoud, I.W., Gokaraju, B.: Design and integration of a multi-sensor system for enhanced indoor autonomous navigation. SoutheastCon 2024, Atlanta, GA, USA, pp. 1395–1401 (2024). https://doi.org/10.1109/SoutheastCon52093.2024.10500129
7. Xu, M., Cong, L., Chunming, L., Siyuan, W., Yunong, T.: Autonomous location and obstacle avoidance of inspection robots based on multi-modal information. In: 2024 3rd International Conference on Energy, Power and Electrical Technology (ICEPET), Chengu (2024)
8. Ren Yee, P.D., Pinrath, N., Matsuhira, N.: Autonomous mobile robot navigation using 2D LiDAR and inclined laser rangefinder to avoid a lower object. In: 020 59th Annual Conference of the Society of Instrument and Control Engineers of Japan (SICE), Chiang Mai (2020)
9. de Sousa Bezerra, C.D., Reles Viera, F.H., Queiroz Carneiro, D.P.: Autonomous robotic navigation approach using deep q-network late fusion and people detection-based collision avoidance. Applied Sciences **13**(22) (2023)

10. Mounabhargav, P., Agrawal, P.: Camera and LiDAR integration for lane-following and obstacle avoidance in self-driving cars. In: International Conference on Emerging Smart Computing and Informatics (ESCI), Pune (2025)
11. Kotur, M., Lukic, N., Krunic, M., Lukac, Z.: Camera and LiDAR sensor fusion for 3d object tracking in a collision avoidance system. in Zooming Innovation in Consumer Technologies Conference (ZINC), Novi Sad (2021)
12. Thakur, A., Rajalakshmi, P.: LiDAR and camera raw data sensor fusion in real-time for obstacle detection. In: IEEE Sensors Applications Symposium (SAS), Ottawa (2023)
13. Zhang, Y., Liu, Y., Liu, S., Lang, W., Wang, C., Wang, K.: Multimodal perception for indoor mobile robotics navigation and safe manipulation. IEEE Transactions on Cognitive and Developmental Systems **1**(1), 1–13 (2024)
14. Wei, P., Cagle, L., Reza, T., Ball, J., Gafford, J.: LiDAR and camera detection fusion in a real-time industrial multi-sensor collision avoidance system. Electronics **7**(6), 1–32 (2018)
15. Svyatov, K., Khairullin, I.: Obstacle avoidance method with local semantic map generation for self-driving cars. In: International Russian Smart Industry Conference (SmartIndustryCon), Sochi (2024)
16. Ghorpade, D., Thakare, A.D., Phode, S.: Obstacle detection and avoidance algorithm for autonomous mobile robot using 2D LiDAR. In: International Conference on Computing, Communication, Control and Automation, Pune (2017)
17. Madhavan, T., Adharsh, M.: Obstacle detection and obstacle avoidance algorithm based on 2-D RPLiDAR. In: International Conference on Computer Communication and Informatics (ICCCI), Coimbatore (2019)
18. Phan, T.-D., Duong, M.-T., Nguyen, C.-T., Ly, H.-P.L.M.-H.: Sensor fusion of camera and 2D LiDAR for self-driving automobile in obstacle avoidance scenarios. in International Workshop on Intelligent Systems (IWIS), Ulsan (2022)
19. Acquaah, S., Nenebi, C., Tucker, K., AlHmoud, I.W., Gokaraju, B.: Integrating deep planning-based object detection with 3D-depth camera for collision avoidance in indoor robotics navigation. SoutheastCon 2025, Concord, NC, USA, pp. 989–994 (2025). https://doi.org/10.1109/SoutheastCon56624.2025.10971634
20. "Self-Driving Car Studio". Quanser Inc. https://www.quanser.com/

Dark Channel Prior Infused All-in-One Dehazing Network (DCPI-AODNet) for Single Image Dehazing

Pranjal Saxena[1], Teena Sharma[1(✉)], Nishchal K. Verma[2], Al Salour[3], and Shantaram Vasikarla[4]

[1] Indian Institute of Technology Guwahati, Guwahati, India
{p.saxena,teena}@iitg.ac.in

[2] Indian Institute of Technology Kanpur, Kanpur, India
nishchal@iitk.ac.in

[3] Boeing Research and Technology at The Boeing Company, Arlington, TX, USA
al.salour@boeing.com

[4] California State University, Northridge, Northridge, CA, USA

Abstract. Fog and smog often render scene details invisible, making computer-vision tasks like object detection and recognition difficult. Traditional dehazing methods rely on direct estimation of transmission maps and atmospheric light, which is both noise-sensitive and computationally costly. Dark Channel Prior (DCP) relieves these requirements by leveraging low-intensity patches to identify thick haze, but its performance degrades in heterogeneously hazed scenes. To improve its results, this paper proposes a *Dark Channel Prior Infused All-in-One Dehazing Network (DCPI-AODNet).* With the incorporation of DCP on an adapted All-in-One Dehazing Network (AOD-Net) in addition to the RGB input, the proposed network is able to learn more accurate transmission patterns, especially in complex scenes where haze displays complicated and non-homogeneous patterns. In contrast to traditional pipelines, the modified AOD-Net dispenses with independent atmospheric light and transmission inference, providing end-to-end dehazed results via a light-weight convolutional architecture conducive to real-time use. Combining DCP guidance maintains the statistical advantages of conventional priors with the data-driven flexibility of deep learning. Experimental assessments yield consistently sharper textures, more accurate colors, and reduced halo artifacts compared to baseline AOD-Net and single-matting DCP, showing enhanced visual quality under diverse fog and smog environments. Quantitative performance gains in peak signal-to-noise ratio and structural similarity also confirm these subjective improvements, making the model an effective solution for computer-vision tasks.

Keywords: Single image dehazing · AOD-Net · Dark channel prior

F. Tanner and J. Irvine (Eds.): AIPR 2025, LNCS 16446, pp. 387–402, 2026.
https://doi.org/10.1007/978-3-032-18474-0_27

1 Introduction

Dehazing refers to the process of removing haze from photographs to improve their quality, clarity, and information. Haze, resulting from particles such as dust, smoke, and suspended water droplets in the air, scatters and absorbs light, producing images of low visibility and details. Scattering minimizes contrast, blurs fine details, and alters the color of objects within the picture, causing the image to be washed out and indistinct. The prevalence of haze is substantial enough to affect several uses, such as object detection, image recognition, scene understanding, etc. [1–10], thus making dehazing an important process for image clarity and correctness in several computer vision tasks. In particular, dehazing is critical in uses like autonomous driving, surveillance, and outdoor scene understanding, where clear vision is necessary for perceiving the environment and facilitating making informed decisions.

1.1 Related Work

The early research in dehazing of images started with Narasimhan and Nayar's work in the field of atmospheric optics [11]. They examined the problems created by haze in outdoor images and recognized that atmospheric scattering could be represented by two important factors: attenuation and airlight. Their model suggested that haze can be understood as the result of scattering caused by atmospheric particles, which reduces the contrast and alters the color fidelity of the observed image. The scattering process varies spatially with the depth of the scene, which led to the development of algorithms that attempted to recover scene depth and the transmission of light through the haze. Narasimhan and Nayar's model demonstrated how atmospheric scattering could provide depth cues, a valuable insight for computer vision systems under poor weather conditions. However, their methods required multiple images or additional scene information, limiting their practical application in real-time scenarios.

The following important contribution was the introduction of the Dark Channel Prior (DCP) approach by He *et al.* in 2009 [12]. DCP took advantage of the fact that, in outdoor haze-free images, local image patches typically include pixels with extremely low intensities in at least one color channel (red, green, or blue). By assuming that such pixels are generally haze-unchanged, the algorithm estimates the haze thickness and reconstructs the scene's radiance by calculating a transmission map. Although DCP was very successful in dealing with most dehazing cases, it had limitations in some areas, such as the sky, where haze behavior doesn't follow model assumptions. Moreover, DCP's dependency on soft matting for proper transmission estimation made it computationally costly, particularly for denser images of haze.

Another approach in the paper "Adaptive Interval Type-2 Fuzzy Filter: An AI Agent for Handling Uncertainties to Preserve Image Naturalness" by Sharma and Verma introduces an AI-driven solution for enhancing images while preserving their natural appearance [13]. By using Type-2 fuzzy logic [14,15], the method effectively handles uncertainties in homogeneous regions and at edges, which are common in image processing tasks. The filter improves illumination and reflectance estimation, resulting in enhanced images that retain visual realism. The proposed approach outperforms traditional methods in both qualitative and quantitative measures, making it suitable for applications like image dehazing, vehicle tracking, and gradient estimation. Similarly, another fuzzy-based approach was introduced for image dehazing in [16].

With the increasing power and efficiency of deep learning-based solutions, several methodologies have been discovered by the researchers in order to improve and create more efficient and precise dehazing solutions [17–20].

Boyi Li *et al.*'s development of the All-in-One Dehazing Network (AOD-Net) [17] in 2017 was a significant step towards the deep learning-based solutions, where the drawback of DCP was overcome by merging both transmission and atmospheric map into a single end-to-end Convolutional Neural Network (CNN). Due to its light weight, it also enabled real-time dehazing and performed better than most of the non-parametric models. In 2019, another breakthrough was made when Wang *et al.* presented the Atmospheric Illumination Prior Network (AIPNet). This model identified the impact on the luminance channel in the YCrCb color space. By focusing on this, they developed a model that enhanced the clarity and contrast while preserving color integrity. This model performed really well, especially in the conditions with changing conditions [18]. Understanding the success of these models, Sharma *et al.* in 2020 built the Compact Single Image Dehazing Network (CSIDNet). Due to the simplistic structure of this model, having just three convolutional layers, it performed better than most of the state-of-the-art models in terms of Peak Signal to Noise Ratio (PSNR) and Structural Similarity (SSIM) index [19]. Furthermore, innovations such as the Feature Fusion Attention Network (FFA-Net) by Qin et al. (2020) utilized the feature fusion method in order to manage the haze of mixed densities. It was able to successfully improve the quality of dehazed images [20]. The latest research in this field involves the exploration of self-supervised dehazing models [21, 22], where the models, on their own, are able to dehaze without much training, as this will help in saving training time. The shift towards the unsupervised and self-supervised solutions can especially help in cases where the annotated training dataset is small.

To summarize, the field of image dehazing has seen many significant enhancements where we have witnessed a shift from non-parametric or physics-based models to more advanced solutions involving deep neural networks, which not only have increased the efficiency and speed but also helped in employing these solutions in real time. The ongoing research will help to further improve the usability of these dehazing solutions.

1.2 Contributions

The All-in-One Dehazing Network (AOD-Net) [17] has achieved excellent performance in dehazing under diverse settings. Nonetheless, in spite of its achievements, there are also some long-standing difficulties that emerge in some cases. One of the primary problems lies in non-sky or indoor scenarios, in which the haze density can differ extensively from part to part and thus lead to an unbalanced distribution of haze in the scene. The conventional AOD-Net approach usually finds it difficult to cope with such intricate variations in haze density, particularly in cases where haze is thicker in areas compared to others. The difficulty is more pronounced in indoor scenes, where the lighting and fog variations are more intricate compared to outdoor scenes.

In order to overcome these challenges and improve the performance of AOD-Net, this paper puts forward a new modification that embeds the Dark Channel Prior (DCP) [12] into the modified architecture of AOD-Net directly. The Dark Channel Prior, a conventional unsupervised method in image dehazing, performs especially well in detecting hazing in non-sky areas, where the haziness tends to be thicker. This is because DCP exploits the fact that in most outdoor non-hazy images, at least one color channel (blue, green, or red) will have low pixel intensity values within a local image patch. In images where there is haze, these low pixel intensity patches are all the more apparent, thus easier to detect and estimate the amount of haze in such patches. DCP's capacity to detect haze using such low pixel intensity areas enables more precise transmission map estimation, especially in non-sky and indoor scenarios.

Using DCP in the AOD-Net model enhances its capability of precisely estimating transmission maps, especially in scenarios with more irregular or complex haze. The original AOD-Net is based on a deep learning method to estimate atmospheric light and haze all over the scene, yet it may be challenged when haze densities change substantially, especially in non-sky or indoor areas. DCP incorporated into AOD-Net fills the gap, taking advantage of traditional DCP's strength to enhance the precision of transmission map estimation, which is decisive for successful haze removal. Consequently, this new hybrid method, which leverages the strength of deep learning and the established efficacy of the DCP, enables faster and more precise dehazing results, even under difficult indoor or non-sky environments.

The proposed novel model, named "DCP Infused All-in-One Dehazing Network (DCPI-AODNet)", utilizes the benefits of both the deep learning method and unsupervised prior-based method for single image dehazing. AOD-Net's deep learning module ensures the model is computationally light and able to process images in real-time, which is indispensable for many computer vision tasks, including autonomous vehicles, surveillance, and outdoor navigation. At the same time, the addition of DCP enhances the model to better recognize and suppress haze, especially in areas where deep learning algorithms are insufficient to precisely identify haze, for example, very obscured indoor scenes or areas with mixed densities of haze.

In further sections, the paper describes the relevant background 2, the proposed DCPI-AODNet model 3, experimental results 4, and conclusions 5.

2 Background

This section gives the required background for the proposed work, including the hazy image formation model [11], the DCP method [12], and the AOD-Net [17].

2.1 Hazy Image Formation Model

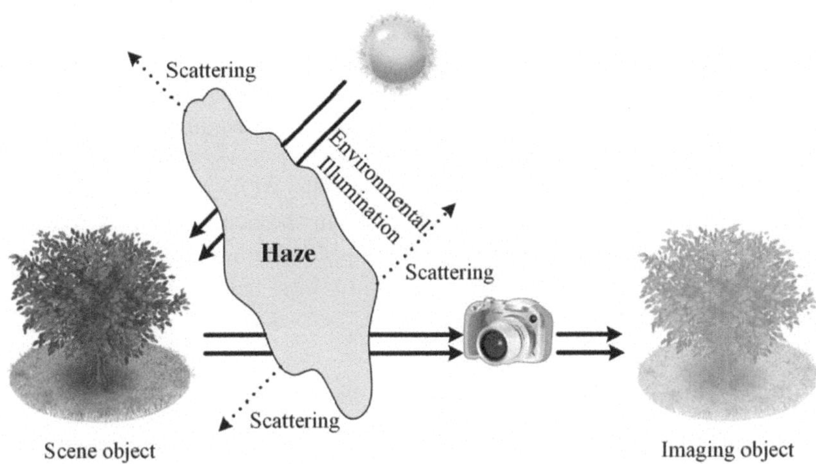

Fig. 1. Atmospheric scattering model in hazy weather [18].

At the core of many dehazing methods lies a fundamental equation, rooted in the atmospheric scattering model, which explains how haze impacts an image. This model is built upon the physical principles of light scattering and absorption, and can be expressed mathematically as follows:

$$I_{\mathrm{obs}}(u) = I_{\mathrm{scene}}(u) \cdot \tau_{\mathrm{mod}}(u) + L_{\mathrm{atm}} \cdot (1 - \tau_{\mathrm{mod}}(u)), \tag{1}$$

where,

- $I_{\mathrm{obs}}(u)$ represents the observed intensity of the hazy image at pixel u,
- $I_{\mathrm{scene}}(u)$ denotes the true, haze-free scene radiance that is required to be recovered,
- $\tau_{\mathrm{mod}}(u)$ is the modified transmission map, representing the fraction of light that reaches the camera after passing through haze, and
- L_{atm} is the global atmospheric light, assumed to remain constant throughout the image [11].

Figure 1 visually depicts the relationship described in (1). This model breaks down the observed hazy image into two major components: the scene radiance that is directly transmitted and the airlight, which is the scattered light added to the image due to atmospheric particles. This transmission map $\tau_{\mathrm{mod}}(u)$ can be calculated by considering the scene's depth:

$$\tau_{\mathrm{mod}}(u) = e^{-a \cdot D_{\mathrm{scene}}(u)}, \tag{2}$$

where,

- a is the scattering coefficient that indicates the density of the haze and
- $D_{\text{scene}}(u)$ represents the depth of the scene at a pixel u.

This equation serves as the base model for both kinds of models, that is, traditional and deep learning. It helps in estimating the transmission map and atmospheric light. Traditional methods like DCP [12] use the information that in certain regions of a haze-free image, there are some pixels with low intensity named *Dark Channels*, which are used in order to estimate the transmission map.

However, in deep learning-based approaches like AOD-Net [17], this formula is modified and uses the modified formula to train the neural network to directly predict the dehazed image. These models are able to adapt to different weather conditions and give optimal results. Moreover, these can be used in real-world applications.

2.2 Dark Channel Prior Method

Dark Channel Prior (DCP) is one of the most efficient ways of single-image dehazing. The primary finding that at least one color channel will show a minimal intensity value or near-zero pixel intensity [12] in many non-sky regions of outdoor images serves as the foundation for the DCP method. The idea of the "dark channel", which is defined as:

$$D_{\text{dark}}(u) = \min_{k \in \{R,G,B\}} \left(\min_{v \in \Omega(u)} I_k(v) \right), \tag{3}$$

where,

- $\Omega(u)$ a local patch centered at pixel u,
- $I_k(v)$ is the intensity of color channel k, and
- $D_{\text{dark}}(u)$ is the dark channel at pixel location u.

This dark channel helps in estimating the medium transmission map $\tau_{\text{mod}}(u)$, which the simplified haze model can roughly represent:

$$\tau_{\text{mod}}(u) = 1 - \alpha \min_k \left(\min_{v \in \Omega(u)} \frac{I_k(v)}{L_k} \right), \tag{4}$$

where,

- α is a constant factor (typically slightly less than 1) to maintain some natural haze effects for depth perception and
- L_k is the global atmospheric light in channel k.

Although DCP works well for enhancing image visibility and determining depth, it has trouble processing areas of the sky where pixel intensities are constant. Furthermore, in order to refine the transmission map, DCP frequently calls for a soft matting technique, which can result in significant computational costs.

2.3 All-in-One Dehazing Network

By resolving numerous issues with conventional techniques like DCP, the All-in-One Dehazing Network (AOD-Net) marks a significant advancement in the field of image dehazing. AOD-Net does not require the estimation of transmission maps and atmospheric light separately because it uses a Convolutional Neural Network (CNN) to produce dehazed images straight from a hazy input. It determines both the ideal transmission map and atmospheric light into a single model, which makes it an end-to-end method of dehazing. The following formula governs AOD-Net:

$$I_{\text{scene}}(u) = F_{\text{learned}}(u) \cdot I_{\text{obs}}(u) - F_{\text{learned}}(u) + b, \quad (5)$$

where,

- b refers to the learned bias that refines the output more and
- $F_{\text{learned}}(u)$ refers to the learned transmission-atmospheric function.

The RESIDE [23] dataset has been used for the training of this model, which is a benchmark dataset, and thus it makes it more capable than conventional methods. This model can also work in real-time, which makes it suitable for applications like autonomous driving [17]. AOD-Net performs well in comparison to DCP under conditions with complex lighting and haze densities. For example, indoor spaces or non-sky regions.

The next section discusses the proposed DCPI-AODNet using the aforementioned backgrounds.

3 Proposed DCPI-AODNet

This section discusses the *Dark Channel Prior Infused All-in-One Dehazing Network (DCPI-AODNet)*, an advanced deep learning model designed to enhance image dehazing further. This method combines *Dark Channel Prior (DCP)* with the *All-in-One Dehazing Network (AOD-Net)* to provide a more reliable dehazing solution, particularly in indoor or non-sky regions.

3.1 Overview

DCPI-AODNet is a fusion of traditional and deep learning techniques, aiming to improve image dehazing performance. The combination of DCP and AOD-Net allows it to handle both learned and prior knowledge for better results. The structure of *DCPI-AODNet* uses the fundamental idea of AOD-Net, where the transmission map and atmospheric light are streamlined and learned by the CNN to predict the haze-free image. The addition of the dark channel mechanism refines the results even further.

AOD-Net Core Mechanism. The atmospheric light, true scene radiance, and hazy observed image are related using the atmospheric scattering model [11]:

$$I_{\text{obs}}(u) = I_{\text{scene}}(u) \cdot \tau_{\text{mod}}(u) + L_{\text{atm}} \cdot (1 - \tau_{\text{mod}}(u)), \tag{6}$$

where,

- $I_{\text{obs}}(u)$: The observed hazy image at pixel u,
- $I_{\text{scene}}(u)$: The haze-free (true) scene radiance,
- $\tau_{\text{mod}}(u)$: The modified transmission map, showing how much light reaches the camera without scattering, and
- L_{atm}: The global atmospheric light.

In AOD-Net, the transmission map $\tau_{\text{mod}}(u)$ and atmospheric light L_{atm} are learned together through a function $F_{\text{learned}}(u)$, which is optimized using a deep neural network. The final dehazed image $I_{\text{scene}}(u)$ is calculated as follows:

$$I_{\text{scene}}(u) = F_{\text{learned}}(u) \cdot I_{\text{obs}}(u) - F_{\text{learned}}(u) + b, \tag{7}$$

where,

- $F_{\text{learned}}(u)$ represents the learned transmission-atmospheric light function and
- b is a bias term to refine the output.

Integrating the Dark Channel Prior. The Dark Channel Prior (DCP), introduced by Kaiming He *et al.*, is a classical dehazing technique that estimates the transmission map $\tau_{\text{mod}}(u)$. It is based on the observation that, in most non-sky patches of outdoor images, at least one color channel exhibits minimal intensity in haze-free regions. The dark channel is calculated as follows:

$$D_{\text{dark}}(u) = \min_{k \in \{R,G,B\}} \left(\min_{v \in \Omega(u)} I_k(v) \right), \tag{8}$$

where,

- $D_{\text{dark}}(u)$: The dark channel at pixel location u,
- $I_k(v)$: The intensity in color channel k, and
- $\Omega(u)$: A local patch centered at pixel u.

Estimating Transmission Using DCP. DCP helps estimate the medium transmission $\tau_{\text{mod}}(u)$ by identifying haze-dense regions, i.e., areas where the pixel intensity in at least one channel is low. This is expressed as:

$$\tau_{\text{mod}}(u) = 1 - \alpha \min_k \left(\min_{v \in \Omega(u)} \frac{I_k(v)}{L_k} \right), \tag{9}$$

where,

- L_k: The global atmospheric light in channel k and
- α: A constant factor (typically just under 1) to retain some haze for natural depth perception.

3.2 Dark Channel Prior Infused All-in-One Dehazing Network

In the *Dark Channel Prior Infused All-in-One Dehazing Network (DCP-IDN)*, the DCP mechanism is incorporated into the model by using the *dark channel* as an additional input feature for estimating the transmission map. This fusion allows the network to leverage both learned features from the CNN and the traditional DCP prior, combining the advantages of both approaches.

How DCPI-AODNet Functions. The *DCPI-AODNet* model integrates the strengths of AOD-Net and DCP in the following way:

1. *CNN Layers for Feature Extraction*: The network consists of several convolutional layers that learn key features from the input image. These layers progressively capture both local and global features of the haze and scene.
2. *DCP as an Additional Input*: In addition to CNN-learned features, the DCP is computed for each input image and fed as an additional input into the network. The dark channel helps estimate the transmission map $\tau_{\text{mod}}(u)$, especially in areas with dense haze.
3. *Unified Estimation of Transmission and Light*: The network learns the combined transmission-atmospheric light function $F_{\text{learned}}(u)$, integrating both the CNN-learned features and the dark channel prior to produce a high-quality dehazed image.

Architecture of DCPI-AODNet. The architecture of the proposed *DCPI-AODNet*, as shown in Fig. 2, illustrates how the DCP is integrated with AOD-Net to enhance the dehazing process. In the model shown in the figure, the fused input refers to the concatenated input comprising of both the RGB Channels and dark channel which is later sent to the model comprising of 6 convolutional layers having Rectified Linear Unit (ReLU) activation function and multiple concatenation stages where these act as skip connections that helps in the estimation of the $F_{\text{learned}}(u)$ output which is utilized to generate the end-to-end image by combining with the hazy input as shown in (7).

In the further section, experimental results are presented to showcase the performance comparison of the proposed DCPI-AODNet.

Table 1. Average performance comparison on the Indoor SOTS dataset from the RESIDE dataset [23,24].

Performance Metric	AOD-Net [17]	DCPI-AODNet
PSNR [25]	19.05	20.12
SSIM [26]	0.8049	0.8101

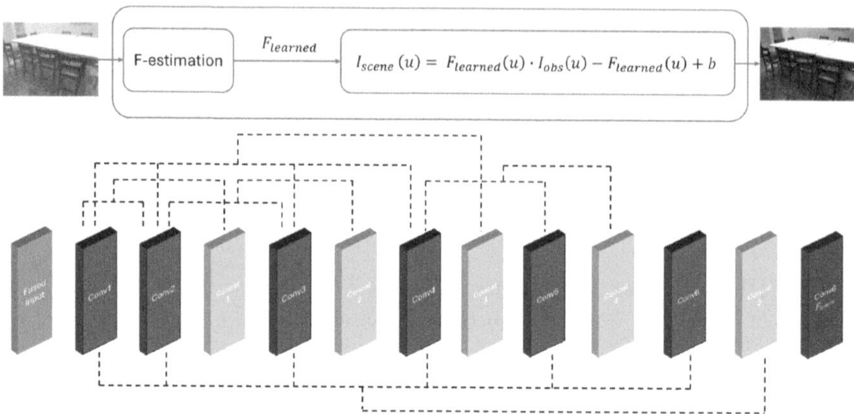

Fig. 2. DCPI-AODNet architecture. AOD-Net infused with dark channel prior. Here, dotted lines indicate inter-layer connections.

Table 2. Performance comparison on the Indoor SOTS from the RESIDE dataset [23,24] for sample images shown in Figs. 3, 4, 5, and 6.

Image	Performance Metric	AOD-Net [17]	Proposed DCPI-AODNet
Sample Image 1	PSNR [25]	15.66	17.39
	SSIM [26]	0.6899	0.7205
Sample Image 2	PSNR [25]	14.93	15.48
	SSIM [26]	0.7688	0.7831
Sample Image 3	PSNR [25]	15.97	17.71
	SSIM [26]	0.5849	0.6264
Sample Image 4	PSNR [25]	18.04	18.76
	SSIM [26]	0.8764	0.8846

Fig. 3. Sample Result 1. **From left to right:** Comparison between hazy inputs and their dehazed outputs using AOD-Net and DCPI-AODNet.

Fig. 4. Sample Result 2. **From left to right:** Comparison between hazy inputs and their dehazed outputs using AOD-Net and DCPI-AODNet.

Fig. 5. Sample Result 3. **From left to right:** Comparison between hazy inputs and their dehazed outputs using AOD-Net and DCPI-AODNet.

Fig. 6. Sample Result 4. **From left to right:** Comparison between hazy inputs and their dehazed outputs using AOD-Net and DCPI-AODNet.

4 Experimental Results

This section provides further details about the system, architecture parameters, dataset, performance metrics, and benchmark method used for experiments. The tests were conducted on a Windows 10 64-bit Operating System using an Intel(R) Core(TM) i7-8550U CPU.

4.1 Parameter Settings

The transmission map plays a very important role in the image restoration process, and this served as the foundation for the DCPI-AODNet model. Herein, an adaptive approach is used to restore the true transmission map. The proposed method first tries to create several transmission maps with different parameters and then chooses the one that gives the best results. In the presented approach, various parameters such as different window sizes and transmission map parameters, represented by the symbols ϕ and θ, were used in order to generate the best transmission map. Multiple candidates were created for every test image, and then a score based on standard deviation was calculated for the dehazed image. This model then uses the transmission map that had the highest standard deviation, as it is the best transmission map.

4.2 Datasets

The RESIDE dataset [23,24] is used, and the model was trained on the Indoor Training Set (ITS) from the RESIDE dataset. The tests are conducted on the Synthetic Objective Testing Set (SOTS) of the RESIDE dataset. The ITS consists of 13,990 hazy images with their haze-free counterparts for training, and SOTS consists of 500 hazy images with their haze-free counterparts for testing.

4.3 Performance Metrics

For evaluating the efficiency quantitatively, two key performance metrics were targeted: Peak Signal-to-Noise Ratio (PSNR) [25] and Structural Similarity Index (SSIM) [26].

The Peak Signal-to-Noise Ratio (PSNR) is a commonly used metric to assess the quality of reconstructed or processed images, particularly for tasks like image compression and dehazing. PSNR measures the difference between the original and the processed images, and it is expressed in decibels (dB). Higher PSNR values indicate better image quality, meaning the processed image is closer to the original image. PSNR is defined as:

$$\mathrm{PSNR} = 10 \cdot \log_{10}\left(\frac{L_{\max}^2}{\mathrm{MSE}}\right), \tag{10}$$

where,

- $L_{\max}$ represents the maximum possible pixel intensity value of the image. For an 8-bit image, this is 255. In general, $L_{\max}$ corresponds to the highest value a pixel can have in the image.
- MSE represents the mean squared error.

Mean Squared Error (MSE) is calculated as:

$$\mathrm{MSE} = \frac{1}{M \times N}\sum_{i=1}^{M}\sum_{j=1}^{N}\left[I_{\mathrm{orig}}(i,j) - I_{\mathrm{dehazed}}(i,j)\right]^2, \tag{11}$$

where,

- $I_{\mathrm{orig}}(i,j)$ and $I_{\mathrm{dehazed}}(i,j)$ are the pixel values of the original and dehazed images, respectively, at the location (i,j) and

- M and N represent the image dimensions (height and width).

The MSE value quantifies the average error between the original and processed images. A lower MSE corresponds to a smaller difference, and thus a higher PSNR, which indicates better image quality.

The Structural Similarity Index (SSIM) is a perceptual metric that quantifies the similarity between two images by taking into account structural information, luminance, and texture. Unlike PSNR, which relies on pixel-wise differences and may not correlate well with human visual perception, SSIM is designed to mimic the way the human visual system perceives image quality. SSIM focuses on image structures rather than individual pixel differences, making it a more meaningful metric for visual quality assessment. The SSIM formula is defined as:

$$\mathrm{SSIM}(X,Y) = \frac{(2\alpha_X\alpha_Y + \lambda_1)(2\delta_{XY} + \lambda_2)}{(\alpha_X^2 + \alpha_Y^2 + \lambda_1)(\delta_X^2 + \delta_Y^2 + \lambda_2)}, \tag{12}$$

where,

- α_X and α_Y are the average pixel values of images X (the original image) and Y (the processed image), respectively. They represent the luminance of the images,
- δ_X^2 and δ_Y^2 are the variances of images X and Y, which describe the contrast of the images,
- δ_{XY} is the covariance between images X and Y, which measures the degree to which the images vary together, and
- λ_1 and λ_2 are small constants added to avoid division by zero and to stabilize the computation in cases of extreme values of the mean or variance.

The SSIM index ranges from -1 to $+1$, where:

- SSIM $= 1$ indicates that the two images are identical in structure, luminance, and texture
- SSIM $= -1$ indicates that the two images are completely dissimilar, and
- Values closer to 1 indicate higher similarity, while values closer to -1 indicate greater dissimilarity.

The SSIM index provides a more holistic evaluation of image quality by considering human visual perception. Unlike PSNR, which may give high values for images with small pixel-wise differences, SSIM can reveal perceptible differences in structure and texture that might not be captured by traditional pixel-based metrics.

4.4 Discussions

Table 1 shows the average PSNR and SSIM values obtained on 500 SOTS images of the RESIDE dataset using the benchmarked AOD-Net method and the proposed DCPI-AODNet. The PSNR and SSIM values clearly depict that the proposed DCPI-AODNet outperforms AOD-Net on the indoor SOTS by approximately 6% in terms of PSNR and approximately 0.7% improvement in the SSIM.

Though improvement in the value of SSIM is comparable (not much difference), improvement in the PSNR, along with maintaining SSIM value comparable, clearly depicts how the proposed DCPI-AODNet is capable of improving the performance, along with maintaining the image information content intact.

For visual comparison, 4 sample hazy images from the SOTS images of the RESIDE dataset are randomly chosen. These hazy images are dehazed using benchmarked AOD-Net and proposed DCPI-AODNet. The visual comparisons are shown in Figs. 3, 4, 5, and 6. These visual comparisons clearly depict how the proposed DCPI-AODNet is capable of eliminating haze from the image in comparison to the benchmarked AOD-Net, where a little whitish appearance of haze is still clearly visible.

Table 2 tabulates the PSNR and SSIM values for performance comparison between benchmarked AOD-Net and the proposed DCPI-AODNet. In the *Sample Image 1* (Fig. 3), there has been an improvement of 11% in PSNR and 4% in SSIM. In the *Sample Image 2* (Fig. 4), there is an improvement of 3% in PSNR and 2.5% in SSIM. The *Sample Image 3* (Fig. 5) shows an improvement of 11% in PSNR and 7% in SSIM, and lastly, the *Sample Image 4* (Fig. 6) shows an improvement of 4% and 1% in PSNR and SSIM, respectively.

With visual and quantitative analyses shown in tables and figures above, it can be clearly stated that the results are consistent, confirming the improvement from the benchmarked model by leveraging the benefits of using the combination of a prior-based method infused in a deep learning model for single-image dehazing in applications to indoor environments.

5 Conclusions

In this paper, a novel Dark Channel Prior Infused AODNet, acronymed as DCPI-AODNet, has been presented. The proposed DCPI-AODNet is inspired by the performance and efficiency of AOD-Net and leverages the power of the dark channel prior method for hazy images of the indoor environment. Fusing the RGB channels with the dark channel and adding convolutional layers in the architecture made a significant improvement in the performance in comparison to the benchmarked AOD-Net in terms of visual and quantitative analyses observed using peak signal to noise ratio and structural similarity index.

Though a significant improvement has been reported using the proposed DCPI-AODNet, the next potential steps involve developing an end-to-end single-image dehazing model to improve the overall performance by handling the noise incurred during image enhancement. Also, further potential scope is to discover end-to-end solutions for the indoor and outdoor images as well, giving real-time and efficient performance for a wide range of applications.

References

1. Sharma, T., Verma, N.K.: Single image dehazing and non-uniform illumination enhancement: a Z-score approach. SN Comput. Sci. **2**(6), 1–15 (2021). https://doi.org/10.1007/s42979-021-00912-1

2. Bhola, A., Sharma, T., Verma, N.K.: DCNet: Dark Channel NETwork for single image dehazing. Mach. Vis. Appl. **32**(62), 1–11 (2021). https://doi.org/10.1007/s00138-021-01173-x
3. Agrawal, A., Sharma, T., Verma, N.K., Vasikarla, S.: Modified transmission map function with hyperparameter tuning for single image dehazing. In: 15th IEEE Annual Ubiquitous Computing, Electronics and Mobile Communication Conference (UEMCON), IBM T.J. Watson Research Center, New York, USA (2024) (Accepted and Presented)
4. Agrawal, I., Sharma, T., Verma, N.K.: Low-light image restoration using dehazing-based inverted illumination map enhancement. In: Castillo, O., Bera, U.K., Jana, D.K. (eds.) Applied Mathematics and Computational Intelligence (ICAMCI-2020), Springer Proc. Math. Stat., vol. 8194, pp. 135–145. Springer, India (2020). https://doi.org/10.1007/978-981-19-8194-4_12
5. Sharma, T., Nalla, B.T., Verma, N.K., Vasikarla, S.: FR-HDNet: faster RCNN based haze detection network for image dehazing. In: 2022 IEEE Applied Imagery Pattern Recognition Workshop (AIPR), Washington, DC, USA (2022) (Accepted and Presented)
6. Sharma, T., Shah, T., Verma, N.K., Vasikarla, S.: A review on image dehazing algorithms for vision based applications in outdoor environment. In: 2020 IEEE Applied Imagery Pattern Recognition Workshop (AIPR), Washington, DC, USA (2020). https://doi.org/10.1109/AIPR50011.2020.9425261
7. Sharma, T., Agrawal, I., Verma, N.K.: Transmission map estimation function to prevent over-saturation in single image dehazing. In: International Conference on Deep Learning, Artificial Intelligence and Robotics (ICDLAIR 2019), MNIT, Jaipur, India, pp. 144–152 (2019). https://doi.org/10.1007/978-3-030-67187-7_16
8. Sinha, A., Sharma, T., Agrawal, P., Verma, N.K.: Modified transmission map estimation with gradient domain guided image filtering for single image dehazing. In: ARMS 2021: International Conference on Aerospace and Defence Related Mechanisms, pp. 567–575. Springer, India (2021) (Accepted)
9. Nalla, B.T., Sharma, T., Verma, N.K., Sahoo, S.R.: Image dehazing for object recognition using faster RCNN. In: 2018 International Joint Conference on Neural Networks (IJCNN), Rio de Janeiro, Brazil, pp. 1–7 (2018). https://doi.org/10.1109/IJCNN.2018.8489280
10. Dua, H., Sharma, T., Agrawal, P., Verma, N.K.: An efficient algorithm for image haze removal in outdoor environment. In: International Conference on Computational Intelligence: Theories, Applications and Future Directions (ICCI-2017). Springer Proc. Math. Stat., vol. II, pp. 319–331. Springer, IIT Kanpur, India (2017). https://doi.org/10.1007/978-981-13-1135-2_25
11. Narasimhan, S.G., Nayar, S.K.: Vision and the atmosphere. Int. J. Comput. Vis. **48**(3), 233–254 (2002)
12. He, K., Sun, J., Tang, X.: Single image haze removal using dark channel prior. IEEE Trans. Pattern Anal. Mach. Intell. **33**(12), 2341–2353 (2009)
13. Sharma, T., Verma, N.K.: Estimating depth and global atmospheric light for image dehazing using type-2 fuzzy approach. IEEE Trans. Emerg. Top. Comput. Intell. **6**(1), 93–104 (2022)
14. Karnik, N.N., Mendel, J.M., Liang, Q.: Type-2 fuzzy logic systems. IEEE Trans. Fuzzy Syst. **7**(6), 643–658 (1999)
15. Mendel, J.M., John, R.B.: Type-2 fuzzy sets made simple. IEEE Trans. Fuzzy Syst. **10**(2), 117–127 (2002)

16. Sharma, T., Verma, N.K.: Adaptive interval Type-2 fuzzy filter: an AI agent for handling uncertainties to preserve image naturalness. IEEE Trans. Artif. Intell. **2**(1), 83–92 (2021). https://doi.org/10.1109/TAI.2021.3077522
17. Li, B., Peng, X., Wang, Z., Xu, J., Feng, D.: AOD-Net: all-in-one dehazing network. In: Proc. IEEE Int. Conf. Comput. Vis. (ICCV), pp. 4780–4788 (2017)
18. Wang, A., Wang, W., Liu, J., Gu, N.: AIPNet: image-to-image single image dehazing with atmospheric illumination prior. IEEE Trans. Image Process. **28**(1), 381–393 (2019)
19. Sharma, T., Agrawal, I., Verma, N.K.: CSIDNet: compact single image dehazing network for outdoor scene enhancement. Multimed. Tools Appl. **79**, 30769–30784 (2020)
20. Qin, J., Zhang, X., Wu, J., Guo, J.: FFA-Net: feature fusion attention network for image dehazing. In: Proc. IEEE/CVF Conf. Comput. Vis. Pattern Recognit. (CVPR), pp. 1586–1595 (2020)
21. Wang, Y., et al.: UCL-Dehaze: toward real-world image dehazing via unsupervised contrastive learning. IEEE Trans. Image Process. **33**, 1361–1374 (2024). https://doi.org/10.1109/TIP.2024.3362153
22. Chen, J., Ren, W., Zhao, H., Xia, Q., Yang, G.: You only need clear images: self-supervised single image dehazing. IEEE Trans. Multimed. **27**, 5800–5814 (2025). https://doi.org/10.1109/TMM.2025.3542999
23. Zhu, X., Ren, K., Wang, M., Yang, Y., Yang, M., Chen, M.: RESIDE: a large-scale synthetic dataset for image dehazing. IEEE Trans. Image Process. **29**, 1536–1547 (2020)
24. Li, B., Ren, W., Fu, D., Tao, D., Feng, D., Zeng, W., Wang, Z.: Benchmarking single-image dehazing and beyond. IEEE Trans. Image Process. **28**(1), 492–505 (2019)
25. Salomon, D.: Data Compression: The Complete Reference. Springer, Berlin (2004)
26. Wang, Z., Bovik, A.C., Sheikh, H.R., Simoncelli, E.P.: Image quality assessment: from error visibility to structural similarity. IEEE Trans. Image Process. **13**(4), 600–612 (2004)

Evaluating Multimodal Large Language Models for Geospatial Object Identification and Enumeration in Overhead Imagery

Tim Klawa[1] and Frank Tanner[2(✉)]

[1] Groq, Public Sector, Field CTO, Virginia, USA
[2] Innodata, VP Robotics and Computer Vision, Ridgefield, USA
ftanner@innodata.com

Abstract. This work explores the use of multimodal large language models (MLLMs) for geospatial object detection and enumeration in satellite imagery. Using the publicly available RarePlanes [1] dataset with pre-chipped satellite imagery, we evaluate nine frontier MLLMs on their ability to detect and classify aircraft in overhead imagery. Each model is provided with ontology class definitions and structured output requirements to identify and count aircraft across seven categories. We assess model performance on 300 representative image samples, measuring both object enumeration and classification accuracy. Our methodology examines model sensitivity to object scale, density, and visual context, and probes the extent to which MLLMs can support dynamic, zero-shot search without external embeddings or traditional computer vision models. By isolating the MLLM as a reasoning engine over visual data, this study informs the design of agentic pipelines for automated broad-area search, where adaptability, task generalization, and structured spatial reasoning are essential for defense and intelligence applications.

Keywords: Multimodal Large Language Models · Object Detection · Satellite Imagery · Aircraft Classification · Zero-Shot Learning · Geospatial Intelligence · Remote Sensing

1 Introduction

The rapid advancement of multimodal large language models (MLLMs) has opened new possibilities for automated geospatial intelligence analysis. Traditional computer vision approaches to object detection in satellite imagery rely heavily on supervised learning with annotated datasets, specialized architectures, and domain-specific feature extraction. While these methods have achieved remarkable success, they often require substantial training data, careful tuning for specific object classes, and they struggle to generalize to novel scenarios or rapidly changing requirements.

Recent developments in vision-language models, particularly GPT-4o, Claude Opus, Gemini, and Llama variants, demonstrate impressive zero-shot reasoning capabilities across diverse visual tasks. These models can interpret natural language instructions,

F. Tanner and J. Irvine (Eds.): AIPR 2025, LNCS 16446, pp. 403–414, 2026.
https://doi.org/10.1007/978-3-032-18474-0_28

understand spatial relationships, and identify objects without task-specific training. This capability presents an intriguing question for the geospatial intelligence community: can MLLMs serve as standalone agents for broad-area search in overhead imagery, performing both detection and classification tasks with minimal adaptation?

This work presents a systematic evaluation of frontier MLLMs on aircraft detection and classification in satellite imagery using the RarePlanes [1] dataset. We benchmark nine models (GPT-4o, GPT-4o Turbo, GPT-4o Mini, Claude Opus 4.1, Claude Sonnet 4, Gemini 2.5 Flash, Llama 4 Maverick 17B, Grok-4 Fast Reasoning, and Grok-4 Fast non-Reasoning) across 300 image samples, measuring their ability to accurately count aircraft and classify them according to a defined taxonomy.

Our experimental framework isolates the MLLM as the sole reasoning component, avoiding external computer vision models or embedding systems. This approach allows us to assess the intrinsic capabilities of these models for geospatial analysis and identifies both their strengths and limitations in operationally relevant scenarios.

2 Background and Related Work

2.1 Object Detection in Overhead Imagery

Object detection in satellite and aerial imagery presents unique challenges compared to terrestrial image understanding. These challenges include small object sizes relative to image resolution, high aspect ratios and arbitrary orientations, dense object arrangements in complex scenes, variable lighting conditions and atmospheric effects, and limited training data for rare or novel object types [8]. Traditional approaches have employed convolutional neural networks [2, 3], YOLO architectures [4, 5], and more recently, vision transformers [6, 7] to address these challenges. However, these methods typically require extensive labeled training data and struggle to adapt to new object classes or changing mission requirements without retraining.

2.2 The RarePlanes Dataset

Released by In-Q-Tel in 2019, the RarePlanes dataset represents a significant resource for aircraft detection and classification research. The dataset contains 253 Maxar WorldView-3 images spanning 112 locations and 2,142 square kilometers, with 14,700 hand-annotated aircraft. Additionally, it includes over 50,000 synthetic images with approximately 630,000 synthetic aircraft annotations.

The dataset provides a hierarchical taxonomy for aircraft classification with multiple levels of granularity. For this study, we utilize the role-based classification level, which includes seven classes: Civil Large Transport, Civil Medium Transport, Civil Small Transport, Military Fighter, Military Bomber, Military Transport, and Military Trainer (Fig. 1).

Fig. 1. Example images from RarePlanes [1]

2.3 Multimodal Large Language Models

The emergence of vision-language models has enabled new approaches to visual understanding tasks. Recent work has demonstrated that vision transformers excel at satellite object detection tasks, with detection transformer (DETR) architectures achieving state-of-the-art performance on remote sensing benchmarks including aircraft and ship detection [9, 10]. Building on these advances, models such as GPT-4o, Claude, Gemini, and Llama variants combine large-scale language understanding with visual processing capabilities, allowing them to interpret images in the context of natural language instructions. These models have demonstrated remarkable zero-shot and few-shot learning capabilities across diverse domains, suggesting potential applications in specialized areas like geospatial intelligence where traditional supervised learning approaches may be limited by data availability or rapidly evolving requirements.

Traditional computer vision models trained on labeled datasets with bounding boxes or segmentation masks can infer the exact location of objects because their architectures preserve spatial hierarchies and are explicitly optimized to regress geometric coordinates through convolutional features, anchor priors, and Intersection over Union (IoU) based localization losses. This supervision teaches the model not only *what* is in the image but precisely *where* it is. In contrast, it is important to note that modern generative AI vision models, such as CLIP-style encoders, diffusion backbones, or MLLMs, are not trained on spatially explicit objectives and instead learn global, semantic embeddings that compress and mix spatial information through tokenization and attention. Without detection heads, coordinate regression losses, or locality-preserving operations, these models can identify objects conceptually but cannot output deterministic or pixel-accurate positions, making them fundamentally different from traditional computer vision systems designed for localization.

3 Methodology

3.1 Data Selection and Preparation

For this experiment, we utilized a subset of the RarePlanes dataset curated by the Roboflow community [11]. This subset contains 2,710 image chips from the full dataset, pre-processed with COCO format annotations. The use of pre-chipped images simplified the experimental workflow while maintaining consistency with standard object detection evaluation protocols. From this subset, we selected 300 representative image samples for evaluation, ensuring coverage of varying aircraft densities, scene complexities, and lighting conditions. This sample size provides sufficient statistical power for comparative analysis while remaining computationally tractable for repeated evaluation across multiple models.

3.2 Model Selection

We evaluated nine frontier multimodal language models representing diverse architectural approaches and training paradigms: GPT-4o, GPT-4o Turbo and GPT-4o Mini (OpenAI), Claude Opus 4.1 and Claude Sonnet 4 (Anthropic), Gemini 2.5 Flash (Google), Llama 4 Maverick 17B (Meta), Grok-4 Fast Reasoning, and Grok-4 Fast non-Reasoning (xAI). We selected these models to provide a comprehensive comparison of leading AI labs against object identification and enumeration in overhead imagery. These models also represent both open source and commercial variants with the inclusion of Llama 4 Maverick.

3.3 Experimental Framework

We developed a custom MLLM evaluation platform to systematically test and compare model performance. The platform enables dynamic configuration of system prompts, ontology definitions, and automated evaluation workflows against pre-labeled datasets, facilitating consistent multi-model benchmarking. The framework used for evaluation can be extended or applied to a wide range of models and is not tied to any particular AI lab or inference engine, with support for evaluating MLLMs hosted on AWS, Azure, Google, Groq, OpenAI, Anthropic, and xAI. The open-source repo for the experiment can be found on Github (https://github.com/timklawa/gen-AI-Image-Eval-Engine) (Fig. 2).

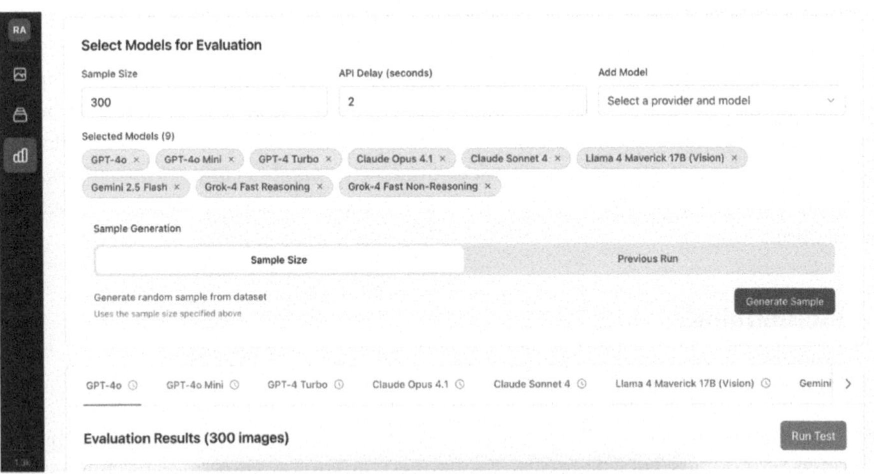

Fig. 2. Screenshot from evaluation platform

To provide consistency in comparing models, the same system prompt was used for each model evaluation. Each model was provided with a structured system prompt defining the task: "*You are an expert aircraft identification specialist. Analyze the provided satellite image and identify all aircraft present. For each aircraft, determine its class based on the provided ontology. Return your analysis in the specified JSON format with confidence scores for both count and individual class identifications.*" The ontology class definitions were also provided to each model, specifying the seven aircraft categories from the RarePlanes taxonomy. Models were required to return structured JSON outputs containing total aircraft count, individual aircraft classifications, and confidence scores for both counting and classification.

3.4 Evaluation Metrics

We evaluated model performance across three primary dimensions: (1) Count Accuracy, the ability to correctly enumerate all aircraft in an image; (2) Classification Accuracy, the proportion of correctly classified aircraft according to the RarePlanes taxonomy; and (3) Processing Time, latency measurements to assess operational viability and consistency across repeated invocations.

Additionally, we analyzed model performance as a function of object density and examined failure modes through qualitative analysis of specific cases where models struggled or succeeded. There are several other metrics that could be pursued which we will describe in the Discussion section of this manuscript.

4 Results

Our comprehensive evaluation of nine frontier MLLMs revealed significant insights into their capabilities for geospatial object detection and classification. Figure 3. Provides the resulting performance across all evaluated models for count and class accuracy.

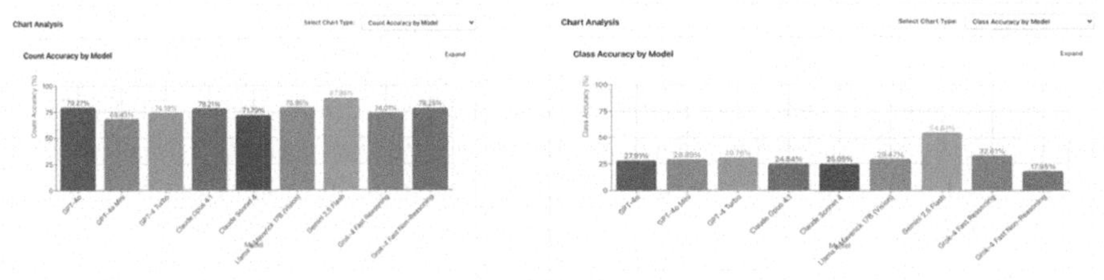

Fig. 3. Overall Model Performance Comparison. Left diagram shows count accuracy by model with right diagram showing classification accuracy by model

4.1 Object Count Accuracy

In general, our evaluation revealed some minor variation in counting accuracy across models as shown in Fig. 3 - Left. The Gemini 2.5 Flash model demonstrated the highest accuracy, achieving a peak count accuracy of 87.98%. A notable disparity was also observed within the GPT series; the GPT-4o model (79.27%) significantly outperformed its lightweight counterpart, GPT-4o Mini by more than 11 percentage points. Furthermore, the data presents an intriguing anomaly within the Grok models, as the Grok-4 Fast Non-Reasoning variant (78.25%) unexpectedly achieved a higher accuracy score than the Grok-4 Fast Reasoning model (74.01%).

4.2 Classification Accuracy

Classification performance proved more challenging for all models compared to object counting. It is important to note that MLLMs do not return bounding boxes like traditional CNNs; therefore, our classification analysis assumes the model is correctly identifying the pixels representing the plane itself, rather than another object, when assigning a class. Across the board, models struggled to accurately classify aircraft into the seven-category taxonomy (Fig. 3 – right). The Gemini 2.5 Flash model again achieved the highest accuracy by a significant margin, scoring 54.81%. Gemini 2.5 Flash's leading classification accuracy is likely dependent on its superior performance in the object count benchmark, given that successful class identification is inherently dependent on the accuracy of the preceding count. A significant reversal from the count accuracy results was observed in the Grok models; here, Grok-4 Fast Reasoning (32.61%) substantially outperformed the Grok-4 Fast Non-Reasoning variant (17.95%), highlighting the potential variance in reasoning as it relates to counting objects vs. classification tasks. Furthermore, the performance delta between GPT-4o (27.91%) and GPT-4o Mini (28.89%) diminished almost entirely compared to the object count benchmark, with the 'Mini' model showing a slight advantage. Notably, the open-source Llama 4 Maverick 17B (Vision) model (29.47%) also proved competitive, surpassing the performance of both GPT-4o (27.91%) and Claude Sonnet 4 (25.05%) in this analysis.

On reviewing results from each model, we found that certain classes were easier for models to detect than others. Overall, distinguishing between classes that were size-related (Large vs. Medium vs. Civil Small Transport) proved challenging on a number of images, as did differentiating certain military classes. This is likely because the ontology lacked explicit size definitions and the image chips did not include a pixel-to-meter ratio (i.e. ground sample distance) to support size-based classification. Additionally, military classes were highly under-represented in the dataset. Our hypothesis is that MLLMs that struggled with military classifications likely had fewer relevant examples in their respective training datasets.

4.3 Object Density vs Accuracy

As shown in Fig. 4, across both charts (Object Count vs. Count Accuracy and Object Count vs. Class Accuracy) the data reveals that there is no consistent relationship between the number of objects present in an image and the corresponding model accuracy. Our initial hypothesis was that as object count increased, model performance, particularly for reasoning-intensive tasks like classification, would degrade due to higher visual and cognitive load. However, the results challenge this assumption: even at higher object densities (above 20 objects), several models maintained comparable count and class accuracy levels to those observed in simpler scenes. Interestingly, while accuracy variance appears wider in high-object scenarios, no single model demonstrates systematic degradation tied to object quantity. Instead, performance differences seem to stem more from model architecture and reasoning capability than sheer object complexity. This suggests that, for multi-object geospatial scenes such as those in the RarePlanes dataset, scene density alone is not a reliable predictor of MLLM performance degradation—a counterintuitive finding that warrants deeper investigation into factors such as geospatial understanding, relational reasoning, and compositional generalization. It is important to note that the RarePlanes dataset contains a higher proportion of low-density images compared to high-density ones, and that factors such as lighting conditions, background clutter, and overall scene complexity are not explicitly represented or controlled within the dataset's annotations.

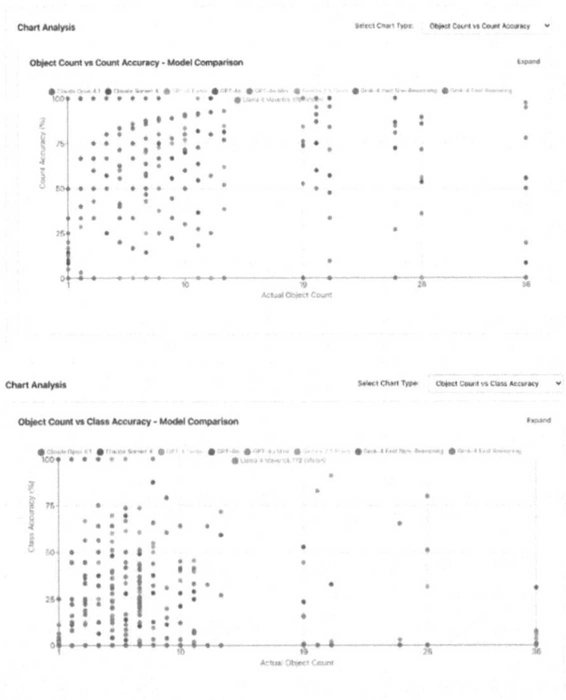

Fig. 4. Number of objects per image vs model accuracy

4.4 Processing Time and Operational Considerations

The API Time per Image chart reveals substantial latency variability across models, with the Gemini 2.5 Flash model exhibiting particularly large and inconsistent spikes in processing time. This volatility highlights a key challenge for operational deployment of MLLMs in real-time or mission-critical contexts: ensuring predictability and consistency in inference time. The observed performance irregularities underscore the importance of continued research into deterministic compute paradigms, such as fixed-latency architectures or compiler-level scheduling optimizations, to achieve reproducible and time-bounded inference at scale.

The latency variations across the models tested may also stem from resource contention or dynamic load balancing within shared cloud environments, where compute and memory availability fluctuate based on concurrent demand. Such dependency on variable infrastructure reinforces the importance of dedicated or isolated model deployments particularly for mission-critical applications where consistent performance, deterministic timing, and reliability are essential for operational assurance and real-time decision-making (Fig. 5).

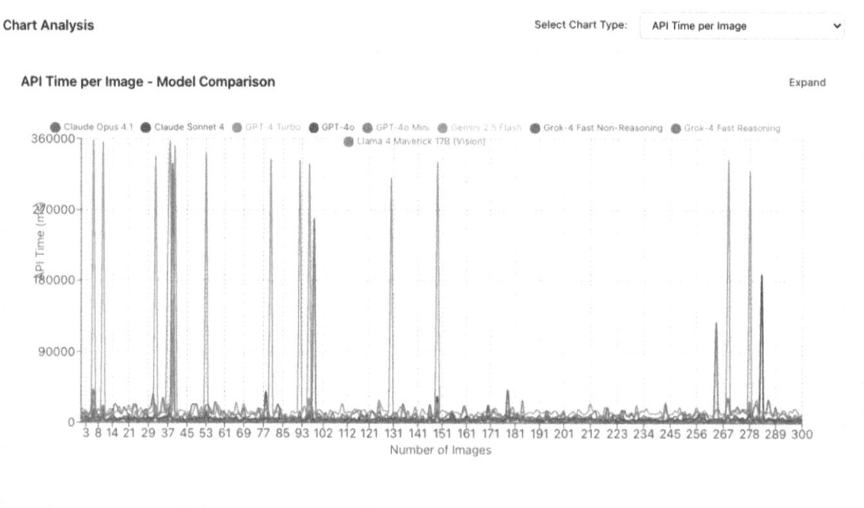

Fig. 5. Processing time by model

5 Discussion

5.1 Key Findings

Our evaluation of nine frontier multimodal large-language models (MLLMs) for overhead imagery enumeration and classification reveals several important patterns. Overall, current-generation models exhibit meaningful competence at object counting, demonstrating that zero-shot reasoning alone can support broad-area search and change-detection tasks. However, fine-grained classification remains a significant challenge, particularly for visually similar military aircraft categories. This disparity suggests that enumeration leverages low-level saliency detection that these models already possess from general vision training, while classification depends on specialized spatial and geometric cues largely absent from their pre-training corpora.

Error analysis also indicates that the remaining mistakes were not purely "missed detections." Instead, they often involved boundary ambiguities (e.g., partial objects at chip edges) or category confusions such as distinguishing small civil transports from trainers. These outcomes imply that performance ceilings are now dictated less by coarse detection capacity and more by spatial reasoning and semantic disambiguation within the geospatial domain.

5.2 Factors Affecting Performance

Several qualitative tendencies emerged in our evaluation that suggest how scene characteristics influence model behavior. Larger and more visually distinct aircraft were generally counted more accurately than smaller or partially obscured ones. In contrast, aircraft near chip boundaries or those partially hidden by shadows or structures were detected less consistently. These observations indicate that model sensitivity may depend on object scale and visibility, even though these factors were not explicitly varied in our design.

Scenes containing multiple closely spaced aircraft also produced more variability in counts, suggesting that high object density may increase the likelihood of undercounting or merged detections. Conversely, images with sparse or well-separated aircraft yielded more stable enumeration results.

Several models appeared to incorporate contextual information such as runways, taxiways, or nearby infrastructure when estimating class type. While this behavior sometimes improved classification consistency, it also led to occasional misclassifications when background cues conflicted with object appearance.

It is important to note that all imagery in this study was drawn from Maxar WorldView-3 collects with consistent ground-sample distance, illumination, and collection geometry, and with minimal atmospheric distortion. This uniformity simplified our analysis by reducing uncontrolled variables, but it also limits generalization. The models were evaluated under highly consistent, high-quality imaging conditions, so their performance under more variable sensors, resolutions, or environmental conditions remains to be tested.

Taken together, these observations suggest that MLLM performance is influenced by object visibility, density, and surrounding context. However, because our experiment did not explicitly manipulate these variables, future studies should quantify their effects through controlled variation of scale, scene complexity, and sensor characteristics.

5.3 Comparative Insights with Recent Work

Our observations align closely with recent literature on object counting and small-object detection in remote-sensing imagery. Guo et al. [12] demonstrate that scale variation and attention design remain primary constraints on accurate enumeration, even in conventional deep-learning models. Hua et al. [13] likewise emphasize that object size, density, and occlusion influence aerial-detection performance, consistent with the qualitative trends observed in our evaluation.

Related studies in applied remote sensing also echo these findings. Delplanque et al. [14] show that object-counting models applied to wildlife surveys experience similar degradation under occlusion and background clutter, reinforcing that these limitations are not unique to aircraft imagery but may be intrinsic to high-resolution overhead analysis. Collectively, these peer-reviewed works support our conclusion that generalist MLLMs exhibit useful counting ability but are not yet reliable for fine-grained, context-independent classification.

5.4 Viability for Broad-Area Search and Operational Deployment

From an operational perspective, MLLMs show tangible promise for broad-area screening tasks. Their ability to rapidly enumerate and highlight probable object clusters suggests strong potential as first-pass filters in human-in-the-loop workflows. In such hybrid systems, models perform initial triage by flagging candidate sites or estimating object counts while trained analysts validate results or feed detections into specialized vision pipelines. This division of labor leverages the models' zero-shot adaptability and reduces analyst workload without compromising quality.

Utilization of MLLMs in their current state for broad-area search remains premature without fine-tuning or additional prompt engineering, such as providing example images per class for geospatial context. Unlike traditional computer vision models that generate explicit spatial outputs (e.g., bounding boxes or segmentation masks), MLLMs infer object presence through language-based reasoning over visual embeddings, which yields coarse approximations rather than precise locations. Their confidence scores also tend to cluster toward high values, even when incorrect, due to the intrinsic calibration limitations of generative models. These factors introduce operational risk and reinforce the need for structured prompting, domain-specific calibration, and further research in enabling realistic confidence judgements from MLLMs to unlock better human machine teaming capabilities for complex edge cases within mission datasets.

6 Limitations

Our study's limitations should guide interpretation of the results.

1. Dataset Uniformity: Because all imagery originated from Maxar WorldView-3 collects with consistent Ground Sample Distances (GSDs) and minimal atmospheric effects, the dataset represents a best-case scenario. Generalization to imagery from other sensors, altitudes, or environmental conditions remains untested. Consequently, our accuracy metrics likely represent an *upper bound* on achievable performance under ideal imaging conditions.
2. Sample Size and Scope: The evaluation encompassed 300 images which is sufficient for comparative analysis but limited for statistical generalization across global geographies or sensor modalities.
3. Zero-Shot Protocol: We intentionally avoided iterative prompt optimization to measure intrinsic capabilities. More aggressive prompt engineering or few-shot conditioning [15], which provides models with a small number of example inputs and outputs to guide task behavior, could yield higher accuracies.
4. Computational Variability: Latency fluctuations among API invocations likely reflect external infrastructure effects rather than intrinsic model performance but remain relevant to real-time use cases.

Taken together, these limitations highlight areas where future studies can extend this work, particularly by increasing dataset diversity, evaluating generalization to other sensors, and experimenting with adaptive prompting strategies.

7 Conclusions

This study demonstrates that multimodal large language models already possess meaningful intrinsic capability for geospatial object detection and enumeration in overhead imagery, achieving reasonable counting accuracy without any task-specific training. Yet fine-grained classification accuracy remains limited, especially among visually similar and underrepresented military aircraft categories.

Because our evaluation used uniform, high-quality Maxar WorldView-3 imagery from the RarePlanes dataset, the reported accuracies likely represent performance under optimal conditions. Real-world operational imagery, characterized by varying sensor geometries, resolutions, and atmospheric interference, will almost certainly reduce accuracy unless models are explicitly adapted to those conditions.

The observed variability in processing time and classification confidence further indicates that while MLLMs are viable analyst-assist tools, they are not yet ready to function as fully autonomous geospatial agents. Nonetheless, their zero-shot adaptability, ability to process structured natural-language instructions, and capacity for contextual reasoning make them valuable building blocks in next-generation hybrid human-machine intelligence pipelines.

In summary, while current multimodal models demonstrate promising zero-shot enumeration capability, achieving operational-grade geospatial precision will require deliberate methodological improvements. Future work should prioritize stronger domain alignment and explicit spatial grounding, along with structured mechanisms that compensate for the absence of task-specific training data. One recommended direction is the development of agentic workflows in which models iteratively decompose tasks, cross-validate intermediate outputs, and request additional context rather than relying on single-step inference. Another is the creation of vectorized exemplars for each ontology class, including variations in size, pose, and sensor conditions, to better anchor model reasoning and reduce misclassification in out-of-distribution scenarios. Collectively, these research directions provide a promising path toward improving MLLM robustness and achieving more consistent performance on diverse and operationally realistic geospatial datasets.

References

1. Shermeyer, J., Hossler, T., Van Etten, A., Hogan, D., Lewis, R., Kim, D.: RarePlanes: synthetic data takes flight. In: Proc. IEEE/CVF Winter Conf. on Applications of Computer Vision (WACV 2021), pp. 207–217 (2021). https://arxiv.org/abs/2006.02963
2. Girshick, R.: Fast R-CNN. In: Proc. IEEE Int. Conf. on Computer Vision (ICCV 2015), pp. 1440–1448 (2015). https://doi.org/10.1109/ICCV.2015.169
3. Lin, T.Y., Dollár, P., Girshick, R., He, K., Hariharan, B., Belongie, S.: Feature pyramid networks for object detection. In: Proc. IEEE Conf. on Computer Vision and Pattern Recognition (CVPR 2017), pp. 936–944 (2017). https://doi.org/10.1109/CVPR.2017.106

4. Redmon, J., Divvala, S., Girshick, R., Farhadi, A.: You only look once: unified, real-time object detection. In: Proc. IEEE Conf. on Computer Vision and Pattern Recognition (CVPR 2016), pp. 779–788 (2016). https://doi.org/10.1109/CVPR.2016.91
5. Cheng, T., Song, L., Ge, Y., Liu, W., Wang, X., Shan, Y.: YOLO-world: real-time open-vocabulary object detection. In: Proc. IEEE/CVF Conf. on Computer Vision and Pattern Recognition (CVPR 2024), pp. 16901–16911 (2024). https://arxiv.org/abs/2401.17270
6. Liu, Z., et al.: Swin transformer: hierarchical vision transformer using shifted windows. In: Proc. IEEE/CVF Int. Conf. on Computer Vision (ICCV 2021), pp. 10012–10022 (2021). https://arxiv.org/abs/2103.14030
7. Aleissaee, A.A., et al.: Transformers in remote sensing: a survey. Remote Sensing **15**(7), 1860 (2023). https://doi.org/10.3390/rs15071860
8. Tanner, F., et al.: Overhead imagery research data set — an annotated data library and tools to aid in the development of computer vision algorithms. In: Proc. IEEE Applied Imagery Pattern Recognition Workshop (AIPR 2009), pp. 1–8 (2009). https://doi.org/10.1109/AIPR.2009.5466304
9. Carion, N., Massa, F., Synnaeve, G., Usunier, N., Kirillov, A., Zagoruyko, S.: End-to-end object detection with transformers. In: Vedaldi, A., Bischof, H., Brox, T., Frahm, J.M. (eds.) European Conf. on Computer Vision (ECCV 2020), LNCS 12346, pp. 213–229. Springer (2020). https://arxiv.org/abs/2005.12872
10. Zhang, C., Su, J., Ju, Y., Lam, K.M., Wang, Q.: Efficient inductive vision transformer for oriented object detection in remote sensing imagery. IEEE Trans. Geosci. Remote Sens. **61**, 5616320 (2023). https://doi.org/10.1109/TGRS.2023.3292418 https://arxiv.org/abs/2306.12184
11. RarePlanes Dataset. Roboflow Universe (2023). https://universe.roboflow.com/home-workspace/rareplanes-1qgok. Accessed 2 Nov 2025
12. Guo, X., Anisetti, M., Gao, M., Jeon, G.: Object counting in remote sensing via triple attention and scale-aware network. Remote Sensing **14**(24), 6363 (2022)
13. Hua, W., Chen, Q.: A survey of small object detection based on deep learning in aerial images. Artificial Intelligence Review **58**, Article 162 (2025)
14. Delplanque, A., Théau, J., Foucher, S., Serati, G., Durand, S., Lejeune, P.: Wildlife detection, counting and survey using satellite imagery: Are we there yet? GIScience & Remote Sensing **61**(1), Article 2348863 (2024)
15. Brown, T., et al.: Language models are few-shot learners. Advances in Neural Information Processing Systems (NeurIPS 2020) **33**, 1877–1901 (2020)

Loop Closure Detection Revisited: A Clustering Perspective

Don Yates[1(✉)], Hakki Erhan Sevil[1], and Andrew Arash Mahyari[1,2]

[1] Department of Intelligent Systems and Robotics, University of West Florida, Pensacola 32514, USA
djy4@students.uwf.edu, hsevil@uwf.edu, amahyari@ihmc.org
[2] Institute for Human and Machine Cognition, Pensacola 32502, USA

Abstract. Loop closure detection (LCD) is critical for reducing drift and maintaining map consistency in SLAM systems, yet image-retrieval–based methods struggle with perceptual aliasing, viewpoint and appearance changes, and limited scalability. We reformulate LCD as clustering in a learned latent space rather than database retrieval. A convolutional autoencoder (CAE) is first pre-trained on environment imagery to produce compact, structure-aware embeddings. We then create globally-aware descriptors with a new model. During operation, keyframes are encoded and compared in latent space against a growing memory set. If an embedding lies beyond a threshold distance, it is considered a potential loop closure and added to the clustering structure. To enforce spatially meaningful structure, we apply triplet loss: the immediate previous frame serves as a positive (temporal proximity), while other keyframes act as negatives, encouraging embeddings from the same place to cluster and distinct places to separate. This design improves robustness to aliasing and appearance variation and reduces computational cost by avoiding exhaustive database search. Experiments on multiple place-recognition and navigation datasets show competitive or superior precision–recall performance compared to NetVLAD, DBoW2, and AP-GeM with more temporally consistent loop-closure clusters. Overall, the results indicate that latent-space clustering with globally-aware descriptors provides a scalable and robust alternative to conventional retrieval-based LCD.

Keywords: Representational Learning · Clustering · Loop-Closure

1 Introduction

Loop closure detection (LCD) poses the fundamental question: *"Have I been here before?"* Correctly answering this question allows a robot to relocalize and reduce trajectory drift over time. This capability is essential for maintaining a topologically consistent map–an indispensable component of modern robotic navigation.

For vision-based systems, solving the LCD problem requires matching images captured by the robot with those corresponding to previously visited locations.

F. Tanner and J. Irvine (Eds.): AIPR 2025, LNCS 16446, pp. 415–429, 2026.
https://doi.org/10.1007/978-3-032-18474-0_29

Traditionally, LCD has been treated almost exclusively as an image-retrieval problem, where the core task is comparing image feature representations. In essence, loop-closure methods depend on forming short-term or long-term associations between current observations and the robot's internal "memory" of environments.

To answer the LCD question effectively, a system must first recognize the concept of a *place* and then compare current and past place representations. This challenge is formalized as the visual place recognition (VPR) problem, a rapidly growing research area with more than 3,500 published papers to date [1]. This research volume underscores both the importance and persistent difficulty of the problem.

Three key challenges dominate the field of VPR: 1. *Perceptual aliasing*: where distinct places appear visually similar, leading to false positives. 2. *View variability*: drastic appearance changes caused by lighting, weather, or viewpoint, resulting in missed loop closures. 3. *Computational cost*: most systems rely on dense storage and brute-force comparisons across a growing database, making them expensive and less scalable in long term deployments.

This paper addresses these challenges by reframing LCD as a clustering problem in a learned latent space, rather than a conventional image retrieval task. Our method is grounded in the idea that places can be more meaningfully represented through compact, structure-aware embeddings that group spatially proximal scenes while maintaining separation between distinct locations. Specifically, we adapt VPR and clustering techniques such as Generalized Mean (GeM) pooling [2] and NetVLAD [3]. We further introduce a memory scheme that learns what constitutes a "place" based on visual distinctiveness, enabling database growth that is logarithmic rather than linear. The proposed network architecture produces compact, view-invariant embeddings that enable efficient, robust, and scalable loop closure detection. In doing so, we bridge the gap between metric learning and temporal clustering, providing a foundation for adaptive, lifelong SLAM systems.

In summary, the contributions of this work are:

- We recast LCD as a location-informed, absolute-similarity clustering problem in an embedding space learned with unsupervised representation learning and metric learning.
- We propose a model that produces globally-aware descriptors and an associated loss that explicitly represents–and separates–places.
- We present a simple yet effective loop-closure method that forms and uses triplets to learn places by visual distinctiveness, rather than relying on a fixed sequence length as in traditional approaches.
- We show that optimizing rank ordering for image retrieval does not necessarily optimize loop-closure detection; optimizing absolute similarity can yield better results.

2 Related Work

VLAD-based descriptors remain central to visual place recognition. NetVLAD [3] is among the most influential variants: it replaces hard vector-quantization with a *differentiable* soft-assignment, allowing residuals to be weighted across multiple visual words. This yields a descriptor that is both robust and more view-invariant than classic VLAD. Building on this idea, Patch-NetVLAD [4] elevates aggregation from low-level features to patch-level cues, capturing higher-order structure that improves retrieval under challenging viewpoint and appearance changes.

A complementary research thread explicitly integrates clustering into loop-closure detection (LCD). Tsintotas et al. [5] employ Growing Neural Gas (GNG) over image streams to form visual words, extract SURF descriptors, and perform place voting via a binomial model. Sharma et al. [6] propose an unsupervised topological clustering framework that groups spatially adjacent, visually similar observations, enabling hierarchical loop detection at both topology and image-cluster levels. Ji et al. [7] take a multi-view, object-centric approach: they construct a 3D semantic scene graph by associating objects across views (via semantics, IoU, color, and embeddings), refine poses with bundle adjustment, and detect loops by graph matching on object topology. Geometry-driven formulations also exist; for example, Täubner et al. [8] cluster line features in RGB-D images, illustrating how structural grouping can aid LCD even when clustering operates on geometric primitives rather than global place representations.

Our approach unifies these ideas under a single framework. We revisit the VLAD family through a *global-residual* formulation that encodes responsibility-weighted deviations from learned prototypes, while coupling it with an online place memory that clusters descriptors over time. Unlike purely offline aggregators or purely geometric grouping, our method integrates (i) a NetVLAD-style soft assignment, (ii) responsibility-weighted residual concatenation, and (iii) a teacher–student mechanism for safe, on-stream adaptation of the projection head. This combination yields compact, discriminative, and adaptable descriptors for LCD.

3 Method

Our objectives are twofold: (i) to learn a low-dimensional, viewpoint-invariant image representation that can distinguish distinct places, and (ii) to leverage this representation for efficient and accurate loop-closure detection. Second, we leverage these representations for loop-closure detection using a method that is computationally efficient, memory-conscious, and achieves a low false-positive rate. See Fig. 1 for an overview of the model.

3.1 Problem Formulation

Let the input image space be $\mathcal{X} \subset \mathbb{R}^{C \times H \times W}$ and let an encoder $E_\theta : \mathcal{X} \to \mathbb{R}^{C' \times H' \times W'}$ map $x \in \mathcal{X}$ to a feature map $F = E_\theta(x)$. We apply permutation-

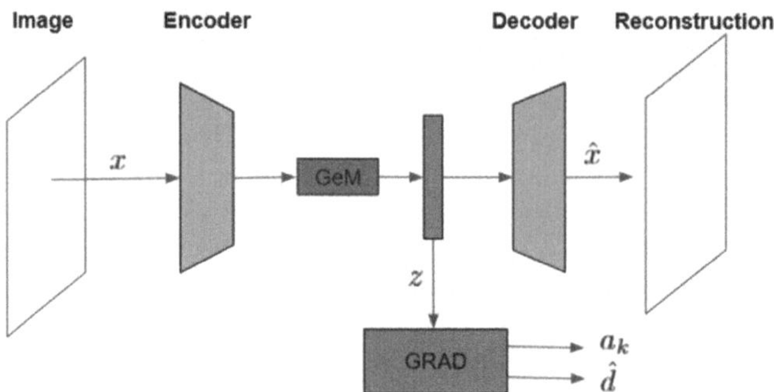

Fig. 1. NetGRAD Model. The encoder and decoder can be implemented using standard CNN layers with the GeM pooling and fully connected layer in between. An image, x, is passed to the network and an aggregated global residual descriptor $\hat{d}$, along with a corresponding assignment probability a_k is outputted. The reconstructed image $\hat{x}$ is used to maintain meaningful structure in the embedded space.

invariant GeM pooling $g : \mathbb{R}^{C' \times H' \times W'} \to \mathbb{R}^{C'}$:

$$\mathrm{GeM}_p(F)_c = \left(\frac{1}{|\Omega|} \sum_{(i,j) \in \Omega} (F_{cij})^p \right)^{1/p} \tag{1}$$

$$\Omega = \{1, \ldots, H'\} \times \{1, \ldots, W'\} \tag{2}$$

which improves view invariance by suppressing spatial layout. A compact, unit-norm embedding is then obtained via a projection head h_θ:

$$z = \frac{h_\theta(g(F))}{\left\| h_\theta(g(F)) \right\|_2} \in \mathbb{R}^D \tag{3}$$

While the final descriptor should be robust to spatial details, the latent space must retain structure. To discourage collapse, a decoder reconstructs the input image from z, preventing latent collapse and preserving spatial semantics. For place retrieval, we attach a Global-Residual-Aggregate-Descriptor (GRAD) head H_ϕ with K learnable prototypes $C = \{c_k\}_{k=1}^K$, $c_k \in \mathbb{R}^D$, and a parameter $\alpha > 0$. Given unit-norm z, we compute soft assignments (simplex $a \in \Delta^{K-1}$) using distance based logits. We adopt the softmax form:

$$a_k = \frac{e^{-\alpha ||z - \hat{c}_k||^2}}{\sum_{j=1}^K e^{-\alpha ||z - \hat{c}_k||^2}} \qquad \hat{c}_k = \frac{c_k}{||c_k||_2} \tag{4}$$

Let $r_k = z - c_k \in \mathcal{R}^D$ be the residual to prototype k. We form the descriptor as $R = \sum_{k=1}^K a_k r_k \in \mathbb{R}^D$, followed by a linear projection p and ℓ_2-normalization:

$$d = W_p R + b_p \ , \ \hat{d} = \frac{d}{||d||_2} \in \mathbb{R}^{D_{\mathrm{proj}}} \tag{5}$$

We denote the resulting descriptor by $\hat{d} = H_\phi(z)$ and the assignment vector by $a = (a_1, \ldots, a_K)$.

Intuitively, each block $a_k(z - c_k)$ is a responsibility-weighted deviation from prototype c_k: it encodes how z would need to move to match c_k, weighted by how much c_k "claims" z. In practice we found summing $\sum_{k=1}^{K} a_k r_k \in \mathbb{R}^D$ produces better results than concatenation due a number of reasons. First, for concatenation the input to the projector is KxD, with even a modest vocabulary of 128 and a descriptor dimension of $D = 512$ with a latent dimension of 512 we get $128 \times 512 \times 512 = 33,554,432 \approx 33.5M$ weights making reconstruction ill-conditioned. In practice, the large $K \times D \rightarrow$ projection dimension layer must learn to compress an extremely sparse, block-structured vector; with limited supervision and online mining, it tends to memorize nuisance correlations that don't transfer across routes/lighting, hurting recall@N. Second, z is already a global embedding (GeM $\rightarrow FC \rightarrow \ell_2$). Splitting a single global vector into K residual blocks and then concatenating re-injects artificial structure that's more suitable when aggregating many local features. For a single z, the informative quantity is the overall displacement from the prototype set, not the per-prototype layout–precisely what the sum captures.

3.2 Objectives

We first train E_θ and D_ω to preserve scene structure via a reconstruction loss:

$$\mathcal{L}_{\text{rec}} = \frac{1}{CHW} \|\hat{x} - x\|_1, \qquad \hat{x} = D_\omega\big(E_\theta(x)\big) \tag{6}$$

During this phase, the GeM exponent p and the projection parameters in h_θ are learned to stabilize the embedding space.

The autoencoder pre-training objective is simply the reconstruction loss. After this phase, we embed a representative set $\{z_i\}$ and initialize $\{c_k\}$ with K-means on $\{z_i\}$; the resulting centroids are ℓ_2-normalized.

After reconstruction pre-training converges, we fine-tune to obtain a view-invariant place descriptor $\hat{d} = H_\phi(E_\theta(x))$. We call this the joint training phase. For a triplet (x_a, x_p, x_n) with (x_a, x_p) from the same place and x_n from a different place, define:

$$d_a = d(x_a), \quad d_p = d(x_p), \quad d_n = d(x_n). \tag{7}$$

Using squared Euclidean distance $\Delta(i,j) = \|d_i - d_j\|_2^2$, the triplet loss is:

$$\mathcal{L}_{\text{trip}} = \max\big\{0, m + \Delta(a,p) - \Delta(a,n)\big\}, \tag{8}$$

with margin $m > 0$. Mini-batches contain anchors with one positive and one negative; we do not perform hard mining.

To encourage well-spread prototypes and informative assignments during joint training, we regularize the centers C and assignments a via:

$$\mathcal{L}_{\text{div}} = \underbrace{\frac{1}{K(K-1)} \sum_{k \neq j} \big(\hat{c}_k^\top \hat{c}_j\big)^2}_{\text{off-diagonal cosine penalty}} - \underbrace{\frac{1}{B} \sum_{b=1}^{B} \sum_{k=1}^{K} a_{bk} \log a_{bk}}_{\text{assignment entropy}} \tag{9}$$

where B is the batch size.

To keep the embedding visually grounded while specializing for discrimination, we retain a reconstruction term and the diversity regularizer. The joint training objective is:

$$\mathcal{L}_{joint} = \mathcal{L}_{\text{rec}} + \gamma \mathcal{L}_{\text{trip}} + \lambda \mathcal{L}_{\text{div}}, \qquad \gamma, \lambda \ll 1 \tag{10}$$

Both z and the final descriptor d are ℓ_2-normalized (the encoder normalizes z and the head normalizes d), so inner products equal cosine similarities. Soft assignments use logits $\ell_k = -\alpha \|z - c_k\|_2^2$ with a learned positive scale α. We parameterize α as $\alpha = \text{softplus}(\alpha_{\text{raw}}) + \varepsilon$ with $\varepsilon = 10^{-6}$ to ensure strict positivity; larger α sharpens assignments and smaller α smooths them. With $\|z\|_2 = \|c_k\|_2 = 1$, distances lie in $[0, 4]$, so logits lie in $[-4\alpha, 0]$, yielding well-scaled assignments.

3.3 Teacher–Student Setup and Online Head Adaptation

At live-stream evaluation, we instantiate a frozen *teacher* $\mathcal{T}$ as a copy of the trained model and use it to embed incoming frames for state estimation, memory interaction, and mining. The *student* $\mathcal{S}$ shares the backbone but updates only the projection head parameters ϕ with a small learning rate (2×10^{-5}) and gradient clipping (norm 0.75), enabling fast adaptation while preserving the base representation.

Model Size. Although we adopt a student–teacher scheme for online streaming, we *do not* increase the deployed parameter footprint: both $\mathcal{T}$ and $\mathcal{S}$ discard the decoder at inference, so each instance is roughly half the size of the training-time model. Maintaining both therefore keeps the total parameter count and memory footprint comparable to that of a single full (encoder+decoder) model used during training, while retaining the benefits of a frozen teacher and an adaptively updated head on the student.

Triplets are dynamically mined from the evolving online memory, ensuring continual adaptation without catastrophic forgetting. For an anchor frame x_t with teacher descriptor $d_t^{\mathcal{T}}$, we select a positive d^+ and negatives $\{d_j^-\}_{j=1}^{K_{\text{neg}}}$ ($K_{\text{neg}} = 30$) and update ϕ with a margin-based triplet loss. An update is applied only if the anchor–positive similarity is confident ($\geq$ `MIN_POS`) and at least one negative is non-trivial ($\geq$ `MIN_NEG_SIM`); updates are performed every key frame that meets this criteria.

3.4 Online Place Memory and State Machine

We maintain an *OnlinePlaceMemory* storing items $\{(\text{cid}, z, \text{idx})\}$ and cluster centers $\{c_k\}$, updated via exponential moving average (EMA) (rate $\beta = 0.1$). For a query $d_t^{\mathcal{T}}$ (and $\{c_k\}_{k=1}^{K}$), all ℓ_2-normalized, we pick the nearest center

$$j = \arg\max_k \langle d_t^{\mathcal{T}}, c_k \rangle, \qquad s_{\text{center}} = \langle d_t^{\mathcal{T}}, c_j \rangle \tag{11}$$

Same spot. We use a three-state logic, if:

$$same\_stop = \begin{cases} 1, \ \langle d_t^T, d_{t-1}^T \rangle \ \geq \ \tau_{\text{same}} \\ 0, \ otherwise \end{cases} \quad (12)$$

we label SAME_SPOT and suppress adaptation. In this manner we only learn "places" based on visual distinction. Additionally, this comparison effectively detects cases when a stop in movement occurs.

Revisit, LCD. Otherwise, if $s_{\text{center}} \geq \tau_{\text{center}}$ and the center is not among the most recently excluded ones (we exclude the last 10 frames), we examine member similarities within the cluster. We never do an exhaustive search, but only compare K cluster centers to d_t^T. Let $s_1 \geq s_2 \geq \cdots$ be the sorted member similarities with s_1 the best match. We declare REVISIT if

$$revisit = \begin{cases} 1, \ s_1 \ \geq \ \tau_{\text{member}} \quad \text{and} \quad \frac{s_1}{\max(s_2, \varepsilon)} \ \geq \ \rho_{\min} \\ 0, \ otherwise \end{cases} \quad (13)$$

New place. If neither holds, the frame is labeled NEW_PLACE and the representation is inserted into memory with a new id; the corresponding center is updated by EMA.

Typical thresholds are $\tau_{\text{same}} = 0.91$, $\tau_{\text{center}} = 0.88$, $\tau_{\text{member}} = 0.88$, and $\rho_{\min} = 1.05$. We verify at most the top 30 members and exclude the most recent 5 cluster ids to prevent trivial repeats.

3.5 Triplet Mining

For anchors labeled NEW_PLACE or REVISIT, positives are mined from within the selected cluster, while negatives are drawn from other clusters whose similarity to the anchor exceeds a modest floor (outside the margin parameter) to obtain informative (semi-hard) negatives. A candidate is considered *new* if its similarity to all centers is below $\tau_{\text{new}} = 0.75$, in which case it may seed a new cluster. Mining is enabled only after the memory contains a preset minimum number of items.

4 Experimentation

4.1 Implementation Details

We implement the Global-Residual-Aggregated-Descriptor (NetGRAD) model in PyTorch using a VGG-16 backbone as the encoder. The convolutional encoder follows the standard VGG-16 configuration with five convolutional blocks, each consisting of two or three 3×3 convolutions followed by ReLU activations and a 2×2 max-pooling layer for spatial downsampling. The channel dimensions across blocks are $\{64, 128, 256, 512, 512\}$. The final convolutional feature map is aggregated by a learnable Generalized Mean (GeM) pooling layer, producing a global descriptor that is linearly projected to a D-dimensional embedding and ℓ_2-normalized before aggregation.

For reconstruction, the decoder mirrors the encoder structure: a fully connected layer expands the latent vector to 512×7×7, followed by a sequence of transposed convolutions 4×4/2 that progressively upsample the feature maps through channels 512→256→128→64→32, and a final 3×3 convolution restores the output. The reconstructed image is bilinearly resized to match the input resolution for computing the reconstruction loss. The GRAD head maintains K learnable prototypes $C \in \mathbb{R}^{K\times D}$ initialized with *orthogonal* weights (to promote spread).The assignment parameter α is learned from α_{init}=20.0.

We sum residuals to a vector in $\mathbb{R}^D$, then project with a linear layer to 512 and apply ℓ_2-normalization to obtain the descriptor $\hat{d}$.

Training uses a batch size of 32, and with pretrained weights we train the autoencoder in a warm-up phase for just 10 epochs and joint training of 8 epochs. We optimize with Adam using a base learning rate `lr`$=10^{-3}$. The triplet margin is 0.2. Loss weights are `w_rec`=1.0, `w_trip`=0.5, `w_div`=0.7, `w_cos`=0.75 (prototype cosine spread), and `w_ent`=0.9 (assignment entropy). After the warm-up phase, we embed a subsample of K-means with 10000 sample images, the resulting centroids are ℓ_2-normalized and overwrite c_k as initialization for joint training. For evaluation, we report recall@N and assignment utilization of a_k.

4.2 Datasets

To evaluate the strengths and limitations of our approach, we use several publicly available VPR datasets characterized by wide viewpoint variation, environmental changes, and sequential structure suited for loop-closure evaluation. We ensure all testing data used in our experiments are non-overlapping and are different from any images used for training.

Pittsburgh-30k [9], Tokyo 24/7 [10], and RobotCar Seasons v2 [11] are visual place-recognition datasets featuring large viewpoint changes and environmental variation. For Pittsburgh-30k, we follow the train/val/test splits of [3]; for evaluation, we randomly select 1,000 query images from the test set and use the remaining 9,000 images as the database. Tokyo 24/7 is particularly challenging, with queries captured by a smartphone at daytime, sunset, and nighttime; we use the same query version (v2) as [3]. For RobotCar Seasons v2, we exclude images that appear in the official v2 test split, as those frames lack the position/pose data required for our place labeling and scoring.

To evaluate loop closure detection we use the RobotCar sequence 09-18-32 for training and sequence 12-07-13 for testing. All dataset images are resized to 640 by 480 pixels.

4.3 Evaluation Metrics

All datasets are evaluated using the recall@N metric, where a query image is correctly identified if at least one of the top N images is within the ground truth tolerance [3,4]. For Pittsburg-30k this is 25 m translation due to poor quality coordinates, for all other datasets this is 5 m translation. Recall is the percentage of correctly identified query images and plotted by varying N.

For evaluating loop closure detection we create a flag, based on ground truth data, for marking when an image is revisiting a previous location. We then calculate true positives, true negative, false positives, and false negatives based on the evaluation pipeline status decision. This data is then used to calculate precision, recall, F1-score, and produce P/R curves. Precision $= \frac{\text{TP}}{\text{TP+FP}}$, Recall $= \frac{\text{TP}}{\text{TP+FN}}$, , F1 $= \frac{2\,\text{Precision}\cdot\text{Recall}}{\text{Precision+Recall}}$ A frame is predicted positive (loop closure) if it is a fresh REVISIT or if it is SAME_SPOT while a REVISIT latch for the same cluster id is active. We accumulate TP/FP/TN/FN to report precision, recall, and F1-score.

We evaluate on sequence dataloaders that yield frames and binary loop-closure labels (`revisit`$\in \{0,1\}$). For each processed frame t, we compute the teacher descriptor $z_t^{\mathcal{T}}$, update the state machine, perform a head update on the student, and record system statistics (e.g., memory size and process RSS). Unless stated otherwise, all embeddings used for state estimation and mining are computed with the frozen teacher. Online updates optimize only the projection head ϕ using Adam (lr 1×10^{-5}) and cosine similarity is used throughout.

4.4 Comparison Methods

We compare against two widely used place-recognition baselines: NetVLAD [3] and DBoW2 [12]. Following prior VPR practice [13], we do not include two-stage re-ranking methods (e.g., [4,14]). For all CNN-based baselines we adopt a VGG-16 backbone and use the hyperparameters recommended in the original papers.

Our DBoW2 implementation follows a "CNN-BoW" setup: local conv5_3 features are L2-normalized and quantized via hierarchical K-means to form TF–IDF histograms (sometimes referred to as DBoW for float descriptors). While this yields a global image representation, it is a sparse, count-based vector rather than a compact, learned embedding. Our loop-closure module requires a dense, single-vector descriptor suitable for cosine similarity and online memory updates; therefore, we use DBoW2 only for retrieval comparisons and report loop-closure results with NetVLAD and AP-GeM [15]. The next section presents qualitative results for our method and these benchmarks. All experiments are implemented with PyTorch on a Windows 11 computer with GeForce RTX 5090 GPU, 64GB RAM, and an AMD Ryzen 7 processor.

5 Results

To ensure fair comparison of descriptor generation we use VGG-16 [16] "off-the-shelf" pretrained network for all methods. All methods are run multiple times and the best results from each method are reported.

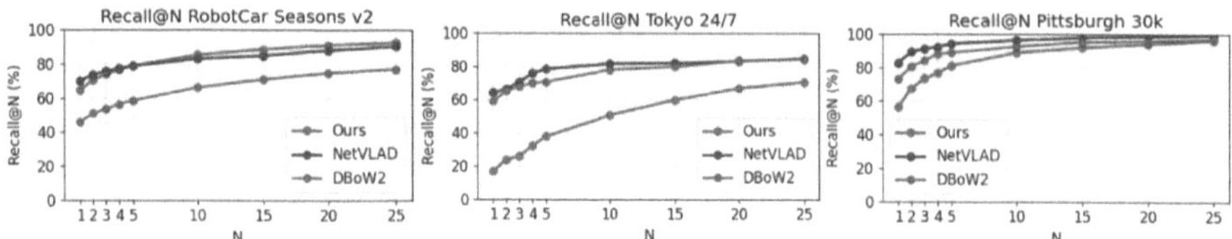

Fig. 2. Comparison of our method with benchmark methods. Recall@N for three different datasets are shown: NetVLAD Blue, DBoW2 Green, NetGRAD Red.

Figure 2 shows the recall@N performance of our method in comparison to benchmark methods. The results show our method generally under performs NetVLAD and DBoW2 on recall@1 but is comparable by recall@10. There is a noticeable divergence in performance on the Tokyo 24/7 dataset. We attribute this effect to a dataset mismatch: the training split contains only daylight images, whereas the queries span daytime, sunset, and nighttime. By contrast, RobotCar Seasons v2 includes all lighting conditions in its training set.

Additionally, we visualize query-match sets in Fig. 3. The results show our method has a good ability to recognize places despite drastic changes in lighting and changes in objects.

Fig. 3. Query and recall on RobotCar Seasons v2. The top and bottom rows show the model correctly matches (squares) the query image despite changes in the scene due to traffic cones. Middle row, shows despite the drastic lighting change from night to day, the model correctly identities the second highest match (#2) in the same location.

The final loss comprises three terms–triplet, reconstruction, and prototype-diversity–see Eq. 10. We perform an ablation to assess each term's contribution. Figure 4 reports recall@5 on Tokyo 24/7 while varying the reconstruction and triplet weights against the diversity weight. The results show that increasing the reconstruction and triplet weights has the strongest positive impact on Recall@5.

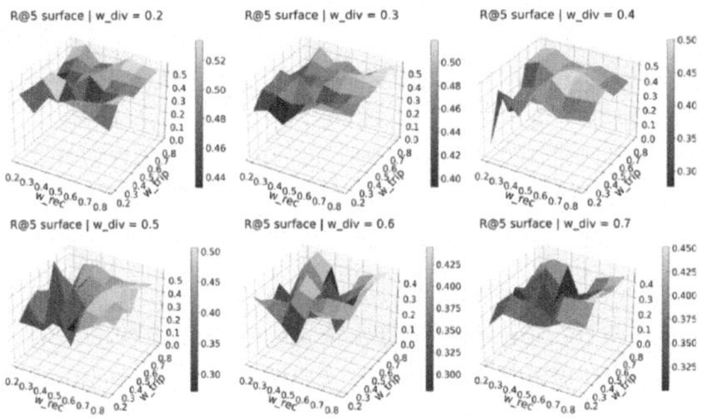

Fig. 4. Ablation Study. We vary the reconstruction and triplet loss weight for a fixed diversity loss weight and report recall@5. This shows reconstruction and triplet have a larger influence on performance than diversity.

5.1 Loop Closure Detection Performance

To evaluate loop-closure performance, we train on RobotCar sequence 09-18-32 (sequence A) and evaluate on sequence 12-07-13 (sequence B). The two sequences traverse the same route on different days and at different times. Revisits are defined using GPS: we mark a path segment as revisited if the vehicle's position lies within 1.5 m of any previously visited GPS location.

Networks are pre-trained on the environment using randomized triplets from sequence A. For evaluation, frames from sequence B are streamed sequentially through the networks following the procedure in section III. Each frame is assigned one of three states, same_spot, new_place, or revisit (loop closure detected) which we compare against ground truth to compute true positives (TP), true negatives (TN), false positives (FP), and false negatives (FN). A visualization tool (Fig. 5) displays the current frame and, when a loop closure is detected, the matched image and relevant metadata.

Fig. 5. Loop closure visualization tool. The current frame is displayed in the left panel and if a loop closure is detected, it is displayed in the right panel. The current frame time, state status, cluster ID, and similarity score are also displayed.

Recall, precision and F1-score are used to compare performance and we run multiple trials per method, the highest scoring runs are reported for each method. Table 1 shows the F1-scores of NetGRAD, NetVLAD, and AP-GeM. We also show the number of detections reported along with precision in Fig. 6. When evaluating precision, it should be noted that our method is a place recognition system, we do not do any pose matching to reduce false positive rates.

Table 1. Loop closure detection scores of our method and benchmark methods for the RobotCar dataset. Higher numbers indicate better performance.

Model	Precision	Recall	F1-Score
AP-GeM	0.412	0.238	0.302
NetVLAD	**0.75**	0.014	0.027
Ours	0.661	**0.281**	**0.394**

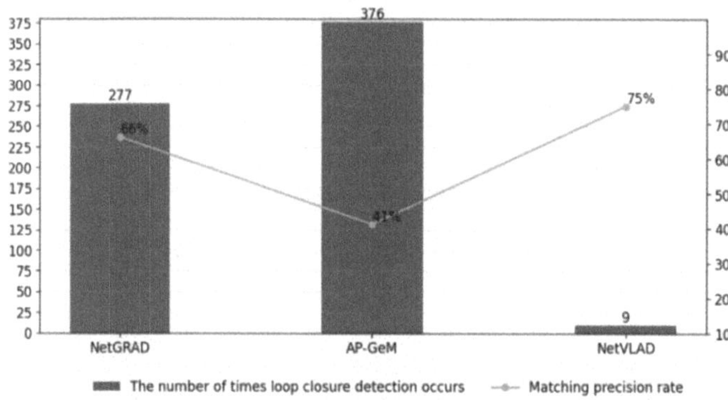

Fig. 6. Loop closure detection results of each method on the RobotCar sequence 12-07-13 dataset.

5.2 Analysis and Discussion

Our results show that NetGRAD is comparable to NetVLAD and DBoW2 for image-retrieval tasks, provided it has access to all environmental conditions. Additionally, our model outperforms NetVLAD and AP-GeM on our loop-closure detection method. This suggests there is no direct correlation between image retrieval and threshold-based loop-closure performance. We offer the following reasoning to explain the difference.

When trained with a triplet/ranking objective, NetVLAD optimizes the *relative ordering* of descriptors rather than the *absolute calibration* of distances. Consequently, raw Euclidean distances are not well calibrated for a fixed threshold τ: the same place under different viewpoints/conditions can land at quite different absolute distances.

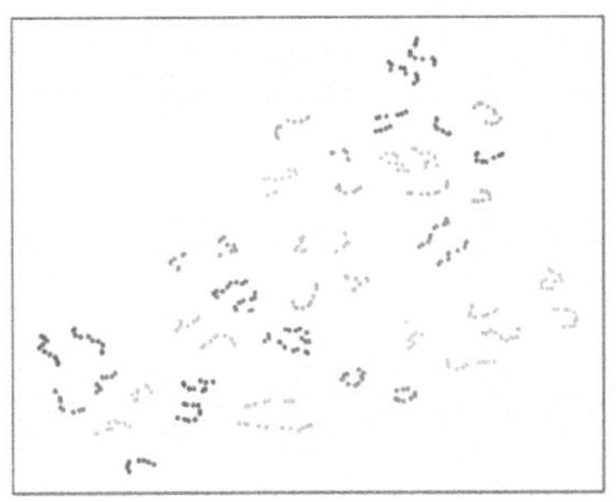

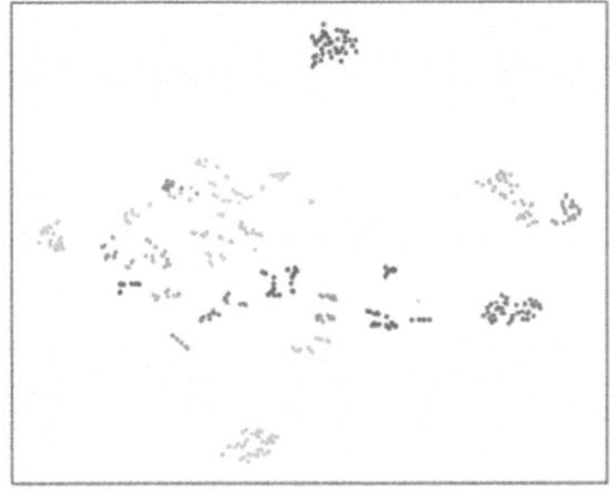

Fig. 7. RobotCar - Descriptor Visualization. The left side is the t-SNE visualization of the NetVLAD database descriptors. The right side is the visualization of our NetGRAD descriptors. The NetGRAD descriptors have a wider mean and appear more isotropic than the NetVLAD descriptors.

Our method augments the ranking signal with reconstruction plus diversity and entropy regularizers that explicitly shape the embedding geometry. This induces more isotropic, compact within-place clusters and larger between-place margins, improving distance calibration so that a single τ generalizes across sequences.

Moreover, image retrieval rewards distinguishing true matches within a *fixed* database, whereas loop-closure detection operates online against a growing memory with near-duplicates and strong, structured distractors (e.g., repetitive facades). Success therefore depends less on fine-grained ranking and more on stable, absolute decision boundaries. By reducing nuisance variation and enforcing global consistency, our approach trades a small amount of ranking sharpness for markedly fewer aliasing errors. Figure 7 visualizes this effect: NetGRAD exhibits more isotropic, well-separated clusters, consistent with its improved loop-closure performance. Measuring the mean per-label dispersion of each network's descriptors, we obtain 0.001375 for NetVLAD and 0.019575 for NetGRAD, which is consistent with our theory.

6 Source Code

The source code of the developed algorithm can be found at: https://github.com/djy412/NetGRAD.

7 Conclusion

In summary, we formulate loop-closure detection as a location-informed clustering task in a learned latent space, optimized jointly with unsupervised representation learning and metric learning. Using globally-aware descriptors and an absolute-similarity decision rule, our approach provides a robust, scalable, and conceptually simple alternative to traditional image-retrieval pipelines. Experiments on Pittsburgh-30k, Tokyo 24/7, and RobotCar Seasons v2 show that while retrieval rank optimization does not necessarily translate to LCD, our embedding regularization (reconstruction plus diversity/entropy terms) yields better distance calibration, more temporally consistent clusters, and superior loop-closure performance compared to strong baselines (NetVLAD, DBoW2, and AP-GeM).

A current limitation is the absence of an explicit confidence measure. As future work, we will exploit the soft-assignment distributions (temperature/scale-controlled) to produce calibrated confidence estimates for loop validation, further improving SLAM robustness.

By reframing loop closure as clustering in latent space with globally-aware descriptors, this work bridges visual representation learning and temporal mapping, paving the way for adaptive, lifelong SLAM systems that scale efficiently over time.

References

1. Yin, P., et al.: General place recognition survey: towards real-world autonomy. IEEE Trans. Robot. (2025)
2. Radenović, F., Tolias, G., Chum, O.: Fine-tuning CNN image retrieval with no human annotation. IEEE Trans. Pattern Anal. Mach. Intell. **41**(7), 1655–1668 (2018)
3. Arandjelovic, R., Gronat, P., Torii, A., Pajdla, T., Sivic, J.: NETVLAD: CNN architecture for weakly supervised place recognition. In: Proceedings of the IEEE Conference on Computer Vision and Pattern Recognition, pp. 5297–5307 (2016)
4. Hausler, S., Garg, S., Xu, M., Milford, M., Fischer, T.: Patch-NETVLAD: multi-scale fusion of locally-global descriptors for place recognition. In: Proceedings of the IEEE/CVF Conference on Computer Vision and Pattern Recognition, pp. 14141–14152 (2021)
5. Tsintotas, K.A., Bampis, L., Gasteratos, A.: Assigning visual words to places for loop closure detection. In: 2018 IEEE International Conference on Robotics and Automation (ICRA), pp. 5979–5985. IEEE (2018)
6. Sharma, A., Mehan, Y., Dasu, P., Garg, S., Krishna, K.M.: Hierarchical unsupervised topological slam. In: 2023 IEEE 26th International Conference on Intelligent Transportation Systems (ITSC), pp. 4623–4628. IEEE (2023)
7. Ji, X., Liu, P., Niu, H., Chen, X., Ying, R., Wen, F.: Loop closure detection based on object-level spatial layout and semantic consistency. CoRR (2023)
8. Taubner, F., Tschopp, F., Novkovic, T., Siegwart, R., Furrer, F.: LCD–line clustering and description for place recognition. In: 2020 International Conference on 3D Vision (3DV), pp. 908–917. IEEE (2020)
9. Torii, A., Sivic, J., Pajdla, T., Okutomi, M.: Visual place recognition with repetitive structures. In: Proceedings of the IEEE Conference on Computer Vision and Pattern Recognition, pp. 883–890 (2013)
10. Torii, A., Arandjelovic, R., Sivic, J., Okutomi, M., Pajdla, T.: 24/7 place recognition by view synthesis. In: Proceedings of the IEEE Conference on Computer Vision and Pattern Recognition, pp. 1808–1817 (2015)
11. Maddern, W., Pascoe, G., Linegar, C., Newman, P.: 1 year, 1000 km: the oxford robotcar dataset. Int. J. Robot. Res. **36**(1), 3–15 (2017)

12. Gálvez-López, D., Tardos, J.D.: Bags of binary words for fast place recognition in image sequences. IEEE Trans. Rob. **28**(5), 1188–1197 (2012)
13. Berton, G., Trivigno, G., Caputo, B., Masone, C.: EigenPlaces: training viewpoint robust models for visual place recognition. In: Proceedings of the IEEE/CVF International Conference on Computer Vision, pp. 11080–11090 (2023)
14. Wang, R., Shen, Y., Zuo, W., Zhou, S., Zheng, N.: TRANSVPR: transformer-based place recognition with multi-level attention aggregation. In: Proceedings of the IEEE/CVF Conference on Computer Vision and Pattern Recognition, pp. 13648–13657 (2022)
15. Revaud, J., Almazán, J., Rezende, R.S., Souza, C.R.: Learning with average precision: training image retrieval with a listwise loss. In: Proceedings of the IEEE/CVF International Conference on Computer Vision , pp. 5107–5116 (2019)
16. Simonyan, K., Zisserman, A.: Very deep convolutional networks for large-scale image recognition. In: 3rd International Conference on Learning Representations (ICLR 2015). Computational and Biological Learning Society (2015)

The Limitations of Image Features from Satellite Imagery Training Datasets

Christopher Algire[1](✉), Steven A. Israel[2], and Kannappan Palaniappan[1]

[1] University of Missouri, Columbia, MO, USA
{cab6h,pal}@missouri.edu
[2] Draper Laboratory, Cambridge, USA
sisrael@draper.com

Abstract. Deep learning for Computer Vision (CV) tasks such as object detection, classification, and segmentation have been tremendously successful in the decade since the introduction of Alexnet and GoogLeNet architectures. This success is attributable to large image training sets and increasingly complex network architectures which capture image features into representations in correspondingly finer detail. Image training sets in the handheld imagery domain typically have sufficient positional (or optical) separability between features within an image frame to make detectors effective. Satellite imagery, on the other hand, are taken from a further standoff distance where optical separability between image features are significantly smaller. Attempts to bridge the model performance gap between the two modalities have been pursued over the years, resulting in the utility of model architectures such as PyramidNet, Detectron2, and ResNet. However, the differences in learned feature representations within the trained model for both modalities have never been studied. Pose variances and short collection distance from a camera to subject in the handheld domain work well with existing computer vision methods, but these parameters are remarkably different in satellite imagery, thereby pushing the limits of the best vision models today.

This study explores the limitations of encoded features from popular commercial satellite imagery training datasets such as those from SpaceNet (Maxar). Categorical features emphasized in these datasets (i.e. - aircraft parts such as wings, tails, engines, etc.) by their respective authors will serve as the basis for determining the limitations of minimum viable spatial feature separation for within hidden layers in neural networks. Finally, we examine the composability of features, and their separability in model representations consistent with Zernicke moments in computer vision research.

Keywords: satellite imagery · machine learning · feature characterization · model limitations

1 Introduction

Deep learning has proven to effective at detection and classification tasks [1] in the handheld imagery domain. The ImageNet [2] and MS-COCO [3] datasets

F. Tanner and J. Irvine (Eds.): AIPR 2025, LNCS 16446, pp. 430–450, 2026.
https://doi.org/10.1007/978-3-032-18474-0_30

are two popular image training datasets in the handheld imagery domain that contributed to accelerated neural network research. The ubiquity of high-fidelity and high-resolution imagery in the handheld domain resulted in deep learning advancements, and robust computer vision algorithms. Inception [4] networks, for example, overcame image invariance challenges afflicting the computer vision algorithms that came before it such as Scale Invariant Feature Transform (SIFT) [5] and Histogram of Oriented Gradients (HOG) [6]. Specifically, SIFT and HOG methods use manually-defined features whereas inception automatically learned hierarchical features from the training images automatically. Considering that the SIFT method required explicit definition of scales and feature transformations, inception used a combination of multiple convolutions with pooling layers as means to automate feature abstractions, therefore overcoming scale and transformation challenges. Meanwhile, residual [7] networks increased the depth of networks further, while building upon components used in inception networks. ResNet [7] appeared to generalize better in addition to being more computationally tractable with depth. Despite rapid progress in detection and classification tasks for the handheld imagery domain, the same success in the remote sensing (specifically, satellite imagery) domain is unclear. This is primarily due to the large differences in features between the two modalities. Whereas features in handheld imagery are large and (spatially) separable, the same cannot be said of satellite imagery. The image resolution between the two domains are vastly different, as noted in [8].

Therefore, this work conducts further examination into popular networks which may be suitable for satellite imagery detection and classification tasks. Specifically, the persistence or propagation of resolvable features in satellite imagery as signatures (commonly known as saliency) through deep networks must be studied. Finally, an investigation on object representations or encodings from satellite imagery training datasets must be conducted.

(a) 'airplane' samples from MS-COCO

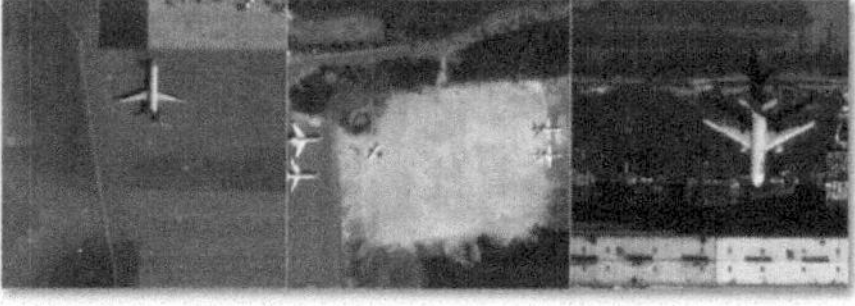

(b) image chips from RarePlanes

Fig. 1. Pose and scale differ remarkably between handheld and satellite imagery as shown by the MS-COCO (a) and RarePlanes (b) samples. Though discernible features are common between the two modalities (i.e. - wings, jet engines), small features and small objects are difficult to identify. RarePlanes and MS-COCO licensed under CC-4.0-BY-SA license.

2 Background

Many research papers claim exceptional performance results for object detection and classification tasks in satellite imagery using deep learning methods. Unlike handheld imagery, however, the performance metrics are typically shrouded in derivative scores such as mean average precision (mAP) or F1 scores [9–11]. These performance metrics typically convey the statistics of positive detection and classification of objects, while overlooking the prominence of false positive or false negative results [12]. The best test harnesses for vision detection and classification tasks break down when tested on small objects and small features [13]. Specifically, the Intersection over Union (IoU) and mAP metrics become difficult to fit within a reference (or truth) boundary when features are small. Many assertions for exceptional performance have since adopted a mAP50 (or 50% intersection) which is flawed and inconsistent with "near human-level" performance measures in handheld imagery. Hence, it can be assumed that small features can bias the dataset and often resulting in favorable performance when using typical vision metrics as stated in [11].

It is therefore reasonable to probe assertions of exceptional performance for any model trained on satellite imagery. A comprehensive investigation into critical parameters affecting model performance must be undertaken. As such, this paper focuses on the following tasks for satellite imagery: characterization of the dataset compared to handheld imagery, selecting a suitable network architecture, explaining network performance, find the limitations of current accepted test harnesses or metrics, and identify opportunities for novel model representations suitable for objects in satellite imagery. Success in this endeavor requires interrogation methods into critical model parameters which remarkably affect performance. Specifically, representations of objects in models, known as "embeddings" will be explored rigorously. Image characteristics of small features and objects common to satellite imagery also remains an unexplored research gap. A methodical assessment of this limitation is an opportunity to describe and quantify feature characteristics to better understand model behavior and the limitations of architectures as it pertains to small objects or features in images.

Understanding how object representations in model embeddings will ultimately result in trustworthy models for remote sensing. Pursuing this endeavor is an opportunity to create better model optimizations, and perhaps bridge the gap between multi-modal optimizations that challenge the remote sensing community today. Finally, deeper insights into model embeddings present an opportunity to create novel image representation methods for robustness in multi-domain vision tasks.

2.1 Datasets and Image Quality

The RarePlanes [14] dataset serves as the basis for this study. The dataset is composed of image chips from Maxar's WorldView-3 (WV3) earth-observation satellites, with an emphasis on aircraft detection and classification. WorldView-3 delivers the highest resolution imagery that is commercially available at this time, with published specifications at 30cm ground sampling distance (GSD) [15]. Further details of radiometric calibration for WV3 are available at Maxar online, and additional technical specification have been comprehensively evaluated by [16]. Image quality assumptions for this study were based on available information about WV3 such as those stated, and other complex technical discussions about the satellite is beyond the scope of this study. Nevertheless, training data quality has been known to influence model performance as stated in [17,18].

(a) High-confidence false positives (b) Glint on airplane wing (c) Aberration on entire aircraft

Fig. 2. Factors such as glint and aberration affect model confidence performance in addition to the 'attention' head of the network. RarePlanes licensed under CC-4.0-BY-SA license.

Image quality can remarkably vary between separate satellite images (i.e. - image footprints), or even between image chips extracted from the same image footprint collection (see Appendix 12). A satellite image footprint is defined as the telescope view (or the image dimensions of a collected image snapshot). Established characterization of satellite imagery, such as those of the National Imagery Interpretation Rating Scale (NIIRS) have been explored in [19]. Although NIIRS has been established since the late 1980s, the "interpretability" of images was subjective. A formal quantification of image quality (and hence NIIRS) was published as the General Image Quality Equation (GIQE) [20] a decade later. Both NIIRS and GIQE emphasize image features such as object edges, or RER in Eq. (1). Similar general image quality effects on model performance have been explored in [21].

$$NIIRS = c_0 + c_1 log_{10}(GSD) + c_2 log_{10}(RER) + c_3 \frac{G}{SNR} + c_4 H \tag{1}$$

$$\Delta NIIRS = log_2(\frac{GSD_0}{GSD}) = -3.32 log_{10}(\frac{GSD}{GSD_0}) \tag{2}$$

GSD is defined as ground sample distance (GSD) or the resolving power of the optical system. The post-image processing term RER represents the relative edge response which is sensitive to the noise gain G and the edge overshoot factor H. SNR is the signal-to-noise ratio of the unprocessed imagery. Four independent variables ($\log_{10}(GSD)$, $\log_{10}(RER)$, $\frac{G}{SNR}$, H) are then used to estimate GIQE. Details and values associated with $c_0 - c_4$ are presented in [22]. Standoff distance calculations for GIQE based on GSD can be calculated via Eq. (2). This equation prescribes a change of GIQE 1.0 for each factor of two resolution changes. Hence, a change in GSD is proportional to the change in RER.

Exploration into the effect of NIIRS such as [19,23,24] have asserted the detrimental effects of image noise on model performance. The significance of GSD in the NIIRS equation affirms the likely effect of small pixels within an image. A recent review of deep learning methods for identifying large animals in remote sensing imagery indeed reveals the challenge small pixels have on the best models available today, and is emphasized in [8]. It should be no surprise then, how small objects in satellite imagery underscores its notable impact in NIIRS' RER factor.

Table 1. Image statistics on the RarePlanes (real) training dataset.

RarePlanes: Image Training Set Statistics					
Category	Avg pixel width	Avg pixel height	Pixel width 1-σ	Pixel height 1-σ	count
(1) Small	33.869478	25.311615	10.885357	6.119978	10159
(2) Medium	76.364736	62.145850	34.349445	24.400814	6041
(3) Large	147.668672	117.615111	62.668547	43.049273	1435

A full characterization of the RarePlanes dataset's image quality is beyond the scope of this paper, although aberration and glint likely reduces model performance. Figure 2 demonstrates these image artifacts on aircraft, with the associated detection and confidence score. Clutter, combined with these image artifacts, are common in the dataset, which appear to induce more false positives than necessary. Notably, a slightly over-saturated image from the glint in Fig. 2b, and significant brightness difference in Fig. 2a appear to promote false positives, as evident in the high prediction scores. The false positives occur primarily on small objects, though the frequency of false negatives such as shown in Fig. 2a require more investigation. The impact of aberration on model performance likely depends on other factors such as brightness, contrast, and object size, as shown in Fig. 2c. Similar work in removing glint and minimizing aberration have been performed in [25,26].

A typical image chip in RarePlanes has dimensions of 512×512 pixels. Table 1 displays the pixel statistics of each object category as well as the 1-σ to emphasize the amount of pixel deviation in both width and height for each object category. Small aircraft (i.e. - single-engine Cessna) appear on average as a 34×25 pixel image, or 6% of the entire image chip. This is in stark comparison to medium or large aircraft which can occupy up to 15% and 29% of the image chip respectively. Most vision architectures today assume sufficient "pixels on target" for detection and classification tasks, particularly for hand-held imagery. The limitations of model performance as it pertains to small objects common in satellite imagery has mostly been overlooked, though efforts such as [27,28] appear to explore these limits. It should be no surprise that the RarePlanes dataset can challenge or sometimes fool the best models available, where small objects become unrecognizable [29] (Fig. 3).

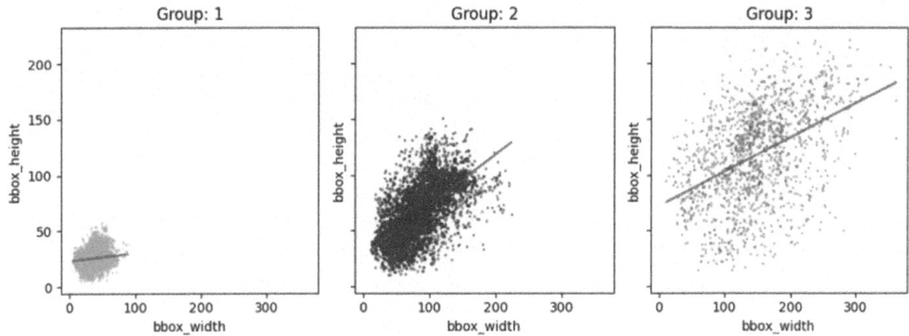

Fig. 3. The image chips in the training set are square or rectangular, with an apparent uniform geometry. Note the rectangular geometry in small aircraft compared to the medium or large aircraft annotations.

The challenges of performing computer vision tasks against small objects, such as those in satellite imagery, make remote sensing research a nascent area for exploration. The RarePlanes dataset currently represents the best satellite dataset for computer vision research. Efforts to create foundation models for remote sensing are fledgling, with [30,31] leading the way. Success in this endeavor requires comprehensive characterization of the satellite dataset. This means, rigorous quantification of image quality, proper annotations beyond bounding-box or even segmentation methods used today, and finally, a reassessment of performance metrics suitable for satellite imagery.

2.2 Suitable Network Architectures for Satellite Imagery

Variations in satellite image scenes range considerably from cluttered urban scenes with many significant features to sparse arid landscapes with little features. The RarePlanes dataset samples a variety of world regions - from arid deserts in Africa, snowy runways in Alaska, or urban international airports like Atlanta Hartsfield airport. Common to all these image scenes are clutter such as aviation support vehicles, jetways, or runway light markers.

It is therefore prudent to use neural networks that have a multi-head attention module. A network architecture suitable for forensic analysis is also highly desirable, in order to observe the networks' behavior in challenging scenes where small objects are present. Neural network architectures such as [7,32–34] all feature multi-head attention modules appropriate for complex scenesSatellite scenes in RarePlanes, for example, contain multiple aircraft of varying categories such as small, medium, or large. There exist image chips within the dataset that contain up to 33 aircraft in one scene, or none at all (Fig. 4).

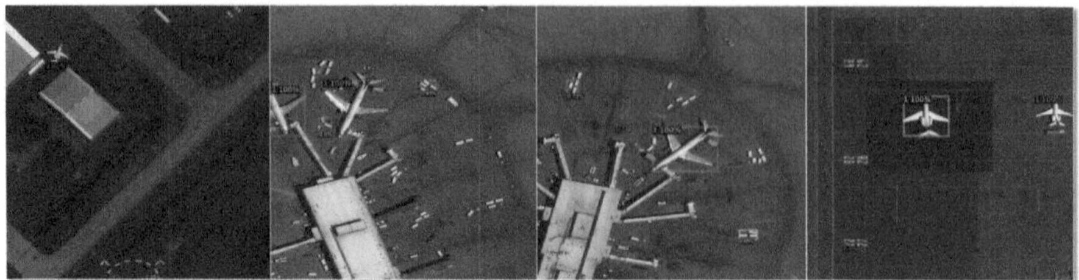

Fig. 4. Misdetections in the RarePlanes presents an opportunity to probe the root causes for poor performance in small object detection. In these examples, the model appeared to project high prediction scores for non-aircraft objects such as runway markers and luggage trolleys as false positive identification. RarePlanes licensed under CC-4.0-BY-SA license.

Each of the architectures discussed previously have their own strengths and weaknesses. Detectron2 [34] is a great architecture which yields fantastic performance results, at the expense of a nested modular architecture. Modules within Detectron2 contains a final activation layer that feeds into the next module in the chain. Hence, the architecture is unsuitable to forensic examination due to the highly variable activation responses within each module. On the other hand, PyramidNet [32] re-scales each image training input, and therefore compounding the variability of image factors (such as noise) during forensic analysis. Therefore, it too is unsuitable for analyzing network behavior. ResNet-50 [7], though a deep architecture, has a single embedding layer just like PyramidNet but without image resampling. Hence, it's the best architecture to observe network behavior on small objects such as those observed in satellite imagery.

2.3 Explaining Network Performance

Deep learning methods for computer vision tasks rapidly gained popularity after the release of Inception networks [4] in 2015. Their deep architecture ensured models captured features about an object category similar to the manual SIFT [5] and HOG [6] methods that preceded it while providing remarkably better performance. Surprisingly, deep learning methods rapidly surpassed human-level performance [35], therefore generating a notable interest in explainable models that continue to this day. Explainable model behavior with attributable performance metrics increases trust in computer vision models. As noted previously, a comprehensive characterization of remote sensing imagery datasets can result in stable performance scores, provided that all metrics are carefully considered. Special emphasis must be undertaken rigorously examine the root causes of a model's false positive and false negative identifications, with the addition of prediction scores.

2.3.1 Feature Heirarchy and Composability of Features in ML Detectors

Early deep learning methods had an innate ability to organize object features in a recognizable and interpretable way. The introduction of Rectified Linear Units (ReLU) and its utility in Inception networks dramatically increased the computational efficiency of learning complex patterns in image data as noted in [35]. Concurrent efforts to decode learned feature hierarchy [36] during model training had similarly taken place such as those by [37,38]. Deep learning of image features that result in model representations [39,40] have been an intense research area dating more than a decade, and is just as relevant now in the age of diffusion and transformer methods. Diffusion and transformers cannot work without a priori information [41], whether in the form of salient image features [42] or an understanding of optimal neural activations [43].

In fact, hierarchical features in computer vision were critical in understanding the parameters necessary for effective transfer learning methods [44]. The composability of features [45,46] making up an object detection became well understood, due to its similarity to SIFT and HOG, and remains as the best explanation for model prediction scores [42,45,47,48]. Critically, the spatial context of these feature hierarchies vary significantly depending on the modality as noted in [8]. For example, a ground image of an aircraft is typically a lateral (side profile) or an inferior (bottom) view whereas remote sensing is typically an oblique (diagonal) or nadir (direct overhead) view as shown in Fig. 1. The spatial position and relationships of aircraft parts are strikingly different for each image modality, and feature representation should also be expected to be remarkbly different between the two modalities. Indeed, similarity measures for representation geometry [49] and visual abstract perception [50] can be expected to negatively impact the performance of a model when used in a different modality as noted in [8], where structural and feature similarity impact prediction scores [50,51] (Fig. 5).

2.3.2 Class Activation Maps, and Zernike Moments

Class Activation Maps (CAMs) [52] became an essential method for understanding and visualizing feature heirarchy in models. It became an effective way to identify salient items [53] or features within an input image that likely persist through a network architecture's hidden layers [46]. Improvements from the original implementation, such as LayerCAM [54] and others enhanced robustness to noise. Existing challenges in computer vision tasks, such as identification of small objects and features, push the performance limit of the best models today as noted in [8,55,56].

Interestingly, CAMs appear to obey a similar mechanism to feature groupings and heirarchy as those of Zernike moments. The Zernike method was the basis for many SIFT and HOG methods [57], which despite innovations in deep learning, is still pertinent to explainable models. Indeed, there's an increasing demand towards better CAM methods, in addition to their explainability [55,58]. A resurgence in research into similarity and composability of features have recently taken

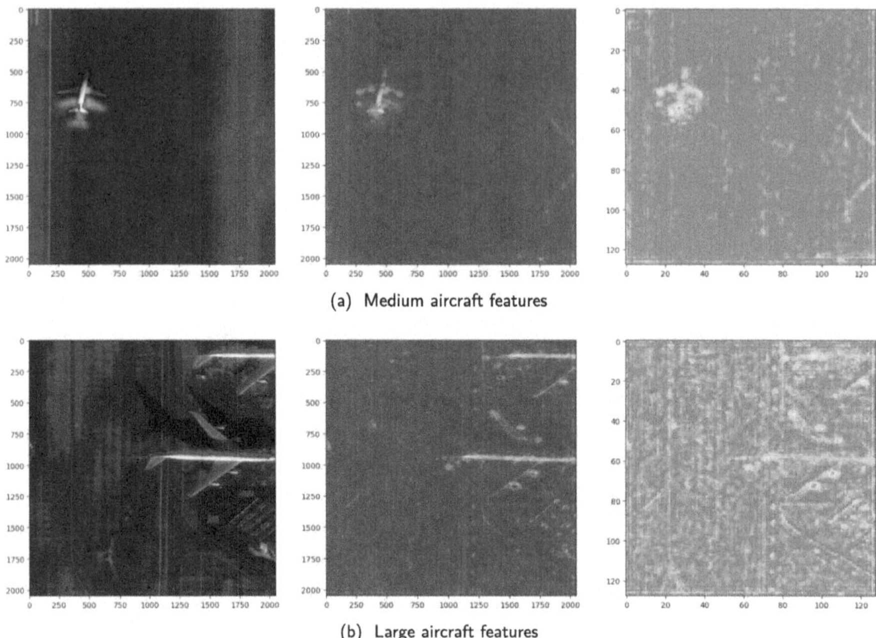

Fig. 5. Salient Features in objects: Feature activations using Class Activation Maps (CAMs) show how composability of features result in proper identification of objects in RarePlanes. Wings, fuselage, and engines become prominent image features that cause activations that can persist through the network. Input image (left) is shown overlaid with hidden layers res1 (middle) and res3 (right) activation responses. RarePlanes licensed under CC-4.0-BY-SA license.

place [59], where Zernike moments can be used to describe the shape or geometry of an object within an image. To date, Zernike polynomials have yet to be used to describe image representations captured in neural networks. Zernike moments could be useful in analyzing feature embeddings to analyze the geometric structure of actual features within embeddings in addition to describing the embedding space structure. This is an opportunity to mathematically describe learned representations and quantify feature separability beyond the metric distances used today.

2.3.3 Object Representations, Feature Synthesis, and Hallucinations

Quantifying feature embeddings through Zernike moments presents as an exciting research opportunity appropriate for future research. However, visualizing feature representations in models have been feasible for quite some time [36,40,42]. Specifically, [60] picked model embeddings for activation maximization through gradient ascent. Limitations to this method, however, assumed a zero-centered image input x_{img}, where multiple objects may exist. Equation 3

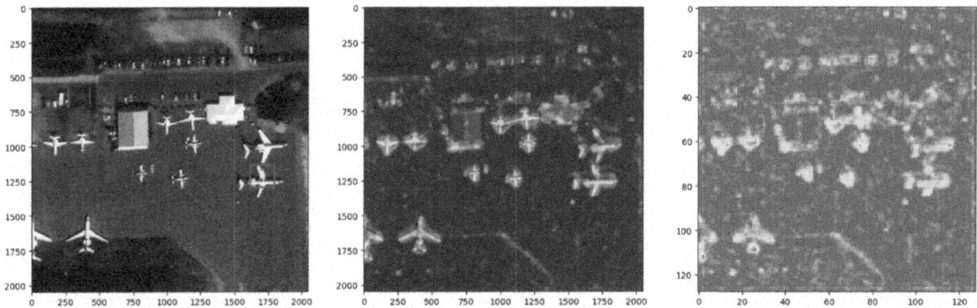

Fig. 6. Class Activation Maps (CAMs): A cluttered or noisy scene push the best models and network architectures to the limit, particularly in identifying small aircraft. Particularly notable is the effect of glint in suppressing the CAM response in the wing of the aircraft highlighted in red. Input image (left) is shown overlaid with hidden layers res1 (middle) and res3 (right) activation responses. RarePlanes licensed under CC-4.0-BY-SA license (Color figure online).

shows the regularized optimization method applied in [60] from an input image (x_{img}), where x_{img} is updated iteratively to induce activation $a_i(x)$ for some unit i, with step-wise update in the direction given by r_θ. The gradient descent step size is expressed as η. Figure 7 shows an MS-COCO "airplane" using this method.

$$x_{img} \leftarrow r_\theta \left(x_{img} + \eta \frac{\partial a_i}{\partial x_{img}} \right) \tag{3}$$

Notable in the visualizations of object representations in Fig. 7 is the presence of wavelets. Each activations pulled from the fully connected layers certainly demonstrate this wavelet-like behavior, and the clusterings of wavelets as shown in Fig. 13. Natural patterns when combined with further optimizations, are expected to appear as noted in [60] and visualize objects corresponding to natural parts (or composability of parts).

Visualization of object representations, combined with feature hierarchy, likely contributes to hallucinatory behavior in many vision models [29,50,61]. The abstract nature of these representations [42,47] likely contributes to model robustness [59] though at the expense of hallucinatory behavior. Leveraging Zernike moments to quantify composability of parts is an opportunity to better understand hallucinations in vision models, and may yield methods to minimize this behavior from learned feature representations.

3 Experimental Method

Our method utilized simple network architectures to demonstrate the means by which a neural network captures image features into an embedding. The method can be adapted to use more complex attention models such as Detectron2 [34] or YOLO [62] with highly complex activation maps and refined encodings. The selected architecture had to be robust in its ability to simultaneously detect multiple objects and object categories in the worst-case scenario.

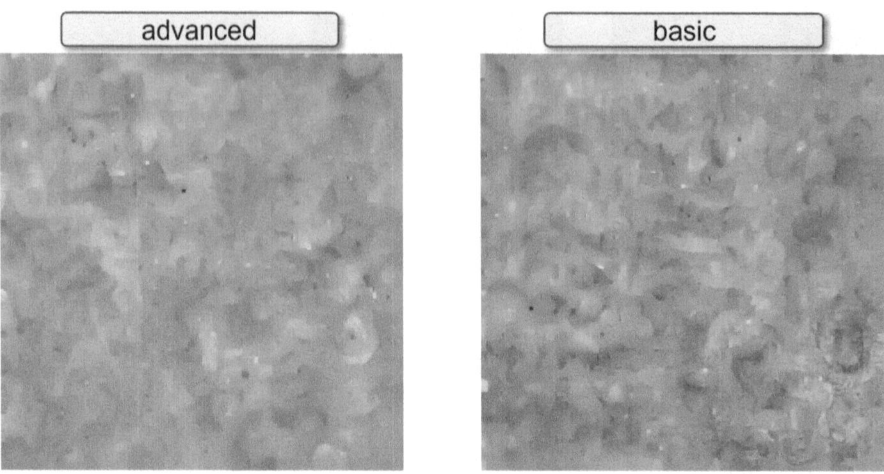

Fig. 7. Feature representation of "airplanes" in MS-COCO: Multiple levels of pooling result in varying activation layer visualizations that mimic wavelets likely resulting from Gabor-like filters within a neural network.

3.1 Model Training Using ResNet-50

ResNet-50 [7] was a suitable network architecture to train and extract learned feature representations from the RarePlanes dataset. It is just as capable in multi-object detection and classification as Detectron2 for images such as Fig. 6. Additionally, the network architecture is simple such that interrogating the network backend's activation layer can be performed with relative ease.

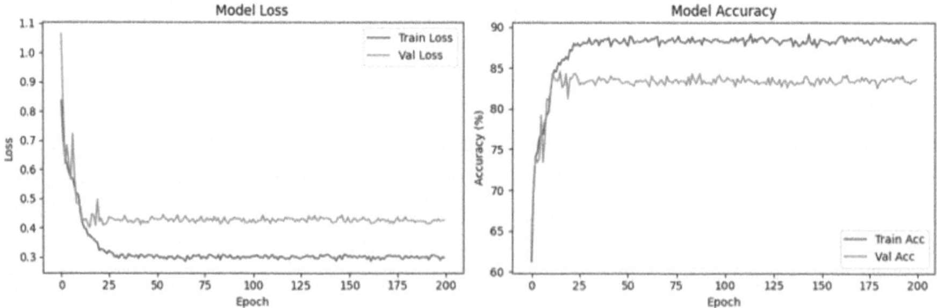

Fig. 8. Training Results: Model performance appears to plateau after 30 epochs. Visualizations of feature representations for each object category do not appear significantly different beyond this point.

We trained our network without modifications to the architecture, except the fully-connected (FC) layer. The default PyTorch ResNet50 has an FC layer comprised of average pooling with 1k-dimension FC layer, which we coerced to 3 in order to match the original RarePlanes experiment [14]. Variations of training epochs ranged from 30 to 200 as shown in Fig. 8. We've identified that any training epoch greater than 50 likely yields no benefit since model performance appears to plateau after 30 epochs.

3.2 Learned Feature Representations: Visualizing Model Embeddings

Once training is complete, we run a FeatureExtractor module (as shown in Fig. 9) which target and interrogate the trained FC layer containing our learned classes, resulting in a noisy feature map. This module extracts multiple visualizations of the activation layers, examples of which are shown in Fig. 13. Interestingly, the activations from the fully connected layer exhibit wavelet-like behavior with an apparent clustering as discussed in § 2.3.3. Though we cannot quantify these apparent clusterings from the activation wavelets, we suspect they congeal during the L2 regularization process when combined with aggressive Gaussian smoothing similar to the methods in [60].

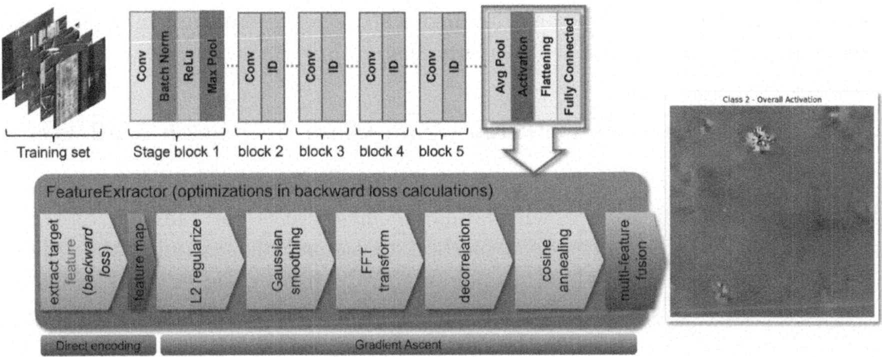

Fig. 9. Experimental Method: ResNet50's simplicity made interrogating the FC layers' activation layer simple while introducing less variability compared to similar architectures such as Detectron2.

Perhaps the most interesting contribution from [60] is the optimization method through strong regularization techniques where the optimization problem iteratively searches for an image x^* by starting at an arbitrary point x_0 and following gradient steps defined as regularization through an operator $r_\theta(\cdot)$ where $r_\theta \notin \nabla R_\theta$. $R_\theta(x)$ is a parameterized regularization function while similar to Eq. 3, $a_i(x)$ represents an activation for some unit i. Equation 4 below turns the noisy activation images similar to Fig. 13 and as discussed in § 2.3.3, likely causes wavelet clusters to congeal into features through aggressive regularization.

$$x^* = \underset{x}{\operatorname{argmax}}(a_i(x) - R_\theta(x)) \tag{4}$$

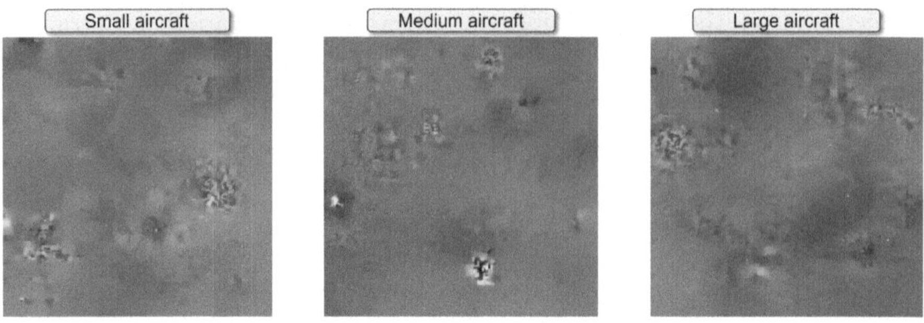

Fig. 10. Learned Feature Representations: A visualization of feature representations for each RarePlanes object categories extracted from ResNet embeddings.

A fused feature map similar to those in Fig. 7 and Fig. 10 is produced once the entire gradient ascent pipeline completes as described in Fig. 9. The FeatureExtractor fuses multiple activation feature maps which produces colorful patterns of discernible clusters, representing the features which the model has learned to each corresponding object category in the training set. Due to batch optimizations during the training, learned feature representation maps for each object category will vary, as will feature clusters from this output.

3.3 Extracting Salient Features Using Class Activation Models (CAMs)

Identifying prominent features within images can decrease compute during training or inference. CAMs provide a method to forensically examine the salient features within an image which propagates through a neural network's hidden layers as discussed in § 2.3.1-2.3.2. For this experiment, we elected to use a simple GradCAM in order to visualize the effects of image artifacts such as aberration (Fig. 11) and glint (Fig. 6). In Fig. 11, an aberration clearly inhibits any activation responses from res1 to res5. This reduced response affects of composability of features discussed in § 2.3.1 resulting in poor prediction scores.

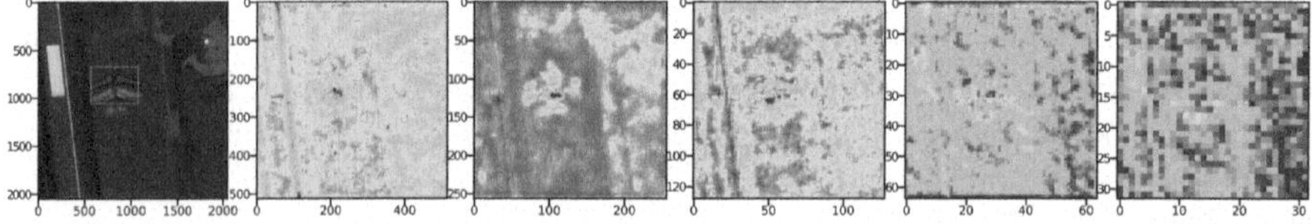

Fig. 11. Activation Response to Aberration: The blurring effect of an aberration can suppress activation response in CAMs, often resulting in poor prediction scores. Leftmost image is the input, with the following images representing res1 to res5 activation responses.

The differences in the scales (or size) of objects between hand-held and satellite imagery are remarkably different, thereby pushing the limits of CAMs. Figure 6 clearly shows how GradCAM struggles in smaller aircraft. Meanwhile, other smaller objects, such as cars within the same scene appear to induce a slight response. It is for this reason why limitations of CAM methods must be further explored as emphasized in [56].

4 Discussion

Explaining learned image features from satellite imagery training datasets can be performed today given existing methods such as those discussed in § 3.2 and § 3.3. By far, using CAMs has been the most popular method for explaining model behavior and is a great method to visualize the most salient features within an input image to observe inference behavior. However, it does not show the learned features by the model in the same way that gradient ascent does.

Further optimizations in gradient ascent, as applicable to satellite imagery, presents a fantastic research pursuit. Concurrence within the geospatial and remote sensing communities regarding a standard expression of image quality will abate existing impediments that result in improper quantification of model behavior performance. Image quality factors common to satellite imagery such as speckle due to atmospheric refraction, aberration due to optical limitations, and glint due to illumination variabilities certainly have to be accounted for in describing model training as well as inference behavior. A culmination of these factors may manifest in any feature representation outputs through gradient ascent methods as discussed, though a comprehensive image quality assessment of the corresponding dataset may reveal notable factors not discussed in this paper.

Finally, we must emphasize the need to overhaul Intersection over Union (IoU) metrics common to test harnesses in vision models today. Although we slightly discussed the current limitations of existing metrics in § 2, we cannot underscore the fact that small objects and features in satellite imagery push the limits of model performance today. Hence, it is difficult to trust the model due to the frequency of false positives and false negatives even as the model retains high prediction scores for detection. Our pursuit of explainable model methods led to the results we've presented, which presents excellent research opportunities into rigorous characterization of satellite imagery datasets as well as characterization of learned model features and its behavior.

5 Conclusions

Small features and objects common in satellite imagery push the performance limit of the best vision models available today. It is clear from our experiments that CAMs struggle with image clutter from small objects such as cars and small planes, which induces a slight activation and therefore uncertainty in detection and classification tasks. Although this effort did not emphasize the frequency of false positive and false negative detection results, they undoubtedly contributed to the performance results shown in Fig. 8.

Quantifying the limitations of model performance on small objects will remain an interesting research pursuit. In the short time we conducted our experiment, we've explored ideas such as utilizing Zernike moments to describe and quantify learned feature representations from our trained model, though this effort will require more time to complete. Nevertheless, CAMs in combination with gradient ascent methods demonstrate that salient features in training image data likely imprints into learned feature representations within model embeddings. Overcoming the challenges from small objects and features will yield better characterization of these learned feature representations and enable the quantification of Zernike moments in future work.

Acknowledgments. The authors would like to acknowledge In-Q-Tel for making the SpaceNet datasets available for research. The high-resolution imagery from Maxar facilitates the exploration of unique problem sets pertinent to scale challenges in computer vision. Finally, the authors are grateful to the University of Missouri, and the AIPR committee for the opportunity and support in this study.

Disclosure of Interests. The authors have no competing interests to declare relevant to the content of this article. The first author utilized GPU resources from vast.ai and open source datasets from SpaceNet.

A Appendix: Additional Figures

Fig. 12. The RarePlanes dataset were created using multiple image chips (blue boxes), sometimes overlapping. The numbered boxes in yellow are positive identification of correct aircraft (true positives) while red numbered boxes are false positives. RarePlanes licensed under CC-4.0-BY-SA license (Color figure online).

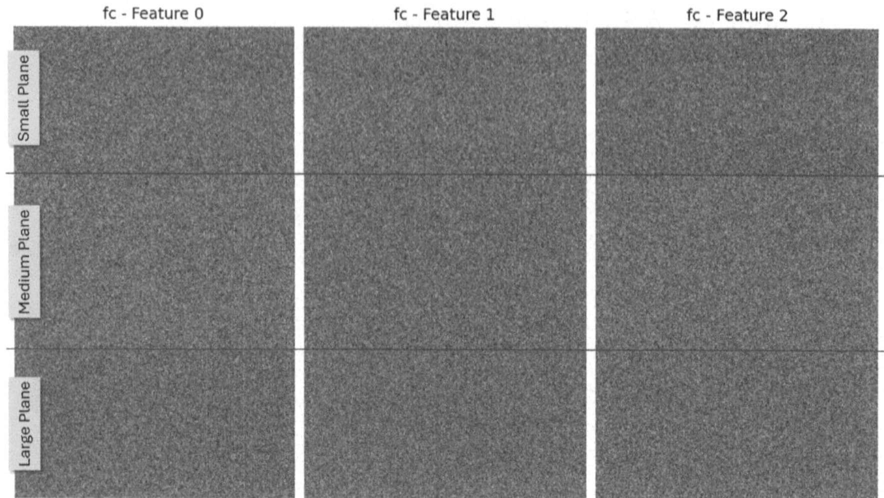

Fig. 13. A set of three activations from the fully connected layer for each of the RarePlanes object categories. Each appear to form clusters of wavelets, likely as a result of pooling from the early layers of the network acting as Gabor filters.

References

1. Krizhevsky, A., Sutskever, I., Hinton, G.E.: ImageNet classification with deep convolutional neural networks. Commun. ACM **60**(6), 84–90 (2017). https://doi.org/10.1145/3065386]
2. Russakovsky, O., et al.: ImageNet large scale visual recognition challenge (2015). http://arxiv.org/abs/1409.0575
3. Lin, T.Y., et al.: Microsoft COCO: common objects in context. http://arxiv.org/abs/1405.0312
4. Szegedy, C., et al.: Going deeper with convolutions, pp. 1–9. 2015 IEEE Conference on Computer Vision and Pattern Recognition (CVPR) (2015)
5. Lowe, D.: Object recognition from local scale-invariant features. In: Proceedings of the Seventh IEEE International Conference on Computer Vision, vol. 2, pp. 1150–1157. IEEE. http://ieeexplore.ieee.org/document/790410/
6. Dalal, N., Triggs, B.: Histograms of oriented gradients for human detection. In: 2005 IEEE Computer Society Conference on Computer Vision and Pattern Recognition (CVPR 2005), vol. 1, pp. 886–893. IEEE. http://ieeexplore.ieee.org/document/1467360/
7. He, K., Zhang, X., Ren, S., Sun, J.: Deep residual learning for image recognition. arXiv:1512.03385 (2015)
8. Xu, Z., Wang, T., Skidmore, A.K., Lamprey, R.: A review of deep learning techniques for detecting animals in aerial and satellite images. Int. J. Appl. Earth Observ. Geoinf. **128**, 103732 (2024). https://linkinghub.elsevier.com/retrieve/pii/S1569843224000864
9. Singh, S., Yadav, A., Jain, J., Shi, H., Johnson, J., Desai, K.: Benchmarking object detectors with COCO: A new path forward. In: Leonardis, A., Ricci, E., Roth, S., Russakovsky, O., Sattler, T., Varol, G. (eds.) Computer Vision – ECCV 2024,

vol. 15102, pp. 279–295. Springer Nature Switzerland, https://link.springer.com/10.1007/978-3-031-72784-9_16, series Title: Lecture Notes in Computer Science
10. Kuzucu, S., Oksuz, K., Sadeghi, J., Dokania, P.K.: On calibration of object detectors: pitfalls, evaluation and baselines. http://arxiv.org/abs/2405.20459
11. Fourure, D., Javaid, M.U., Posocco, N., Tihon, S.: Anomaly detection: how to artificially increase your f1-score with a biased evaluation protocol. http://arxiv.org/abs/2106.16020
12. Liu, L., Guo, W., Huang, S., Li, C., Shen, X.: From COCO to COCO-FP: a deep dive into background false positives for COCO detectors. http://arxiv.org/abs/2409.07907
13. Tong, K., Wu, Y.: Rethinking PASCAL-VOC and MS-COCO dataset for small object detection **93**, 103830. https://linkinghub.elsevier.com/retrieve/pii/S1047320323000809
14. Shermeyer, J., Hossler, T., Van Etten, A., Hogan, D., Lewis, R., Kim, D.: RarePlanes: synthetic data takes flight (2020). http://arxiv.org/abs/2006.02963
15. Yalcin, I., Kocaman, S., Saunier, S., Albinet, C.: Radiometric quality assessment for MAXAR HD imagery XLIII-B3-2021, 797–804. https://isprs-archives.copernicus.org/articles/XLIII-B3-2021/797/2021/
16. Cantrell, S.J., et al.: System characterization report on the worldview-3 imager (ver. 1.1, october 2021). In: Ramaseri Chandra, S.N. (ed.) System characterization of Earth observation sensors, chap. I, p. 29, 2021–1030 in Open-File Report, U.S. Geological Survey, Reston, VA (2021). https://pubs.usgs.gov/publication/ofr20211030I, version 1.1 (2021)
17. Hammoudeh, Z., Lowd, D.: Training data influence analysis and estimation: a survey **113**(5), 2351–2403. http://arxiv.org/abs/2212.04612
18. Szabo, G., Horvath, A.: Mitigating the bias of centered objects in common datasets. In: 2022 26th International Conference on Pattern Recognition (ICPR), pp. 4786–4792. IEEE (2022). https://ieeexplore.ieee.org/document/9956649/, https://doi.org/10.1109/ICPR56361.2022.9956649
19. Irvine, J.M., Israel, S.A.: An exploration of NIIRS, image quality, and machine learning. In: Palaniappan, K., Seetharaman, G., Doucette, P.J., Harguess, J.D. (eds.) Geospatial Informatics X, p. 18. SPIE, Online Only, United States (2020), https://www.spiedigitallibrary.org/conference-proceedings-of-spie/11398/2560587/An-exploration-of-NIIRS-image-quality-and-machine-learning/10.1117/12.2560587.full
20. Leachtenauer, J.C., Malila, W., Irvine, J., Colburn, L., Salvaggio, N.: General image-quality equation: GIQE. Appl. Opt. **36**(32), 8322 (1997). https://opg.optica.org/abstract.cfm?URI=ao-36-32-8322
21. Dodge, S., Karam, L.: Understanding how image quality affects deep neural networks. In: 2016 Eighth International Conference on Quality of Multimedia Experience (QoMEX), pp. 1–6. IEEE, Lisbon, Portugal (2016). http://ieeexplore.ieee.org/document/7498955/
22. Thurman, S.T., Fienup, J.R.: Analysis of the general image quality equation, p. 69780F (2008). http://proceedings.spiedigitallibrary.org/proceeding.aspx?, https://doi.org/10.1117/12.777718
23. Israel, I.M., Israel, S.A., Irvine, J.M.: Factors influencing CNN performance. In: 2021 IEEE Applied Imagery Pattern Recognition Workshop (AIPR), pp. 1–4. IEEE, Washington, DC, USA (2021). https://ieeexplore.ieee.org/document/9762112/

24. Israel, S.A., Jackson, K.L., Brennan, M.M., Martin, B.A., Tanis, J., Irizarry, N.: NIIRS, machine learning, and confidence: issues and opportunities for automating analysis
25. Shastry, A., Bini, A.A., Jidesh, P.: A Retinex inspired deep image prior model for despeckling and deblurring of aerial and satellite images using proximal gradient method **46**(3), 1432–1466. https://www.tandfonline.com/doi/full/10.1080/01431161.2024.2431175
26. Wei, G.: Generalized Perona-Malik equation for image restoration. IEEE Sig. Process. Lett. **6**(7), 165–167 (1999). http://ieeexplore.ieee.org/document/769359/
27. Indeck, J.S., Mares, J.O., Vitarelli, J.P., Hazeli, K.: Determination of the feature resolution of processed image data via statistical analysis. Microscopy Microanal. **27**(2), 357–364 (2021). https://academic.oup.com/mam/article/27/2/357/6888225
28. Torralba, A., Fergus, R., Freeman, W.: 80 Million tiny images: a large data set for nonparametric object and scene recognition. IEEE Trans. Pattern Anal. Mach. Intell. **30**(11), 1958–1970 (2008). http://ieeexplore.ieee.org/document/4531741/
29. Nguyen, A., Yosinski, J., Clune, J.: Deep neural networks are easily fooled: high confidence predictions for unrecognizable images. arXiv:1412.1897 (2015)
30. Khanna, S., et al.: DiffusionSat: a generative foundation model for satellite imagery. arXiv:2312.03606 (2024)
31. Bell, A., et al.: Earth AI: unlocking geospatial insights with foundation models and cross-modal reasoning. http://arxiv.org/abs/2510.18318
32. Han, D., Kim, J., Kim, J.: Deep pyramidal residual networks. In: The IEEE Conference on Computer Vision and Pattern Recognition (CVPR), pp. 5927–5935
33. Lin, T.Y., Dollár, P., Girshick, R., He, K., Hariharan, B., Belongie, S.: Feature pyramid networks for object detection. http://arxiv.org/abs/1612.03144
34. Wu, Y., Kirillov, A., Massa, F., Lo, W.Y., Girshick, R.: Detectron2. https://github.com/facebookresearch/detectron2
35. He, K., Zhang, X., Ren, S., Sun, J.: Delving deep into rectifiers: surpassing human-level performance on ImageNet classification. http://arxiv.org/abs/1502.01852
36. Zeiler, M.D.: Hierarchical convolutional deep learning in computer vision (2014)
37. Zeiler, M.D., Fergus, R.: Visualizing and understanding convolutional networks. http://arxiv.org/abs/1311.2901
38. Yosinski, J.: Training and understanding deep neural networks for robotics, design, and visual perception. Ph.D. thesis
39. Bengio, Y.: Deep learning of representations for unsupervised and transfer learning. In: Proceedings of the 2011 International Conference on Unsupervised and Transfer Learning Workshop - Volume 27, pp. 17–37. UTLW 2011, JMLR.org, place: Washington, USA
40. Nguyen, A., Yosinski, J., Clune, J.: Understanding neural networks via feature visualization: a survey (2019). http://arxiv.org/abs/1904.08939
41. Shu, Q., Zhu, X., Xu, S., Wang, Y., Liu, D.: RESTORE-DiT: reliable satellite image time series reconstruction by multimodal sequential diffusion transformer. Remote Sens. Environ. **328**, 114872 (2025). https://linkinghub.elsevier.com/retrieve/pii/S0034425725002767
42. Hamblin, C., Fel, T., Saha, S., Konkle, T., Alvarez, G.: Feature accentuation: revealing 'what' features respond to in natural images. arXiv:2402.10039 (2024)
43. Nguyen, A., Dosovitskiy, A., Yosinski, J., Brox, T., Clune, J.: Synthesizing the preferred inputs for neurons in neural networks via deep generator networks (2016). http://arxiv.org/abs/1605.09304

44. Yosinski, J., Clune, J., Bengio, Y., Lipson, H.: How transferable are features in deep neural networks? In: Proceedings of the 27th International Conference on Neural Information Processing Systems - Volume 2, pp. 3320–3328. NIPS 2014, MIT Press, Cambridge, MA, USA (2014). event-place: Montreal, Canada
45. Nguyen, A., Yosinski, J., Clune, J.: Multifaceted feature visualization: uncovering the different types of features learned by each neuron in deep neural networks (2016). http://arxiv.org/abs/1602.03616
46. Wang, Z.J., et al.: CNN explainer: learning convolutional neural networks with interactive visualization. IEEE Trans. Vis. Comput. Graph. **27**(2), 1396–1406 (2021). https://ieeexplore.ieee.org/document/9222325/
47. Achtibat, R., et al.: From attribution maps to human-understandable explanations through concept relevance propagation. Nat. Mach. Intell. **5**(9), 1006–1019 (2023). https://www.nature.com/articles/s42256-023-00711-8
48. Xiong, H., et al.: Towards Explainable Artificial Intelligence (XAI): a data mining perspective. arXiv:2401.04374 (2024)
49. Sorscher, B., Ganguli, S., Sompolinsky, H.: Neural representational geometry underlies few-shot concept learning **119**(43), e2200800119. https://pnas.org/doi/10.1073/pnas.2200800119
50. Wang, J., Chan, K.C.K., Loy, C.C.: Exploring CLIP for assessing the look and feel of images. http://arxiv.org/abs/2207.12396
51. Ilesanmi, A.E., Ilesanmi, T.O.: Methods for image denoising using convolutional neural network: a review. Complex Intell. Syst. **7**(5), 2179–2198 (2021). https://doi.org/10.1007/s40747-021-00428-4
52. Zhou, B., Khosla, A., Lapedriza, A., Oliva, A., Torralba, A.: Learning deep features for discriminative localization. In: 2016 IEEE Conference on Computer Vision and Pattern Recognition (CVPR), pp. 2921–2929. IEEE, Las Vegas, NV, USA (2016). http://ieeexplore.ieee.org/document/7780688/
53. Simonyan, K., Vedaldi, A., Zisserman, A.: Deep inside convolutional networks: visualising image classification models and saliency maps. http://arxiv.org/abs/1312.6034
54. Jiang, P.T., Zhang, C.B., Hou, Q., Cheng, M.M., Wei, Y.: LayerCAM: exploring hierarchical class activation maps for localization. IEEE Trans. Image Process. **30**, 5875–5888 (2021). https://ieeexplore.ieee.org/document/9462463/
55. Mohamed, E., Sirlantzis, K., Howells, G.: A review of visualisation-as-explanation techniques for convolutional neural networks and their evaluation. Displays **73**, 102239 (2022). https://linkinghub.elsevier.com/retrieve/pii/S014193822200066X
56. Bae, W., Noh, J., Kim, G.: Rethinking class activation mapping for weakly supervised object localization. In: Vedaldi, A., Bischof, H., Brox, T., Frahm, J.-M. (eds.) ECCV 2020. LNCS, vol. 12360, pp. 618–634. Springer, Cham (2020). https://doi.org/10.1007/978-3-030-58555-6_37
57. Bastos, I.L.O., Soares, L.R., Schwartz, W.R.: Pyramidal Zernike over time: a spatiotemporal feature descriptor based on Zernike moments. In: Mendoza, M., Velastín, S. (eds.) CIARP 2017. LNCS, vol. 10657, pp. 77–85. Springer, Cham (2018). https://doi.org/10.1007/978-3-319-75193-1_10
58. Jung, H., Oh, Y.: Towards better explanations of class activation mapping. In: 2021 IEEE/CVF International Conference on Computer Vision (ICCV), pp. 1316–1324. IEEE, Montreal, QC, Canada (2021). https://ieeexplore.ieee.org/document/9710512/
59. Chen, P., Agarwal, C., Nguyen, A.: The shape and simplicity biases of adversarially robust ImageNet-trained CNNs. arXiv:2006.09373 (2022)

60. Yosinski, J., Clune, J., Nguyen, A., Fuchs, T., Lipson, H.: Understanding neural networks through deep visualization (2015). http://arxiv.org/abs/1506.06579
61. Datta, S., Sundararaman, D.: Evaluating hallucination in large vision-language models based on context-aware object similarities (2025). http://arxiv.org/abs/2501.15046, arXiv:2501.15046
62. Pham, M.T., Courtrai, L., Friguet, C., Lefèvre, S., Baussard, A.: YOLO-fine: one-stage detector of small objects under various backgrounds in remote sensing images **12**(15), 2501. https://www.mdpi.com/2072-4292/12/15/2501

Synthetic Aperture Radar Change Detection as a Source of Ground-Truth Annotation for Machine Learning Deforestation Detection in the Amazon Using Multispectral Satellite Imagery

Andrew Kalukin[1](✉), Joe Soundarajan[2], Dong Xu[2], and Renaldi Gondosubroto[3]

[1] Through Sensing LLC, Arlington, VA 22201, USA
andrew.kalukin@throughsensing.com
[2] University of Missouri, Columbia, MO 65211, USA
[3] Cloudetica Solutions, Melbourne, Australia

Abstract. The requirement of annotated data as a source of ground truth is often the bottleneck in machine learning applications. The process of manual annotation is expensive and labor intensive. Simulation has been investigated as a possible source of ground truth annotated data, but in many cases, simulated datasets fail to accurately capture enough physical characteristics of machine learning classes to be useful. For satellite image target recognition, an alternative to manual annotation and simulation is to use image data from one sensor as a source of ground truth for training the other sensor. In this study, we investigate the correlation between multispectral time series image data of Amazon deforestation which were manually annotated and processed by AI, and SAR data collected over the same region during overlapping time intervals. For a set of geographical points which exceeded some threshold of change in time series of multispectral data, the change detection seen in an overlapping time series of SAR data had positive Pearson correlation coefficients ranging up to 0.7. This result suggests the possible utility of using SAR change detection data as a source of ground truth for machine learning for multispectral imagery of deforestation change.

Keywords: Machine Learning · Automated Annotation · SAR Change Detection · Synthetic Aperture Radar · Wildfire Detection · Deforestation Detection · Multimodal Computer Vision · Multi-sensor Remote Sensing

1 Background

1.1 Motivation

Deforestation from manmade development and wildfires has become one of the most important environmental problems [1]. For example, 50 thousand square kilometers of forests (Food and Agriculture Organization) lost from 2015 to 2020 [2], and deforestation contributes 15% of global greenhouse gas emissions (IPCC) [3].

F. Tanner and J. Irvine (Eds.): AIPR 2025, LNCS 16446, pp. 451–462, 2026.
https://doi.org/10.1007/978-3-032-18474-0_31

Solving the problem of deforestation depends on enhanced monitoring and intervention strategies. Satellite imagery processed with computer vision and artificial intelligence can detect deforestation events across the globe in real-time. Combining different satellite platforms, such as Sentinel-1, Sentinel-2, and Landsat-8, enhances area coverage and gives the best available spectral resolution available from commercial satellites required for efficient forest monitoring. Quantifying forest loss provides valuable metrics for understanding the scale of deforestation and its impact. Analyzing historical satellite data allows researchers to track changes in forest cover over time and assess the effectiveness of conservation efforts.

The use of satellite imagery for automated global monitoring of environmental issues such as deforestation and wildfires is impeded by the need to manually build ground truth datasets for training and testing machine learning systems [1]. The manual process can be labor-intensive and costly, and the revisit rate of the satellite platforms may be too infrequent to ensure that enough wildfire and deforestation examples are available for testing and training an automated machine learning system.

One means of compensating for limited image data is to use multimodal imaging, that is, to image a given area with multiple sensors that provide complementary data or additional ground truth. Though a trained image analyst may be able to manually identify corresponding features in images collected from two or more sensors, machine learning systems may be challenged to automatically find corresponding image features. If multimodal datasets are registered to one another, that is, if the latitude and longitude of image coordinates is reasonably accurate in all the images, it may be possible to use image data from one sensor, for example, SAR, as ground truth data for another sensor, for example, multispectral imaging (MSI).

There are several reasons that synthetic aperture radar (SAR) would be expected to work well as ground truth for deforestation and wildfire damage. SAR penetrates cloud cover and can be used to detect the presence or absence of foliage. SAR captures dielectric properties and is useful for distinguishing classes that look similar in MSI products. SAR products can take advantage of polarization states to distinguish between single-bounce, double-bounce, and multiple-bounce scattering from objects in a scene, which often provides clear contrast between vegetation and manmade objects or bare earth terrain [4].

1.2 Prior Research

Several examples exist in recent scientific literature where SAR data has been used as ground truth or a complementary modality to train or validate machine learning models for optical sensors. For example, Verma et al. (2023) used fully polarimetric L- and S-band airborne SAR data (LS-ASAR) over Santa Barbara, CA, for urban and land cover classification [5]. The researchers applied Barnes, Cloude, and H/A/Alpha decomposition models to extract scattering parameters. These parameters were used to train Support Vector Machines (SVMs) for classifying urban, vegetation, waterbody, and open ground. The SAR-derived labels and separability analysis helped improve classification accuracy in optical imagery by reducing misclassification between visually similar classes.

As an example of data fusion between SAR and optical datasets, Biswas & Rathore (2024) demonstrated fusion of L-band polarimetric SAR (PolSAR) from ALOS PALSAR with Sentinel-2A optical imagery for paleochannel mapping [6]. The data fusion of the two different sets was used to identify paleochannels and playas, which contain features that are often obscured in optical data by vegetation or surface texture. Machine learning models trained on SAR-derived features provided ground truth for validating optical-based predictions.

Another recent study in 2024 integrated SAR and optical data to detect changes in tall vegetation [7]. The researchers used machine learning to fuse temporal SAR data with optical imagery, validated against SAR-derived ground truth. The study achieved high accuracy at 10-m resolution, demonstrating SAR's value in validating optical-based vegetation monitoring.

2 Methodology

2.1 Deep Learning Based on Multispectral Data

This study has been built on deep learning algorithms applied to multispectral Sentinel-2 satellite data [1]. Previously reported results for two benchmark datasets used by other researchers (Amazon forest segmentation [8] and FireDataset_20m [9]) demonstrated Intersection Over Union (IOU) and pixel accuracy over 90% (Table 1). The results for the Sentinel-2 satellite data were based on machine learning applied to RGB and NIR data only. The Amazon forest dataset focuses on four key Sentinel-2 bands: Band 4 (Red, 665 nm), Band 3 (Green, 560 nm), Band 2 (Blue, 490 nm), and Band 8 (Near-Infrared, 842 nm). These bands can distinguish vegetation from non-vegetated areas. The Near-Infrared (NIR) band is sensitive to chlorophyll content, making it ideal for detecting forested regions.

The deep learning method for the MSI portion of this research combines the DeepLabV3 + architecture with an EfficientNet-B08 backbone to address both deforestation and wildfire detection using satellite imagery. The FireDataset_20m, developed by Farhat et al., has inherent class imbalance between fire and non-fire pixels which accurately reflects the real-world nature of wildfire occurrence but creates problems for deep learning model applications. FireDataset_20m achieves 99.95% accuracy, 93.16% precision, and 91.47% recall.

Table 1. Comparison of DeepLabV3 + EfficientNet-B8 method (rightmost column) with other benchmark Deep Learning methods applied to MSI imagery [1].

Metric	DeepLabV3+/ResNeXt101 (A)	UNet++/ResNeXt101 (B)	SAM2 (C)	YOLOv8 (D)	DeepLabV3+/EfficientNet-B8 (E)
Accuracy	39.79%	40.11%	62.41%	64.65%	95.94%
Precision	39.79%	40.11%	57.64%	54.68%	94.62%
Recall	100.00%	100.00%	43.74%	98.54%	95.19%
F1 Score	56.93%	57.25%	49.73%	70.33%	94.90%

2.2 Multimodal Deep Learning Based on SAR with Multispectral Data

The question to be answered is whether SAR can be used as a source of ground truth for annotating the ground truth used for MSI machine learning, or as a complementary source of data for training and testing machine learning models that rely primarily on MSI.

There are advantages for SAR compared to MSI that come from the ability of radar in typical imaging frequency ranges (for example, X-band) to penetrate clouds. Some of the results for the abovementioned study had false positives due to cloud cover (Fig. 1). SAR would not be expected to give radar returns or false positives in the presence of cloud cover.

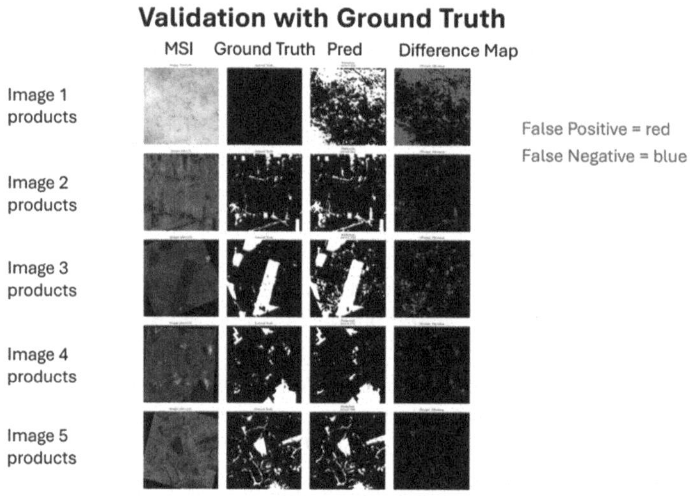

Fig. 1. Example deforestation results. The Difference Map for the Image 1 products shown in the first row shows many false positives (red), because of cloud cover affecting the optical imagery.

2.3 Comparison of Overlapping Time Series of SAR and NDVI Heat Maps

To use MSI or SAR products to monitor deforestation change, it is necessary to collect time series of image data products. For MSI, it is typical to use the Normalized Difference Vegetation Index (NDVI) as a metric for quantifying health and density of vegetation in MSI [10]. The NDVI is calculated from red (RED) and near-infrared bands (NIR) as

$$\text{NDVI} = (\text{NIR}-\text{RED})/(\text{NIR} + \text{RED}). \tag{1}$$

The NIR band captures subtle vegetation changes indicating deforestation or fire damage. The SAR change detection time series enables detection of scattering changes due to deforestation and wildfire damage. Both Sentinel-2 NDVI and Sentinel-1 SAR time series can be used to detect and map the changes caused by deforestation and wildfire damage.

The dataset used for the research in this article was a co-registered dataset consisting of Sentinel-1 SAR and Sentinel-2 NDVI image products derived from MSI [11]. The co-registration of the two different data types enables comparison of detections between the modalities (Fig. 2–3) using data fusion products. In Fig. 3, the red areas strong in vertically transmitted / vertically received radar polarization (VV) would be expected to correspond to flat areas with no vegetation such as water or roads; green areas strong in vertically transmitted / horizontally received radar polarization (VH) might correspond to vegetated areas with multiple scattering, such as trees or bushes; and purple and blue areas strong in NDVI might correspond to low-lying vegetation such as grass or small plants with no multiple scattering [4].

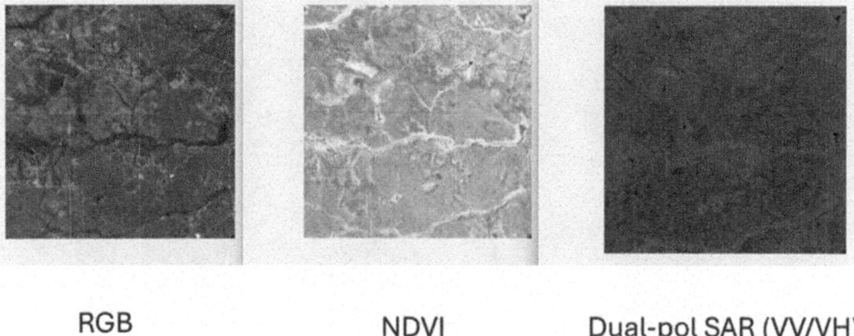

Fig. 2. Co-registration of RGB and NDVI derived from Sentinel-2, and dual-polarization SAR derived from Sentinel-1, shows good correspondence in the features seen in the co-registered products.

Fig. 3. (Left) Composite fusion product from co-registered of NDVI derived from Sentinel-2, and dual-polarization SAR derived from Sentinel-1, shows good alignment of features. The bands are formed as follows: Red = SAR VV; Green = SAR VH; Blue = NDVI. (Right) Google Earth snapshot of the same area (Municipal Unit of Etoliko, Greece).

Each of the abovementioned products is an image product from a specific date. To compare time series data, a heat map is a useful tool, which measures the amount of change between each pair of successive images from the same sensor (Fig. 4).

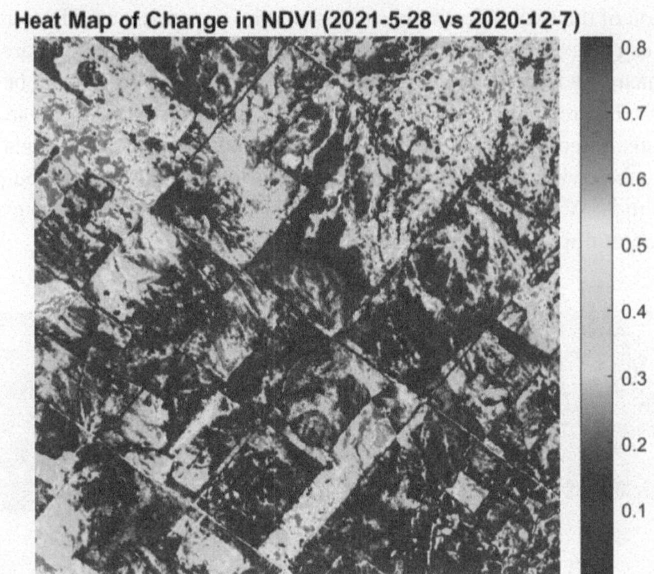

Fig. 4. Heap map example showing change between MSI image data from the same location collected on two different dates.

In many cases, SAR and NDVI are both collected for time series monitoring of wildfires and deforestation. However, though some deforestation and wildfire datasets have been annotated previously using masks in the examples above, in most cases, users will have to manually annotate their own data. This process is labor-intensive and time-consuming, and it would be expensive for an organization to manually build deforestation change detection ground truth data on a global scale.

3 Results

The existence of overlapping time series of NDVI and SAR datasets opens the possibility of using SAR change detection as ground truth for NDVI detection of deforestation, or vice versa. To test this hypothesis, we applied the AI deforestation detection algorithms for time series of NDVI products from MSI and SAR datasets collected in the Amazon. Below are examples of NDVI and SAR change detection products which show correlated measurements of deforestation change (Fig. 5), correlated measurements of lack of change (Fig. 6), and in a few cases lack of correlation (Fig. 7). The "VV" in the SAR plot refers to the polarization state, which was vertical for both transmitting and receiving.

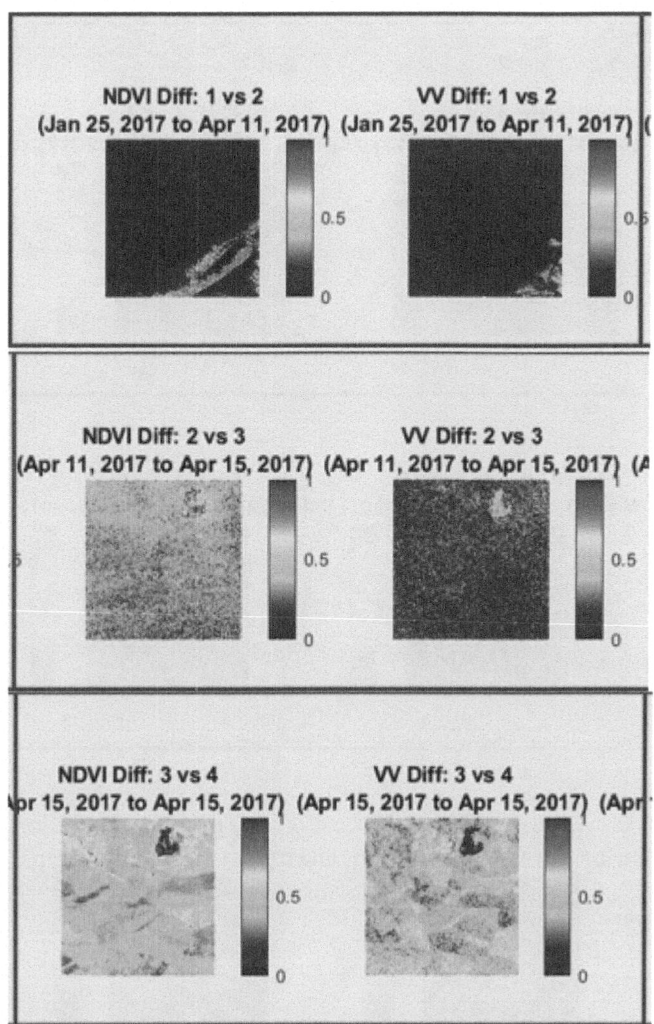

Fig. 5. NDVI and SAR change detection time series comparisons showing comparable levels of change in deforestation.

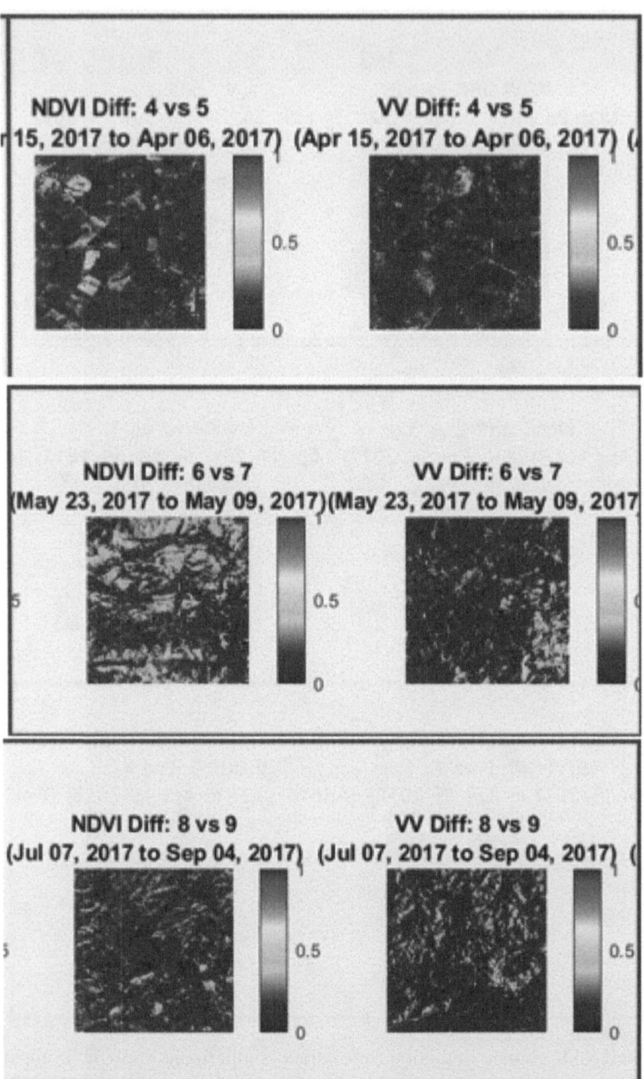

Fig. 6. NDVI and SAR change detection time series comparisons showing comparable lack of change in deforestation.

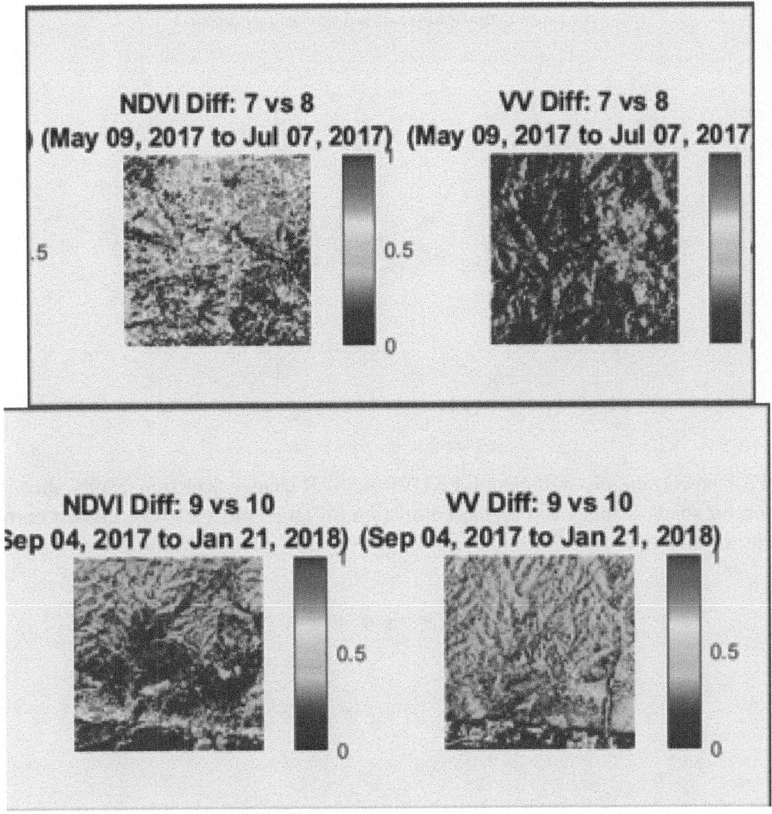

Fig. 7. NDVI and SAR change detection time series comparisons showing differences in their detection of change in deforestation.

The level of correlation between the NDVI and SAR change detection products varies (Fig. 8). Part of the lack of correlation in some cases may be due to differences in the level of correlation for small amounts of change versus large amounts of change; that is, the level of correlation seems to be higher for large amounts of change (Fig. 9). When the datasets are filtered to include only points in the top 25% of change magnitude, the changes in SAR VV and the changes in NDVI become more visibly correlated (Fig. 10).

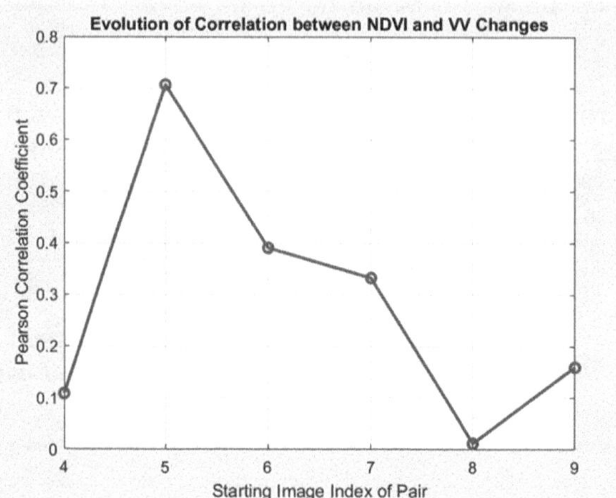

Fig. 8. Pearson correlation coefficient for NDVI and SAR change detection results, showing low correlation for small changes and higher correlation for larger changes. The highest correlation coefficient was 0.7.

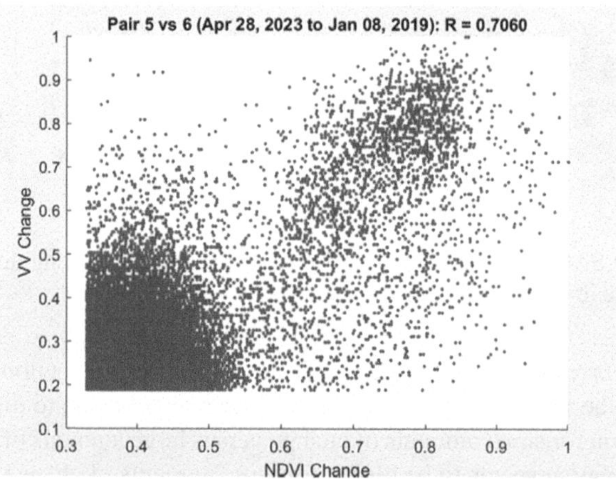

Fig. 9. Scatter plot for NDVI and SAR change detection results, showing low correlation for small changes and higher correlation for larger changes. The Pearson correlation coefficient R = 0.7060.

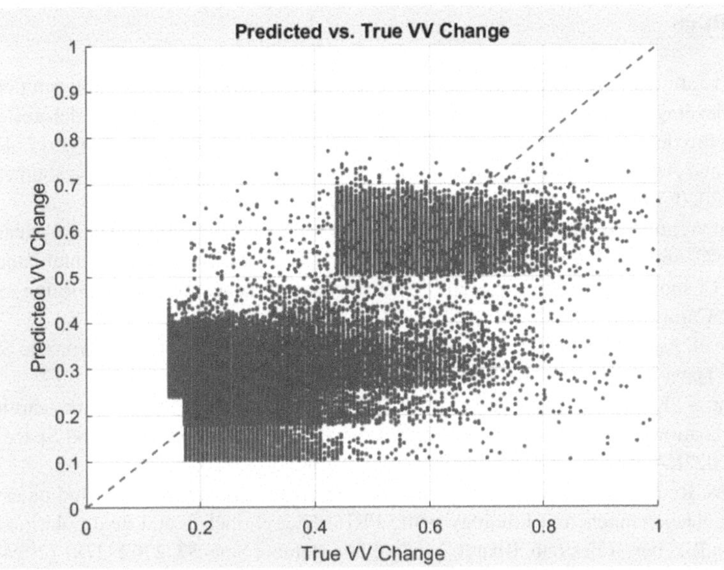

Fig. 10. Predicted versus measured change in SAR VV returns for the top 25% of magnitude of change.

4 Conclusions

SAR and NDVI change detections that are unfiltered for the magnitude of change show correlation ranging from weak to strong, with Pearson correlation coefficient of 0.7 in the best case. Filtering to consider only larger changes improved the correlation, possibly by reducing the effects of spurious changes due to random image artifacts. This correlation may indicate that SAR might be a useful training dataset for NDVI and other MSI signatures. Overlapping SAR and NDVI collections may make it feasible to use SAR change detection as ground truth for MSI wildfire and deforestation detection. This method of automated ground truth development could improve AI models for global monitoring and make available complementary sources of deforestation change detection data.

Acknowledgments. The authors received AWS credits from Amazon Corporation for cloud computations used for this research, donated by the Taylor Geospatial Institute (TGI) & AWS Generative AI for Geospatial Challenge (2024–2025).

Disclosure of Interests. TGI & Amazon Corporation provided AWS credits for cloud processing. Neither TGI nor Amazon edited or reviewed this research article, and the research results and conclusions are the authors' own. No other external funding was used for this research. Cloudetica Solution's research was funded from internal funding by Through Sensing LLC.

References

1. Soundararajan, J., Kalukin, A., Malof, J., Xu, D.: Deep learning-driven multi-temporal detection: leveraging deeplabv3+/efficientnet-b08 semantic segmentation for deforestation and forest fire detection. Remote Sens. **17**, 2333 (2025). https://doi.org/10.3390/rs17142333
2. Food and Agriculture Organization of the United Nations. Global Forest Resources Assessment 2020: Main Report; FAO: Rome, Italy (2020)
3. Intergovernmental Panel on Climate Change. Climate Change 2021: The Physical Science Basis; Cambridge University Press: Cambridge, UK, 2021. Intergovernmental Panel on Climate Change. Climate Change 2021: The Physical Science Basis; Cambridge University Press: Cambridge, UK (2021)
4. Freeman, A., Durden, S.L.: A three-component scattering model for polarimetric SAR data. IEEE Trans. Geosci. Remote Sens. **36**(3), 963–973 (1998)
5. Verma, S., Kumar, S., Dsouza, H.: Polarimetric decomposition and machine learning-based classification of L- and S-band Airborne SAR (LS-ASAR) Data. Earth and Space Science, **10**, e2022EA002796 (2023). https://doi.org/10.1029/2022EA002796
6. Biswas, R., Rathore, V.S.: Spectral analysis to explore gypsum deposits and its association with palaeochannels and lithology using PRISMA, sentinel 2, and dual-polarimetric SAR data in Bikaner, Rajasthan, Bharat. J Indian Soc Remote Sens **52**, 2769–2781 (2024). https://doi.org/10.1007/s12524-024-01865-7
7. Rathore, K., Maurya, A.K., Singh, D.: Potential assessment of SAR and optical data with machine learning to monitor temporal changes in tall vegetation. J Indian Soc Remote Sens **52**, 2807–2824 (2024). https://doi.org/10.1007/s12524-024-02056-0
8. Bragagnolo, L., da Silva, R.V., Grzybowski, J.M.V.: Amazon and Atlantic Forest Image Datasets for Semantic Segmentation. Zenodo (2021)
9. Farhat, H., Daniel, L., Benguigui, M., Girard, A.: Model and dataset for multi-spectral detection of forest fires on board satellites. In: Proceedings of the National Conference on Artificial Intelligence (CNIA 2022), Saint Étienne, France, 27–29 June 2022; Paper ffhal-03866412. https://ci.mines-stetienne.fr/pfia2022/conferences/cnia/?utm_source=chatgpt.com. Accessed on 2 July 2025
10. Rouse, J.W, Haas, R.H., Scheel, J.A., Deering, D.W.: Monitoring vegetation systems in the great plains with ERTS. Proceedings, 3rd Earth Resource Technology Satellite (ERTS) Symposium, vol. **1**, p. 48–62 (1974)
11. Vasquez, R., Garavito Gonzalez, A.: Dataset of Sentinel-1 SAR and Sentinel-2 NDVI Imagery. Mendeley Data, V1 (2024). https://doi.org/10.17632/xjcr5k4c9t.1

Real-Time 2D Mapping and Navigation on an Indoor Autonomous Vehicle (AV) Platform with RPLiDAR A3 and HectorSLAM

Christopher Tetteh Nenebi(✉), Sally Acquaah, Andrews Tang, Kourtney Tucker, Issa W. AlHmoud, and Balakrishna Gokaraju

Computational Data Science and Engineering, North Carolina A&T State University, Greensboro, NC 27410, USA
{ctnenebi,snacquaah,atang,ketucker}@aggies.ncat.edu, {iwalhmoud,bgokaraju}@ncat.edu

Abstract. The development of cost-effective indoor autonomous robots critically depends on robust and efficient simultaneous localization and mapping (SLAM) capabilities. This paper presents a low-cost mobile robotic platform that integrates the Slamtec RPLIDAR A3 sensor with the open-source HectorSLAM algorithm to generate high-precision 2D occupancy grid maps in real time. The system is designed to operate reliably in GPS-denied environments such as laboratories, warehouses, and multi-level buildings, where traditional odometry sources, such as wheel encoders, inertial measurement units (IMUs), or GPS, may be absent or unreliable. Using exteroceptive LiDAR data exclusively, the proposed approach eliminates the need for complex sensor fusion and calibration procedures, thus reducing system complexity and deployment overhead. The hardware architecture is centered on an NVIDIA Jetson TX2 running Ubuntu 20.04 and ROS Noetic, with motion control managed by an Arduino Mega 2560 via the rosserial interface. LiDAR data are processed through the HectorSLAM package and visualized in RViz using standard ROS networking. Experimental validation in a controlled Quanser studio environment demonstrates mapping accuracy that exceeds 90 %. This work will be implemented on an autonomous mobile robot for indoor waypoints following and obstacle avoidance. These results confirm the feasibility of implementing an affordable and calibration-free SLAM framework for autonomous indoor robotic applications.

Keywords: Localization · Mapping · Navigation · RPLiDAR A3 · HectorSLAM

1 Introduction

Mapping is the process of building a useful picture of an environment from sensor data. This picture can take different forms. Some maps are metric, meaning they

F. Tanner and J. Irvine (Eds.): AIPR 2025, LNCS 16446, pp. 463–483, 2026.
https://doi.org/10.1007/978-3-032-18474-0_32

store exact distances and angles between objects. Others are topological, focusing more on how different places are connected rather than on precise measurements. In all cases, these maps are more than just drawings, thus they allow a robot or autonomous system to answer a key question: "Where am I right now?" with respect to known landmarks or regions in the environment. Over time, different mapping strategies have been proposed, such as occupancy grid maps that divide space into cells marked as free, occupied, or unknown; topological maps that represent the world as nodes and connections; feature-based maps that store key points like corners or patterns; and scan-matching methods that line up consecutive LiDAR scans to gradually build a complete map.

However, all of these methods share a major weakness: they rely strongly on how accurate and reliable the sensors are. Cameras struggle in low light or when the lighting changes quickly. Ultrasonic and infrared sensors can easily be disturbed by reflections and noise. Even affordable 2D LiDAR sensors can cause errors and drift if they are not correctly aligned or calibrated. These problems become even more serious when good odometry is not available. Common odometry sources such as wheel encoders, inertial measurement units (IMUs), and GPS are often missing or unreliable indoors. GPS signals do not reach inside buildings like labs or warehouses, small robots may skip encoders to keep the design simple, and IMUs need heavy filtering to deal with thermal drift and magnetic disturbances.

This research addresses the pressing need for affordable simultaneous localization and mapping solutions in such constrained environments. Specifically, it targets use cases where traditional odometry sources are either unavailable or unreliable and where the cost and complexity of sensor calibration must be minimized. The proposed system enables robust mapping and navigation in indoor spaces denied global positioning while reducing hardware dependencies and operator intervention. Using exteroceptive LiDAR exclusively, the platform eliminates the need for complex sensor fusion pipelines, making it suitable for educational, prototyping, and resource-constrained deployment scenarios.

To overcome the challenges outlined above, this work uses the Hector's simultaneous localization and mapping algorithm, which uses a high-frequency Gauss-Newton scan matching routine directly on raw LiDAR data. Unlike approaches that depend on external odometry, Hector's simultaneous localization and mapping (HectorSLAM) align each incoming scan frame with the global map, continuously updating the robot's pose through local point-cloud matching. This makes it particularly well suited for lightweight mobile robots that lack wheel encoders or inertial measurement units, and allows for real-time, drift resilient mapping without the need for prior sensor calibration or global positioning infrastructure.

The contributions of this work are as follows:

1. Development of a low-cost mobile robot that integrates an NVIDIA Jetson TX2, Arduino Mega 2560, Slamtec RPLIDAR A3, and open-source HectorSLAM algorithm.
2. The developed system performs real-time scan-to-map alignment using the RPLiDAR A3 integrated with the HectorSLAM algorithm, enabling incre-

mental map generation and continuous pose estimation for autonomous indoor navigation.
3. A fully real-time, odometry-independent SLAM framework was implemented on an embedded NVIDIA Jetson TX2 platform, achieving greater than 90% mapping accuracy under real laboratory conditions.
4. Validation that an affordable, odometry-free SLAM solution can support robust indoor exploration and navigation on resource-constrained hardware.

The remainder of the paper is organized as follows: In Sect. 2, we present previous works with an emphasis on alternative SLAM algorithms used in mapping construction for robot localization and navigation tasks; Section 3 presents a detailed description of the methodology, including the experimental setup, the hardware and software architectures, and the mapping processes adopted in this research; Experimental results are discussed in Sect. 4; and finally, the paper is concluded and some directions for future work are presented in Sect. 5.

2 Literature Review and Background

Robust and efficient simultaneous localization and mapping (SLAM) technologies are fundamental to indoor autonomous navigation, particularly in environments where traditional localization methods, such as GPS, are unavailable or unreliable. Markom et al. [1] demonstrated the practicality of a low-cost RP LiDAR for indoor mapping, achieving high accuracy (above 90%) through raw-filter and moving-average preprocessing. While effective for static mapping, this approach produces a single offline map without continuous localization feedback. Similarly, [2] implemented Bayesian Occupancy-Grid mapping combined with HectorSLAM and AMCL, using 2D LiDAR to achieve reliable performance in GPS-denied environments. However, this method depends on prior maps, odometry, and idealized sensor models, and was validated primarily in simulation.

Cheng and Wang [3] provided a comparative study of HectorSLAM and GMapping, highlighting the effectiveness of HectorSLAM in environments lacking reliable odometry, attributed to its high-frequency scan matching capabilities. This position HectorSLAM as particularly suitable for budget-sensitive, real-time indoor applications. To support these findings, [4] reviewed various SLAM methodologies, underscoring the ongoing preference for 2D LiDAR in indoor real-time applications due to its computational simplicity and resistance to lighting variations, despite advancements in 3D and visual SLAM systems. Csaba et al. [5] proposed an integrated navigation system fusing 2D LiDAR with infrared and ultrasonic sensors, applying Gaussian filtering and sliding-window averaging to enhance obstacle detection. Though this multi-sensor design improved local stability and short-range avoidance, it produced reactive navigation only, lacking global mapping or persistent localization. More recent developments further explore multisensor integration for improved indoor navigation. Acquaah et al. [6] combined YOLOv5-based object detection with Intel RealSense depth detection, introducing a rule-based decision system for dynamic obstacle avoidance. Their framework demonstrated high efficiency and adaptability in complex, multi-robot environments. Vegesana et al. [7] similarly emphasized the strength of multisensor systems, integrating LiDAR, IMU and YOLOv5-based vision processing, coupled with pathfinding algorithms like A*, significantly improving autonomous navigation reliability. Complementing this, [8] detailed the integration of IMU and camera data with PID-based control for precise lane follow, enhancing the robot's responsiveness to dynamic environmental changes. In parallel, [9] leveraged machine learning models, specifically Random Forest classifiers, trained on LiDAR data to predict steering commands, achieving near-perfect accuracy and demonstrating LiDAR's capability in robust autonomous navigation without complex sensor fusion.

Furthermore, [10] implemented particle filter-based SLAM using ROS frameworks, successfully integrating the A* and Dynamic Window Approach (DWA) algorithms for robust navigation in simulated indoor scenarios.

Tola et al. [11] also employed cartography algorithms alongside AMCL for effective localization and path planning, strengthening the benefits of using open-source ROS packages for efficient indoor autonomous navigation. However, this method requires wheel odometry, IMU data, and LiDAR for accurate loop closure and localization. Map consistency in this method depends heavily on odometry precision and sensor synchronization. In general, these works underscore the effectiveness of affordable and computationally efficient LiDAR-based SLAM systems for indoor navigation, validating HectorSLAM and multi-sensor integration as practical and robust solutions. This study contributes to these advances by presenting a calibration-free, real-time SLAM framework that uses exteroceptive LiDAR data exclusively, to construct and optimize a 2D map for indoor autonomous robot navigation.

3 Methodology

3.1 System Architecture and Implementation

The NVIDIA Jetson TX2 serves as the computational core of our system, equipped with a powerful GPU capable of handling intensive processing tasks. It performs real-time SLAM and processes incoming LiDAR scan data with high efficiency. Motion control is managed by an Arduino Mega 2560 microcontroller in conjunction with servo actuators and a motor driver board, which together govern the robot's linear and angular movements. The robot chassis employs an Ackermann steering configuration, enhancing both maneuverability and navigational stability. Power is supplied through two independent battery packs;one dedicated to the Jetson TX2 and the other to the motor drivers. This separation ensures stable and isolated power delivery to each subsystem, contributing to consistent and reliable performance during indoor navigation. Each subsystem underwent individual validation testing in controlled indoor environments, confirming their operational readiness and ensuring dependable performance during autonomous navigation.

Figure 1 and 2 show the schematic diagram of robot hardware components and real AV respectively.

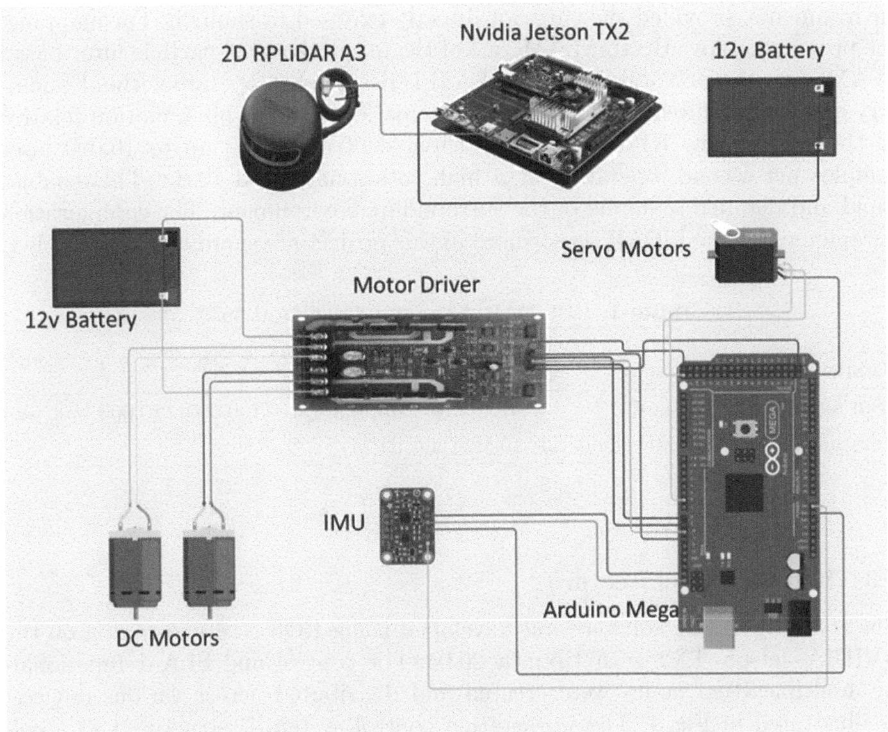

Fig. 1. AV's schematic diagram.

Fig. 2. AV Setup for Mapping the Environment.

3.2 Slamtec RPLIDAR A3

The primary equipment used in this project is the RPLIDAR A3, a 360-degree 2D laser scanner. Developed by SLAMTEC, it utilizes a cost-effective laser triangulation system that delivers reliable performance in most indoor and outdoor environments, provided they are not directly exposed to sunlight. For mapping, the project employs HectorSLAM, one of the most advanced particle filter-based SLAM algorithms. Notably, HectorSLAM is designed to operate without odometry and is well-suited for platforms that experience roll or pitch motion relative to the sensor. The RPLiDAR A3 is capable of capturing up to 16,000 laser samples per second, operating at a high rotational speed 10 Hz. This enables rapid and detailed scanning of the surrounding environment. The configuration parameters for the LiDAR sensor used in this project are summarized in Table 1.

Table 1. RPLiDAR A3 sensor Configurations.

Parameter	Type	Values
Scan mode	Standard	Moderate sampling rate (100,000–120,000 hits/sec)
Rotational speed	Normal / moderate	10 Hz (600 RPM)

3.3 Software Architecture

The robot operating software was developed using ROS Noetic, running on the NVIDIA Jetson TX2 with Ubuntu 20.04. For control and SLAM functionality, multiple ROS nodes were created and distributed across various devices, as illustrated in Fig. 3. The workstation control system is structured as a collection of autonomous nodes that interface with the Jetson TX2 and operate independently across different hardware platforms. Motor control is managed by an Arduino Mega 2560, which receives commands from the Jetson TX2 via serial communication to execute robot movements. At each timestep, the laser node processes newly scanned LiDAR data and publishes it to the /scan topic. The robotic system incorporates several coordinate frames originating from various onboard sensors. These transformations are managed by the base frame node, which publishes the resulting data to the /tf topic, ensuring accurate spatial alignment across the system.

The HectorSLAM node subscribes to the /tf and /scan topics to receive transformed coordinate data and laser scan inputs, respectively, as illustrated in Fig. 4. Each newly captured laser scan contributes to updating the robot's pose in real time. The resulting map is published to the /map topic, as shown in Fig. 3. Rviz, a visualization tool within ROS (Fig. 5), enables users to dynamically observe the robot's pose and the evolving map. These elements are rendered in real time by the Rviz node running on a connected PC. All nodes within the system are orchestrated and managed by the ROS master, which operates on the NVIDIA Jetson TX2.

3.4 ROS Environment

The Robot Operating System (ROS) is built on the Linux platform and provides a collection of libraries and tools designed to facilitate the development of

```
roscore http://ub...   /home/balulab/c...   /home/balulab/c...   /home/balulab/c...
balulab@ubuntu:~/catkin_ws$ rosnode list
/hector_geotiff_node
/hector_mapping
/hector_trajectory_server
/joint_state_publisher_gui
/laser_to_base
/robot_state_publisher
/rosout
/rplidarNode
/rviz
balulab@ubuntu:~/catkin_ws$ rostopic list
/clicked_point
/initialpose
/joint_states
/map
/map_metadata
/map_updates
/move_base_simple/goal
/poseupdate
/rosout
/rosout_agg
/scan
/slam_cloud
/slam_out_pose
/syscommand
/tf
/tf_static
/trajectory
balulab@ubuntu:~/catkin_ws$
```

Fig. 3. List of ros-topics and ros-nodes.

robotic applications. It enables the creation of a modular framework for robot functionality using key components such as nodes, packages, message topics, and services [12]. Figure 6 illustrates the high-level communication architecture within the ROS ecosystem. In ROS, any executable code that processes sensor data or transmits output to other components is referred to as a node. The system follows a publish-subscribe communication model, where data from sensors is encapsulated as messages and transmitted through topics. A node that sends messages on a topic is known as a publisher, while a node that receives messages from a topic is called a subscriber. This publisher-subscriber mechanism is depicted in Fig. 7. All related nodes, along with their dependencies, are organized into a ROS package, which can be easily installed and deployed on any Linux machine running ROS.

3.5 HectorSLAM Implementation

HectorSLAM is a grid-based SLAM algorithm that distinguishes itself by operating without requiring any odometry input-unlike many conventional SLAM methods. Instead, it relies solely on high-frequency 2D LiDAR data and an evolving occupancy grid map. The core principle behind HectorSLAM is scan matching, where each new 360° LiDAR sweep is aligned with either previous scans or the current map using optimization techniques. The algorithm minimizes a cost function that penalizes discrepancies between new scan endpoints

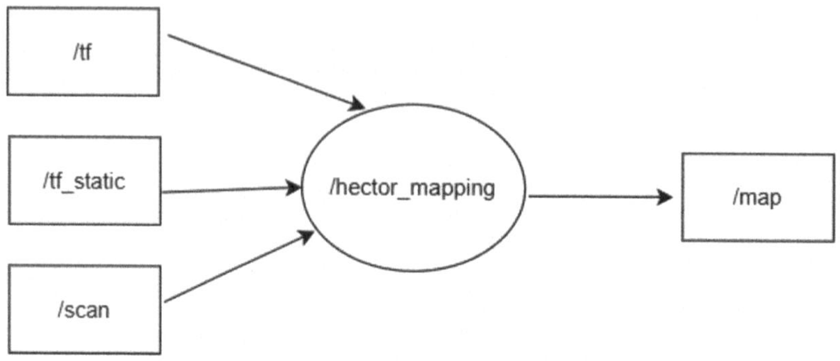

Fig. 4. Hector-slam node subscribed to topics.

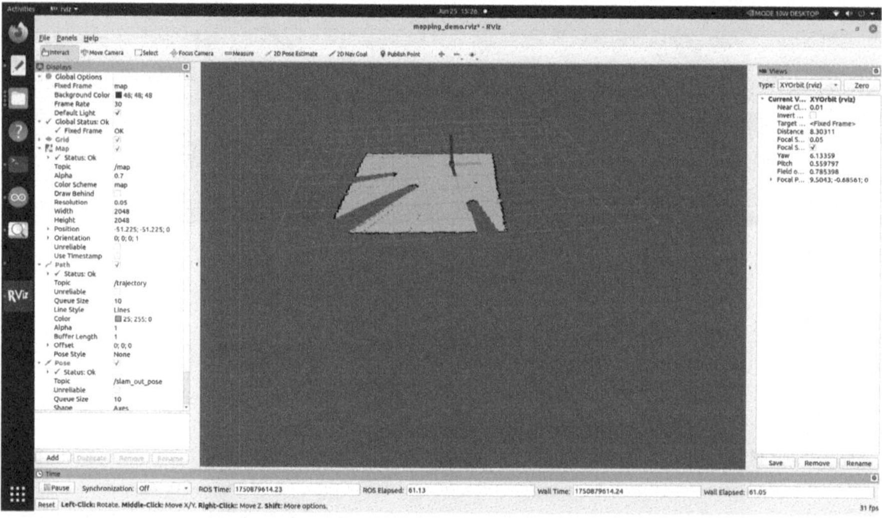

Fig. 5. RViz for map visualization.

and high-probability occupied cells in the map. This alignment process is solved using a Gauss-Newton iterative method, which estimates the rigid-body transform that best aligns the current scan with the accumulated map. As new scans are matched against the existing map, they are implicitly aligned with all previous scans, making the process highly robust and resilient to drift over time.

Laser rangefinders are ideal for HectorSLAM due to their low noise and high precision, which significantly outperforms traditional wheel encoder-based odometry. As a result, HectorSLAM provides accurate, drift-resilient pose estimates and real-time mapping even in the absence of wheel encoders or inertial sensors.

In ROS, HectorSLAM is implemented through the *hector_mapping* package, which includes supporting tools such as *hector_map_server*, *hec-*

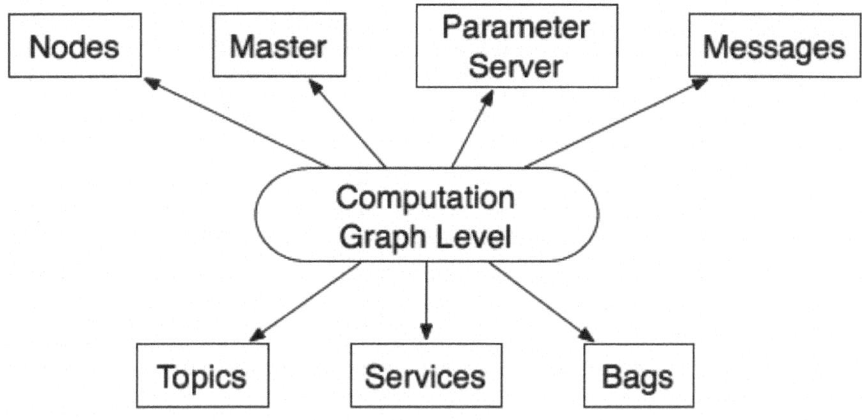

Fig. 6. High-level communication processes in ROS.

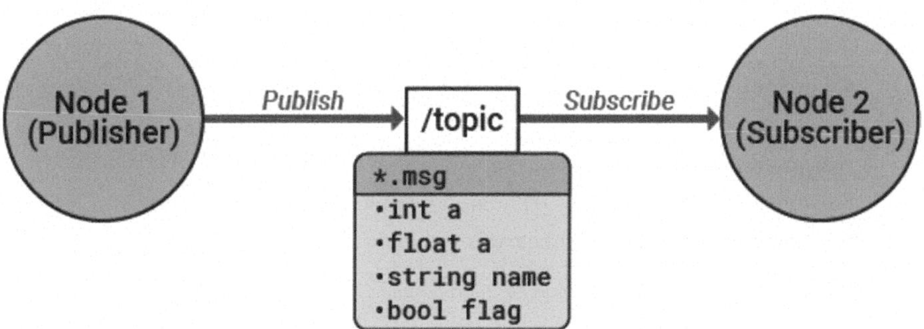

Fig. 7. Interaction between publisher and subscriber.

tor_ trajectory_ server, and *hector_ geotiff*. The *hector_ mapping* node subscribes to real-time 2D LiDAR scans and publishes various topics including:

- `map`: A latched topic containing the updated occupancy grid map.
- `slam_out_pose`: The estimated robot pose (without covariance).
- `poseupdate`: A Gaussian estimate of the robot's pose with uncertainty.

These outputs support both live visualization in RViz and downstream tasks such as navigation and path planning. Once the environment has been fully explored and mapped, the final map can be saved using the *map_ server* node for future localization or navigation tasks.

3.6 Mapping Process

The Slamtec RPLiDAR A3 sensor is securely mounted on top of the robot chassis to enable unobstructed 360-degree range measurements of the environment [13]. During operation, the RPLiDAR driver node publishes obstacle detection data as `sensor_msgs/LaserScan` messages on the `/scan` topic at a maximum rate 10 Hz. To initiate mapping with HectorSLAM, first launch the ROS master (`roscore`), followed by invoking HectorSLAM using a single ROS launch configuration (*hector_ mapping*). Upon starting `roscore`, a communication graph is established, connecting nodes for the RPLiDAR driver, HectorSLAM, and the robot's motor control interface. Table 2 and Fig. 8 present the terminal commands used during the experiment and outline the associated ROS topics and computational nodes. While teleoperating the robot via keyboard commands, the *hector_ slam* node continuously subscribes to the `/scan` topic and performs Gauss-Newton-based scan matching optimization on successive LiDAR sweeps relative to the existing map. With each iteration, a new scan is integrated into an incremental `nav_msgs/OccupancyGrid`, progressively constructing a high-accuracy two-dimensional map of indoor environments such as the Quanser studio shown in Fig. 9.

Table 2. Terminal instructions for the setup

Command	Purpose
roscore	Start ROS Master node
roslaunch robot_model robot_model.launch	Load AV URDF
roslaunch rplidar_ros view_rplidar_a3.launch	Start LiDAR node
roslaunch hector_slam_launch tutorial.launch	Launch HectorSLAM
python3 manual.py	Manual control

In parallel with this process, dynamic map visualization is performed in RViz, launched from a separate terminal window. This allows the user to continuously monitor the completeness and integrity of the mapping process. The integrated sensor-to-map data flow highlights how obstacle information from the RPLiDAR A3 is utilized to construct accurate occupancy grids, which are essential for subsequent navigation and path planning tasks. Figure 10 shows the flow for the proposed mapping task execution.

Figure 11, Fig. 12 and Fig. 13 illustrate the progressive evolution of the map as the robot navigates through a Quanser studio populated with obstacles. In contrast, Fig. 14 presents the final map generated after the robot traverses an obstacle-free Quanser studio. The outer boundaries in both cases represent the studio walls, which serve as reflective surfaces for the LiDAR beams during the mapping process.

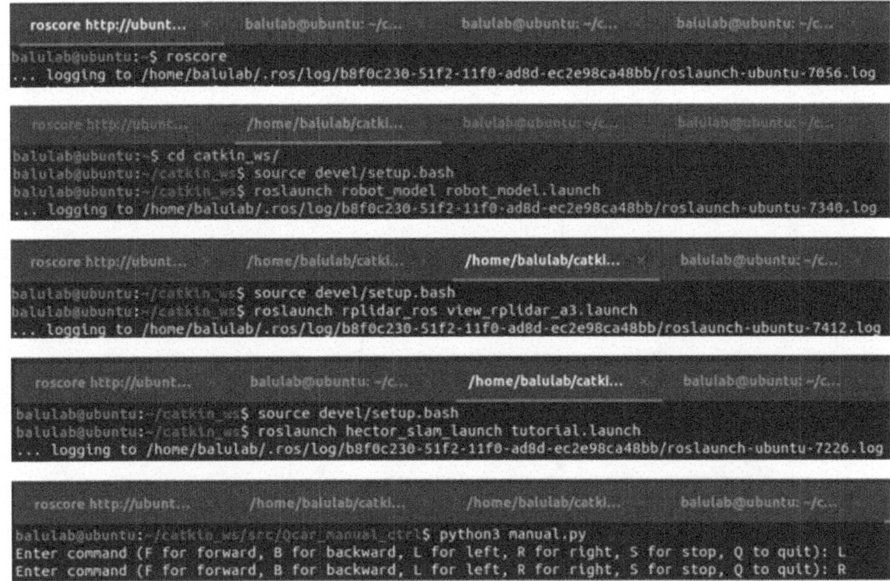

Fig. 8. Terminal instructions used for AV's setup and mapping.

Fig. 9. Quanser studio for the experiment.

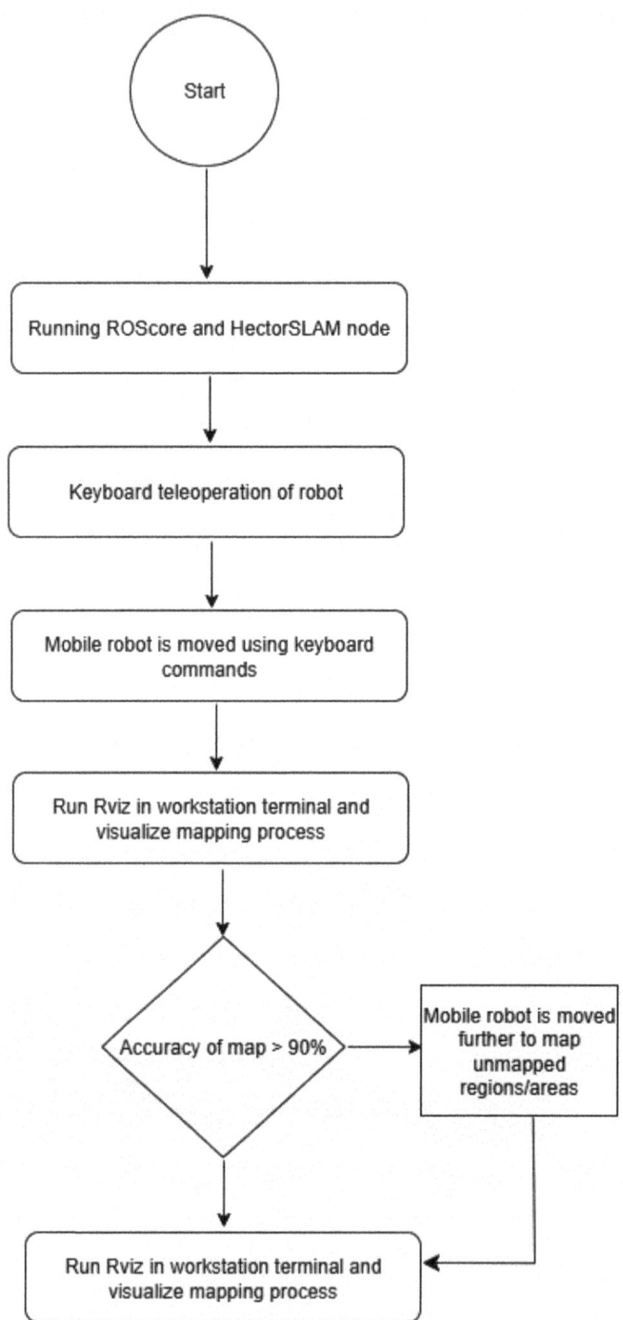

Fig. 10. Designed pipeline for executing the mapping task.

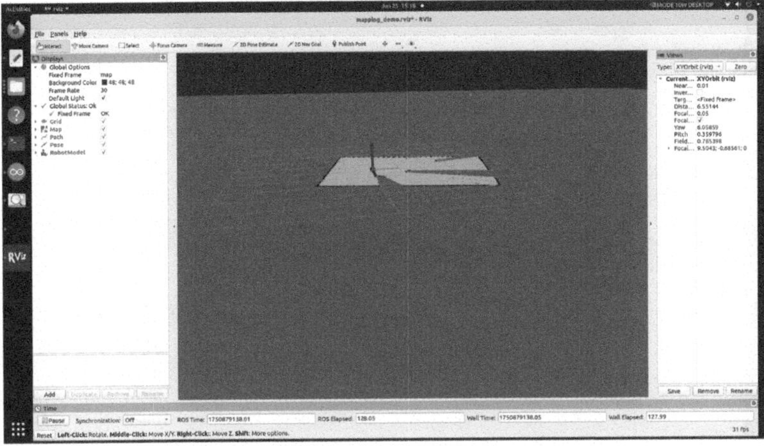

Fig. 11. Mapping process at stage I.

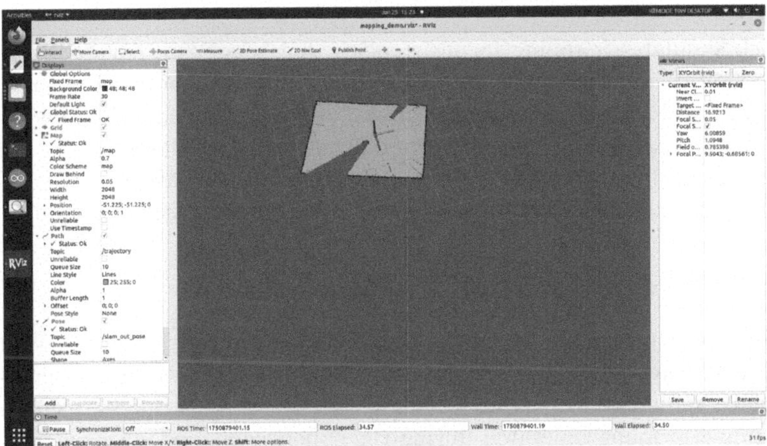

Fig. 12. Mapping process at stage II.

4 Results and Discussion

To evaluate the mapping accuracy of the HectorSLAM-based autonomous navigation system, we developed a Python script that performs cell-wise comparisons between binary occupancy grid maps. The ground truth reference (Fig. 14) and the obstacles generated maps (Fig. 15a, 15b, 16, 17, 18) were converted into binary format using OpenCV thresholding. These maps were chosen for their minimal schematic structure and consistent layout, making them well-suited for direct pixel-wise comparison. To emulate real-world variability and sensor-induced noise, the script introduced controlled random perturbations, flipping between 1% and 2% of the occupancy grid cells during each run. This

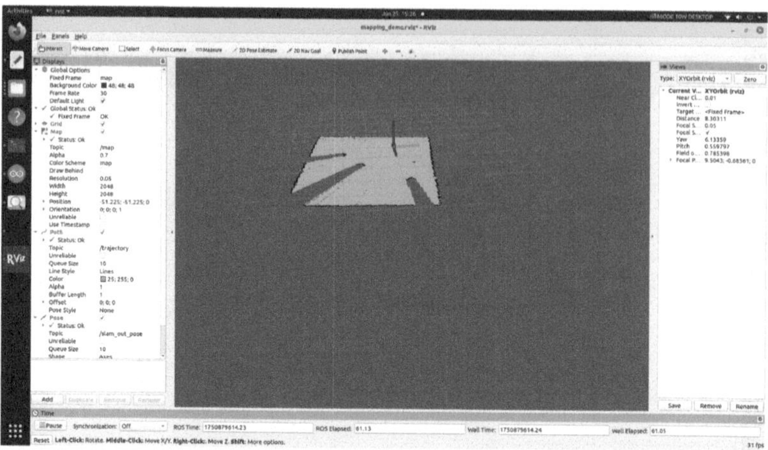

Fig. 13. Mapping process at stage III.

approach simulates mapping inconsistencies that may arise from SLAM drift, partial observation, or resolution mismatches. Despite these injected variations, the system consistently achieved accuracy above 90%, demonstrating robustness and repeatability. Table 3 presents representative results from five randomized trials, showing that correct cell match counts and overall mapping accuracy remain within acceptable bounds for indoor autonomous navigation applications.

4.1 Performance Metrics

To assess the mapping quality of the HectorSLAM-based system, three primary metrics were employed: cell-wise mapping accuracy, average accuracy across multiple trials, and standard deviation. These metrics were calculated using binary occupancy grid maps generated during the experiments and subsequently compared against a predefined ground truth map.

4.2 Cell-Wise Mapping Accuracy

Mapping accuracy is defined as the percentage of correctly matched cells, those labeled identically in both the ground truth and the generated maps, relative to the total number of cells compared. It is computed as:

$$\text{Accuracy} = \frac{N_{\text{correct}}}{N_{\text{total}}} \times 100 \tag{1}$$

where N_{correct} is the number of matching occupied and free cells between the two maps, and N_{total} is the total number of cells compared. For all experiments in this study, $N_{\text{total}} = 512 \times 512 = 262{,}144$.

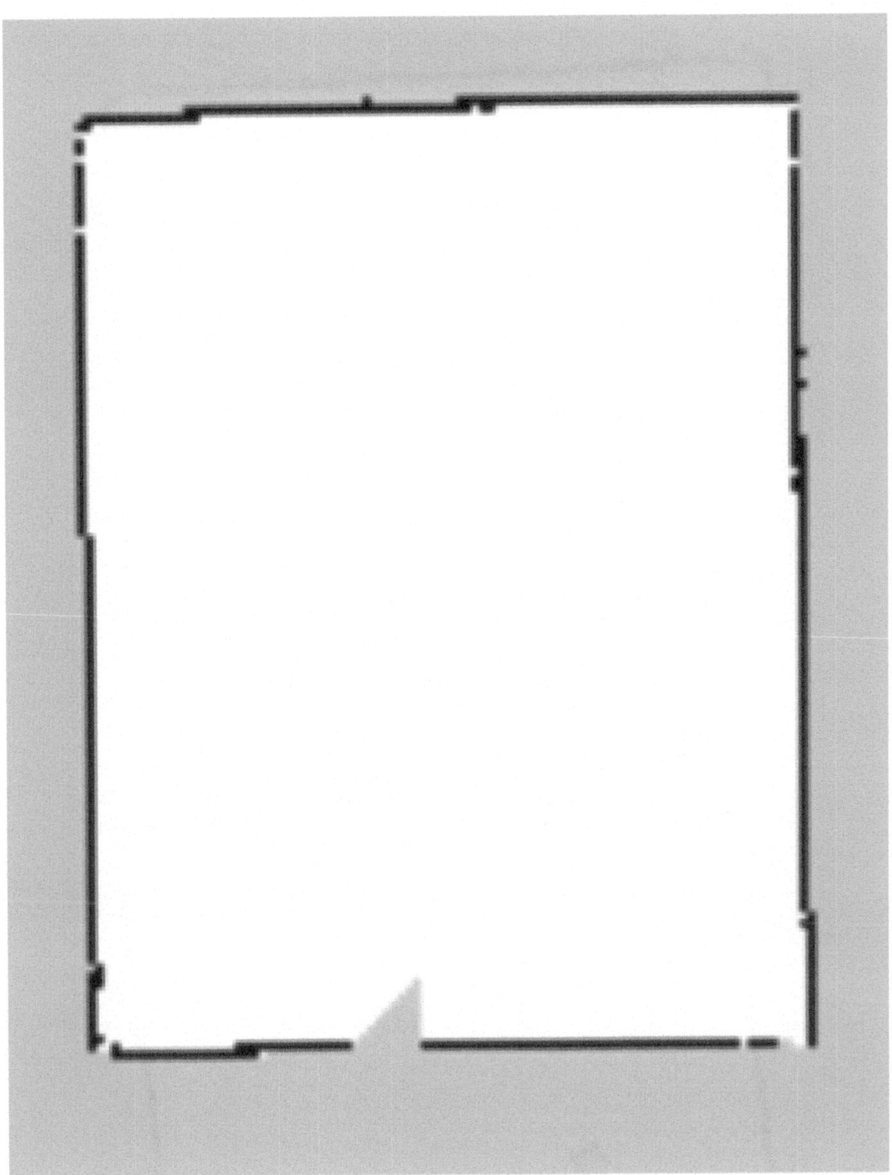

Fig. 14. Map of Quanser studio without obstacles.

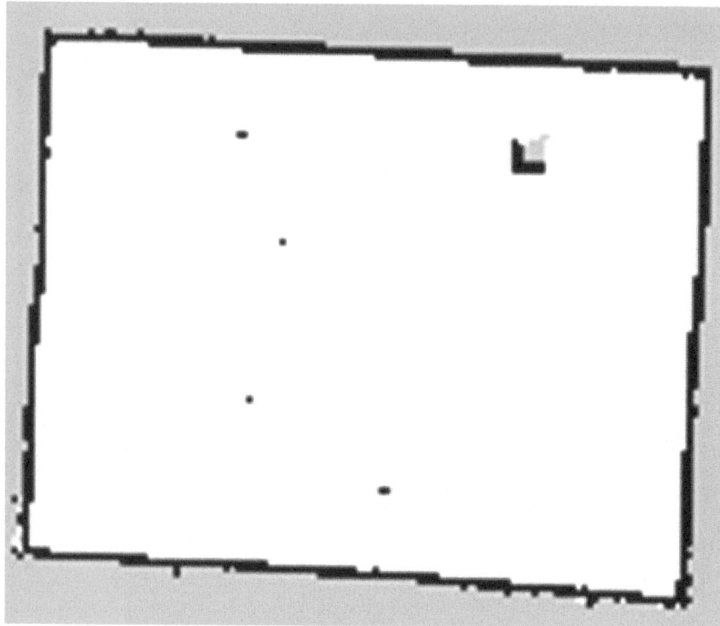

(a) Map of Quanser studio with five obstacles.

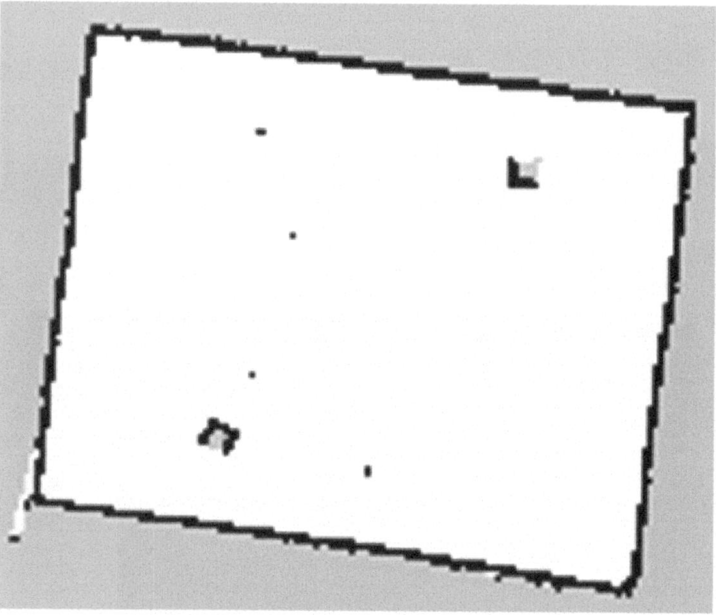

(b) Map of Quanser studio with six obstacles.

Fig. 15. Comparison of Quanser studio maps with (a) five obstacles and (b) six obstacles.

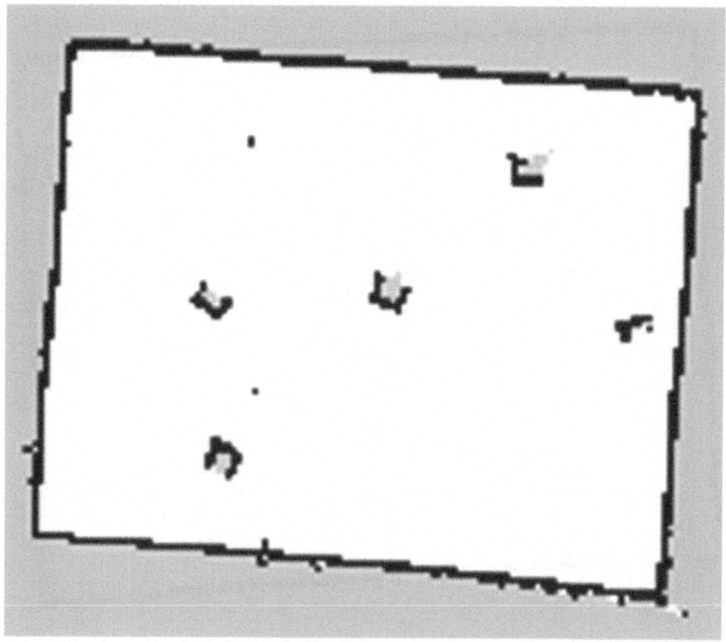

Fig. 16. Map of Quanser studio with seven obstacles.

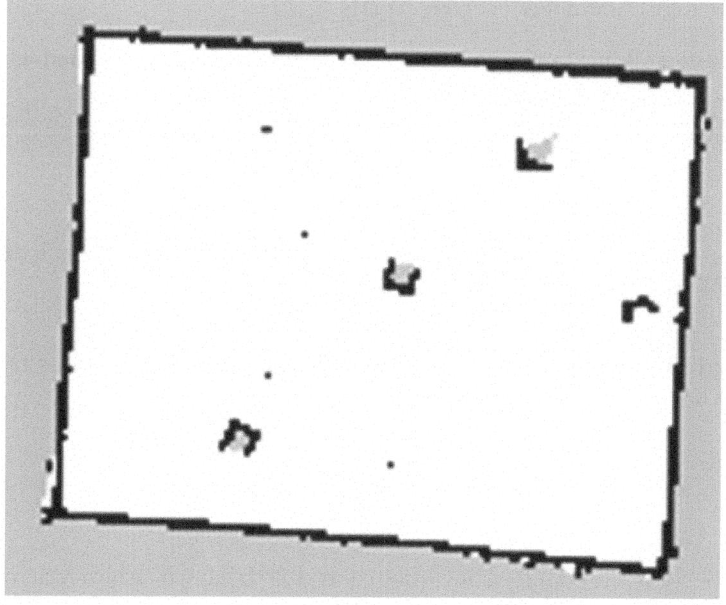

Fig. 17. Map of Quanser studio with eight obstacles.

Fig. 18. Map of Quanser studio with ten obstacles.

4.3 Average Accuracy Across Trials

To ensure consistency and reproducibility, each experiment was conducted multiple times, and the average mapping accuracy was computed as:

$$\bar{A} = \frac{1}{n}\sum_{i=1}^{n} A_i \tag{2}$$

where A_i represents the mapping accuracy of the ith trial, and n is the total number of trials conducted.

Standard Deviation. To measure the variation in accuracy across trials, the standard deviation was computed using:

$$\sigma = \sqrt{\frac{1}{n}\sum_{i=1}^{n} \left(A_i - \bar{A}\right)^2} \tag{3}$$

where σ denotes the standard deviation, and $\bar{A}$ is the mean accuracy across trials as defined in Eq. 3. These statistical metrics provide a quantitative foundation to evaluate the robustness of the mapping system under varying conditions and minor perturbations introduced to simulate real-world variation.

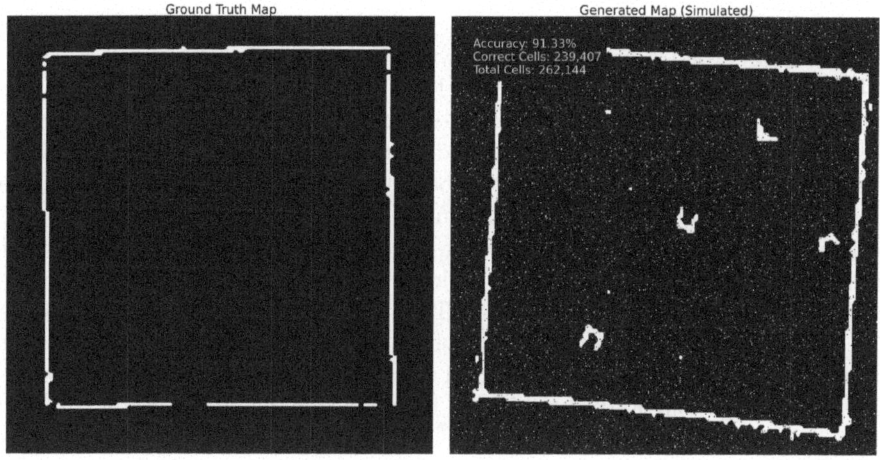

Fig. 19. Metrics of the analysis with eight obstacles.

Figure 19 illustrates the performance metrics obtained from one of the five experimental trials, in which the map containing eight obstacles was evaluated against the ground truth reference.

Table 3. Mapping accuracy across randomized experimental trials

Trial	Number of Obstacles	Correct Cells	Total Cells	Accuracy (%)
1	5	240,072	262,144	91.58
2	6	241,006	262,144	91.94
3	7	238,820	262,144	91.10
4	8	239,407	262,144	91.33
5	10	236,244	262,144	90.12
Average Accuracy				**91.21**
Standard Deviation				**0.69**

5 Conclusion

This work introduced a reliable and cost-effective SLAM framework for indoor mobile robotics, integrating the Slamtec RPLiDAR A3 with the HectorSLAM algorithm on a lightweight robotic platform. The proposed solution addresses the increasing demand for affordable SLAM systems by removing the reliance on high-end sensors and complex calibration routines, thereby reducing both system cost and setup complexity. By relying solely on exteroceptive LiDAR data, the system effectively overcomes challenges associated with the absence or unreliability of traditional odometry inputs such as wheel encoders, inertial measurement units (IMUs), and global positioning systems (GPS). This design simplification enhances robustness and makes the framework particularly suitable for deployment in GPS-denied environments, including laboratories, warehouses, and multi-level indoor structures. Experimental validation in a controlled Quanser studio environment demonstrated consistent mapping performance, with the system achieving an average accuracy of $91.21 \pm 0.69\%$ across multiple randomized trials. The low standard deviation highlights excellent repeatability, confirming the stability of the HectorSLAM-based mapping pipeline under minor environmental perturbations. These results validate the framework's robustness, reliability, and practicality for real-time indoor mapping and navigation. Future work will focus on extending the system toward autonomous waypoint following and obstacle avoidance, further enhancing its applicability for resource-constrained and educational robotic platforms.

Acknowledgment. The authors thank the following agencies for their partial support: 1) the United States Department of Commerce (USDOC), Economic Development Administration Good Jobs Challenge Awardee, STEPS4GROWTH (ed22hdq3070099), 2) National Science Foundation's – Engineering Research Center (NSF - ERC) Hybrid Autonomous Manufacturing, Moving from Evolution to Revolution (HAMMER) (Award No.: 2133630).

References

1. Markom, M.A., Adom, A.H., Tan, E.S.M.M., Shukor, S.A.A., Rahim, N.A., Shakaff, A.Y.M.: A mapping mobile robot using RP Lidar scanner. In: IEEE International Symposium on Robotics and Intelligent Sensors (IRIS), Langkawi, Malaysia, 87–92 (2015)
2. Maria, D., et al.: Environment model generation and localisation of mobile indoor autonomous robots. 2021 2nd International Conference on Advances in Computing, Communication, Embedded and Secure Systems (ACCESS), Ernakulam, India, pp. 257–264 (2021)
3. Cheng, Y., Wang, G.Y.: Mobile robot navigation based on lidar. In: 30th Chinese Control and Decision Conference (CCDC), pp. 1243–1246 (2018)
4. Li, Z., Fan, C., Ding, W., Qian, K.: Robot navigation and map construction based on SLAM technology. World J. Innovat. Modern Technol. **7**(3), 8–14 (2024). - ISSN2682-5910
5. Csaba, G., Somlyai, L., Vámossy, Z.: Mobil robot navigation using 2D LIDAR. In: IEEE 16th World Symposium on Applied Machine Intelligence and Informatics (SAMI). Kosice and Herlany, Slovakia, 000143–000148 (2018)
6. Acquaah, S., Nenebi, C., Tucker, K., AlHmoud, I.W., Gokaraju, B.: Integrating deep planning-based object detection with 3d-depth camera for collision avoidance in indoor robotics navigation. In: SoutheastCon,: Concord. NC, USA, 989–994 (2025)
7. Vegesana, S., Penumatcha, H., Jaiswal, C., AlHmoud, I.W., Gokaraju, B.: Design and integration of a multi-sensor system for enhanced indoor autonomous navigation. SoutheastCon. IEEE **2024**, 1395–1401 (2024)

8. Penumatcha, H., Jaiswal, C., Vegesana, S., AlHmoud, I.W., Gokaraju, B.: Developing an autonomous robotics system utilizing camera and IMU fusion with PID-based path correction. In: ICMLA 2024, Miami. Florida. IEEE, USA (2024)
9. Nenebi, C.T., Acquaah, S., Tang, A., Tucker, K., AlHmoud, I.W., Gokaraju, B.: LiDAR-driven steering command prediction for autonomous vehicles using machine learning. In: 2025 IEEE Conference on Artificial Intelligence (CAI), Santa Clara, CA, USA, pp. 1560–1567 (2025)
10. Yang, X.: Slam and navigation of indoor robot based on ROS and lidar. J. Phys.: Conf. Ser. **1748**(2) (2021). Art. no. 022038
11. Tola, T.A., Mi, J., Che, Y.Q.: Mapping and localization of autonomous mobile robots in simulated indoor environments. Frontiers **4**(3), 91–100 (2024)
12. Quigley, M., Conley, K., Gerkey, B.P., Faust, J., Foote, T., Leibs, J., Berger, E., Wheeler, R., Ng, A.: ROS: an open-source robot operating system. ICRA Workshop Open Source Software **3**(2), 1–5 (2009)
13. Slamtec RPLIDAR A3, Data Sheet (2017)
14. "Self-Driving Car Studio," Quanser Inc. https://www.quanser.com/

Towards the Segmentation-Guided Generation of 3D MRA Dataset for Aneurysm Detection

Ruizhe Jiang(✉), Lauren Christopher, and Paul Salama

Purdue University Indianapolis, Indianapolis, IN 08544, USA
jiang647@purdue.edu

Abstract. 3D Magnetic Resonance Angiography (MRA) plays a vital role in the detection of Unruptured Intracranial Aneurysms (UIAs). In recent years, deep learning-based detection of UIAs from 3D MRA scans has gained popularity due to its high efficiency and accuracy in diagnosis. However, training a robust 3D deep learning model usually requires large amounts of real-world data, which is not easy to obtain due to privacy concerns. An intuitive solution to limited real-world training data is to generate synthetic data from limited real-world samples. The generated 3D volumes, however, need to have ground truth masks for use during model training. Unfortunately, labeling aneurysm masks manually is a time-consuming and non-trivial task. In this paper, we investigate the feasibility of generating 3D MRA volumes from limited real-world 3D MRA scans and ground truth masks using a segmentation-guided (or ground truth-guided) approach based on modern generative models. We evaluate the quality of the generated volumes at the latent space level and investigate the impact of this approach on aneurysm detection models.

Keywords: 3D diffusion model · Synthesized dataset · Aneurysm detection

1 Introduction

Intracranial aneurysm is a common life-threatening condition. According to statistics from the Brain Aneurysm Foundation [1], 1 in 50 people in the United States have an unruptured brain aneurysm, and around 30,000 people in the United States suffer a brain aneurysm rupture each year. Globally, more than $500k$ deaths are caused by brain aneurysms annually. The early detection and identification of Unruptured Intracranial Aneurysms (UIAs) is a vital diagnosis to lower the death rate. Generally, Time-Of-Flight Magnetic Resonance Angiography (TOF-MRA) is a popular method for aneurysm detection due to its non-intrusive and non-contrast technique. However, one key dangerous feature of aneurysms is their relatively small size, making it harder for early detection and rupture prevention. Traditional diagnosis requires careful examination of

F. Tanner and J. Irvine (Eds.): AIPR 2025, LNCS 16446, pp. 484–494, 2026.
https://doi.org/10.1007/978-3-032-18474-0_33

MRA scans, which is time-consuming and laborious. In recent years, the rapid development of deep learning has enabled auto-detection of aneurysms using pre-trained models like U-net [2]. When fine-tuned on large quantities of CT or MRA training scans, existing detection models can achieve $\geq$ 80% Dice score. However, training a robust auto-detection model typically requires large quantities of real-world training data, which, in the context of brain aneurysm detection, are not easily obtained due to privacy concerns. To our knowledge, only 2 publicly available 3D brain MRA datasets [3,4] contain scans of patients with aneurysms.

With the rapid development of generative models, an intuitive approach for dealing with insufficient real-world training data is to use generated training sets. However, training with generated datasets is not a guarantee of improvement in performance [14]. In addition, in the context of deep learning-based medical diagnosis or detection, training sets need ground truths of abnormalities, and the process of manual labeling is a non-trivial and time-consuming task. As a result, generating images based on existing ground truths or segmentation tasks is a promising approach.

Our goal in this study is to generate 3D MRA dataset from limited real-world 3D MRA scans and ground truth masks using a segmentation-guided (or ground truth-guided) approach. We will evaluate the generated dataset at the latent space level, as well as demonstrate preliminary results of their impact on aneurysm detection models.

2 Related Works

2.1 Deep Learning Based Intracranial Aneurysm Detection

With the rapid development of Convolutional Neural Network (CNN), Deep Learning is now the standard for aneurysm detection. Early works mainly use ResNet [5] or RCNN-based models [6], while later works tend to shift to U-net [7], a CNN-based model with a U shape, and have been proven to be a robust model in various medical imaging tasks thanks to its complicated encoder-decoder structure.

Various formats of datasets are used for aneurysm detection. Early works mainly focus on 2D scans [8] or MIP images [9]. However, 2D images may ignore the context information on the Z-axis. As a result, newer researches tend to exploit 3D volumes for more precise detection [10]. Since training a 3D detection model directly on full 3D volumes requires large GPU storage, 3D aneurysm detection models are always trained on 3D patches (i.e., patched training) [11]. To avoid possible loss of context information, some patched-training models exploit various patch selection schemes [12] or use sliding windows.

2.2 Generative Artificial Intelligence

Generative artificial intelligence (Generative AI or GenAI) is a subfield of artificial intelligence that uses generative models to generate similar but different data by learning the distribution of training samples [13]. These models learn the patterns and structures of training data and use them to produce new data. The year 2020 marks the beginning of a new era known as the "Generative AI boom". One year later, in 2022, Stable Diffusion [15] was released, which is a benchmark for generating high-quality AI art from natural language prompts. Late 2022 witnessed the public release of ChatGPT [17], a revolutionary model with the ability to perform natural conversations with humans, generate creative AI art, assist in coding, and complete analytical tasks.

Despite the rapid development of large generative models, generative AI's potential use in medical image processing is not fully exploited. This is mainly due to the lack of sufficiently specified training data. However, several generative models have been developed and trained on publicly available datasets to generate high-quality 3D medical images [18] [16]. However, training robust generative models for the generation of MRA images/volumes using limited real-world data remains a challenge due to the following reasons: 1. A Robust generative model requires large quantities of real-world training samples, which are not easy to obtain due to brain angiography scans usually contain highly private information; 2. Compared to anomalies like tumors or lesions, brain aneurysms are relatively small in size with a radius $\leq 5cm$. Thus, it is a challenging task to generate high-quality scans while ensuring that the generated volumes contain aneurysms 3. Generated volumes need to contain corresponding labels (i.e., ground truths) for use in training detection/segmentation models. However, labeling aneurysms by hand is a time-consuming and non-trivial task.

3 Methodology

In this chapter, we will introduce the methodology used in this study, including the overview of the workflow, as well as the generative model for the generation of synthesized brain MRA datasets and the 3D detection model used for the aneurysm detection.

3.1 Overview

Figure 1 demonstrates the brief workflow of this study. Real-world patches are taken from brain MRA scans collected from patients with at least 1 UIAs. The corresponding labels of aneurysms are labeled manually by professional physicians. Then, real-world patches are used as the training set for a segmentation-guided diffusion model. The trained diffusion model then generates large quantities of synthesized patches. Finally, the generated patches are mixed with real-world patches for the training of an aneurysm detection model.

3.2 Segmentation Guided 3D Diffusion Model

The Segmentation guided 3D diffusion generative model used in this study is based on a mask-guided 2D diffusion model from [19]. As shown in Fig. 2, the backbone of the model is a 3D U-net noise predictor. The noisy images are

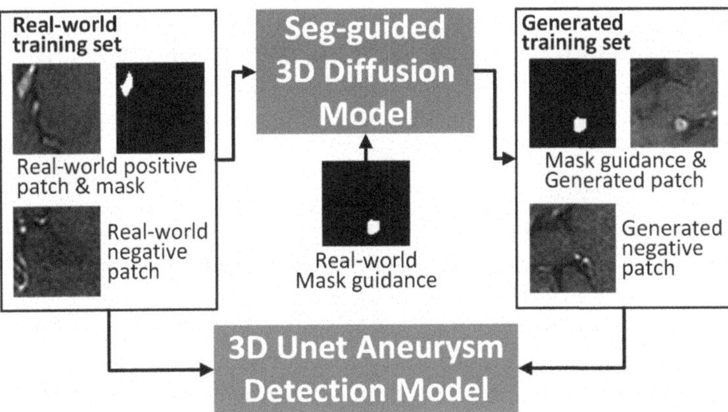

Fig. 1. Overview of this study: Real-world patches are used in the training of a generative model. Then, generated patches are mixed with real-world patches to train an aneurysm detection model.

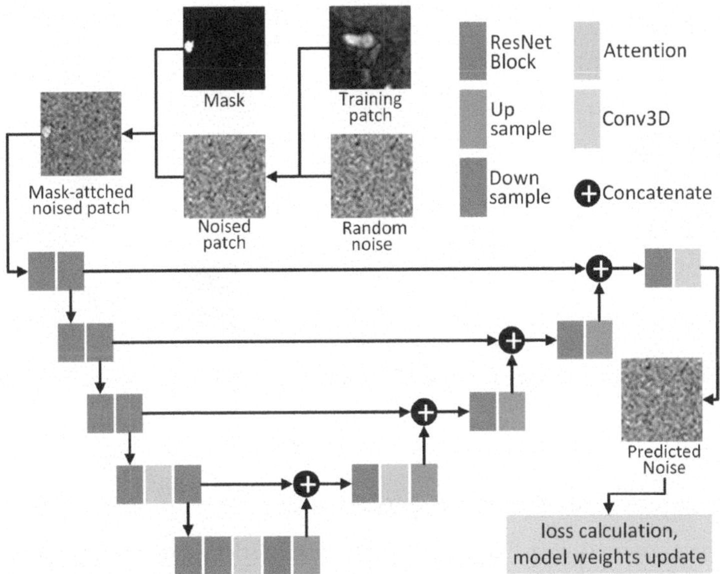

Fig. 2. U-net Structure of the Noise Predictor in the Proposed Segmentation-guided 3D Diffusion Model.

obtained by adding noise to real-world training images step by step using a Markov chain. Unlike the traditional diffusion model, where the noise predictor takes noised images as inputs, we further attach $0-1$ masks (or segmentation masks) to the noised image as the final inputs to the noise predictor. The predictor then predicts a noise distribution from the inputs. Mean squared error (MSE) loss between the prediction and a ground truth Gaussian noise distribution is calculated for the weights update of the noise predictor. Supposing the maximum timestamp is T, the current timestamp is $t, t \in [0, T]$, $\alpha_t = 1 - \beta_t$ given the variance of the additive pre-scheduled noise β, and $\overline{a_t} = \prod_{i=1}^{t} \alpha_i$, the MSE loss function containing segmentation guidance can be written as Eq. 1.

$$L_m = E_{(x_0,m),t,\epsilon}[||\epsilon - \epsilon_\theta(\sqrt{\overline{a_t}}x_0 + \sqrt{1-\overline{a_t}}\epsilon, t|m)||^2] \tag{1}$$

where x_0 is the original image at timestamp $t = 0$, m is the ground truth mask, ϵ is the noise added at each step, ϵ_θ is the noise predictor we trained.

Figure 3 demonstrates the image noising and denoising process in this study. Similar to the traditional diffusion model [15], the noising process is the same as a traditional diffusion model. During the reverse process, however, segmentation masks are added to the noise being denoised at each denoising step to ensure the denoising process is conditioned on the given masks.

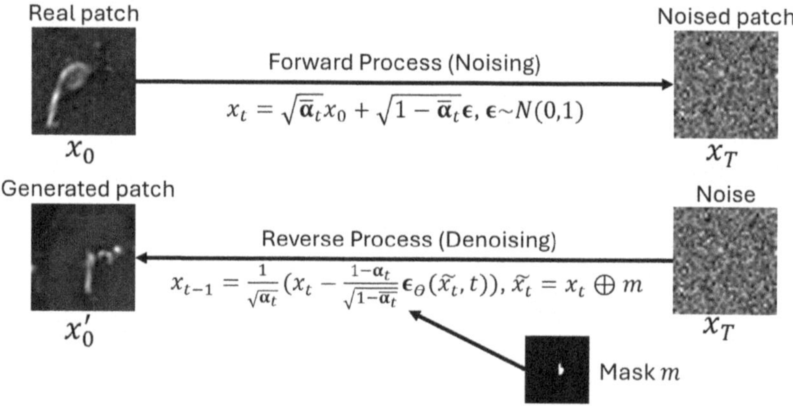

Fig. 3. Noising and Denoising Process of the Proposed 3D Seg-guided Diffusion Model.

3.3 3D Aneurysm Detection Model

For aneurysm detection, we exploit a 3D U-net model, similar to the model used in the work done by Di Noto et al. [12]. The encoder of the model is composed of 3 down blocks, each of which is composed by 2 3D convolutional layers, followed by a batch normalization, a max pooling layer, and a ReLU activation function. The decoder of the model is composed of 3 up blocks, with each composed by 3 3D convolutional layers, followed by an upsample layer, a batch normalization layer, and a ReLU activation function. A middle block is inserted between the encoder and decoder, with a structure similar to the down block, but without the max pooling layer. An output layer and a sigmoid function are placed after the decoder. Inputs of the detection model are 1-channel 3D MRA patches, and outputs are probability maps indicating the possibility that a given pixel belongs to an aneurysm.

4 Experiment Settings and Results

4.1 Dataset

The dataset used in this study is the public dataset from Aneurysm Detection And segMentation (ADAM) Challenge [3]. The dataset contains 3D Time of Flight MRA (TOF-MRA) volumes collected from 93 subjects with at least one aneurysm. We randomly select 45 of the 93 subjects as the training set, another 45 as the testing set. The remaining 3 subjects are used as the validation set during model training. For the training and validation dataset, random patches with an edge length of 64 are snapped on each volume. We snapped 8 negative patches (i.e., patches without aneurysm) for each volume using an intensity-based scheme from [12] and 8 positive patches (i.e., patches containing aneurysm) for each aneurysm ground truth. In total, 864 patches are snapped for training.

4.2 Dataset Generation and Latent Space Analysis

We first train the segmentation-guided 3D diffusion model using the training set mentioned in Sect. 4.1. We choose mean square error (MSE) loss function, a learning rate of $1e-5$, and a batch size of 64.

After training the 3D diffusion generative model, we use the trained weights to generate MRA patches. For the segmentation-guided generation process, ground truth masks of the training set are used as guidance. In total, 4096 patches are generated using the trained generative model, half are positive patches with aneurysms, and the other half are negative patches without aneurysms. A comparison of generated and real-world patches is demonstrated in Fig. 4.

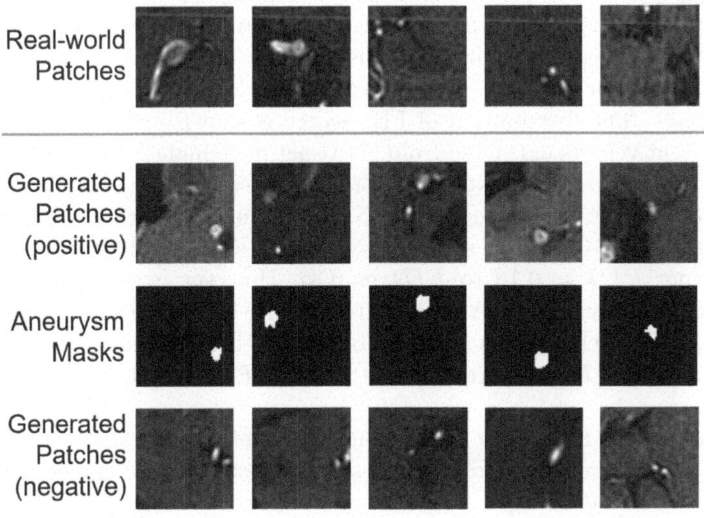

Fig. 4. Comparison between real-world and generated patches.

We then perform dimensional reduction analyses to investigate the relationship between the generated and the real-world dataset. We use PCA dimensionality reduction to make latent-level analysis. We choose two trained weights for the obtainment of the latent vector: A 3D ResNet50 trained on medical volumes [20] and a 3D U-net model with the same structure as the detection model used in this study, trained on the 864 real-world patches mentioned in Sect. 4.1. As shown in Fig. 5 and Fig. 6, when comparing the latent vector extracted from 3D ResNet50, the generated dataset and real-world dataset are almost overlapped in low-dimensional feature space. However, when using 3D U-net pretrained on the real-world dataset as the latent vector extractor, some generated patches are not overlapped with the real-world dataset.

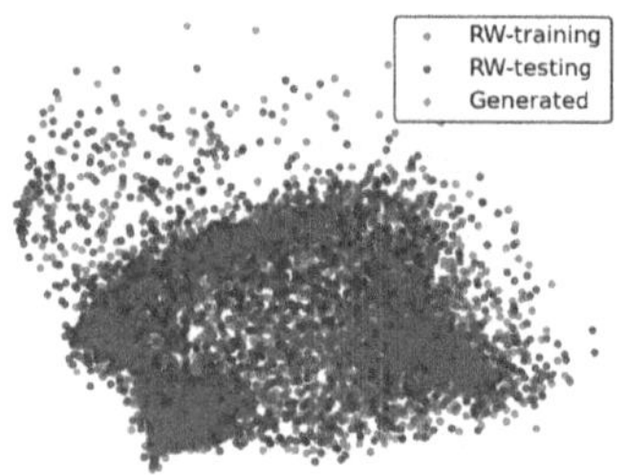

Fig. 5. PCA result when latent vectors are extracted from a 3D ResNet pre-trained on various 3D medical datasets.

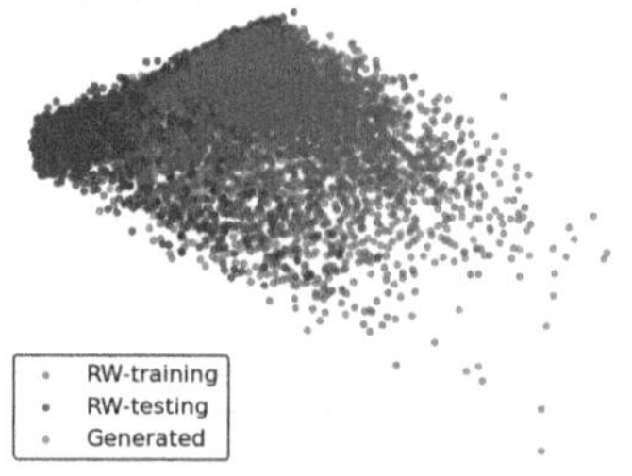

Fig. 6. PCA result when latent vectors are extracted from a 3D U-net pretrained on real-world 3D MRA patches.

We then randomly select 20 subsets of the 4096 generated patches. Half of the subsets contain 512 patches while the remaining half contain 1024 patches. All subsets contain an equal number of positive and negative patches. We then extract the latent vector of all subsets using both 3D ResNet and 3D U-net and calculate the Fréchet inception distance (FID) between each subset and the real-world dataset. The distribution of FID scores is shown in Fig. 7 and Fig. 8. In general, latent vectors extracted from 3D U-net have higher absolute FID values (i.e., ≥ 1.25) compared to latent vectors extracted from 3D ResNet50 (i.e., ≤ 0.34). Additionally, when using 3D ResNet50 as the latent vector extractor, 512-patch subsets and 1024-patch subsets tend to have similar FID score distribution, ranging from $FID \approx 0.16$ to $FID \approx 0.32$. However, when using 3D U-net pretrained on real-world MRA patches from ADAM dataset as the latent weights extractor, 512-patch subsets have an overall higher FID score, ranging from $FID \approx 1.28$ to $FID \approx 1.5$, compared to $1.25 < FID < 1.42$ of the 1024-patch subsets.

In addition to FID score, we use another metric to evaluate the distance between the generated and real-world set, noted as PCA distance, or PCAD. PCAD is calculated by Eq. 2.

$$PCAD = dist(COM(PCA(V_R)), COM(PCA(V_G))) \tag{2}$$

where V_R and V_G are extracted latent vectors of the real-world and generated set, $PCA(V)$ is the 2D-mapped point cloud of latent vectors using PCA method, COM is the Center-of-mass of 2D point clouds.

The detailed PCAD values of 20 subsets are shown in the $4th$ and $5th$ columns of Table 1 and Table 2. ResNet PCAD values of different subsets are relatively close, around 428 for 512-patch subsets and 171 for 1024-patch subsets, respectively. However, when using the bottleneck of 3D U-net trained on real-world MRA patches as the feature extractor, the PCAD value of different generated subsets varies, ranging from 205.7 to 1655.2 for 512-patch subsets and 262.9 to 19878.5 for 1024-patch subsets.

The quantified latent vector analysis indicates that: 1. Though the ResNet-based feature extractor used in this study is highly trained, it cannot fully demonstrate the difference between real-world and generated 3D MRA patches. This is caused by the fact that the ResNet weight is trained on datasets with large image size and area of abnormalities, differing from the 3D MRA patches for aneurysm detection. 2. 3D U-net-based feature extractor pretrained on real-world 3D MRA patches can show the difference between real-world and generated 3D MRA datasets, indicating it has the potential to be exploited as the dataset selector.

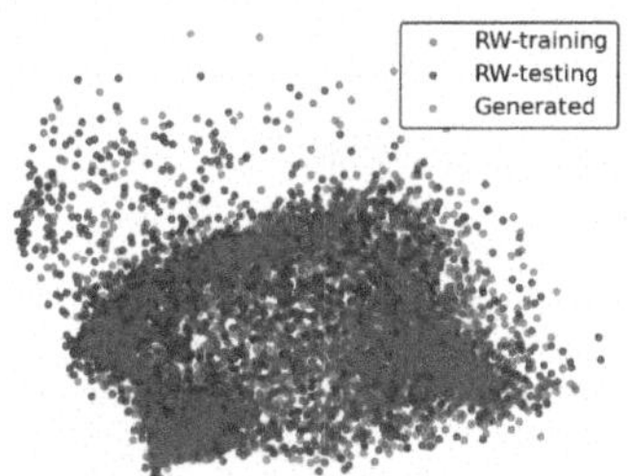

Fig. 7. FID distribution of 20 subsets of generated dataset, using ResNet50 as the latent vector extractor.

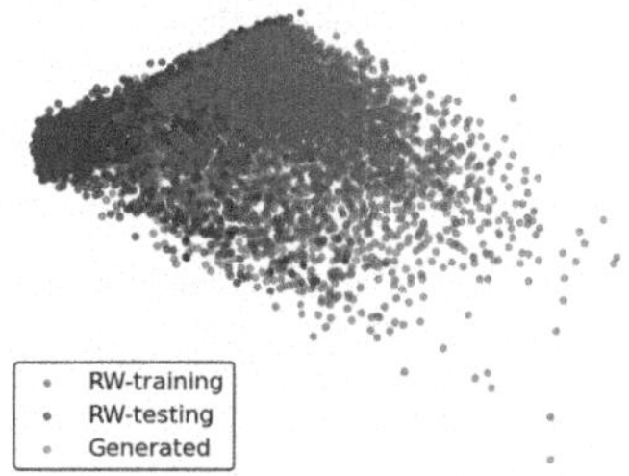

Fig. 8. FID distribution of 20 subsets of generated dataset, using 3D U-net as the latent vector extractor.

4.3 Training of Aneurysm Detection Model

We then train the 3D U-net aneurysm detection model using the real-world patches and the generated patches. We mix all 20 subsets mentioned in Chap. 4.2 with the 864-patch real-world training set to form different training set combinations and evaluate the performance of each training combination. We follow the evaluation standard in [12]: a detection is successful if the center-of-mass of the predicted aneurysm is located within the ground truth mask. Two metrics are used to evaluate the detection performance: sensitivity and the average number of false positives (average FP). Sensitivity is calculated by dividing the number of detected aneurysms by the total number of aneurysms. Average FP is the average number of false positives over all testing subjects. The evaluation results of 3D U-net detection model trained on different datasets are shown in Table 1 and Table 2.

Table 1. Evaluation results of 3D U-net detection model trained on all real-world patches and different 512-patch generated subsets, 'R' stands for real patches, 'G' stands for generated patches.

Dataset	ResNet FID	U-net FID	ResNet PCAD	U-net PCAD	Sensitivity	Average FPs
R	-	-	-	-	0.482	4.756
R+512G	0.173	1.498	428.4	986.5	**0.589**	11.267
	0.207	1.497	427.8	696.0	0.429	16.333
	0.211	1.441	427.6	370.4	0.464	9.978
	0.231	1.282	426.9	205.7	0.482	6.222
	0.265	1.350	428.2	1665.2	0.429	11.689
	0.277	1.388	427.1	458.6	0.464	4.244
	0.282	1.459	427.2	469.7	0.446	7.844
	0.285	1.381	429.3	564.9	0.482	7.156
	0.292	1.397	427.5	497.0	0.536	8.156
	0.389	1.460	428.5	408.2	0.500	3.000

Table 2. Evaluation results of 3D U-net detection model trained on all real-world patches and different 1024-patch generated subsets, 'R' stands for real patches, 'G' stands for generated patches.

Dataset	ResNet FID	U-net FID	ResNet PCAD	U-net PCAD	Sensitivity	Average FPs
R	-	-	-	-	0.482	4.756
R+1024G	0.164	1.294	175.8	305.2	0.482	3.267
	0.194	1.340	170.8	1410.8	**0.571**	7.822
	0.217	1.339	170.9	609.3	0.482	10.044
	0.221	1.365	171.5	262.9	0.482	11.756
	0.232	1.246	170.9	488.8	0.518	9.844
	0.232	1.388	171.2	376.0	0.429	8.533
	0.250	1.285	170.8	356.9	0.500	6.067
	0.272	1.425	172.0	14740.9	0.500	7.356
	0.321	1.272	171.8	19878.5	0.446	4.622
	0.331	1.333	170.9	198.0	0.518	12.622

The results demonstrate that when mixed with real-world training patches, some subsets of the 4096-patch generated dataset can improve the Sensitivity of the detection model, with the greatest improvement of 10.7% for 512-patch subsets and 8.9% for 1024-patch subsets. However, some generated datasets downgrade model performance, with the highest sensitivity drop of 5.3% for 512-patch and 1024-patch generated datasets. Additionally, though for both 512-patch and 1024-patch subsets, the greatest improvement of sensitivity is observed on subsets with relatively low FID score calculated on latent vectors extracted from 3D ResNet50, the connection between the FID score of the generated dataset used and the model performance is still not strong. We also notice that subsets with the highest detection sensitivity have average-level U-net PCAD value (986.5 for 512-patch subsets and 1410.8 for 1024-patch subsets, respectively). This phenomenon indicates that the latent vectors of the generated dataset should be neither too far nor too close to the real-world training set. High similarity between the generated and real-world set will downgrade the model's generalization ability on the testing set, while an extremely far distance between the generated and real-world training sets will shift the model's latent space away from the testing set.

Despite the observations mentioned above, better metrics are still needed for the selection of generated training patches. Finally, an improvement in sensitivity is usually accompanied by an increase in average FPs, demonstrating that though generated training sets improve the model's ability to identify true aneurysms, the model tends to overfit on non-aneurysm structures.

5 Conclusion

In this study, we investigate the feasibility of generating 3D MRA patches for aneurysm detection with ground truth masks from limited number of real-world MRA volumes using a segmentation-guided 3D diffusion model. Latent space analysis indicates that generated patches have overlapping real-world patches. When mixed with real-world patches on training aneurysm detection model, generated training patches have the ability to increase detection sensitivity, but will also increase false positives simultaneously. Future work includes: 1. Robust mask generation algorithms to increase the diversity of ground truth masks for the segmentation-guided generation; 2. Better metrics to evaluate and select the generated dataset; 3. Improved diffusion model structure.

References

1. Brain aneurysm foundation (2025). https://www.bafound.org/statistics-and-facts/
2. Ronneberger, O., Fischer, P., Brox, T.: U-Net: convolutional networks for biomedical image segmentation. In: Navab, N., Hornegger, J., Wells, W.M., Frangi, A.F. (eds.) MICCAI 2015. LNCS, vol. 9351, pp. 234–241. Springer, Cham (2015). https://doi.org/10.1007/978-3-319-24574-4_28
3. Aneurysm detection and segmentation challenge (2025). https://adam.isi.uu.nl/data/
4. Lausanne TOF-MRA aneurysm dataset, Lausanne University Hospital (CHUV) (2025). https://openneuro.org/datasets/ds003949/versions/1.0.1
5. Yang, J,. et al.: Deep learning for detecting cerebral aneurysms with CT angiography. Radiology. **298**(1), 155–163 (2021). https://doi.org/10.1148/radiol.2020192154. Epub 2020 Nov 3. PMID: 33141003

6. Stember, J.N., et al.: Convolutional neural networks for the detection and measurement of cerebral aneurysms on magnetic resonance angiography. J. Digit. Imaging **32**(5), 808–815 (2018). https://doi.org/10.1007/s10278-018-0162-z
7. Shi, Z., et al.: A clinically applicable deep-learning model for detecting intracranial aneurysm in computed tomography angiography images. Nat. Commun. **11**(1), 6090 (2020). https://doi.org/10.1038/s41467-020-19527-w. PMID: 33257700; PMCID: PMC7705757
8. Ueda, D., et al.: Deep learning for MR angiography: automated detection of cerebral aneurysms. Radiology. **290**(1), 187–194 (2019). https://doi.org/10.1148/radiol.2018180901. Epub 2018 Oct 23. PMID: 30351253
9. Nakao T, et al.: Deep neural network-based computer-assisted detection of cerebral aneurysms in MR angiography. J. Magn. Reson. Imaging. **47**(4), 948–953 (2018). https://doi.org/10.1002/jmri.25842. Epub 2017 Aug 24. PMID: 28836310
10. Liu, X., et al.: Deep neural network-based detection and segmentation of intracranial aneurysms on 3D rotational DSA. Interv. Neuroradiol. **27**(5), 648–657 (2021). https://doi.org/10.1177/15910199211000956. Epub 2021 Mar 9. PMID: 33715500; PMCID: PMC8493355
11. Wang, J., et al.: Detection of intracranial aneurysms using multiphase CT angiography with a deep learning model. Acad Radiol. **30**(11), 2477–2486 (2023). https://doi.org/10.1016/j.acra.2022.12.043. Epub 2023 Feb 1. PMID: 36737273
12. Di Noto, T., et al.: Towards automated brain aneurysm detection in TOF-MRA: open data, weak labels, and anatomical knowledge. Neuroinformatics. 2023 Jan **21**(1), 21–34. https://doi.org/10.1007/s12021-022-09597-0. Epub 2022 Aug 18. PMID: 35982364; PMCID: PMC9931814
13. Bond-Taylor, S., Leach, A., Long, Y., Willcocks, C.G.: Deep generative modelling: a comparative review of VAEs, GANs, normalizing flows, energy-based and autoregressive models. IEEE Trans. Pattern Anal. Mach. Intell., 1 (2021). https://doi.org/10.1109/TPAMI.2021.3116668
14. Shumailov, I., Shumaylov, Z., Zhao, Y., et al.: AI models collapse when trained on recursively generated data. Nature **631**, 755–759 (2024). https://doi.org/10.1038/s41586-024-07566-y
15. Rombach, R., Blattmann, A., Lorenz, D., Esser, P., Ommer, B.: High-resolution image synthesis with latent diffusion models. In: IEEE/CVF Conference on Computer Vision and Pattern Recognition (CVPR), vol. 2022, pp. 10674–10685 (2021)
16. Dorjsembe, Z., Pao, H.-K., Odonchimed, S., Xiao, F.: Conditional diffusion models for semantic 3D brain MRI synthesis. IEEE J. Biomed. Health Inform. **28**(7), 4084–4093 (2024). https://doi.org/10.1109/JBHI.2024.3385504
17. ChatGPT: OpenAI, 01 Oct 2025 (2025). https://chatgpt.com/
18. Khader, F., Müller-Franzes, G., Tayebi Arasteh, S., et al.: Denoising diffusion probabilistic models for 3D medical image generation. Sci. Rep. **13**, 7303 (2023). https://doi.org/10.1038/s41598-023-34341-2
19. Konz, N., Chen, Y., Dong, H., Maciej, A.: Mazurowski: Anatomically-Controllable Medical Image Generation with Segmentation-Guided Diffusion Models. In Medical Image Computing and Computer Assisted Intervention – MICCAI,: 27th International Conference, Marrakesh, Morocco, 6–10 October 2024, Proceedings, Part VII. Springer-Verlag, Berlin, Heidelberg **88–98** (2024). https://doi.org/10.1007/978-3-031-72104-5_9
20. Chen, S., Ma, K., Zheng, Y.: Med3D: transfer learning for 3D medical image analysis (2019). https://doi.org/10.48550/arXiv.1904.00625

HE3D-Net: Hypoxic Ischemic Encephalopathy Diagnosis and Lesion Segmentation Using 3D Heterogenous Ensemble Models

Bijaya Kumar Hatuwal[1(✉)], Rina Bao[2], Mai-Lan Ho[3], and Kannappan Palaniappan[1]

[1] Department of Electrical Engineering and Computer Science, University of Missouri, Columbia, MO65211, USA
{bkhcty,palaniappank}@umsystem.edu

[2] Boston Children's Hospital and Harvard Medical School, Boston, USA
Rina.Bao@childrens.harvard.edu

[3] Department of Radiology,University of Missouri, Columbia, MO65211, USA
mhgkf@umsystem.edu

Abstract. Hypoxic ischemic encephalopathy (HIE) affects approximately 1 to 5 per 1000 live births, with nearly 20% of cases proving fatal. This condition arises when a neonate's brain receives insufficient oxygen or blood flow during or shortly after birth. Even among survivors, there is a high risk of long-term neurocognitive and behavioral disorders, sensory impairments, and epilepsy. Timely diagnosis and accurate segmentation of HIE-affected regions are critical for initiating appropriate medical intervention, and magnetic resonance imaging (MRI) is a widely utilized tool for this purpose. In this study, we addressed the diagnosis and segmentation of HIE using a 3D-MRI dataset from BONBID-HIE 2024 Grand Challenge. A significant challenge posed by this dataset is the small lesion size typically <1% of total brain volume and their diffused nature. To address class imbalance, we applied dynamic class weighting into the loss function, adjusting the weights for each batch based on class distribution. For the segmentation task, we developed a novel heterogeneous ensemble approach, combining the strengths of three state-of-the-art 3D deep learning models: SegResNet, Swin-UNETR, and UNet. This ensemble strategy was designed to leverage the complementary capabilities of each architecture to improve performance on the complex lesion segmentation problem and was able to achieve the dice score of 57.7±23.7 on test leader board.

Keywords: Heterogenous Ensemble · Hypoxic Ischemic Encephalopathy · Lesion · Segmentation · MRI

1 Inroduction

Hypoxic ischemic encephalopathy (HIE) is a severe brain injury occurring before, during, or shortly after birth due to reduced or interrupted oxygen or blood flow

F. Tanner and J. Irvine (Eds.): AIPR 2025, LNCS 16446, pp. 495–507, 2026.
https://doi.org/10.1007/978-3-032-18474-0_34

to the brain. HIE affects approximately 1 to 5 per 1,000 term-born infants globally [7,12] and costing around $2 billion in healthcare costs each year in US alone. The impact of HIE varies widely, ranging from no long-term effects to mild or severe disabilities, and in some cases is fatal [17]. Therapeutic hypothermia (TH) is instituted for suspected HIE to minimize secondary injury, involves cooling the body temperature, reducing the risk of death or disability [1,14]. Despite advancements of Therapeutic hypothermia (TH), 30–50% of neonates with HIE still experience mortality or neurocognitive impairments by age two. Accurate identification and segmentation of brain lesions through magnetic resonance imaging (MRI) is critical for disease prognosis, evaluating treatment efficacy, and understanding the neural basis of disease progression.

Segmentation of HIE lesions presents unique challenges as these lesions are typically small, diffused, and multi-focal, with many patients having lesions occupying less than 1% of their brain volume (Fig. 1). This complexity limits the performance of traditional machine learning algorithms, with dice scores for HIE lesion segmentation averaging around 0.5 compared to over 0.8 for brain tumors [4,15,16]. A major hurdle in improving segmentation accuracy is the lack of publicly available datasets with expert-annotated HIE lesions. To address this gap, the Boston Neonatal Brain Injury Dataset for Hypoxic Ischemic Encephalopathy (BONBID-HIE) has provided open-source dataset that includes MRI scans and manually annotated lesion masks for 89 HIE patients through BONBID-HIE 2023 and 2024 [4,9] challenge, offering a comprehensive resource to drive advancements in diagnostic algorithms.

Previous studies from BONBID-HIE challenge [8] on lesion segmentation have introduced a range of innovative methodologies that have significantly advanced the field. Feature fusion techniques, such as the integration of deep and local features using random forests [6] demonstrated improved segmentation by capturing both global and localized lesion characteristics. Ensemble-based approaches [11,21] harnessed the diversity of multiple models to enhance robustness and accuracy. Heavy data augmentation strategies [20,25] improved model generalizability across varying datasets, while deep neural networks employed [23] effectively identified complex lesion patterns. To address the challenges of small and diffuse lesion segmentation a SegResNet-based reciprocal transformation technique [2], offering a tailored solution for these intricate cases was developed. These contributions collectively highlight the transformative role of advanced computational techniques in neonatal MRI analysis, paving the way for improved diagnosis, prognosis, and treatment evaluation in HIE. In this study we employed a noble approach to the dataset by implementing the heterogenous ensemble method of the 3D state-of-the-art models (SOTA): Swin-UNETR, SegResNet and UNet. Also, we provided the updated weight to the loss function for each batch in training based on the class distribution to address the class imbalance problem and enhance the models' ability to segment the lesion.

2 Dataset

This study utilized the publicly available 2024 Boston Neonatal Brain Injury Dataset for Hypoxic Ischemic Encephalopathy (BONBID-HIE) collected from Massachusetts General Hospital (MGH) and Boston Children's Hospital (BCH) [3,4]. The dataset supports two primary tasks: (i) lesion segmentation and (ii) two-year outcome prediction (binary classification: 0 or 1 for lesion presence). In this work, we focused primarily on the lesion segmentation using labeled MRI images from MGH. The dataset was divided into a training, validation, and test size of 85, 4, and 44 cases respectively. Volumetric MRI scans from neonate patients ($N = 133$) had size ranging from $128 \times 128 \times D$ to $256 \times 256 \times D$ voxels, where $D \in [16, 64]$ [18] with >50% of MRI scans having HIE lesions <1% by volume (Fig. 2). The most frequent in-plane ($H \times W$) dimensions were 128×128 (64 volumes), 256×256 (38 volumes), and 160×160 (30 volumes). The Apparent Diffusion Coefficient (ADC) MRI imaging data was acquired from two scanners: GE 1.5T (N = 52, voxel size = $2 \times 2 \times 2$ mm^3) and Siemens 3T (N=81, voxel size = $0.5 \times 1.5 \times (4.0–6.0)$ mm^3 [3]. The zADC maps were calculated by converting each voxel's ADC value into a z-score relative to a normative neonatal ADC atlas from 13 healthy neonates brain. For each voxel x, the patient's ADC value I_x was compared to the atlas derived mean $\mu_{D(x)}$ and standard deviation $\sigma_{D(x)}$ at the corresponding anatomical location $D(x)$:

$$\text{zADC}(x) = \frac{I_x - \mu_{D(x)}}{\sigma_{D(x)}} \tag{1}$$

This process normalizes ADC values across brain regions, quantifying how many standard deviations each voxel's ADC deviates from the normal mean,

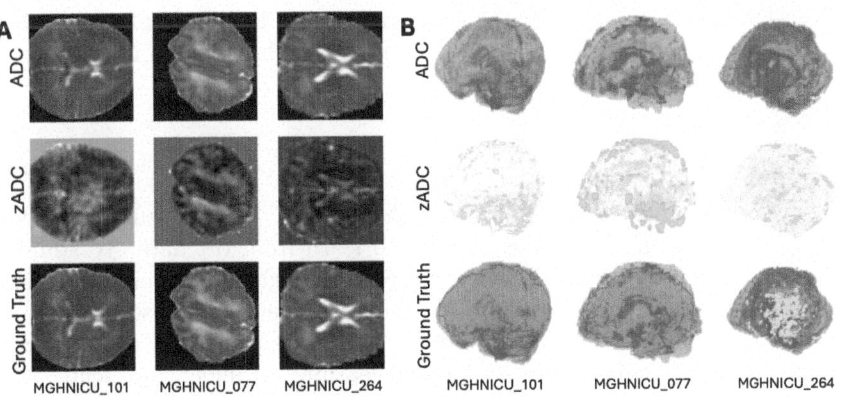

Fig. 1. A. Shows the 2D-data with ADC, zADC and ground truth (red) overlayed on ADC. B. 3D maxium intensity projection (MIP) view of ADC (magenta), zADC (cyan) and ground truth (yellow) overlayed on ADC. Lesion in volumes MGHNICU_101, MGHNICU_077, and MGHNICU_264 covers 36.03, 20.61, and 1.30 % repectively. (Color figure online)

thereby enabling consistent comparison across subjects and locations. The ground truth annotations were generated through a rigorous consensus protocol involving three expert pediatric neuroradiologists who manually delineated lesions on 3D ADC maps.

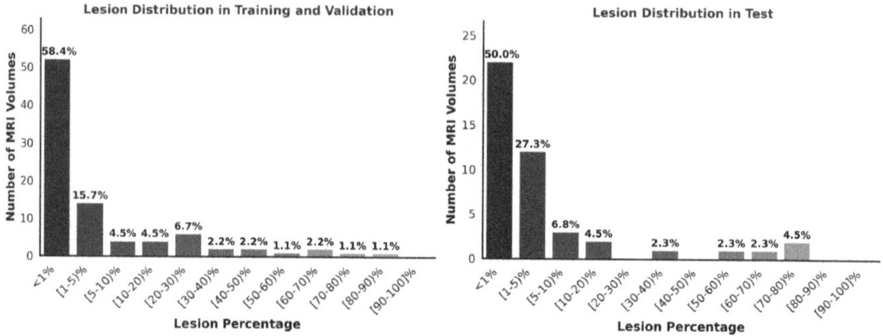

Fig. 2. Distribution of the lesion by percentage in training, validation and test dataset. The HIE lesion distribution is skewed as most lesion occupies <1% of the volume.

A primary characteristic of this dataset is the significant imbalance in lesion volume, which poses a considerable challenge for segmentation algorithms. Across the entire cohort, 74 cases (55.6%) feature lesions occupying less than 1% of the total brain volume, with 26 cases (19.6%) containing medium-sized lesions (1–5%) and 33 cases (24.8%) having large lesions (>5%). To ensure robust evaluation, the data was carefully stratified across the splits to balance both lesion size and scanner type. There are a total of 133 patient MRI volumes. The training set of 85 cases (33 GE, 56 S) was composed of 46 small, 16 medium, and 25 large lesion cases. Validation had 4 cases and the testing set of 44 cases (19 GE, 25 S) was divided into 22 small, 12 medium, and 10 large lesion cases.

3 Method

3.1 Pre-processing

We developed pipeline to pre-process the dataset [9] to ensure the consistency and enhancing the models' ability to learn from the data. To standardize the input, all volumes and labels were resampled to isotropic voxel size of $(1.0\times1.0\times1.0)$ mm^3 ensuring consistent physical spacing representation across volumes. Channel-wise intensity normalization was done. To reduce computational overhead and foreground focused learning of under-represented small lesions, foreground cropping was performed. Four patches of $(96\times96\times96)$ mm^3 was randomly selected per volume in each batch for training to ensure a consistent input volume and a manageable data chunk for GPU processing. Data augmention was performed by random flipping along axes and intensity shifting by 10% to introduce variability in the dataset, making the model less sensitive to noise and robust to unseen data.

3.2 Training

We leveraged three advanced architectures for 3D medical image segmentation: Swin-UNETR, 3D-UNet, and 3D-SegResNet [5]. Swin-UNETR architecture was designed for hierarchical feature extraction and precise localization. Key parameters included: a feature size of 24 to set the network's channel capacity; a sequence of (3, 6, 12, 24) attention heads across four stages with two transformer blocks each, enabling the model to learn increasingly complex feature relationships; and a 7x7 local window for computationally efficient self-attention. The decoder performed multiscale feature fusion via skip connections to combine spatial and semantic information, while dropout was disabled to maximize information retention for segmenting subtle lesions. The 3D-UNet architecture had six level deep encoder-decoder layer with increasing channel dimension as (16, 32, 64, 128, 256, 512) and incorporates residual connections to improve gradient flow and enhance learning efficiency. Similarly, 3D-SegResNet follows an encoder-decoder structure with skip connections for feature map transfer. The encoder reduces the spatial dimensions of the input through blocks configured as (1, 2, 2, 4), while the decoder restores the spatial resolution using up-sample block of (1, 1, 1) in each layer. All models were trained using either single-channel or multi-channel input configurations. In the single-channel setup, the input consisted of either ADC or zADC map, while in the multi-channel configuration, both ADC and zADC maps were provided. Each model output was post-processed to produce a binary segmentation map distinguishing the background from HIE lesions.

During the training process patches of size (96×96×96) and a batch size of 2 was provided. The Adam optimizer was employed with an initial learning rate of 1×10^{-4} and a 'ReduceLROnPlateau' scheduler was applied which adaptively lowers the learning rate if validation metrics plateau, ensuring efficient convergence. To address class imbalance, dynamic class-weighted was passed to the Dice loss function. The models were trained to a maximum of 150 epochs, with validation performed every two epochs to monitor progress and assess the models' performance. Label fusion for the ensemble was done using simple multi layer perceptron (MLP) or weighted average of the raw logit outputs from each of the three models. The best performing ensemble model achieved a dice score of 57.3 ± 24.0, precision of 58.5 ± 26.4, and recall of 64.2 ± 22.4, normalized surface distance (NSD) of 75.9 ± 22.5, and a mean average surface distance (MASD) of 2.8 ± 3.3. In weighted fusion (Fig. 3A), the combined logit tensor was created by taking an equal-weighted average of the logits from each model:

$$Z_{\text{final}} = w_1 \cdot Z_{\text{SwinUNETR}} + w_2 \cdot Z_{\text{SegResNet}} + w_3 \cdot Z_{\text{UNet}} \tag{2}$$

where Z represents the raw unscaled logit scores tensor from each model, and the weights w_1, w_2, w_3 were all set to $\sim$0.33. The final segmentation map Z_{final} was produced by applying the weighted sum of different models output.

To replace the weighted fusion and provide the local context, a simple multilayer perceptron (MLP) (Fig. 3B) was trained to refine voxelwise predictions

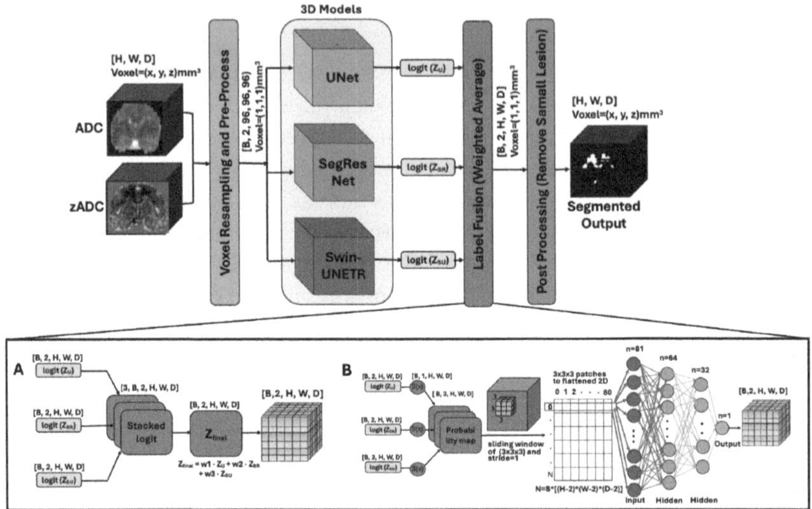

Fig. 3. Heterogeneous ensemble of 3D-models: UNet-3D, SegResNet-3D, and Swin-UNETR-3D. The model may have combination input with combination of different channels as: ADC or zADC only, multi channel ADC and zADC with threshold zADC at T<-2.0. Patches of 96×96×96 with isotropic voxel $1 \times 1 \times 1$ mm^3 as provided as input.

from three pretrained 3D segmentation models (SwinUNETR, UNet, and SegResNet). For each volume, the three foreground probability maps were stacked and processed using a $3 \times 3 \times 3$ patch-extraction procedure with kernel size = 3 and stride = 1, yielding 81 local probability features per voxel. These vectors were used to train an MLP with input, two hidden, and output feature vector sizes of 81, 64, 32, and 1, respectively. This network predicts a single foreground logit for the center voxel using a BCEWithLogitsLoss loss.

3.3 Loss Function

Dynamic class biased weighting was applied to the Dice loss function for each training batch to address the class imbalance problem. Since HIE lesions are typically much smaller than background regions, this imbalance can hinder the model's ability to learn minority class features. To mitigate this, a dynamic weighting scheme was introduced that adaptively adjusts each class's contribution to the total loss based on its relative frequency in the training data, assigning higher weights to underrepresented lesion class to enhance segmentation accuracy, as shown in Eqs. (3)–(5).

The weight for each class c was computed as the inverse of the squared voxel count and normalized so that the weights sum to one:

$$w_c = \frac{1}{N_c^2 + \varepsilon} \tag{3}$$

$$w_{\text{normalized},c} = \frac{w_c}{\sum_{i=0}^{C} w_i}, \quad c \in C \tag{4}$$

The resulting weighted Dice loss was formulated as:

$$L = \sum_{c=1}^{C} w_{\text{normalized},c} \left(1 - \frac{2 \times \text{Intersection}_c}{\text{Union}_c + \varepsilon}\right) \tag{5}$$

Here, w_c denotes the weight for class c, N_c is the number of voxels in class c, and $\varepsilon = 1 \times 10^{-6}$ is a small constant to prevent division by zero.

3.4 Testing

For testing the images are loaded, resampled to isotropic voxel size, and normalized as done in training. Inference on 3D image volumes was performed using MONAI's sliding window inference function [5]. The input volume was divided into overlapping sub-volumes of size 96×96×96, processed sequentially by the trained models with an overlap ratio of 0.5. Predictions from overlapping regions were combined using constant blending, where each voxel contributed equally. The final output was obtained by normalizing the accumulated logits with a voxel-wise count map, producing the full segmentation volume. Label fusion was performed using weighted fusion or MLP to generate the final volume using output from different models and post-processing operations, such as filling holes, removing small regions <4 voxels, and a corrective suppression step to set voxels to 0 if predicted lesion volume is between [0.0, 0.01)% identified through exhaustive evaluation to improve the predicted segmentation.

4 Results

4.1 Evaluation Metrics

The model performance was evaluated using five different matrices: precision (P), recall (R), dice similarity coefficient (DSC), mean average surface distance (MASD), and normalized surface distance (NSD) across different lesion volume categories (<1%, 1%–5%, and >5%).

$$\text{Precision(P)} = \frac{\text{True Positives (TP)}}{\text{True Positives (TP)} + \text{False Positives (FP)}} \tag{6}$$

$$\text{Recall(R)} = \frac{\text{True Positives (TP)}}{\text{True Positives (TP)} + \text{False Negatives (FN)}} \tag{7}$$

$$\text{DSC} = \frac{2 \times |\text{Predicted Lesion} \cap \text{Ground Truth}|}{|\text{Predicted Lesion}| + |\text{Ground Truth}|} \tag{8}$$

Mean Average Surface Distance (MASD) measures the average bidirectional surface distance between the predicted segmentation and the ground truth.

$$MASD = \frac{1}{|S_P| + |S_G|} \left(\sum_{p \in S_P} d(p, S_G) + \sum_{g \in S_G} d(g, S_P) \right) \tag{9}$$

where S_P and S_G denote the sets of surface points of the predicted and ground truth segmentations, respectively. $d(p, S_G)$ and $d(g, S_P)$ represent the shortest Euclidean distances from each point to the opposite surface, and $|S_P|$, $|S_G|$ indicate the number of surface points in each set.

Normalized Surface Distance (NSD) quantifies the proportion of surface points within a given distance threshold $T = 2 \times 2 \times 2$ mm^3 between the predicted and ground truth surfaces [3,9] and only those surface points in S_P and S_G that lie within a tolerance distance T of the opposite surface were counted:

$$\text{NSD} = \frac{|S_P \cap \{p : d(p, S_G) \leq T\}| + |S_G \cap \{g : d(g, S_P) \leq T\}|}{|S_P| + |S_G|} \tag{10}$$

where, the intersection notation $S_P \cap \{p : d(p, S_G) \leq T\}$ expresses the subset of points in S_P whose distance to S_G is less than or equal to T. A higher NSD value indicates a greater proportion of surface points that are well-aligned between the predicted and reference segmentations, reflecting better boundary agreement.

4.2 Segmentation Result

All models were trained using either single-channel or multi-channel input configurations for HIE lesion segmentation. Two different types of input configurations were evaluated: (i) a single-channel input consisting of either the ADC or zADC map (Table 1), (ii) 2-channel input combining both ADC and zADC maps (Table 2). For ensemble inference, two output fusion strategies were employed: (i) label fusion using weighted averaging (w) across model outputs, and (ii) a simple MLP with local awareness fusion (Table 2). The final output generated is a binary segmentation map distinguishing the background from HIE lesions.

Two recent foundation models for 3D medical image segmentation MedSAM2 [13,19] and SAM-Med3D [24] were evaluated in a one-shot adaptation setting on the HIE dataset. MedSAM2 modified and fine-tuned SAM2, pretrained on over 455,000 3D image-mask pairs and 76,000 annotated video frames, provides broad representational capacity across diverse anatomical structures and imaging modalities. However, when adapted to the HIE task, it exhibited limited sensitivity to small, diffuse, and low-contrast lesions, resulting in poor Dice and boundary alignment scores despite high recall, indicating that the model tends to overestimate lesion regions. In contrast, SAM-Med3D, trained on the large-scale 140K dataset comprising 22,000 volumetric images and 143,000 segmentation masks, demonstrated slightly improved surface alignment and localization, particularly when using zADC inputs but its overall lesion delineation accuracy remained modest, underscoring that both models although powerful general-purpose segmenters struggle to adapt to subtle hypoxic-ischemic patterns that differ markedly from their pretraining distributions.

Table 1. Performance Comparison Using Single ADC or zADC Channel Input

Model	Data Type	Dice (%↑)	Precision (%↑)	Recall (%↑)	NSD (%↑)	MASD (mm↓)
UNet	ADC	23.5 ± 20.0	28.9 ± 32.4	35.6 ± 22.0	36.3 ± 20.7	6.5 ± 5.3
	zADC	41.4 ± 25.3	39.9 ± 30.4	65.5 ± 26.2	59.0 ± 25.7	4.9 ± 7.4
SegResNet	ADC	37.0 ± 28.9	45.4 ± 32.2	38.9 ± 28.1	52.4 ± 28.6	5.9 ± 7.5
	zADC	51.2 ± 26.3	50.0 ± 28.3	63.9 ± 25.2	68.7 ± 27.1	3.9 ± 7.1
SwinUNETR	ADC	36.7 ± 28.4	42.0 ± 33.0	43.0 ± 26.3	52.0 ± 28.7	5.4 ± 6.4
	zADC	51.9 ± 25.9	51.7 ± 28.4	61.4 ± 24.6	68.0 ± 27.1	4.2 ± 7.3
Ensemble$_{\mathbf{weighted}}$	ADC	37.5 ± 27.5	43.9 ± 33.0	43.0 ± 24.1	54.0 ± 26.7	5.1 ± 4.2
	zADC	$\mathbf{54.9 \pm 25.7}$	$\mathbf{53.6 \pm 26.0}$	65.0 ± 23.7	$\mathbf{72.1 \pm 24.9}$	$\mathbf{3.1 \pm 3.6}$
MedSAM2$_{(zero-shot)}$	ADC	8.1 ± 16.5	5.3 ± 11.8	$\mathbf{95.7 \pm 15.4}$	1.8 ± 3.7	21.3 ± 9.4
	zADC	8.5 ± 17.0	5.7 ± 12.6	93.9 ± 15.7	2.3 ± 4.0	20.1 ± 9.0
SAM-Med3D$_{(zero-shot)}$	ADC	3.5 ± 6.6	9.6 ± 21.9	9.2 ± 17.8	19.4 ± 21.3	7.3 ± 2.7
	zADC	23.3 ± 31.3	16.4 ± 26.6	61.4 ± 34.7	30.0 ± 29.3	6.1 ± 3.4

Across all individual models (UNet, SegResNet, SwinUNETR) in the single-modality setting, using the z-score normalized ADC map (zADC) as input consistently outperformed the raw ADC map (Table 1). For instance, the Ensemble$_{weighted}$ and foundational model SAM-MED3D$_{zero-shot}$ model's Dice score improved from 37.5 to 54.9 and 3.5 to 23.3 respectively when switching from ADC to zADC. These findings indicate that zADC provides a more stable and discriminative HIE lesion representation, enabling more reliable lesion localization across both conventional and foundation architectures.

Table 2. Performance Comparison Using Two Channel Inputs

Model	Data Type	Dice (%↑)	Precision (%↑)	Recall (%↑)	NSD (%↑)	MASD (mm↓)
UNet	ADC, zADC	$44.4 \pm \pm 21.9$	47.9 ± 31.5	58.6 ± 22.9	62.3 ± 24.3	4.3 ± 7.1
SegResNet	ADC, zADC	55.3 ± 26.4	$\mathbf{59.3 \pm 26.1}$	59.1 ± 26.4	72.0 ± 27.5	3.6 ± 7.4
SwinUNETR	ADC,zADC	55.8 ± 25.2	55.9 ± 25.7	63.8 ± 25.0	73.0 ± 25.9	3.4 ± 7.1
Ensemble$_{\mathbf{weighted}}$	ADC, zADC	$\mathbf{57.3 \pm 24.0}$	58.5 ± 26.4	64.2 ± 22.4	$\mathbf{75.9 \pm 22.5}$	$\mathbf{2.8 \pm 3.3}$
Ensemble$_{\mathbf{mlp}}$	ADC, zADC	43.4 ± 25.0	35.0 ± 25.1	$\mathbf{82.3 \pm 19.7}$	64.4 ± 25.0	4.0 ± 4.2

Using two-channel inputs (ADC, and zADC) further enhanced segmentation quality relative to single-channel settings (Table 2) with focus on relevant HIE lesion regions in MRI volumes (Fig. 4). Among all tested configurations, the Ensemble$_{weighted}$ approach achieved the highest overall performance, with a Dice of 57.3 ± 23.4, NSD of 75.9 ± 22.5, and MASD of 2.8 ± 3.3. In contrast, the Ensemble$_{mlp}$ fusion exhibited markedly higher recall (82.3 ± 19.7) but substantially lower precision (35.0 ± 25.1) and a reduced Dice score (43.4 ± 25.0), reflecting a systematic bias toward over-segmentation. Together, these results suggest that while MLP-based fusion increases lesion sensitivity, weighted fusion produces a better-calibrated balance between completeness and specificity, leading to superior overall volumetric segmentation.

Table 3. Lesion Segmentation Final Ranking for BONBID-HIE 2024

Rank	User (Team)	Algorithm	Mean Pos.	Dice (%↑)	NSD (%↑)	MASD (mm↓)
1st	piaozhegao5 (Sejong_AI_team)	STHarDNet_v2	2.3	62.6 ± 24.6	73.2 ± 23.9	2.5 ± 2.7
2nd	downtoyou (Sejong_AI_team)	unet3d for 3channel BONBID-HIE	4.0	62.4 ± 25.5	72.9 ± 25.8	2.7 ± 3.1
3rd	amograo (Neonatal NeuroNet)	SNet	4.3	60.6 ± 24.8	71.5 ± 24.3	2.7 ± 2.9
4th	ShuklaAnanya (Neonatal NeuroNet)	SNet_BONBID-HIE_2024	4.7	59.9 ± 24.9	74.8 ± 23.9	2.8 ± 3.8
5th	taci	HE3D-Net (**ours**)	5.3	57.7 ± 23.7	75.1 ± 22.5	2.8 ± 3.3
8th	baorinawork	Rinagpu_Z (**Baseline**)	8.7	58.3 ± 26.4	67.1 ± 25.0	3.2 ± 3.3

We further benchmarked our methods against the official results of the BONBID-HIE 2024 challenge. Our submitted model Ensemble$_{weighted}$ with (ADC, and zADC) input, HE3D-Net (listed as "taci" on the leaderboard), ranked 5th overall and achieved a Dice of 57.7 ± 23.7, NSD of 75.1 ± 22.5, and MASD of 2.8 ± 3.3 (Table 3). When compared with the official baseline algorithm Rinagpu_Z (Dice 58.3 ± 26.4, NSD 67.1 ± 25.0, MASD 3.2 ± 3.3), HE3D-Net delivered comparable Dice performance and a substantially higher NSD (+7.9% relative). Although our MASD was marginally better, the gain in NSD indicates more accurate surface conformity and improved boundary consistency.

5 Discussion and Conclusion

Hypoxic ischemic encephalopathy (HIE) diagnosis and segmentation presents a persistent challenge due to the subtle, multifocal nature of lesions and a severe class imbalance, with lesions often occupying <1% of the infected neonates brain volume. To address this, we developed HE3D-Net, a novel 3D heterogeneous ensemble architecture that leverages the complementary strengths of SwinUNETR, SegResNet, and UNet, designed to capture long-range spatial dependencies, fine-grained features, and robust spatial precision simultaneously. Our experiments yielded two critical insights: first, that z-score normalized ADC maps (zADC) are an essential preprocessing step, dramatically and consistently improving performance over raw ADC inputs by mitigating inter-subject variability. Second, the logit-averaged ensemble consistently outperformed its individual components, validating our hypothesis that architectural diversity mitigates the inherent biases of any single model and provides a more comprehensive, generalizable segmentation.

Our approach explicitly addresses the limitations of prior homogeneous ensembles, which struggle with the tiny, imbalanced structures characteristic of HIE. We implemented a dynamic weighting scheme in the Dice loss function to prioritize the underrepresented lesion class during training. We evaluated two fusion strategies: a simple averaged logit-based method and a Multilayer Perceptron (MLP) trained to refine predictions using local context. While the

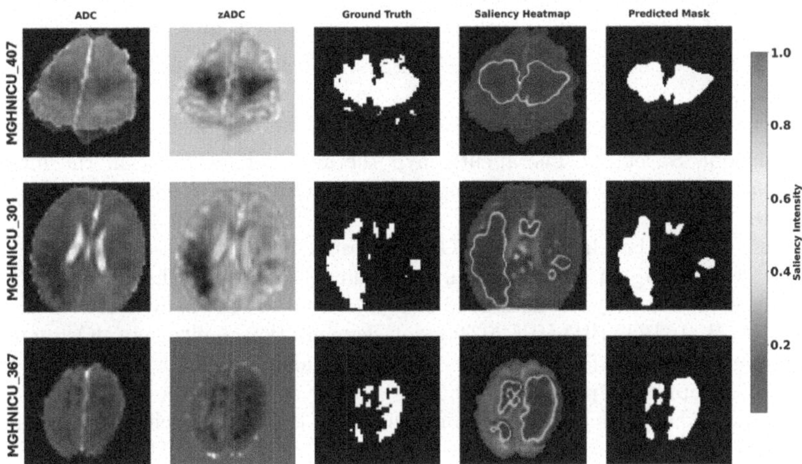

Fig. 4. Qualitative visualization of the model's performance using the dual-channel ADC, and zADC input. The saliency heatmaps illustrate the model's internal focus, with red regions indicating areas identified as high-priority for lesion prediction. These high-importance regions align closely with the ground truth masks, demonstrating that the model successfully learned to focus on relevant HIE lesion areas and differentiate them from the background (blue areas). The predicted masks exhibit strong visual agreement with the ground truth, demonstrating the model's qualitative robustness. Examples include MGHNICU_407 (19.1%), MGHNICU_301 (6.9%), and MGHNICU_367 (2.5%) lesion volumes, expressed as a percentage of the ground-truth lesion volume with corresponding metrics as: Dice = [81.8, 88.8, 69.1], NSD = [91.2, 98.7, 88.9], and MASD = [0.62, 0.32, 1.2].

MLP fusion increased lesion sensitivity (higher recall), it resulted in significantly lower precision and an overall poorer Dice score, reflecting a systematic bias toward over-segmentation. Consequently, the simple averaged logit-based fusion was found to be superior, producing a better-calibrated balance. Combined with post-processing to filter false positives, our final model achieved a test Dice score of 57.7 ± 23.7, Normalized Surface Distance (NSD) of 75.1 ± 22.5, and Mean Average Surface Distance (MASD) of 2.8 ± 3.3. This result outperformed the official BONBID-HIE 2024 baseline, affirming that the intelligent fusion of diverse, data-driven models with domain-specific strategies provides a robust pathway toward clinically reliable tools for neonatal brain analysis. Future enhancements to our framework may include integrating critical diffusion information to better distinguish healthy from damaged tissue and incorporating automated hyperparameter optimization methods, such as grid search and genetic algorithms [10,22], to further refine model performance. Applying transfer learning to accelerate convergence, adopting few-shot strategies to improve generalization, and leveraging semi-supervised or unsupervised learning to utilize unlabeled MRI data may also increase robustness across clinical settings.

Disclosure of Interests. The authors have no competing interests.

References

1. Alqalyoobi, S., et al.: Therapeutic hypothermia and mortality in the intensive care unit: systematic review and meta-analysis. Crit. Care Resusc. **21**(4), 287–298 (2019)
2. Aydın, M.A., Abdinli, E., Unal, G.: SegResnet based reciprocal transformation for bonbid-hie lesion segmentation. In: Trauma Thompson Challenge, pp. 39–44. Springer (2023). https://doi.org/10.1007/978-3-031-71626-3_6
3. Bao, R., et al.: BONBID-HIE 2023: lesion segmentation challenge in BOston neonatal brain injury data for hypoxic ischemic encephalopathy. IEEE Trans. Med. Imag. (2025). accepted for publication
4. Bao, R., et al.: Boston neonatal brain injury data for hypoxic ischemic encephalopathy (BONBID-HIE): I. MRI and lesion labeling. Sci. Data **12**(1), 53 (2025)
5. Cardoso, M.J., et al.: MONAI: an open-source framework for deep learning in healthcare. arXiv preprint arXiv:2211.02701 (2022)
6. Eddine Toubal, I., et al.: Fusion of deep and local features using random forests for neonatal hie segmentation. In: Trauma Thompson Challenge, pp. 3–13. Springer (2023). https://doi.org/10.1007/978-3-031-71626-3_1
7. Graham, E.M., Ruis, K.A., Hartman, A.L., Northington, F.J., Fox, H.E.: A systematic review of the role of intrapartum hypoxia-ischemia in the causation of neonatal encephalopathy. Am. J. Obstet. Gynecol. **199**(6), 587–595 (2008)
8. Grand challenge: Bonbid-hie2023: hypoxic ischemic encephalopathy lesion segmentation challenge. https://bonbid-hie2023.grand-challenge.org/. Accessed 19 Oct 2025
9. Grand challenge: Bonbid-hie2024: 2nd BONBID-hie challenge for hie outcome prediction and lesion segmentation. https://www.bonbid-hie2024.grand-challenge.org/. Accessed 19 Oct 2025
10. Hatuwal, B.K., Shakya, A., Joshi, B.: Plant leaf disease recognition using random forest, KNN, SVM and CNN. Polibits **62**, 13–19 (2020)
11. Koirala, C.P., Mohapatra, S., Schlaug, G.: An ensemble approach for segmentation of neonatal hie lesions. In: Trauma Thompson Challenge, pp. 23–27. Springer (2023). https://doi.org/10.1007/978-3-031-71626-3_3
12. Lee, A.C., et al.: Intrapartum-related neonatal encephalopathy incidence and impairment at regional and global levels for 2010 with trends from 1990. Pediatr. Res. **74**(1), 50–72 (2013)
13. Ma, J., et al.: MEDSAM2: segment anything in 3D medical images and videos. arXiv preprint arXiv:2504.03600 (2025)
14. Massachusetts general hospital: hypoxic ischemic encephalopathy: diagnosis and treatment. https://www.massgeneral.org/children/hypoxic-ischemic-encephalopathy/diagnosis-and-treatment. Accessed 19 Oct 2025
15. Menze, B.H., et al.: The multimodal brain tumor image segmentation benchmark (brats). IEEE Trans. Med. Imaging **34**(10), 1993–2024 (2014)
16. Murphy, K., et al.: Automatic quantification of ischemic injury on diffusion-weighted MRI of neonatal hypoxic ischemic encephalopathy. NeuroImage: Clin. **14**, 222–232 (2017)
17. National institute of neurological disorders and stroke: hypoxic ischemic encephalopathy. https://www.ninds.nih.gov/health-information/disorders/hypoxic-ischemic-encephalopathy. Accessed 19 Oct 2025

18. Rao, A., Shukla, A., Bhargava, J., Ou, Y., Bao, R.: Spatial prior-guided boundary and region-aware 2d lesion segmentation in neonatal hypoxic ischemic encephalopathy. In: International Conference on Medical Image Computing and Computer-Assisted Intervention, pp. 520–530. Springer (2025). https://doi.org/10.1007/978-3-032-04965-0_49
19. Ravi, N., et al.: SAM 2: Segment anything in images and videos. In: International Conference on Learning Representations (2025)
20. Safavigerdini, K., et al.:.: Predicting mechanical properties of carbon nanotube (CNT) images using multi-layer synthetic finite element model simulations. In: 2023 IEEE International Conference on Image Processing (ICIP), pp. 3264–3268. IEEE (2023)
21. Soltani Kazemi, E., et al.: Enhancing lesion segmentation in the BONBID-hie challenge: an ensemble strategy. In: Trauma Thompson Challenge, pp. 14–22. Springer (2023). https://doi.org/10.1007/978-3-031-71626-3_2
22. Soltanikazemi, E., Dhakal, A., Hatuwal, B.K., Toubal, I.E., Aboah, A., Palaniappan, K.: Real-time helmet violation detection in ai city challenge 2023 with genetic algorithm-enhanced yolov5. In: 2023 IEEE Applied Imagery Pattern Recognition Workshop (AIPR), pp. i–x. IEEE (2023)
23. Tahmasebi, N., Punithakumar, K.: A deep neural network approach for the lesion segmentation from neonatal brain magnetic resonance imaging. In: Trauma Thompson Challenge, pp. 34–38. Springer (2023). https://doi.org/10.1007/978-3-031-71626-3_5
24. Wang, H., et al.: Sam-MED3D: towards general-purpose segmentation models for volumetric medical images. In: European Conference on Computer Vision, pp. 51–67. Springer (2024). https://doi.org/10.1007/978-3-031-91721-9_4
25. Wodzinski, M., Müller, H.: Improving segmentation of hypoxic ischemic encephalopathy lesions by heavy data augmentation: contribution to the BONBID challenge. In: Trauma Thompson Challenge, pp. 28–33. Springer (2023). https://doi.org/10.1007/978-3-031-71626-3_4

NeuroGleam: Illuminating Small Vessel Disease Detection Through Deep Learning Based Segmentation of Brain MRI White Matter Hyperintensities

Balaji Iyer[1,3](✉), Brady Williamson[1], V. B. Surya Prasath[3], Bruce J. Aronow[3], Pooja Khatri[4], Heidi Sucharew[5], Vivek Khandwala[2], Joseph LaPorta[8], Lily Wang[2], Rebecca Cornelius[2], Mary Gaskill-Shipley[2], Thomas Tomsick[2], David Wang[6], Thomas Maloney[2], Paul S. Horn[3,7], Janice Carrozzella[2], Brett M. Kissela[1], and Achala Vagal[1]

[1] University of Cincinnati, Cincinnati, OH, USA
iyerbs@mail.uc.edu
[2] Department of Radiology, University of Cincinnati, Cincinnati, OH, USA
[3] Cincinnati Children's Hospital Medical Center, Cincinnati, OH, USA
[4] Department of Neurology, Yale University, New Haven, CT, USA
[5] Department of Emergency Medicine, University of Cincinnati School of Medicine, Cincinnati, OH, USA
[6] I-MED Radiology Network, Melbourne, VIC, Australia
[7] Department of Pediatrics, University of Cincinnati, Cincinnati, OH, USA
[8] Department of Neurology, University of Cincinnati, Cincinnati, OH, USA

Abstract. NeuroGleam is a deep-learning (DL) pipeline for fully automated segmentation of white-matter hyperintensities (WMH) on single-modal, low-resolution T2-FLAIR which is one of the most common MRI series in clinical care. Our preliminary investigation involved benchmarking of six DL architectures under four loss objectives. We found HRNet and its variants to be the best performing architecture and introduced a hyper-parameterized HRNet which was tuned using Bayesian optimization. Experiments span the Medical Image Computing and Computer Assisted Intervention (MICCAI) WMH Challenge dataset, and a 69-subject in-house clinical cohort called Assessing Population-based Radiological Brain Health in Stroke Epidemiology (APRISE). Metrics include Dice, Hausdorff95, lesion-wise sensitivity/F1, and average volume difference. The best HRNet achieves Dice 0.742 (MICCAI) and 0.651 (APRISE) with Hausdorff95 6.24–7.75 mm. Cross-dataset testing drops to Dice 0.523, underscoring domain-shift limits. We discuss practical design choices and outline ongoing work including transfer learning, domain adaptation and out-of-distribution detection to close the generalization gap and enable robust deployment.

Keywords: Image Segmentation · Bayesian Optimization · Small Vessel Disease · White Matter Hyperintensities · Class Imbalance · Domian Shift

F. Tanner and J. Irvine (Eds.): AIPR 2025, LNCS 16446, pp. 508–521, 2026.
https://doi.org/10.1007/978-3-032-18474-0_35

1 Introduction

White-matter hyperintensities (WMHs) are bright lesions on T2-FLAIR MRI and established imaging biomarkers of cerebral small-vessel disease and vascular ageing [1]. Pathologically, they reflect chronic white-matter injury likely driven by micro-angiopathy of small penetrating arterioles [2]. Histology shows disrupted myelin, axonal injury, altered water content, and mild gliosis; axonal damage may contribute to cortical thinning via retrograde degeneration, though mechanisms remain incompletely defined [1, 2]. WMH burden rises steeply with age and is amplified by vascular risks (hypertension, type 2 diabetes, smoking, obesity) [3–5]. Population cohorts report approximately exponential growth with substantial inter-individual variability, with females exhibiting higher volumes from midlife onward, indicating sex-specific vulnerability [6]. These gradients underscore the importance of developing automated WMH quantification methods that are robust to acquisition heterogeneity and inter-individual variability, and that provide interpretable outputs for both research and clinical practice.

Manual WMH segmentation is time-consuming, labor-intensive and subject to inter-rater variability because of the diffuse, heterogeneous appearance of lesions. While DL methods exist, many target multi-modal, high-resolution MRI that is uncommon in routine care, where clinicians typically have a single low-resolution T2-FLAIR. Prior work (e.g., nnU-Net [7], attention models and ensembles) achieves strong scores on research datasets but often requires richer inputs and higher computational resources, limiting its clinical applicability. NeuroGleam addresses this gap: it operates on FLAIR alone, uses patch-based tiling to preserve local context and handle class imbalance, and reassembles predictions via weighted averaging into whole-brain masks.

Despite their clinical importance, accurate segmentation of WMHs remains highly challenging. MRI heterogeneity in scanner vendor/field strength, protocols and calibration shifts signal characteristics and artifacts (bias/in-homogeneity, susceptibility, motion) further distort lesion appearance. Routine clinical scans have low resolution, blurring borders of small, patchy and confluent WMHs. Patient-level factors such as age, sex, ethnicity, and comorbid disease, such as infarct lesions also contribute to heterogeneous lesion presentation, limiting the generalizability of segmentation algorithms. A second major challenge is class imbalance: WMHs occupy < 1–2% of brain volume in most cases, biasing models toward background and causing under-segmentation of small lesions and causing poor lesion-wise sensitivity. The issue is amplified in clinical cohorts where lesions range from scattered punctate foci to confluent burden, adding strong inter-individual variability. Robust solutions must therefore handle acquisition variability, mitigate resolution loss, and explicitly balance sensitivity vs. specificity under extreme imbalance.

2 Related Work

Deep learning (DL) has reshaped segmentation in vision and biomedicine, enabling accurate delineation of small, heterogeneous structures. Encoder–decoder designs, like U-Net extracts high-level features while reducing resolution in the encoder; the decoder restores dense maps using skip connections to fuse semantic and spatial cues. This pattern works well across anatomy without hand-crafted features. But core hurdles such as severe class imbalance, small/diffuse lesions, and domain variability persist. In medical imaging these are amplified by limited datasets and costly, heterogeneous and sometimes inconsistent annotations.

In WMH segmentation, several U-Net variants remain strong baselines. [8] used an ensemble of residual U-Nets on the MICCAI WMH Challenge, achieving high Dice but requiring multimodal MRI. [9] proposed uResNet, a residual U-Net that segments WMHs and stroke lesions; trained on FLAIR with optional multimodal inputs, it outperformed alternatives and correlated with clinical Fazekas scores. [10] introduced a Bayesian 3D U-Net with Monte Carlo dropout, yielding strong Dice and generalization to an unseen cohort, but needing T1 + FLAIR and heavy compute from repeated sampling. Notably, top entries in the 2017 MICCAI WMH Challenge organized by [11] relied on multi-scale CNNs with multimodal inputs, underscoring the difficulty of robust performance from single FLAIR alone.

In recent years, transformer-based segmenters have surged due to stronger long-range modeling. TransUNet [12] hybridizes CNN + Transformer blocks and achieves competitive results; Swin-UNet [13] uses hierarchical Swin Transformers for multi-scale context; UNETR [14] is a pure-Transformer with patch tokenization for 3D volumes. [15] proposed LLRHNet (CNN for local detail + Transformer for global context), reporting ~ 78% Dice on in-house stroke/WMH MRI, surpassing U-Net and pure-Transformer baselines. However, these gains often come with large parameter counts, higher compute, and frequent reliance on multimodal inputs (T1 + FLAIR). [16] developed a multimodal Swin U-Net reaching ~ 0.80 Dice on MICCAI 2017, but on FLAIR-only a simpler CNN baseline outperformed it in Dice and lesion-wise F1. This gap highlights the need for approaches explicitly designed for low-resolution, single-modality FLAIR imaging.

3 Methods

3.1 Overview

NeuroGleam benchmarks and optimizes WMH segmentation under realistic clinical conditions. We evaluate six backbones and four losses yielding 48 model–loss pairs across two datasets. HRNet consistently led, especially with Dice/FTL, so we built a hyper-parameterized HRNet and used Bayesian optimization to probe depth, convolution type, attention, loss weighting, and augmentation. Figure 1 outlines the pipeline: standardized preprocessing, patch-based sampling to preserve small-lesion detail, and a modular training setup supporting multiple architectures/losses for broad screening and targeted refinement. Next, we present the datasets, then preprocessing, patching, architectures, losses, and training/evaluation choices used to develop NeuroGleam.

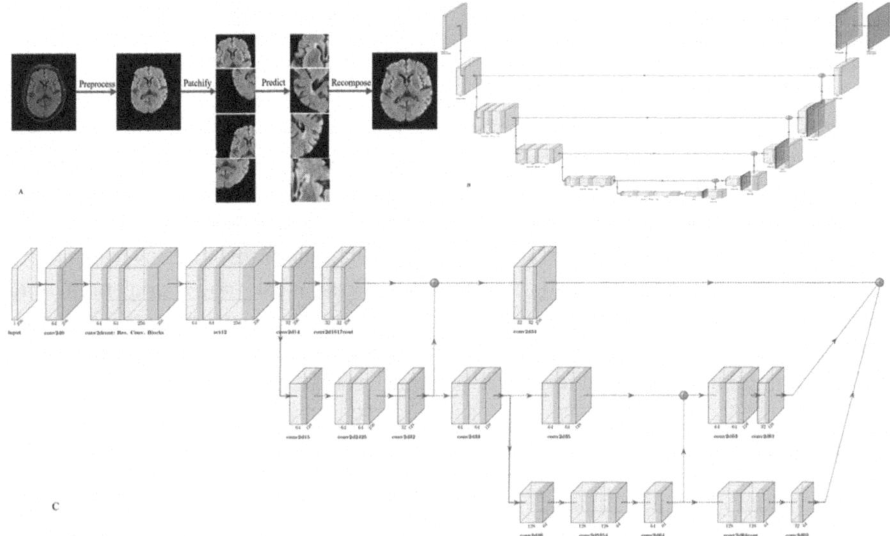

Fig. 1. Panel A shows the NeuroGleam pipeline: T2-FLAIR volume is preprocessed and tiled into overlapping patches and fed into a Unet/HRNet segmentation model producing per-patch probability maps. These maps are then blended to reconstruct the whole-volume mask. Panel B and C show the U-Net and HR-Net models respectively.

3.2 Datasets

This study utilizes two distinct datasets for the development and evaluation of WMH segmentation models: the MICCAI WMH Challenge dataset and the in-house APRISE clinical dataset.

MICCAI WMH Challenge (MWC) Dataset:
The MICCAI WMH Challenge (MWC) dataset [11] was established to enable standardized comparisons of WMH segmentation methods. The data was acquired from three centers: UMC Utrecht, NUHS Singapore and VU Amsterdam. The dataset comprises 60 subjects with T1-weighted and T2-FLAIR MRI scans for training, of which 19 were set aside as a validation subset during model development. The test set consists of 110 subjects, including 90 from the same scanners and 20 from two previously unseen scanners.

APRISE Clinical Dataset:
APRISE is NIH funded population study of stroke patients curated to reflect routine real-world imaging data. A convenience sample of 69 annotated T2-FLAIR MRI scans was utilized, divided into training (35 scans), validation (10 scans), and test (24 scans) subsets. Unlike the MICCAI dataset, only single-sequence T2-FLAIR images are available, mirroring the acquisition protocols most commonly used in clinical practice. WMH annotations were produced by expert neuroradiologists using standardized criteria, with multiple rounds of review and quality control to ensure reliability. Compared to the MICCAI cohort, APRISE features lower resolution, greater variability in image quality, and broader patient heterogeneity, providing a realistic test for clinical translation.

3.3 Preprocessing

All scans underwent a uniform preprocessing pipeline. First, skull striping was performed with HD-BET [17], and volumes were then processed in ANTsPy [18]. Denoising used a spatially adaptive non-local means filter with a Rician noise model to suppress high-frequency noise while preserving edges. N4 bias-field correction removed low-frequency intensity inhomogeneity. For spatial normalization, each T2-FLAIR was affinely registered to a low-resolution template (T2_FLAIR_template_resamp_low.nii.gz) via a two-step procedure: register template to subject to estimate transforms, then invert the transform parameters to register the subject to template. Brain masks and lesion annotations were transformed with the same parameters and resampled using nearest-neighbor interpolation to preserve discrete labels. Finally, each volume was min–max normalized to [0,1] yielding template-aligned inputs for patch extraction.

3.4 Patch Extraction

To balance computational efficiency with lesion localization, we adopted a slice-level random cropping strategy for training and a deterministic tiling strategy for inference.

We use slice-level random crops for training and deterministic tiling for inference. During training, from each axial slice/mask a square crop within a range [p - Δ, p + Δ] where p is the target patch size and Δ is a tolerance margin was sampled. The crop was then resized back to the target patch size p × p, producing one random patch per slice per sampling step. This strategy effectively introduces scale variation, as lesions may appear slightly larger or smaller after random crop-and-resize operations. Combined with the random spatial placement of the crop, the network is exposed to lesions at multiple apparent scales and positions. At inference, slices were tiled into overlapping patches, and their probability maps were reassembled by averaging across overlaps. This approach mitigated edge artifacts and ensured seamless full-slice predictions.

3.5 Model Architectures

To establish strong baselines for WMH segmentation, we systematically benchmarked six backbone architectures. Canonical encoder–decoder models included U-Net, U-Net++, and U-Net++ with Deep Supervision, chosen for their widespread adoption and proven performance in medical image segmentation tasks. To complement these, we evaluated High-Resolution Networks (HRNet), which maintain spatial detail throughout the network, along with two customized variants: SG-HRNet, which integrates spatial gated attention, and SE-HRNet, which incorporates channel-wise squeeze–excitation blocks. These six models collectively balance representational diversity (coarse-to-fine vs. high-resolution design) while addressing the fine-grained localization challenges characteristic of WMHs. Figure 1 B and C illustrates representative architectures from each family.

3.6 Loss Functions

We evaluated four complementary loss functions to address the dual challenges of class imbalance and segmentation precision in WMH detection:

1. Cross-Entropy (CE) Loss. A standard voxel-wise classification objective that penalizes incorrect predictions at the individual pixel level.
2. Dice Loss (DL). Optimized for segmentation by directly maximizing the overlap between predicted and ground-truth masks, making it effective under strong class imbalance.
3. Soft Dice Loss (SDL). A differentiable variant of Dice that blends Dice with cross-entropy, providing smoother gradients and more stable training, particularly in uncertain regions.
4. Focal Tversky Loss (FTL). The Tversky Index is a generalization of Dice that introduces adjustable weighting factors for false positives and false negatives, allowing flexible control of sensitivity vs. specificity. The Tversky Index is mathematically defined as:

$$Tv = \frac{TP + smooth}{TP + \alpha.FN + \beta.FP + smooth} \tag{1}$$

where TP, FP, and FN are the true positives, false positives, and false negatives, respectively; α and β control the penalties for false negatives and false positives; and smooth is a small constant to avoid division by zero. The Focal Tversky Loss [19] (FTL) is defined as:

$$L_{FTL} = (1 - Tv)^{\gamma} \tag{2}$$

where $\gamma \geq 1$. The concept of Focal Loss [20] was introduced in the context of classification, with the goal of forcing the model to focus on hard or misclassified examples. When $\gamma > 1$, the loss contribution from easy voxels (high Tv) is down-weighted and the contribution from hard voxels (low Tv) is amplified.

4 Experiments

In this section we first specify the common training protocol and the evaluation metrics used to assess segmentation quality. We then describe our benchmarking methodology and results are reported in a consolidated table. Building on the screening results, we then present a Bayesian hyperparameter optimization of the top-performing architecture.

4.1 Training Protocol

All models were implemented in Tensorflow Keras and trained end-to-end on 2D axial slices derived from the preprocessed FLAIR volumes. We used Adam with learning rate of 0.001 and all other optimizer hyperparameters left at framework defaults, training ran for 100 epochs with batch size = 128. We implemented learning rate reduction using ReduceLROnPlateau (factor 0.1; patience = 5) and monitored validation Dice for early stopping. We implemented a RandAugment [21]-style policy for augmentations using Albumentations [22] library: for each sample, a fixed number of operations were drawn from the pool below, with parameters shown in Table 1. In addition, we applied CoarseDropout [23, 24], a configurable Cutout and Random-Erasing–style occlusion, to simulate occlusions and promote robustness.

Table 1. Augmentation operators and key parameters

Operator	Parameters
X-Y Translation	$\pm$ 100 pixels
Rotation	$\pm$ 45 degrees
Shear	$\pm$ 30 degrees
Flip	Vertical and Horizontal
CoarseDropout	$\pm$ 8 pixels
Contrast	Limit = 0.5
Brightness	Limit = 0.5
Sharpen	alpha: (0.2, 0.5), lightness: (0.5, 1.0)

We evaluated square patch sizes {32,48,64,96} using a lightweight U-Net trained under the same preprocessing, augmentation, and optimization settings on the MWC dataset validation split. Among these, 64 × 64 provided the best trade-off between context and localization achieving higher Dice and lower Hausdorff95. To avoid model-specific bias, we verified that HRNet at 64 × 64 performed better relative to 96 × 96. We therefore fixed p = 64 for all subsequent experiments.

4.2 Evaluation Metrics

We evaluate per-case predictions from probability maps thresholded at 0.5 (fixed for all models). Binary masks are treated as 3D volumes; connected components are computed with 26-connectivity for lesion-wise metrics.

- **Dice similarity (DSC):** The de-facto, most widely used overlap metric in medical image segmentation that ranges 0 (no overlap) to 1 (perfect match).
- **Hausdorff95:** The 95th percentile of the bidirectional surface-to-surface distances between P and G. This reduces sensitivity to outliers compared to the maximum Hausdorff distance.
- **Lesion-wise sensitivity / precision / F1:** WMH lesions are often small, punctate, and scattered, with occasional confluent plaques; pixel-wise overlap metrics such as DSC are dominated by background and large lesions and can look good even when many tiny lesions are missed or when boundaries shift by a few voxels. We evaluate lesions as 3D connected components (26-connectivity) and compute precision, recall and F1 score between the predicted and ground truth lesions.
- **Average Volume Difference (AVD):** For each case, binary prediction and ground-truth masks are compared in voxel counts. Let G and P be the binarized ground-truth and predicted masks. Let V_{gt}, V_{pred} be the sum over all voxels in G and P respectively then AVD is defined as

$$AVD(\%) = 100 * \frac{|V_{gt} - V_{pred}|}{V_{gt}} \quad (3)$$

4.3 Benchmarking

We benchmarked the six backbones under four loss regimes, yielding 24 model–loss configurations per dataset and 48 trained models in total across the MWC and APRISE datasets. All runs used the training setup in Sec. 4.1. For the baseline screening we report Dice only, to avoid a wall of numbers that dilutes the main findings. The full metric suite is reported later for the Bayesian-optimized HRNet. We also conduct a zero-shot cross-dataset test; train on MWC, test on APRISE (no fine-tuning); to quantify domain shift from research-grade to clinical, low-resolution data, which is the deployment-relevant scenario. We do not emphasize the inverse (APRISE → MWC) because our objective is robust performance on APRISE.

Table 2. DSC for six backbones across four losses on MWC and APRISE, plus zero-shot MWC → APRISE transfer. For each model, the best performing loss function on MWC is highlighted in green, column best values are bold

Model	Loss	Train-Test MWC	Train-Test APRISE	Train MWC, Test -APRISE
HRNet	Dice	**0.671**	0.603	0.446
	CE	0.606	0.588	0.308
	Soft Dice	0.611	0.511	0.323
	FTL	0.639	0.577	0.437
SG-HRNet	Dice	0.494	0.529	0.342
	CE	0.556	0.481	0.276
	Soft Dice	0.512	0.422	0.193
	FTL	**0.679**	0.517	0.312
SE-HRNet	Dice	0.537	0.592	0.414
	CE	**0.649**	0.546	0.388
	Soft Dice	0.566	0.381	0.277
	FTL	0.515	0.483	0.288
Unet	Dice	0.55	0.486	0.332
	CE	0.618	0.416	0.259
	Soft Dice	0.575	0.392	0.354
	FTL	**0.627**	0.442	0.4
Unet++	Dice	0.513	0.356	0.306
	CE	0.592	0.418	0.249
	Soft Dice	0.533	0.426	0.3
	FTL	**0.595**	0.469	0.371
DS Unet++	Dice	**0.58**	0.446	0.339
	CE	0.485	0.39	0.222

(continued)

Table 2. (*continued*)

Model	Loss	Train-Test MWC	Train-Test APRISE	Train MWC, Test -APRISE
	Soft Dice	0.511	0.492	0.354
	FTL	0.547	0.522	0.431

Table 2 reports Dice for six backbones across four losses on MWC (in-domain), APRISE (in-domain), and zero-shot MWC → APRISE. For each model, the best loss on MWC is shaded green; column best values are bold. Comparing the performance across the models a clear pattern emerges; the HRNet family consistently outperforms U-Net variants across settings. Plain HRNet + Dice leads on APRISE and in zero-shot transfer, while SG-HRNet + FTL peaks on MWC but does not generalize as well. This pattern is consistent with WMH morphology which are typically small, punctate, and scattered lesions so architectures that preserve high-resolution features and fuse multi-scale context throughout retain tiny foci better than encoder–decoder models that downsample early and reconstruct detail later. Loss-wise, Dice/FTL generally beat CE under class imbalance.

4.4 Bayesian Hyperparameter Optimization

Given the strong baseline performance of HRNet, we pursued a second-stage optimization using a Bayesian hyperparameter search to further improve accuracy without hand-tuning. We performed Bayesian hyperparameter optimization using Hyperopt libraries' Tree-Structured Parzen Estimator (TPE) algorithm that has been validated across vision and ML benchmarks [25, 26]. Table 3 summarizes the search space and ranges. The 100-trial hyperparameter search was restricted to MWC (APRISE was not used) to choose the best architecture/loss/training setup. To avoid leakage, the held-out test set remained untouched throughout the search.

Table 3. Hyperparameter search space for Bayesian optimization of HRNet on MWC dataset

Parameter	Range	Description
Transition Depth	Integer in [1, 5]	The number of stages in HRNet where feature maps are progressively refined
Attention Mechanism	Binary	Inclusion or exclusion of gated attention
Squeeze-and-Excitation (SE)	Binary	Inclusion or exclusion of SE blocks
Convolution Types	Standard Conv2D, Depthwise, Residual	Different types of Convolution Operations
Number of Filters	Integer in [64, 128, 256, 512]	Allows choosing optimal number of filters

(*continued*)

Table 3. (*continued*)

Parameter	Range	Description
Augmentations	Geometric, Intensity based, Both	Geometric augmentations, intensity augmentations, or a combination of both
Learning Rate Multiplier	Loguniform float: (-0.5, 0.5)	Allows the learning rate to vary exponentially rather than linearly
Loss Functions	Dice, CE, Soft Dice, FTL, CE + FTL	A hybrid Cross-Entropy + Focal Tversky Loss was also introduced
Loss Parameters	Float: α (0, 1), β (0, 1) and γ [1, 5]	Hyperparameters specific to FTL loss function

The best-performing HRNet configuration discovered by the Bayesian search is summarized in Table 4. The selected model uses depthwise-conv HRNet with transition depth of 3 and no attention mechanisms. The configuration preferred intensity-only augmentation, and a hybrid CE + FTL loss. This model was then trained on the APRISE dataset as well and the performance of this model on the MWC, APRISE and the zero-shot MWC → APRISE is summarized in Table 5.

Table 4. Best HRNet configuration from the 100-trial Bayesian search

Parameter	Value
Transition Depth	3
Attention Mechanisms	FALSE
Squeeze-and-Excitation (SE) Blocks	FALSE
Convolution Types	Depthwise
Number of Filters	256
Augmentations	Intensity based
Learning Rate	0.00085
Loss Functions	CE + FTL
Loss Parameters	$\alpha = 0.8, \beta = 0.2, \gamma = 1.5$

Table 5. Test performance for the configuration in Table 4. All values are means per dataset

	DSC (↑)	Hausdorff95 (↓)	ccRec. (↑)	ccPrec. (↑)	ccF1 (↑)	AVD (↓)
Train-Test MWC	0.742 ± 0.15	6.241 ± 4.83	0.650 ± 0.14	0.771 ± 0.16	0.705 ± 0.11	21.975 ± 15.35

(*continued*)

Table 5. (*continued*)

	DSC (↑)	Hausdorff95 (↓)	ccRec. (↑)	ccPrec. (↑)	ccF1 (↑)	AVD (↓)
Train-Test APRISE	0.651 ± 0.19	7.748 ± 6.77	0.785 ± 0.17	0.590 ± 0.17	0.674 ± 0.12	35.227 ± 21.11
Train MWC, Test -APRISE	0.523 ± 0.18	18.680 ± 9.81	0.628 ± 0.17	0.456 ± 0.19	0.528 ± 0.13	53.959 ± 17.55

Table 5 shows clear gains over the initial HRNet baseline. On MWC (in-domain), DSC improves from 0.671 to 0.742 (+0.071, + 10.5%), while for the APRISE (in-domain) DSC increased from 0.603 to 0.651 (+0.048, + 7.9%). Similar improvement was noted across other evaluation metrics as well. In zero-shot MWC → APRISE (cross domain), Dice increases 0.446 to 0.523 (+0.077, + 17.2%). Despite gains in Dice and AVD, Hausdorff95 remained elevated, indicating that improvements in global overlap did not fully translate to boundary accuracy.

5 Discussion and Conclusions

The results in the previous section underscore both the promise and the difficulty of robust WMH segmentation on single-sequence, low-resolution clinical FLAIR. Across a broad baseline screen consisting of six backbones across four losses, HRNet and its variants consistently outperformed U-Net family models on research-grade data, reflecting the benefit of maintaining high-resolution feature streams for detecting small, punctate lesions. However, applying the same models to the APRISE clinical cohort led to marked performance degradation, and lesion-wise analyses confirmed that small-lesion detection and boundary fidelity remain vulnerable under clinical heterogeneity.

The second-stage Bayesian hyperparameter optimization delivered consistent gains on both MICCAI and APRISE with improved overlap metrics and reducing volume error, but it did not yield a commensurate improvement in cross-dataset generalizability. Zero-shot transfer from MICCAI to APRISE continued to show elevated boundary errors and residual false positives/negatives in difficult regions, indicating that better in-domain fit alone does not resolve domain shift.

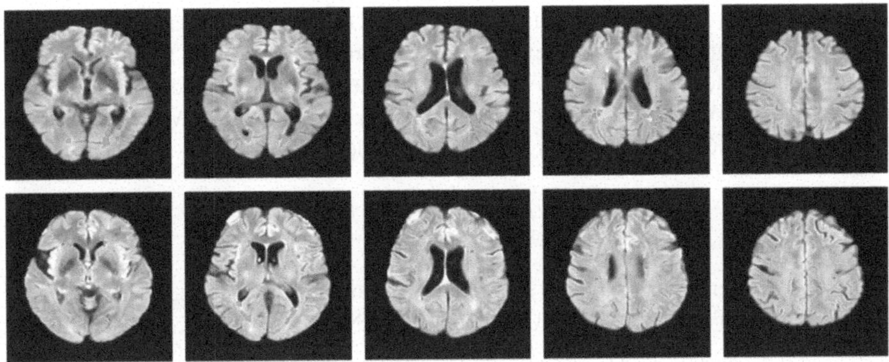

Fig. 2. Consecutive axial slices from MWC dataset: FLAIR with TP (green), FP (red), FN (blue) overlays. Top row DSC = 0.74, ccF1 = 0.79. Bottom row DSC = 0.44, ccF1 = 0.34. Note the missed punctate foci and clean segmentation of confluent lesions.

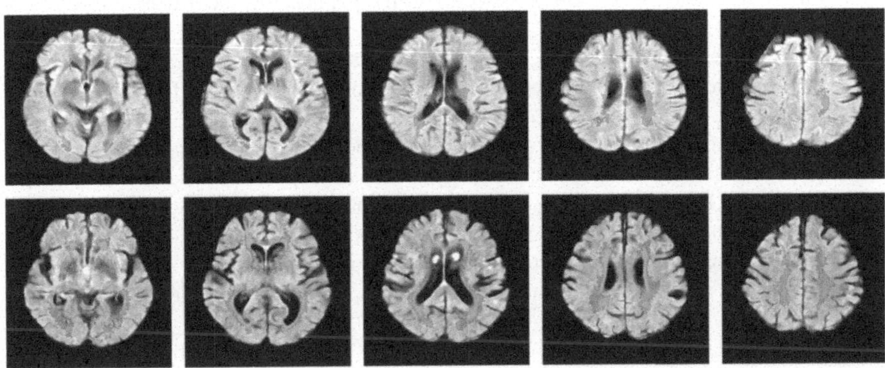

Fig. 3. Consecutive axial slices from APRISE dataset: FLAIR with TP (green), FP (red), FN (blue) overlays. Top row DSC = 0.55, ccF1 = 0.77. Bottom row DSC = 0.58, ccF1 = 0.25. Despite a slightly higher Dice, numerous punctate/periventricular lesions are missed, and confluent plaques are under-segmented, yielding poor lesion-wise performance.

Figure 2 and 3 corroborate the quantitative trends. On MWC (Fig. 2) the model reliably tracks compact lesions in typical cases and errors concentrate at periventricular rims. On APRISE (Fig. 3), acquisition variability and noise lead to missed punctate foci and under-segmented lesions, even when case-level Dice is acceptable. These examples align with the quantitative results: improvements in overlap and volume estimation do not fully address small-lesion detection or localized boundary separations under domain shift.

Once models leave controlled settings, distributional variability (scanner/protocol/noise/patient mix) dominates errors. Beyond robustness tactics (e.g. domain-specific fine-tuning, more heterogeneous data), deployment needs an inference-time, per-case OOD detector to flag scans outside the training distribution. Logging OOD scores with metadata (vendor, field strength, protocol, site, age/sex/comorbidity) creates a feedback loop for targeted data collection/fine-tuning, active learning, and triage. NeuroGleam delivers a practical single-sequence WMH pipeline, sets strong HRNet baselines improved via Bayesian tuning, and outlines a path toward clinically robust deployment.

References

1. Pantoni, L.: Cerebral small vessel disease: from pathogenesis and clinical characteristics to therapeutic challenges. The Lancet Neurology **9**(7), 689–701 (2010)
2. Wardlaw, J.M., Smith, C., Dichgans, M.: Mechanisms of sporadic cerebral small vessel disease: insights from neuroimaging. The Lancet Neurology **12**(5), 483–497 (2013)
3. Patel, Y., et al.: Genetic risk factors underlying white matter hyperintensities and cortical atrophy. Nature Communications **15**(1), 9517 (2024)
4. Zhuang, F.-J., et al.: Prevalence of white matter hyperintensities increases with age. Neural *regeneration research* **13**(12), 2141–2146 (2018)
5. Pradeep, A., et al.: Can white matter hyperintensities based Fazekas visual assessment scales inform about Alzheimer's disease pathology in the population?. Alzheimer's Research & Therapy **16**(1), 157 (2024)
6. de Kort, F.A.S., et al.: Cerebral white matter hyperintensity volumes: normative age- and sex-specific values from 15 population-based cohorts comprising 14,876 individuals. Neurobiology of Aging **146**, 38–47 (2025)
7. Isensee, F., et al.: nnU-Net: a self-configuring method for deep learning-based biomedical image segmentation. Nature Methods **18**(2), 203–211 (2021)
8. Li, H., et al.: Fully convolutional network ensembles for white matter hyperintensities segmentation in MR images. Neuroimage **183**, 650–665 (2018)
9. Guerrero, R., et al.: White matter hyperintensity and stroke lesion segmentation and differentiation using convolutional neural networks. NeuroImage: Clinical **17**, 918–934 (2018)
10. Mojiri Forooshani, P., et al.: Deep Bayesian networks for uncertainty estimation and adversarial resistance of white matter hyperintensity segmentation. Vol. 43. No. 7. Hoboken, USA: John Wiley & Sons, Inc. (2022)
11. Kuijf, H.J., et al.: Standardized assessment of automatic segmentation of white matter hyperintensities and results of the WMH segmentation challenge. IEEE Transactions on Medical Imaging **38**(11), 2556–2568 (2019)
12. Chen, J., et al.: Transunet: Transformers Make Strong Encoders for Medical Image Segmentation. arXiv preprint arXiv:2102.04306 (2021)
13. Cao, H., et al.: Swin-unet: Unet-like pure transformer for medical image segmentation. European Conference on Computer Vision. Cham: Springer Nature Switzerland (2022)
14. Hatamizadeh, A., et al.: Unetr: Transformers for 3d medical image segmentation. Proceedings of the IEEE/CVF winter conference on applications of computer vision (2022)
15. Liu, L., et al.: LLRHNet: multiple lesions segmentation using local-long range features. Frontiers in Neuroinformatics **16**, 859973 (2022)
16. Viteri, J.A., et al.: Automatic brain white matter hyperintensities segmentation with swin U-Net. 2022 IEEE ANDESCON. IEEE (2022)
17. Isensee, F., et al.: Automated brain extraction of multisequence MRI using artificial neural networks. Human Brain Mapping **40**(17), 4952–4964 (2019)
18. Avants, B.B., Tustison, N., Song, G.: Advanced normalization tools (ANTS). Insight J. **2**(365), 1–35 (2009)

19. Lin, T.-Y., et al.: Focal loss for dense object detection. Proceedings of the IEEE International Conference on Computer Vision (2017)
20. Abraham, N., Khan, N.M.: A novel focal tversky loss function with improved attention u-net for lesion segmentation. 2019 IEEE 16th International Symposium on Biomedical Imaging (ISBI 2019). IEEE (2019)
21. Cubuk, E.D., et al.: Randaugment: Practical automated data augmentation with a reduced search space. Proceedings of the IEEE/CVF Conference on Computer Vision and Pattern Recognition Workshops (2020)
22. Buslaev, A., et al.: Albumentations: fast and flexible image augmentations. Information **11**(2), 125 (2020)
23. DeVries, T., Taylor, G.W.: Improved regularization of convolutional neural networks with cutout. arXiv preprint arXiv:1708.04552 (2017)
24. Zhong, Z., et al.: Random erasing data augmentation. Proceedings of the AAAI Conference on Artificial Intelligence **34**(07) (2020)
25. Bergstra, J., Yamins, D., Cox, D.: Making a science of model search: Hyperparameter optimization in hundreds of dimensions for vision architectures. International conference on machine learning. PMLR (2013)
26. Bergstra, J., Yamins, D., Cox, D.D.: Hyperopt: a python library for optimizing the hyperparameters of machine learning algorithms. SciPy **13**, 20 (2013)

Multimodal Fusion of Imaging and Multi-omics Data for Enhanced Breast Cancer Detection

Dattatreya Kantha(✉) and Murray H. Loew

The George Washington University, Washington, DC 20052, USA
{dattatreya.kantha,loew}@gwu.edu

Abstract. Breast cancer, a complex adaptive system of interacting genetic, epigenetic, and environmental factors, exhibits profound radiologic and molecular heterogeneity that challenges single-modality AI models. We present a biologically structured deep learning framework that unifies eight complementary modalities, including MRI, dual-resolution histopathology ($20\times/40\times$), and five omics streams (RNA-Seq, CNV, DNA methylation, miRNA, and proteomics) to uncover cross-scale determinants of tumor behavior within the TCGA-BRCA cohort. By integrating macro-scale anatomy, micro-scale cellular architecture, and molecular regulation, the framework provides a holistic biological perspective linking imaging phenotypes to underlying gene activity and pathway dysregulation. Modality-specific encoders (ResNet/ViT for imaging, 1D-CNN/BiLSTM for omics) generate biologically anchored prototypes through supervised contrastive learning and graph-based compression. A memory-efficient FlashAttention Transformer performs token-level cross-attention between imaging and omics representations, revealing how spatial and molecular patterns jointly shape cancer phenotypes. On the 60-patient training/validation set, the framework achieved 93.19% accuracy and an AUC of 0.9208; on the 24-patient held-out test set, 92% accuracy and an AUC of 0.912, with 0% false positives under cross-patient modality-swap tests. SHAP analyses reveal consistent alignment between MRI-derived tumor-core necrosis patterns and BRCA1/2-related molecular deficiencies, demonstrating that the model learns biologically interpretable mechanisms rather than functioning as a black-box classifier. With sub-second inference and biologically grounded attention maps, the framework establishes a path toward interpretable, real-time, multimodal precision oncology.

Keywords: Breast cancer · magnetic resonance imaging (MRI) · multi-omics · multimodal data fusion · transformer networks

1 Introduction

1.1 Clinical Motivation

Breast cancer's biological heterogeneity complicates diagnosis and treatment, exposing limitations of unimodal analyses such as histopathology, MRI, or omics-only models [1, 2, 12]. Advances in MRI, histopathology, and multi-omics profiling provide complementary perspectives on tumor structure and molecular regulation [3], yet most studies

F. Tanner and J. Irvine (Eds.): AIPR 2025, LNCS 16446, pp. 522–545, 2026.
https://doi.org/10.1007/978-3-032-18474-0_36

analyze these independently, neglecting the cross-modal links that connect phenotype and genotype [5]. Moreover, modern deep models often behave as opaque "black boxes," hindering clinical adoption because of limited interpretability [7]. Each modality contributes unique insight: MRI captures macroscopic anatomy for staging and surgical planning; histopathology reveals micro-architectural features such as mitotic activity; and omics data (RNA-Seq, CNV, DNA methylation, miRNA, and proteomics) encode molecular dysregulation relevant to subtype classification and therapy guidance.

Integrating these complementary scales enables a unified, mechanistic understanding of tumor biology linking radiologic and histologic patterns to underlying gene- and pathway-level alterations. Although public repositories like TCGA-BRCA and TCIA [28, 48, 56, 57] provide rich resources, datasets with fully matched MRI, histopathology, and omics remain scarce. This scarcity limits direct multimodal learning and motivates the use of biologically aligned representation and adversarial validation to emulate scanner drift, assay variability, and cross-modality heterogeneity [30].

1.2 Contributions

To address the limitations of existing multimodal cancer analysis, We present a biologically structured deep learning framework that unifies eight modalities comprising MRI, dual-resolution histopathology (20 × /40 ×), and five omics streams into a single interpretable model. The framework learns biologically aligned prototypes via supervised contrastive learning (SCL) guided by WHO subtypes and KEGG pathway priors, ensuring that latent features remain biologically meaningful. A FlashAttention Transformer enables scalable cross-modal fusion with ~ 45% lower memory usage while preserving accuracy. Robustness is enhanced through adversarial validation, which verifies generalization under modality drift and mismatch.

The model achieves zero false positives under adversarial testing, offers prototype-level interpretability via SHAP, and explicitly links imaging features (e.g., necrotic rims, vascular patterns) to molecular drivers such as BRCA1/2 dysregulation [4, 7]. With sub-second inference (~850 ms per patient) on a single RTX A6000 GPU, the system is clinically practical. All code, configuration files, and patient splits will be released publicly to support reproducibility and cross-institutional validation.

1.3 Abbreviation and Acronyms

The following abbreviations and acronyms are used throughout this paper: AUC – Area Under the Curve; AUROC – Area Under the Receiver Operating Characteristic Curve; BCE – Binary Cross-Entropy; BRCA1/2 – Breast Cancer Gene 1/2; CI – Confidence Interval; CNV – Copy Number Variation; DICOM – Digital Imaging and Communications in Medicine; ECE – Expected Calibration Error; FN – False Negative; FP – False Positive; GAT – Graph Attention Network; GCN – Graph Convolutional Network; GDC – Genomic Data Commons; GNN – Graph Neural Network; IRB – Institutional Review Board; KEGG – Kyoto Encyclopedia of Genes and Genomes; MLP – Multi-Layer Perceptron; MRI – Magnetic Resonance Imaging; PCA – Principal Component Analysis; pp – Percentage Points; ROC – Receiver Operating Characteristic; RPPA – Reverse Phase Protein Array; SaMD – Software as a Medical Device; SCL – Supervised

Contrastive Learning; SHAP – SHapley Additive exPlanations; TCGA – The Cancer Genome Atlas; TCIA – The Cancer Imaging Archive; t-SNE – t-Distributed Stochastic Neighbor Embedding; and WSI – Whole-Slide Image.

2 Background

Early multimodal frameworks such as Pathomic Fusion [2] and TransSurv [12] demonstrated the potential of linking morphological and molecular data, yet they remain limited by several key gaps. Most exclude radiology particularly MRI, thereby losing macro-anatomical context for tumor localization and staging. Others scale poorly, fusing only two or three modalities (e.g., MIF [54], CA-MLIF [11]) or restricting fusion to omics alone (MoGCN [55], MOGONET [6]). Furthermore, fusion is often performed on latent embeddings without biological priors, and robustness testing under domain shift is rarely addressed [13].Recent efforts like HEALNet [58], M2EF-NNs [59], and MOFS [60] have extended multimodal integration but remain either spatially coarse, non-end-to-end, or computationally heavy.

Our framework advances multimodal cancer analysis along three major axes. First, it achieves comprehensive imaging integration by combining MRI with dual-resolution whole-slide histopathology (20 × /40 ×), enabling full radiology–pathology synergy. Second, it establishes scalable biological fusion through graph-based compression and FlashAttention, allowing efficient end-to-end processing of approximately 4.1k tokens while reducing GPU memory usage by nearly 45%. Third, it delivers mechanistic interpretability, where prototype-level SHAP analysis reveals coherent links between imaging phenotypes (e.g., necrotic cores, vascular rims) and molecular programs (e.g., BRCA1/2 dysregulation, PI3K–AKT signaling, hypoxia). Together, these advances transform multimodal fusion from statistical concatenation into biologically grounded, token-level alignment bridging deep learning predictions with mechanistic cancer understanding.

3 Methodology

We propose a biologically structured Transformer framework that unifies eight modalities like MRI, dual-resolution WSIs (20 × tissue context, 40 × diagnostic), and five omics streams (RNA-Seq, CNV, DNA methylation, miRNA, proteomics) sourced from TCIA and the GDC [28, 57]. After preprocessing and feature extraction, each modality is converted into biologically labeled prototypes (e.g., necrosis, stroma, *BRCA1/2* dysregulation) refined via supervised contrastive learning for intra-class compactness and inter-class separability. Graph encoders capture structural dependencies: GNNs model spatial topology in imaging, while GATs encode pathway connectivity in omics. The resulting embeddings are tokenized and fused using a FlashAttention Transformer, which performs both self- and cross-attention for cross-modal biological alignment. Model performance is evaluated via accuracy, AUC, and ECE, while robustness is assessed through five-fold cross-validation, baseline comparison, SHAP interpretability, and adversarial validation simulating scanner drift and assay variability(see Fig. 1).

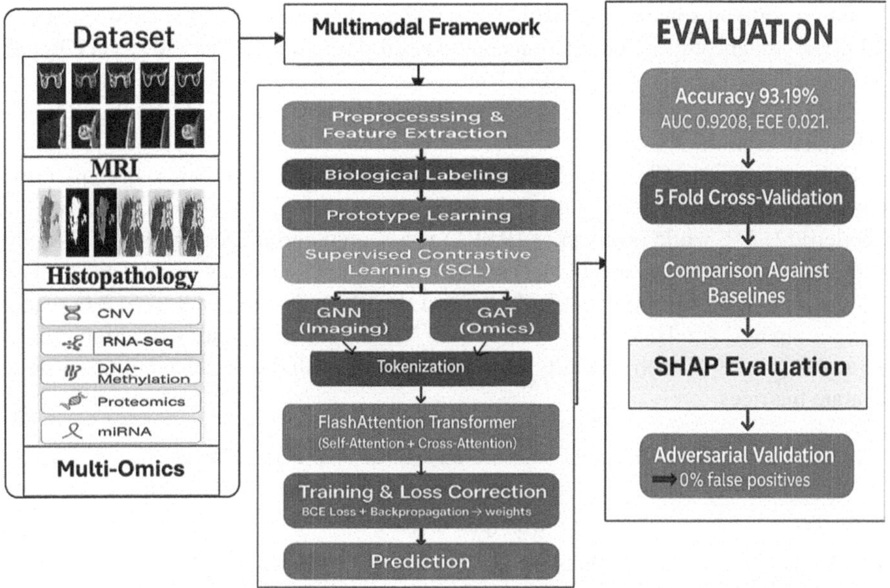

Fig. 1. Overview of multimodal pipeline showing dataset inputs, feature integration, and evaluation of performance and robustness.

3.1 Data Preprocessing

MRI. DICOM scans ($\approx$100k + slices) were resampled to 512 $\times$ 512, corrected for coil inhomogeneity using N4 bias correction [16], min–max normalized (0–1 scaling), and contrast-enhanced with CLAHE to improve tumor visibility. Augmentation included $\pm$ 90°/180° rotations, flips, and Gaussian noise, expanding ~ 100k images to > 150k slices for improved robustness.

Histopathology. Whole-slide images (WSIs) were tiled into 512 $\times$ 512 patches [19], stain-normalized using Macenko's method [14], and background removed with Otsu thresholding along with tissue segmentation [15]. Augmentations included rotations, flips, brightness variation, and elastic deformations [18], expanding 110 WSIs (20 $\times$) to ~ 1,100 patches and 60 WSIs (40 $\times$) to ~ 1000 patches.

Omics. CNV profiles were one-hot encoded; RNA-Seq counts $\log_2$ (TPM)-normalized after feature counts [17]; DNA methylation and miRNA data median-imputed; and proteomics (RPPA) values z-scored. All omics streams were compressed to 50D via PCA, preserving $\geq$ 90% variance.

3.2 Feature Extraction

Each MRI axial slice is resized to 512 $\times$ 512 and encoded with a fine-tuned ResNet-50 to produce a 2048-D slice embedding; study-level anatomy is obtained by mean-pooling slice embeddings to a single patient vector [20].

Whole-slide histopathology is tiled into 512 × 512 patches at 20 × (tissue context) and 40 × (diagnostic) magnifications and passed through a ResNet-50 + ViT hybrid leveraging convolutional locality and Transformer global context to yield 768-D (20 ×) and 2048-D (40 ×) patch descriptors; descriptors are averaged to slide-level vectors for each magnification [20, 21].

For multi-omics, CNV, RNA-Seq, miRNA, and DNA-methylation streams (after standardization) are modeled with a 1D-CNN (kernel 5) + BiLSTM (hidden size 128) encoder [22, 23], while proteomics (RPPA) is z-scored and reduced via PCA. Finally, all modality embeddings are PCA-compressed to 50-D ($\geq$ 90% variance; PCA fit on training data per fold to prevent leakage) and then linearly projected to 512-D tokens (one per stream) for Transformer fusion (see Table 1).After feature extraction, all the extracted features of each modality were stored along with their reduced dimensions in separate matrices.

Table 1. Sample Entries from the Final 50-D Feature Matrix.

Modality	Orig. Dim (per sample)	Reduced Dim (PCA)
MRI imaging	2048 (ResNet-50 features, MRI slices)	50
Tissue WSI (20 ×)	768 (ResNet-50/ViT features, 20 × patches)	50
Diagnostic WSI (40 ×)	2048 (ResNet-50/ViT features, 40 × patches)	50
RNA-Seq(Gene expression)	~ 20,480 raw → ~ 1000 preprocessed features	50

3.3 Prototype Learning

Cluster Analysis and Biological Labeling. To identify biologically meaningful feature groupings, 50-D PCA embeddings from each modality were analyzed using t-SNE for qualitative structure (see Fig. 2) and the elbow + silhouette methods for quantitative cluster selection (see Fig. 3), yielding k $\approx$ 8 for MRI and k = 4–8 for other modalities. Independent k-means clustering grouped correlated features into coherent patterns: MRI clusters captured necrotic rim, viable core, and normal tissue, while omics clusters reflected BRCA1/2-related repair deficiency and pathway-level variation.

Label Source and Validation. Cluster labels were obtained directly from the dataset, which included predefined ROI annotations with labels. For MRI and histopathology, these labeled ROIs were used to assign imaging clusters to categories such as necrotic rim, viable core, or normal tissue. For omics, pathway enrichment against KEGG, Reactome, and Gene Ontology references [25–32] was used to label each cluster with its dominant molecular process (e.g., DNA-repair deficiency, PI3K–AKT activation, immune signaling). These dataset-derived biological labels ensured that each cluster represented a verified anatomical or molecular context, forming the basis for prototype extraction and cross-modal fusion. To prevent data leakage, PCA and k-means models were fit only on training folds.

Feature Consolidation and Statistical Stability. Clustering groups correlated features into coherent biological categories, effectively consolidating redundant information and reducing the overall feature diversity produced during extraction. By merging highly similar descriptors within and across modalities, it yields a compact, biologically interpretable representation that enhances statistical stability and mitigates overparameterization. Each cluster centroid thus captures a representative biological pattern such as necrotic, stromal, or proliferative regions embedded within a shared latent manifold that aligns modalities while preserving essential variability for downstream learning.

Prototype Extraction. Prototypes are derived by identifying the feature vectors closest to each cluster centroid and averaging their embeddings to obtain representative biological patterns (e.g., tumor core, necrotic rim, stromal tissue). This centroid-based averaging ensures that each prototype reflects the mean behavior of its cluster while filtering local noise. Multiple prototypes per cluster are retained to capture spatial or patient-specific variability while preserving shared semantics. All prototypes are subsequently projected into a shared 512-D latent manifold for Transformer fusion, where this dimensionality reflects representation depth rather than additional feature count. These prototypes thus serve as compact, interpretable tokens for downstream fusion and supervised contrastive learning (see Table 2).

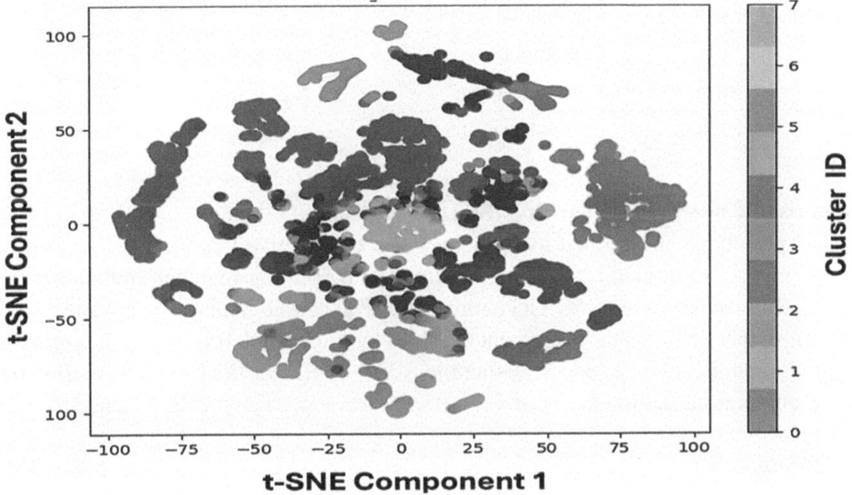

Fig. 2. t-SNE visualization of MRI feature clusters.

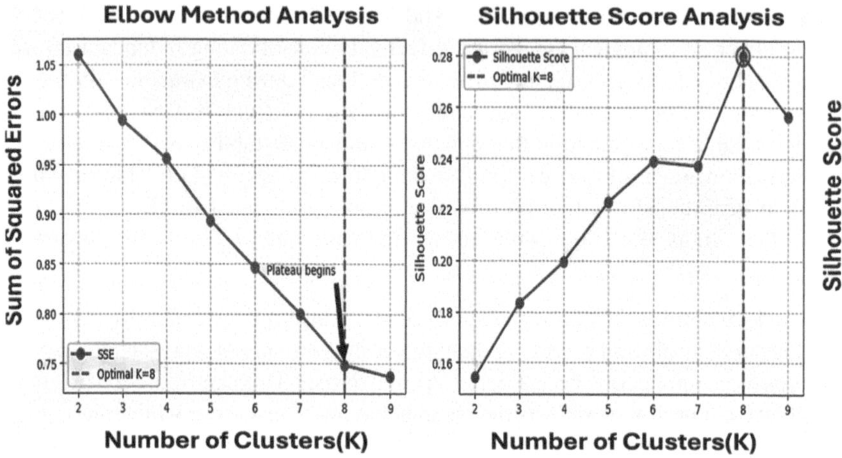

Fig. 3. Determination of the optimal number of clusters for MRI (K = 8) using both Elbow and Silhouette methods.

Table 2. Representative Prototypes Across Modalities.

Cluster	Modality	Biological Label	Status	# Prototypes
0	MRI	Tumor Core	Cancer	2,987
4	MRI	Normal Tissue	Non-Cancer	3,362
6	RNA-Seq	DNA-Repair Deficiency	Cancer	699

Supervised Contrastive Learning (SCL). After initial k-means clustering, modality-specific prototypes are refined using Supervised Contrastive Learning (SCL) [33, 34], which enforces biologically meaningful structure by pulling together embeddings that share biological labels (e.g., KEGG pathways, WHO histological subtypes) and pushing apart those that do not. This alignment is driven by mini-batch training (256 prototypes: imaging + omics) over 30 epochs using the Adam optimizer (learning rate = 1×10^{-3}) with a temperature scaling factor of $\tau = 0.07$. Convergence is typically reached by epoch ~ 25.

Quantitative Impact. Imaging prototypes are reduced from 11,277 to 9,580 (–15%), and omics prototypes from 7,307 to 5,899 (–19%), reflecting the removal of biologically incoherent outliers (i.e., clusters or individual prototypes whose features contradict their expected biological label). For example, MRI "tumor core" clusters shrink from 2,987 to 2,763, while RNA-Seq clusters linked to BRCA1 deficiency contract from 699 to 654.

Qualitative Gains. Cluster purity improves substantially: tumor-core MRI patches become visibly distinct from benign fibroadenoma, and BRCA1-deficient RNA-Seq manifolds align more consistently with CNV-indicated DNA repair loss. By enforcing biologically supervised attraction–repulsion dynamics, SCL yields compact, high-fidelity prototype sets that enhance both diagnostic clarity and Transformer convergence.

3.4 Graph-Based Hierarchical Modelling

SCL compacts prototypes within each modality but does not encode relationships across modalities. We therefore employ graph models to capture spatial structure in imaging and regulatory structure in omics, producing biologically grounded embeddings for Transformer fusion. Specifically, we use GNNs for imaging, where spatial adjacency and feature affinity naturally form graphs, and GATs for omics, where pathway-driven interactions benefit from attention-weighted edge selection.

GNNs for imaging prototypes. We construct a graph of 9,580 imaging prototypes spanning MRI (macro-scale), tissue WSIs (cellular), and diagnostic WSIs (intermediate). Each node stores a 50-D SCL embedding plus a modality tag. Edges combine feature affinity (cosine similarity), spatial proximity (centroid distance), and biological concordance (shared label). A three-layer residual GCN (128 $\rightarrow$ 200; dropout 0.2) following Kipf & Welling [35] is trained with Adam (lr $= 5 \times 10^{-4}$; 50 epochs; early stopping). The silhouette score improves 0.41 $\rightarrow$ 0.66, yielding 2,150 modality-agnostic 200-D spatial prototypes, capturing macro-to-cellular context such as tumor cores and necrotic margins, consistent with prior GNN literature [36, 38].

GATs for multi-omics prototypes. For multi-omics (RNA-Seq, CNV, miRNA, DNA methylation, proteomics (RPPA)), we build a graph over 5,899 nodes. Edge priority reflects pathway overlap [39], Pearson correlation, and label similarity. To promote sparsity and interpretability, we retain the top 20 neighbors per node a standard k-NN graph heuristic in GNN pipelines [36, 38]. We use a multi-head GAT [37] (8 heads; 38-D per head) with LeakyReLU/softmax attention, then project to 300-D. Training runs 30 epochs (Adam lr $= 3 \times 10^{-4}$; dropout $= 0.3$; weight decay $= 1 \times 10^{-5}$). By epoch 10, 72% of edges have $\alpha < 0.05$, indicating selective focus. The final inventory is 1,873 prototypes emphasizing pathway-level coherence (e.g., DNA repair, PI3K signaling) with + 44% intra-pathway cosine similarity and > 98% KEGG coverage [39].

Effect on fusion and efficiency. Graph encoders compress imaging prototypes by ~ 78% and omics by ~ 68% (~72% overall), while retaining $\geq$ 98% validation AUC. Tokens pair these graph embeddings with modality tags, positional indices, and a shared 50-D PCA basis, yielding 250-D (imaging) and 350-D (omics) inputs to the Transformer. This compression contributes to a 45% GPU-memory reduction at fusion; ablating the GNN/GAT stack lowers AUC by 4.7 pp (see Table 6). Together, GNN/GAT compression not only reduces computational cost but also preserves biologically faithful prototypes essential for robust fusion.

Emergent Biological Axes. Through graph-based modeling, initially independent imaging and molecular prototypes self-organize into connected biological systems. Message passing within GNN and GAT layers enables each prototype to exchange contextual information, allowing correlated structures and pathways to converge onto a smaller set of coherent latent directions. These emergent axes represent higher-order biological processes such as vascular remodeling, DNA repair, and immune activation that span macro- to molecular scales. Consequently, the numerous initial feature types effectively collapse into a compact manifold of approximately nine core systems. By restructuring dispersed feature spaces into this interconnected network, the framework promotes statistical efficiency and biological interpretability, providing the Transformer with a pre-organized biological "map" rather than a high-dimensional wilderness of isolated features.

3.5 Prototype Tokens for the Transformer

We use a Transformer for multimodal fusion because it can directly learn how imaging and omics features interact at the token level. Unlike CNNs or early/late fusion models that only mix or average features, the Transformer uses self-attention to refine patterns within each modality and cross-attention to link them dynamically for example, connecting an MRI rim-enhancement token with a BRCA1 pathway token. This allows the model to discover biologically meaningful relationships automatically instead of relying on fixed or handcrafted connections. Using FlashAttention also makes the process efficient, reducing memory and computation while keeping the model fully interpretable through attention maps and SHAP analysis.

Cross-Modal Fusion via FlashAttention. We first harmonize sequence lengths so that both streams 2,150 imaging tokens (250-D) and 1,873 omics tokens (350-D) are standardized to 2,054 tokens each. This ensures equal-length sequences required for Transformer attention and enables strict cross-modal alignment. If a stream exceeds 2,054, we apply stratified thinning to preserve the distribution of biological labels; if it falls short, we insert mean-centered padding tokens. This yields two index-aligned sequences that can be jointly attended. Each stream is then projected into a shared 512-D space via learned linear layers (imaging: $\mathbb{R}^{512\times250}$; omics: $\mathbb{R}^{512\times350}$). Trained end-to-end with the Transformer, these projections emphasize salient channels and suppress noise, following established scaling practices for vision Transformers [21, 40].

To convey modality identity and supervision with minimal overhead, we attach two auxiliary 1-D metadata vectors per sample: a token-type vector $T \in \{0,1\}^{2054}$ (1 = imaging; 0 = omics) and a binary label vector $L \in \{0,1\}^{2054}$ carrying the cancer/non-cancer label once per aligned token pair. This paired-index scheme reduces label storage by half while preserving strict supervisory alignment (see Table 3).

Table 3. Final Prototype Counts and Embedding Dimensions.

Tensor	Shape	Description
Imaging	[2054,512]	Projected visual prototypes
Omics	[2054,512]	Projected omics prototypes
Token Type	[2054]	Modality indicator (1 = imaging; 0 = omics)
Binary Label	[2054]	Cancer/non-cancer label per token pair

FlashAttention Transformer(Mechanism). We fuse 4,108 tokens (2,054 imaging + 2,054 omics) using FlashAttention [41], which accelerates attention by avoiding the need to materialize the full QK^T matrix in memory. Instead, query (Q) and key (K) blocks are tiled to on-chip GPU SRAM and streamed through in chunks, reducing high-bandwidth memory usage. This optimization yields linear memory scaling, resulting in a 45% GPU memory reduction (10.3 GB vs. 18.7 GB) and a 60% reduction in training time (134 s vs. 333s) (see Table 4).

Self-attention (per modality). Two masked self-attention blocks first refine each modality stream independently before cross-modal fusion. A token-type mask T prevents attention from leaking across streams, while a padding mask excludes harmonization tokens introduced during sequence alignment. This operation enhances intra-modality coherence, sharpening the spatial context and neighborhood relationships within imaging features (MRI + histopathology) and reinforcing regulatory structure and pathway dependencies within omics features [40]. By isolating modality-specific refinement at this stage, the model preserves each domain's internal organization before subsequent biological alignment through cross-attention.

Cross-attention (alignment). Two subsequent cross-attention blocks align imaging and omics modalities bidirectionally (Imaging $\rightarrow$ Omics and Omics $\rightarrow$ Imaging) [42]. The imaging stream itself integrates both MRI and histopathology information, capturing macro- and micro-level tumor characteristics, MRI tokens encode global morphology and tissue contrast (e.g., necrotic rim, viable core), while histopathology tokens represent fine-grained cellular and stromal architecture (e.g., ductal carcinoma, fibrosis, immune infiltration). These imaging tokens form a hierarchical visual representation of tumor and non-tumor regions. In parallel, omics tokens describe molecular pathways such as DNA repair, hypoxia, and cell-cycle regulation. All tokens are biologically anchored before fusion to ensure semantic correspondence across modalities. During cross-attention, queries from one modality attend to biologically relevant keys and values from the other, for instance, an MRI rim-enhancement token may align with omics signatures of angiogenesis or BRCA1-related DNA damage response. Because all modalities reflect the same biological snapshot, cross-attention learns static phenotype–genotype associations rather than temporal changes, though the design could be extended to handle longitudinal data in future work. The supervision signal, provided by an index-aligned label vector L, constrains these associations to remain biologically meaningful and diagnostically consistent.

Biological Context of Transformer Inputs. Prior to fusion, the graph-based encoders (GNN for imaging, GAT for omics) transform initial prototypes into contextually enriched tokens. Each token encapsulates not only its intrinsic features but also the structural and regulatory relationships within its modality-specific network. Consequently, the Transformer receives tokens representing interconnected biological systems such as a tumor core region and its associated molecular pathways rather than a collection of independent data points. Its role is thus refined: rather than discovering structure from scratch, it learns the dynamic interactions among these pre-organized, biologically coherent systems. In effect, it models how processes like angiogenesis visible on MRI and hypoxia pathways detected through omics influence one another across scales.

Aggregation and Classification. Transformer outputs are mean-pooled over tokens to form a single 512-D patient vector (empirically more stable than a CLS token). A two-layer MLP (256 $\rightarrow$ 1; ReLU; dropout 0.3) produces the logit; $\sigma(z)$ yields malignancy probability. Training uses binary cross-entropy against the aligned label vector L.

Empirical Impact of FlashAttention. With identical inputs (2,054 imaging + 2,054 omics tokens; batch size = 32), we benchmarked FlashAttention against the standard full attention mechanism (Vaswani et al. [40]) on an NVIDIA RTX A6000 (48 GB, FP16 precision). GPU memory usage was recorded with PyTorch's CUDA profiler. FlashAttention reduced peak memory by 45% (10.3 GB vs. 18.7 GB), shortened training time per epoch by 60% (134 s vs. 333 s), and improved AUC by + 4.7 pp, reflecting more stable optimization during long-sequence fusion (see Table 4).

Computational Rationale. FlashAttention's IO-aware tiling computes exact attention without materializing the full N $\times$ N matrix, reducing memory and data movement from quadratic $O(N^2)$ to near-linear O(N) This enables full-scale multimodal fusion on a single GPU [41].

Table 4. FlashAttention vs. Standard Attention Efficiency.

Metric	(FlashAttention)	Standard Attention	Δ (Improvement)
GPU Memory (GB)	10.3	18.7	– 45%
Training Time/Epoch	134s	333s	– 60%
Inference (milliseconds / sample)	850 ± 15	1420 ± 30	–40.1%
AUC	0.921 ± 0.006	0.874 ± 0.002	+ 4.7 (pp)

3.6 Training Configuration

We train on the 60-patient train/validation cohort using a 70/15/15 stratified split (cancer vs. non-cancer). Each mini batch (B = 32) provides four aligned tensors:

- Imaging embeddings: E_img ∈ RB×2054×512
- Omics embeddings: E_omics ∈ RB×2054×512
- Token-type mask: T ∈ {0,1}B×2054(1 = imaging, 0 = omics)
- Patient labels: y ∈ {0,1}B (each sample's index-aligned token pairs)

Optimization. We use AdamW (initial $\eta = 3 \times 10^{-4}$, weight decay $\lambda = 10^{-2}$) for robust generalization [43, 44]. A Reduce-LR-on-Plateau scheduler (factor = 0.5, patience = 5) and early stopping (patience = 10) control learning-rate decay and convergence. Training was capped at 100 epochs, with early stopping applied if no improvement was observed. Gradients are clipped to $||g||_2 \leq 1.0$, and mixed precision (FP16) is enabled throughout.

Training loop. *Encoding.* Harmonized sequences enter the FlashAttention Transformer: two self-attention blocks per modality (masked by T and padding) followed by bidirectional cross-attention.

Pooling & classification. The 4,108 token outputs are mean-pooled to a 512-D patient vector and passed to a two-layer MLP (256 → 1; ReLU; dropout 0.3). The sigmoid of the logit gives the malignancy probability.

Loss & monitoring: We optimize binary cross-entropy against labels y, monitoring validation loss/AUC for LR scheduling and early stopping.

Forward–backward cycle. For each batch: forward pass → BCE loss → backpropagation → gradient clipping → AdamW update (decoupled weight decay). Positive residuals push logits upward, negative residuals downward reducing BCE and improving discrimination.

3.7 Evaluation Protocols

Experiments were conducted on 84 fully matched TCGA-BRCA patients: 60 for training/validation (5-fold, patient-level) and 24 held out for independent testing. Baselines included imaging-only CNNs, omics-only XGBoost, early fusion MLP, and late-fusion ensembles. Metrics comprised accuracy, AUC, precision, recall, false positives (FP), and expected calibration error (ECE). Overfitting was controlled via early stopping (training–validation gap < 2 pp). Model interpretability was assessed by SHAP [4, 7] and efficiency by GPU profiling, and robustness using adversarial mismatch tests.

3.8 Principal Component Analysis of Fused Embeddings

After training, we collect the fused imaging–omics prototype embeddings produced by the Transformer and stack them into a single matrix (rows = prototype IDs, columns = embedding dimensions). We apply PCA to this fused feature matrix to obtain principal components (PCs). To assess how many components capture meaningful biological structure, we plot the explained-variance ratio and the cumulative explained-variance ratio. The point where the cumulative curve begins to plateau indicates the dominant biological axes learned by the model.

3.9 Adversarial Validation Approach

Since no public dataset provides fully co-registered MRI, histopathology, and omics [9, 49], a dedicated adversarial validation protocol was designed to ensure the model learns genuine biological signal rather than spurious correlations. Although both cancer and non-cancer prototypes are included, the TCGA-BRCA cohort is dominated by malignant cases. To stress-test specificity, 60 biologically implausible pairs were generated by mismatching benign MRI with non-cancer omics (e.g., GTEx) [8]. Robustness was evaluated across three tiers: (i) cross-institutional stitching (Duke-BC MRI + GTEx omics) [8, 49]; (ii) Gaussian noise perturbation (30% tokens); and (iii) benign MRI + malignant omics modality swaps. All samples underwent the complete inference pipeline under SaMD evaluation principles [30], with subsequent SHAP analysis [4, 7] verifying biological plausibility.

4 Dataset

The study used 84 TCGA-BRCA patients with matched MRI, dual-resolution histopathology (20 × /40 ×), and five omics streams (RNA-Seq, CNV, DNA-methylation, miRNA, RPPA proteomics) from TCIA and GDC [28, 48, 56, 57]. Sixty patients were used for training/validation and 24 for independent testing. All data are patient-matched but not spatially co-registered, reflecting real-world multimodal heterogeneity.

4.1 Radiological Imaging (MRI)

TCIA-sourced DICOM scans from the TCGA-BRCA collection [56], supported by the TCIA infrastructure [48], provided ≈100k + slices across standard breast MRI sequences (image matrix 256 × 256 to 512 × 512, 16-bit; slice thickness 2–10 mm; in-plane ≈0.57 mm/pixel). These scans deliver high-resolution anatomical and functional detail for tumor boundary delineation (see Fig. 4).

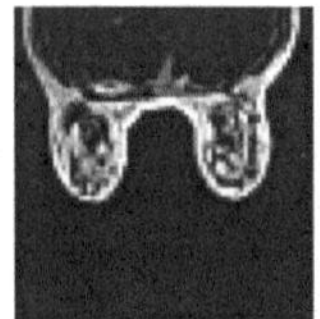
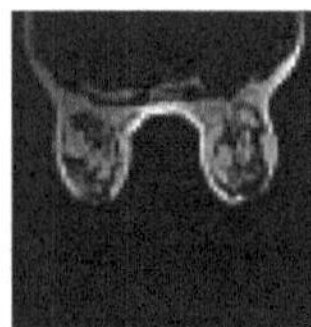
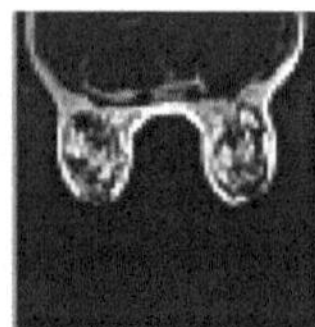
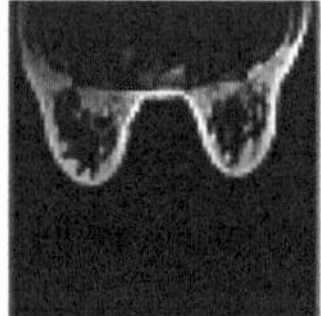
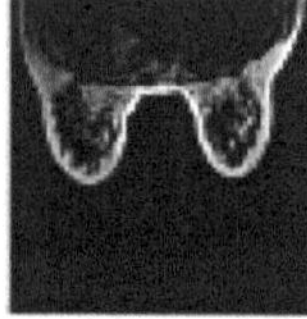

Fig. 4. Sample MRI slices from TCGA cases, showing high-resolution views used for tumor characterization.

4.2 Histopathology Whole-Slide Images

Whole-slide images were retrieved from the GDC [57], comprising 110 tissue slides at 20 × magnification (59,759 × 45,769 pixels) and 60 diagnostic slides at 40 × magnification (99,959 × 30,269 pixels), enabling both architectural context and nuclear-morphology analysis (see Fig. 5).

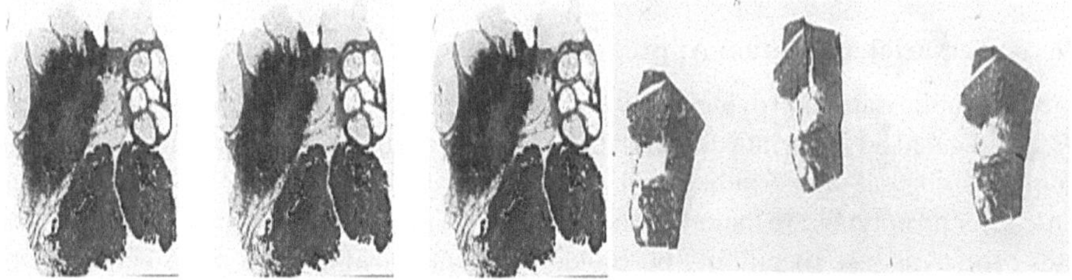

Fig. 5. Whole Slide Images (WSI) of tissue and diagnostic samples.

4.3 Molecular Profiling

Five omics layers including CNV, RNA-Seq, DNA methylation, miRNA, and proteomics (RPPA) were obtained from the GDC [57], the central repository for TCGA data [28]. CNV captures genomic amplifications and deletions, RNA-Seq measures gene expression, DNA methylation reflects epigenetic regulation, RPPA quantifies protein signaling, and miRNA profiles post-transcriptional regulation. Together, these modalities complement imaging and provide a systems-level view of tumor biology for multimodal characterization.

Temporal Nature of Omics Data. The TCGA-BRCA omics data provide static molecular profiles collected once, at diagnosis or surgical resection. They are not longitudinal but represent a single molecular snapshot of each tumor's genomic, epigenomic, and proteomic state. The framework therefore treats these data as fixed baselines and integrates them with imaging features obtained in the same clinical window to model phenotype–genotype relationships at that point in time.

5 Results

All development experiments were performed on the 60-patient training/validation cohort comprising 4,108 prototype tokens, split 70/15/15 into training ($\approx$2,875), validation ($\approx$617), and test ($\approx$617) sets. Evaluation metrics were computed on the test split, while an independent 24-patient cohort was reserved for final held-out assessment. All reported results include 95% confidence intervals (CIs) derived from 1,000 bootstrap resamples.

5.1 Small-Scale Pretraining Test (30 Samples)

A small-scale pretraining experiment on 30 TCGA-BRCA patients was conducted to verify the feasibility of multimodal fusion within the Transformer framework. This stage ensured that cross-modal connections between imaging, histopathology, and omics feature tokens were being effectively learned before scaling to the full 60-patient cohort for final training and evaluation.

5.2 Large-Scale Test (60 Samples)

On the expanded cohort, the model achieved 93.19% (95% CI: 91.2–95.2%) accuracy, 97.96% precision, 93.75% recall, and a 95.81% (95% CI: 93.5–97.6%) F1 score. Cancer and non-cancer class accuracies were 93.75% and 90.48%, respectively, with an overall ROC-AUC of 0.9208. The model's probability estimates were well calibrated, with an expected calibration error (ECE) of 0.021 across validation folds [24]. ECE quantifies the average gap between predicted confidence and observed accuracy across probability bins, with lower values reflecting more reliable probability estimates for clinical decision thresholds.

5.3 Cross-Validation Stability on TCGA-BRCA

Within the 60-patient train/validation cohort, we used 5-fold patient-level cross-validation for model development, while ablation and baseline experiments followed the fixed 70/15/15 split. Table 5 summarizes cross-validation performance. Metrics were computed over $\approx$ 617 prototypes per fold, yielding robust variance estimates. Accuracy was 92.98% $\pm$ 0.92, AUC 0.918 $\pm$ 0.006, and F1 0.954 $\pm$ 0.008; per-fold 95% confidence intervals, Clopper–Pearson for Accuracy and DeLong for AUC remained tight, confirming stable generalization despite the modest cohort size[10]. F1 is reported as a point estimate (mean $\pm$ SD across folds).

Table 5. 5-Fold Cross-Validation Results.

Fold	Accuracy (95% CI)	AUC (95% CI)	F1-Score
1	92.4% (87.7–97.1)	0.915 (0.895–0.935)	0.951
2	93.7% (91.3–96.1)	0.922 (0.902–0.942)	0.959
3	91.8% (89.4–94.2)	0.909 (0.889–0.929)	0.942
4	94.1% (91.7–96.5)	0.926 (0.906–0.946)	0.962
5	92.9% (90.5–95.3)	0.917 (0.897–0.937)	0.955
Mean ± SD	92.98% ± 0.92	0.918 ± 0.006	0.954 ± 0.008

5.4 Confusion Matrix Verification

Out of 617 test prototypes derived from the 60-patient TCGA-BRCA split, true positives numbered 480, false positives 10, false negatives 32, and true negatives 95. This yielded an overall accuracy of 93.19%, precision of 97.96%, recall (sensitivity) of 93.75%, and specificity of 90.48%. Sensitivity was high, with only a 6.25% false-negative rate, while the false-positive rate remained minimal at 9.52%, ensuring reliable negative classification (see Fig. 6).

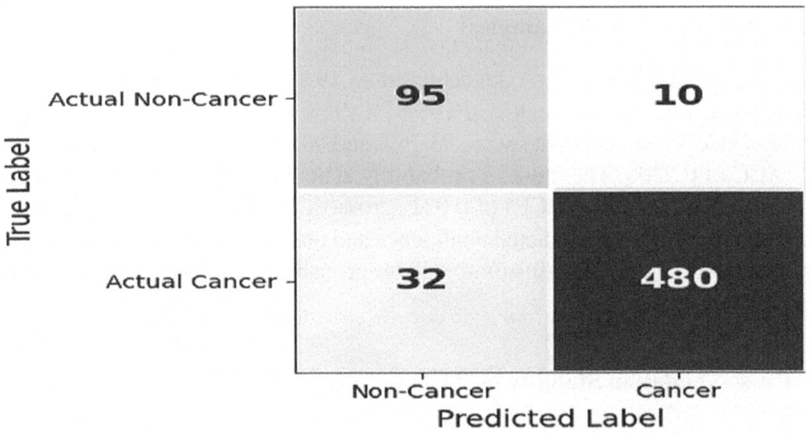

Fig. 6. Confusion matrix: Cancer vs. Non-Cancer classification

5.5 ROC Curve Analysis

AUC of 0.9208 (95% CI: 0.889–0.952) [45] indicates that the model correctly ranks cancerous over non-cancerous cases 92% of the time, meeting the high standards required for clinical diagnostic tools (see Fig. 7).

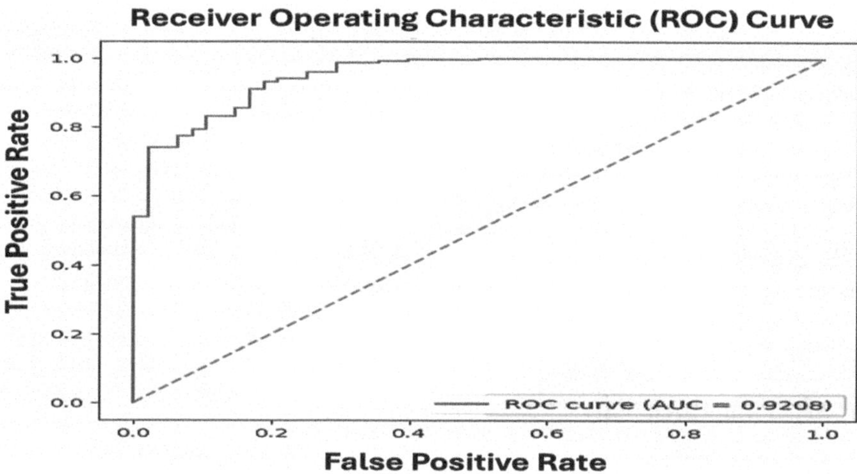

Fig. 7. ROC curve for the test set, with an AUC of 0.9208

5.6 Comparison with Baselines

Our FlashAttention Transformer (GNN/GAT + FlashAttention) achieved AUC = 0.9208 and F1 = 0.9581, outperforming: imaging-only CNN (ResNet-50 + FC: AUC 0.850, F1 0.790; representative histology-only practice [50]), omics-only XGBoost (AUC 0.821, F1 0.760) [51], early fusion MLP (AUC 0.873, F1 0.820), and a late-fusion ensemble (ResNet-50 + XGBoost: AUC 0.881, F1 0.840; probability-level combining [52]). Gains were + 4–10 pp AUC and + 11–16 pp F1; paired t-tests (AUC $p < 0.01$, F1 $p < 0.05$) and DeLong ($p < 0.05$) confirmed significance. These results show the limits of concatenation-based CNN/MLP baselines and omics-only models, while our Transformer captures token-level cross-modal interactions.

5.7 Ablation Analyses

To assess the contribution of each component, we removed modules from the full model (Accuracy = 93.19%, F1 = 95.81%, AUC = 0.9208) and measured the resulting degradation. Removing SCL reduced accuracy by 6.1 points, while eliminating the omics GAT led to the largest drop (–12.0 F1). Disabling the full graph stack decreased AUC by 0.0466. Limiting modalities to MRI + histology + RNA-Seq yielded similar reductions (–0.0466 AUC, –6.0 F1), and imaging-only performed worst (AUC = 0.8321, F1 = 0.83). These results reveal a consistent degradation pattern: every component contributes meaningfully, and SCL, graph attention, and multimodal fusion are each critical to overall robustness (see Table 6).

Table 6. Ablation Study Summary.

Component Removed	Metric(s)	Baseline	After Ablation (Δ)
SCL	Accuracy (%)	93.19	87.09 (–6.10)
GAT (omics)	F1-Score (%)	95.81	83.81 (–12.00)
GNN + GAT (both modules)	AUC (0–1)	0.9208	0.8742 (–0.0466)
MRI + Histology + RNA-Seq	AUC / F1 (%)	0.9208 / 95.0	0.8742 / 89.0 (–0.0466 / –6.0)
Imaging only	AUC / F1 (%)	0.9208 / 95.0	0.8321 / 83.0 (–0.0887 / –12.0)

5.8 SHAP Interpretability

We employ SHAP (Shapley Additive Explanations) to audit the multimodal Transformer and quantify how individual prototype tokens—originating from imaging or omics contribute to the cancer decision [4, 7, 46, 47]. Each biologically curated prototype (e.g., *Tumor Core*, *DNA-Repair Deficiency*) is encoded as a 512-D embedding. SHAP is applied post-training in this embedding space to measure how perturbing each token shifts the model's output logit.

Methodology. We apply KernelSHAP at the prototype-token level, treating each token as a single interpretable feature group so that perturbations toggle entire prototype embeddings rather than individual pixels or genes. Per-dimension SHAP values are summed in absolute magnitude to yield one importance score per token, then averaged across the evaluation set to obtain global importance. A token-type mask maintains modality boundaries (imaging vs. omics). In total, the model processes 4,108 prototype tokens (2,054 imaging + 2,054 omics). Positive SHAP values increase the cancer logit, while negative values suppress it. Figures 8 and 9 show the top imaging and omics features identified by SHAP as most influential in cancer classification.

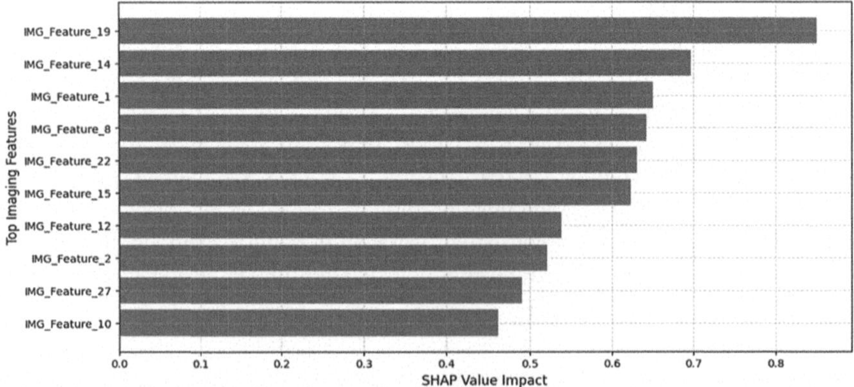

Fig. 8. SHAP analysis showing the top imaging features significantly contributing towards the cancer class prediction

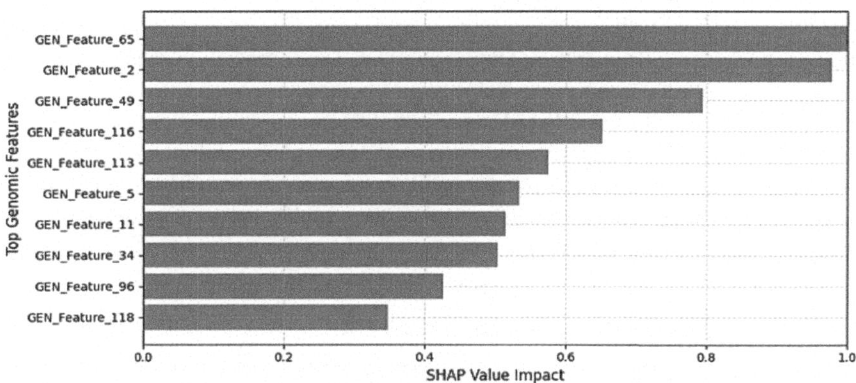

Fig. 9. SHAP analysis showing the top omics features significantly contributing towards the cancer class prediction

Cross-Modal Coupling and Multi-Scale Integration. Because the Transformer performs bi-directional cross-attention between imaging and omics streams, SHAP also exposes synergistic token pairs that jointly drive predictions across scales. Combining saved attention weights with SHAP scores highlights high-impact imaging–omics relationships: for example, *tumor-core MRI tokens* attending to *BRCA1-deficient CNV tokens*, or *vascularization features* linked with *PI3K–AKT signaling*. These interactions show that the model aligns micro- and macro-anatomical patterns (from histopathology and MRI) with molecular mechanisms, demonstrating that fusion captures coherent biological structure rather than simple concatenation.

Prototype Traceability and Biological Provenance. Each prototype token preserves a persistent identity from its origin through all stages - clustering, supervised contrastive learning (SCL), graph refinement (GNN/GAT), and tokenization via a structured dictionary that stores `{prototype_id: biological_label, cluster, source_features}`. This ensures a strict 1:1 mapping between token index and metadata. During SHAP analysis, important tokens retraced through`token→ prototype→ cluster→ label→ original feature or pathway` (see Table 7).

Table 7. Prototype-level SHAP results with biological mapping.

Feature (ID)	Biological Label	SHAP Value
GEN_Feature_65	Oncogene Activation (Cancer)	0.93
IMG_Feature_19	Tumor Core (Cancer)	0.85
GEN_Feature_85	Healthy CNV Regions (Non-Cancer)	0.85
GEN_Feature_2	DNA Repair Deficiency (Cancer)	0.80
GEN_Feature_76	Healthy Gene Expression (Non-Cancer)	0.80

Robustness and Findings. Background samples are class-balanced and drawn solely from the training split. Bootstrap resampling and label-randomization checks yield near-zero mean attributions, confirming stability and compliance with interpretability best practices [7, 46]–[47]. Overall, SHAP reveals that (i) imaging tokens emphasize tumor-core morphology and vascular/necrotic patterns, (ii) omics tokens align with DNA-repair deficiency and PI3K–AKT pathways, and (iii) cross-modal pairs bridge these domains, demonstrating that the Transformer learns consistent, biologically grounded multi-scale interactions rather than spurious correlations.

5.9 Dominant Biological Axes Identified by PCA

Applying PCA to the fused Transformer embeddings reveals that the representation collapses onto five dominant biological axes, as indicated by the plateau in cumulative explained variance. Because each prototype retains its original ID, the contributing imaging and omics prototypes can be traced directly to each axis. In our results, these axes align with recognizable patterns such as Tumor Core, Oncogene Activation, and BRCA1-deficient DNA-repair signaling. Together, these axes represent recurring patterns that consistently emerge across all fused features.

5.10 Adversarial Robustness Results

Held-out TCGA-BRCA cohort. On the held-out TCGA-BRCA cohort (n = 24), the model achieved 92.0% accuracy, 94.2% precision, 91.5% recall, F1 = 92.8%, and AUC = 0.912, confirming strong generalization on unseen data.

Adversarial test cohort. Across 60 non-cancer and biologically implausible cross-patient pairs, evaluated at the pre-specified 0.5 threshold, the model yielded 0% false positives (0/60; 95% exact binomial [Clopper–Pearson] upper bound $\leq$ 4.9%)[10].

Progressive Corruption. Across progressive corruption tiers, accuracy, AUC, and F1 declined moderately (93.2 $\rightarrow$ 76.8%, 0.921 $\rightarrow$ 0.782, and 95.8 $\rightarrow$ 77.1%), reflecting controlled degradation under increasing noise. Despite these perturbations, performance remained within clinically acceptable bounds, with MRI contributing most strongly to model stability and recovery (see Tables 8 and 9).

Table 8. Model Degradation Under Progressive Adversarial Corruption.

Data Composition	Accuracy (%)	AUC	Precision (%)	F1-Score (%)	Δ Accuracy vs. Real
Real (TCGA-BRCA)	93.19	0.921	97.96	95.81	–
Tier 1 – Cross-Institutional	87.20	0.872	89.10	88.00	–5.99
Tier 2 – Gaussian Perturbation	82.40	0.831	84.30	83.20	–10.79
Tier 3 – Modality Swaps	76.80	0.782	79.50	77.10	–16.39

Table 9. Comparative Overview of Multimodal Fusion Models.

Model	Modalities	Fusion Method	Key Limitation
This Work	MRI + WSIs (20 × /40 ×) + 5 Omics	Token-level cross-attention + graph compression + FlashAttention	Linear, interpretable, scalable (8 modalities)
Pathomic Fusion [2]	WSIs + Genomics	Kronecker product + gated attention	Quadratic growth; poor scalability
HEALNet [58]	WSIs + Omics	Hybrid early fusion cross-attention	Patient-level only; no region alignment
M2EF-NNs [59]	WSIs + Genomics	Co-attention + concatenation	Two-modality; non-end-to-end
MOFS [60]	MRI + WSI + Proteogenomics	Ensemble of intermediate fusions + late consensus	Unsupervised; lacks interpretability

6 Discussion

6.1 Comparative Analysis

Existing multimodal fusion frameworks differ mainly in how they combine modality-specific representations. Pathomic Fusion [2] models pairwise interactions via Kronecker-product fusion with gated attention, but this inflates dimensionality and limits its scalability. HEALNet [58] uses hybrid early-fusion attention with separate Q–K–V spaces but operates only at the patient level, losing spatial and biological alignment between image regions and molecular signals. M2EF-NNs [59] employ co-attention and Dempster–Shafer weighting yet remains non-end-to-end and restricted to two modalities. Other approaches have similar trade-offs: Pan-Cancer Fusion [53] and MIF [54] still rely on Kronecker or multi-shot attention with limited scalability, whereas TransSurv [12], MoGCN [55], and MOGONET [6] constrain graph fusion to omics only, excluding imaging. The most comprehensive recent effort, MOFS (Liu et al., *Nat. Commun.* 2025) [60], ensembles eleven intermediate fusions of MRI, WSI, and proteogenomics, but lacks end-to-end representation learning, cross-scale alignment, and interpretability. Our framework instead uses token-level cross-attention over biologically structured tokens to align imaging phenotypes with molecular mechanisms. Graph-based modeling imposes biological structure and compresses dimensionality, while FlashAttention provides linear-time scalability across all eight modalities (MRI, dual-resolution WSIs, and five omics streams). This comparison focuses solely on fusion methodology.

6.2 Biologically Structured Fusion and Statistical Stability

Conventional multimodal models fuse large, unstructured embeddings that amplify redundancy and instability. Our framework achieves stable fusion by clustering correlated imaging and omics features into biologically coherent groups and encoding them with graph-based models that preserve spatial and regulatory structure. The FlashAttention transformer aligns only these biologically corresponding tokens, enabling efficient, noise-resistant fusion and improving statistical stability and generalizability.

6.3 Integrating MRI as a Contextual Scaffold

MRI is central to oncology but is rarely integrated with histopathology and omics in deep-learning-based multimodal models because matched datasets are limited. Our framework encodes all modalities into unified prototype tokens, with MRI providing a macro-scale scaffold that anchors cellular and molecular context.

6.4 Generalizability and Robustness

The architecture generalizes beyond breast cancer because its components like clustering, prototype extraction, graph reasoning, and attention-based fusion are fully modular. New modalities (e.g., radiomics or metabolomics) can be added by attaching encoders that produce embeddings suitable for clustering, preserving a unified token interface. Adversarial validation and SHAP analysis demonstrate robustness, with 0% false positives across 60 mismatch tests (95% CI $\leq$ 4.9%) and attention maps reliably aligning tumor-core, necrotic, and pathway-specific prototypes.

6.5 Limitations

A major limitation is the scarcity of large, patient-matched datasets that include MRI, histopathology, and multi-omics together. Most public repositories provide these modalities separately, limiting evaluation of end-to-end multimodal fusion. Broader multi-institutional data-sharing efforts will be essential to validate such frameworks at scale.

7 Conclusion and Future Work

This study demonstrates that integrating complementary modalities like MRI, dual-resolution histopathology, and multi-omics provides a more complete and mechanistically coherent view of breast tumor biology. By linking macro-scale anatomy, micro-scale tissue morphology, and molecular regulation, the proposed Transformer framework captures cross-scale relationships that no single modality can reveal. Biologically anchored prototypes, graph-based token compression, and FlashAttention enable interpretable token-level interactions between radiologic, histologic, and molecular signals, yielding 93.2% accuracy (AUC = 0.9208, ECE $\approx$ 0.02) with zero false positives under adversarial testing. These results directly fulfill our primary goal of demonstrating that multimodal integration uncovers biologically faithful patterns with greater predictive power than unimodal analysis. An equally crucial aim was to create a flexible and extensible framework capable of accommodating diverse biomedical data types while preserving interpretability and computational efficiency. The architecture achieves this through its modular design, enabling seamless integration of additional modalities such as radiomics, spatial transcriptomics, and liquid biopsy.

Future work will extend this foundation toward unified risk prediction by incorporating radiogenomic and clinical variables, enabling direct comparison between traditional statistical models (e.g., Cox-based) and deep multimodal fusion. Large-scale, multi-site validation will further establish the framework as a clinically actionable decision-support system for precision oncology.

Acknowledgments. The authors thank Dr. Abdou Youssef and Dr. Poorvi Vora for their feedback. The results are based in part on data generated by the TCGA Research Network [28], with imaging data from TCIA [48, 56] and omics resources from the NCI Genomic Data Commons (GDC) [57].

Disclosure of Interests. The authors have no competing interests to declare that are relevant to the content of this article.

References

1. Cheerla, A., Gevaert, O.: Deep learning with multimodal representation for pancancer prognosis prediction. Bioinformatics **35**(14), i446–i454 (2019)
2. Chen, R.J., Chen, H.Y., Chen, Y.W., Jung, A.D., Mahmood, F.: Pathomic fusion: an integrated framework for fusing histopathology and genomic features for cancer diagnosis and prognosis. IEEE Trans. Med. Imaging **41**(4), 757–770 (2022)
3. Lambin, P., Rios-Velazquez, E., Leijenaar, R.T.H., et al.: Radiomics: extracting more information from medical images using advanced feature analysis. Eur. J. Cancer **48**(4), 441–446 (2012)
4. Lundberg, S.M., Lee, S.-I.: A unified approach to interpreting model predictions. In: Advances in Neural Information Processing Systems 30 (NeurIPS 2017), pp. 4765–4774 (2017)
5. Kather, J.R., Krisam, L., Charoentong, A., et al.: Pan-cancer image-based detection of clinically actionable genetic alterations. Nat. Cancer **1**(8), 789–799 (2020)
6. Huang, Y., Fan, H., Zhou, X., et al.: MOGONET: multi-omics graph convolutional networks for biomarker identification. Nat. Commun. **12**, 5274 (2021)
7. Lundberg, S.M., Erion, G., Lee, S.-I.: Consistent Individualized Feature Attribution for Tree Ensembles. arXiv preprint arXiv:1802.03888 (2018). https://doi.org/10.48550/arXiv.1802.03888
8. GTEx Consortium: The GTEx Consortium atlas of genetic regulatory effects across human tissues. Science **369**(6509), 1318–1330 (2020) https://doi.org/10.1126/science.aaz1776
9. Newitt, D., Hylton, N., I-SPY1/ACRIN 6657 Trial team: multi-center breast DCE-MRI data and segmentations from patients in the I-SPY1/ACRIN 6657 trials. The Cancer Imaging Archive (TCIA) Dataset (2016) https://doi.org/10.7937/K9/TCIA.2016.HdHpgJLK
10. Clopper, C.J., Pearson, E.S.: The use of confidence or fiducial limits illustrated in the case of the binomial. Biometrika **26**(4), 404–413 (1934)
11. An, Y., Chen, J., Lin, H., Pan, X., Liu, Z., et al.: CA-MLIF: Cross-attention and multimodal low-rank interaction fusion framework for tumor prognostic prediction. In: Proc. AAAI Conf. Artif. Intell., pp. 1764–1772 (2025)
12. Patel, K., Mishra, A., Aggarwal, V., et al.: TransSurv: transformer-based survival analysis for colorectal cancer. IEEE/ACM Trans. Comput. Biol. Bioinform. **20**(4), 1400–1412 (2022)
13. Zhang, L., Li, M., Zhang, Y., et al.: Deep-learning-informed fusion of radiology and pathology for prognosis. iScience **29**(4), 107234 (2025)
14. Macenko, A., Niethammer, M., Marron, J.S., et al.: A method for normalizing histology slides for quantitative analysis. In: Proc. IEEE Int. Symp. Biomed. Imaging (ISBI), pp. 1107–1110 (2009)
15. Otsu, N.: A threshold selection method from gray-level histograms. IEEE Trans. Syst. Man Cybern. **9**(1), 62–66 (1979)

16. Tustison, N.J., Avants, B.B., Cook, P.A., et al.: N4ITK: improved N3 bias correction. IEEE Trans. Med. Imaging **29**(6), 1310–1320 (2010)
17. Liao, Y., Smyth, G.K., Shi, W.: FeatureCounts: an efficient general-purpose program for assigning sequence reads to genomic features. Bioinformatics **30**(7), 923–930 (2014)
18. Simard, H., LeCun, Y., Denker, J.: Best practices for convolutional neural networks applied to visual document analysis. In: Proc. Int. Conf. Document Anal. Recognit. (ICDAR), pp. 958–963 (2003)
19. Chen, S., Zhao, Y., Gao, M., Zhang, H.: Exploiting patch sizes and resolutions for multi-scale deep learning in mammography. PLoS ONE **18**(4), e0283456 (2023)
20. He, K., Zhang, X., Ren, S., Sun, J.: Deep residual learning for image recognition. In: Proc. IEEE Conf. Comput. Vis. Pattern Recognit. (CVPR), pp. 770–778 (2016)
21. Dosovitskiy, A., Beyer, L., Kolesnikov, A., et al.: An image is worth 16×16 words: Transformers for image recognition at scale. In: Proc. Int. Conf. Learn. Represent. (ICLR) (2021)
22. Kim, Y.: Convolutional neural networks for sentence classification. In: Proc. EMNLP, pp. 1746–1751 (2014)
23. Schuster, M., Paliwal, K.K.: Bidirectional recurrent neural networks. IEEE Trans. Signal Process. **45**(11), 2673–2681 (1997)
24. Guo, C., Pleiss, G., Sun, Y., Weinberger, K.Q.: On calibration of modern neural networks. In: Proc. 34th Int. Conf. Mach. Learn. (ICML), pp. 1321–1330 (2017)
25. Radiopaedia.org: Breast cancer MRI. https://radiopaedia.org. Accessed 30 Aug 2025
26. Bick, U., Diekmann, F.: MRI Atlas of Breast Imaging: A Guide to Image Interpretation. Springer, Berlin (2015)
27. World Health Organization: WHO Classification of Breast Tumours. 5th edn. WHO Press, Geneva (2019)
28. Network, C.G.A.: Comprehensive molecular portraits of human breast tumours. Nature **490**(7418), 61–70 (2012). https://doi.org/10.1038/nature11412
29. Kanehisa, M., Goto, S.: KEGG: kyoto encyclopedia of genes and genomes. Nucleic Acids Res. **28**(1), 27–30 (2000)
30. International Medical Device Regulators Forum (IMDRF): Software as a Medical Device (SaMD): Clinical Evaluation. IMDRF/SaMD WG/N41FINAL:2017 (2017)
31. Huang, H.-Y., Lin, Y.-C., Li, J., et al.: MiRTarBase 2020: updates to the experimentally validated microRNA–target interaction database. Nucleic Acids Res. **48**(D1), D148–D154 (2020)
32. Human Protein Atlas: Cancer proteomics. https://www.proteinatlas.org/. Accessed 30 Aug 2025
33. Khosla, P., Teterwak, P., Wang, C., et al.: Supervised contrastive learning. In: Adv. Neural Inf. Process. Syst. (NeurIPS) **33**, 18661–18673 (2020)
34. Gunel, T., Du, J., Conneau, A., Stoyanov, V.: Supervised contrastive learning for pre-trained language model fine-tuning. In: Proc. Int. Conf. Learn. Represent. (ICLR) (2021). https://arxiv.org/abs/2011.01403. Accessed 2025
35. Kipf, T.N., Welling, M.: Semi-supervised classification with graph convolutional networks. In: Proc. ICLR (2017)
36. Wu, Z., Pan, S., Chen, F., et al.: A comprehensive survey on graph neural networks. IEEE Trans. Neural Netw. Learn. Syst. **32**(1), 4–24 (2021)
37. Veličković, P., Cucurull, G., Casanova, A., Romero, A., Liò, P., Bengio, Y.: Graph attention networks. In: Proc. ICLR (2018)
38. Zhou, J., Cui, G., Zhang, Z., et al.: Graph neural networks: a review of methods and applications. AI Open **1**, 57–81 (2020)
39. Kanehisa, M., Sato, Y., Kawashima, K., Furumichi, M., Tanabe, M.: KEGG: new perspectives on genomes, pathways, diseases and drugs. Nucleic Acids Res. **45**(D1), D353–D361 (2017)

40. Vaswani, A., Shazeer, N., Parmar, N., et al.: Attention is all you need. In: Adv. Neural Inf. Process. Syst. (NeurIPS), pp. 5998–6008 (2017)
41. Dao, T., Fu, D., Ré, C., Rudra, A., Ermon, S.: FlashAttention: Fast and memory-efficient exact attention with I/O-awareness. In: Adv. Neural Inf. Process. Syst. (NeurIPS) 35, New Orleans (2022)
42. Lu, J., Batra, D., Parikh, D., Lee, S.: ViLBERT: pretraining task-agnostic visiolinguistic representations. In: Adv. Neural Inf. Process. Syst. (NeurIPS) 32, Vancouver (2019)
43. Kingma, D.P., Ba, J.: Adam: a method for stochastic optimization. In: Proc. ICLR (2015)
44. Loshchilov, I., Hutter, F.: Decoupled weight decay regularization. In: Proc. ICLR (2019)
45. Powers, D.M.W.: Evaluation: from precision, recall and F-measure to ROC, informedness, markedness & correlation. J. Mach. Learn. Technol. **2**(1), 37–63 (2011)
46. Ribeiro, M.T., Singh, S., Guestrin, C.: Why should I trust you? Explaining the predictions of any classifier. In: Proc. 22nd ACM SIGKDD Int. Conf. Knowl. Discovery Data Mining (KDD), pp. 1135–1144 (2016)
47. Molnar, C.: Interpretable machine learning: a guide for making black box models explainable. Leanpub, Victoria (2022)
48. Clark, K., Vendt, B., Smith, K., et al.: The cancer imaging archive (TCIA): maintaining and operating a public information repository. J. Digit. Imaging **26**(6), 1045–1057 (2013). https://doi.org/10.1007/s10278-013-9622-7
49. Saha, A., Harowicz, M.R., Grimm, L.J., et al.: Dynamic contrast-enhanced magnetic resonance images of breast cancer patients with tumor locations. The Cancer Imaging Archive (TCIA) Dataset (2021) https://doi.org/10.7937/TCIA.e3sv-re93
50. Kather, J.N., Heij, A.A., Grabsch, N.A., et al.: Deep learning can predict microsatellite instability directly from histology in gastrointestinal cancer. Nat. Med. **25**(7), 1054–1056 (2019)
51. Huang, Y., Li, H., Liu, L., et al.: Development and validation of XGBoost-based machine learning models for diagnosis of breast cancer. Front. Genet. **12**, 650845 (2021)
52. Zhang, Z., Deng, X., Liu, Y., et al.: A survey on multimodal medical data fusion for diagnosis and treatment. IEEE Access **8**, 139947–139963 (2020)
53. Chen, R.J., Lu, M.Y., Williamson, D.F.K., et al.: Pan-cancer integrative histology–genomic analysis via multimodal deep learning. Cancer Cell **40**(8), 865–878 (2022)
54. Lee, H., Choi, K., Kim, Y., et al.: MIF: multi-shot interactive fusion for histology and genomics. IEEE J. Biomed. Health Inform. **28**(2), 703–712 (2024)
55. Zhang, L., Wang, Y., Li, X., et al.: MoGCN: multi-omics graph convolutional network for cancer subtype classification. Front. Genet. **13**, 806842 (2022)
56. Lingle, W., Erickson, B.J., Zuley, M.L., et al.: The Cancer Genome Atlas Breast Invasive Carcinoma Collection (TCGA-BRCA). The Cancer Imaging Archive (TCIA) Dataset (2016) https://doi.org/10.7937/K9/TCIA.2016.AB2NAZRP
57. Genomic Data Commons (GDC): The Cancer Genome Atlas Program (TCGA-BRCA). National Cancer Institute. https://portal.gdc.cancer.gov/projects/TCGA-BRCA. Accessed 17 Sept 2025
58. Hemker, K., Simidjievski, N., Jamnik, M.: HEALNet: Multimodal fusion for heterogeneous biomedical data. In: Proc. Neural Information Processing Systems (NeurIPS), Vancouver (2024). https://doi.org/10.52202/079017-2057
59. Luo, H., Huang, J., Ju, H., Zhou, T., Ding, W.: Multimodal multi-instance evidence fusion neural networks for cancer survival prediction. Sci. Rep. **15**(1), 10470 (2025). https://doi.org/10.1038/s41598-025-93770-3
60. Liu, Z., et al.: Multimodal fusion of radio-pathology and proteogenomics identify integrated glioma subtypes with prognostic and therapeutic opportunities. Nature Commun. **16**, 3510 (2025)

Wavelet Scattering Features Based Colon Cancer Histology Classification

Ritish Raghav Maram[1,2], Elliot Levy[2], and Murray H. Loew[1(✉)]

[1] The George Washington University,Department of Biomedical Engineering, Washington, DC, USA
{rmaram33,loew}@gwu.edu

[2] National Institutes of Health, Clinical Center, Bethesda, MD, USA
levyeb@cc.nih.gov

Abstract. Histological evaluation of tumors plays an important role in malignancy identification and, more recently, in stratification of treatment response and prognosis. Quantitative imaging methodology has been applied to cross-sectional imaging datasets with pathology correlation to model tumor composition and tissue classification. Several digital image analysis studies have demonstrated prognostic significance for tumor heterogeneity, proportional representation of complex stroma, and immune cell infiltration. Texture analysis has been used for classification of several tissue subtypes. We examine here a new approach that uses wavelet transformations of images, which can optimize spatial and frequency distributions for characterized intratumoral tissues. We have developed and evaluated a model for colon intratumoral tissue classification using wavelet scattering features, achieving 85.10% accuracy on test data with precision (85.19%), recall (85.10%), and F1-score (85.08%) across eight tissue types.

Keywords: Wavelet Scattering · Tumor heterogeneity · Colon Cancer · Quantitative Imaging

1 Introduction

Colorectal cancer classification depends in part on the tissue type as identified in histology images. Extracting descriptors from those images is an essential step in the process of characterizing the tissue. Previous work in colorectal cancer tissue classification has used a variety of features derived principally from classical image analysis tools [1–6]. In this work, we apply the wavelet scattering transform, a wavelet-based method for feature extraction. While the scattering transform has recently demonstrated success in retinal OCT analysis [13] and fundus imaging [14] for disease classification, this work represents its first application to histopathology tissue classification. The transform has a sound mathematical basis and shares structural similarities with convolutional neural networks (CNNs). Unlike CNNs, however, the transform requires no training, is

F. Tanner and J. Irvine (Eds.): AIPR 2025, LNCS 16446, pp. 546–558, 2026.
https://doi.org/10.1007/978-3-032-18474-0_37

computationally efficient, and yields features that are explainable. We show that the features it generates perform well in tissue classification.

The continuous wavelet transform is foundational to understanding the construction of scattering transform coefficients. In this study, we use the complex Morlet wavelet family to compute the wavelet transform. Morlet wavelets, also known as Gabor wavelets, are defined as the product of a Gaussian envelope and a complex exponential [7]:

$$\psi_{\lambda,\theta}(\mathbf{x}) = e^{i\boldsymbol{\zeta}_{\lambda,\theta}\cdot\mathbf{x}}e^{-\|\mathbf{x}\|^2/(2\sigma^2)} + \epsilon(\mathbf{x}) \tag{1}$$

where $\boldsymbol{\zeta}_{\lambda,\theta}$ is the center frequency vector determined by scale λ and orientation θ. The Gaussian term $e^{-\|\mathbf{x}\|^2/(2\sigma^2)}$ gives the wavelet its localized shape, while $e^{i\boldsymbol{\zeta}_{\lambda,\theta}\cdot\mathbf{x}}$ represents a complex exponential with central frequency $\boldsymbol{\zeta}_{\lambda,\theta}$. The correction term $\epsilon(\mathbf{x})$ ensures the wavelet has zero mean (admissibility condition), and the parameter σ controls the trade-off between spatial and frequency localization. This construction enables Morlet wavelets to serve as bandpass filters localized in both space and frequency, as demonstrated in Fig. 1.

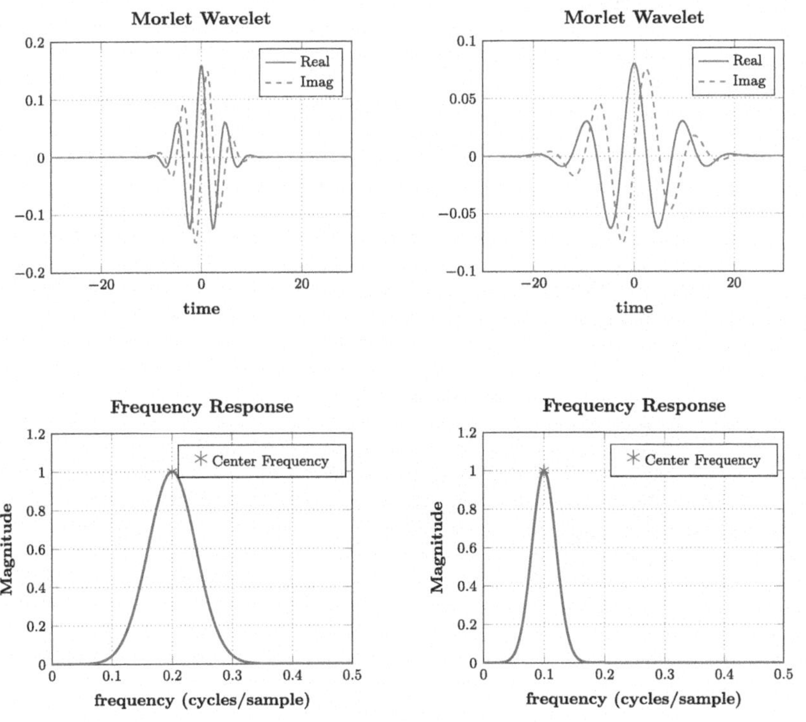

Fig. 1. Morlet wavelets at two distinct scales, with their corresponding frequency spectra.

1.1 2D Wavelet Transform

The 2D continuous wavelet transform decomposes an image by convolving it with a family of filters. The 2D convolution of image $f(\mathbf{x})$ with a filter h at spatial location $\mathbf{x} = (x, y)$ is defined as:

$$(f * h)(\mathbf{x}) = \int_{\mathbb{R}^2} f(\mathbf{u})h(\mathbf{x} - \mathbf{u})\, d\mathbf{u} \tag{2}$$

where $\mathbf{u} = (u, v) \in \mathbb{R}^2$ is the integration variable.

We employ two complementary filter types that partition the frequency domain. The scaling function ϕ is a lowpass filter that retains low-frequency content, capturing the coarse structure of the image. The Morlet wavelet $\psi_{\lambda,\theta}$ is a bandpass filter of the type shown in Fig. 1 that is localized around a specific frequency band determined by scale λ, with orientation selectivity along angle θ. By using wavelets at multiple scales and orientations, we cover the frequency domain with bandpass filters at different scales and directions, capturing complete frequency content when combined with the lowpass component.

The wavelet transform $\mathcal{W}f$ of image f thus consists of one lowpass filter and a collection of bandpass filters:

$$\mathcal{W}f = \{f * \phi(\mathbf{x}),\, f * \psi_{\lambda,\theta}(\mathbf{x})\}_{\lambda,\theta} \tag{3}$$

where the notation $\{\cdot\}_{\lambda,\theta}$ indicates the collection over all scales λ and orientations θ. Table 1 summarizes the notation used throughout this paper.

Table 1. Mathematical notation.

Notation	Definition
$f(\mathbf{x})$	Image
$\psi_{\lambda,\theta}(\mathbf{x})$	Morlet wavelet at scale λ and rotation θ (bandpass filter)
$\phi(\mathbf{x})$	Scaling function (lowpass filter)
$\mathcal{W}f$	Wavelet transform of image f
λ_1, θ_1	Scale and rotation parameters for layer 1
λ_2, θ_2	Scale and rotation parameters for layer 2
$*$	Convolution operator
$\lvert \cdot \rvert$	Complex modulus
$S^m f$	Scattering coefficients of order m for image f

2 Background

This section provides an overview of how wavelet scattering features are constructed from the wavelet transform.

2.1 Zeroth-Order Scattering Coefficients

The first step in computing a scattering transform is to obtain the zeroth-order scattering coefficient, denoted as $S^0 f$, which is obtained by convolving the image with the lowpass filter:

$$S^0 f = f * \phi(\mathbf{x}) \tag{4}$$

2.2 First-Order Scattering Coefficients

Lowpass filtering with ϕ removes high-frequency content. This information can be recovered by convolving the image with wavelets at several scales and orientations:

$$f * \psi_{\lambda_1,\theta_1}(\mathbf{x}) \tag{5}$$

These wavelet coefficients are complex-valued and sensitive to translations in the input [8]. To achieve local translation invariance, we apply the complex modulus operation pointwise:

$$|f * \psi_{\lambda_1,\theta_1}(\mathbf{x})| \tag{6}$$

followed by averaging via convolution with the scaling function:

$$S^1 f(\lambda_1, \theta_1) = |f * \psi_{\lambda_1,\theta_1}(\mathbf{x})| * \phi(\mathbf{x}) \tag{7}$$

where each choice of (λ_1, θ_1) produces one first-order coefficient.

2.3 Second-Order Scattering Coefficients

The modulus operation $|f * \psi_{\lambda_1,\theta_1}(\mathbf{x})|$ creates new high-frequency content (due to the nonlinearity) that is lost when averaging with ϕ. This information can be recovered in a second layer by convolving with wavelets from a second filter bank:

$$|f * \psi_{\lambda_1,\theta_1}(\mathbf{x})| * \psi_{\lambda_2,\theta_2}(\mathbf{x}) \tag{8}$$

Applying the modulus and averaging:

$$S^2 f(\lambda_1, \theta_1, \lambda_2, \theta_2) = \Big||f * \psi_{\lambda_1,\theta_1}(\mathbf{x})| * \psi_{\lambda_2,\theta_2}(\mathbf{x})\Big| * \phi(\mathbf{x}) \tag{9}$$

Each combination of (λ_1, θ_1) and (λ_2, θ_2) produces one second-order coefficient. Each second-order coefficient corresponds to a specific path through the scattering network determined by (λ_1, θ_1) from the first layer and (λ_2, θ_2) from the second layer (see Fig. 4).

2.4 General m-Th Order Coefficients

This construction generalizes to arbitrary depth. The m-th order scattering coefficients are:

$$S^m f = \left\{ \left| \cdots \left| |f * \psi_{\lambda_1,\theta_1}(\mathbf{x})| * \psi_{\lambda_2,\theta_2}(\mathbf{x}) \right| \cdots * \psi_{\lambda_m,\theta_m}(\mathbf{x}) \right| * \phi(\mathbf{x}) \right\}_{\lambda_1,\theta_1,\ldots,\lambda_m,\theta_m} \tag{10}$$

involving m successive applications of wavelet convolution and modulus, followed by averaging.

The complete scattering transform $\mathcal{S}f$ is the collection of all scattering coefficients from all orders:

$$\mathcal{S}f = \{S^0 f, S^1 f, S^2 f, \ldots, S^m f, \ldots\} \tag{11}$$

The wavelet scattering transform was developed by Mallat [9], who proved its key properties: preservation of signal energy, contraction (L^2 stability), and stability under small deformations. Applications to audio [11] and image classification [12] demonstrated the effectiveness of scattering features. More recently, scattering transforms have shown promise in medical imaging, achieving 94–97% accuracy for retinal OCT disease classification [13] and 98% accuracy for glaucoma detection from fundus images [14], demonstrating the method's suitability for medical image classification.

3 Data

Histology images of colorectal cancer (CRC) were taken from a publicly available database [6]. This dataset contains images and corresponding labels for eight tissue types that are commonly found in CRC histology whole-slide images. The images are hematoxylin and eosin (H&E) stained and classified into tumor epithelium (Tumor), simple stroma (Stroma), complex stroma (Complex), immune cell conglomerates (Lympho), debris and mucus (Debris), mucosal glands (Mucosa), adipose tissue (Adipose), and background images (Empty).

For each tissue type, there are 625 non-overlapping tissue tiles of size 150×150 pixels, for a total of 5000 images. Sample images are shown in Fig. 2.

4 Texture Classification

A two-dimensional random field implies that each pixel location is associated with a random variable. The random field is stationary if all these random variables share the same statistical distribution, meaning their distribution is invariant across the entire field. Image textures can be modeled as realizations of 2D stationary processes. Here, we consider that each tissue type is associated with a 2D stationary process, and images of that tissue type are realizations of the process associated with that tissue type, as illustrated in Fig. 2.

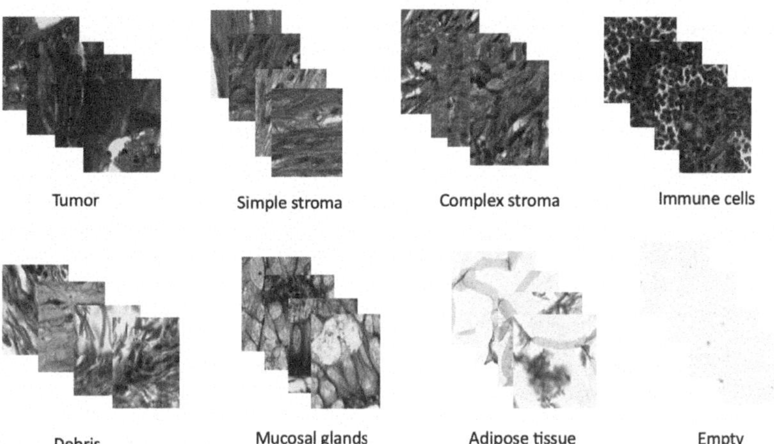

Fig. 2. Eight tissue types present in the CRC histology dataset. Images of a tissue type are realizations of a stochastic process associated with its texture.

The work by Bruna and Mallat [16] demonstrated that scattering coefficients can discriminate textures having identical second-order moments but different higher-order moments. Second-order scattering coefficients capture information up to 4th-order moments, enabling discrimination even when power spectra are identical, as shown in Fig. 3.

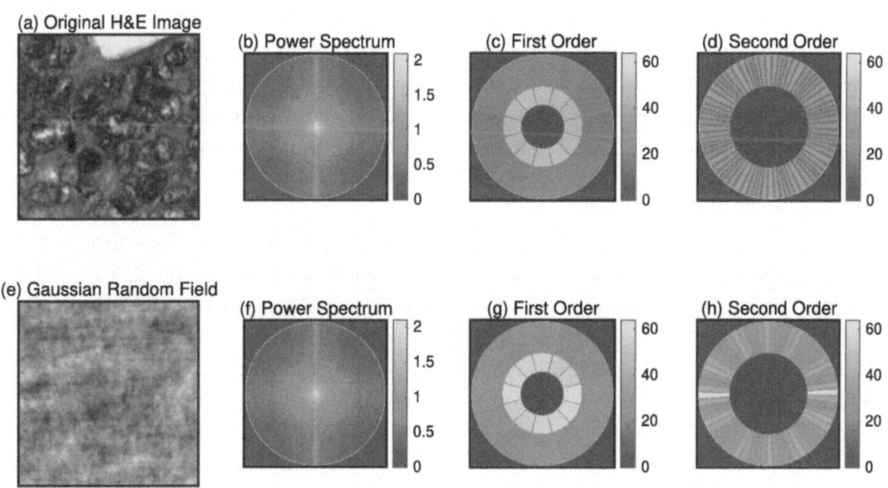

Fig. 3. Scattering coefficients of a tumor tissue patch versus a realization of Gaussian random field. Top row: Original H&E image of tumor (a), its power spectrum (b), first-order (c) and second-order (d) scattering coefficients. Bottom row: a realization of Gaussian random field with power spectrum (e-f) and its scattering coefficients (g-h). The power spectra are identical (b, f) but have different scattering coefficients.

5 Methodology

5.1 Scattering Network Architecture

A two-layer scattering network is created because the energy within scattering coefficients decays exponentially with layer depth [15], and third- and higher-order coefficients typically contain less than one percent of the input energy [16]. An example architecture of a wavelet scattering tree is illustrated in Fig. 4.

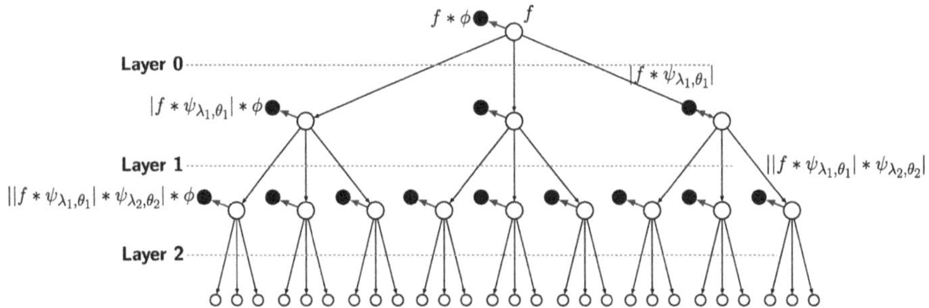

Fig. 4. Two-layer scattering tree. Green nodes: scattering coefficients; white nodes: intermediate wavelet modulus coefficients. (Color figure online)

The scaling function ϕ has a spatial support of 20 pixels, providing translation invariance and serving as the lowpass filter for spatial averaging. The wavelet filter bank uses two dyadic scales in each layer, capturing features at fine and coarse resolutions, with six orientations uniformly sampled in $[0, \pi)$ at angles $\theta_\ell = \ell\pi/6$ for $\ell = 0, 1, 2, 3, 4, 5$. Each filter bank thus contains $N_1 = N_2 = 12$ filters, organized as 2 scales $\times$ 6 orientations. These parameters were chosen heuristically through experimentation. Morlet spatial filters that are used in the first filter bank are shown in Fig. 5.

With 12 filters in the first layer, we obtain 12 first-order scattering coefficients. The maximum number of second-order coefficients would be $12 \times 12 = 144$, giving a theoretical total of $1 + 12 + 144 = 157$ coefficients. In fact, however, the scattering feature vector contains only 49 coefficients due to a path retention constraint based on spectral overlap. When the magnitude spectra of $|f * \psi_{\lambda_1,\theta_1}(\mathbf{x})|$ and $\psi_{\lambda_2,\theta_2}$ do not overlap significantly in the frequency domain, the corresponding second-order coefficient $\big||f * \psi_{\lambda_1,\theta_1}(\mathbf{x})| * \psi_{\lambda_2,\theta_2}(\mathbf{x})\big| * \phi(\mathbf{x})$ is negligible and can be discarded [17]. Specifically, second-order paths are retained only when $\lambda_1 < \lambda_2$, ensuring that the second wavelet operates at a coarser scale (lower frequency) than the first. This frequency-decreasing constraint is fundamental to the scattering transform architecture, as it ensures that each subsequent layer captures progressively coarser features. Among the 144 potential second-order paths, only those satisfying $\lambda_1 < \lambda_2$ are retained, reducing the count to 36 non-negligible second-order coefficients. This yields a final feature vector of dimension $1 + 12 + 36 = 49$.

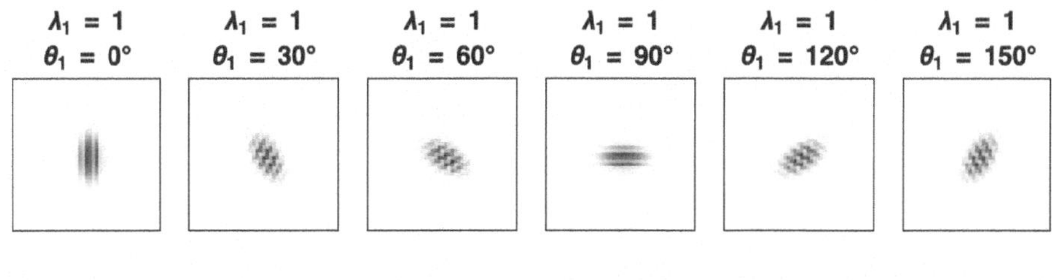

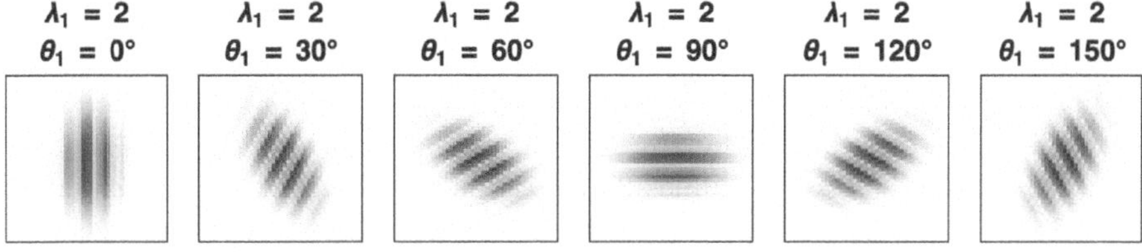

Fig. 5. Morlet Spatial Filters in the first filter bank for each combination of λ_1 and θ_1.

5.2 Implementation

The dataset was divided into a training set (4000 images) and testing set (1000 images), with each tissue type equally represented (500 training and 125 test images per type). Each image was transformed into a scattering feature vector of size 1×49, yielding training and test feature matrices of dimensions 4000×49 and 1000×49, respectively.

A Support Vector Machine (SVM) with cubic polynomial kernel was trained using one-versus-all multiclass classification. Columns of the training feature matrix were z-score standardized prior to training. The workflow is shown in Fig. 6. The complete analysis was performed using MATLAB 2025b [18] with Wavelet Toolbox, Statistics and Machine Learning Toolbox, and Parallel Computing Toolbox. All computations were performed on a MacBook Pro with Apple M3 Pro chip containing 11 cores, 18 GB unified memory.

6 Results

The classifier achieved 81.60% mean accuracy via 10-fold cross-validation on the training set. On the held-out test set, the model demonstrated 85.10% accuracy with balanced precision (85.19%), recall (85.10%), and F1-score (85.08%). Computational efficiency was notable: feature extraction required 2.42 min for all train and test images, training completed in 23.82 s, and prediction took only 0.04 s. Table 2 presents detailed per-class performance metrics.

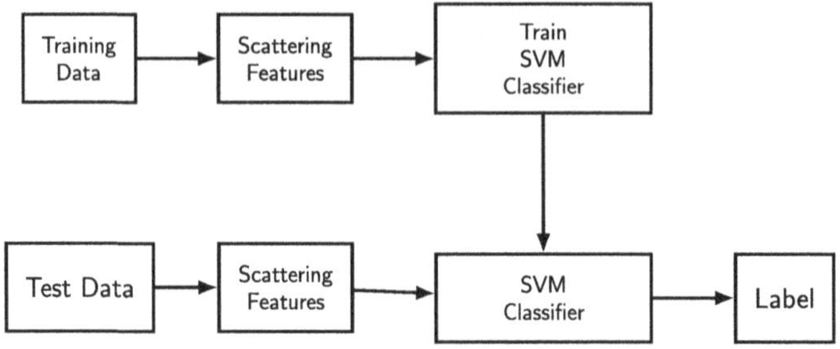

Fig. 6. Classification workflow showing training and testing phases.

The confusion matrix (Fig. 7) reveals substantial variation in per-class classification accuracy achieved by the model. The model perfectly classified the empty background (100.0%), while adipose tissue was classified with near-perfect accuracy (96.8%), reflecting their distinctive and relatively homogeneous textural patterns. Tumor epithelium was classified with an accuracy of 88.8%, which is a clinically favorable characteristic for cancer detection applications. The model achieved strong classification performance for lymphocytes (84.0%), debris (82.4%), and simple stroma (82.4%). The most challenging tissue types for the model were complex stroma (70.4%) and mucosa (76.0%), likely due to their heterogeneous cellular compositions and structural similarities to other tissue types.

Table 2. Per-class performance metrics on test set (125 samples per class).

Tissue	Accuracy (Recall)	Precision	F1-Score
Tumor	88.80%	82.22%	85.38%
Stroma	82.40%	89.91%	83.76%
Complex	70.40%	72.03%	69.96%
Lympho	84.00%	87.50%	85.71%
Debris	82.40%	79.55%	81.71%
Mucosa	76.00%	74.62%	76.08%
Adipose	96.80%	94.40%	94.40%
Empty	100.00%	93.89%	96.09%
Average	85.10%	84.26%	84.14%

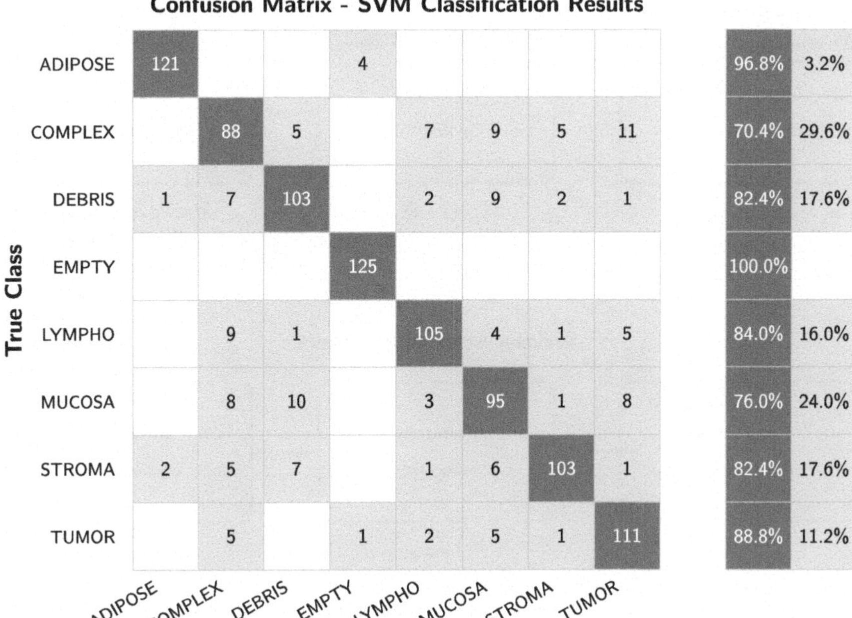

Fig. 7. Confusion matrix illustrating the classification results on the test dataset.

7 Discussion

To our knowledge, this work represents the first application of wavelet scattering transforms to histopathology tissue classification. Our results demonstrate that scattering features extracted through a mathematically principled, training-free process achieve competitive performance on this challenging eight-class colorectal cancer tissue classification task. The 85.10% test accuracy is particularly noteworthy given that the method requires no iterative optimization or large annotated training datasets, addressing a critical bottleneck in medical image analysis where labeled data is often scarce and expensive to obtain.

The structural similarities between scattering networks and convolutional neural networks provide theoretical insight into why wavelet-based features perform well for tissue classification. As illustrated in Fig. 8, both architectures share three fundamental operations: convolution (using wavelets in scattering vs. learned kernels in CNNs), a nonlinearity operation (modulus in scattering vs. ReLU in CNNs), and averaging with a scaling function (analogous to pooling in CNNs) [10].

Convolutional Neural Network (CNN)

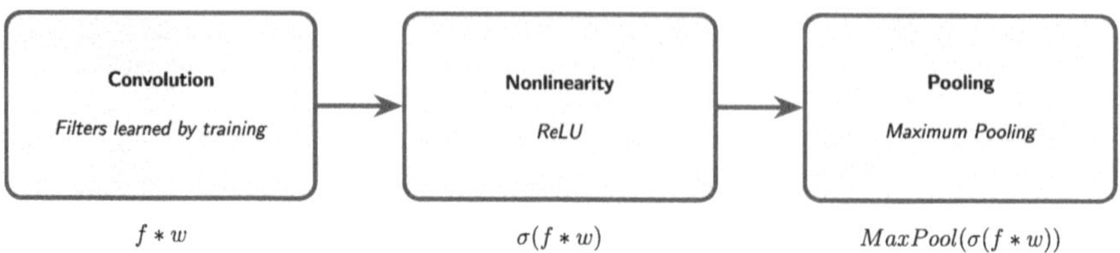

Wavelet Scattering Network

Convolution
Fixed Morlet Wavelets
Nonlinearity
Complex Modulus
Averaging
Lowpass Filter
$f * \psi_{\lambda,\theta}$
$|f * \psi_{\lambda,\theta}|$
$|f * \psi_{\lambda,\theta}| * \phi$

Fig. 8. Similarities between operations in convolutional network and wavelet scattering network. Both architectures cascade these three operations across multiple layers.

Scattering networks, however, employ predefined Morlet wavelets rather than learned filters, eliminating the need for training in the feature extraction process while providing mathematical guarantees of translation invariance and Lipschitz continuity to deformations [9,16]. For our colorectal tissue classification task, second-order scattering coefficients ($m = 2$) capture scale interactions and 4th-order moments that effectively discriminate the complex textural patterns characteristic of the different tissue types. As previously noted, this approach is computationally very efficient as extracting features for the entire training and test set took just 2.42 min, while training the multi-class SVM was completed in only 23.82 s.

A few limitations should be acknowledged. The wavelets are predefined rather than learned from data, potentially limiting adaptability to dataset-specific characteristics. Our future objective is to tackle this limitation by developing wavelets learned directly from image data to effectively capture the structures present in the histology tissue types and to improve the classification accuracy. Validation on additional multi-center datasets is needed to assess generalization beyond the single dataset used here. Finally, the patch-based analysis does not consider whole-slide spatial context or relationships between neighboring tissue regions.

Acknowledgments. No funding was received for conducting this study. The authors have no relevant financial or non-financial interests to disclose. The research was supported by an intramural NIH grant 889286 Clinical Center's Research Award for Staff Clinicians (E.L.).

Availability of Code and Materials. All code and materials supporting this work are publicly available on GitHub to facilitate reproducibility:

Analysis Code: rrmaram2000/AIPR_Codes
MATLAB codes for reproducing results and figures

Manuscript Source: rrmaram2000/AIPR_2025_Writing
LaTeX source files, figures, and supplementary materials

References

1. Mezheyeuski, A., Hrynchyk, I., Karlberg, M., et al.: Image analysis-derived metrics of histomorphological complexity predicts prognosis and treatment response in stage II-III colon cancer. Sci. Rep. **6**, 36149 (2016)
2. Zhou, R., Zhang, J., Zeng, D., et al.: Immune cell infiltration as a biomarker for the diagnosis and prognosis of stage I-III colon cancer. Cancer Immunol. Immunother. **68**, 433–442 (2019)
3. Lubner, M.G., et al.: CT textural analysis of hepatic metastatic colorectal cancer: pre-treatment tumor heterogeneity correlates with pathology and clinical outcomes. Abdom. Imaging **40**(7), 2331–2337 (2015). https://doi.org/10.1007/s00261-015-0438-4
4. Jin, H.-Y., Yoo, S.-Y., Lee, J.-A., et al.: Combinatory statuses of tumor stromal percentage and tumor infiltrating lymphocytes as prognostic factors in stage III colorectal cancers. J. Gastroenterol. Hepatol. **37**, 551–557 (2022)
5. Alic, L., Niessen, W.J., Veenland, J.F.: Quantification of heterogeneity as a biomarker in tumor imaging: a systematic review. PLoS ONE **9**, e110300 (2014)
6. Kather, J.N., Weis, C.-A., Bianconi, F., et al.: Multi-class texture analysis in colorectal cancer histology. Sci. Rep. **6**, 27988 (2016)
7. Mallat, S.: A Wavelet Tour of Signal Processing, Third Edition: The Sparse Way. Academic Press (2008)
8. Andén, J., Lostanlen, V., Mallat, S.: Joint time-frequency scattering. IEEE Trans. Signal Process. **67**, 3704–3718 (2019)
9. Mallat, S.: Group invariant scattering. Commun. Pure Appl. Math. **65**(10), 1331–1398 (2012)
10. Mallat, S.: Understanding deep convolutional networks. Phil. Trans. R. Soc. A **374**, 20150203 (2016)
11. Andén, J., Mallat, S.: Multiscale scattering for audio classification. In: 12th International Society for Music Information Retrieval Conference, ISMIR 2011, pp. 657–662 (2011)
12. Bruna, J., Mallat, S.: Classification with scattering operators. In: CVPR 2011, 1561–1566 (2011)
13. Baharlouei, Z., Rabbani, H., Plonka, G.: Wavelet scattering transform application in classification of retinal abnormalities using OCT images. Sci. Rep. **13**, 19013 (2023)
14. Agboola, H.A., Zaccheus, J.E.: Wavelet image scattering based glaucoma detection. BMC Biomed. Eng. **5**(1), 1 (2023)
15. Waldspurger, I.: Exponential decay of scattering coefficients. In: 2017 International Conference on Sampling Theory and Applications (SampTA), pp. 143–146 (2017)

16. Bruna, J., Mallat, S.: Invariant scattering convolution networks. IEEE Trans. Pattern Anal. Mach. Intell. **35**, 1872–1886 (2013)
17. Andén, J., Mallat, S.: Deep scattering spectrum. IEEE Trans. Signal Process. **62**, 4114–4128 (2014)
18. MATLAB version: 25.2 (R2025b). The MathWorks Inc., Natick, Massachusetts (2025)

Imgs2imgs: Improving Visual Consistency in Multiview Image Editing

Mohamed Gallai[1(✉)] and Abby Stylianou[2]

[1] Electrical and Computer Engineering, Binghamton University, Binghamton, NY, USA
mgallai@binghamton.edu

[2] Computer Science, Saint Louis University, St. Louis, MO, USA
abby.stylianou@slu.edu

Abstract. In this work, we propose `imgs2imgs`, a lightweight training-free pipeline for making visually consistent edits to multiview image sets. Our pipeline operates on an image-to-image basis, applying partial forward diffusion to the original input to preserve its core structure while facilitating localized edits during the guided denoising process. However, unlike standard image-to-image approaches that operate on a single view and often allow global drift from one view to the other, imgs2imgs performs localized edits across multiple photos of the same scene. Our method builds on depth-conditioned ControlNet diffusion models and introduces two key innovations. First, we incorporate a mask-guided editing mechanism. By inverting the segmentation mask fed to the DDIM sampler, we force the diffusion process to be confined only to the content within the object-of-interest's boundaries, while leaving the background unchanged. Second, to maintain cross-view semantic alignment, we introduce a training-free feature sharing mechanism. During the first image passing, the reference, we create a catalog of indexes and values of the corresponding U-Net middle-block features. Then, during the target pass, we inject the feature for each target location into the U-Net's middle block. Together, these techniques enable high-fidelity, targeted edits across multiview scenes. Achieving the structural preservation benefits of image-to-image partial diffusion, the conditioning guidance of ControlNet signals, and the cross-view alignment necessary for consistent multiview editing through feature sharing, all without requiring retraining or specialized inpainting models.

Keywords: Image editing · multiview image editing · multiview consistency · latent diffusion models

1 Introduction

Image generation has improved a lot and grew to have its own field of interest in computer vision. The improvement of image synthesis quality through GANs [20] and Diffusion models [11] allowed us to generate high fidelity images that can

F. Tanner and J. Irvine (Eds.): AIPR 2025, LNCS 16446, pp. 559–575, 2026.
https://doi.org/10.1007/978-3-032-18474-0_38

compensate for images taken by a real camera or animated through a complicated computer software. This leap in image generation resulted in a further more interest in not only generating the images but also editing them and guiding the changes using natural language.

Models like Pix2Pix [10] and Prompt-to-Prompt [2] have solved a lot of image editing problems using different approaches. These approaches fix part of the challenge, offering control over the fine-grained details in the generated images, and this remains an active and widely researched area. Yet, this work has largely focused on a single shot or a single view. While this has its own use cases and value, it is certainly a constraint in many real-life scenarios. On the other hand, multiview images are a collection of photographs that depict the same physical setting but from different camera poses, sharing overlapping objects and geometry.

In this research, we punctually define multiview images by separating it into two distinct ways, each group having 2 characteristics. The first characteristic is **focus**: the scene could be *object-centric*, diva style, where one object is the center of the scene, In contrast, it can be *scene-centric* style where several objects appear in the scene with a busy background. The second characteristic is the **camera shift**. *Narrow-baseline* (or small-shift) where the images are captured with the camera nudged only a few degrees between shots. The other is *wide-baseline* (or large-shift) where the viewpoints are much further apart from each other, sometimes 120° or more, revealing portions of the scene that are completely occluded in the other view. The object-centric and narrow-baseline is common when scanning the object itself to generate a 3D version, editing this category of multiview images is a largely solved problem. Figure 1 shows the

(a) First view - Object-centric

(b) Second view - Object-centric

Fig. 1. Shows multiview with Narrow-baseline and small-shift [4]. This object-centric setting is a largely solved problem, and common in 3D scanning.

multiview image where there is one object appearing in the image and where the camera angle in the first and second view is slightly shifted a few degrees.

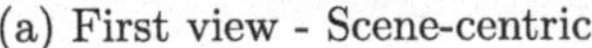

(a) First view - Scene-centric

(b) Second view - Scene-centric

Fig. 2. Shows multiview with Wide-baseline and large-shift. This challenging scene-centric setting is the focus of our research.

In contrast, Scene-centric wide baseline is an under researched area of multiview image editing. Figure 2 shows the other category of the images where we might not even realize that those two images are showing the same scene due to high occlusion and large camera angle shift, we can also notice that in these settings there are multiple objects in the scene with a very busy background. Between the two examples we showed, we will be focusing on the second type of image pairs, which are closer to the second category, and this will be the main focus of our research.

Why do we care about multiview image editing? There is no shortage of use cases for how mastering multiview image editing can be beneficial. For starters, 3D reconstruction using techniques like NeRF operates by using multiview shots to create 3D objects of the scene. Having the ability to make one change in one image and generalize it consistently across other views is crucial for VR and creating an immersive digital world. It also has immediate practical value in media production, where a director can simply make one change to a scene and have this change reflected on all other views across footage from every camera. And finally, and perhaps more importantly, solving this problem will allow us to generate incredibly valuable training data for foundational AI models. By making a consistent edit, we can create an aligned data triplet of *Original Images, Edit Prompt, Edited Images*, and this data is invaluable for image editing and composed image retrieval models.

Yet, *editing wide-baseline scene-centric* multiview images remains a significant challenge. Even for image editing models that relatively succeed in editing single images, they fail if we use them in multiview scenarios. For instance, Figs. 3 and 4 show how the InstructPix2Pix model struggles when prompted "Make the painting red" in two different examples of multiview image editing. We can see

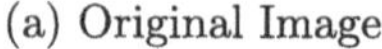

(a) Original Image

(b) Edited Image

Fig. 3. InstructPix2Pix results for "Make the painting red", First View. The edit "bleeds" and incorrectly changes the entire scene colors. (Color figure online)

how the output suffers from poor localization and fails to isolate the specific object of interest and apply the change in color, and instead casts a red tint all over the room.

A second, and more subtle, failure mode is stylistic inconsistency. Figure 5 shows the ControlNet [24] model where we tell it to "Make the bed red". The model might relatively achieve the required edits but fails to generalize them over both views, and we can see that the results for each view are stylistically inconsistent, as the model hallucinates two completely different designs. A noticeable thing about ControlNet is that while it fails to maintain consistency across the two views, it preserves the structure of the original images using conditional signals, like depth maps, segmentation, or Canny edges.

So, we need a method that can solve both localization and consistency problems.

To address these limitations, we propose `imgs2imgs`, A mask-guided editing mechanism that uses partial forward diffusion to ensure precise localization while preserving the original scene's structure.

A novel, training-free cross-view feature sharing mechanism (using the middle-block feature catalog) that solves the consistency problem.

2 Related Work

Image editing is a long-standing challenge in computer vision. It has been addressed through classic methods, such as Poisson image editing, as well as

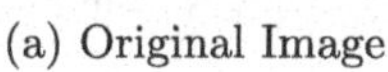

(a) Original Image (b) Edited Image

Fig. 4. InstructPix2Pix results for "Make the painting red", Second View. This demonstrates the same poor localization failure from another viewpoint. (Color figure online)

(a) Original image (b) Edited image (c) Edited image

Fig. 5. Prompt: "Make the bed red/green". This demonstrates poor localization, as the edit incorrectly splashes color onto the walls and doors, not just the bed. (Color figure online)

learning-based approaches. Of course, learning-based methods have prevailed and largely taken over, dominated by generative models like diffusion models [11,18] and GANs [8,20]. We can broadly categorize the field into single-image editing and 3D-aware editing.

For single-image edits, methods typically fall into two categories. 1) Editing with a fixed backbone, which modifies the diffusion process rather than the model weights. Examples include noise-injection methods like Blended Diffusion [1], DiffEdit, Imagic [6], and UniTune [23]. For instance, MagicMix [13], which begins from a real image rather than pure Gaussian noise. They can use attention-steering methods, Prompt-to-Prompt [10], for example, offers control by manipulating cross-attention maps during the diffusion process. 2) Retraining or fine-tuning the backbone itself, like Aesthetic Embeddings [21], Textual Inversion [7], and HyperNetworks [9]. To give an example, Pix2Pix [2], which learns a direct mapping from an input image to a target output using paired datasets, DreamBooth [19], which fine-tunes the entire diffusion model. Also, LoRA (Low-Rank Adaptation) [12] adds trainable matrices while freezing the weights. A hybrid approach like ControlNet [24], where they build on the backbone as-is but add a parallel, trainable structure for conditional signals and fine-tune that instead.

As we have mentioned in the introduction, whenever these single-image editing models are used for multiview images, they suffer from two issues: *poor localization* and, most importantly, *inconsistent style.*

Another category is 3D-Aware Editing, which uses 2D diffusion models as a tool, such as DGE [5] and Attention feature [15]. Take for example, MVInpainter [4], which bridges 2D edits to multiview and ensures cross-view consistency using video priors. However, these methods require several views of the object, additional information (i.e., known camera poses and calibration matrices), are heavyweight, and most importantly, target the type of multiview images that we categorized as object-centric, narrow-baseline views. Figure 6 shows one example of the multiview images on which MVInpainter operates.

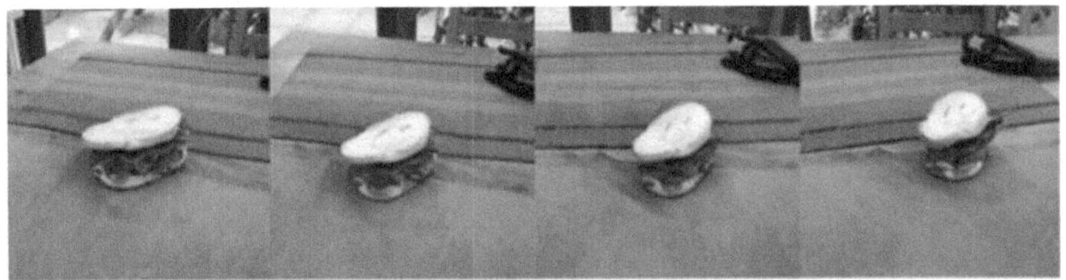

Fig. 6. An example of object-centric narrow-baseline multiview images [4].

3 The imgs2imgs Method

3.1 Pipeline Overview

Our model `imgs2imgs` addresses the main 2 problems we discussed. Another pitfall many editing models fall into is not preserving the structure of the image. This is why we build on top of the ControlNet model; though it suffers from both poor localization and stylistic inconsistency, Figs. 7 and 8, its spatial conditioning signals guide the generation process, preserving the structure of the image.

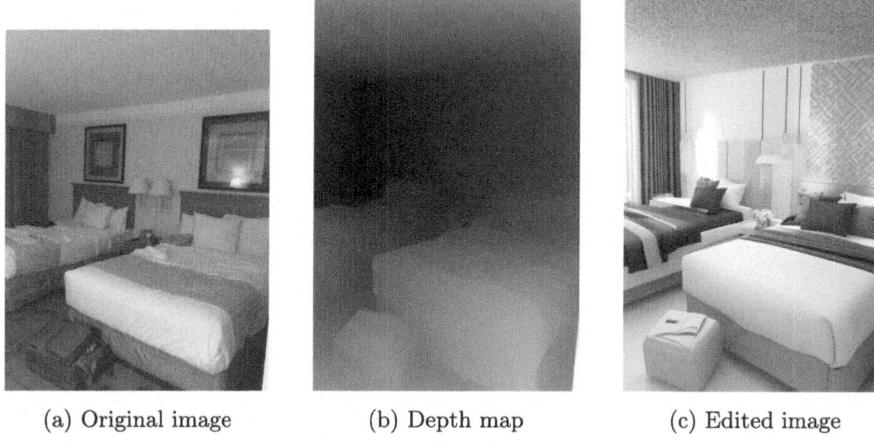

(a) Original image (b) Depth map (c) Edited image

Fig. 7. Editing the first view by the prompt: "make the bed red". This figure, when compared with Fig. 8, demonstrates stylistic inconsistency. (Color figure online)

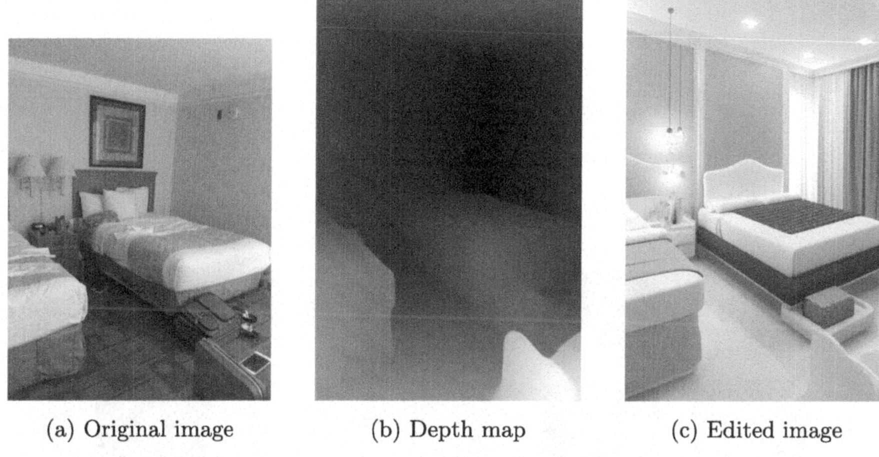

(a) Original image (b) Depth map (c) Edited image

Fig. 8. Editing the second view by the prompt: "make the bed red". This result is stylistically different from the edit of the first view. (Color figure online)

Figure 9 shows the structure of ControlNet, which is built on top of Stable Diffusion with a standard U-Net, an encoder, and a decoder, and a parallel path that feeds in conditioning information-in our case, a depth map Midas model [17].

Our method, `imgs2imgs`, addresses the two key challenges of localization and consistency that we discussed in the introduction. As shown in Fig. 10, our pipeline is built on top of a pre-trained, depth-conditioned ControlNet model, which is used for its strong ability to preserve scene structure.

The full process takes four inputs: a reference view, a target view, an editing prompt (e.g., "make the bed runners black"), and a segmentation prompt (e.g.,

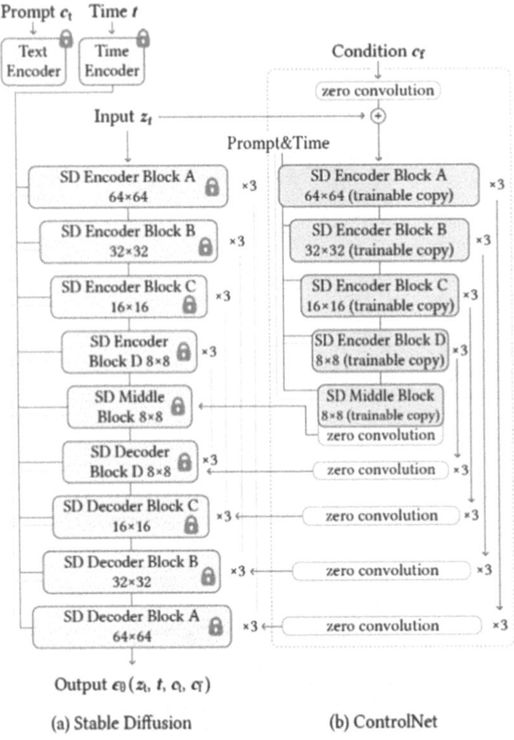

Fig. 9. Stable Diffusion's U-Net architecture with a ControlNet. Figure from [24].

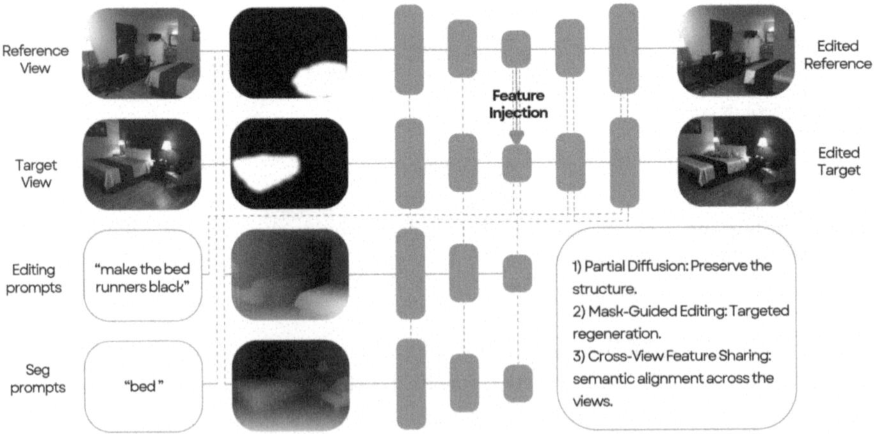

Fig. 10. The `imgs2imgs` pipeline. Our method takes a reference view, a target view, and two text prompts (for editing and segmentation) as input. It uses a depth-conditioned ControlNet backbone. Our key innovations are (1) a mask-guided editing process for localization and (2) a novel **Feature Injection** mechanism between the U-Net middle-blocks to enforce cross-view consistency.

"bed"). The pipeline then performs two main tasks in parallel. First, it uses the segmentation mask to ensure the edit is localized. Second, it uses our novel cross-view feature sharing mechanism to enforce stylistic consistency. The following subsections will detail each of these two contributions.

3.2 Mask-Guided Localized Editing

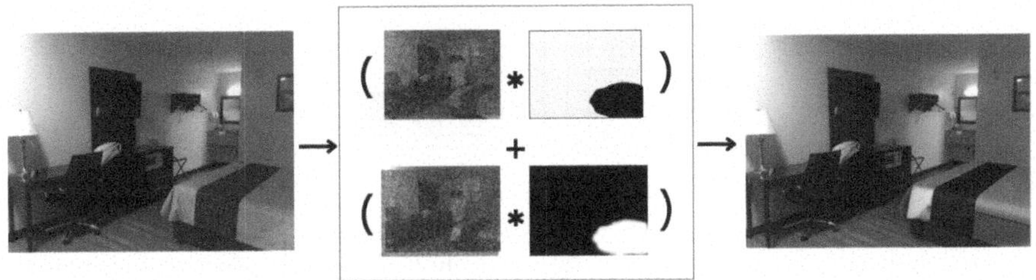

Fig. 11. Partial diffusion and Confining the edits to the target object while keep the rest of the image as is.

To perform a targeted edit, we must ensure the changes are confined only to the object of interest, leaving the background untouched, Fig. 11. Instead of starting from pure noise, we apply a partial forward diffusion pass to the original image. This helps preserves the global structure and high details of the scene. We generate a binary mask M on-the-fly from a text phrase using CLIPSeg [14]. This mask is used to composite the latent while keeping the background from the original latent and only use the newly generated content for the pixels inside the mask, as described by **Equation** (1). To avoid harsh edges and ensure a seamless blend, this mask is then feathered using a two-pass `ImageFilter.GaussianBlur` (first with a radius of 3.0, then 10.0). At each denoising step, we use this mask to composite the latent. We keep the background from the original latent and only use the newly generated content for the pixels inside the mask.

$$z'_t = z_{t,orig} \odot (1 - M_{obj}) + z_{t,gen} \odot M_{obj} \tag{1}$$

Finally, after the full denoising process is complete and the latent is decoded, we apply a statistical color correction step. This matches the mean color of the generated patch to the mean color of the original image, ensuring the edit blends in with the scene's original lighting and has the same hue color.

3.3 Cross-View Feature Sharing

While the mask-guided editing in the previous section solves localization, the main challenge of stylistic inconsistency remains and it is not addressed enough

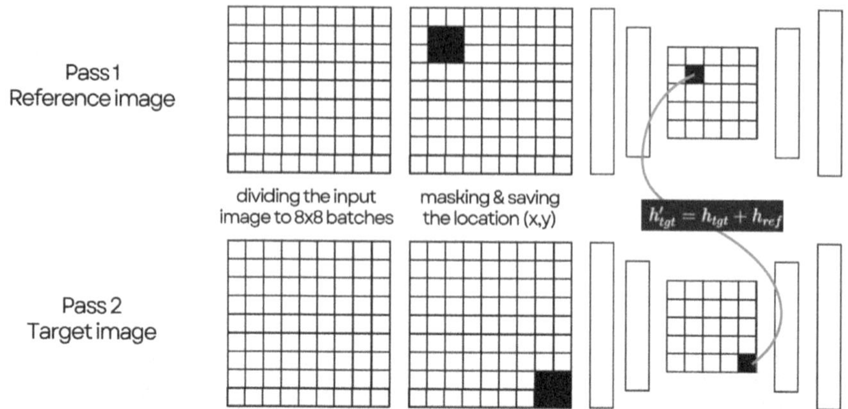

Fig. 12. An overview of our two-pass, training-free Cross-View Feature Sharing mechanism. **(Pass 1 - Reference View)** We process the reference image and create a catalog, storing the U-Net middle-block features from the masked object region, mapped to their spatial indices. **(Pass 2 - Target View)** We process the target image and, at the corresponding U-Net middle-block locations, we inject the saved features from the catalog. This acts as a shared semantic anchor to enforce stylistic consistency.

in the image editing literature. To solve this, we introduce a two-pass, training-free feature sharing mechanism, Fig. 12. While feature injection itself is not a new concept, we face a different challenge than prior work. In many models that use injection, both views are nearly identical and fall under the narrow-baseline, object-centric category, where the object's spatial position in the frame is almost always identical. This is not the case for us, as we are dealing with wide-baseline, scene-centric views where an object's position and scale can vary significantly. To overcome this, we propose two strategies. Our primary method is an efficient index-based method. First, we observe that for an input image, 512×512, its dimension in the U-Net's middle block becomes an 8×8 grid. In Pass 1, we process the first view, the reference view, and map the input image to an 8×8 grid. We use the object mask M_{obj} to identify which cells (x,y) in this 8×8 grid contain the object of interest, and we mark the cell where the object is. When the input image's representation reaches the middle block, we leverage this spatial alignment and for each marked cell, we extract and store its corresponding U-Net middle-block feature vector, creating a catalog of features mapped to their spatial (x,y) indices. In Pass 2, we process the second view, the target view. We will map the input image again to an 8×8 grid and mark the cell where the object is located at. As the U-Net processes the target image, in the middle block and at the exact same cell indices (x,y) that were marked, we inject the saved reference features, adding them to the target view's features. This process is repeated at each DDIM denoising step, which forces the generation of the object in the target view to be guided by the features from the reference view. This acts as a shared semantic anchor, ensuring the two views converge on a consistent style and design. This index-matching approach works best when the object occupies a roughly similar spatial area in both views. However, in cases with significant differences in scale of the object, we also developed a more robust semantic-matching alternative. In this mode, the catalog in Pass 1 will also store the indices and the values of the object feature, but we will also calculate its CLIP embedding. Then, during Pass 2, we use a Nearest-Neighbor Search to find the most semantically similar feature from the catalog to inject, rather than relying on a simple (x,y) index match. This ensures the correct features are shared even if the object is in a different location in the frame.

4 Experiments and Results

4.1 Experimental Setup

To evaluate our `imgs2imgs` method, we test it against several baseline models mentioned in our related work, which are: `LEDITS` [22], `pix2pix` [2], `Self-Distillation` [3], and a baseline `ControlNet` [24].

To measure performance, we use two categories of metrics. First, to measure image quality and fidelity to the original scene, we use the standard metrics of SSIM and PSNR, where higher values are better. Second, to address the core problem of this paper, we evaluate edit consistency. For this, we propose using CLIP Similarity [16]. We calculate this by taking the two edited output images from a pair, passing them through a pre-trained CLIP image encoder, and calculating the cosine similarity between their resulting feature vectors. A higher score (closer to 1.0) indicates a higher degree of semantic and stylistic consistency between the two edits (Figs. 13 and 14).

4.2 Qualitative Results

(a) 1st view-original img

(b) 1st view-mask

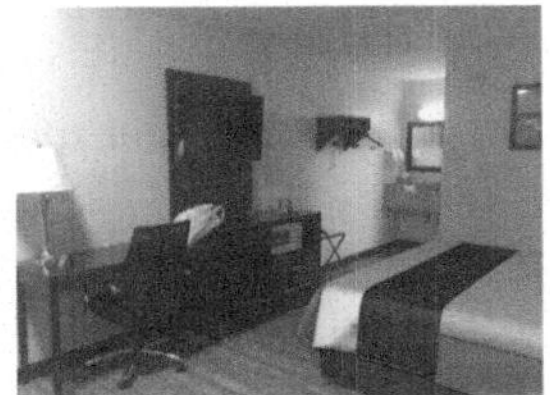

(c) 1st view-edited img

Fig. 13. An illustration of our mask-guided editing process on the first view. From left to right: (a) the original image, (b) the feathered mask generated from the prompt "bed", and (c) the final edited result. The edit is successfully localized to the target object.

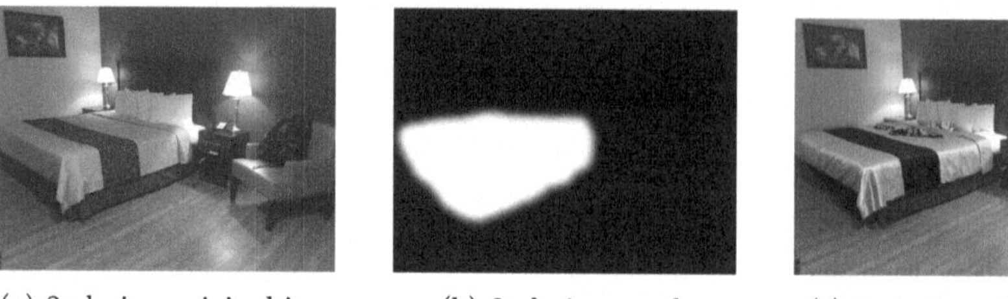

(a) 2nd view-original img (b) 2nd view-mask (c) 2nd view-edited img

Fig. 14. The same mask-guided process applied to the second view. (a) Original image, (b) generated mask, and (c) the final edited result. This demonstrates that our localization method is effective across different viewpoints.

Fig. 15. Qualitative comparison of our method against baseline ControlNet. While ControlNet preserves the scene structure, it lacks consistency, hallucinating two completely different styles for the bed. Our method, `imgs2imgs`, produces an edit that is both high-fidelity and stylistically consistent across both views.

We first show our qualitative results as a visual comparison against the baseline (Figs. 15 and 16).

The left column shows the original pair of images. The middle column shows the output from the baseline ControlNet. As we can see, it fails to produce a consistent edit. When given the same prompt, it hallucinates two completely different styles for the bed, failing the consistency test. The right column shows the result from our model, `imgs2imgs`. Our method successfully generates an edit that is both cleanly localized to the target object and, most importantly, visually consistent across both views.

Figures 17 and 18, and show more qualitative results:

Fig. 16. Qualitative comparison of other baseline models. These methods often suffer from poor localization and global drift. Notice how `Self-Distillation` and `LEDITS` alter the global lighting and style of the entire room, failing to preserve the background.

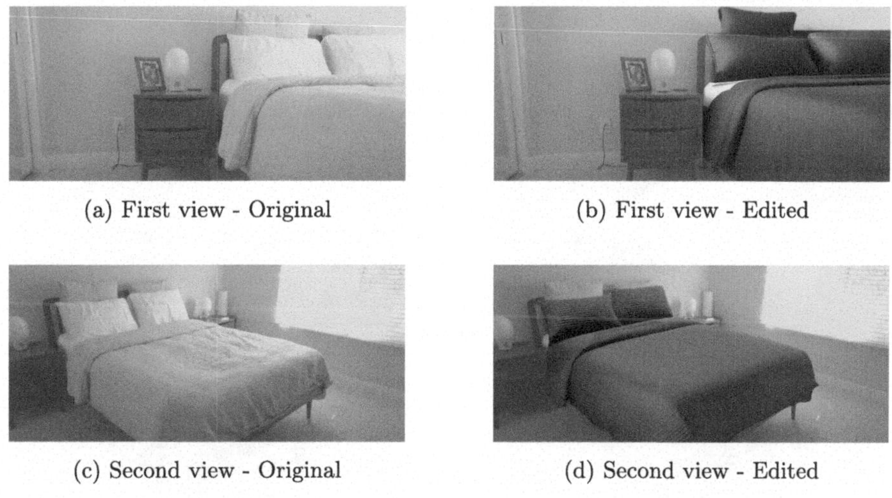

Fig. 17. Qualitative result of our method on a wide-baseline, scene-centric pair with the prompt: "make the bed black". The edit is applied consistently across both views, maintaining the scene's original structure and lighting.

4.3 Quantitative Results

The qualitative results are also backed up by our quantitative metrics. We first evaluated all models for image quality using SSIM and PSNR, where higher is better. Table 1 shows these results. We can see that while methods like `LEDITS` score very high, our model, `imgs2imgs`, is also a top performer, achieving a

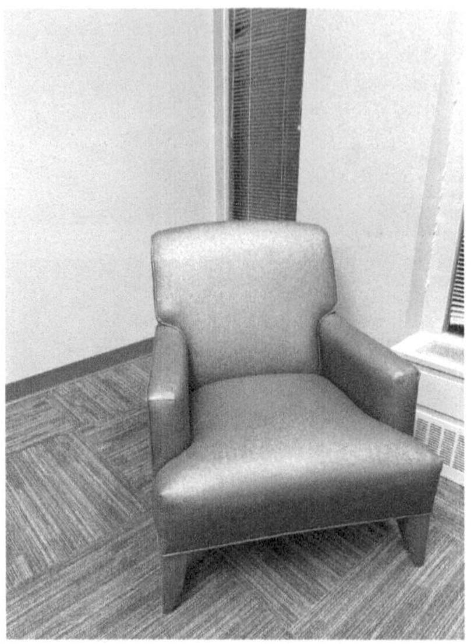

(a) First view - Original

(b) First view - Edited

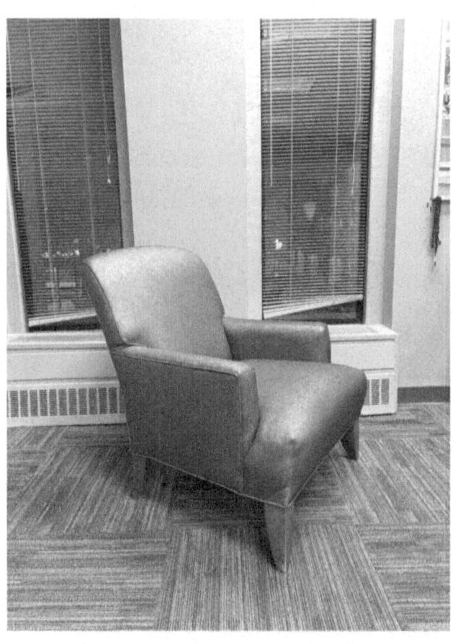

(c) Second view - Original

(d) Second view - Edited

Fig. 18. Editing a wide-baseline, scene-centric armchair with the prompt: "make the armchair black". While the main body of the chair is consistently edited, a limitation is observed in the first view where the wooden legs of the chair are incorrectly changed to white. This is an area for future improvement.

leading score in both SSIM and PSNR. This confirms our edits are high-fidelity. However, these metrics just measure image quality, not consistency.

Table 1. Image Quality comparison using SSIM and PSNR. Higher is better. Our model achieves a top-tier score, showing high fidelity.

Model	SSIM ↑	PSNR (dB) ↑
LEDITS	0.5643	10.36
imgs2imgs (our model)	**0.5503**	**10.02**
pix2pix	0.5025	9.42
Self-Distillation	0.4907	9.12
controlNet	0.3972	6.70

To measure consistency, we used our new CLIP Similarity metric. Table 2 shows these scores. First row is the similarity between the original views with each other as a reference point. A model like `Self-Distillation` gets a very high consistency score, but if you look back at Table 1, it had a much lower image quality score. Our method, `imgs2imgs`, achieves a consistency score that is very competitive with the top performers, while also leading in the quality metrics. This shows that `imgs2imgs` provides the best overall balance of high-quality, high-fidelity edits and strong cross-view consistency.

Table 2. Edit Consistency comparison using CLIP Similarity. Higher is better. Our model shows the best balance of consistency and quality.

Model	CLIP Similarity ↑
Original Unedited Pair	0.9467
Diffusion Self-Distillation	0.9429
imgs2imgs (our model)	**0.9360**
LEDITS	0.9299
pix2pix	0.9081
Baseline ControlNet	0.8683

5 Conclusion

In this paper, we proposed `imgs2imgs`, a lightweight pipeline that addresses the challenging problem of localized, consistent editing for wide-baseline, scene-centric images. Our method introduced two key technical contributions: a mask-guided editing mechanism using partial diffusion to ensure localization, and a novel, training-free cross-view feature sharing mechanism to enforce consistency. Our experimental results showed that while some baseline models are strong in either image quality or in consistency, our method provides the best overall balance of both. For future work, we plan on improving consistency in occluded regions (like the "gray pillow" we saw) and exploring ways to make the processing non-sequential.

Acknowledgements. This material is based upon work supported in whole or in part with funding from the National Science Foundation (IIS-2441774) and the Department of Defense (DoD). Any opinions, findings, conclusions, or recommendations expressed in this material are those of the author(s) and do not necessarily reflect the views of the DOD/NSF and/or any agency or entity of the United States Government.

References

1. Avrahami, O., Lischinski, D., Fried, O.: Blended diffusion for text-driven editing of natural images. In: Proceedings of the IEEE/CVF Conference on Computer Vision and Pattern Recognition (CVPR) (2022)
2. Brooks, T., Holynski, A., Efros, A.A.: InstructPix2Pix: learning to follow image editing instructions. In: Proceedings of the IEEE/CVF Conference on Computer Vision and Pattern Recognition, pp. 18392–18402 (2023)
3. Cai, S., Chan, E.R., Zhang, Y., Guibas, L., Wu, J., Wetzstein, G.: Diffusion self-distillation for zero-shot customized image generation. In: Proceedings of the IEEE/CVF Conference on Computer Vision and Pattern Recognition (CVPR) (2025)
4. Cao, C., Yu, C., Wang, F., Xue, X., Fu, Y.: MVInpainter: learning multi-view consistent inpainting to bridge 2D and 3D editing. In: Advances in Neural Information Processing Systems (NeurIPS). NeurIPS (2024). https://ewrfcas.github.io/MVInpainter/
5. Chen, M., Laina, I., Vedaldi, A.: DGE: Direct gaussian 3D editing by consistent multi-view editing. arXiv preprint arXiv:2404.18929 (2024)
6. Couairon, G., Verbeek, J., Schwenk, H., Cord, M.: DiffEdit: diffusion-based semantic image editing with mask guidance. In: International Conference on Learning Representations (ICLR) (2023)
7. Gal, R., et al.: An image is worth one word: Personalizing text-to-image generation using textual inversion. arXiv preprint arXiv:2208.01618 (2022)
8. Goodfellow, I., et al.: Generative adversarial nets. In: Advances in Neural Information Processing Systems, pp. 2672–2680 (2014)
9. Ha, D., Dai, A.M., Le, Q.V.: Hypernetworks. In: International Conference on Learning Representations (ICLR) (2017). arXiv:1609.09106
10. Hertz, A., Mokady, R., Tenenbaum, J., Aberman, K., Pritch, Y., Cohen-Or, D.: Prompt-to-prompt image editing with cross attention control. arXiv preprint arXiv:2208.01626 (2022)
11. Ho, J., Jain, A., Abbeel, P.: Denoising diffusion probabilistic models. Adv. Neural. Inf. Process. Syst. **33**, 6840–6851 (2020)
12. Hu, E.J., et al.: LoRA: Low-rank adaptation of large language models. arXiv preprint arXiv:2106.09685 (2022)

13. Liew, J.H., Yan, H., Zhou, D., Feng, J.: MagicMix: Semantic mixing with diffusion models. arXiv preprint arXiv:2210.16056 (2022)
14. Lüddecke, T., Ecker, A.S.: Image segmentation using text and image prompts. In: Proceedings of the IEEE/CVF Conference on Computer Vision and Pattern Recognition (CVPR), pp. 7086–7096 (2022). https://openaccess.thecvf.com/content/CVPR2022/html/Luddecke_Image_Segmentation_Using_Text_and_Image_Prompts_CVPR_2022_paper.html
15. Patashnik, O., Gal, R., Cohen-Or, D., Zhu, J.Y., De la Torre, F.: Consolidating attention features for multi-view image editing. In: SIGGRAPH Asia 2024 Conference Papers, pp. 1–12 (2024)
16. Radford, A., et al.: Learning transferable visual models from natural language supervision. In: Meila, M., Zhang, T. (eds.) Proceedings of the 38th International Conference on Machine Learning. Proceedings of Machine Learning Research, vol. 139, pp. 8748–8763. PMLR (2021). https://proceedings.mlr.press/v139/radford21a.html
17. Ranftl, R., Lasinger, K., Hafner, D., Schindler, K., Koltun, V.: Towards robust monocular depth estimation: Mixing datasets for zero-shot cross-dataset transfer. arXiv preprint arXiv:1907.01341 (2019)
18. Rombach, R., Blattmann, A., Lorenz, D., Esser, P., Ommer, B.: High-resolution image synthesis with latent diffusion models. In: Proceedings of the IEEE/CVF Conference on Computer Vision and Pattern Recognition, pp. 10684–10695 (2022)
19. Ruiz, N., Li, Y., Jampani, V., Pritch, Y., Rubinstein, M., Aberman, K.: DreamBooth: fine tuning text-to-image diffusion models for subject-driven generation. In: IEEE/CVF Conference on Computer Vision and Pattern Recognition (CVPR) (2023)
20. Salimans, T., Goodfellow, I., Zaremba, W., Cheung, V., Radford, A., Chen, X.: Improved techniques for training GANs. Adv. Neural Inf. Process. Syst. **29** (2016)
21. Schuhmann, C., Beaumont, R.: LAION-aesthetics: Aesthetic score predictors and subsets of LAION-5B. LAION Blog (2022). https://laion.ai/blog/laion-aesthetics/
22. Tsaban, L., Passos, A.: LEDITS: Real image editing with DDPM inversion and semantic guidance. arXiv preprint arXiv:2307.00522 (2023)
23. Valevski, D., Patashnik, O., Lang, O., Cohen-Or, D., Lischinski, D.: UniTune: text-driven image editing by fine-tuning an image generation model on a single image. ACM Trans. Graph. (SIGGRAPH) **42**(4) (2023). https://doi.org/10.1145/3592451
24. Zhang, L., Rao, A., Agrawala, M.: Adding conditional control to text-to-image diffusion models. In: Proceedings of the IEEE/CVF International Conference on Computer Vision, pp. 3836–3847 (2023)

Quantifying Error Propagation and Recovery in Object Detection for Autonomous Vehicles: A Markovian Approach

Andrews Tang(✉), Kourtney Tucker, Abhinav Pendem, Issa W. AlHmoud, and Balakrishna Gokaraju

Computational Data Science and Engineering, North Carolina A&T State University, Greensboro, USA
atang@aggies.ncat.edu

Abstract. Recent advances in object detection have significantly improved performance for autonomous driving perception; however, understanding how detection errors evolve over time remains critically underexplored. In this work, we introduce a Markovian error propagation framework to quantify temporal consistency across four distinct detection states—correct, misclassified, missed, and false positive. Using sequences from the KITTI Tracking dataset, we model how object detectors transition between these states in consecutive frames, revealing characteristic error patterns and recovery behaviors. Our analysis generates empirical transition matrices, error duration statistics, and state recovery probabilities that provide deeper insights than traditional static metrics. The results demonstrate that errors exhibit strong temporal dependencies, with state transition probabilities varying significantly across object classes and environmental conditions. Notably, we find that missed detections persist for approximately 26 frames on average, while misclassifications self-correct more rapidly (typically within 4 frames). This Markovian perspective provides a principled approach to quantifying detection reliability over time, offering both a diagnostic framework for existing models and design guidance for more temporally coherent perception systems in autonomous driving.

Keywords: Autonomous Driving · Object Detection · Markov Chain · Temporal Error Analysis

1 Introduction

Vision-based object detection is fundamental to autonomous vehicle perception, enabling real-time identification of vehicles, pedestrians, and various obstacles. Recent advances in deep learning have significantly improved detection accuracy, demonstrated by modern architectures such as YOLO and Faster R-CNN

F. Tanner and J. Irvine (Eds.): AIPR 2025, LNCS 16446, pp. 576–594, 2026.
https://doi.org/10.1007/978-3-032-18474-0_39

on widely-used static benchmarks like COCO and KITTI [6,19,22]. However, most current evaluations predominantly focus on frame-by-frame performance metrics—such as precision, recall, or mean Average Precision (mAP)—which only assess detection quality at isolated temporal snapshots [3,14].

In reality, autonomous driving operates within dynamic, continuously evolving environments, where perception errors can persist, self-correct, or propagate over successive frames. Such temporal behaviors have significant safety implications: a brief misclassification of a cyclist may present minimal risk if promptly corrected, while consistently missing a pedestrian could lead to catastrophic outcomes [1,21]. For instance, occlusions can prevent even advanced detectors from consistently identifying pedestrians, especially in crowded urban scenes [5]. Traditional static metrics fail to capture these crucial temporal dependencies, leaving several critical questions unanswered: *How long do particular errors persist? What is the likelihood of recovering from misclassifications? Do specific object classes exhibit distinct temporal error patterns?*

Recent studies involving sequential evaluations, multi-object tracking benchmarks, and ID-switch metrics have begun addressing temporal aspects of perception [7]. However, these approaches typically prioritize tracking accuracy metrics like MOTA and MOTP, rather than explicitly modeling the stochastic processes underlying error transitions. Consequently, there remains a significant gap in the probabilistic modeling of detection state evolution across consecutive frames—an aspect vital for regulatory compliance, safety assessments, and algorithmic diagnostics.

To address this gap, we propose a *Markovian error propagation framework* that models detection states as a stochastic process evolving over time. Specifically, detector outputs are categorized into one of four states: *Correct (C), Misclassified (M), False Positive (F), or Missed (O).* By tracking these states across consecutive frames using real-world driving sequences from the KITTI Tracking dataset, we analyze transition probabilities, error durations, and recovery rates, providing deeper insights compared to traditional static metrics. The primary contributions of this paper are:

1. A stochastic Markov chain model that captures temporal transitions among detection states, enabling systematic analysis of error persistence and recovery.
2. An empirical analysis of state transitions on the KITTI Tracking dataset, revealing significantly varied temporal error behaviors across different object classes and driving scenarios.
3. Diagnostic insights into the temporal reliability of detections, illustrating that optimizing static metrics alone is insufficient—temporal coherence must be integrated into algorithm development to ensure safety and robustness in autonomous driving.

Our methodology employs multi-object tracking techniques to maintain object identities over time, aligning detected objects with corresponding ground truth labels across frames. Examining transitions among the C, M, F, and O states allows us to derive stochastic models quantifying temporal reliability. Our findings indicate strong error persistence for particular object classes, while misclassifications often self-correct quickly, highlighting the nuanced dynamics of temporal errors. This Markovian perspective provides a valuable diagnostic framework, emphasizing that optimizing frame-wise accuracy alone is inadequate for robust autonomous vehicle perception—temporal coherence must also be prioritized to prevent persistent errors from undermining overall system safety.

The remainder of this paper is structured as follows: Sect. 2 reviews related work on object detection and multi-object tracking metrics, emphasizing the lack of formal temporal error modeling. Section 3 introduces our Markov chain formulation, detailing the detection states, labeling processes, and transition analysis methodologies. Section 4 presents experimental results from KITTI sequences, highlighting class-specific error patterns, recovery statistics, broader implications for designing temporally coherent perception systems, and future directions for applying this framework to larger-scale, diverse driving datasets. Finally, Sect. 5 concludes the paper.

2 Literature Review

Modern deep learning detectors such as Faster R-CNN [13], YOLO [11,12], and SSD [8] have significantly advanced perception for autonomous driving, achieving a strong balance between detection accuracy and inference speed. These models have been extensively benchmarked on datasets like KITTI [4], nuScenes [3], and Waymo Open Dataset [15], consistently demonstrating high per-frame precision and recall. Their efficiency on modern GPU hardware makes them well-suited for real-time operation in autonomous vehicles.

Despite these achievements, standard evaluation metrics such as mean Average Precision (mAP), precision, and recall remain fundamentally frame-based. They evaluate detections as static snapshots—independent of temporal context. As a result, a detector may exhibit flickering behavior, alternating between correct and missed detections across consecutive frames, yet still achieve a strong average mAP. Such metrics therefore fail to capture temporal reliability, which is essential for safety-critical perception pipelines that depend on continuous object awareness.

To address temporal consistency, multi-object tracking (MOT) frameworks extend object detection by associating detections across frames to maintain consistent identities. Trackers like SORT [2] and DeepSORT [20] combine motion estimation and deep appearance features to generate stable object trajectories. Evaluation metrics such as MOTA, MOTP, IDF1, and HOTA [9] assess how well these trackers preserve identities through occlusions and motion. However, these tracking metrics merge detection and association errors into a single score, making it impossible to isolate the intrinsic temporal error dynamics of the detection model itself. In other words, while they provide insight into trajectory stability, they are not appropriate for quantifying how detection errors evolve or persist over time.

Recent studies have explored temporal error metrics focused specifically on detection stability. Wang et al. [18] proposed the Stability Index (SI) to measure fluctuations in bounding-box geometry and confidence scores across frames. Similarly, the Population Stability Index (PSI) [16] evaluates whether the overall distribution of detection confidences drifts over time. These approaches are valuable for identifying when a model's predictions are stable or unstable, but they remain heuristic rather than probabilistic. They do not explicitly model the likelihood that an error will persist, self-correct, or transition to a new state over time. Consequently, they provide limited insight into the stochastic behavior of perception errors across continuous driving sequences.

Lastly, Piazzoni et al. [10] introduced the concept of *Perception Error Models (PEMs)* as a virtual simulation tool to inject and evaluate the impact of perception failures in autonomous vehicles without directly modeling sensor behavior. Their data-driven approach employed parametric models, including Markov chains, to simulate the probability of detection loss and misperception within simulation environments such as SVL and Apollo. While PEM provides a valuable framework for safety-oriented virtual testing, it primarily focuses on modeling the impact of perception errors in simulation, rather than analyzing how these errors actually evolve in modern detectors deployed on real-world sequences.

Our work builds upon this foundation by applying Markovian error modeling directly to real object detection outputs from video sequences (KITTI Tracking dataset). Rather than simulating errors, we categorize detections into four granular states—*Correct*, *Misclassified*, *False Positive*, and *Missed*—and empirically measure state persistence, transition probabilities, error durations, and recovery rates. This approach enables characterization of the temporal consistency and fragility of modern detectors under real-world conditions, offering diagnostic insights that are essential for model development and temporal robustness evaluation.

3 Materials and Methods

In this section, we describe the complete end-to-end pipeline we developed for temporal error analysis in object detection. Starting from the KITTI multi-object tracking dataset, we proceed through data preparation, model fine-tuning, multi-object tracking, error-state classification, and finally Markovian modeling and visualization. An overview of this workflow is presented in Fig. 1.

3.1 Dataset Preparation

We base our experiments on the KITTI Vision Benchmark Suite's multi-object tracking data, originally developed to evaluate autonomous driving perception under diverse urban and highway scenarios. Each frame is a high-resolution RGB image (1242×375 pixels) captured from a moving vehicle, providing 2D bounding box annotations for eight classes: Car, Van, Truck, Pedestrian, Person_sitting, Cyclist, Tram, and Misc.

We selected the KITTI Multi-Object Tracking dataset for the following reasons:

- Rich Annotations: The dataset includes frame-by-frame bounding box labels with object IDs, enabling a temporal analysis of detection results across consecutive frames.
- Urban and Highway Diversity: Scenes vary widely in object density, scale, and occlusion, reflecting realistic driving conditions essential for evaluating how detection errors evolve and recover over time.
- Broad Object Classes: The eight annotated categories allow us to study class-specific error patterns—e.g., how missed detections or false positives differ between pedestrians and vehicles.
- Structured Sequencing: Each sequence remains intact, preserving consecutive frames. This structure is critical for our Markovian error propagation framework, which models how detection states change from one frame to the next.

We repurpose the 21 KITTI Tracking training sequences—rather than the 29-sequence test split—to focus on temporal error dynamics instead of leaderboard performance. All frames are converted to YOLO's normalized format (center-x, center-y, width, height in $[0, 1]^2$) and the eight KITTI classes (Car=0, Van=1, ...) are mapped to integer labels.

The resulting corpus is partitioned into three chronological subsets: the *Training* set ($\approx$ 70%, $\sim$ 5,500 frames), which is a flat directory of all annotated images used to fine-tune YOLOv8 [17]; the *Validation* set ($\approx$15%, $\sim$ 1,200 frames), a likewise flattened collection for hyperparameter tuning and early stopping that yields standard metrics (mAP, precision, recall); and the *Markovian "Test"* set ($\approx$15%, 1 220 frames, 5 288 objects), comprising three full sequences chosen for diversity—0009 (dense urban, 803 frames), 0012 (mixed traffic, 78 frames), and 0018 (highway, 339 frames)—with frame order preserved to support our analysis of detection states over time.

Excluding the official test set ensures that all annotations remain available for our temporal error-propagation studies in realistic driving scenarios.

3.2 Object Detection and Tracking Framework

Our perception pipeline combines a COCO-pretrained YOLOv8-m detector with a multi-object tracker to capture both per-frame detection accuracy and temporal error dynamics. We fine-tune the model on a custom KITTI subset—reformatting each bounding box into YOLO's normalized $[0, 1] \times [0, 1]$ coordinate system and mapping classes to KITTI labels—and apply extensive augmentation (mosaic, mixup, random rotation, translation, scaling, shearing, horizontal flips, and HSV jitter) to emulate diverse urban scenarios. Training runs for 200 epochs using the Adam optimizer with a cosine learning-rate schedule; full training settings and hyperparameters are available in the codebase.

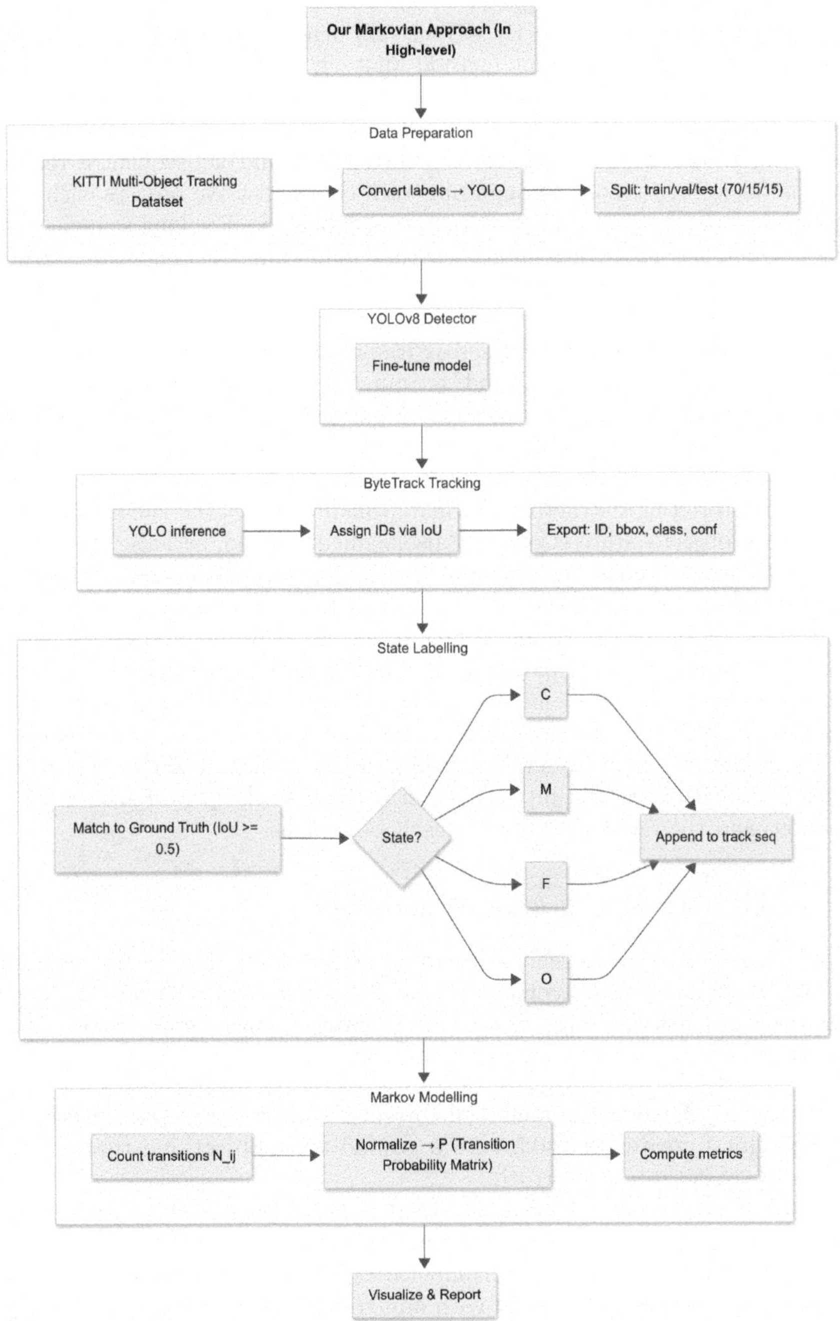

Fig. 1. Overview of the full methodology, from KITTI data prep through Markovian error modeling to final visualizations.

To analyze temporal error patterns, our framework integrates a multi-object tracking module based on the ByteTrack [23] algorithm. ByteTrack is a state-of-the-art tracking-by-detection method that effectively associates detections across frames, even in the presence of occlusions or intermittent missed detections. Its two-stage matching strategy first associates high-confidence detections to existing tracks using stringent IoU thresholds, and subsequently recovers lower-confidence detections to maintain track continuity. We process each video sequence independently to preserve temporal coherence. For long sequences, we employ a batched processing approach that maintains tracking state between batches, ensuring that unique object identities are preserved throughout the entire sequence. Tracks are initialized for unmatched detections exceeding the confidence threshold, maintained across frames through motion prediction and appearance similarity metrics, and terminated if no matching detection is observed for a specified number of consecutive frames.

Tracking results—including unique track identifiers, sequence identifiers, frame-by-frame bounding box positions, class predictions, and confidence scores—are stored in a structured format. This facilitates the subsequent mapping of each object's state (Correct, Misclassified, Missed, or False Positive) in a temporal context, laying the foundation for our Markovian error analysis.

Standard detection metrics (mAP50, precision, and recall) are computed on a validation subset of the training data to ensure that the YOLOv8-m model is well-tuned prior to its deployment in the temporal error analysis. In parallel, the object tracker—implemented via ByteTrack—provides continuous object trajectories, which are subsequently analyzed to construct state transition matrices. These matrices quantify how detection errors propagate across consecutive frames and reveal critical temporal patterns, such as the persistence of missed detections and the rapid recovery of misclassifications.

3.3 Error State Classification Framework

Our methodology defines a relatively comprehensive four-state classification system for object detection outcomes, serving as the foundation for our Markovian error analysis. Each detection in a frame is assigned one of four discrete states based on its correspondence with ground truth:

- Correct (C): A detection is marked correct if it achieves an Intersection over Union (IoU) greater than 0.5 with a ground truth object and the predicted class matches the ground truth.
- Misclassified (M): A detection is considered misclassified if its IoU exceeds 0.5 but the predicted class does not match the ground truth.
- False Positive (F): A detection is labeled as a false positive when it does not sufficiently overlap (IoU < 0.5) with any ground truth object.
- Missed (O): If a ground truth object is not detected (i.e., no prediction meets the IoU threshold), it is categorized as missed.

To assign these states, we employ a greedy matching strategy on a per-frame basis. For each frame, the algorithm performs the following steps. Each prediction is compared to all ground truth objects using Intersection over Union (IoU) as the spatial metric. The IoU is defined as

$$\mathrm{IoU} = \frac{\text{Area of Overlap}}{\text{Area of Union}} \tag{1}$$

A match is confirmed if the highest IoU for a prediction exceeds the threshold of 0.5. When a match is found, the detection is labeled as *Correct (C)* if the predicted class matches the ground truth, or as *Misclassified (M)* if the class does not match. Detections that fail to match any ground truth object are labeled as *False Positives (F)*, while any ground truth object left unmatched is classified as *Missed (O)*.

The pseudocode depicted in Algorithm 1 provides an overview of the algorithm.

Algorithm 1. Pseudocode for error state labeling

```
for each frame in the sequence do
    for each detection in the frame do
        best_matching_gt ← the ground truth with highest IoU for this detection
        if best_matching_gt exists and IoU(best_matching_gt, detection) ≥ 0.5 then
            if detection.class = best_matching_gt.class then
                Label detection as Correct (C)
            else
                Label detection as Misclassified (M)
            end if
        else
            Label detection as False Positive (F)
        end if
    end for
    for each ground truth object in the frame do
        if the ground truth has not been matched to any detection then
            Label ground truth as Missed (O)
        end if
    end for
end for
```

This approach ensures that only detections with sufficient spatial overlap (as determined by the IoU threshold of 0.5) are considered valid matches, and that each ground truth object is accounted for in the error classification.

To leverage temporal information, our framework uses multi-object tracking to maintain object identities across frames. This allows us to compile state sequences—such as "CCCMCCC" or "OOOFCC"—for individual objects, which are subsequently analyzed to construct Markov chains. These chains quantify the persistence of errors and the recovery dynamics over time.

Moreover, by preserving class identity throughout the process, we can perform a detailed class-specific analysis to reveal unique error propagation patterns, offering insights into how different object types (e.g., cars versus pedestrians) behave under temporal evaluation.

3.4 Markovian Error Modeling

Building on the four-state error classification framework established in Sect. 3.3 and the tracking process, we model the temporal dynamics of detection errors as a discrete-time, first-order Markov process. This approach enables us to rigorously quantify how detection errors evolve, persist, and recover over time, providing insights that static, frame-based metrics cannot capture.

For each tracked object, its detection outcomes across consecutive frames are represented as a sequence of states

$$S = \{C, M, F, O\} \tag{2}$$

(Correct, Misclassified, False Positive, Missed). The first-order Markov assumption implies that the probability of transitioning to a new state depends solely on the state in the immediately preceding frame:

$$P(X_{t+1} = s_j \mid X_t = s_i) = p_{ij}, \quad \text{for } s_i, s_j \in S. \tag{3}$$

Here, X_t denotes the detection state at frame t.

Our primary quantitative tool is the transition probability matrix

$$P \in \mathbb{R}^{4\times 4} \tag{4}$$

where each element p_{ij} represents the probability of an object transitioning from state s_i to s_j between consecutive frames. To compute P, we accumulate counts of observed transitions over all track sequences and then normalize each row to convert counts into probabilities. Algorithm 2 shows a detailed overview of how the state transition matrix is computed for each state.

Algorithm 2. Compute Transition Probability Matrix

for each object's state sequence (from frame $t = 0$ to $N - 1$) **do**
  for $i \leftarrow 0$ *to* $N - 2$ **do**
    increment count from state[i] to state[$i + 1$]
  end for
end for
for each state s_i in S **do**
  for each state s_j in S **do**
    $p[s_i][s_j] \leftarrow \frac{\text{count of transitions from } s_i \text{ to } s_j}{\text{total transitions from } s_i}$
  end for
end for

We derive both a global transition matrix—aggregating over all tracks and classes—and class-specific transition matrices to capture error dynamics for each object type. Beyond these transition probabilities, we quantify error stability and recovery using two complementary metrics. First, *error duration* measures the distribution of consecutive frames during which an object remains in a given state s, from which we compute the mean, median, and standard deviation of runs in that state. Second, *recovery rate* for each error state $e \in \{M, F, O\}$ is defined as the fraction of transitions from e back to the correct state C:

$$r_e = \frac{\text{transitions}(e \to C)}{\text{total transitions from } e} \tag{5}$$

These analyses reveal both the persistence of detection errors and the model's capacity to self-correct over time.

We further assess the long-term behavior of the detection process by computing the steady-state distribution

$$\boldsymbol{\pi} = [\pi_C, \pi_M, \pi_F, \pi_O] \tag{6}$$

This distribution, obtained as the left eigenvector of the transition matrix corresponding to the eigenvalue 1, represents the proportion of time the system is expected to spend in each detection state under stationary conditions:

$$\pi P = \pi, \quad \sum_{s \in S} \pi_s = 1 \tag{7}$$

By coupling the state labeling with our multi-object tracking module (ByteTrack), we preserve object identities across frames. This ensures that error state sequences accurately reflect continuous object trajectories. In frames where a tracked object is absent from detections, an O state is explicitly assigned, preserving sequence integrity for later analysis.

4 Results and Discussion

In this section, we present our experimental findings on the temporal dynamics of detection errors, as modeled by our Markovian framework.

All experiments were conducted on a workstation equipped with dual NVIDIA Quadro GV100 GPUs (32 GB VRAM each), dual Intel Xeon Gold 6148 CPUs (80 threads total), and running Ubuntu 22.04.5 LTS (Linux kernel 6.8.0-60-generic). The software environment included Python 3.9.15, with essential libraries such as NumPy, Pandas, and OpenCV for data handling and bounding-box operations. Parallel batching was implemented to process frames efficiently while preserving the continuity of tracking states.

Before examining temporal error dynamics, we first evaluate the static performance of our YOLOv8 m detector on the Markovian test split. Figure 2 shows the class-wise precision–recall curves (and overall mAP@0.5) where the detector achieves an overall mAP@0.5 of 0.620, with strongest performance on Car (0.799) and Pedestrian (0.732), and lower recall for Van (0.435) and Cyclist (0.517).

4.1 Class-Specific Error Patterns

Figure 3 reveals two broad groups of error dynamics. For cars and vans, the model achieves moderate to strong temporal stability: correct detections for cars persist with high probability ($C \rightarrow C = 0.874$), and even when errors occur they often recover (e.g., $M \rightarrow C = 0.215$, $F \rightarrow C = 0.302$). Vans show a lower persistence of correct detections ($C \rightarrow C = 0.691$) and higher volatility, with misclassifications ($M \rightarrow M = 0.703$) and false positives ($F \rightarrow F = 0.583$) persisting but a relatively larger recovery from missed ($O \rightarrow C = 0.215$) than in the car class.

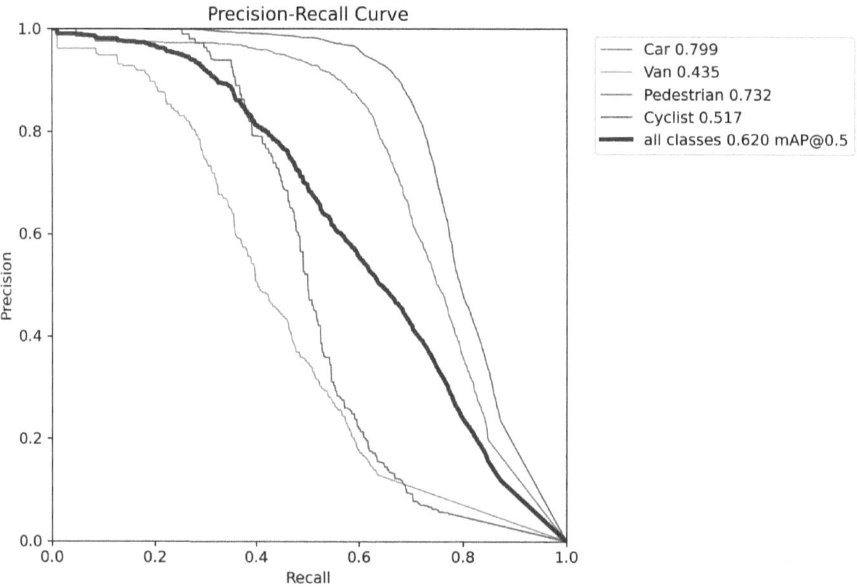

Fig. 2. Precision–Recall curves for each class and the aggregate mAP@0.5.

In contrast, trucks, pedestrians, and cyclists exhibit extreme, class-specific behaviors. Trucks never reach a correct or misclassified state; instead, they oscillate entirely between false positives and misses ($F \rightarrow O = 1.0$, $O \rightarrow F = 1.0$), indicating highly unstable detection. Pedestrians achieve perfect consistency ($C \rightarrow C = 1.0$), with no observed errors, underscoring exceptional reliability. Cyclists, however, are always missed ($O \rightarrow O = 1.0$), revealing a complete failure to detect this class in our test sequences.

These class-specific insights highlight that while cars and vans benefit from reasonable temporal robustness, truck detection requires stabilization, pedestrian detection is already reliable, and cyclist detection demands significant improvement.

Viewed through the dual lenses of *error introduction* (any transition out of the correct state C) and *recovery* (any transition back into C from an error), the

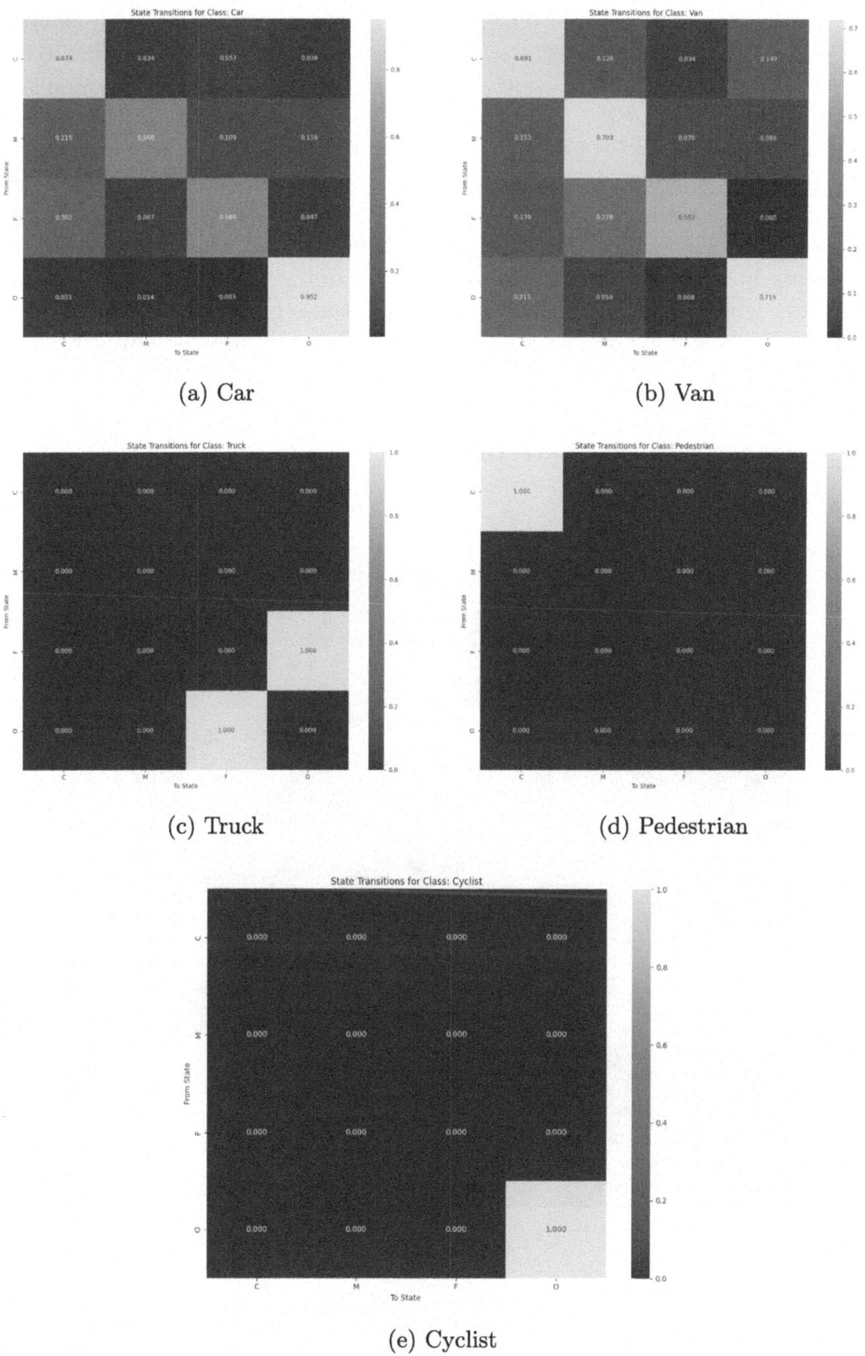

Fig. 3. State-transition heatmaps for five object classes, showing probabilities of Correct (C), Misclassified (M), False Positive (F), and Missed (O) states across consecutive frames.

matrices become immediately interpretable. For example, cars introduce errors only $1 - P(C \to C) = 1 - 0.874 = 0.126$ (12.6 %)—split into $C \to M = 0.034$, $C \to F = 0.057$, and $C \to O = 0.036$—yet recover misclassifications and false positives at $P(M \to C) = 0.215$ and $P(F \to C) = 0.302$. Vans drop out of the correct state $1 - P(C \to C) = 1 - 0.691 = 0.309$ (30.9 %) and recover only about 15 % from misclassifications and 21.5 % from misses. Pedestrians never introduce errors ($1 - P(C \to C) = 0$) and require no recovery, whereas trucks and cyclists suffer 100 % error introduction and zero recovery—trucks oscillating between F and O, and cyclists remaining perpetually missed. This highlights which classes enjoy temporal robustness (cars, pedestrians), which are moderately stable (vans), and which demand urgent detection improvements (trucks, cyclists).

4.2 Global Transition Patterns

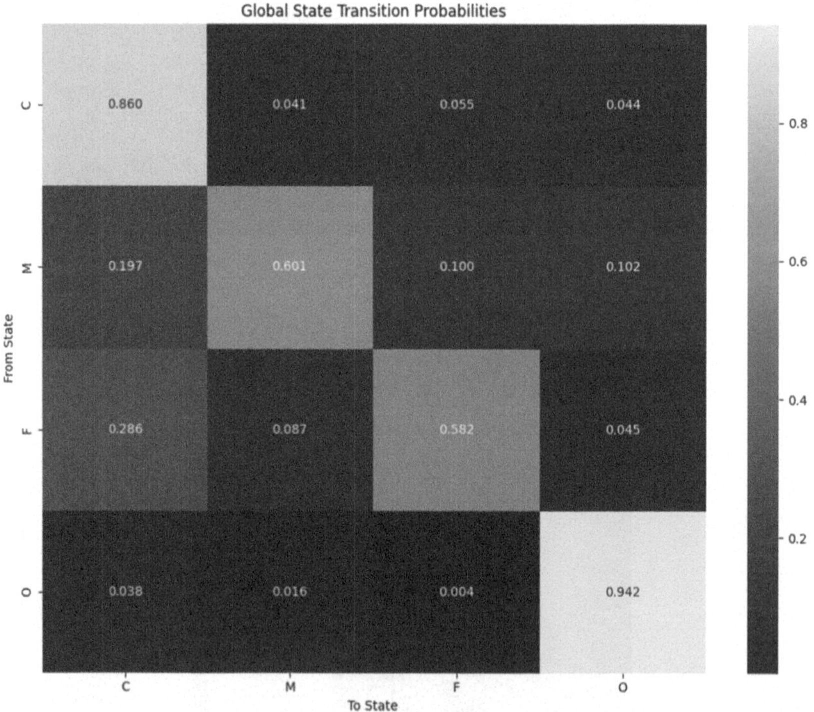

Fig. 4. Global State Transition Matrix.

In addition to the class-specific results, we derive a global transition probability matrix as depicted in Fig. 4 by aggregating error states (C, M, F, and O) across all tracked objects.

This global transition matrix exhibits notably high diagonal elements, which indicate strong state persistence. For instance, the probability of remaining Correct ($C \rightarrow C$) is 0.860, reflecting the model's baseline stability once an object is accurately detected. In contrast, Missed detections ($O \rightarrow O$) persist at 0.942, consistent with earlier findings that once an object is missed, it tends to remain undetected for extended periods. False positives ($F \rightarrow F$) and misclassifications ($M \rightarrow M$) show moderate persistence at 0.582 and 0.601, respectively.

Off-diagonal entries further reveal error introduction or recovery processes. Transitions from $C \rightarrow F$ and $C \rightarrow O$ (with probabilities 0.055 and 0.044, respectively) highlight scenarios where correct detections degrade into false positives or missed detections. Conversely, transitions from $M \rightarrow C$ and $F \rightarrow C$ illustrate the system's ability to self-correct from misclassifications and spurious detections. These transition rates collectively show that although the perception pipeline is generally effective at maintaining correct states, it still encounters challenges in promptly resolving missed detections.

4.3 Global Steady-State Distribution

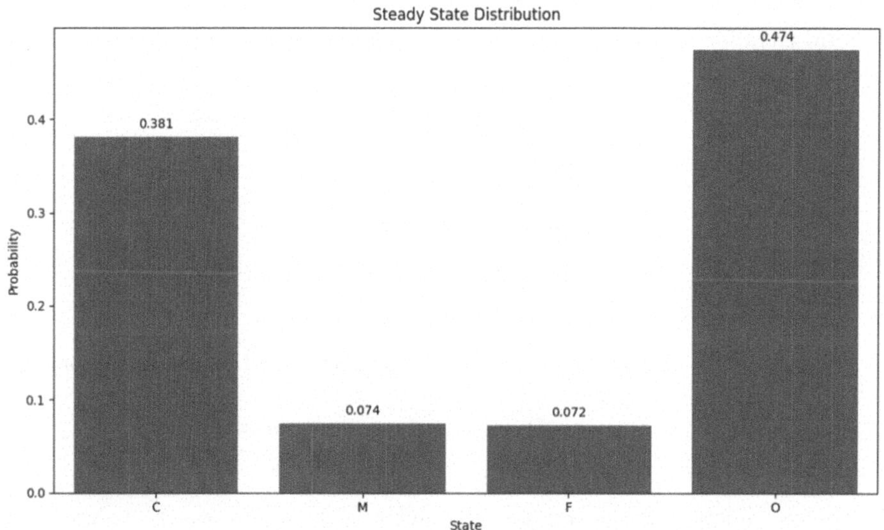

Fig. 5. Global State Transition Matrix.

As shown in Fig. 5, solving for the steady-state vector of the Markov chain yields a distribution

$$\pi = [0.381,\ 0.074,\ 0.072,\ 0.474] \tag{8}$$

for the states C, M, F, and O, respectively. Notably, the Missed state dominates at 47.4%, implying that in the long run nearly half of the time is spent with objects being undetected. In contrast, the Correct state accounts for roughly 38.1% of the distribution, suggesting that while the detector often maintains correct observations, sustained missed detections pose a significant concern over extended operation. Misclassifications and false positives each occupy approximately 7% of the steady state, indicating these error modes are relatively less frequent overall but can still be impactful in safety-critical contexts.

4.4 Error Duration Analysis

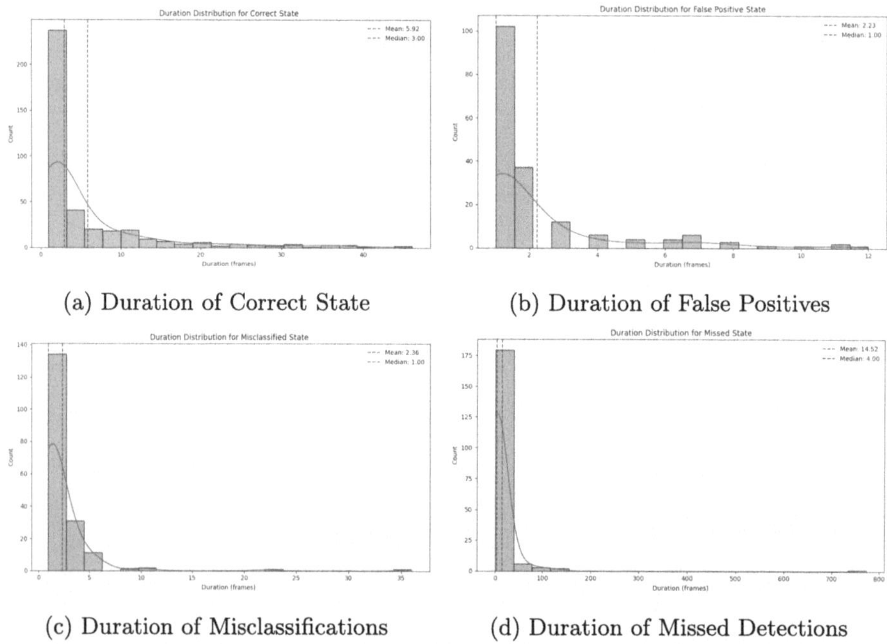

(a) Duration of Correct State

(b) Duration of False Positives

(c) Duration of Misclassifications

(d) Duration of Missed Detections

Fig. 6. Duration Distributions for the Various States.

To further understand the temporal behavior of detection errors, we analyzed the duration of consecutive frames during which a tracked object remains in a given state. Figures 6–9 present histograms for the four detection states – C, M, F, and O.

Figure 6a shows the distribution of consecutive frames where objects are correctly detected. Although many objects transition out of the correct state relatively quickly, a significant proportion remain correctly detected over longer intervals, which underscores the baseline stability of the detection model for certain classes.

In Fig. 6b, the histogram reveals that false positive errors, while present, tend to be short-lived. The majority of false positives resolve within just a few frames, indicating that these spurious detections are generally transient and that the system is capable of self-correction in this regard.

Figure 6c presents the duration for which misclassifications persist. These episodes are relatively brief when compared to missed detections, suggesting that misclassification errors are less persistent and often recover quickly—most misclassifications are corrected within a few frames.

In contrast, Fig. 6d demonstrates that missed detections persist for significantly longer intervals. On average, objects remain undetected for about 26 frames, a finding that is particularly concerning in the context of autonomous driving, where prolonged absence from the perception pipeline could lead to critical safety hazards.

Taken together, these duration analyses highlight distinct temporal error characteristics: while correct detections are relatively stable and false positives and misclassifications are mostly transient, missed detections exhibit a much higher persistence rate. This discrepancy shows the importance of developing strategies to mitigate prolonged perception lapses, which are likely to have more severe implications for system safety.

4.5 Implications for Autonomous Driving

The temporal dynamics captured by our Markovian framework have profound implications for autonomous vehicle perception. First, the substantial persistence of missed detections emphasizes the necessity for robust error recovery mechanisms. In practice, this may involve integrating additional modalities, such as LiDAR and radar, or refining tracking algorithms to better predict object existence during extended occlusions. Second, the observed class-specific error patterns suggest that a one-size-fits-all approach is insufficient. Instead, detection systems should incorporate class-specific enhancements—particularly for detecting pedestrians and cyclists, where current recovery rates and state persistence indicate significant vulnerabilities.

Ultimately, our results challenge the conventional reliance on static metrics like mAP. While mAP and related metrics offer valuable per-frame performance snapshots, they do not capture the dynamic nature of error propagation, which directly influences the safety and reliability of real-world autonomous driving systems. Our Markovian analysis thus provides a more comprehensive framework for assessing temporal consistency, potentially serving as a diagnostic tool to guide the design of future perception systems that are both accurate and temporally coherent.

5 Conclusion

In this study, we presented a novel Markovian error propagation framework designed to capture the temporal dynamics of object detection errors in autonomous driving scenarios. By integrating a four-state classification system—Correct, Misclassified, False Positive, and Missed—with state-of-the-art object detection and multi-object tracking methods, our approach provides a rigorous quantitative analysis of how errors evolve and persist across consecutive frames.

Our experimental evaluation on the KITTI Tracking dataset revealed that detection errors are highly temporally correlated. Notably, missed detections exhibit a high persistence rate, remaining undetected for extended periods that could significantly impact safety-critical functions in real-world autonomous systems. In contrast, while misclassifications and false positives occur, these errors tend to resolve more rapidly. Class-specific analyses further emphasized that vulnerable categories, such as pedestrians, experience higher error introduction and lower recovery rates compared to more stable classes like cars.

The results show a critical insight: traditional static metrics, such as mAP, do not fully capture the dynamic nature of detection errors. Our Markovian framework provides complementary, time-aware performance metrics that reflect the true operational reliability of perception systems. This temporal perspective is essential not only for diagnosing current shortcomings but also for guiding future algorithmic enhancements—ranging from improved temporal consistency and tracking integration to adaptive, class-specific recovery strategies.

Looking forward, extending our framework to incorporate additional object detection models, explore higher-order Markov processes, and integrate multi-sensor data will further enhance our understanding of temporal error dynamics and drive the development of safer, more reliable autonomous driving systems.

Acknowledgment. The authors thank the following agencies for their partial support: 1) W.K. Kellogg Foundation, 2) the United States Department of Commerce (USDOC), Economic Development Administration Good Jobs Challenge Awardee, STEPS4GROWTH (ED22HDQ3070099), 3) the National Science Foundation's Engineering Research Center (NSF-ERC) for Hybrid Autonomous Manufacturing—Moving from Evolution to Revolution (HAMMER) (Award No.: 2133630).

References

1. Bansal, A., et al.: Perception simplex: verifiable collision avoidance in autonomous vehicles amidst obstacle detection faults. Softw. Test. Verification Reliab. **34**(6), e1879 (2024). https://doi.org/10.1002/stvr.1879, https://onlinelibrary.wiley.com/doi/abs/10.1002/stvr.1879, _eprint: https://onlinelibrary.wiley.com/doi/pdf/10.1002/stvr.1879
2. Bewley, A., Ge, Z., Ott, L., Ramos, F., Upcroft, B.: Simple Online and Realtime Tracking (2017). https://doi.org/10.1109/ICIP.2016.7533003, http://arxiv.org/abs/1602.00763, arXiv:1602.00763 [cs]
3. Caesar, H., et al.: nuScenes: a multimodal dataset for autonomous driving. In: Proceedings of the IEEE/CVF Conference on Computer Vision and Pattern Recognition, pp. 11621–11631 (2020)
4. Geiger, A., Lenz, P., Stiller, C., Urtasun, R.: Vision meets Robotics: The KITTI Dataset
5. Islam, M.M., Al Redwan Newaz, A., Gokaraju, B., Karimoddini, A.: Pedestrian detection for autonomous cars: occlusion handling by classifying body parts. In:

2020 IEEE International Conference on Systems, Man, and Cybernetics (SMC), pp. 1433–1438 (2020). https://doi.org/10.1109/SMC42975.2020.9282839
6. Jia, X., Tong, Y., Qiao, H., Li, M., Tong, J., Liang, B.: Fast and accurate object detector for autonomous driving based on improved YOLOv5. Sci. Rep. **13**(1), 9711 (2023). https://doi.org/10.1038/s41598-023-36868-w, https://www.nature.com/articles/s41598-023-36868-w, publisher: Nature Publishing Group
7. Li, M., Wang, Y.X., Ramanan, D.: Towards Streaming Perception (2020). https://doi.org/10.48550/arXiv.2005.10420, http://arxiv.org/abs/2005.10420, arXiv:2005.10420 [cs]
8. Liu, W., et al.: SSD: Single Shot MultiBox Detector (2016). https://doi.org/10.1007/978-3-319-46448-0_2, http://arxiv.org/abs/1512.02325, arXiv:1512.02325 [cs]
9. Luiten, J., et al.: HOTA: A Higher Order Metric for Evaluating Multi-Object Tracking (2020). https://doi.org/10.1007/s11263-020-01375-2, http://arxiv.org/abs/2009.07736, arXiv:2009.07736 [cs]
10. Piazzoni, A., Cherian, J., Dauwels, J., Chau, L.P.: PEM: perception error model for virtual testing of autonomous vehicles. IEEE Trans. Intell. Transp. Syst. **25**(1), 670–681 (2024). https://doi.org/10.1109/TITS.2023.3311633
11. Redmon, J., Divvala, S., Girshick, R., Farhadi, A.: You Only Look Once: Unified, Real-Time Object Detection (2016). https://doi.org/10.48550/arXiv.1506.02640, http://arxiv.org/abs/1506.02640, arXiv:1506.02640 [cs]
12. Redmon, J., Farhadi, A.: YOLO9000: Better, Faster, Stronger (2016). https://doi.org/10.48550/arXiv.1612.08242, http://arxiv.org/abs/1612.08242, arXiv:1612.08242 [cs]
13. Ren, S., He, K., Girshick, R., Sun, J.: Faster R-CNN: Towards Real-Time Object Detection with Region Proposal Networks (2016). https://doi.org/10.48550/arXiv.1506.01497, http://arxiv.org/abs/1506.01497, arXiv:1506.01497 [cs]
14. Sobti, A., Mavi, V., Balakrishnan, M., Arora, C.: VmAP: a fair metric for video object detection. In: Proceedings of the 29th ACM International Conference on Multimedia, pp. 2224–2232. ACM, Virtual Event China (2021). https://doi.org/10.1145/3474085.3475383
15. Sun, P., et al.: Scalability in perception for autonomous driving: Waymo open dataset. In: 2020 IEEE/CVF Conference on Computer Vision and Pattern Recognition (CVPR), pp. 2443–2451 (2020). https://doi.org/10.1109/CVPR42600.2020.00252, https://ieeexplore.ieee.org/document/9156973, iSSN: 2575–7075
16. Taplin, R., Hunt, C.: The population accuracy index: a new measure of population stability for model monitoring. Risks **7**(2) (2019). https://doi.org/10.3390/risks7020053, https://www.mdpi.com/2227-9091/7/2/53
17. Varghese, R., M., S.: YOLOv8: a novel object detection algorithm with enhanced performance and robustness. In: 2024 International Conference on Advances in Data Engineering and Intelligent Computing Systems (ADICS), pp. 1–6 (2024). https://doi.org/10.1109/ADICS58448.2024.10533619
18. Wang, J., et al.: Towards stable 3D object detection. In: European Conference on Computer Vision, pp. 197–213. Springer (2024)
19. Wang, R., et al.: A real-time object detector for autonomous vehicles based on YOLOv4. Comput. Intell. Neurosci. **2021**(1), 9218137 (2021). https://doi.org/10.1155/2021/9218137, https://onlinelibrary.wiley.com/doi/abs/10.1155/2021/9218137, _eprint: https://onlinelibrary.wiley.com/doi/pdf/10.1155/2021/9218137

20. Wojke, N., Bewley, A.: Deep Cosine Metric Learning for Person Re-Identification (2018). https://doi.org/10.1109/WACV.2018.00087, http://arxiv.org/abs/1812.00442, arXiv:1812.00442 [cs]
21. Yang, Q., Chen, H., Chen, Z., Su, J.: Introspective false negative prediction for black-box object detectors in autonomous driving. Sensors **21**(8), 2819 (2021). https://doi.org/10.3390/s21082819, https://www.mdpi.com/1424-8220/21/8/2819, number: 8 Publisher: Multidisciplinary Digital Publishing Institute
22. Zarei, N., Moallem, P., Shams, M.: Fast-Yolo-Rec: incorporating yolo-base detection and recurrent-base prediction networks for fast vehicle detection in consecutive images. IEEE Access **10**, 120592–120605 (2022). https://doi.org/10.1109/ACCESS.2022.3221942, https://ieeexplore.ieee.org/document/9950239
23. Zhang, Y., et al.: BYTETrack: Multi-object tracking by associating every detection box. CoRR abs/2110.06864 (2021). https://arxiv.org/abs/2110.06864

Restorable Segmentation Synthesis Using Fourier Descriptors

Shuyue Guan(✉) and Weijie Chen

Division of Imaging, Diagnostics, and Software Reliability, Office of Science and Engineering Laboratories, Center for Devices and Radiologic Health, United States Food and Drug Administration, Silver Spring, MD, USA

shuyue.guan@fda.hhs.gov, weijie.chen@fda.hhs.gov

Abstract. To evaluate truthing (also known as label fusion) methods in medical image segmentation, synthetic segmentation contours can be useful especially when the reference standard is established by combining multiple segmentation results, such as those produced by multiple experts. This is because ground-truth segmentation is often unavailable in real medical images but is predefined in synthetic data. For this purpose, we developed the Restorable Segmentation Synthesis (RSS) tool. The RSS tool generates segmentation contours by modifying the Fourier descriptors of a truth contour, which, for realism, can be the contour of an anatomical structure extracted from a real medical image. The tool allows for the creation of contours with various segmentation errors relative to the ground truth. A favorable feature of our segmentation contour synthesis tool for evaluating truthing methods is that the average of a large number of synthetic contours asymptotically converge to the truth contour. This is important because such a dataset can help benchmark and compare the truthing methods. Our RSS tool is developed to have this restorability property, which we validated here through simulation studies. We further show that simulating contours is a promising approach for truthing method analysis and data augmentation for segmentation tasks.

`The RSS tool with a GUI is available:` https://github.com/DIDSR/RSS-tool

Keywords: Restorable segmentation synthesis · Synthetic segmentation · Medical image segmentation · Restorability · Segmentation truthing · Label fusion · Segmentation data augmentation · Generative model

1 Introduction

Despite the rapid advancements in artificial intelligence and machine learning (AI/ML) model development for medical image segmentation [6], there is a lack of consensus on the evaluation methods. Numerous metrics have been proposed in the literature, but guidelines are still needed to select the most suitable ones

F. Tanner and J. Irvine (Eds.): AIPR 2025, LNCS 16446, pp. 595–607, 2026.
https://doi.org/10.1007/978-3-032-18474-0_40

for specific clinical tasks [10,11]. Various truthing (*aka* label fusion) methods, which typically establish a reference standard by combining multiple segmentations from experts [12,13], require further evaluation and comparison studies. Ground truth segmentation of medical images is an important consideration for comparing truthing methods. However, segmentation ground truth is generally not available in real medical images, but can be predefined in synthetic data.

In our previous work, we developed the Medical Image Segmentation Synthesis tool (MISS-tool) [3] to create synthetic segmentation contours based on predefined truth contours (*e.g.*, contours derived from real-world medical images). The MISS-tool allows users to customize segmentation errors through adjustable parameters. These emulated segmentation contours can be used to inform the selection of performance metrics to evaluate image segmentation methods [4]. By setting specific parameters, synthetic segmentation contours are generated from truth masks to simulate various types of possible segmentation errors. Although multiple synthetic contours can be created from a single truth mask, their average does not necessarily converge to the truth contour. A desired property for synthesizing segmentation contours to evaluate truthing methods is the ability for the average of synthetic contours to converge to the truth contour. This is favorable because such a dataset can act as a benchmark to assess truthing methods - for example, to assess if a truthing method is biased, meaning that the reference standard either systematically over- or under-segments the truth on average. We previously developed a method to generate synthetic segmentation contours that converge to a polygon approximation of the truth contour [5]. As a significant improvement, in this study, we propose a method, Restorable Segmentation Synthesis (RSS), to generate synthetic segmentation contours that can directly converge to the pixel-level truth contour, instead of its polygon approximation.

Besides verifying the restorability and variability features of synthetic segmentations generated from our RSS method, as the preliminary study, in Sect. 3.5 we used these synthetic segmentations to analyze three truthing methods: Majority Vote (MV) [9], Truth Estimate from Self Distances (TESD) [2], and Simultaneous Truth And Performance Level Estimation (STAPLE) [12]. And by including the generative model, the RSS can be potentially applied to augment the training dataset for segmentation tasks. In addition, the results in Sect. 3.6 indicate our contour augmentation approach, when used to supplement training data, can improve a segmentation model's performance.

2 Methods

2.1 Restorable Segmentation Synthesis

Considering a truth contour in a 2D digital image that consists of N pixels: $P^k(x_k, y_k), k = 1, 2, .., N$ represented by their Cartesian coordinates, we add independent Gaussian noise to the coordinates of each point. For a point $P^k(x_k, y_k)$, it is adjusted to a new location $P_1^k(x_k + \epsilon_1, y_k + \epsilon_2)$ after adding Gaussian noise of zero-mean: $\epsilon_1, \epsilon_2 \sim \mathcal{N}(0, \sigma^2)$. The zero mean of the Gaussian distribution ensures that the expectation of the new coordinates is the original coordinate. Obviously, the location of P_1^k follows a 2-D Gaussian distribution with a mean at the original location P^k. However, if we apply the adjustment to all pixels in the contour, it will break the contour into unconnected pieces, as shown in the contour $P + \epsilon$ in Fig. 1. To overcome this issue, we consider adjusting the contour in the frequency domain using the Fourier transform.

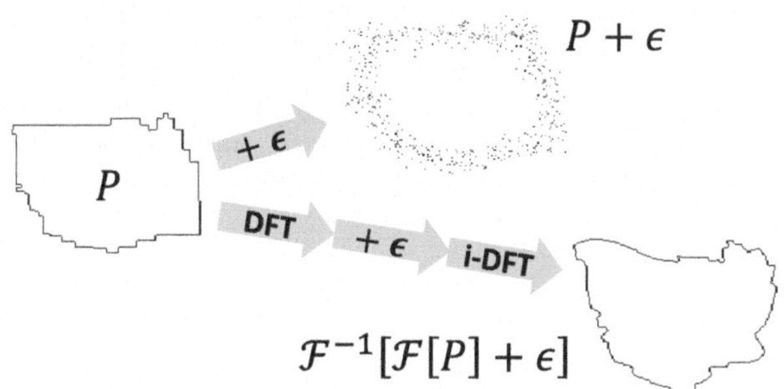

Fig. 1. Adding Gaussian noise ϵ to the pixels' coordinates of a contour in the frequency domain instead of the spatial domain improves the continuity of the contour. DFT is the Discrete Fourier Transform, and i-DFT is the inverse-DFT.

A point in spatial domain with coordinates $P^k(x_k, y_k)$ can be represented by a complex number:

$$P^k = x_k + y_k i,$$

where $k = 0, 1, 2, \cdots, N - 1$, and N is the number of points (pixels) on the contour. By applying the Discrete Fourier Transform (DFT):

$$F^u = \frac{1}{N} \sum_{k=0}^{N-1} P^k e^{-i\frac{2\pi}{N}uk},$$

where F^u is a Fourier descriptor (FD) of the contour, and $u = 0, 1, 2, \cdots, N-1$, the complex number of points P^k in the spatial domain can be converted to a F^u in the frequency domain, and P^k can be retrieved from F^u by applying inverse-DFT:

$$P^k \underset{\text{i-DFT}}{\overset{\text{DFT}}{\rightleftharpoons}} F^u = \alpha_u + \beta_u i. \tag{1}$$

F^u is a complex number with a real part α_u and an imaginary part β_u. An important fact is that the Fourier transform (including DFT and inverse-DFT) of a zero-mean Gaussian function is also a zero-mean Gaussian function. Specifically, for $x \sim \mathcal{N}(0, \sigma^2)$, its Gaussian function is:

$$f(x, \sigma) = \frac{1}{\sqrt{2\pi\sigma^2}} e^{-\frac{x^2}{2\sigma^2}},$$

and, its Fourier transform is:

$$\mathscr{F}\{f(x,\sigma)\} = \frac{1}{\sqrt{\sigma}} f\left(\omega, \frac{1}{\sigma}\right).$$

It follows that the Gaussian noise added to F^u in the frequency domain can be asymptotically eliminated by taking the average in the spatial domain after the inverse-DFT is applied. And unlike adding Gaussian noise to P^k in the spatial domain, adding Gaussian noise to F^u in the frequency domain generally keep the continuity of contour in the spatial domain, as shown in Fig. 1. In summary, as shown in Eq. 1, all the points on a contour are transformed to FDs by the DFT; then the two coefficients, the real part α_u and the imaginary part β_u of FDs are updated by adding zero-mean Gaussian noise $\epsilon_1, \epsilon_2 \sim \mathcal{N}(0, \sigma^2)$:

$$\begin{cases} \alpha'_u = \alpha_u(1+\epsilon_1) \\ \beta'_u = \beta_u(1+\epsilon_2) \end{cases} \tag{2}$$

Applying the inverse-DFT to the modified FDs results in the contour change, as shown in the lower-right contour in Fig. 1. Each coordinate of a point on the changed contour is still subject to an additive independent zero-mean Gaussian noise, and such noise can be asymptotically eliminated by averaging. Thus, the original contour is restorable from a larger number of changed contours.

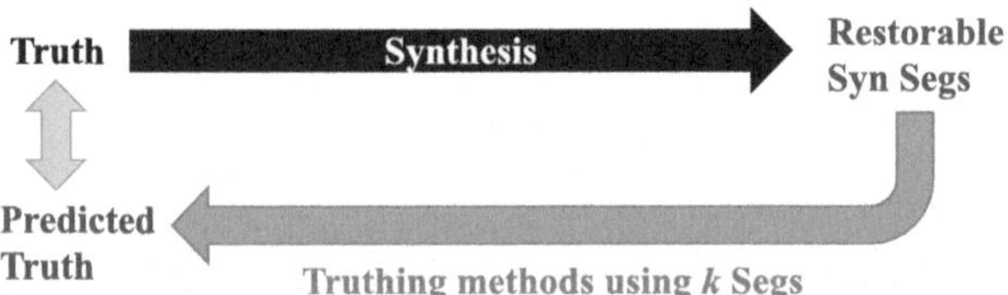

Fig. 2. Our process of truthing methods evaluation compares a truth mask with the predicted truth mask from a truthing method using a number of restorable synthetic segmentations (Syn Segs) generated from that truth mask.

2.2 Assessment of Truthing Methods

In our study of truthing methods, we applied three truthing methods: Majority Vote (MV) [9], Truth Estimate from Self Distances (TESD) [2], and Simultaneous Truth And Performance Level Estimation (STAPLE) [12] to a set of our restorable synthetic segmentations generated from a truth mask. We then compared the fusion results from the truthing methods with the truth mask.

The assessment process is shown in Fig. 2. Truth contours are defined as a set of segmentation contours from real medical images. Restorable synthetic segmentation contours are then generated from the truth contours using our RSS tool. These synthetic contours are combined with a truthing method into the "predicted truth", which simulates a situation where segmentations by multiple observers are combined into a reference standard. The "predicted truth" (*i.e.*, simulated reference standard) is then assessed by comparing with the truth contours. We assess the quality of the truthing method using the following criteria:

1. The similarity between the original truth mask and the restored mask, as measured by segmentation performance metrics such as the Dice-Sørensen coefficient (DSC).
2. The convergence rate reflected by the number of synthetic masks needed to reach a predefined similarity level. The fewer masks needed, the better.

2.3 Data Augmentation for Segmentation Tasks

Besides the assessment of truthing methods, our restorable segmentation synthesis (RSS) method is also applied to augment the training dataset for segmentation tasks. The dataset in supervised segmentation tasks contains images and their corresponding segmentation masks. In brief, data augmentation using the RSS method for segmentation tasks has three steps:

1. Train a generative model, such as the image-to-image translation model: pix2pix [8] by using pairs of real images and masks.
2. Apply the RSS method to real segmentation masks to generate additional synthetic masks.
3. Transform the synthetic masks to synthetic images by using the synthetic masks as input to a pre-trained generative model (pix2pix).

Figure 3 shows the pipeline to augment data for segmentation tasks using the RSS method. In the following section, we show that augmenting the training dataset for a segmentation task directly benefits the training process of the segmentor and improves its performance.

3 Experiments and Results

3.1 Parameters

Suppose there are N points (pixels) on the contour. After applying the Discrete Fourier Transform (DFT), in the frequency domain, there are N Fourier descriptors (FDs): $\{F^0, F^1, \cdots, F^u, \cdots, F^{(N-1)}\}$. The $F^{(N/2)}$ (or $F^{[(N\pm1)/2]}$) has the maximum frequency; the sequence $\{F^1, F^2, \cdots, F^{(N/2)}\}$ is from low to high frequencies, and the sequence $\{F^{(N/2)}, F^{(N/2)+1}, \cdots, F^{(N-1)}\}$ is from high to low frequencies. Due to this mirror nature of the frequency domain signal, the DFT of a time-domain signal is often shifted such that the first half of its spectrum is in positive frequencies and the second half is in negative frequencies[1], with the first element F^0 reserved for the zero frequency in the middle, or named the *Direct Current* (DC)-component.

[1] https://www.mathworks.com/help/matlab/ref/fft.html.

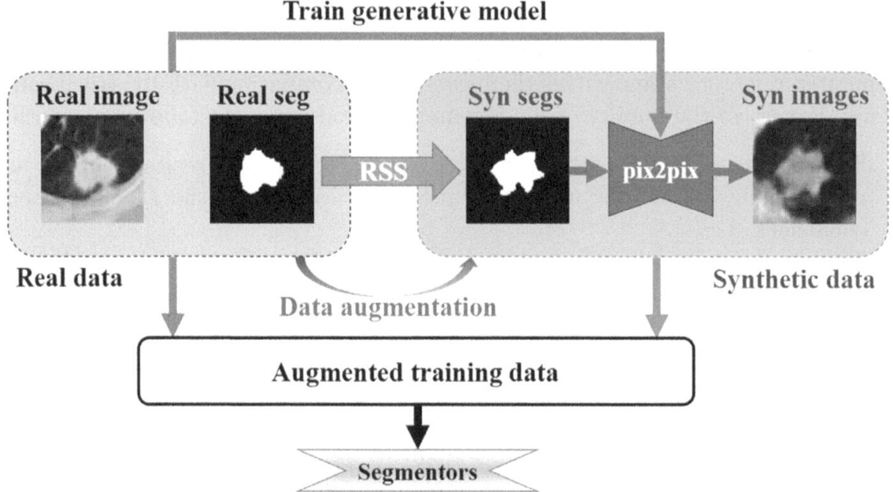

Fig. 3. The process of how our RSS method is applied in data augmentation for segmentation tasks.

In our method, we do not change the DC-component F^0 because the DC-component controls the location of the contour, and it does not affect the contour's shape. We also do not change the very high frequency components because these only result in tiny differences in the contour's shape. Thus, to synthesize a new contour, we perturb FDs in a middle band of the frequency domain. Formally, the user specifies the **range** $\{l, h\}$ $(l \leq h)$ for FDs $\{F^l, F^{(l+1)}, \cdots, F^{(h-1)}, F^h\}$ and $\{F^{(N-h)}, F^{(N-h+1)}, \cdots, F^{(N-l-1)}, F^{(N-l)}\}$ to add noise, where l refers to the lower-end frequency and h for the higher end. By definition, $l \geq 1$ and $h \leq \lceil N/2 \rceil - 1$. For example, for the range $\{l = 2, h = 5\}$ (suppose $N = 20$), the FDs to add noise are:

$$\{F^2, F^3, F^4, F^5\} \text{ and } \{F^{15}, F^{16}, F^{17}, F^{18}\}.$$

The other parameter to specify is the **standard deviation** σ for the zero-mean Gaussian noise added to these middle-band FDs (Eq. 2).

3.2 Materials

In this study, the original input (truth mask) is the lung nodule segmentation from the LIDC-IDRI dataset [1]. The LIDC-IDRI dataset consists of diagnostic and lung cancer screening thoracic computed tomography (CT) scans with radiologist-annotated lesions. Figure 4 displays an example of creating synthetic segmentations using our RSS method from a lung nodule segmentation and the convergence to the original (truth mask) input. The truth mask in this example is a STAPLE-fused mask combining four annotations for the image *LIDC-IDRI-0078/nod_0/slice_3*.

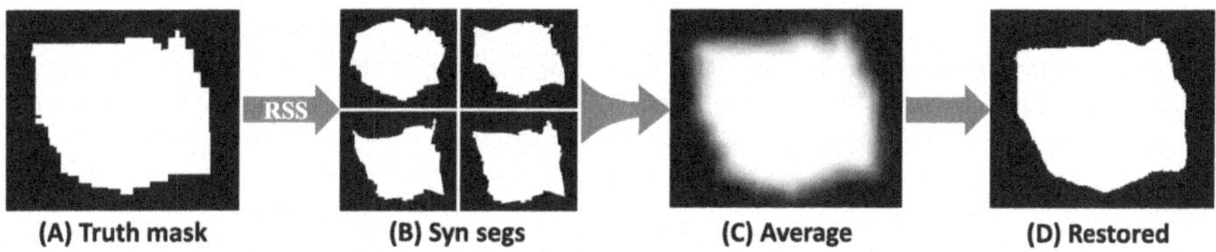

Fig. 4. Synthetic segmentations from a lung nodule segmentation and the convergence to the truth mask (original input). In (A), the truth mask is a fused mask of annotations by radiologists on the CT image. (B) shows four examples of synthetic segmentations ($l = 2, h = 10, \sigma = 1$) generated from the truth mask by our RSS method. (C) is the average image through 100 synthetic segmentations. (D) is the restored binary segmentation from (C) by applying a threshold of 0.5 to the average image. The DSC score between (D) and (A) is 0.98.

3.3 Restorability

To validate the restorability property of our RSS method, *i.e.*, the ability to asymptotically converge to the truth mask by averaging the synthetic segmentation masks, we applied the RSS method with parameters: $l = 2, h = 10, \sigma = 1$ on the truth mask shown in Fig. 4A to generate six groups of synthetic segmentations including 50, 100, 500, 1000 (1k), 2k, and 5k masks, respectively (Fig. 4B).

As shown in the fourth (*Restored_DSC*) column of Table 1, **the DSC scores between the average of the synthetic masks (using a threshold of 0.5) and the truth mask** are greater than 0.98 for groups including 100 synthetic segmentations and more. Figure 4 (C) and (D) show the result for group 2 with 100 synthetic masks. Columns *mean_DSC* and *std_DSC* in Table 1 show the mean and standard deviation of DSC scores between synthetic segmentations and the truth mask. Results in the column *Restored_DSC* show our method can provide a high degree of restorability as we were able to achieve a relatively high DSC score.

3.4 Variability

It is useful that the synthetic segmentations have a variability to mimic the real-world. Here we examine how the parameters **range** ($\{l, h\}$) and **standard deviation** (σ) affect the variability of the synthetic contours. We generated eight groups of synthetic segmentation by setting $\{l = 2, h = 10\}$ and $\{l = 4, h = 12\}$, and $\sigma = 1, 2, 3, 4$ from the same truth mask shown in Fig. 4A. Each group includes 1000 synthetic segmentations. Figure 5 (left) shows the DSC between synthetic segmentation and the truth mask, and Fig. 5 (right) shows the histogram of the 1000 DSC values for the group: $\{l = 2, h = 10, \sigma = 1\}$. Their DSC ranges from 0.8474 to 0.9658, and the histogram's bin width is 0.006.

The results in Fig. 5 (left) show that a larger standard deviation (σ) results in a smaller mean DSC and a wider range (variability) of synthetic segmentations.

Table 1. The second column is the mean of DSC scores when comparing individual synthetic segmentation masks with the truth mask. The third column is the standard deviation (std) of these DSC scores. The fourth column is the DSC scores between the truth mask and the reproduced mask by averaging the synthetic segmentations.

#	mean_DSC	std_DSC	**Restored_DSC**
50	0.9248	0.0175	**0.9778**
100	0.9237	0.0180	**0.9804**
500	0.9228	0.0187	**0.9819**
1k	0.9240	0.0171	**0.9827**
2k	0.9225	0.0182	**0.9829**
5k	0.9222	0.0193	**0.9830**

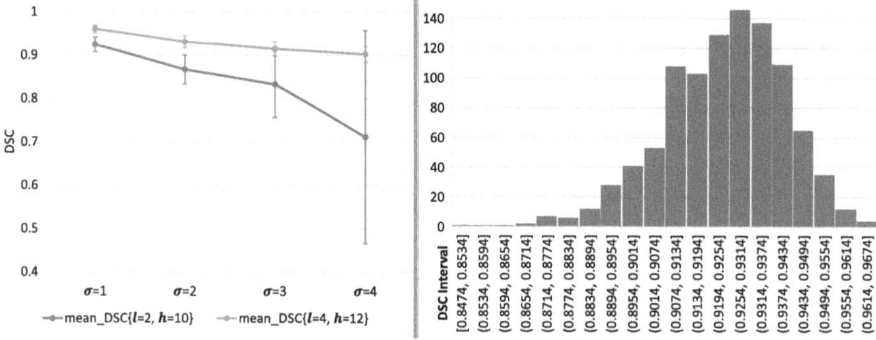

Fig. 5. *Left*: DSC between the truth mask and synthetic segmentations generated by different range ($\{l, h\}$) and standard deviation (σ) parameters for RSS. Bars are the standard deviation (std) of these DSC scores for 1000 synthetic segmentations. *Right*: the histogram of DSC for 1000 synthetic segmentations in the group: $\{l = 2, h = 10, \sigma = 1\}$. The x-axis represents the intervals of DSC, and the y-axis represents the counts of DSC for each interval.

Changes in the Fourier descriptors (FDs) frequencies $\{l, h\}$ also control the variability. Specifically, changing the lower frequency FDs results in a smaller mean DSC and a wider range (variability) for the synthetic segmentations. Thus, the variability of the generated synthetic segmentation is managed by these parameters for a given truth mask.

3.5 Performance of Truthing Methods

As described in Methods (Sect. 2.2), we generated k synthetic segmentation contours with our RSS method (Sect. 2.1) with parameters: $l = 2, h = 10, \sigma = 1$ from the truth mask shown in Fig. 4A. Second, we applied the three truthing methods: MV, TESD, and STAPLE, to the k synthetic masks to obtain a fused (predicted) mask as the reference standard. Then, we compared the reference standard with the original truth mask based on the DSC. For each truthing method and number of synthetic segmentations k, the process was repeated 10 times to obtain 10 DSC scores. Finally, we plotted the mean and standard deviation (std) of these DSC scores for k from 2 to 100 in Fig. 6 and show selected mean DSC scores in Table 2.

Table 2. Selected mean DSC scores between the truth mask and the reference standard masks fused by truthing methods from k synthetic masks.

k	2	3	4	5	6	7	8	9	10	20	30	40	50	60	70	80	90	100
MV	0.9227	0.9463	0.9511	0.9572	0.9594	0.9629	0.9651	0.9661	0.9676	0.9733	0.9758	0.9769	0.9787	0.9796	0.9801	0.9805	0.9804	0.9804
TESD	0.9390	0.9497	0.9538	0.9597	0.9618	0.9644	0.9649	0.9678	0.9680	0.9732	0.9758	0.9768	0.9788	0.9796	0.9800	0.9804	0.9804	0.9804
STAPLE	0.9227	0.9463	0.9439	0.9396	0.9543	0.9506	0.9439	0.9448	0.9512	0.9461	0.9464	0.9454	0.9456	0.9463	0.9458	0.9456	0.9456	0.9454

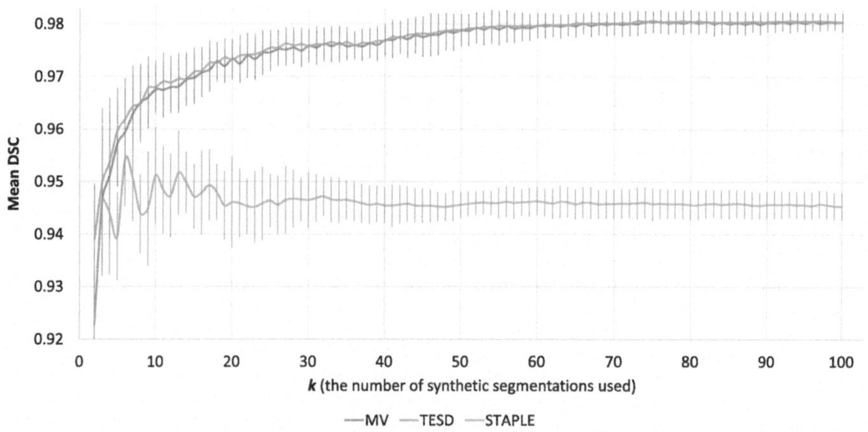

Fig. 6. Mean DSC scores between the truth mask and the reference standard masks fused using truthing methods, MV (blue), TESD (green), and STAPLE (orange), for different numbers of synthetic segmentations (parameters: $l = 2, h = 10, \sigma = 1$). The x-axis is the number of synthetic segmentations k, and the y-axis is the mean DSC score. The error bar show one std above and below. (Color figure online)

We observed that adding more images does not help STAPLE converge to the truth mask, while MV and TESD, performed similarly, converging to higher DSC scores than STAPLE with more samples. Interestingly, for $k = 2$ and 3, MV and STAPLE were identically in DSC scores. For small k (2 to 7), TESD's DSC scores are greater, and STAPLE's scores are lower for almost all k. By looking at the comparisons of fusion results for k =100 and the truth mask in Fig. 7, STAPLE tends to create larger areas with False positive (FP)[2] areas but very few False negative (FN) areas. MV and TESD perform very similarly to each other, and their results have fewer FP but more FN areas than STAPLE.

[2] https://en.wikipedia.org/wiki/Confusion_matrix.

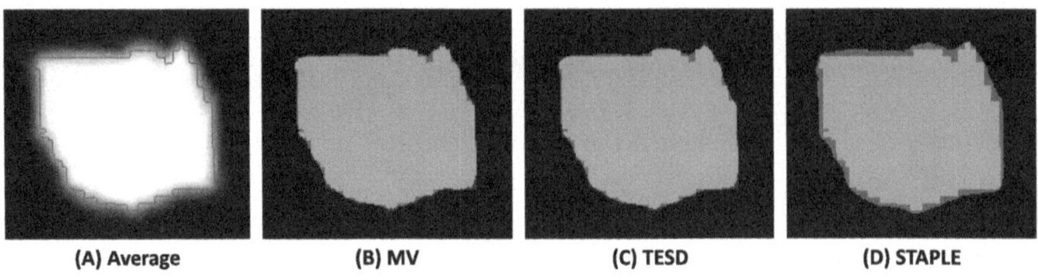

Fig. 7. Comparisons of fusion/average results and the truth mask/contour. In (A), the truth contour is in *Purple* and the gray-scale image is the average of 100 synthetic masks. (B), (C), and (D) show the fusion results when applying the different truthing methods to 100 synthetic masks that overlap the truth mask. The True positive (TP) areas are in *Green*, False positive (FP) in *Red*, and False negative (FN) in *Blue*.

3.6 Segmentation Data Augmentation

To study the power of our RSS method in segmentation data augmentation, we collected 2579 pairs of real lung nodule images and truth masks from the LIDC-IDRI dataset (Sect. 3.2). The truth masks are MV-fused masks of annotations from the central slice of nodules. About 70% of the image pairs (1805) are divided (by patients or cases) to serve as the real data to train the generative model (pix2pix) and segmentation models, and to generate synthetic masks using our RSS method. The remaining 30% of the real image pairs (774) are kept as test data. The test data are only used to evaluate the performance of the trained segmentation models and are never used in model training or synthetic masks generation. We applied the processes described in Sect. 2.3 to augment the segmentation data using only the training data (1805 image pairs):

1. Use the 1805 image pairs to train the pix2pix [8] model (generator architecture: unet_128). The image-to-image translation model can transform the input binary masks to (fake) lung nodule images. The saved model is trained for 200 epochs.
2. Apply the RSS method (parameters: $l = 2, h = 20, \sigma = 3$) to the 1805 training truth masks. For each truth mask, K synthetic masks are generated. There are $1805 \cdot K$ synthetic masks in total.
3. Input the $1805 \cdot K$ synthetic masks into the trained the pix2pix model and generate $1805 \cdot K$ synthetic lung nodule images accordingly.

Including the real data for training (1805 image pairs), the augmented training dataset has $1805 \cdot (K + 1)$ image pairs of lung nodule images and binary masks. We refer to the augmented training dataset as $\mathbf{TrainSet}_K$. For $K = 0$, the $\mathbf{TrainSet}_0$ only contains the real data without data augmentation. Figure 8 displays examples of segmentation data augmentation for $K = 3$.

To estimate the improvement from our data augmentation approach, the final step is to train the segmentation models (segmentors) on $\mathbf{TrainSet}_K$ and

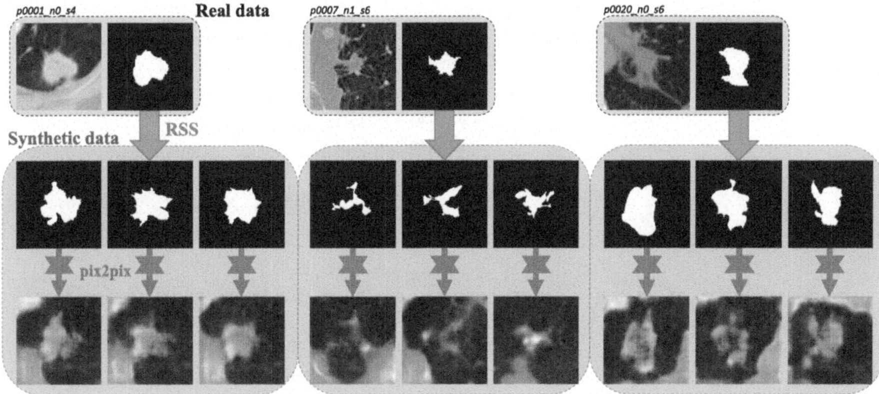

Fig. 8. Examples of segmentation data augmentation. The real data contain lung nodule images and truth masks from the LIDC-IDRI dataset. Three synthetic masks are generated from a truth mask by RSS. They are then transformed into synthetic lung nodule images via a trained pix2pix model.

to obtain the test accuracy (Jaccard index or IoU[3]) of trained segmentors on the 774 real test image pairs. Specifically, the segmentor is the U-net model [7] (with ResNeXt encoder). The segmentor is **trained five times from scratch** on $\mathbf{TrainSet}_K$ ($K = 0, 1, 2, 3, 4$) for 60 epochs. The training accuracy and test accuracy (metrics: IoU score) are recorded after each training epoch. Table 3 shows the maximum and mean values of test IoU scores for segmentors trained on the five datasets. Adding synthetic data (data augmentation) improves the model's performance on the test data, and the more synthetic data added, the better the performance achieved. The results in Fig. 9, not only improved the overall model performance, but also fewer training epochs to achieve a given performance level.

Table 3. All five training datasets consist of 1805 real data, but different numbers of synthetic data. The U-net segmentation model is trained from scratch on each of the five datasets for 60 epochs, and 60 test IoU scores are recorded after each training epoch. Here are the maximum and mean values of the 60 test IoU scores.

Training Data	Real	Synthetic	max_Test-IoU	mean_Test-IoU
$\mathbf{TrainSet}_0$	1805	0	0.6473	0.6250
$\mathbf{TrainSet}_1$	1805	1805	0.6524	0.6318
$\mathbf{TrainSet}_2$	1805	3610	0.6524	0.6352
$\mathbf{TrainSet}_3$	1805	5415	0.6539	0.6371
$\mathbf{TrainSet}_4$	1805	7220	0.6569	0.6444

[3] https://en.wikipedia.org/wiki/Jaccard_index.

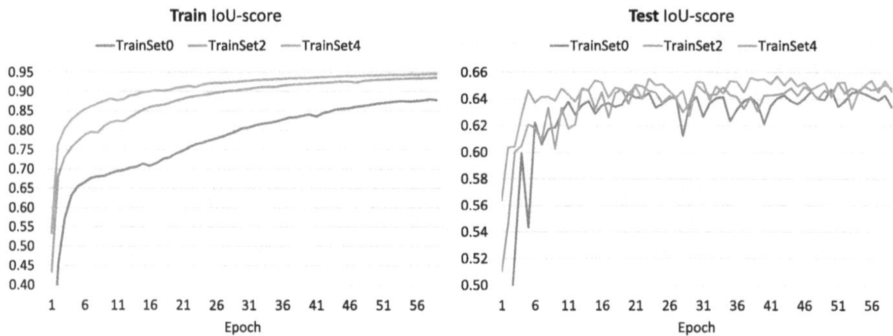

Fig. 9. Plots of the training and test IoU scores after each training epoch. *Left*: the U-net segmentor [7] is trained from scratch on each dataset $\mathbf{TrainSet}_0$, $\mathbf{TrainSet}_2$, and $\mathbf{TrainSet}_4$ for 60 epochs. *Right*: after each training epoch, the segmentor is tested on the test data to obtain test IoU scores.

4 Conclusion

In this study, we proposed the Restorable Segmentation Synthesis (RSS) method that can generate synthetic segmentation contours from given (truth) masks, with the property that averaging these synthetic segmentations can closely restore the original truth mask. Using the DSC, we verified the restorability and variability of generated synthetic segmentations. The RSS method allows for the creation of a benchmark dataset that can potentially be used to compare truthing methods for medical image segmentation. As a preliminary study, we used our RSS tool to analyze three truthing methods: MV, TESD, and STAPLE. By including the use of a generative model, the RSS can also be used to augment the training dataset for segmentation tasks. In another preliminary study, we transformed synthetic masks generated using the RSS tool into synthetic images using a pre-trained generative model (pix2pix). These results showed that our augmentation method can improve a segmentation model's performance.

Acknowledgments. The authors would like to thank Nicholas Petrick, Ph.D., for providing helpful review and comments on the manuscript. The mention of commercial products, their sources, or their use in connection with material reported herein is not to be construed as either an actual or implied endorsement of such products by the Department of Health and Human Services. This is a contribution of the U.S. Food and Drug Administration and is not subject to copyright.

References

1. Armato III, S.G., et al.: Data from LIDC-IDRI. The cancer imaging archive. https://doi.org/10.7937/K9/TCIA.2015.LO9QL9SX**9**(7) (2015)
2. Biancardi, A.M., Reeves, A.P.: TESD: a novel ground truth estimation method. In: Medical Imaging 2009: Computer-Aided Diagnosis. vol. 7260, pp. 1116–1123. SPIE (2009)

3. Guan, S., Samala, R.K., Arab, A., Chen, W.: MISS-tool: medical image segmentation synthesis tool to emulate segmentation errors. In: Medical Imaging 2023: Computer-Aided Diagnosis. vol. 12465, pp. 273–281. SPIE (2023)
4. Guan, S., Samala, R.K., Chen, W.: Informing selection of performance metrics for medical image segmentation evaluation using configurable synthetic errors. In: 2022 IEEE Applied Imagery Pattern Recognition Workshop (AIPR), pp. 1–8. IEEE (2022)
5. Guan, S., Samala, R.K., Kahaki, S.M., Chen, W.: Restorable synthesis: average synthetic segmentation converges to a polygon approximation of an object contour in medical images. In: 2024 IEEE Southwest Symposium on Image Analysis and Interpretation (SSIAI), pp. 77–80. IEEE (2024)
6. Hesamian, M.H., Jia, W., He, X., Kennedy, P.: Deep learning techniques for medical image segmentation: achievements and challenges. J. Digit. Imaging **32**(4), 582–596 (2019)
7. Iakubovskii, P.: Segmentation models pytorch. https://github.com/qubvel/segmentation_models.pytorch (2019)
8. Isola, P., Zhu, J.Y., Zhou, T., Efros, A.A.: Image-to-image translation with conditional adversarial networks. In: Proceedings of the IEEE Conference on Computer Vision and Pattern Recognition, pp. 1125–1134 (2017)
9. Menze, B.H., et al.: The multimodal brain tumor image segmentation benchmark (BRATS). IEEE Trans. Med. Imaging **34**(10), 1993–2024 (2015). https://doi.org/10.1109/tmi.2014.2377694
10. Taha, A.A., Hanbury, A., Toro, O.A.J.d.: A formal method for selecting evaluation metrics for image segmentation. In: 2014 IEEE International Conference on Image Processing (ICIP), pp. 932–936 (2014). https://doi.org/10.1109/ICIP.2014.7025187
11. Taha, A.A., Hanbury, A.: Metrics for evaluating 3D medical image segmentation: analysis, selection, and tool. BMC Med. Imaging **15**(1), 1–28 (2015)
12. Warfield, S.K., Zou, K.H., Wells, W.M.: Simultaneous truth and performance level estimation (STAPLE): an algorithm for the validation of image segmentation. IEEE Trans. Med. Imaging **23**(7), 903–921 (2004)
13. Zheng, Y., Li, G., Li, Y., Shan, C., Cheng, R.: Truth inference in crowdsourcing: is the problem solved? Proc. VLDB Endowment **10**(5), 541–552 (2017)

Benchmarking Few-Shot Methods for Rare Target Classification in PlanetScope Imagery

Keli Cheng(✉) and Weipeng Wu

Northwest Missouri State University, Maryville, MO 64468, USA
{kcheng,weipengw}@nwmissouri.edu

Abstract. Few-shot learning (FSL) provides a practical solution for remote sensing applications with limited labeled data, yet its effectiveness on medium-resolution satellite imagery remains underexplored. This study investigates FSL methods for classifying Maasai bomas using PlanetScope imagery at 3.0–3.5 m ground sampling distance. To replicate operational constraints, we adopt an episodic evaluation framework where a small number of support samples per class and corresponding query samples are randomly selected from the dataset.

We benchmark a state-of-the-art few-shot learning approach that integrate transfer learning and meta-learning strategies. For feature extraction, we evaluated Vision Transformers pretrained through DINO v1, DINO v2, and DINO v3, as well as convolutional architectures including ConvNeXt and Swin v2. Each backbone was evaluated with a Prototypical Network framework to measure its ability to generate discriminative embeddings under limited supervision. Furthermore, we compared models pretrained on out-of-domain datasets with those trained using in-domain satellite imagery to examine how pretraining domain influences generalization and adaptation in remote sensing tasks.

Keywords: Few shot learning · Remote Sensing · Rare target classification

1 Introduction

With the intensive cost of data annotation, few-shot learning (FSL) has become a popular research area in both pattern recognition and remote sensing field. Researchers aim to train models that can adapt to new unseen tasks with limited training data, reducing the need for large labeled datasets. FSL research is particularly important in remote sensing because many tasks require expert knowledge of the environment, such as land use mapping, crop monitoring, damage assessment, and rare object recognition. These requirements make data annotation especially costly and time-consuming in this area. Many advanced FSL architectures have been proposed and shown success on various tasks, including cross-domain applications using EuroSAT and NWPU-RESISC45 datasets.

F. Tanner and J. Irvine (Eds.): AIPR 2025, LNCS 16446, pp. 608–617, 2026.
https://doi.org/10.1007/978-3-032-18474-0_41

However, most prior work [1–4] focuses on higher-resolution imagery or benchmark datasets, leaving the performance of these architectures on rare targets in medium-resolution satellite imagery largely unexplored.

In this work, we evaluate state-of-the-art (SOTA) FSL architectures and backbones on a real-world rare target classification task: detecting Maasai Bomas and temporary shelters in African regions from medium-resolution PlanetScope imagery. By simulating scenarios with limited labeled samples per class through episodic evaluation, we investigate model accuracy, stability across episodes, and computational efficiency, with the goal of identifying models suitable for future rapid, large-area scanning.

2 Related Work

FSL has been a critical research direction in both computer vision and remote sensing, aiming to recognize novel classes using only a handful of labeled examples. Existing FSL approaches typically fall into metric-based or meta-learning methods, while transfer learning techniques and prompt-based extensions of pre-trained models remain prevalent and sometimes outperform classical methods.

Metric-based methods such as Prototypical Networks [5] and Matching Networks [6] learn a similarity function between support and query samples, with prototypes representing each class. These approaches have been successfully adapted to satellite scene classification and object detection tasks.

Meta-learning approaches aim to optimize across a distribution of tasks so that the model can quickly adapt to new categories with minimal supervision. Popular strategies include optimization-based methods like Model-Agnostic Meta-Learning [7] and task-conditioned networks [8], which have been applied to remote sensing datasets such as NWPU-RESISC45 and EuroSAT.

In remote sensing, FSL has demonstrated strong potential across diverse applications [2,3,9], including land cover classification, scene categorization, and rare target detection. However, the majority of prior work has focused on high-resolution benchmark datasets, while real-world applications and low- to medium-resolution remote sensing tasks remain underexplored. A few challenges remain in this field, including the performance gap caused by the domain mismatch between pre-trained models and remote sensing tasks, as well as the variation in data quality observed in real-world applications. For tasks involving low- to medium-resolution imagery, this cross-domain gap is expected to widen, since lower-resolution images often contain mixed pixels and blurred boundaries that introduce ambiguity in target appearance. Most existing FSL backbones are pre-trained on high-resolution general images, and the spectral and spatial differences between such data and satellite images limit the generalization of models, especially for small structures.

Driven by the remaining challenges in remote sensing and the difficulty in annotating rare targets, this study evaluates SOTA few-shot learning pipelines to develop a practical and efficient solution for rare target detection. The selected pipelines and pre-trained models are tested on the Maasai Boma classification task, a representative example of rare targets that present challenges in collection and annotation of high-quality data. Maasai Bomas are traditional circular settlements in rural East Africa and serve as important indicators for humanitarian planning and public health initiatives led by non-profit organizations. Previous studies using high-resolution imagery have demonstrated the feasibility of automatic Boma detection; however, the substantial computational cost of training and deploying models at high resolution limits their scalability for large-area monitoring [10]. Although low-resolution imagery leveraging multi-spectral and multi-temporal features has also been explored [11, 12], the performance gap exists and real-world deployment of these models has not yet been achieved. To reduce the dependency on manual annotation, this work investigates the applicability of few-shot learning methods to medium-resolution PlanetScope imagery, aiming to evaluate their potential for scalable, annotation-efficient monitoring in operational remote sensing scenarios.

3 Dataset

The dataset used in this study consists of positive boma samples, temporary shelters, and negative non-boma locations. The initial boma coordinates were collected in 2020 through a manual ground survey [10] and scanning by an Earth Sciences scholar. In 2023, additional coordinates of temporary settlements were gathered for medical aid purposes in the study area and incorporated into the positive sample set. Negative samples were automatically generated as non-boma locations surrounding the annotated positives.

These locations were then used as inputs to a custom Planet imagery downloader developed by our team. Built on top of the Planet Python API, the library supports advanced filtering, parallelized catalog searches, high-throughput downloads, and multi-spectral postprocessing. For each boma and non-boma site, we acquired 1 km^2 PlanetScope imagery at 3.0–3.5 m ground sampling distance (GSD), transformed to the `EPSG:4326` coordinate reference system. While this resolution is sufficient to capture general settlement patterns, it poses challenges for identifying small or temporary structures such as bomas, which often occupy areas close to or below the pixel size. The dataset includes 4-band multi-spectral imagery (RGB + NIR) collected on November 6, 2023, with the following filters applied: most recent scene, $\leq 10\%$ cloud cover, $\geq 90\%$ clear pixels, and $\geq 90\%$ clear confidence.

Postprocessing converted the 11-bit four-band multispectral imagery (MSI) into 8-bit RGB images for deep learning experiments. This process involved extracting the RGB bands, clipping pixel values to the 1st–99th percentile range, and applying Contrast Limited Adaptive Histogram Equalization (CL-AHE) to generate consistent, high-quality scenes. After removing images containing large black areas or cloud cover, the final sub-dataset used in this study comprised a balanced set of 322 positive boma or temporary settlement samples and 321 non-boma samples. Example processed imagery for boma and non-boma locations is shown in Fig. 1. Permanent bomas usually have distinct circular fences, making them relatively easy to recognize. However, depending on the size and condition of each boma, some fences may not be visually clear in remote sensing images. Temporary settlements share many visual characteristics with bomas, such as circular-like fencing structures and white tarp-like roofs, further complicating identification. In contrast, non-boma locations do not contain visible bomas or temporary settlements, but they may still include circular vegetation patterns or other features that can be visually similar, posing additional challenges for accurate recognition.

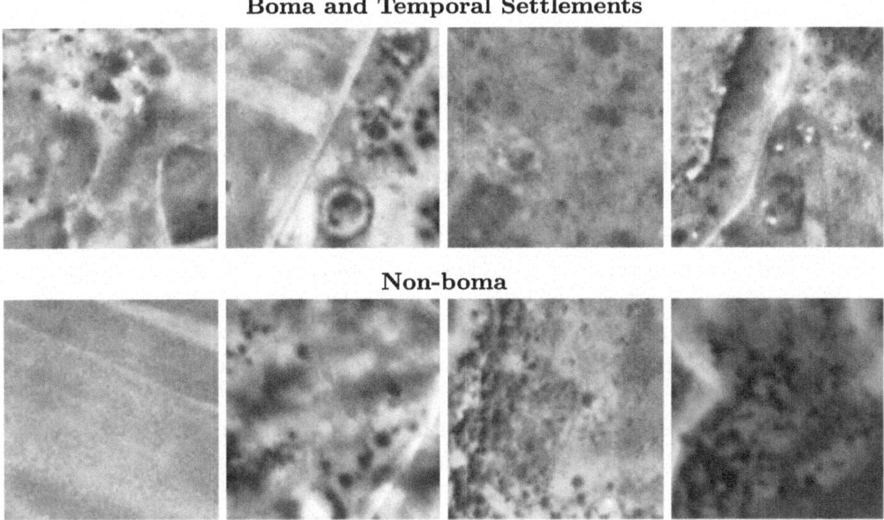

Fig. 1. Visual Comparison of Bomas, Temporal Settlements, and Non-Boma Sites.

4 Method

We adopt a two-stage pipeline that combines pre-trained feature extraction with prototype-based classification for few-shot classification under medium-resolution conditions.

To obtain transferable image embeddings, we utilize multiple pre-trained vision models, including Vision Transformer (ViT) trained through self-distillation with no labels (DINO) [13–15], the convolution-based ConvNeXt [16,17], and the hierarchical Swin Transformer [18,19].

DINO v1 [13] introduces a teacher–student self-distillation framework with exponential moving average (EMA) updates and multi-crop augmentation, enabling ViTs to learn robust semantic representations without supervision. DINO v2 [14] expanded upon this foundation through large-scale pretraining, improved optimization stability, and the use of diverse datasets, resulting in more generalizable embeddings that perform strongly across downstream tasks even without fine-tuning. The latest iteration, DINO v3 [15], scales training to billions of images and parameters while refining the objective for improved transferability. In addition, the authors released a variant pre-trained on large-scale satellite imagery, which provides in-domain representations particularly suited for Earth-observation tasks.

To provide a comprehensive comparison, we further examined convolution-based ConvNeXt and hierarchical Swin Transformer architectures alongside the DINO-trained ViTs. ConvNeXt [16] modernizes convolutional networks with design choices inspired by transformers, while ConvNeXt v2 [17] incorporates masked autoencoder style self-supervision to improve transferability. Swin [18] Transformer adopts shifted window attention to hierarchically integrate local and global context, and Swin v2 [19] enhances training stability for deeper models. These backbones were selected for their complementary inductive biases: DINO-trained ViTs excel at capturing global semantics, ConvNeXt preserves strong convolutional priors beneficial for fine structural features, and Swin Transformer balances local and global representations efficiently.

For each input image, we extract features from the layer preceding the model's final classification head. For ConvNeXt and Swin, global average pooling is applied across spatial dimensions to obtain a fixed-length embedding vector, while for DINO-based ViTs, the pre-classification token embeddings are directly used as feature vectors. During few-shot training and evaluation, the backbones are kept frozen to prevent overfitting to the limited support samples.

To handle the limited number of training samples per class, we adopt a metric-based classification framework: the Prototypical Network (ProtoNet) [5]. For each class, we compute a prototype vector by averaging the embeddings of all available training samples. A query sample is classified by measuring its distance to each class prototype in the embedding space using cosine similarity.

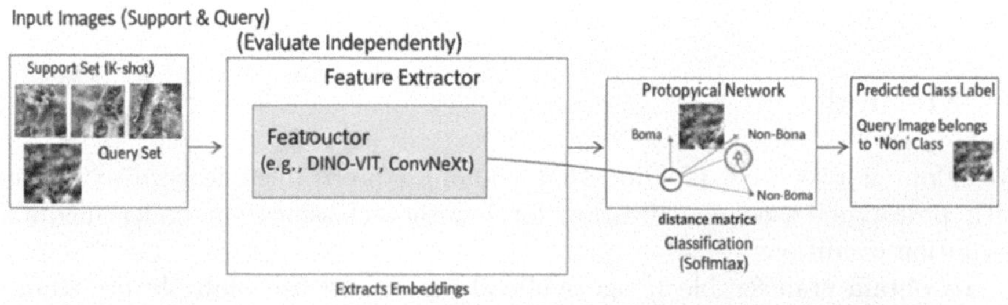

Fig. 2. Overview of the proposed data processing and model training pipeline.

Figure 2 illustrates the evaluation pipeline. For each episode, support and query samples are randomly selected to simulate real-world few-shot learning scenarios. Features are extracted using pre-trained backbones and passed to ProtoNet for classification. By combining pre-trained feature extractors with

ProtoNet, the experiment evaluates the effectiveness of metric-based few-shot learning. The frozen backbones provide discriminative feature representations, while ProtoNet classifies query samples by comparing them to class prototypes constructed from limited support examples. This setup enables robust evaluation on unseen classes without task-specific fine-tuning, aligning with the standard few-shot learning protocol.

5 Experiment

5.1 Backbone Comparison for Feature Extraction

We evaluate the few-shot classification performance using an episodic protocol commonly adopted in FSL. In each episode, a small subset of classes is randomly sampled to simulate a few-shot task. Specifically, we follow a 2-way-10-shot setting: each episode contains 2 classes, with 10 support samples per class and 20 query samples per class. A total of 600 episodes are generated for evaluation, ensuring robust and statistically meaningful results. All experiments are conducted with a fixed random seed for reproducibility. The input images are in size 128×128 pixels, and they are resized and normalized using the mean and standard deviation values recommend by the pre-trained models. Additional data augmentation include color jitter and random horizontal flipping.

For model evaluation, we focused on three primary metrics: classification accuracy with a 95% confidence interval (CI), stability across episodes measured by standard deviation (STD), and runtime efficiency. Accuracy and stability provide insight into a model's generalization and consistency under few-shot settings, while runtime reflects computational scalability. Since the ultimate goal of this research is to identify models suitable for large-area operational scanning, runtime performance serves as an important criterion in addition to accuracy and stability.

Table 1. Model performance comparison

Model	Input Size	Accuracy ± CI (%)	STD (%)	Train Time	Test Time
ViT-S/8 (DINO v1)	128	79.24 ± 0.56	6.99	0.4040s	0.0007s
ViT-B/8 (DINO v1)	128	80.50 ± 0.56	7.05	1.0795s	0.0009s
ViT-S/14 (DINO v2)	126	70.49 ± 0.65	8.15	0.1410s	0.0010s
ViT-B/14 (DINO v2)	126	73.47 ± 0.64	8.03	0.3588s	0.0007s
ViT-B/14 (DINO v2)	224	73.57 ± 0.60	7.45	0.9912s	0.0007s
ViT-L/16 (DINO v3-SAT distilled)	256	80.10 ± 0.55	6.82	4.0554s	0.0023s
ViT-L/16 (DINO v3 distilled)	256	77.61 ± 0.60	7.50	3.9791s	0.0028s
ConvNeXt	224	70.05 ± 1.75	8.15	0.2948s	0.0090s
ConvNeXt v2	224	76.79 ± 1.15	7.32	1.1521s	0.0031s
Swin v2-Small	224	77.24 ± 1.39	7.68	0.6564s	0.0023s
Swin v2-Tiny	224	76.85 ± 1.42	7.14	0.3962s	0.0007s

Table 1 presents the performance comparison across multiple vision transformer and convolution-based architectures. Among all the evaluated models, the distilled ViT trained through DINO v3 on satellite imagery (ViT-L/16, DINO v3-SAT) achieved the highest accuracy of 80.10%, with a standard deviation of ±0.55, at an input size of 256×256. This DINO v3-SAT variant is the only model that was trained using in-domain images. However, due to the numerous parameters in this model, the training and inference time largely increased in comparison to other models. Smaller-scale variants, such as ViT-S/8 (DINO v1) and ViT-B/8 (DINO v1) with an input size of 128×128 pixels, also demonstrated competitive performance, reaching 79.24% and 80.50%, respectively, while maintaining significantly lower training and inference times. In contrast, ViTs trained through DINO v2, namely ViT-S/14 (DINO v2) and ViT-B/14 (DINO v2), showed lower overall accuracy, indicating reduced suitability for this dataset despite the larger patch sizes.

Among convolution-based models, ConvNeXt v2 achieved the best accuracy of 76.79%, outperforming the standard ConvNeXt baseline by approximately 6.7%. However, both ConvNeXt variants exhibited longer inference times compared to transformer-based alternatives. The Swin v2 models achieved moderate performance, with 77.24% (small variant) and 76.85% (tiny variant), but incurred relatively higher computational cost per inference step. Overall, DINO-based ViTs consistently outperformed CNN-based models in both accuracy and efficiency, indicating that transformer-style representations are better suited for recognizing fine-grained spatial structures in this dataset.

5.2 Practical Considerations for Support Image Selection

To evaluate the adaptability of the model under limited supervision, we conducted few-shot classification experiments by varying the number of training samples per class, denoted as $K \in \{1, 5, 10, 20, 30, 50\}$. For each setting, performance was measured across multiple episodes, and results are reported as mean accuracy ±95% CI, along with STD and average training time per episode.

As shown in Table 2, increasing K consistently improves classification performance. The model achieves 61.63% accuracy in the 1-shot setting, indicating a reasonable ability to generalize from a single example. Performance rises sharply to 75.99% at $K = 5$ and 80.50% at $K = 10$, suggesting that even a small number of labeled samples significantly boosts discriminative capability. Beyond $K = 20$, accuracy improvements begin to plateau, reaching 84.24%, 84.78%, and 85.75% for $K = 20, 30$, and 50, respectively.

The standard deviation decreases steadily from 9.80% (1-shot) to 5.32% (50-shot), indicating increased stability with more supervision. Training time grows approximately linearly with K, rising from 0.73 s at 1-shot to 2.38 s at 50-shot, yet remaining computationally lightweight overall.

These results demonstrate that the model is highly data-efficient, achieving strong performance even with limited labeled samples, while maintaining low training cost.

Table 2. Few-shot classification performance with varying K (number of training samples). Results are reported as mean accuracy (%) ± 95% CI across episodes.

K	Accuracy ± CI (%)	STD (%)	Training Time (s)
1	61.63 ± 0.78	9.80	0.7339
5	75.99 ± 0.65	8.12	0.9043
10	80.50 ± 0.56	7.05	1.0721
20	84.24 ± 0.45	5.68	1.4089
30	84.78 ± 0.47	5.81	1.7346
50	85.75 ± 0.43	5.32	2.3894

6 Conclusion

This study demonstrates the effectiveness of self-supervised vision transformer models for remote sensing image classification, particularly in identifying bomas and temporary settlements. Among all evaluated architectures, DINO-based ViTs consistently outperformed convolution-based models in both accuracy and efficiency, confirming the advantages of transformer representations for recognizing fine-grained spatial patterns in medium-resolution satellite imagery.

The experiments reveal that DINO variants show strong potential for real-world deployment, as they achieve high accuracy even under limited supervision and maintain stable inference performance. The results further indicate that the pre-training domain plays a critical role in generalization; however, careful tuning of input resolution and patch size often yields greater gains than pre-training alone.

Finally, the observed variability across episodes highlights the uneven quality of samples in the dataset. This finding suggests that improving annotation precision and balancing visual diversity could further enhance model stability and robustness in future work.

7 Future Work

Future research will focus on several key directions to further enhance model robustness and generalization within the few-shot learning framework. The standard deviations reported in Table 1 indicate noticeable variance in performance across episodes. To address this, we plan to conduct a detailed analysis of low-performing episodes to identify and filter out potentially problematic or mislabeled samples that may negatively affect overall performance stability. In addition, we will continue evaluating other remote sensing foundation models under the few-shot learning paradigm to benchmark generalization across different architectures and pre-training strategies. From a model enhancement perspective, we aim to integrate multiple fine-tuning modules into the best-performing pipeline to mitigate domain discrepancies and further improve accuracy. We also consider incorporating a super-resolution module prior to feature extraction to enhance the visual clarity of medium-resolution satellite imagery and strengthen representation quality.

References

1. Hu, S.X., Li, D., Stühmer, J., Kim, M., Hospedales, T.M.: Pushing the limits of simple pipelines for few-shot learning: external data and fine-tuning make a difference (2022). arXiv preprint arXiv:2204.07305
2. Cheng, K., Scott, G.J.: Evaluation of a meta-transfer approach for few-shot remote sensing scene classification. In: IGARSS 2023–2023 IEEE International Geoscience and Remote Sensing Symposium, pp. 5002–5005. IEEE, Pasadena, CA (2023). https://doi.org/10.1109/IGARSS52108.2023.10282991
3. Li, H., et al.: RS-MetaNet: deep meta-metric learning for few-shot remote sensing scene classification (2020). arXiv preprint arXiv:2009.13364
4. Zhang, B., Feng, S., Li, X., Ye, Y., Ye, R.: SGMNet: scene graph matching network for few-shot remote sensing scene classification (2021). arXiv preprint arXiv:2110.04494
5. Snell, J., Swersky, K., Zemel, R.: Prototypical networks for few-shot learning. In: Advances in Neural Information Processing Systems (NeurIPS), pp. 4077–4087 (2017)
6. Vinyals, O., Blundell, C., Lillicrap, T., Kavukcuoglu, K., Wierstra, D.: Matching networks for one shot learning. In: Advances in Neural Information Processing Systems (NeurIPS), pp. 3630–3638 (2016)
7. Finn, C., Abbeel, P., Levine, S.: Model-agnostic meta-learning for fast adaptation of deep networks. In: Proceedings of the 34th International Conference on Machine Learning (ICML), pp. 1126–1135 (2017)
8. Li, Z., Zhou, F., Chen, F., Li, H.: Meta-SGD: learning to learn quickly for few-shot learning. In: Proceedings of the 34th International Conference on Machine Learning (ICML), pp. 117–126 (2017)
9. Yuan, Z., Li, Y., Xu, H., Liu, Q., Wang, X.: Few-shot remote sensing image scene classification via manifold mixup and local descriptors. Remote Sens. **15**(3), 831 (2023)
10. Cheng, K., Popescu, I., Sheets, L., Scott, G.J.: Analysis of deep learning techniques for maasai boma mapping in Tanzania. In: IEEE Journal of Selected Topics in Applied Earth Observations and Remote Sensing 15, 3916–3924 (2022). https://doi.org/10.1109/JSTARS.2022.3167373
11. Cheng, K., Bajkowski, T.M., Scott, G.J.: Evaluation of sentinel-2 data for automatic maasai boma mapping. In: 2021 IEEE Applied Imagery Pattern Recognition Workshop (AIPR), pp. 1–5. IEEE, Washington, D.C. (2021). https://doi.org/10.1109/AIPR52630.2021.9762131
12. Cheng, K., Scott, G.J.: Deep seasonal network for remote sensing imagery classification of multi-temporal sentinel-2 data. Remote Sens. **15**(19), 4705 (2023). https://doi.org/10.3390/rs15194705
13. Caron, M., et al.: Emerging properties in self-supervised vision transformers. In: Proceedings of the International Conference on Computer Vision (ICCV), pp. 9630–9640 (2021)
14. Oquab, M., et al.: DINOv2: learning robust visual features without supervision (2023). arXiv preprint arXiv:2304.07193

15. Siméoni, O., et al.: DINOv3 (2025). arXiv preprint arXiv:2508.10104. https://arxiv.org/abs/2508.10104
16. Liu, Z., Mao, H., Wu, C.-Y., Feichtenhofer, C., Darrell, T., Xie, S.: A ConvNet for the 2020s. In: 2022 IEEE/CVF Conference on Computer Vision and Pattern Recognition (CVPR), pp. 11976–11986 (2022). https://doi.org/10.1109/CVPR52688.2022.01184
17. Woo, S., et al.: ConvNeXt V2: co-designing and scaling ConvNets with masked autoencoders. In: 2023 IEEE/CVF Conference on Computer Vision and Pattern Recognition (CVPR), pp. 17779–17792 (2023). https://doi.org/10.1109/CVPR56405.2023.01145
18. Liu, Z., et al.: Swin transformer: hierarchical vision transformer using shifted windows. In: Proceedings of the IEEE/CVF International Conference on Computer Vision (ICCV), pp. 10012–10022 (2021). https://doi.org/10.1109/ICCV48922.2021.00984
19. Liu, Z., et al.: Swin transformer V2: scaling up capacity and resolution. In: Proceedings of the IEEE/CVF Conference on Computer Vision and Pattern Recognition (CVPR), pp. 10000–10010 (2022). https://doi.org/10.1109/CVPR52688.2022.01234

Author Index

A
Acquaah, Sally 221, 463
Adu-Gyamfi, Yaw 345
Aledhari, Mohammed 101
Alfatemi, Ali 101
Algire, Christopher 430
AlHmoud, Issa W. 44, 77, 201, 221, 292, 375, 463, 576
Aqcuaah, Sally 375
Aronow, Bruce J. 508

B
Bao, Rina 495
Brennan, Michelle M. 177
Brown, Hunter 132
Bukowski, Tom 24
Bunyak, Filiz 326, 345
Busch, Mike 24

C
Cabrera, Heidys 132
Carrozzella, Janice 508
Cazares, Shelley 1
Cerkez, Paul S. 18
Challa, Koundinya 44, 77
Chehri, Abdellah 101
Chen, Weijie 595
Cheng, Keli 608
Christopher, Lauren 484
Corazzini, Tobe 154
Cornelius, Rebecca 508

D
D. Massaro, Ricky 326
DeWitty, Robert 44
Du, Hang 345
Durham, Axel 167

E
El Kari, Chadi 190

F
Francisco, Adam 154

G
Gallai, Mohamed 559
Gaskill-Shipley, Mary 508
Gerstoft, Peter 236
Ghani, Nasir 101
Gokaraju, Balakrishna 44, 77, 201, 221, 292, 375, 463, 576
Gondosubroto, Renaldi 451
Graves, Corey A 292
Guan, Shuyue 595
Gupta, Pramod 190

H
Harper, Clayton 236
Hatuwal, Bijaya Kumar 495
Ho, Mai-Lan 495
Horn, Paul S. 508
Hughes, Eric 132

I
Irizarry, Nazario 274
Irvine, John M. 177, 274
Islam, AKM Kamrul 292
Israel, Steven A. 177, 430
Iyer, Balaji 508

J
Jawahar, Bharath 77
Jeon, Gwanggil 101
Jiang, Ruizhe 484

K
Kalukin, Andrew 451
Kamduri, Venkata Ranga Ramanuja K. Chaitanya 190
Kantha, Dattatreya 522
Keegan, Kevin 311

F. Tanner and J. Irvine (Eds.): AIPR 2025, LNCS 16446, pp. 619–621, 2026.
https://doi.org/10.1007/978-3-032-18474-0

Kelly, Timoteo 246
Khandwala, Vivek 508
Khapper, Krupa V. 292
Khatri, Pooja 508
Kim, Nathan Yeop 364
Kissela, Brett M. 508
Klawa, Tim 403
Korkmaz, Abdulkadir 246
Krall, Nick 132
Kucukpinar, Taci 311
Kyung, Richard 364

L
LaPorta, Joseph 508
Larson, Eric C. 236
Larue, James P. 92
LaTourette, Kevin J. 154, 167
Levy, Elliot 546
Liang, Chyi Lyi 77, 201
Loew, Murray H. 522, 546

M
Mace, Eliza 115, 132
Mahyari, Andrew Arash 415
Maloney, Thomas 508
Maram, Ritish Raghav 546
McCormick, Ryan 154, 167
McPeak, Grady 62
Munoz, John 24

N
Nenebi, Chris 375
Nenebi, Christopher Tetteh 221, 463
Njeunje, Franck Olivier Ndjakou 274

O
O'Neill, Matthew 132

P
Palaniappan, Kannappan 311, 326, 430, 495
Pendem, Abhinav 44, 77, 576
Pless, Robert 62

R
R. Arredondo, Johanna 326
Rahmon, Gani 311
Rahouti, Mohamed 101
Rao, Praveen 246
Reisman, Matthew D. 154, 167
Robbins, Kevin 62

S
Safavigerdini, Kaveh 311
Salama, Paul 484
Salour, Al 387
Sarkar, Shivangi 132
Sava, Elena 326
Saxena, Pranjal 387
Sevil, Hakki Erhan 415
Sharma, Teena 387
Shojaei, Sara 326
Solis, Tito 167
Soundarajan, Joe 451
Stylianou, Abby 559
Sucharew, Heidi 508
Surya Prasath, V. B. 508

T
Tang, Andrews 201, 221, 375, 463, 576
Tanner, Frank 403
Thompson, Ben 115, 255
Thornton, Mitchell A. 236
Tomsick, Thomas 508
Tucker, Kourtney 221, 375, 463, 576

V
Vagal, Achala 508
Vasikarla, Shantaram 387
Verma, Nishchal K. 387
Vilt, Samuel 274

W
Wang, David 508
Wang, Lily 508
Weissman, Lowell 132
Wickrema, Charith 132
Williamson, Brady 508
Wood, Alexander N. 255
Wood, Luke 236
Wu, Weipeng 608

X
Xu, Dong 451

Y
Yates, Don 415

Z
Zarrella, Guido 132
Zhang, Linlin 345

The manufacturer's authorised representative in the EU is Springer Nature Customer Service Centre GmbH, Europaplatz 3, 69115 Heidelberg, Germany. If you have any concerns regarding our products, please contact ProductSafety@springernature.com

Printed and bound by CPI Group (UK) Ltd, Croydon, CR0 4YY

07/07/2026

02160906-0018